# BYZANTINES AND CRUSADERS IN NON-GREEK SOURCES
## 1025–1204

PROCEEDINGS OF THE BRITISH ACADEMY · 132

# BYZANTINES AND CRUSADERS IN NON-GREEK SOURCES 1025–1204

Edited by

## MARY WHITBY

Published for THE BRITISH ACADEMY
by OXFORD UNIVERSITY PRESS

*Oxford University Press, Great Clarendon Street, Oxford* OX2 6DP

*Oxford New York*
*Auckland Bangkok Buenos Aires Cape Town Chennai*
*Dar es Salaam Delhi Hong Kong Istanbul Karachi Kolkata*
*Kuala Lumpur Madrid Melbourne Mexico City Mumbai Nairobi*
*São Paulo Shanghai Singapore Taipei Tokyo Toronto*

*Published in the United States*
*by Oxford University Press Inc., New York*

*© The British Academy 2007*

*Database right The British Academy (maker)*

*First published 2007*

*British Library Cataloguing in Publication Data*
*Data available*

*Library of Congress Cataloging in Publication Data*
*Data available*

*ISBN 978–0–19–726378–5*
*ISSN 0068–1202*

*Typeset by*
*J&L Composition, Filey, North Yorkshire*
*Printed in Great Britain*
*on acid-free paper by*
*The Cromwell Press Limited*
*Trowbridge, Wilts*

# Contents

vi *Contents*

# Notes on Contributors

**Michael Angold** is Professor Emeritus of Byzantine History at the University of Edinburgh.

**Michel Balard** is Professor of Medieval History at the University of Paris 1 Panthéon-Sorbonne and president of the Society for the Study of the Crusades and the Latin east.

**Averil Cameron** is Warden of Keble College, Oxford and former chair of the committee of the Prosopography of the Byzantine World project.

**Krijnie Ciggaar** is actively engaged in publishing on relations between Byzantium and western Europe; she is currently working in particular on Antioch during the period 969–1268.

**Nicholas de Lange** is Professor of Hebrew and Jewish Studies at the University of Cambridge and editor of the *Bulletin of Judaeo-Greek Studies*.

**Peter Edbury** is a professor in the Cardiff School of History and Archaeology, University of Cardiff.

**Simon Franklin** is Professor of Slavonic Studies at the University of Cambridge and a Fellow of Clare College, Cambridge.

**Tim Greenwood** is Lecturer in Byzantine and Eastern Christian Studies in the Department of Mediaeval History, University of St Andrews.

**Carole Hillenbrand** is Professor of Islamic History at the University of Edinburgh.

**Joshua Holo** is Associate Professor of Jewish History at the Hebrew Union College–Jewish Institute of Religion, Los Angeles, California.

**Michael Jeffreys** is Research Manager for the Prosopography of the Byzantine World project; until 2000 he was Professor of Modern Greek at the University of Sydney.

**Jeremy Johns** is Director of the Khalili Research Centre for the Art and Material Culture of the Middle East, and Lecturer in Islamic Archaeology in the Oriental Institute, University of Oxford.

**Stephen H. Rapp Jr.** is Associate Professor of Medieval Eurasian and World History at Georgia State University, Atlanta, and is director of the Program in World History and Cultures.

**Jonathan Riley-Smith** is the recently retired Dixie Professor of Ecclesiastical History, University of Cambridge.

**Vera von Falkenhausen** is Professor of Byzantine History at the Università di Roma Tor Vergata.

**Witold Witakowski** is Associate Professor at the Institute of Linguistics and Philology, University of Uppsala, Sweden; his research interests are in the fields of Semitic studies, especially Syriac.

# Abbreviations

| | |
|---|---|
| *AI* | *Annales islamologiques* |
| *AOH* | *Acta Orientalia Hungarica* |
| *ASI* | *Archivio storico italiano* |
| *BÉO* | *Bulletin des études orientales* |
| *BF* | *Byzantinische Forschungen* |
| BHG | Bibliotheca Hagiographica Graeca |
| BHL | Bibliotheca Hagiographica Latina |
| *BIFAO* | *Bulletin de l'Institut français d'archéologie orientale du Caire* |
| *BJGS* | *Bulletin of Judaeo-Greek Studies* |
| *BMGS* | *Byzantine and Modern Greek Studies* |
| *BSOAS* | *Bulletin of the School of Oriental and African Studies* |
| *BZ* | *Byzantinische Zeitschrift* |
| *Byz* | *Byzantion* |
| CCCM | Corpus Christianorum, Continuatio Mediaevalis |
| *CM* | *Classica et Mediaevalia* |
| CSCO | Corpus Scriptorum Christianorum Orientalium |
| CSCO, SS | Corpus Scriptorum Christianorum Orientalium, Scriptores Syri |
| *DOP* | *Dumbarton Oaks Papers* |
| *EHR* | *English Historical Review* |
| *HUCA* | *Hebrew Union College Annual* |
| *JAOS* | *Journal of the American Oriental Society* |
| *JESHO* | *Journal of the Economic and Social History of the Orient* |
| *JHS* | *Journal of Hellenic Studies* |
| *JJS* | *Journal of Jewish Studies* |
| *JMH* | *Journal of Medieval History* |
| *JÖB* | *Jahrbuch der österreichischen Byzantinistik* |
| *JQR* | *Jewish Quarterly Review* |
| *JRAS* | *Journal of the Royal Asiatic Society* |
| *JSAI* | *Jerusalem Studies in Arabic and Islam* |
| *JSS* | *Journal of Semitic Studies* |
| MGH | Monumenta Germaniae Historica, ed. G.H. Pertz and others (Hanover, Weimar, Stuttgart and Cologne, 1826–) |

| | |
|---|---|
| MGHS | Monumenta Germaniae Historica, Scriptores, 38 vols. so far (1826–) |
| MGHS in usum scholarum | Scriptores Rerum Germanicarum in usum scholarum separatim editi, 75 vols. so far (1839–) |
| MGHS rer. Germ. n.s. | Scriptores Rerum Germanicarum. Nova series, 18 vols. so far (1922–) |
| *MGWJ* | *Monatsschrift für Geschichte und Wissenschaft des Judentums* |
| *PAAJR* | *Proceedings of the American Academy for Jewish Research* |
| PBW | Prosopography of the Byzantine World |
| PG | Patrologia Graeca |
| PL | Patrologia Latina |
| PO | Patrologia Orientalis |
| *RÉA* | *Revue des études arméniennes* |
| *RÉB* | *Revue des études byzantines* |
| *RÉI* | *Revue des études islamiques* |
| *RÉJ* | *Revue des études juives* |
| *RHC* | *Recueil des historiens des croisades* |
| *RHC Oc* | *Recueil des historiens des croisades. Historiens occidentaux*, ed. Académie des Inscriptions et Belles-Lettres, 5 vols. (Paris, 1844–95) |
| *RHGF* | *Recueil des historiens des Gaules et de la France*, ed. M. Bouquet and M.-J.-J. Brial, 24 vols. (Paris, 1738–1904) |
| *RRH* | R. Röhricht, ed., *Regesta Regni Hierosolymitani (MXCVII–MCCXCI)* (Innsbruck, 1893; additamentum 1904; repr. New York, 1960) |
| *ROL* | *Revue de l'Orient latin* |
| *RSBN* | *Rivista di studi bizantini e neoellenici* |
| *RSI* | *Rivista storica italiana* |
| *UEAI* | *Union européenne des Arabisants et Islamisants* |
| *VV* | *Vizantiiskii vremmennik* |
| *WZKM* | *Wiener Zeitschrift für die Kunde des Morgenlandes* |

# Preface

IT HAS BEEN A PLEASURE AND A PRIVILEGE to edit this volume. I have learned a great deal from the scholars who have contributed and have been assisted by their courteous and patient discussion with a non-specialist on numerous points of detail. I would particularly like to single out Jeremy Johns who produced the chapter on Arabic sources for Sicily with great efficiency at extremely short notice. I have enjoyed the support of stalwart colleagues on the Prosopography of the Byzantine World project:* the original idea for this book came from Michael Jeffreys, and he and Tassos Papacostas have always been ready to listen and discuss issues. Tassos has also cheerfully provided a great deal of advice and practical help; it was he who found the striking cover image. At an earlier stage their predecessors, John Martindale and Dion Smythe were my kindly mystagogues in the art of prosopography. Harold Short, Director of the Centre for Computing in the Humanities at King's College London, under whose aegis the prosopography project falls, has been consistently supportive, characteristically optimistic and always ready with a practical suggestion. In particular he offered the services of the Centre for work on the maps and put me in touch with Martyn Jessop who began the task. The final artwork was produced by Hafed Walda, who collaborated enthusiastically with Tassos to produce excellent clear results from diverse and sometimes difficult raw materials. James Rivington, Publications Officer at the British Academy, has been upbeat and imaginative, while Colin Baldwin has been a patient copy-editor. I am grateful to Tony Eastmond for advice on a cover image, to Alicia Correa for taking on the task of compiling the index, and to George Molyneaux for meticulous checking of it. My own work has been partly funded by a British Academy Larger Research Grant, one of many debts over a long period that the British prosopography project owes to the Academy. Finally I would like to pay tribute to Averil Cameron for firm but generous leadership, common sense and extraordinary humanity.

Mary Whitby
October 2006

*http://www.pbw.kcl.ac.uk

# Maps

*Note*
As far as possible spelling follows that of the *Oxford Dictionary of Byzantium* and the *Encyclopaedia of Islam* (2nd edn.) as appropriate. Maps 1–4 draw on maps found in the *Oxford Dictionary of Byzantium* and Map 9 on one in the *Encyclopaedia of Islam*; Map 5 was prepared by Paolo Vitti.

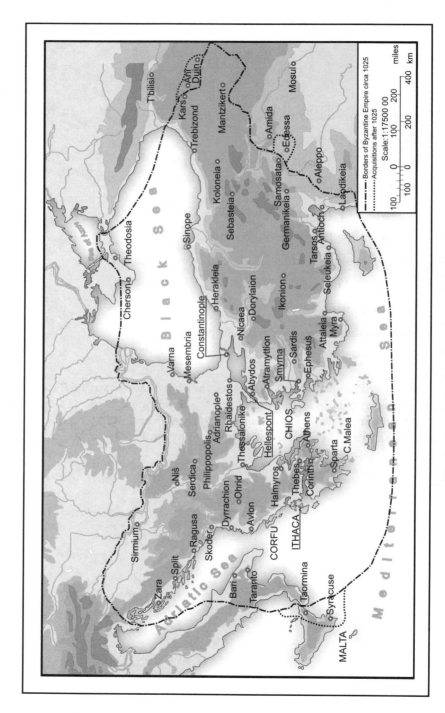

**Map 1.** Boundaries of the Byzantine empire in 1025

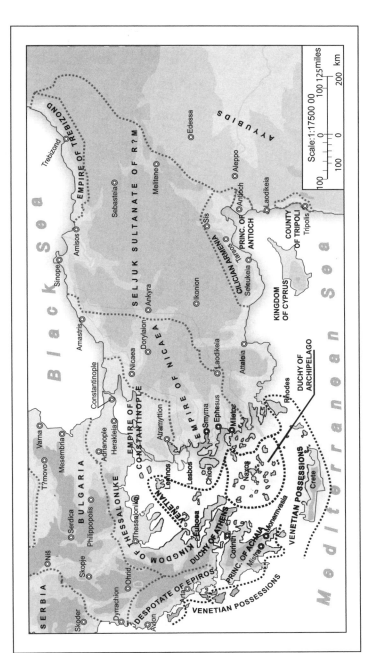

Map 2.   The Byzantine world, 1204–61

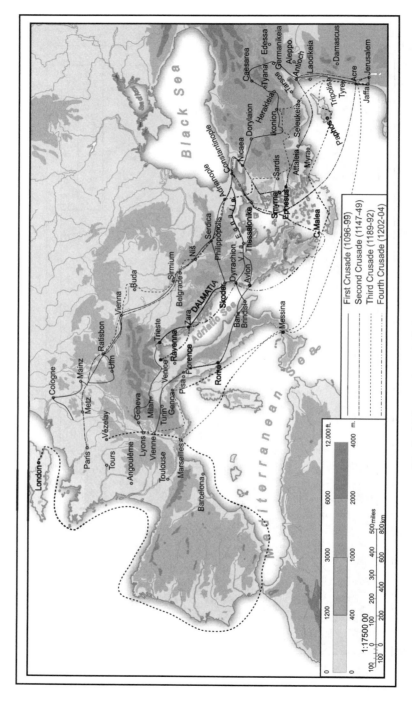

**Map 3**  Main crusader and pilgrim routes, 1025–1204

**Map 4.** The Near East in the crusader period

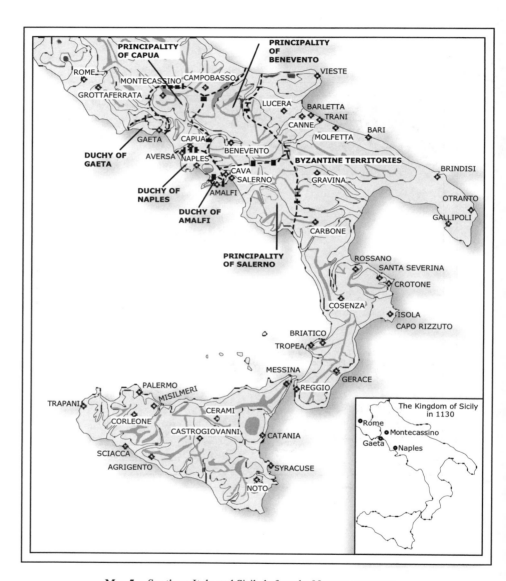

**PRINCIPALITY OF CAPUA**

**PRINCIPALITY OF BENEVENTO**

ROME

MONTECASSINO   CAMPOBASSO   VIESTE

GROTTAFERRATA

LUCERA   BARLETTA
TRANI

CANNE

GAETA   CAPUA   MOLFETTA   BARI

**DUCHY OF GAETA**

AVERSA   NAPLES   BENEVENTO

**BYZANTINE TERRITORIES**

CAVA   BRINDISI

SALERNO   GRAVINA

**DUCHY OF NAPLES**

AMALFI   OTRANTO

GALLIPOLI

**DUCHY OF AMALFI**

CARBONE

**PRINCIPALITY OF SALERNO**

ROSSANO
SANTA SEVERINA

CROTONE

COSENZA

ÍSOLA
CAPO RIZZUTO

BRIATICO

TROPEA

MESSINA

GERACE

PALERMO   REGGIO

MISILMERI

TRAPANI

CERAMI

CORLEONE

CASTROGIOVANNI   CATANIA

SCIACCA

AGRIGENTO   SYRACUSE

NOTO

The Kingdom of Sicily
in 1130

Rome

Montecassino

Gaeta   Naples

**Map 5.**   Southern Italy and Sicily before the Norman conquest

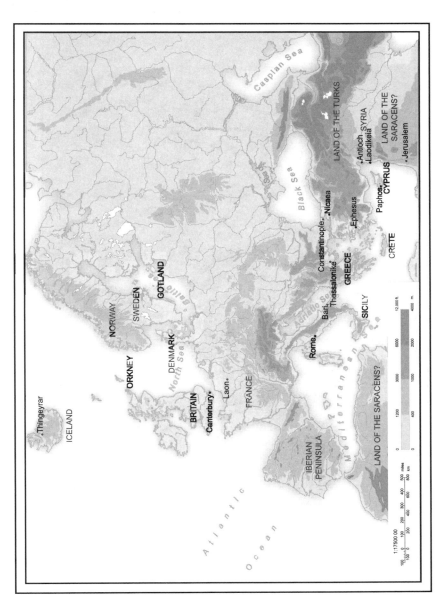

**Map 6.** North-western Europe and Byzantium

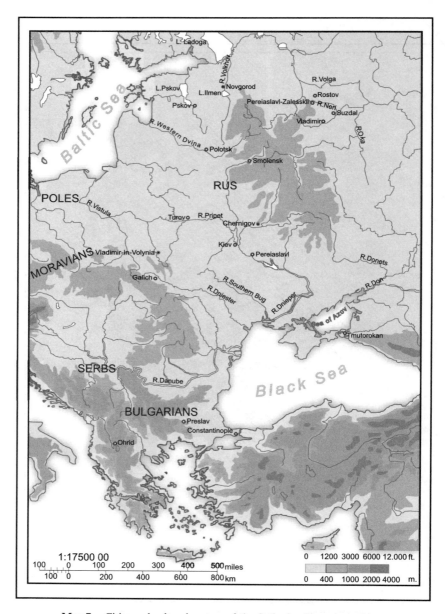

**Map 7.** Cities and cultural centres of the Orthodox Slavonic world

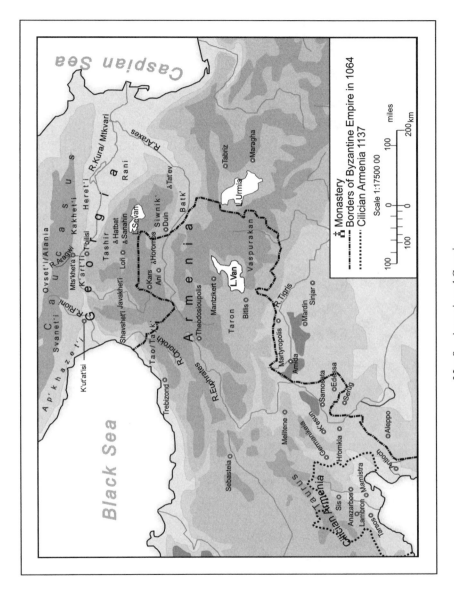

**Map 8.** Armenia and Georgia

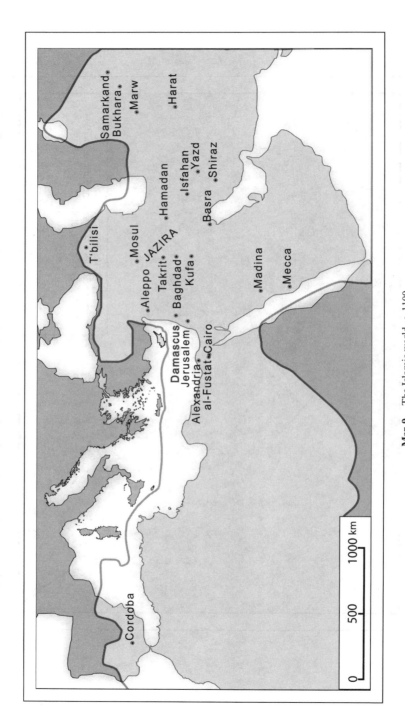

**Map 9.** The Islamic world, c. 1100

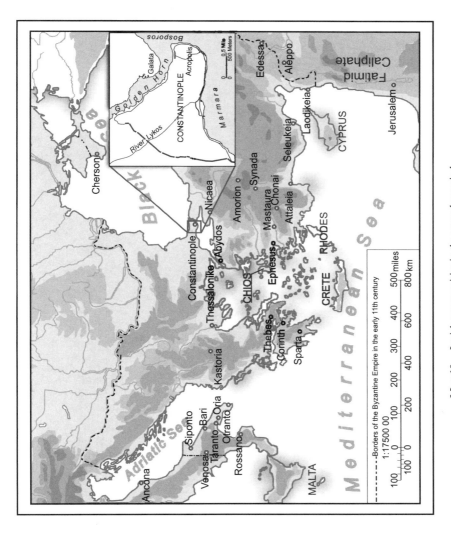

**Map 10.** Jewish communities in the crusader period

# Introduction

THE CRUSADES HAVE ACQUIRED A NEW AND URGENT RELEVANCE in relation to the events of the past few years, as a result of which western and eastern, and indeed Christian and Muslim, relations have again become tense and uncertain. In addition, the eight hundredth anniversary in 2004 of the sack of Constantinople by the Fourth Crusade in 1204 stimulated several conferences and academic essays. That event came as an enormous psychological shock to the Byzantines, who were driven from the capital city in which they had lived for nearly nine hundred years, and hardly less so to the westerners. The Byzantines set up a court in exile at Nicaea in Asia Minor, while the crusaders were left to form a Latin government in Constantinople, the fabled capital of an ancient and prestigious empire whose riches they had desired but which they did not understand. The city's greatest treasures were looted and its most sacred relics carried off to western Europe where they served to bolster the claims of Louis IX, later St Louis, to a sacral kingship meant to evoke and surpass that of the Byzantine emperors.

This violent clash of east and west was the dramatic culmination of a tension which had been felt since before the First Crusade in 1095. The ✳ arrival of western knights in Byzantine territory on their way to the Holy Land confronted the Byzantines with a variety of difficult decisions. The Byzantine historian Anna Komnene presents us with a highly prejudiced and hostile view of the newcomers, in a narrative designed to show her father the Emperor Alexios I Komnenos in the best possible light. In fact his position was unenviable as he tried to deal with these difficult and potentially uncom- ✳ fortable allies. The story was more complex than Anna suggests; yet the fact was that from now on the Byzantines had somehow to deal with the unwelcome fact of western intrusion into their own territory, at a time when they were also experiencing encroachment by the Turks. Indeed, the Byzantine emperor himself in 1095 asked Pope Urban for help against the Seljuks, and pledged Byzantine assistance to the crusaders. However it was not solely a matter of expeditions launched in the name of religion and with the aim of recovering the Holy Land. The Byzantine empire in this period was in practice experiencing the impact of an aggressive expansion of western Europe, which inevitably disturbed the geopolitical balance.[1] It is hardly surprising to find that the two sides did not understand each other. On the other hand, it

---

[1] See R.D. Bartlett, *The Making of Europe. Conquest, colonization and cultural change, 950–1350* (Princeton, 1993); D. Abulafia, *The Mediterranean in History* (London, 2003).

is also true that the mutual hostility present in some of the contemporary sources can make it difficult to appreciate the influence and interaction which were also part of the story. There are lessons for today in contemplating these complex and changing relationships.

Recent scholarship has done something to redress the excessively western perspective of research on the period covered by the crusades.[2] It has also questioned the applicability of the term 'crusade' for every expedition which set out, mostly for the east, after 1095, as well as the appropriate numbering of the major crusading ventures.[3] However, this book goes considerably further, by showing that the issue is not simply one of west and east, Latin and Greek.[4] The changes in the Islamic world clearly need to be part of the story too: the parameters of world power were changing. In order to do justice to the subject, it is necessary to realise the full complexity of the late medieval world, both eastern and western, in the eleventh and twelfth centuries, and this entails coming to grips with historical sources extant in a whole variety of languages.

The starting-point of the book came from ongoing work on Byzantine prosopography, that is, the attempt to collect and analyse all known information about Byzantine individuals. This is the aim of related projects in Britain and in Germany, which were set up with the aim of covering between them the whole of the Byzantine empire from AD 641 to 1261.[5] As work proceeded on the British project for the period AD 1025–1261, and especially in view of contemporary events, it became clear that it was necessary to widen the scope of the research to match the enormously more complicated world in which the Byzantines found themselves, in particular the interplay between east and west that now came more sharply into relief. Contrary to popular perceptions, the

---

[2] See especially Angeliki E. Laiou and Roy Parviz Mottahedeh, eds., *The Crusades from the Perspective of Byzantium and the Muslim World* (Washington, 2001).

[3] See Giles Constable, 'The historiography of the crusades', in Laiou and Mottahedeh, eds., *Crusades*, 1–22.

[4] For the complex questions of western influences on Byzantium during the eleventh and twelfth centuries, see A. Kazhdan, 'Latins and Franks in Byzantium: perception and reality from the eleventh to the twelfth century', in Laiou and Mottahedeh, eds., *Crusades*, 83–100.

[5] John Martindale, ed., *Prosopography of the Byzantine Empire*, vol. 1 (641–867) (Aldershot, 2001) [CD ROM]; work in progress: http://www.pbw.kcl.ac.uk. This project, now renamed Prosopography of the Byzantine World (PBW) in recognition of its expanded scope, has been mainly financed by the Arts and Humanities Research Council and is also a British Academy Research Project. F. Winkelmann, R.-J. Lilie, C. Ludwig, T. Pratsch, I. Rochow and others, eds., *Prosopographie der mittelbyzantinischen Zeit*, Abt. I, *641–867: Prolegomena, Bde I–VI* (1998–2002); work in progress: http://www.bbaw.de/forschung/pmbz. This project is funded by the Berlin-Brandenburgische Akademie der Wissenschaften. The Palaiologan period is covered by E. Trapp, with R. Walther, H.-V. Beyer, K. Sturm-Schnabel, E. Kislinger, I.Gh. Leontiades, S. Kaplaneres and others, eds., *Prosopographisches Lexikon der Palaiologenzeit*, 12 fascicles with index, addenda and corrigenda (Vienna, 1976–96).

Byzantine empire was not simply a Greek empire; moreover it was surrounded and impacted on by a variety of other peoples and states. It was soon realised that no adequate, and certainly no accessible, guides existed to much of the necessary source material in other relevant languages. Thus it was necessary to commission a range of specialists who might fill this need. The essays in this volume, all by leading scholars, present, in many cases for the first time, both overviews of particular bodies of material and detailed analytical bibliographical guides to the historical sources from particular areas or in specific languages. It would be hard to underestimate either the difficulty or the value of this undertaking. The volume provides an entirely new scholarly guide, which will at the same time serve to underline the fact that a traditionally western-centric approach to this period is no longer acceptable. In historical writing, as well as in modern political and cultural relations, it is necessary to try to do justice to all the available evidence and perspectives.

The foundations for this volume were laid by a colloquium generously hosted by the British Academy in December 2002, and organised by Professors Judith Herrin and Michael Jeffreys on behalf of the Prosopography of the Byzantine World (PBW).[6] It has been edited by Dr Mary Whitby, who has been a member of the research team of PBW since 1999. As the current chair of the committee of PBW (the change of title from Prosopography of the Byzantine Empire to Prosopography of the Byzantine World follows the principles set out above), I would like to pay tribute to Mary Whitby's skills as editor in putting together such a complex volume, with contributions by specialists in such a wide variety of fields. I would also like to thank the British Academy once again for its support of this part of the research of the project, and indeed for its continued support of the PBW project. Lastly our thanks are again due to the Academy's Publications Committee for accepting the volume as a British Academy publication.

Averil Cameron

---

[6] For the history of the project, see also Averil Cameron, ed., *Fifty Years of Prosopography. The Later Roman Empire, Byzantium and beyond* (Oxford, 2003).

# 1

# PBW: the Project and the Colloquium

## MICHAEL JEFFREYS

THE PROJECT 'PROSOPOGRAPHY OF THE BYZANTINE WORLD' (PBW) appears on many of the pages of this volume, occasionally explicitly, more often by implication. PBW is a British Academy project now largely funded by the Arts and Humanities Research Council, though it has also recently received, after competitive application, valuable additional support from the Academy under different programmes. The geographical limits of the project's Byzantine world are those of the great empire left by Basil II in 1025, as distinct from the shrinking limits of the actual Byzantine empire in the period under consideration. Like all projects involving the Middle East, PBW has re-examined its definitions and scope in the light of events in the first five years of the twenty-first century: the main result of this review was the colloquium which led to this book, for which participants were asked to consider inhabitants of and visitors to the Byzantine world in the period 1025–1204.

Prosopography is the study of a defined group of people as individuals and members of families. It concentrates on personal activities and family identities, thus cutting through generalisations and stereotypes. It is a particularly valuable method of historical research for periods like that under study, when large armies are on the move in east and west and some are settling in newly conquered lands. Some sources for the period speak of the clash of irreconcilable religions and civilisations, and it is true that two major lines on the modern cultural map were confirmed at this time—those between Muslims and Christians and between the Orthodox east of Europe and the non-Orthodox west. But it is important to compare this dimension of struggle with personal enmities and compromises, as individuals at all social levels who were caught up in the changes found ways to survive and make life tolerable, or exploited the situation to their advantage. The mission of the PBW database is to give broad on-line access to these personalities and narratives, providing simple answers to simple questions, but also giving the opportunity to formulate and test quite complex hypotheses.

A considerable shift in PBW's original focus was already plain in the planning of the colloquium. Previously it had only one centre, Byzantium. Yet the first four numbered crusades are probably the four most important events in

*Proceedings of the British Academy* **132**, 1–4. © The British Academy 2007.

the Byzantine world during the period from 1095 to 1204: the Fourth Crusade in fact was the greatest disaster in Byzantine history. The westerly movement of the Turks in the eleventh century is both a major destructive force for Byzantium and also (to an extent which remains controversial) a primary cause of the crusades. Thus it would be impossible to write PBW without giving a very prominent place to crusading issues. All the Turkish invaders and conquerors of Asia Minor during this period, like all the western pilgrims and crusaders, were visitors to the Byzantine world, and many remained as residents. All have a place in the PBW database. The capitals of the Seljuk Turks of Konya and the Danishmendids of Niksar (Neokaisareia in Pontos) were part of that world. Of the Christian states in the east, Antioch and Edessa were within the empire of Basil II and so within PBW's definition of the Byzantine world, though Jerusalem and much of Tripolis had not been recovered after being lost to the first Arab expansion of the seventh century. Yet many events in the history of Jerusalem directly concerned Byzantium, or involved travellers who used (and abused) Byzantine roads and harbours to reach there, or included residents of the Byzantine world from Antioch or Edessa, or showed Jerusalem residents active inside that world, in Antioch or Edessa to Jerusalem's north. Only details of the history of Jerusalem which were purely internal or involved those to its east and south are not strictly Byzantine.

From the perspective of 2002–5 it makes no sense to prepare a prosopography which covers ninety per cent of crusading activity in the east without adding the last ten per cent. The crusaders were thus included in the colloquium title. Some speakers were invited to address crusading history directly, others to make it a part of their presentations on other groups of sources. The inclusion of Tripolis and Jerusalem in the Byzantine world was an arbitary yet natural corollary, and it has clear positive results. Byzantium, the major regional power of 1025, is the only sizeable platform available from which to survey the crusading period with a degree of impartiality between polarised eastern and western viewpoints. Admittedly Byzantium was staunchly Christian, but it lost many eastern provinces to the Muslim Turks in the eleventh century, while its capital and some western provinces fell to the crusaders in 1204, so that it came to look on both these enemies with equal horror. There was always tension between Orthodox Byzantines and the non-Orthodox crusaders, especially near Constantinople.

Participants in the colloquium were asked to assess the importance for the Byzantine and crusader world of the particular sources they were invited to discuss. The geographical extent of that world had been defined as the limits of Basil II's empire of 1025, but the criteria for membership of this Byzantine world became a major theme of the colloquium. Some speakers produced explicit advice on the problems posed by their sources or populations; others described their material in a more general way, leaving PBW to work out its policies accordingly. Among articles giving direct advice may be mentioned those on Armenian and Georgian sources, where rulers and aristocratic groups often had parallel Byzantine identities; on southern Italy, where Byzantine forms were taken over as markers of distinction for a decidedly non-Byzantine Norman nobility; on visitors from northern Europe, some of whom served as mercenaries of Byzantium; and on Slavic lands, where an ecclesiastical hierarchy centred on Constantinople (and including some confirmed Greek-speakers) may be seen partially to byzantinise a population which in other respects cannot be described as Byzantine.

The above comments may help to explain the scope of this volume and the different emphases of different chapters. It may also be of interest to set out the conclusions PBW drew from the papers and from the extensive discussion which occurred in the framework of the colloquium.

The first and most obvious was a clear imperative to aim at the inclusion of sources other than those in Greek, together with some Latin and a limited representation from other languages—the texts for whose study PBW was originally funded. Special importance should be given to Arabic sources, because of their large numbers and their political importance, both in the medieval period and in the twenty-first century. An application to the Leverhulme Trust has in fact now enabled the funding of a sister project to PBW, devoted to Arabic sources.

The second was a need to present the actual project within the perspective of a wider ideal project covering all the sources in all available languages. PBW should publish results in a framework to contrast that ideal with the partial work which had been funded and achieved. A good deal of time has in fact been spent in the construction of chronological tables to show the sources read and those (from the ideal project) not yet studied. These tables will form one of the points of entry to the prosopography.

The third was a response to the extreme difficulty of making a binary division between possible candidates for a place in the prosopography, finding secure definitions to include some in the Byzantine world and exclude others. Outside the central area of Byzantium, the Byzantine identity of most individuals is best assessed as a point on a continuum of possibilities rather then decided simply in the positive or negative. The solution to this problem, reached in discussions at the colloquium, has been to convert this theoretical problem into a practical issue of timetabling the work. The boundaries of the Byzantine world have been set very wide, including those with even slight claims to membership and hence giving greater flexibility. Then work on the prosopography can be prioritised to move approximately from the secure identifications to the insecure, following the guidelines set out in this volume.

Finally, the colloquium suggested the metaphor of an umbrella for the overall form to be adopted by the prosopography. The umbrella would consist of different-sized panes of cloth spreading out from a single point of definition, the Byzantine world. Each pane would represent one (or sometimes more) of the categories of sources represented by the chapters of this book. Each would demand different skills (especially languages and cultural sensitivities), and would become a distinct project or project module. At the same time, all the modules together would make up a single large-scale enterprise, an integrated whole to be consulted for fully rounded answers to users' questions. PBW is now approaching the end of the Greek pane of the umbrella, with some contributions to others. At the same time it is seeking to encourage and facilitate a concerted attempt to complete the other panes. In this endeavour its researchers will be among the first and most avid readers of this excellent book. The progress of the project will be recorded on the PBW website, where it is also proposed in due course to maintain updated versions of the bibliographies in this volume. The URL is: http://www.pbw.kcl.ac.uk

# 2

# Pilgrims and Crusaders in Western Latin Sources

## JONATHAN RILEY-SMITH

### PILGRIMAGES AND CRUSADES TO THE EAST

THE YEAR 1025 COINCIDED WITH the recommencement of western pilgrimages to Palestine on a large scale after a hiatus caused by the Fatimid caliphate's persecution of Christians in Palestine from 1009 and the closing of the route through the Empire by the Greek government in 1017. In 1026 there was a pilgrimage, said to be of 700 persons, financed by the duke of Normandy and led by Richard, the abbot of St Vanne of Verdun, and his bishop. They were joined on the road by pilgrims from northern France and by a large party, mostly from Angoulême and led by Count William IV Taillefer but also including the magnate Eudes of Déols from near Paris. Thereafter there was hardly a year when we do not have evidence for pilgrims to Jerusalem; and there were certain periods when the stream became a flood. The year 1033 was believed to be the thousandth anniversary of Christ's crucifixion and throughout the decade, during which the shrines in Jerusalem were partially restored by the Byzantine emperor,[1] pilgrims from many parts of the west were converging on the city. The next major wave appears to have surged east in the 1050s. Then in 1064 there was a large pilgrimage, recruited in France and Germany and motivated by the belief that Good Friday 1065 fell on exactly the same day of the year as had the crucifixion. The German contingent, led by the bishop of Bamberg, accompanied by the archbishop of Mainz, the bishops of Utrecht and Regensburg, and the empress's chaplain, was estimated—probably grossly overestimated—to contain between 7,000 and 12,000 persons. In the 1070s passage across Asia Minor, now being overrun by nomadic Turks, must have become much more difficult, but the traffic does not seem to have lessened. It certainly increased from the middle of the 1080s, the best known pilgrimage being that of Count Robert I of Flanders in 1085.

---

[1] Martin Biddle, *The Tomb of Christ* (Stroud, 1999), 77–81.

*Proceedings of the British Academy* **132**, 5–21. © The British Academy 2007.

A popular route in the eleventh century was through Rome to southern Italy and then, after crossing the Adriatic from Bari, along the old imperial road, the via Egnatia, to Constantinople. But the conversion of Hungary made the land passage through central Europe more secure; pilgrims no longer had to take even the short Adriatic crossing. A third route ran through Dalmatia before joining the via Egnatia. These three roads to Constantinople—down Italy to Bari and across to Greece; by way of Hungary and Bulgaria; and through Dalmatia—were to be used by the armies of the First Crusade. From Constantinople most eleventh-century pilgrims seem to have taken the old imperial highway to the east. It ran to Antioch, from where they travelled south down the Syrian and Palestinian coasts to Jerusalem. The journey to the Holy Land could be made surprisingly quickly. In 1026 William Taillefer left Angoulême on 1 October and reached Jerusalem just over five months later, in the first week of the following March. Lampert of Hersfeld departed from Aschaffenburg in late September 1058 and was back almost a year later. Gunther of Bamberg left Jerusalem for home on 25 April 1065 and had reached Hungary by the time of his death on 23 July.[2]

After the conquest of Palestine by the First Crusade pilgrim traffic naturally grew and although many western pilgrims were now going directly to the east by sea, a substantial number still travelled by way of Constantinople, where, with much of Asia Minor under Turkish control, many of them hired ships for the rest of the journey. This was the route taken in 1172 by the pilgrimage of Henry the Lion, duke of Saxony. Henry was accompanied by perhaps as many as 1,500 persons: senior churchmen, nobles, knights, *ministeriales* and *servi*.[3]

The First Crusade, which swept eastwards in at least four waves, was in one sense the last great eleventh-century pilgrimage, but it also instituted a series of crusades, or war-pilgrimages, to the east: in 1107, 1108, 1122, 1128, 1139, 1147 (the Second Crusade), 1177, 1189 (the Third Crusade), 1197 and 1202 (the Fourth Crusade). In addition there were papal summonses, the effects of which have not yet been properly researched, in 1157, 1165, 1166, 1173 (probably), 1181 and 1184. Some of the minor crusades were transported the whole way by sea, but must have taken on water at Crete, Rhodes or Cyprus. The First Crusade and those of 1107, 1122, 1147, 1189 and 1202 definitely entered Greek territory. Meanwhile the military orders, or

---

[2] Jonathan Riley-Smith, *The First Crusaders* (Cambridge, 1997), 25–39.
[3] See Einar Joransson, 'The Palestine pilgrimage of Henry the Lion', in James Lea Cate and Eugene N. Anderson, eds., *Medieval and Historical Essays in Honor of James Westfall Thompson* (Chicago, 1938), 146–225.

at any rate the Hospital of St John of Jerusalem, had representatives in Constantinople.[4]

## PREVIOUS ATTEMPTS TO LIST INDIVIDUALS

The first edition of Professor Hans Mayer's *Bibliographie* itemises seventy-three books and articles on crusaders from localities or on families in the Low Countries, Germany, England, France, Italy and Scandinavia.[5] Of these the best known is Reinhold Röhricht's listing of German pilgrims and crusaders travelling to Palestine between 650 and 1291.[6] More titles, although harder to find, are indexed in Mayer's more selective bibliography, which was published in 1989.[7] Some attempts have also been made with respect to individual crusades: before 1204 the two that spring to mind are my own for the First and the 1107 Crusades[8] and Jean Longnon's for the Fourth.[9] I believe that Jonathan Phillips is now trying to do the same for the Second. But none of these could claim to be definitive.

## WESTERN SOURCES

Leaving aside the extensive body of vernacular literature, the western sources for crusaders and pilgrims can be divided into the two categories, often defined typologically as 'narrative or literary' and 'non-narrative and record', or, alternatively, 'library' and 'archive' sources.[10] But one should not distinguish these types too strictly, since examples which should fall into one category are often to be found in the other.

---

[4] See Jonathan Riley-Smith, *The Knights of St John in Jerusalem and Cyprus, c.1050–1310* (London, 1967), 359–60.

[5] Hans Eberhard Mayer, *Bibliographie zur Geschichte der Kreuzzüge* (Hanover, 1960), 116–19.

[6] Reinhold Röhricht, *Die Deutschen im Heiligen Lande* (Innsbrück, 1894).

[7] Hans Eberhard Mayer and Joyce McLellan, 'Select bibliography of the crusades', in Kenneth M. Setton, ed.-in-chief, *A History of the Crusades*, vol. 6 (Madison, 1989), 650–1.

[8] Riley-Smith, *The First Crusaders*, 196–246.

[9] Jean Longnon, *Les compagnons de Villehardouin* (Geneva, 1978).

[10] See Raoul Charles van Caenegem, *Guide to the Sources of Medieval History* (Amsterdam, 1978), 15–16.

**Library Sources**

(i)    There are many accounts of crusades or pilgrimages, some incorporated into chronicles and *gesta*, some independent.

(ii)   There are briefer references in annals and chronicles.

(iii)  There are family histories, the fashion for which developed in the twelfth century.

(iv)   There are letters, written not only by crusaders on the march, of course, but also by leading figures in the west, such as Ivo of Chartres, Bernard of Clairvaux and Peter the Venerable.

(v)    There are pilgrim itineraries.

(vi)   There is important hagiographical material.

There are fewer references to crusaders in western miracle collections than one might imagine—at least a trawl through the *Acta Sanctorum* proved to be fairly disappointing—but pilgrimage, and above all crusade, resulted in large numbers of relics being transferred to the west and these *translationes*, and the *miracula* associated with them, contain details of the individuals involved in relic-collecting in the east. For example, a contemporary account of the theft of an arm of St George from an Orthodox monastery in Syria during the First Crusade, and its eventual arrival at Anchin in Flanders, contains the names of five crusaders. Three, all chaplains in Count Robert of Flanders's household, are unknown and this source provides the only evidence for the fourth, Gerard of Buc the castellan of Lille, taking part in the expedition.[11]

Most of the accounts in this category have been published in reasonably good editions and there are translations of the eye-witness narratives of the major crusades (few more than adequate; none to be trusted) and of the pilgrim itineraries. There are, moreover, good commentaries on some of them[12] and useful guides to the material, particularly in Mayer's bibliographies. But it would never be enough to read only the authoritative edition of a narrative, because individual crusaders and pilgrims can often be found in variant readings. They have also made their way into later histories, the authors of which have used different manuscripts of the eye-witness accounts from those which have survived. Although one always has to bear in mind that names could be introduced at a later date for domestic or political reasons, much precious information can lie hidden in second-hand accounts of the First Crusade

---

[11] 'Narratio quomodo relliquiae martyris Georgii ad nos aquicinenses pervenerunt', *RHC Oc* 5. 248–52. For relics of the True Cross, see especially Anatole Frolow, *La relique de la Vraie Croix*, Archives de l'Orient chrétien 7 (Paris, 1961) and *Les reliquaires de la Vraie Croix*, Archives de l'Orient chrétien 8 (Paris, 1965).

[12] See especially Verena Epp, *Fulcher von Chartres* (Düsseldorf, 1990).

such as those of Guibert of Nogent or Baldric of Bourgeuil, in which the basic material, drawn from the *Gesta Francorum*, has been supplemented by the author's own knowledge or by traditions in the locality in which he lived, or, as in the case of Baldric, by local traditions in a region in which one of the manuscripts of his work was copied.

The difficulties faced in relation to narrative and hagiographical sources are well known and are common to Byzantinists and western historians. A particular problem, however, relates to family histories. Serious critical treatment of these has only recently begun.[13] They have obvious failings, including the authors' determination to present their ancestors or those of their patrons in the best possible light by making them crusaders when they were not. Assertions can sometimes be confirmed. The family of Arnold II of Ardres was maintaining a century later that he had taken part in the First Crusade and that his name was not to be found in the long lists of knights recorded in the epic, *La chanson d'Antioche*, because he had refused to bribe the author to include it. The family was probably right, at least in believing that Arnold had been a crusader, because a charter seems to show him to have been in the entourage of Count Robert of Flanders on an early stage of the march.[14] But in many cases we are at a loss to know whether family recollections are accurate or not.

### Archival Material

(i)    The continuous run of surviving papal registers begins only with Pope Innocent III, although these are very incomplete and there have been several large-scale projects aiming to provide comprehensive lists of all extant papal charters for the period 1198–1417.[15] For a hundred years, moreover, the *Pius-Stiftung für Papsturkunden*, one of those monumental nineteenth-century enterprises, has been publishing critical editions of all papal letters from before Innocent's accession in 1198.[16]

---

[13] See Léopold Genicot, *Les généalogies*, Typologie des sources du Moyen Âge occidental 15 (Turnhout, 1975); Georges Duby, 'French genealogical literature', in Cynthia Postan, tr., *The Chivalrous Society* (London, 1977), 149–57; Jean Dunbabin, 'Discovering a history for the French aristocracy', in Paul Magdalino, ed., *Perceptions of the Past in the Twelfth Century* (London, 1992), 1–14; Thomas N. Bisson, 'Princely nobility in an age of ambition', in Anne J. Duggan, ed., *Nobles and Nobility in Medieval Europe: concepts, origins, transformations* (Woodbridge, 2000), 101–13. Nicholas Paul, a research student of mine, is blazing a trail on this topic.

[14] See Riley-Smith, *The First Crusaders*, 2–3.

[15] See Caenegem, 256–7.

[16] See Caenegem, 213–14.

(ii)   The court and chancery records of secular governments become increasingly important from the later twelfth century, particularly with respect to England where they come into their own with the preparations for the Third Crusade.[17] The English ones are calendared, but the calendars are inaccurate and misleading. It is essential to use them only as guides to the originals, which must be read.

(iii)   There are regional and local ecclesiastical *acta*. By the late twelfth century diocesan materials are becoming more frequent although the lines of episcopal registers only get going in the thirteenth century. There are a few lists of crusaders, often compiled with the purpose of getting laggards to fulfil their vows, such as those drawn up in England in the later twelfth century, although there is no evidence that these men ever went.[18]

(iv)   *Rotuli mortuorum*, necrologies and obit lists sometimes contain references to the deaths of benefactors on the march and to gifts made by crusaders and pilgrims on their return.

(v)   Crusaders' testaments, drawn up both in the east and in the west, are to be found incorporated into narrative accounts or in cartularies.

(vi)   Then there are charters. I use the word in a broad sense to include *cartae* proper and *notitiae*, and everything in between.[19] Although the contribution charters can make declines during the twelfth century, at the time of the First Crusade they are very important and they remain significant for the Fourth. Charters relate mostly to endowments for prayer made before departure and on return or to arrangements made to finance participation, but they sometimes contain unusual details relating to the course of crusades. Peter Jordan of Châtillon fell ill at Antioch, probably during the epidemic of typhoid or malaria which broke out in July 1098, and in this state he was received and tonsured by a monk 'in the name and to the honour of God and St Paul'. Recovering his health, he forgot his profession and continued with his crusade, but a few days after he had got home to France he began to feel ill again and, believing the return of illness to be a sign from God, he sent for monks of the abbey of Cormery, which seems to have been the nearest to him dedicated to St Paul, and asked to be received into their community. One result was the charter recording Peter Jordan's experiences in the east, his admission and his entry gift. At Antioch he must have been professed into the

[17] For England and the crusades, see Simon Lloyd, *English Society and the Crusade 1216–1307* (Oxford, 1988); Christopher Tyerman, *England and the Crusades 1095–1588* (Chicago, 1988).
[18] See Jonathan Riley-Smith, *What were the Crusades?* (3rd edn., Basingstoke, 2002), 69.
[19] See Marcus Bull, 'The diplomatic of the First Crusade', in Jonathan Phillips, ed., *The First Crusade. Origins and impact* (Manchester, 1997), 35–54.

Greek monastery of St Paul. This is the only evidence after the ninth century for the continuing existence of that famous community.[20]

But the usefulness of charters varies from region to region. Coverage is not uniform. There has been destruction, of course, but local factors, including scribal practices, also play a part. The names of many more first crusaders from the Limousin survive than from most other regions of France. But a comparison of recruitment among the greater lords in Limousin with that in other regions does not suggest that the nobles of Limousin were much more enthusiastic than those elsewhere. Champagne also contributed a respectable body of nobles and the reason we know the names of many more ordinary crusading knights from Limousin may simply be that Champagne was a rich region, the lords of which could afford to subsidise their followers, whereas the knights of Limousin, living in a poor one, had to dispose of property to finance themselves, generating the charters which provide the evidence for their participation. The knight Raymond of Curemonte, for example, going in the viscount of Turenne's party, raised cash for the journey on his own account in a pledge authorised by the viscount himself, who promised to make sure that its terms were not infringed by Raymond's relations. The absence of material from Normandy, from where we know a large force left for the east in 1096, may be because Duke Robert II, who had borrowed a huge sum of money from his brother King William II of England, could subsidise his followers. And a similar ability to subsidise on the part of Raymond IV of St Gilles may account for relatively little information surviving from Languedoc.

The scarcity of early evidence relating to crusaders in England and Germany may also be a consequence of scribal conventions which favoured brief statements of legal fact, eschewing references to motives, as opposed to the more expansive and informative style employed in much of France, Lorraine and imperial Burgundy, even if not in all of it. It was pointed out long ago by Professor Giles Constable that a marked increase of grants around 1100 to the Cluniac house of Domène in Burgundy and to the cathedral of Grenoble may have been linked to the needs of the crusade, but the Domène cartulary contains few references to it and there is only one relevant charter in that of Grenoble.[21] The reasons for the development throughout the French-speaking lands from the mid-eleventh century of what Dominique Barthélemy has called *narrativité* are debatable, but *narrativité* certainly helps

---

[20] Jean-Jacques Bourassé, ed., *Cartulaire de Cormery* (Tours, 1861), 104. For the monastery of St Paul in Antioch, see Claude Cahen, *La Syrie du nord à l'époque des croisades et la principauté franque d'Antioche* (Paris, 1940), 334, n. 19.

[21] See Riley-Smith, *The First Crusaders*, 3–4.

us, because so many details are provided by it. In an age when charter-
writers were looking for striking events to jog the memories of those called
to witness the authenticity of a deed years later, the crusade, or the part taken
in it by a local worthy, could be used as a reference point even for those who
were not involved.[22] Of the 658 individuals I have identified as certain or
probable recruits for the First Crusade, 241, or nearly 37%, are known only
from charters.[23]

But charters are especially hard to interpret. By the time they reach us
many of them are shadows of their former selves, mutilated or corrupted,
and the issue of authenticity arises time and time again. Many of them were
edited in the nineteenth century by local history societies and the standard of
editing is variable. And the number of them potentially relevant to crusade
or pilgrimage is vast. When I researched the reasons why men and women
were recruited for the First Crusade I read over seven hundred cartularies
and collections of documents. I concentrated on those relating to France
and England, but I made substantial inroads into the German, Spanish and
Italian charter collections as well. Even so I do not think I had even covered
half the available material when I decided to start writing on the basis of
what I had to hand; otherwise I could never see myself finishing. And I was
using only edited documents: I had not begun to make use of the many
cartularies which are still unpublished.

## RESEARCHING INDIVIDUALS

Collecting the names of men and women from whatever sources has to be
only the start of a process of research. It is often hard to date the act of pilgrimage or crusade precisely, because in many cartularies the dating clauses
were omitted when the charters were copied and in necrologies and obit lists
the date given is always the day, never the year. And identification can be
exceptionally difficult. Much of the information that comes to hand turns out
to be unusable. Many individuals, for example, are referred to only by their
Christian names and it is not often that another closely related charter
enables one to attach a more informative toponym. And toponyms themselves pose problems. It is all too easy to suppose that one is faced by the
member of a family of lords when in fact the toponym concerned simply
indicates a place of residence. This is not to suggest that locations are
unimportant; they can in fact be vital, even though it can be very hard to

---

[22] Bull, 'The diplomatic', 36–44.
[23] Riley-Smith, *The First Crusaders*, 197–232.

distinguish between, say, all the Rocheforts and Châteauneufs in France. There can also be variety in the use made of toponyms with reference to the same individual: the notorious first crusader Thomas of Marle, for example, can also be found called Thomas of Coucy and Thomas of La Fère. And there is the use of the same forenames by successive or alternate generations. It follows that it is imperative that one should at least try to create a pedigree for each man or woman, together with the kindred most closely associated, so that he or she can be approximately dated. Identification can often only be established after a long process of detailed, time-consuming and very boring research into family, place of residence and career, but I have come to believe that without the additional material a name alone, followed by a list of references, is even less useful to the historian than a butterfly pinned to a board is to a collector. It is only when individuals are placed in the context of kindred, society and region that sense can be made of them. And knowledge of background can be rewarding in all sorts of unexpected ways. How far, for example, was the Greeks' surprisingly rough treatment of Hugh of Vermandois on the First Crusade a result of their knowledge that his mother was Anna of Kiev?

It is not always easy, moreover, to establish whether we are faced by a crusader or a pilgrim, since in many charters the man or woman is referred to non-committally as *Hierosolymam pergens* or *petens* or *tendens* or *proficiscens* or *iturus*. In the past I assumed that when, for instance, the distinctly non-military verb *ambulare* was used of the journey to Jerusalem, or the motive was given as *orationis gratia*, the reference was probably to a pilgrim. This was helpful with respect to the First Crusade, but the twelfth century was marked by occasions on which pilgrims, having fulfilled their vows, took up arms for the rest of their stay in Palestine, and this led to ambivalent language being used of them.[24] In many charters the march is described by the neutral words *iter* or *via*, which had long histories in the language of pilgrimage. Faced by a record such as that of a gift by Astanove II of Fézensac in *c*.1098 which was made 'on the day of his *peregrinatio* when he took the *iter* to Jerusalem' and bereft of any other evidence, one can say only that Astanove was probably a crusader.[25] It is not often that the addition of a defining phrase clarifies the issue, as in a charter announcing how Quino son of Dodo planned to join the 'Jerusalem journey undertaken with force

[24] Jonathan Riley-Smith, 'An army on pilgrimage', to be published in proceedings of a conference held in Huesca in 1999.
[25] C. Lacave La Plagne Barris, ed., *Cartulaires du chapitre de l'église métropolitaine Sainte-Marie d'Auch* (Paris and Auch, 1899), 57.

of arms'.[26] Of course from the point of view of the Prosopography of the Byzantine World why men or women were within the bounds of the Byzantine empire is less important than the fact that they *were* there. But it is precisely on the question of their presence that so many charters let us down. Unless the scribe was good enough to let us know or a narrative account provides us with more material the identification of a crusader in a charter is often no evidence that he joined a campaign, only that he intended to do so. I am not certain that even half the 241 first crusaders I found referred to only in charters actually left home.

# BIBLIOGRAPHY

## WESTERN SOURCES IN LATIN

### LIBRARY SOURCES

#### The More Important Accounts of Crusades or Pilgrimages

There is hardly a narrative source of the twelfth century which does not make some reference to crusades and pilgrimages to the east and in this bibliography I will list only the more important sources. A way into other references to crusades is to follow those in Reinhold Röhricht, *Geschichte des Königreichs Jerusalem 1100–1291* (Innsbruck, 1898), because Röhricht seems to have ploughed his way through all available chronicles and annals searching for evidence.

*1. Accounts of Pilgrimages*
Pilgrimages from western Europe in the early eleventh century are referred to by, among others, Adhémar of Chabannes, *Chronicon*, ed. Jules Chavanon (Paris, 1897), and Ralph Glaber, *Historiarum libri quinque*, ed. and tr. John France (Oxford, 1989). The great German pilgrimage of 1064 is described in the *Annales altahenses maiores*, ed. Edmund L.B. Ab Oefele, MGHS in usum scholarum (Hanover, 1891), and by Lampert of Hersfeld, *Opera*, ed. Oswald Holder-Egger, MGHS in usum scholarum (Hanover and Leipzig, 1894), who went on it.

Pilgrimage itineraries of the twelfth century have been collected and translated by John Wilkinson, *Jerusalem Pilgrimage 1099–1185*, Hakluyt Society (London, 1988). The important accounts of Saewulf, John of Würzburg and Theoderic have been re-edited in *Peregrinationes tres*, ed. Robert B.C. Huygens, CCCM 139 (Turnhout, 1994).

A probable eye-witness account of the pilgrimage of Henry the Lion in 1172 was written by Arnold of Lübeck, *Chronica Slavorum*, ed. Johann M. Lappenberg, MGHS in usum scholarum (Hanover, 1868), 10–31.

---

[26] André Lesort, ed., *Chroniques et chartes de l'abbaye de Saint-Mihiel*, Mettensia 6 (Paris, 1909–12), 191.

## 2. Accounts of the First Crusade

Eye-witness accounts are:

Caffaro di Caschifellone, 'De liberatione civitatum orientis', ed. Luigi T. Belgrano, *Annali genovesi* 1, Fonti per la storia d'Italia 11 (Genoa, 1890), 3–75

Ekkehard of Aura, 'Hierosolymita', *RHC Oc* 5, 1–40

Fulcher of Chartres, *Historia Hierosolymitana*, ed. Heinrich Hagenmeyer (Heidelberg, 1913); tr. Frances R. Ryan in Harold S. Fink, ed., *A History of the Expedition to Jerusalem 1095–1127* (Knoxville, 1969)

*Gesta Francorum et aliorum Hierosolimitanorum*, ed. and tr. Rosalind M.T. Hill (London, 1962)

Peter Tudebode, *Historia de Hierosolymitano itinere*, ed. John H. and Laurita L. Hill (Paris, 1977); variant ms. in *RHC Oc* 3, tr. John H. and Laurita L. Hill (Philadelphia, 1974)

Raymond of Aguilers, *Liber*, ed. John H. and Laurita L. Hill (Paris, 1969); variant ms. in *RHC Oc* 3, tr. John H. and Laurita L. Hill (Philadelphia, 1968)

Almost as good, because he used first-class sources, is Albert of Aachen, 'Historia Hierosolymitana', *RHC Oc* 4, 265–713. A new edition and translation by Susan Edgington is in preparation for Oxford Medieval Texts.

Important contemporary and theologised narratives are:

Baldric of Bourgueil, bishop of Dol, 'Historia Jerosolimitana', *RHC Oc* 4, 1–111

Guibert of Nogent, *Dei gesta per Francos*, ed. Robert B.C. Huygens, CCCM 127a (Turnhout, 1996)

Ralph of Caen, 'Gesta Tancredi', *RHC Oc* 3, 587–716

Robert of Rheims, 'Historia Iherosolimitana', *RHC Oc* 3, 721–882

See also:

Bartolf of Nangis, 'Gesta Francorum Iherusalem expugnantium', *RHC Oc* 3, 487–543

Gilo of Paris, *Historia vie Hierosolymitane*, ed. and tr. Christopher W. Grocock and J. Elizabeth Siberry, Oxford Medieval Texts (Oxford, 1997)

'Historia peregrinorum euntium Jerusolymam', *RHC Oc* 3, 169–229

'Narratio floriacensis de captis Antiochia et Hierosolyma et obsesso Dyrrachio', *RHC Oc* 5, 356–62

'Versus de viris illustribus dioecesis tarvanensis in sacra fuere expeditione', ed. Edmond Martène and Ursin Durand, *Veterum scriptorum . . . amplissima collectio* 5 (Paris, 1729), col. 540

## 3. Accounts of the Second Crusade

The following are eye-witness narratives:

Raol, *De expugnatione lyxbonensi*, ed. and tr. Charles W. David (New York, 1936); repr. with foreword by Jonathan Phillips (New York, 2001). Raol's identity was established by Harold Livermore, 'The "Conquest of Lisbon" and its author', *Portuguese Studies* 6 (1990), 1–16

Eudes of Deuil, *De profectione Ludovici VII in orientem*, ed. and tr. Virginia G. Berry (New York, 1948)

Otto of Freising, *Chronica*, ed. Adolf Hofmeister, MGHS in usum scholarum (Hanover and Leipzig, 1912)

## 4. Accounts of the Third Crusade

The more important Latin narratives are:

'Historia de expeditione Friderici imperatoris', ed. Anton Chroust, *Quellen zur Geschichte des Kreuzzuges Kaiser Friedrichs I*, MGHS rer. Germ n.s. 5 (Berlin, 1928), 1–115

'Historia peregrinorum', ed. Anton Chroust, *Quellen zur Geschichte des Kreuzzuges Kaiser Friedrichs I*, MGHS rer. Germ n.s. 5 (Berlin, 1928), 116–72

*Itinerarium peregrinorum et gesta regis Ricardi*, ed. William Stubbs, *Chronicles and Memorials of the Reign of Richard I*, vol. 1, Rolls Series 38 (London, 1864), which is linked to the eye-witness Anglo-Norman doggerel of Ambroise.

Ralph of Diceto, *Opera historica*, ed. William Stubbs, 2 vols., Rolls Series 68 (London, 1876)

Rigord, *Gesta Philippi Augusti*, ed. H. François Delaborde, *Oeuvres de Rigord et Guillaume le Breton*, vol. 1 (Paris, 1882)

Roger of Howden, *Chronica*, ed. William Stubbs, 4 vols., Rolls Series 51 (London, 1868–71). Roger Howden was definitely present in Palestine. The passages relating to the crusade in the *Gesta regis Henrici secundi*, ed. William Stubbs, 2 vols., Rolls Series 49 (London, 1867), may well have been his more immediate account of events.

## 5. Accounts of the Fourth Crusade

The more important Latin narratives are:

Gunther of Pairis, *Hystoria constantinopolitana*, ed. Peter Orth, Spolia Berolinensia 5 (Hildesheim and Zürich, 1994); tr. Alfred J. Andrea, *The Capture of Constantinople* (Philadelphia, 1997); and the three anonymous narratives, the 'Devastatio constantinopolitana' and those relating to the participation of the bishops of Halberstadt and Soissons. All three have been ed. and tr. by Alfred J. Andrea in *Contemporary Sources for the Fourth Crusade*, The Medieval Mediterranean 29 (Leiden, 2000).

## 6. Family Histories

Among those of interest are:

'Chronica de gestis consulum andegavorum', ed. Louis Halphen and René Poupardin, *Chroniques des comtes d'Anjou et des seigneurs d'Amboise* (Paris, 1913), 25–73

'Gesta ambaziensium dominorum', ed. Louis Halphen and René Poupardin, *Chroniques des comtes d'Anjou et des seigneurs d'Amboise* (Paris, 1913), 74–132

Geoffrey of Vigeois (Geoffrey of Brueil), 'Chronica', ed. Philippe Labbé, *Novae bibliothecae manuscriptorum librorum* 2 (Paris, 1657), 279–329; also ed. *RHGF* 10. 267–8; 11. 288–9; 12. 421–51; 18. 211–23

Gislebert of Mons, *Chronicon hanoniense*, ed. Léon Vanderkindere, *La Chronique de Gislebert de Mons* (Brussels, 1904)

Lambert of Ardres, 'Historia comitum ghisnensium', MGHS 24, 557–642

Orderic Vitalis, *Historia aecclesiastica*, ed. and tr. Marjorie Chibnall, 6 vols. (Oxford, 1969–79)

## 7. Letters

For the First Crusade, see:

*Die Kreuzzugsbriefe aus den Jahren 1088–1100*, ed. Heinrich Hagenmeyer (Innsbruck, 1901)

For the Fourth Crusade, see:

Hugh of St Pol, 'Letter': variants in R. Pokorny, 'Zwei unedierte Briefe aus der Frühzeit des lateinischen Kaiserreichs von Konstantinopel', *Byz* 55 (1985), 204 and 'Annales colonienses maximi', MGHS 17, 813; tr. Alfred J. Andrea in *Contemporary Sources for the Fourth Crusade*, The Medieval Mediterranean 29 (Leiden, 2000), 186–201

Baldwin of Flanders in *De Oorkonden der graven van Vlaanderen*, ed. Walter Prevenier, vol. 2 (Brussels, 1964), 564–77

Letters from crusaders in Palestine are to be found calendared in *Regesta Regni Hierosolymitani 1097–1291*, comp. Reinhold Röhricht (Innsbruck, 1893), *Additamentum* (Innsbruck, 1904).

## 8. Hagiographical Material and Relics

*Acta Sanctorum quotquot toto orbe coluntur*, ed. Société des Bollandistes, 70 vols. so far (Antwerp, Brussels, Tongerloe, 1643–)

I have found the following to be useful with regard to the First Crusade:

'De reliquiis sanctissimi crucis et dominici sepulchri Scaphusam allatis', *RHC Oc* 5, 335–9

'Historia de translatione sanctorum magni Nicolai … ejusdem avunculi, alterius Nicolai, Theodorique … de civitate mirea in monasterium S. Nicolai de Littore Venetiarum', *RHC Oc* 5, 253–92

'Miracula S.Nicolai conscripta a monacho beccensi', ed. Bollandists, *Catalogus codicum hagiographicorum latinorum antiquiorum saeculo XVI qui asservantur in Bibliotheca nationali parisiensi*, vol. 2 (Brussels, 1890)

'Narratio quomodo relliquiae martyris Georgii ad nos aquicinenses pervenerunt', *RHC Oc* 5, 248–52

'Pancharta caduniensis seu Historia sancti sudarii Jesu Christi', *RHC Oc* 5, 299–301

'Passiones Beati Thiemonis', *RHC Oc* 5, 203–23

'Qualiter reliquiae B.Nicolai episcopi et confessoris ad Lotharingiae villam, quae Portus nominatur, delatae sunt', *RHC Oc* 5, 293–4

'Qualiter tabula S.Basili continens in se magnam dominici ligni portionem Cluniacum delata fuerit, tempore Pontii abbatis', *RHC Oc* 5, 295–8

'Tractatus de reliquiis S.Stephani Cluniacum delatis', *RHC Oc* 5, 317–20

# ARCHIVAL MATERIAL

## Papal Letters

A guide to papal correspondence is:

*Regesta pontificum romanorum*, comp. Philipp Jaffé, 2nd edn. Wilhelm Wattenbach, Samuel Löwenfeld *et al.*, 2 vols. (Leipzig, 1885–8)

Letters of individual popes are collected in the volumes of the Patrologiae cursus completus. Series latina, comp. Jacques P. Migne, 221 vols. and 4 vols. of indexes (Paris, 1841–64).

Others are to be found in:

*Acta pontificum romanorum inedita*, ed. Julius von Pflugk-Harttung, 3 vols. (Tübingen and Stuttgart, 1881–6)

Calixtus II, *Bullaire*, ed. Ulysse Robert, 2 vols. (Paris, 1891)

Eugenius III, 'Quantum praedecessores', ed. Peter Rassow, *Neues Archiv* 45 (1924), 302–5

Innocent III, *Register*, ed. Othmar Hageneder *et al.*: vols. 1–7 (Graz, 1964–) are relevant.

*Papsturkunden für Kirchen im Heiligen Lande*, ed. Rudolf Hiestand, *Vorarbeiten zum Oriens Pontificius* 3 (Göttingen, 1985)

*Papsturkunden für Templer und Johanniter*, ed. Rudolf Hiestand, 2 vols., *Vorarbeiten zum Oriens Pontificius* 1–2 (Göttingen, 1972–84)

'Papsturkunden in Deutschland', ed. Albert Brackmann, *Nachrichten von der Gesellschaft der Wissenschaften zu Göttingen. Phil.-hist. Kl.* (1902), 193–223; (1904), 94–138

*Papsturkunden in Portugal*, ed. Carl Erdmann, *Abhandlungen der philologisch-historischen Klasse der Akademie der Wissenschaften zu Göttingen*, n.s. 20.3 (Berlin, 1927)

*Papsturkunden in England*, ed. Walther Holtzmann, 3 vols., *Abhandlungen der philologisch-historischen Klasse der Akademie der Wissenschaften zu Göttingen*, n.s. 25; 3rd ser. 14, 33 (Berlin and Göttingen, 1930–52)

'Papsturkunden in Florenz', ed. Wilhelm Wiederhold, *Nachrichten von der Gesellschaft der Wissenschaften zu Göttingen. Phil.-hist. Kl.* (1901), 306–25

*Papsturkunden in Frankreich*, ed. Wilhelm Wiederhold, Hermann Meinert, Johannes Ramackers and Dietrich Lohrman, 11 vols., *Nachrichten von der Gesellschaft der Wissenschaften zu Göttingen. Phil.-hist. Kl.*, Beihefte 1906–7, 1910, 1913 and *Abhandlungen der philologisch-historischen Klasse der Akademie der Wissenschaften zu Göttingen*, 3rd ser. 21, 23, 27, 35, 41, 95 (Berlin and Göttingen, 1906–76)

*Papsturkunden in den Niederlanden*, ed. Johannes Ramackers, *Abhandlungen der philologisch-historischen Klasse der Akademie der Wissenschaften zu Göttingen*, 3rd ser. 8–9 (Berlin, 1933–4)

'Papsturkunden in Italien', ed. Paul Kehr, *Nachrichten von der Gesellschaft der Wissenschaften zu Göttingen. Phil.-hist. Kl.* (1896), 277–308, 357; (1897), 175–216, 223–33, 349–89; (1898), 6–97, 237–334, 349–96; (1899), 197–249, 251–337; (1900), 1–75, 111–269, 286–344, 360–436; (1901), 57–115, 117–70, 196–228, 239–71; (1902), 67–167, 169–92, 393–558; (1903), 1–161, 505–641; (1904), 139–203; (1905), 321–80; (1908), 223–304; (1909), 435–517; (1910), 229–88; (1911), 267–335; (1912), 321–83, 414–80; (1924), 156–93

*Papsturkunden in Spanien*, ed. Paul F. Kehr, 2 vols. *Abhandlungen der philologisch-historischen Klasse der Akademie der Wissenschaften zu Göttingen*, n.s. 18.2, 22.1 (Berlin, 1926–8)

*Regesta pontificum romanorum:*
  *Germania pontificia*, ed. Albert Brackmann *et al.*, 7 vols. (Berlin and Göttingen, 1911–87)
  *Italia pontificia*, ed. Paul F. Kehr *et al.*, 10 vols. (Berlin and Zürich, 1906–75)

## Secular Court and Chancery Records

Here is a selection of useful material:
*Actes des comtes de Flandre 1071–1128*, ed. Fernand Vercauteren (Brussels, 1938)
Conrad III, *Urkunden*, ed. Friedrich Hausmann, MGH. *Die Urkunden der deutschen Könige und Kaiser* 9 (Vienna, Cologne, and Graz, 1969)
*Curia Regis Rolls, 1194–5*, ed. Frederic W. Maitland (London, 1891)
*The Great Rolls of the Pipe* (London, 1844–)
*I Libri Iurium della Repubblica di Genova*, ed. Dino Puncuh, Antonella Rovere *et al.*, 8 vols. so far, Pubblicazioni degli Archivi di Stato, Fonti 12 (Rome, 1992–)
Louis VI, *Recueil des actes de Louis VI*, ed. Jean Dufour, 4 vols., Chartes et diplômes relatifs à l'histoire de France (Paris, 1992–4)
Louis VII, 'Epistolarum regis Ludovici et variorum ad eum volumen', *RHGF* 16 (1878)
Philip I, *Recueil des actes de Philippe I$^{er}$, roi de France (1059–1108)*, ed. Maurice Prou, Chartes et diplômes relatifs à l'histoire de France (Paris, 1908)
Philip II, *Recueil des actes de Philippe Auguste*, ed. Henri-François Delaborde, Charles Petit-Dutaillis, Jacques Boussard and Michel Nortier, 4 vols., Chartes et diplômes relatifs à l'histoire de France (Paris, 1916–79)
*Regesta regum Anglo-Normannorum 1066–1154*, ed. Henry William Carless Davis *et al.*, 5 vols. (Oxford, 1913–69)
*Rotuli Curiae Regis*, ed. Francis Palgrave (London, 1835)
*Urkunden zur älteren Handels- und Staatsgeschichte der Republik Venedig*, ed. Gottlieb Lukas Friedrich Tafel and Georg Martin Thomas, 3 vols., Fontes Rerum Austriacarum. 2 Abt. Diplomataria et acta 12–14 (Vienna, 1856–7)

The notarial registers recording commerce are full of information. Not much from Venice survives before 1200, but see:
'Le Carte del mille e del millecento che si conservano nel R. Archivio notarile di Venezia', ed. Antonio Baracchi and Rinaldo Fulin, *Archivio veneto* 6 (1873), 293–307; 7 (1874), 80–98, 352–69; 8 (1874), 134–53; 9 (1875), 99–115; 10 (1875), 332–51; 20 (1880), 51–80, 314–30; 21 (1881), 106–20; 22 (1881), 313–32
*Documenti del commercio veneziano nei secoli XI–XIII*, ed. Raimondo Morozzo della Rocca and Antonino Lombardo, 2 vols., Regesta Chartarum Italiae 28–9 (Rome and Turin, 1940)
*Nuovi doumenti del commercio veneto dei secoli XI–XIII*, Deputazione di storia patria per le Venezie: Monumenti storici n.s. 7 (Venice, 1953)

In Genoa on the other hand, a wealth of notarial material survives. It is being edited on behalf of the R. Deputazione di storia patria per la Liguria in the series Notai liguri del secolo XII e XIII (Genoa, 1938 to the present).

## Ecclesiastical Acta

Episcopal registers do not begin until outside the period. Some early English cases are listed in *Select Cases from the Ecclesiastical Courts of the Province of Canterbury, c.1200–1301*, ed. Norma Adams and Charles Donahue (London, 1981).

There are, however, disparate collections, which can mostly be found listed under towns in the guides to charter collections. A few are given here, as examples:

### Le Mans

*Actus pontificum Cenomannis in urbe degentium*, ed. Gustave and Ambroise Ledru, Archives historiques du Maine 2 (Le Mans, 1901)

*Cartulaire de l'évêché du Mans*, ed. Bertrand de Broussillon, 2 vols., Archives historiques du Maine 1, 9 (Le Mans, 1900–8)

*Chartularium insignis ecclesiae cenomanensis quod dicitur Liber albus capituli*, ed. René Jean François Lottin, Institut des provinces de France, *Mémoires*, 2nd ser., 2 (Paris, 1869)

### Genoa

*Liber privilegiorum ecclesiae ianuensis*, ed. Dino Puncuh, Fonte e studi di storia ecclesiastica 1 (Genoa, 1962)

## Rotuli Mortuorum, Necrologies and Obit Lists

See Nicolas Huyghebaert, *Les documents nécrologiques*, Typologie des sources du Moyen Âge occidental (Turnhout, 1972)

The only attempts I know to catalogue the necrologies of countries systematically are:
Léopold Delisle, *Rouleux des morts du IX^e au XV^e siècle* (Paris, 1886)
*Inventaire des obituaires belges*, publ. Commission royale d'histoire (Brussels, 1899)

An ambitious scheme in France, although proceeding very slowly, is the series *Obituaires*, published by the Recueil des historiens de France (Paris, 1902–). Among the provinces so far treated are Lyon, Rodez and Sens. But many necrologies and obituaries are being published locally in France, as is the case elsewhere, for instance in Italy and Germany.

## Charters

There is as yet no complete guide to cartularies and collections of documents, not even to printed ones and one still has to turn to unreliable works such as Laurent Henri Cottineau, *Répertoire topo-bibliographie des abbayes et prieurés*, 3 vols. (Farnborough, 1935–7, 1970)

As far as I can understand it there is no general guide to the rich collections in Italy.

The situation in France is somewhat better. The standard guide is:
Henri Stein, *Bibliographie générale des cartulaires français ou relatifs à l'histoire de France* (Paris, 1907)

supplemented by:

Ferdinand Lot *et al.*, 'Liste des cartulaires et recueils contenant des pièces antérieures à l'an 1000', *Bulletin Du Cange* 15 (1940)

—— 'Liste des cartulaires et recueils contenant des pièces antérieures à l'an 1100', *Bulletin Du Cange* 22 (1952)

Even more useful when completed will be:

Jacqueline Le Braz, *Répertoire de cartulaires de l'ancienne France*, which is appearing diocese by diocese.

*Abbayes et prieurés de l'ancienne France. Recueil historique des archevêqués, abbayes et prieurés*, which is appearing province by province. This remarkable project was begun in 1726 by Dom Beaunier. Fourteen vols. have been published so far of a new edition (1905–).

For Germany:

*Deutschlands Geschichtsquellen im Mittelalter. Die Zeit der Sachsen und Salier,* ed. Wilhelm Wattenbach, Robert Holtzmann and Franz-Joseph Schmale, 5 vols. so far (Darmstadt, 1967–), parts of which cover England and Italy into the early twelfth century as well as Germany.

For Iberia:

*Codiphis. Catálogo de colecciones diplomáticas hispano-lusas de época medieval*, comp. José Angel García de Cortezar, José Antonio Munita and Luis Javier Fortún, 2 vols. (Santander, 1999)

An introduction to English cartularies is:

Godfrey Rupert Carless Davis, *Medieval Cartularies of Great Britain. A short catalogue* (London, 1958)

# 3

# Crusader Sources from the Near East (1099–1204)

## PETER EDBURY

LITERARY EVIDENCE COMPOSED IN LATIN OR FRENCH in the principalities founded by the crusaders in the Levant can and does contribute significantly to our knowledge of the Byzantine world. It is of course a major source for the prosopography of the Latin east itself, and, to a more limited extent, can be utilised in research into Byzantine prosopography.

As is well known, at the very end of the eleventh century and in the early years of the twelfth, western Europeans took control of substantial areas of the Near East, including large tracts of territory that had been ruled by the Byzantines until after 1071. The crusaders were to hold Antioch and the surrounding area of northern Syria continuously from 1098 until 1268. They occupied Edessa until 1144 and a wide area to the north of Antioch including Marash (Germanikeia)[1] and the plain of Cilicia until the late 1130s or the 1140s. Most of this territory they had won from the Turks who themselves had only acquired it a few years before the First Crusade. In some places, however, the crusaders supplanted Armenians who had taken control in the aftermath of Mantzikert and the collapse of Byzantine authority in eastern Anatolia in the 1070s. Elsewhere, notably at Latakia (Laodikeia), the crusaders ousted Byzantine garrisons. Much later, in 1191, the crusaders were to take control of Cyprus, a Byzantine province where a few years earlier a member of the imperial family, Isaac Doukas Komnenos, had seized power in defiance of the authorities in Constantinople.

But even those areas further south that came under crusader rule and that had not been in Byzantine hands since the Arab conquests of the seventh century contained a substantial Orthodox population. Traditionally the emperors had posed as protectors of the Christian communities in the Holy Land, and so, for instance, in the mid-eleventh century Constantine IX Monomachos had contributed to the rebuilding of the Holy Sepulchre. This

---

[1] For Marash, see G. Beech, 'The crusader lordship of Marash in Armenia Cilicia, 1104–1149', *Viator* 27 (1996), 35–52.

*Proceedings of the British Academy* **132**, 23–38. © The British Academy 2007.

concern was to continue after the founding of the Kingdom of Jerusalem, as is shown for example by the bilingual Latin and Greek inscriptions from the 1160s that record Manuel I Komnenos's sponsorship of the new mosaic work adorning the Church of the Nativity in Bethlehem.[2]

So what sort of evidence do we have? There are no twelfth-century letter collections from the Latin east, but nevertheless a number of letters written in the east have survived. Those relating to the period of the First Crusade were assembled and published in 1901 by Heinrich Hagenmeyer, and among the letters in this collection are some that contain invaluable contemporary evidence for relations between the crusaders and Alexios Komnenos.[3] A number of letters from prominent figures in the east to King Louis VII of France (1137–80) were included in the collection made at the time by his chancellor, Hugh of Campo-Florido, and these were published in volume 16 of Bouquet's *Recueil des historiens des Gaules et de la France*. These letters contain important information for the period from the mid-1150s to the late 1160s, but Byzantium is only referred to obliquely.[4] Other letters survive as singletons, sometimes because they were copied into chronicles or other writings, and occasionally they refer to Byzantine affairs. Thus for example, in about 1176 Patriarch Aimery of Antioch wrote to Hugh Eteriano requesting information about the history, theology and spirituality of the Orthodox church,[5] and, in a letter evidently dating to 1189, Queen Sibylla, the wife of Guy of Lusignan, complained to Frederick Barbarossa of Isaac II Angelos's alliance with Saladin.[6]

More plentiful are charters and other legal documents. Inevitably the survival of such material is patchy. Venice, Genoa, Pisa and Amalfi have all preserved charters conferring commercial privileges on their nationals,[7] while Marseilles has a splendid collection of mostly forged charters supposedly

---

[2] For the text, mentioning Ephraim the mosaicist, Manuel, King Amaury and Ralph, the Latin bishop of Bethlehem, see D. Pringle, *The Churches of the Crusader Kingdom: a corpus* (Cambridge, 1993–), vol. 1, 154.

[3] H. Hagenmeyer, ed., *Die Kreuzzugsbriefe aus den Jahren 1088–1100* (Innsbruck, 1901). See also P. Riant, 'Inventaire critique des lettres historiques des croisades', *Archives de l'Orient latin* 1 (1881), nos. 90, 91, 107, 109, 122, 125.

[4] 'Ludovici VII et variorum ad eum epistolae', *RHGF* 16, 1–170.

[5] E. Martène and U. Durand, eds., *Thesaurus novus anecdotorum*, 5 vols. (Paris, 1717), vol. 1, 479–81. See B. Hamilton, 'Aimery of Limoges, Latin patriarch of Antioch (*c*.1142–*c*.1196) and the unity of the churches', in K. Ciggaar and H. Teule, eds., *East and West in the Crusader States: context, contacts, confrontations*, vol. 2, Orientalia Lovaniensia Analecta 92 (Leuven, 1999), 1–12.

[6] *RRH* 681.

[7] For editions, see M.L. Favreau-Lilie, *Die Italiener im Heiligen Land vom ersten Kreuzzug bis zum Tode Heinrichs von Champagne (1098–1197)* (Amsterdam, 1989). See also Michel Balard's contribution to this volume.

relating to the twelfth century. (In reality they were concocted in the mid-thirteenth.)[8] Both the Hospitallers and the Teutonic Knights—but not the Templars—managed to transmit a significant part of their archives to posterity.[9] From Jerusalem we have cartularies for the Holy Sepulchre,[10] the abbey of Saint Mary of Josaphat[11] and the order of Saint Lazarus,[12] and from Nicosia in Cyprus there survives the cartulary of the cathedral church of the Holy Wisdom.[13] But, except for a few isolated survivals or a handful of documents from other religious corporations that have been preserved because the property in question later passed to another house,[14] that is all. All the then known documents relating to the Latins in the Levant were calendared by Reinhold Röhricht in 1893 (with a supplement in 1904).[15] Since then no one has undertaken an update of this work, but Hans Mayer's recent two-volume study of the chancery of the kings of Jerusalem contains a useful list of sources, noting those that are spurious, and this can serve as a starting-point for anyone wishing to know which documents have been re-edited since Röhricht's time and what new material has come to light.[16] For many years now Professor Mayer has been preparing a new edition of the extant royal charters from the Kingdom of Jerusalem, a work of scholarship that is eagerly awaited.

These documents have much to tell us about the legal, social and institutional history of the Latin east, and they may on occasion indicate institutional survivals from Byzantine times. They have plenty of prosopographical information for the Latins settled in the Levant, but on the whole they give very few clues about the individual inhabitants of the Empire. Nor is there

---

[8] H.E. Mayer, *Marseilles Levantehandel und ein akkonensisches Fälscheratelier des 13. Jahrhunderts* (Tübingen, 1972).

[9] J. Delaville Le Roulx, ed., *Cartulaire général de l'ordre des Hospitaliers de St-Jean de Jérusalem (1100–1310)*, 4 vols. (Paris, 1894–1906); E. Strehlke, ed., *Tabulae ordinis theutonici* (Berlin, 1869).

[10] G. Bresc-Bautier, ed., *Le cartulaire du chapitre du Saint-Sépulcre de Jérusalem*, Documents relatifs à l'histoire des croisades 15 (Paris, 1984).

[11] H.-F. Delaborde, ed., *Chartes de Terre Sainte provenant de l'abbaye de N.-D. de Josaphat* (Paris, 1880); C. Kohler, ed., 'Chartes de l'abbaye de Notre-Dame de la vallée de Josaphat en Terre-Sainte (1108–1291)', *ROL* 7 (1900), 108–222.

[12] A. de Marsy, ed., 'Fragment d'un cartulaire de l'ordre de Saint-Lazare, en Terre Sainte', *Archives de l'Orient latin* 2 (1884), documents, pp. 121–57.

[13] N. Coureas and C. Schabel, eds., *The Cartulary of the Cathedral of Holy Wisdom of Nicosia*, Cyprus Research Centre Texts and Studies in the History of Cyprus 25 (Nicosia, 1997).

[14] For example, F. Chalandon, 'Un diplome inédit d'Amaury I roi de Jérusalem en faveur de l'abbaye du Temple-Notre-Seigneur', *ROL* 8 (1900–1), 311–17.

[15] R. Röhricht, ed., *Regesta Regni Hierosolymitani (MXCVII–MCCXCI)* (Innsbruck, 1893; additamentum 1904).

[16] H.E. Mayer, *Die Kanzlei der lateinischen Könige von Jerusalem*, MGH, Schriften 40, 2 vols. (Hanover, 1996).

much evidence for relations between the Latins in the east and the Orthodox clergy who lived within their lands. In 1173 Jobert, the master of the Hospitallers, granted the monastery of Saint George at Bait Jibrin to Meletos the Syrian who is described as the 'archbishop of the Syrians and Greeks living in the area of Jabin and Gaza'. It is an interesting document for a number of reasons, not least because it gives the names of Meletos and his clerical entourage in Greek characters.[17] Sadly it is unique. Two kings of Jerusalem, Baldwin III and Amaury, married members of the imperial family. Theodora Komnena, the niece of Manuel I, wed Baldwin III in 1158. Just one document she issued has survived: it is dated 1161. Here Theodora, 'by the grace of God queen of Jerusalem and niece of the lord and most holy Emperor Manuel' gave a house to her servant, Richard the Englishman. The presence of 'Dionisius *miles*' and 'Michael the Greek (*Grifo*) the *panetarius*' in the witness-list perhaps provides a glimpse of the Greeks in her household.[18] Maria Komnena, Manuel's great-niece, married Amaury in 1167. Unlike Theodora, who, shortly after her husband's death in 1163, famously absconded with her kinsman, the future Emperor Andronikos, Maria chose to remain in the east when Amaury died in 1174. She remarried and lived on until at least 1207. However, she appears in disappointingly few surviving documents. Not once is she mentioned in a charter issued by King Amaury; nor does she make any grants herself. Most of the references to her show her signifying her agreement to the *acta* of her second husband, Balian of Ibelin. The one extant document in which Balian in association with Maria initiated a grant includes a certain 'dominus Constantinus' prominently among the witnesses. While we might speculate that this man was a Greek in Maria's service, there is other evidence to suggest that Constantine had a brother named Bohemond, in which case we may safely assume that, despite his Greek name, he was after all a Latin.[19] The Nicosia cartulary provides evidence for the establishment of the Latin diocese of Nicosia in the 1190s and its early endowments, but once again there is little specifically about the Orthodox. The fleeting appearance of the former landowner 'Minas the Turcopole' in the royal grant of 1197 is the sole mention of a Greek before 1204 and prompts more questions than answers.[20]

We now turn from letters and documents to the literary works composed by the Latins in the east. On the one hand there are the historical narratives, most of which are familiar, and about which I shall say more presently; on the other there are various other writings: in 1127 Stephen of Antioch trans-

---

[17] *DCart*, no. 443. For refs., Pringle, *Churches*, vol. 1, 101, no. 32.

[18] de Marsy, 'Fragment d'un cartulaire', no. 20.

[19] *RRH* 597. See Edbury, *John of Ibelin and the Kingdom of Jerusalem* (Woodbridge, 1997), 120, 146–7.

[20] Coureas and Schabel, *Cartulary of Holy Wisdom*, no. 46.

lated the *Kitāb al-Maliki* by the tenth-century medical writer 'Alī ibn al-'Abbas into Latin;[21] while still archdeacon of Antioch the future patriarch Aimery translated parts of the Old Testament into Castilian and added to them some historico-geographical details;[22] Prior Achard of the Templum Domini in Jerusalem wrote his poem on the Temple before 1136 or 1137 when he died, and this work was later continued by his successor Geoffrey;[23] Rorgo Fretellus, the archdeacon of Antioch in the 1140s, composed a description of the Holy Land; and Gerard of Nazareth, bishop of Latakia (Laodikeia) by 1140, wrote about Latin eremitism in the east and other matters. Fretellus' work is one of a number of guides to the Holy Places written in the twelfth century. Several are anonymous; his is, I think, the only one from before 1204 for whom the author is known by name and who was resident in the east.[24] Gerard of Nazareth's writings only survive in fragmentary form as preserved in the twelfth-century section of the mid-sixteenth-century compilation of the Magdeburg Centuriators. How far his actual words have been retained is hard to judge. This is a great pity, as what we know of his writings show them to have been of great interest, not only for the hermits in the east, many of whom lived on the Black Mountain near Antioch, but also for his tract arguing against the refusal of the Orthodox to identify Mary of Bethany with Mary Magdalene.[25]

One feature of Latin literary culture in the Levant in the twelfth century is the marked importance of the principality of Antioch. Patriarch Aimery of Antioch, Stephen of Antioch, Rorgo Fretellus, and Gerard of Nazareth, the bishop of Latakia (Laodikeia), have already been mentioned. Two other literary figures settled in Antioch were the historians Ralph of Caen and Walter the Chancellor. Ralph's biography of Tancred, the ruler of Antioch from 1104 until his death in 1112, breaks off abruptly in 1105. The bulk of the work is concerned with the events of the First Crusade, and, like other Latin historians of that expedition, Ralph exhibits a marked antipathy for Alexios Komnenos. It is unfortunate that the years 1100–5 are passed over

---

[21] B.Z. Kedar, 'Gerard of Nazareth, a neglected twelfth-century writer in the Latin east: a contribution to the intellectual and monastic history of the crusader states', *DOP* 37 (1983), 55, n. 2, citing C.H. Haskins, *Studies in the History of Mediaeval Science* (2nd edn., Cambridge, Mass., 1927), 131–5.

[22] R. Hiestand, 'Un centre intellectuel en Syrie du nord? Notes sur la personnalité d'Aimery d'Antioche, Albert de Tarse et *Rorgo Fretellus*', *Moyen Age* 100 (1994), 8–11.

[23] R. Hiestand, 'Gaufridus abbas Templi Domini: an underestimated figure in the early history of the Kingdom of Jerusalem', in P. Edbury and J. Phillips, eds., *The Experience of Crusading*, vol. 2, *Defining the Crusader Kingdom* (Cambridge, 2003), 48–59, at 49 and nn. 5–6.

[24] P.C. Boeren, ed., *Rorgo Fretellus de Nazareth et sa description de la Terre Sainte: histoire et edition du texte* (Amsterdam, 1980); for a rebuttal of many of Boeren's conclusions, see Hiestand, 'Un centre intellectuel', 19–36.

[25] Kedar, 'Gerard of Nazareth', 53–77.

comparatively briefly.[26] Walter's history is entitled *The Antiochene Wars* and covers events in the principality of Antioch during the periods from 1114 to 1115 and 1119 to 1122. The theme is the war with the neighbouring Muslims and culminates in the major Christian defeat of 1119 when the prince, Roger of Salerno, was killed.[27] The Greeks are rarely mentioned, but, although Walter apparently shared the Latin hostility to the Byzantines, he does on one occasion admit that the Latins treated the indigenous population of Antioch badly.

I know of just four Latin histories composed in the Kingdom of Jerusalem in the twelfth century or the very beginning of the thirteenth. Well known are those by Fulcher of Chartres, who completed his work in the late 1120s,[28] and William of Tyre who finished writing in 1184.[29] Less familiar are the derivative and generally disregarded *Balduini III Historia nicaena vel antiochena* which dates from the mid-1140s and ends with the events of 1123,[30] and the verse history of the siege of Acre of 1189–91 that has been wrongly attributed to 'Haymarus Monachus'. This last work has as its title: *Monachi florentini acconensis episcopi de recuperatione Ptolemaidae liber*. The Latin can be construed in more than one way, but in the absence of any other evidence for a bishop of Acre named Monachus, I would like to suggest that the title should be translated: 'The book concerning the recovery of Ptolemais (i.e. Acre) by a Florentine monk [who is] bishop of Acre'. If I am right, there may well be something in Helen Nicholson's suggestion that the author was in fact Walter of Florence, bishop of Acre from around 1208.[31]

It may seem rather arbitrary to exclude from this survey those narratives of the crusades that were not actually written in the east such as the *Gesta Francorum* which describes the First Crusade and which was evidently used by Fulcher in composing his history, or Odo of Deuil's *De profectione Ludovici VII in orientem* which has so much to say about Byzantium at the

---

[26] Ralph of Caen, 'Gesta Tancredi in expeditione Hierosolymitana', *RHC Oc* 3, 587–716.

[27] H. Hagenmeyer, ed., *Walter the Chancellor, Bella antiochena* (Innsbruck, 1896); tr. T.S. Asbridge and S.B. Edgington, *The Antiochene Wars: a translation and commentary*, Crusade Texts in Translation 4 (Aldershot, 1999).

[28] H. Hagenmeyer, ed., *Fulcher of Chartres, Historia Hierosolymitani* (Heidelberg, 1913); tr. F.R. Ryan and H.S. Fink, *A History of the Expedition to Jerusalem, 1095–1127* (Knoxville, 1969).

[29] R.B.C. Huygens, ed., *Willelmi Tyrensis archiepiscopi Chronicon*, 2 vols., CCCM 63–63a (Turnhout, 1986); tr. E.A. Babcock and A.C. Krey, *A History of Deeds Done Beyond the Sea*, 2 vols., Records of Civilisation and Studies 35 (New York, 1943).

[30] 'Balduini III Historia nicaena vel antiochena', *RHC Oc* 5, 133–86.

[31] W. Stubbs, ed., 'Monachi florentini acconensis episcopi de recuperatione Ptolemaidae liber', in Roger of Howden, *Chronica*, Rolls Series 51, vol. 3 (1870), cv–ccxxxvi. See H.J. Nicholson, *Chronicle of the Third Crusade. A translation of the Itinerarium peregrinorum et Gesta regis Ricardi*, Crusade Texts in Translation 3 (Aldershot 1997), 5, n. 6.

time of the Second Crusade.[32] The fact is that the *Gesta Francorum* stands at the head of a tradition of writing about the crusades that seeks to portray the Byzantines in an extremely poor light—they are weak, treacherous and undependable—and most later Latin narratives either directly or indirectly take their cue from this source.[33] In their account of the First Crusade both Fulcher and, much later, William of Tyre, follow in this tradition. Fulcher has a brief account of Bohemond of Taranto's attack on the Byzantine empire in 1107, giving as his reason the emperor's attacks on pilgrims bound for the Holy Land, and mentions the treaty of Devol the following year. He also notes the death of Alexios Komnenos in 1118. William's history, on the other hand, is the fullest and most significant source for Byzantine history from the Latin east. He is known to have visited Constantinople on at least two occasions, and, as archbishop of Tyre and chancellor of the Kingdom, he would have had contacts with important Byzantines, not least the queen of Jerusalem, Maria Komnena. His history reveals some widely differing approaches to the Empire and its people. On the one hand, as in his descriptions of the First and the Second Crusades, he could be overtly hostile, verging on the xenophobic—in this he would appear to have been the prisoner of his sources. On the other hand, he could show a considerable degree of insight and objectivity, attempting to portray the Byzantines as the allies and supporters of the Latin principalities in the east and exhibiting a sympathetic understanding of the problems the emperors encountered. We have to remember that William was writing between the late 1160s and early 1180s. For much of that time the kings of Jerusalem were looking to the Byzantines for aid, and accordingly William attempts to cast the empire in a favourable light. Even the interventions of John II Komnenos in Antioch between 1137 and 1142 which in fact posed a serious threat to Prince Raymond's sovereignty and to the territorial integrity of the principality are constructed in a positive manner. William gives considerable attention to the Byzantine expeditions to Antioch and to the diplomatic relations between Jerusalem and Constantinople right up to the death of Manuel Komnenos in 1180. The marriage ties between the royal house of Jerusalem and the Komneni, the attempts at military cooperation and King Amaury's state visit to Constantinople in 1171 are all described at length. It was only at the very end that this rosy picture of the Byzantine empire collapses. The *coup d'état* which brought Andronikos to power and the massacre of the Latins in

---

[32] R. Hill, ed. and tr., *Gesta Francorum et aliorum Hierosolimitanorum* (Oxford, 1972); V.G. Berry, ed. and tr., *Odo of Deuil, De profectione Ludovici VII in orientem* (New York, 1948).

[33] J. France, 'The use of the anonymous Gesta Francorum in the early twelfth-century sources for the First Crusade', in A.V. Murray, ed., *From Clermont to Jerusalem: the crusades and crusader societies, 1095–1500* (Turnhout, 1998), 29–42.

Constantinople in 1182 are told in lurid detail. William was not himself an eye witness, but his descriptions do have the advantage of being almost contemporary. The stereotypes of Greeks as perfidious, weak and effeminate are once again highlighted, and it is here, in describing the events of 1182, that William for the first and only time accuses the Greeks of heresy and schism. It is, I would suggest, the outburst of a man who for long had badly wanted to believe that the Latins in the east could work in harmony with the Greeks and who was now undeceived.[34]

Finally, we need to look forward to those literary works written in the thirteenth century that relate to events from before the Fourth Crusade. Now the cultural milieu has changed. Instead of the clerical sources written in the Latin, we have writings clearly intended for a lay audience and written in Old French. The earliest Latin Syrian legal treatises—*Le livre au roi* and the *Assises of Antioch*, preserved only in a translation into Armenian—both date from around 1200.[35] The later thirteenth-century legal treatise by John of Ibelin includes important material on the ecclesiastical and legal structure of the Kingdom of Jerusalem and on the lordships and knights, compiled shortly before the collapse of the Kingdom in 1187.[36] At some point in the opening decades of the thirteenth century, William of Tyre's history was translated into French and various continuations added which brought his account of the affairs of the Latin east closer to the time they were compiled; in one manuscript the narrative extends to 1277.[37] Related to parts of these continuations is an anonymous work which goes by the name of the *Chronique d'Ernoul et de Bernard le Trésorier*.[38] What seems to have happened is that someone took this work, jettisoned the material that came before the point in 1184 where William's narrative ended and bolted what followed onto the French version of his history. The relationship between the *Chronique d'Ernoul* and the various versions of the continuations of the French William

---

[34] For a detailed treatment of these themes, see P.W. Edbury and J.G. Rowe, *William of Tyre: historian of the Latin east* (Cambridge, 1988), ch. 8.

[35] M. Greilsammer, ed., *Le livre au roi*, Documents relatifs à l'histoire des croisades 17 (Paris, 1995); L.M. Alishan, ed., *Assises d'Antioche, reproduites en françois* (Venice, 1876).

[36] P.W. Edbury, *John of Ibelin and the Kingdom of Jerusalem* (Woodbridge, 1997), chs. 4–8.

[37] 'L'estoire de Eracles empereur et la conqueste de la terre d'Outremer', *RHC Oc* 1–2; M.R. Morgan, ed., *La Continuation de Guillaume de Tyr (1184–1197)*, Documents relatifs à l'histoire des croisades 14 (Paris, 1982); P.W. Edbury, *The Conquest of Jerusalem and the Third Crusade: sources in translation* (Aldershot, 1996). For the translation, see J.H. Pryor, 'The *Eracles* and William of Tyre: an interim report', in B.Z. Kedar, ed., *The Horns of Hattin* (Jerusalem, 1992), 270–93.

[38] L. de Mas Latrie, ed., *La chronique d'Ernoul et de Bernard le Trésorier*, Société de l'histoire de France (Paris, 1871).

of Tyre is complex, but there is no need to describe it here.[39] Suffice it to say that both the Continuations and the pre-1184 section of the *Chronique d'Ernoul* have some interesting material on Byzantine relations with the east, although the genealogical details they give for the dynastic crises of the 1180s are seriously awry. There also exist various Old French annals compiled in Latin Syria in the thirteenth century, one of which leaves us in no doubt that the Christians in the east were particularly annoyed that a crusade that was supposed to come to their assistance and win back Jerusalem from the Muslims had instead ended up seizing Constantinople.[40]

# BIBLIOGRAPHY

## HANDBOOKS, SURVEYS, PROSOPOGRAPHIES

H.E. Mayer and J. McLellan, 'Select bibliography of the crusades', in K.M. Setton, ed., *A History of the Crusades*, 6 vols. (Madison, 1969–89), vol. 6, 511–664
An excellent bibliography compiled in the late 1980s. A supplement to cover the enormous output since then is a major desideratum. This work does not fully supersede H.E. Mayer, *Bibliographie zur Geschichte des Kreuzzüge* (Hanover, 1960) and its supplement, H.E. Mayer, 'Literaturbericht über die Geschichte des Kreuzzüge: Veröffentlichungen 1958–1967', *Historische Zeitschrift*: Sonderheft 3 (1969), 641–731.
A.V. Murray, *The Crusader Kingdom of Jerusalem: a dynastic history, 1099–1125* (Oxford, 2000)
A study of the early years of the Kingdom of Jerusalem, with a 'prosopographical catalogue' (pp. 176–238) of 140 individuals associated in some way with the Bouillon-Boulogne dynasty (AD 1096–1118).
R. Röhricht, ed., *Regesta Regni Hierosolymitani (MXCVII–MCCXCI)* (Innsbruck, 1893; additamentum 1904; repr. New York, 1960)
Calendar (in Latin) of all the charters, letters and other documents from or relating to the Latin east then known. Never superseded, but for an indication of new editions and more recent discoveries, see H.E. Mayer, *Die Kanzlei der lateinischen Könige von Jerusalem*. MGH Schriften 40, 2 vols. (Hanover, 1996), vol. 2, 935–79.

---

[39] See P.W. Edbury, 'The Lyon *Eracles* and the Old French Continuations of William of Tyre', in B.Z. Kedar, J. Riley-Smith and R. Hiestand, eds., *Montjoie: Studies in crusade history in honour of Hans Eberhard Mayer* (Aldershot, 1997), 139–53.
[40] R. Röhricht and G. Raynaud, eds., 'Annales de Terre Sainte', *Archives de l'Orient latin* 2 (1884), documents, pp. 427–61; 'Les Gestes des Chiprois', *RHC Documents arméniens*, vol. 2: 653–69, at 663.

## PRIMARY SOURCES

### Letters

H. Hagenmeyer, ed., *Epistulae et chartae ad historiam primi belli sacri spectantes: Die Kreuzzugsbriefe aus den Jahren 1088–1100* (Innsbruck, 1901; repr. Hildesheim, 1973)
A collection, assembled by the editor, of twenty-three letters relating to the period of the First Crusade.

M. Bouquet *et al.*, eds., 'Ludovici VII et variorum ad eum epistolae', in *RHGF* 16, 1–170
A letter collection compiled by Louis VII's chancellor, Hugh of Campo-Florido, dating from the mid-1150s to the late 1160s and including a number from the Latin east.

### Charters

G. Bresc-Bautier, ed., *Le cartulaire du chapitre du Saint-Sépulcre de Jérusalem*, Documents relatifs à l'histoire des croisades 15 (Paris, 1984)
An edition based on two manuscripts (one dating to the 1160s, the other to the 1230s) totalling 185 documents from the beginning of the twelfth century to the mid-thirteenth. This edition has attracted some acerbic criticism (e.g. H.E. Mayer in P. Edbury and J. Phillips, eds., *The Experience of Crusading,* vol. 2, *Defining the Crusader Kingdom* [Cambridge, 2003], 179, n. 1; 183, n. 21). Still of value is the earlier edition: E. de Rozière, ed., *Cartulaire de l'église du Saint Sépulcre de Jérusalem* (Paris, 1849).

N. Coureas and C. Schabel, eds., *The Cartulary of the Cathedral of Holy Wisdom of Nicosia*, Cyprus Research Centre Texts and Studies in the History of Cyprus 25 (Nicosia, 1997)
This edition completely supersedes the earlier piecemeal editing of L. de Mas Latrie and J.L. LaMonte. It comprises a collection of 140 documents from a sixteenth-century manuscript of which 107 date to before 1322 when the original collection was made.

H.-F. Delaborde, ed., *Chartes de Terre Sainte provenant de l'abbaye de N.-D. de Josaphat*, Bibliothèque de l'École française d'Athènes et de Rome 19 (Paris, 1880)
An edition of fifty-nine documents mostly dating to the twelfth century from the abbey's archives in Sicily. (From 1292 the abbey was located in Messina.) Supplemented by C. Kohler, ed., 'Chartes de l'abbaye de Notre-Dame de la Vallée de Josaphat en Terre-Sainte (1108–1291)', *ROL* 7 (1900), 108–222 (summaries and excerpts of eighty-eight documents—not full editions).

J. Delaville Le Roulx, ed., *Cartulaire général de l'Ordre des Hospitaliers de St.-Jean de Jérusalem (1100–1310)*, 4 vols. (Paris, 1894–1906)
A collection of nearly 5,000 documents that relate to the Latin east and western Europe assembled by the editor from the archives in Malta and elsewhere.

A. de Marsy, ed., 'Fragment d'un cartulaire de l'ordre de Saint-Lazare', in *Archives de l'Orient latin* 2 (1884), documents, pp. 121–57

An edition of the surviving portion of a thirteenth-century cartulary comprising forty documents.

H.E. Mayer, *Marseilles Levantehandel und ein akkonensisches Fälscheratelier des 13. Jahrhunderts*. Bibliothek des deutschen historischen Instituts in Rom 38 (Tübingen, 1972)

Includes critical editions of both the mid-thirteenth-century forgeries and the genuine privileges granted to the Commune of Marseilles.

E. Strehlke, ed., *Tabulae ordinis theutonici* (Berlin, 1869); repr. with an introduction by H.E. Mayer (Toronto, 1975)

An edition of various manuscript cartularies that had been bound together into one volume earlier in the nineteenth century: a total of 725 documents relating to the Teutonic order from the twelfth century to the fifteenth.


## Literary Works

### Achard d'Arrouaise, prior of the Templum Domini

Only the first part of this Latin poem on the Templum Domini has been published. The sections by Abbot Gaufridus remain unedited.

*Editions:*

P. Lehmann, ed., 'Die mittelateinischen Dichtungen der Prioren des Tempels zu Jerusalem Acardius und Gaufridus', in E.E. Stengel, ed., *Corona quernea. Festgabe, Karl Strecker zum 80. Geburtstage dargebracht*, MGH, Schriften 6 (Leipzig, 1941), 296–330. (Not seen)

M. de Vogüé, ed., 'Poème sur le Templum Domini', *Archives de l'Orient latin* 1 (1881), 562–79. (Supplemented by A.C. Clark, ed., 'Poème sur le temple de Salomon par Achard d'Arrouaise', *ROL* 12 [1909/11], 263–74, a hitherto unpublished extract from a longer version of this poem.)

*Secondary Literature:*

R. Hiestand, 'Gaufridus abbas Templi Domini: an underestimated figure in the early history of the Kingdom of Jerusalem', in P. Edbury and J. Phillips, eds., *The Experience of Crusading*, vol. 2, *Defining the Crusader Kingdom* (Cambridge, 2003), 48–59

### Gerard of Nazareth

Wrote on eremetism and controversy with the Orthodox. Only fragments preserved by the Magdeburg Centuriators survive.

*Edition:*

Surviving fragments edited in B.Z. Kedar, 'Gerard of Nazareth, a neglected twelfth-century writer in the Latin east: a contribution to the intellectual and monastic history of the crusader states', *DOP* 37 (1983), 55–77

### Rorgo Fretellus

A description of the Holy Places.

*Edition:*
P.C. Boeren, ed., *Rorgo Fretellus de Nazareth et sa description de la Terre Sainte: histoire et edition du texte* (Amsterdam, 1980)

*Secondary Literature:*
R. Hiestand, 'Un centre intellectuel en Syrie du nord? Notes sur la personnalité d'Aimery d'Antioche, Albert de Tarse et *Rorgo Fretellus*', *Moyen Âge* 100 (1994), 7–34
Critical of Boeren's views.

## Historical Narratives Composed in the Latin East, in Latin

### 'Balduini III Historia nicaena vel antiochena'
This is a derivative anonymous work ending with the events of 1123.

*Edition:*
Anonymous, 'Balduini III Historia nicaena vel antiochena', *RHC Oc* 5, 133–86

### Fulcher of Chartres
The author was a participant in the First Crusade who then settled in the east and whose narrative ends with the events of 1127. A well-informed account by a well-educated cleric.

*Edition:*
H. Hagenmeyer, ed., *Fulcheri carnotensis, Historia Hierosolymitani* (Heidelberg, 1913)

*Translation:*
F.R. Ryan and H.S. Fink, *Fulcher of Chartres, A History of the Expedition to Jerusalem, 1095–1127* (Knoxville, 1969; pbk edn., New York, 1973)
Generally reliable.

*Secondary Literature:*
V. Epp, *Fulcher von Chartres: Studien zur Geschichtsschreibung des ersten Kreuzzuges* (Düsseldorf, 1990)

### *Liber monachi florentini* ('Haymarus Monachus')
A Latin narrative poem of 895 lines on the siege of Acre of 1189–91. Riant attributed it to 'Haymarus (Aymar/Heimar) Monachus', the man he believed to be the patriarch of Jerusalem in the 1190s. This attribution, as Stubbs pointed out in the preface to his edition, is wrong. In fact the name 'Haymarus' or 'Aymar' originated in a mistaken transcription of one of the manuscripts of the Old French Continuations of William of Tyre, and internal evidence leaves no doubt that Patriarch Monachus (died 1202) cannot have been the author. 'Monachus' can be a personal name or alternatively can mean 'monk'. As no bishop of Acre named Monachus is known, how the title is to be translated is problematic: 'The Book about the recovery of Acre (Ptolemais) by a Florentine monk who is bishop of Acre' or 'The Book about the recovery of Acre by Monachus the Florentine (a member of the household) of the bishop of Acre'. (It may be relevant to note that Walter, bishop of Acre between 1208 and 1213 was a Florentine.)

*Editions:*

P. Riant, ed., *Haymarus Monachus, De expugnatata Accone liber tetratichus* (Lyon, 1866)

W. Stubbs, ed., 'Monachi florentini acconensis episcopi de recuperatione Ptolemaidae liber', in Roger of Howden, *Chronica*, Rolls Series 51, vol. 3 (1870), cv–ccxxxvi

## Ralph of Caen, *Gesta Tancredi*

A celebration of Tancred's career in the First Crusade and subsequently which breaks off in 1105.

*Edition:*

Ralph of Caen, 'Gesta Tancredi in expeditione Hierosolymitana', *RHC Oc* 3, 587–716

## Walter the Chancellor

A near-contemporary account of the principality of Antioch, 1114–15 and 1119–22.

*Edition:*

H. Hagenmeyer, ed., *Galterii Cancelarii bella antiochena* (Innsbruck, 1896)

*Translation:*

T.S. Asbridge and S.B. Edgington, *Walter the Chancellor, The Antiochene Wars: a translation and commentary,* Crusade Texts in Translation 4 (Aldershot, 1999)
  This translation has an extensive introduction discussing the author, his purpose and the value of his history.

## William of Tyre

William, archbishop of Tyre and chancellor of the Kingdom of Jerusalem, was at work on his history from the late 1160s until 1184. It is by far the most famous and most detailed account of the history of the Latins in the east from the twelfth century and covers the period from the First Crusade to 1184. The author was a well-informed and sophisticated writer who showed a considerable interest in Byzantine affairs.

*Edition:*

R.B.C. Huygens, ed., *Willelmi Tyrensis archiepiscopi Chronicon*, 2 vols., CCCM 63–63a (Turnhout, 1986)
  A full critical edition, utilising all the Latin manuscripts. It supersedes the edition in *RHC Oc*, vol. 1.

*Translation:*

E.A. Babcock and A.C. Krey, *William of Tyre, A History of Deeds Done Beyond the Sea*, Records of Civilisation and Studies 35, 2 vols. (New York, 1943; repr. New York, 1976)
  A generally reliable translation of the nineteenth-century edition in the *RHC Oc*, vol 1. It therefore omits the 'lost' chapter (XIX, 12), first edited in 1962, that describes the author's studies in the west and lists his masters at Paris, Orleans and Bologna.

*Secondary Literature:*

There is a large literature on William and his *magnum opus*. A good starting-point is P.W. Edbury and J.G. Rowe, *William of Tyre: historian of the Latin east* (Cambridge, 1988). For a recent discussion of William and the Byzantine world, see B. Hamilton, 'William of Tyre and the Byzantine empire' in C. Dendrinos *et al.*, eds., *Porphyrogenita: essays on the history and literature of Byzantium and the Latin east in honour of Julian Chrysostomides* (Aldershot, 2003), 221–33.

## Historical Narratives Composed in the Latin East, in Old French

### The Old French Translation of William of Tyre and its Continuations

Some time in the early thirteenth century William's history was translated into French (with some significant departures from his Latin original) and then at different times the text was brought up to date by the addition of various continuations, one of which extends as far as 1277. These continuations have attracted more scholarly attention than the translation itself, and they provide a major source of information for the Latin east at the end of the twelfth century and for much of the thirteenth. The text is usually referred to as 'L'estoire de Eracles empereur' from the fact that the opening sentence mentions the Byzantine emperor Herakleios (610–41) and his wars against the Persians. About 50 manuscript copies survive. There is no modern critical edition.

*Editions:*
'L'estoire de Eracles empereur et la conqueste de la terre d'Outremer', *RHC Oc*, vols. 1–2
> The translation (vol. 1) is printed below the Latin text of William's history on the basis of four manuscripts; the Continuation (vol. 2) provides various versions of the text, albeit in an edition that is generally inadequate.
P. Paris, ed., *Guillaume de Tyr et ses continuateurs: texte français du xiiiᵉ siècle, revu et annoté*, 2 vols. (Paris, 1879–80)
> An edition based on two manuscripts and the *RHC* edition.
M.R. Morgan, ed., *La Continuation de Guillaume de Tyr (1184–1197)*, Documents relatifs à l'histoire des croisades 14 (Paris, 1982)
> An edition of the unique version of the Continuation for the years 1184–97 from the Lyon Bibliothèque de la ville MS 828, together with some textually related passages (for the period 1191–7) from the Florence Biblioteca Medicea-laurenzianam MS Plu. LXI.10. The editor's view that the Lyon text provides the version closest to the original is disputed.

*Translation:*
P.W. Edbury, *The Conquest of Jerusalem and the Third Crusade: sources in translation* (Aldershot, 1996)
> A translation of the Lyon text for 1184–97 as edited by M.R. Morgan (with a selection of other material relating to the same period).

*Secondary Literature:*
P.W. Edbury, 'The Lyon *Eracles* and the Old French Continuations of William of Tyre', in B.Z. Kedar, J.S.C. Riley-Smith and R. Hiestand, eds., *Montjoie. Studies in crusade history in honour of Hans Eberhard Mayer* (Aldershot, 1997), 139–53
> Critical of M.R. Morgan's views.
B. Hamilton, 'The Old French translation of William of Tyre as an historical source', in P. Edbury and J. Phillips, eds., *The Experience of Crusading*, vol. 2, *Defining the Crusader Kingdom* (Cambridge, 2003), 93–112
J.H. Pryor, 'The *Eracles* and William of Tyre: an interim report' in B.Z. Kedar, ed., *The Horns of Hattin* (Jerusalem, 1992), 270–93

## Chronique d'Ernoul et de Bernard le Trésorier

A narrative covering the period from the founding of the Kingdom of Jerusalem to 1229 (or, in some manuscripts, 1231). How much of the text the putative authors in fact wrote is open to question. A version of the later sections (from 1184) was spliced on to the end of the William of Tyre translation to serve as its Continuation. The relationship between the Ernoul–Bernard narrative and the various versions of the William of Tyre Continuations is complex and the subject of some debate.

*Edition:*

L. de Mas Latrie, ed., *La chronique d'Ernoul et de Bernard le Trésorier*, Société de l'histoire de France (Paris, 1871)
   A serviceable edition of the text, although the introduction and commentary are now decidedly dated.

## Annales de Terre Sainte

In the thirteenth century various annals were compiled in the Latin east, and some of this annalistic material subsequently found its way into compilations such as the William of Tyre Continuations, or the so-called *Chronique d'Amadi*, or was translated into Latin and included in Marino Sanuto's *Liber secretorum fidelium crucis*. Despite the brevity of many of the entries, these annals contain much that is of importance.

*Editions:*

R. Röhricht and G. Raynaud, eds., 'Annales de Terre Sainte', *Archives de l'Orient latin* 2 (1884), documents, pp. 427–61
   An edition of two versions of the annals in Old French.
'Les Gestes des Chiprois', *RHC Documents arméniens*, vol. 2, 651–872
   The first section (pp. 653–69) comprises another version of the annals in Old French covering the period 1131–1224. A later editor has inserted annalistic material into the section by Philip of Novara (1220s-1240s), and the influence of the annals is also clear in the final section by the so-called 'Templar of Tyre'.
A. Sánchez Candeira, 'Las cruzadas en la historiografía española de la época: traducción castellana de una redacción desconocida de los "Anales de Tiera Santa"', *Hispania: Revista Española de Historia* 20 (1960), 325–67
   A Spanish translation ending in 1260.

## Legal Treatises

## Le livre au roi

A description of the law and procedures of the High Court of the Kingdom of Jerusalem, securely dated to the period 1197–1205.

*Edition:*

M. Greilsammer, ed., *Le livre au roi*, Documents relatifs à l'histoire des croisades 17 (Paris, 1995)
   A modern, scholarly edition with full introduction and notes (supersedes the edition in *RHC Lois*, vol. 1).

## The *Assises of Antioch*

An early thirteenth-century description of the law and procedures of the High Court and the Burgess Court of the principality of Antioch. Originally written in French, this only survives in an Armenian translation.

*Edition:*

L.M. Alishan, ed., *Assises d'Antioche, reproduites en françois* (Venice, 1876)
   Edition of the Armenian text with a French translation.

*Translation:*

A.A. Papovian, 'Armianskii perevod "Antiokhiiskikh Assiz"', *Vestnik Matenadarana*
   4 (Erevan, 1958), 331–75 (Russian)

## John of Ibelin, *Le livre des assises*

A treatise on the law and procedure of the High Court of Jerusalem completed in the mid-1260s. It contains some important twelfth-century material on the ecclesiastical and legal structure of the Kingdom and on military service in the mid-1180s with lists of named individuals and their obligations.

*Edition:*

P.W. Edbury, ed., *John of Ibelin: le livre des assises* (Leiden, 2003)
   A critical edition that supersedes the edition in *RHC Lois*, vol. 1. The twelfth-century material is at pp. 590–99, 603–16.

*Secondary Literature:*

P.W. Edbury, *John of Ibelin and the Kingdom of Jerusalem* (Woodbridge, 1997)
   Contains extended discussion of the twelfth-century material including a prosopographical catalogue (pp. 141–54) of the knights named in the section on military obligation.

# 4

# Latin Sources and Byzantine Prosopography: Genoa, Venice, Pisa and Barcelona

## MICHEL BALARD

IN A COMMUNICATION WHICH ALAIN DUCELLIER and I presented to the Sixteenth International Congress of Byzantine Studies in Vienna in 1981, we pointed out that, given the extreme poverty of 'Byzantine' archives, anyone who wishes to enhance their understanding of Palaiologan history must turn to the archives of countries that had commercial or political relations with Byzantium.[1] Using examples selected from the holdings of the Italo-Dalmatian archives, we demonstrated the considerable contribution of these sources, which preserve an impressive quantity of unedited or badly edited documents that are indispensable to any economic and social study of the Byzantine world. Is what is true for the last centuries of Byzantium also the case for the times of the Komneni and the Angeli? I would like to show by means of some examples selected from the archives of Genoa, Venice, Pisa and Barcelona in what respects Byzantine prosopography for the twelfth century can be enriched thanks to deeds, which provide information on ambassadors and merchants, as well as certain of those Latins who settled either temporarily or permanently in Constantinople or in the provincial cities of the Empire.

## GENOA

Since I am more familiar with the Genoese archives than with the other collections mentioned above, I will begin with these sources, which are in fact particularly rich. Treaties made with the Empire and instructions given to

---

[1] M. Balard and A. Ducellier, 'L'apport des archives italo-dalmates à la connaissance du Proche-Orient médiéval', in *Akten d. XVI Internationaler Byzantinistenkongress*, vol. 1, Beiheft 2.2 (Vienna, 1981).

*Proceedings of the British Academy* **132**, 39–58. © The British Academy 2007.

ambassadors going to Constantinople were published long ago: these have
just been updated by the *Società ligure di storia patria*. This learned society
has undertaken to publish in a scholarly way the *Libri iurium*, a large collection of documents on the foreign relations of the Commune, a *Codice diplomatico*, which was elaborated in the middle decades of the thirteenth century
on the initiative of a *podesta* with a legal training. The chronological index to
the documents in the eighth volume makes it easy to find the group of texts
which deal with Genoese relations with Byzantium, from the chrysobull of 12
October 1155, the first concession made by Manuel I Komnenos to the
Commune, up to the legal proceedings for the handing over of the Genoese
quarter in Constantinople, which were enacted in favour of the Genoese
ambassador, Ottobono della Croce, by the officers of Alexios III Angelos.[2]
This edition, supplied with all the necessary *apparatus criticus*, supersedes
Lisciandrelli's 1960 publication of the registers of sources, *Materie politiche*,
as well as the incomplete *Codice diplomatico* initiated by Cesare Imperiale di
Sant'Angelo in the 1940s.[3] Apart from the texts of treaties enacted between
Genoa and the Empire, instructions given by the Commune to its ambassadors are particularly interesting: for example for the years 1168–70, when a
first agreement concluded by Amico de Murta was renounced by the
Commune, which acquired a quarter within Constantinople following new
instructions to its ambassador. The directives given to ambassador Grimaldi
who was sent to Constantinople in 1174 are also of great interest.[4] They show
that the Genoese continued to serve the emperor loyally in the expedition to
Cyprus and against the Cumans, and at the same time indicate the areas of
the Empire in which Genoese merchants were trading. The list includes the
names of businessmen who suffered damage at the time of the looting of the
arcade (*embolos*) of Santa Croce in 1162 and that of Koparion in 1170. It is
notable in the first place that the members of three families of the feudal and
merchant aristocracy, della Volta, Mallone and Usodimare, had themselves
alone invested 3,472 *hyperpyra*, that is 11.8% of the total losses suffered by
the Genoese. Secondly, merchants from cities other than Genoa, even from
the Ligurian coast, are rarely attested: commerce with the Empire still
remained an activity of city-dwellers, professional merchants, to whom were
added certain craftsmen tempted by the lucrative enterprise of trade. The
circle of itinerant merchants, seventy-four in ambassador Grimaldi's list,
was seldom opened to non-Genoese and was composed for the most part
of members of the aristocracy under the authority of Italian bishops.

[2] Pallavicino, *I Libri iurium*, vol. 1.8, 151–350.
[3] Lisciandrelli, *Trattati e negoziazioni*; Imperiale di Sant'Angelo, *Codice diplomatico*.
[4] Bertolotto, 'Nuova serie'.

The work either of chancellors of the Commune or of ordinary notaries, the Genoese *Annals* of Caffaro and his continuators represent a useful complement to the diplomatic sources, especially as they report certain episodes concerning relations between the Genoese and the Byzantine east that are otherwise unknown.[5] There is the case, for example, of the naval incident of 1101, narrated by Caffaro in his treatise *De liberatione civitatum orientis*, appended to his *Annals*.[6] According to this author, the Genoese, while returning from the First Crusade, encountered near Ithaca a fleet of sixty Greek warships (*chelandia*) under the command of the *megadoux* Landulfus, also called Kotromil in another passage. Being defeated, the Byzantine admiral requested negotiations. Genoese and Greeks went to Corfu and two ambassadors of the Commune, Raynaldus de Rodulfo and Lambertus Ghetus, left for Constantinople. There is no other contemporary evidence for this naval incident nor for the embassy. Written by Caffaro in about 1155, when Genoese envoys were going on the one hand to Pope Hadrian IV to ask him to uphold the rights of the Commune that had been violated in the east, and on the other to Constantinople to conclude with Manuel I Komnenos the first treaty agreed with Genoa, this mention of a naval conflict in the period of the First Crusade could surely have no other objective than to elevate the great deeds of the Genoese and to recall the antiquity of their relations with Byzantium. In the absence of other evidence, it is likely that the incident is legendary.

In the course of the second half of the twelfth century we learn from the Genoese *Annals* about the embassies exchanged between the Commune and Byzantium: Amico de Murta in 1157, Enrico Guercio in 1160, Corso Sigismondo, Ansaldo Mallone, Nicola de Rodulfo in 1164, Amico de Murta again in 1168 and 1170, Lanfranco Piper in 1186, while in 1170 Genoa received an embassy from the emperor, which consisted of Andronikos Kontostephanos, Theodoros Kastamonites and Georgios Dishypatos. These came to propose a treaty that the Commune rejected, since the reparations offered following the looting of their arcade (*embolos*) in 1162 were judged inadequate. The embassy of 1164 has left no trace, doubtless because of its failure, and likewise the agreement of 1169 which was rejected by the Commune. Analysis of the chrysobull of 1155, however, shows that it is very close to the original text of the treaty, which chancellor Caffaro must have had before him when he was writing. The parallelism between the diplomatic and narrative sources confirms the value of the latter, which furnish details useful for our understanding of Byzantine–Genoese relations.

---

[5] Belgrano and Imperiale di Sant'Angelo, *Annali genovesi*.
[6] Belgrano and Imperiale di Sant'Angelo, *Annali genovesi*, vol. 1, 118.

The Genoese archives are rightly renowned for the wealth of their notarial sources: the historian of the Byzantine east could not do without them in studying the fourteenth and fifteenth centuries, where the volume of unedited documents is significant.[7] This is not the case for the twelfth century. We know that the Genoese notarial archives possess the most ancient notarial cartulary in the Mediterranean world, kept by Giovanni *scriba* between 1155 and 1164.[8] Subsequently the extant notarial documents are interrupted for almost twenty years; they do not begin again until 1182 and survive only in an interrupted sequence up to the beginning of the thirteenth century. Apart from some documents preserved in the collection of the *Notai ignoti* whose state of preservation today prevents all access for researchers, the cartularies prior to 1204 are all published in the series *Notai liguri dei secoli XII e XIII*, which has unfortunately been suspended for half a century.[9] I shall not discuss again the general interest of the Genoese notarial documentation, which has been the object of numerous studies.[10] As far as Byzantium is concerned, the twelfth-century records attest the comparatively limited importance of Genoese investments, far inferior to those directed towards Egypt or Syria–Palestine. V. Slessarev, in an article of 1970,[11] was able to estimate that the cartulary of Giovanni *scriba* revealed only a tenth or even a twentieth of the investments made by the Genoese. Despite reservations due to the unique character of this document for the mid-twelfth century, we have to recognise that between 1155 and 1164, the terminal dates of the cartulary, Genoese investments in the Byzantine empire, known from twenty deeds—that is an average of two a year—represent only a tenth of the sums invested in commerce with Syria and Egypt.[12] However, they bring into prominence the activity of certain individuals belonging to the Genoese aristocracy, such as

---

[7] In addition to Balard, *Romanie génoise*, see G.G. Musso, *Navigazione e commercio genovese con il Levante nei documenti dell'Archivio di Stato di Genoa* (Rome, 1975); G. Airaldi, *Studi e documenti su Genova e l'Oltremare* (Genoa, 1974); L. Balletto, *Genova, Mediterraneo, Mar Nero (secc. XIII–XV)* (Genoa, 1976); L. Balletto, *Liber officii provisionis Romanie (Genova 1424–1428)* (Genoa, 2000); Pistarino, *I 'Gin', Genovesi d'Oriente* and *I Signori*; K.P. Matschke, 'The Notaras family and its Italian connections', *DOP* 49 (1995), 59–72; T. Ganchou, 'Le rachat des Notaras après la chute de Constantinople ou les relations "étrangères" de l'élite byzantine au XVᵉ siècle', in M. Balard and A. Ducellier, eds., *Migrations et diasporas méditerranéennes (Xᵉ–XVIᵉ siècles)* (Paris, 2002), 149–229.

[8] Chiaudano and Moresco, *Il cartolare*.

[9] Chiaudano, *Oberto scriba*; Chiaudano and Morozzo della Rocca, *Oberto scriba*; Hall, Krueger and Reynolds, *Guglielmo Cassinese*; Eierman, Krueger and Reynolds, *Bonvillano 1198*; Hall Cole, Krueger, Reinert and Reynolds, *Giovanni de Guiberto*; Krueger and Reynolds, *Lanfranco*.

[10] See, for example, G. Costamagna, *La triplice redazione dell'instrumentum genovese* (Genoa, 1961) or the presentation of the sources by Abulafia, *The Two Italies*, 11–22.

[11] Slessarev, 'The pound value'.

[12] Bach, *La cité de Gênes*, 50–1; Abulafia, *The Two Italies*, 99.

the three Guercio brothers who were allied to della Volta, and the links maintained by Genoese with the Montferrat family so prominent in Byzantine
affairs.[13] The end of the century is hardly better represented: no contract in
1182, the year of the massacre of Latins in Constantinople; again none in
1184; a modest resumption in 1186 when Genoa sent two ambassadors to
Isaac II Angelos; nothing in 1190, doubtless because of the Third Crusade
when Genoese ships were mobilised in support of Philip II, king of France;
but in contrast a new impetus in 1191, attested by the deeds of Guglielmo
Cassinese, where investments in Constantinople took third place, a little short
of the sums invested in Syria and Sicily.[14] By contrast both in Bonvillano
(1198) and in Giovanni de Guiberto (1200–11), 'Romania' (Byzantium) is
cited in *commenda* contracts only in connection with forbidding itinerant
merchants to go there.[15] The escalation of piracy in the Aegean and the disputes between the Genoese and Alexios III Angelos hampered business,
which did not really recover before 1203 despite the enlargement of the commercial quarter granted to the Commune by the emperor. Genoese
'Romania' only really expanded after 1261. In the twelfth century Venetians
and Pisans outdid the Ligurians and dominated the markets of
Constantinople and the Empire.

## VENICE

The long-standing relationship between Venice and Constantinople needs no
description. From the will of the Doge Giustiniano Partecipazio at the
beginning of the ninth century up to the activities of the businessman
Romano Mairano that can be traced from 1153 to 1201, Venetians never
stopped frequenting Constantinople and the markets of the Empire, favoured
as they were by ancient connections of dependency between the Lagoon and
the Empire and by the privileges that the emperors granted them very early
on. The texts of these chrysobulls, known unfortunately from the Latin translations since the Greek originals are lost, together with the instructions given
to Venetian ambassadors, published in the middle of the nineteenth century
by Tafel and Thomas,[16] have been the subject of a recent publication,
equipped with all the necessary *apparatus criticus*.[17] A great many historians

---

[13] Day, *Genoa's Response*, 47–69, 108–44.
[14] See the tables drawn up by Abulafia, *The Two Italies*, 158, 161, 166, 174, 177, 182.
[15] Eierman, etc., *Bonvillano 1198*, doc. no. 92; Hall Cole, etc. *Giovanni di Guiberto*, doc. nos. 649,
661, 694, 695, 779, 835, 1222, 1281, 1323. Only document no. 1683 relates to an investment in
Thessalonike.
[16] Tafel and Thomas, *Urkunden*.
[17] Pozza and Ravegnani, *I trattati con Bisanzio*.

have commented on the three most famous chrysobulls granted to Venice by Byzantium, but without always seeing their implications. This is the case, for example, with the document of 992, which lowers the duties due from Venetian ships at the Abydos customs-point, forbids the shipowners of the Lagoon from loading merchandise belonging to Amalfitans, Jews, and the Lombards of Bari, who were all considered foreigners, while the Greeks of southern Italy, who were termed 'subjects' (*douloi*), benefit from privileged treatment.[18] The chrysobull of 1082, which for the first time granted large concessions to foreigners in the Empire, inaugurated a new era in relations between Byzantium and Venice and constituted an innovation in the Byzantine economic and fiscal system. In addition it was cited by the rival maritime republics of Genoa and Pisa so as to obtain similar concessions from the Empire. Finally, although the chrysobull of 1198 expanded the list of Byzantine cities and islands that were open to Venetian commerce, the legal privileges that it contains must not be underestimated: for the first time an emperor was forced to admit the exercise of a foreign jurisdiction on imperial soil, in granting Venetian judges the right to settle monetary disputes between Greek litigants and Venetians. Study of the privileges successively granted to Venice by the emperors shows the progressive expansion of Byzantine regions open to Venetian commerce, which was much more favoured than Pisan or Genoese traffic. But it would no doubt be an overestimate to see in the regulatory documents an exact image of reality: the arbitrary measures of Byzantine officials against western merchants and the development of imperial policy very often affected the application of privileges granted by the emperors and reduced the advantage that the Venetians could derive from them.[19]

To these well-known documents it is appropriate to add the publication of the first deeds of the Venetian ducal chancery, many of which concern Venetians in Constantinople very directly. Thus in 1090 the Doge Vitale Falier granted to Carimanno, abbot of San Giorgio Maggiore in Venice, a group of benefits ceded by Alexios I Komnenos to the Commune of Venice, with the exception of those enjoyed by the monastery of San Nicolò del Lido. In 1112, the Doge Ordelafo Falier repaid the expenses of an embassy sent by the patriarch of Grado, Giovanni Gradenigo, to the emperor. In 1145 one of his successors, Pietro Polani, granted to the priest Domenico, prior of the church of Rodosto (Rhaidestos), the right to use his own weights and measures and to enforce their use on Venetian residents. Another chancery document dated September 1170 details the voyage from Constantinople to

---

[18] See D. Jacoby's review of Pozza and Ravegnani, *I trattati*; Lilie, *Handel und Politik*, 8–16, 41–9; Borsari, *Venezia e Bisanzio*, 3–16.
[19] Jacoby, 'Italian privileges'.

Durazzo (Dyrrachion) of three businessmen, Antolino Marino da Mazzorbo, Almenrico Pagano da Murano and Domenico Guido da Torcello, and the will drawn up by the last on the eve of his death in Durazzo. Finally, at a date between September 1196 and September 1197, the Doge Enrico Dandalo gives instructions to his two delegates at the court of Constantinople, Enrico Navigaioso and Andrea Donà: they were to secure the conclusion of peace with the Empire and the reimbursement of moneys due in compensation for losses suffered by Venetian businessmen.[20] One can scarcely hope for more from the chancery documents, now well known and well edited for twelfth-century Venice.

The most precise information on the Venetians either trading or resident in the Empire in the twelfth century comes from the Venetian notarial deeds assembled by Lombardo and Morozzo della Rocca and completed by the scattered deeds preserved among the records of Venetian monasteries.[21] They allow us to retrace the commercial activities of certain grand figures in pre-capitalist Venice—to use Heynen's phrase:[22] Romano Mairano, who under-took his first voyage to Halmyros and Constantinople in 1153, settled for some time in the Byzantine capital from where he organised his business with Smyrna, Acre and Alexandria, escaped the arrest of Venetian merchants in Constantinople in 1171, rebuilt part of his fortune thanks to his activities in Syria, and returned to the Byzantine capital in 1191 when the secular privi-leges of the Venetians were restored.[23] But alongside this character, whose career can be traced in fifty-six documents, one must also cite Dobramiro and Zaccaria Stagnario, the Bettani brothers who owned property in Halmyros and Thebes, Vitale Voltani, who settled in Greece in the 1160s and dominated the oil market in Corinth, Sparta and Thebes, and all those Venetian mer-chants active in the silk trade and in all forms of commerce between the Peloponnese and Constantinople.[24] Although we can hardly take literally the figures given by the *Historia ducum veneticorum*, which claims that close on 20,000 Venetians were present in Constantinople in 1170 and that half of them were imprisoned following the coup ordered by Manuel I Komnenos, it is certain that many Venetians lived outside the quarter reserved for them and some of them had married Greek wives and acquired real estate in the

---

[20] Pozza, *Gli atti originali*, doc. nos. 1, 5, 10, 16, 32.
[21] Lombardo and Morozzo della Rocca, *Documenti del commercio veneziano, Nuovi documenti.* Records of Venetian monasteries: Lanfranchi, ed., *Famiglia Zusto, San Giovanni Evangelista, San Giorgio Maggiore*, vols. 2 and 3.
[22] Heynen, *Zur Entstehung.*
[23] Thiriet, *La Romanie vénitienne*, 46–7; Renouard, *Les hommes d'affaires italiens*, 77–9; Luzzatto, *Storia economica*, 24–5; Borsari, *Venezia e Bisanzio*, 107–30; Ravegnani, 'Il commercio veneziano'.
[24] Jacoby, 'Silk in western Byzantium', 'The Byzantine outsider in trade'.

Byzantine capital.[25] Further research in the records of the *Cancelleria inferiore* in Venice or in those of the great Venetian families could help in identifying innumerable Venetians established in the Empire and would highlight the very large migration of businessmen from the Lagoon to the Byzantine east during the twelfth century, the golden age of Venetian commerce in the Levant.

## PISA

The Venetian sources also provide some information about the Pisans active in the Empire. As far as chancery documents are concerned, we still have to resort to the old edition of G. Müller which provides in order the Greek and Latin texts of the chrysobulls granted by the emperors to Pisa; it has to be supplemented by the 1957 publication of Heinemeyer.[26] The first chrysobull obtained by Pisa in 1111, a copy of which survives in the treaty of Isaac II of 1192, provided for a reduction to four per cent of the rate of the *kommerkion* paid by the Pisans for merchandise imported into the Empire, although the normal rate of ten per cent was retained for goods bought or exported. The text ended with the granting of honorific privileges and a wharf in Constantinople—starting-point for the Pisan colony. John II in 1136 and then Manuel I Komnenos in 1170 did no more than confirm the concessions awarded in 1111 with a new chrysobull. Victims of the riot against foreigners in Constantinople in 1182, it was only ten years later that the Pisans regained their former privileges: from Isaac II they secured the concession that the reduction of the *kommerkion* to a rate of four per cent applied equally to purchases in and exports from the Empire. The possession of the arcade (*embolos*) with shops, churches and a wharf that they held in Constantinople was solemnly confirmed to them. A last chrysobull granted by Alexios III in 1197 has not been preserved.

Treaties, chancery deeds and the Pisan *Annals* of Bernardo Maragone[27] inform us about a certain number of envoys from the Commune to Constantinople: an embassy of eight people in 1111; the meeting in 1136 between Anselm of Havelberg, accompanied by judge Burgundio, and Niketas of Nikomedeia; Bottacci and Coccus in 1161; the consul Albertus and Burgundio, accompanied by the *vicecomes* Marcus in 1170; the prior Plebanus in 1180; judge Sigerius and Rainerius Gaetani in 1192; Albithus and Enricus de Palascio in 1194; and finally Uguccio Lamberti Bononis and

---

[25] Jacoby, 'Migrations familiales', 358–9.
[26] Müller, *Documenti*; Heinemeyer, 'Die Verträger'.
[27] Lupo Gentile, *Bernardo Maragone*.

Petrus Modanis in 1197.[28] The Pisan community in Constantinople, which is also known from certain notarial deeds, was rather large in the time of Manuel I Komnenos if one believes the Genoese chronicler Caffaro, according to whom a thousand or so Pisans attacked the Genoese quarter in 1162. But according to the investigation of the prior of Constantinople, the community consisted of no more than a hundred or so people on the eve of the Fourth Crusade. Among its members one would single out above all the activity of Hugues Ethérien and Leon Toscan, the first author of a theological treatise, *De sancto et immortali deo*, the second interpreter and translator in the service of the emperor.[29] The best known of these Pisans remains, however, Burgundio of Pisa, jurist, politician, diplomat and above all translator of John of Damascus, St John Chrysostom, Nemesius of Emesa and of the medical works of Hippocrates and Galen—such that he had considerable influence on the thinking of Peter Lombard, St Thomas Aquinas and St Bonaventure.[30] But alongside these Pisan businessmen and intellectuals a place must also be given to all those Pisan pirates who infested the approaches to Constantinople at the end of the twelfth century: Fortis, ally of the Genoan Guglielmo Grasso, seized a ship returning from Egypt in 1192, while a number of Pisan pirates lay in ambush at Abydos: their misdeeds justified the demands for compensation presented by a certain Jacobus, envoy of Isaac II Angelos to Pisa in September 1194.[31]

The texts of chrysobulls, diplomatic documents and notarial deeds also supply particulars about the Pisan settlements in the Empire. In connection with the conveyance of the Constantinopolitan revenues of the Commune of Pisa to the Opera del Duomo in 1162, the Pisan quarter on the banks of the Golden Horn is described: it comprised two churches, a hospital and houses and was placed under the responsibility of a *vicecomes* and an *embularius*. After suffering great damage as a result of the insurrection of 1182 against foreigners, the quarter was reconstructed and enlarged in 1192, when it acquired a new wharf, that of the Ikanatissa.[32] The 1192 *practicum tradicionis* lists two churches, St Nicholas and St Peter, a cemetery, a hospital, ovens, a bath, three wells, five money-changers, four wharves and houses, of which some were leased and yielded a considerable revenue.[33] Benjamin of Tudela[34] also describes briefly the Pisan quarter at Halmyros, which included a church

[28] List of ambassadors in Otten, *Les Pisans en Orient*; see also Borsari, 'Pisani a Bisanzio'.
[29] Dondaine, 'Hugues Ethérien'.
[30] Classen, *Burgundio von Pisa*; Vuillemin-Diem and Rashed, 'Burgundio de Pise'; Tangheroni, 'Pisa et la Romània', 80–2.
[31] Dölger, *Regesten*, no. 1612; Müller, *Documenti*, no. 41, pp. 66–7.
[32] Müller, *Documenti*, no. 34, pp. 40–58; see Lilie, *Handel und Politik*, 79–83.
[33] Müller, *Documenti*, no. 46, pp. 74–5.
[34] B. da Tudela, *Itinerario*, tr. G. Busi (Rimini, 1988), 25.

dedicated to St John,[35] while the instructions given to the embassy of 1197 recall the long-standing presence of Pisans at Thessalonike.[36] Rather more details are known, then, about the constituent elements of the Pisan community in Constantinople than about those of the Genoese or even the Venetians.


## BARCELONA


It is also through the mediation of Pisa that the first contacts between Catalonia and Constantinople were established. It is known that in 1171 an embassy from Manuel I Komnenos went to Pisa to establish a network of alliances against Frederick I Barbarossa. The envoys remained for three years on the banks of the Arno; we may suppose that they made use of this time to establish contacts with powers hostile to the German emperor. It was not, however, until after the latter's defeat at Legnano that the Catalans, fearing until then the intervention of the emperor in Provence, decided in 1176 to send a first embassy to Constantinople: this is known from a contract of exchange and the chartering of a shipowner to transport Ramon of Montcada, Guillem of Claramunt and Berenguer of Barcelona to Constantinople. Their objective was to negotiate the marriage of Ramon Berenguer, count of Provence and brother of Alfonso II of Aragon, to an imperial Byzantine princess, Eudokia. She was sent to the west in 1180, but by the time she arrived her intended husband was already married. She was given in marriage to the lord of Montpellier, Guillaume VII, and was then rejected, ending her life in a nunnery.[37]

These are some examples of the information that the Latin sources can provide for the compilation of a Byzantine prosopography for the period of the Komneni. Numerous names are cited, but unfortunately they are often only names, with the exception of a few better-known individuals. Only a thorough collective investigation into the archives of the four great maritime republics of Italy and Catalonia would enable the reconstruction of the career in the Empire of these merchants, artisans, pirates and adventurers, who were seduced by the mirages of the east and the possibilities of gaining wealth that it allowed them to glimpse. The task is not easy for the twelfth century—except perhaps for Venice—since the notarial sources and the private deeds are far from being known exhaustively. But it is beyond doubt that

---

[35] Müller, *Documenti*, no. 18, pp. 20, 22.
[36] Müller, *Documenti*, no. 44, pp. 71–2.
[37] Ferrer i Mallol and Duran i Duelt, 'Un ambaixada catalana'.

any prosopographical enterprise on the history of Byzantium in the twelfth century, a moment when the Empire was genuinely opening up to the western presence, cannot ignore the Latin sources, modest though they may be.

# BIBLIOGRAPHY

## GENOA

### HANDBOOKS, SURVEYS, PROSOPOGRAPHIES (alphabetical order)

G. Airaldi, *Genova e la Liguria nel Medioevo*, Storia degli Stati italiani dal Medioevo all'Unità, UTET Libreria (Turin, 1986)
  Brief survey of Genoese history with a useful bibliography.
M.-G. Canale, *Nuova istoria della Repubblica di Genova, del suo commercio e della sua letteratura dalle origini all'anno 1797*, 4 vols. (Florence, 1858–64)
  First great synthesis of Genoese history.
G.W. Day, *Genoa's Response to Byzantium 1155–1204. Commercial expansion and factionalism in a medieval city* (Urbana and Chicago, 1988)
  A good survey of the politics and economy of the city of Genoa.
T.O. de Negri, *Storia di Genova* (Milan, 1968)
  More detailed than Vitale's work for the Middle Ages.
S.A. Epstein, *Genoa and the Genoese 958–1528* (Chapel Hill and London, 1996)
  Rather a good survey of Genoese history, but with incomplete bibliography.
R. Savelli, *Repertorio degli statuti della Liguria*, Società ligure di storia patria (Genoa, 2003)
  A complete survey of the statutes of every city in Liguria; very detailed for Genoa.
V. Vitale, *Breviario della storia di Genova*, 2 vols. (Genoa, 1955)
  The first volume gives a useful summary of the history of the city, the second a critical bibliography up to the beginning of the 1950s.
*Storia di Genova*, Società ligure di storia patria (Genoa, 2003)

### PRIMARY SOURCES (chronological order)

#### Charters

*Leges municipales*, Monumenta Historiae Patriae, 2 vols. (Turin, 1838)
E. Ricotti, *Liber iurium reipublicae ianuensis*, Monumenta Historiae Patriae, 2 vols. (Turin 1854–7)
  The first edition of Genoese treaties with foreign states. See now the edition by the Società ligure di storia patria (below)
L.-T. Belgrano, 'Registrum curiae archiepiscopalis Ianuae', *Atti della Società ligure di storia patria* 2.2 (1862)

L.-T. Belgrano, 'Prima serie di documenti riguardanti la colonia genovese di Pera', *Atti della Società ligure di storia patria* 13 (1877–84), 97–336

—— 'Seconda serie di documenti riguardanti la colonia genovese di Pera', *Atti della Società ligure di storia patria* 13 (1877–84), 933–1003

G. Bertolotto, 'Nuova serie di documenti sulle relazioni di Genova con l'Impero bizantino', *Atti della Società ligure di storia patria* 28 (1898), 368–405

*Leges genuenses*, Monumenta Historiae Patriae (Turin, 1901)

C. Imperiale di Sant'Angelo, *Codice diplomatico della Repubblica di Genova*, Fonti per la storia d'Italia, 3 vols., nos. 77, 79, 89 (Rome, 1936–42)
An attempt to publish all public charters (tenth to twelfth centuries).

V. Vitale, *Le fonti del diritto marittimo ligure* (Genoa, 1951)
Publication of the main maritime laws of Genoa.

P. Lisciandrelli, *Trattati e negoziazioni politiche della Repubblica di Genova (958–1797)*, *Atti della Società ligure di storia patria* n.s. 1 (Genoa, 1960)
Brief summary of the agreements between Genoa and foreign states.

D. Puncuh, *Liber privilegiorum ecclesiae ianuensis* (Genoa, 1962)
Gives some information about the customs rights awarded to the Genoese church.

D. Puncuh and A. Rovere, *I registri della Catena del Comune di Savona*, 2 vols., *Atti della Società ligure di storia patria* n.s. 26 (Genoa, 1986)
Documents from the second harbour in Liguria, but nothing at all about Byzantium.

A. Rovere, *I Libri iurium della Repubblica di Genova*, Società ligure di storia patria 1.1 (Genoa, 1992)

D. Puncuh, *I Libri iurium della Repubblica di Genova*, Società ligure di storia patria 1.2 (Genoa, 1996)

—— *I Libri iurium della Repubblica di Genova*, Società ligure di storia patria 1.3 (Genoa, 1998)

S. Dellacasa, *I Libri iurium della Repubblica di Genova*, Società ligure di storia patria 1.4 (Genoa, 1998)

E. Madia, *I Libri iurium della Repubblica di Genova*, Società ligure di storia patria 1.5 (Genoa, 1999)

L. Balletto, *Liber officii provisionis Romanie (Genova 1424–1428)* (Genoa, 2000)

M. Bibolini, *I Libri iurium della Repubblica di Genova*, Società ligure di storia patria 1.6 (Genoa, 2000)

E. Pallavicino, *I Libri iurium della Repubblica di Genova*, Società ligure di storia patria 1.7 (Genoa, 2001)

—— *I Libri iurium della Repubblica di Genova*, Società ligure di storia patria 1.8 (Genoa, 2002)


## Narrative Sources

A. Giustiniani, *Annali della Repubblica di Genova* (Genoa, 1537; repr. 2 vols., Genoa, 1854)

U. Foglietta, *Dell'istorie di Genova* (Genoa, 1596)

L.-T. Belgrano and C. Imperiale di Sant'Angelo, eds., *Annali genovesi di Caffaro e de' suoi continuatori*, 5 vols., Fonti per la storia d'Italia (Rome, 1890–1929)

Publication of the official chronicle of Genoa, written by public chancellors in the twelfth and thirteenth centuries.

E. Pandiani, ed., *Bartolomeo Senarega, De rebus genuensibus*, in L.A. Muratori, Rerum Italicarum Scriptores n.s. 24.8 (Bologna, 1932)

G. Monleone, ed., *Iacopo da Varagine e la sua cronaca di Genova dalle origini al MCCXCVII*, 3 vols., Fonti per la storia d'Italia (Rome, 1941)
Chronicle written by the famous archbishop of Genoa, author of the 'Golden Legend'.

G. Petti Balbi, ed., *Georgii et Iohannis Stellae Annales genuenses*, in L.A. Muratori, Rerum Italicarum Scriptores n.s. 17.2 (Bologna, 1975)
Chronicle written by the Stella brothers in the fourteenth century.

## Notarial Deeds

M. Chiaudano and M. Moresco, *Il cartolare di Giovanni scriba*, 2 vols. (Turin, 1935)
Publication of the first notarial cartulary of the Mediterranean world.

M. Chiaudano and R. Morozzo della Rocca, *Oberto scriba de Mercato 1190*, Notai liguri dei secoli XII e XIII, vol. 1 (Genoa, 1938)

M.W. Hall, H.C. Krueger and R.L. Reynolds, *Guglielmo Cassinese 1190–1192*, 2 vols., Notai liguri dei secoli XII e XIII, vol. 2 (Turin, 1938)

J.E. Eierman, H.C. Krueger and R.L. Reynolds, *Bonvillano 1198*, Notai liguri dei secoli XII e XIII, vol. 3 (Genoa, 1939)

M.W. Hall Cole, H.C. Krueger, R.G. Reinert and R.L. Reynolds, *Giovanni de Guiberto 1200–1211*, 2 vols., Notai liguri dei secoli XII e XIII, vol. 5 (Genoa, 1939–40)

M. Chiaudano, *Oberto scriba de Mercato 1186*, Notai liguri dei secoli XII e XIII, vol. 4 (Turin, 1940)

H.C. Krueger, R.L. Reynolds, *Lanfranco 1202–1226*, 3 vols., Notai liguri dei secoli XII e XIII, vol. 6 (Genoa, 1951–3)

D. Puncuh, *Il cartolario del notaio Martino: Savona 1203–1206* (Genoa, 1974)

## SECONDARY LITERATURE (alphabetical order)

D. Abulafia, *The Two Italies. Economic relations between the Norman Kingdom of Sicily and the northern Communes* (Cambridge, 1977)
A full study of Genoese investments in the Mediterranean world in the twelfth century.

E. Bach, *La cité de Gênes au XIIᵉ siècle* (Copenhagen, 1955)
A study of internal political events combined with economic trends.

M. Balard, *La Romanie génoise (XIIᵉ–début du XVᵉ siècle)*, 2 vols., BEFAR 235 (Rome and Genoa, 1978)
A full study of political and economic relations between Genoa and Byzantium.

—— 'Les transports maritimes génois vers la Terre Sainte, XIIᵉ–XIIIᵉ siècle', in G. Airaldi and B.Z. Kedar, eds., *I comuni italiani nel regno crociato di Gerusalemme* (Genoa, 1986), 141–74
A study of types of ship and of their uses on oriental routes.

M. Balard, 'L'emigrazione monferrino-piemontese in Oriente (secoli XII–XIV)', in L. Balletto, ed., *Atti del Congresso internazionale 'Dai feudi Monferrini e dal Piemonte ai nuovi mondi oltre gli oceani' (Alessandria, 2–6 aprile 1990)*, Biblioteca della Società di storia, arte e archeologia per le Province di Alessandria e Asti 27 (Alessandria, 1993), 249–61
A study of emigration to the Orient.

M. Balard, E. Malamut, J.-M. Spieser, eds., *Byzance et le monde extérieur. Contacts, relations, échanges* (Paris, 2005)

L. Balletto, *Genova, Mediterraneo, Mar Nero (secc. XIII–XV)* (Genoa, 1976)

O. Banti, ed., *Amalfi, Genova, Pisa e Venezia. Il commercio con Costantinopoli e il vicino Oriente nel secolo XII* (Pisa, 1998)
Proceedings of a 1995 conference in Pisa, with studies on the trade of the four maritime republics with Constantinople.

E. Bellomo, *A servizio di Dio e del Santo Sepolcro. Caffaro e l'Oriente latino* (Padua, 2003)
A study of Caffaro's works with special reference to the Latin Orient.

C.M. Brand, *Byzantium Confronts the West 1180–1204* (Cambridge, Mass., 1968)
A comparative study of the politics of the Italian republics in relation to Byzantium under the Angeli.

M. Buongiorno, *L'amministrazione genovese nella 'Romania'* (Genoa, 1977)

E.H. Byrne, 'The Genoese colonies in Syria', in *The Crusades and other Historical Essays presented to Dana C. Munro* (New York, 1928), 139–80
A survey of the administration of Genoese colonies in the Near East.

—— *Genoese Shipping in the Twelfth and Thirteenth Century*, Monograph of the Medieval Academy of America 5 (Cambridge, Mass., 1930)
The first study of Genoese voyages to the Orient.

M. Chiaudano, *Contratti commerciali genovesi del secolo XII. Contributo alla storia dell'accomendatio e della societas* (Turin, 1925)

—— 'I "loca navis" nei documenti genovesi dei secoli XII e XIII', in *Studi in onore di E. Besta*, vol. 4 (Milan, 1938), 413–46

—— 'La moneta di Genova nel secolo XII', in *Studi in onore di A. Sapori*, vol. 1 (Milan, 1957), 187–214

K.N. Ciggaar, *Western Travellers to Constantinople. The west and Byzantium 962–1204* (Leiden, 1996)

H.E.J. Cowdrey, 'The Madhia campaign of 1087', *EHR* 92 (1977), 1–29

J. Danstrup, 'Manuel I's coup against Genoa and Venice in the light of Byzantine commercial policy', *CM* 10 (1949), 195–219

G.W. Day, 'Manuel and the Genoese: a reappraisal of Byzantine commercial policy in the late twelfth century', *Journal of Economic History* 37 (1977), 289–301

—— 'Byzantino-Genoese diplomacy and the collapse of Manuel's western diplomacy, 1168–1171', *Byz* 48 (1978), 393–405

R. de Roover, 'The "cambium maritimum" contract according to the Genoese notarial records of the XII[th] and XIII[th] centuries', *Explorations in Economic History* 7 (1969–70), 15–33

C. Desimoni, 'Sui quartieri dei Genovesi a Costantinopoli nel secolo XII', *Giornale ligustico di archeologia, storia e belle arti* (1874), 137–80
First attempt to describe the Genoese quarter in Constantinople.

R. Di Tucci, *Studi sull'economia genovese del secolo XII. La nave e i contratti marittimi. La banca privata* (Turin, 1933)

S. Epstein, *Wills and Wealth in Medieval Genoa, 1150–1250* (Cambridge, Mass., 1984)
A detailed study of Genoese society between the twelfth and thirteenth centuries.

M.-L. Favreau, *Die Italiener im Heiligen Land, vom ersten Kreuzzug bis zum Tode Heinrichs von Champagne, 1098–1197* (Amsterdam, 1989)
An important section is devoted to the Genoese.

A. Greif, 'On the political foundations of the late medieval commercial revolution: Genoa during the twelfth and thirteenth centuries', *Journal of Economic History* 54 (1994), 271–87

W. Heinemeyer, 'Die Verträge zwischen dem oströmischen Reiche und den italienischen Städten Genua, Pisa und Venedig von 10. bis 12. Jahrhundert', *Archiv für Diplomatik* 3 (1957), 79–161

W. Heyd, *Histoire du commerce du Levant au Moyen Âge*, 2 vols. (Leipzig, 1885–6; repr. Amsterdam, 1967)
The first survey of Levantine trade, with an important section on the Genoese.

C.B. Hoover, 'The sea loan in Genoa in the XII[th] century', *Quarterly Journal of Economics* 40 (1925–6), 495–529

D. Jacoby, 'Genoa, silk trade and silk manufacture in the Mediterranean region (ca. 1100–1300)', *Tessuti, oreficerie, miniature in Liguria XIII–XV secolo. Atti del Convegno internazionale di studi Genova–Bordighera, 22–25 mai 1997* (Bordighera, 1999), 11–40
A study of a luxury product with close links to Byzantium.

B.Z. Kedar, 'Mercanti genovesi in Alessandria d'Egitto negli anni sessanta del secolo XI', in *Miscellanea di studi storici*, vol. 2 (Genoa, 1983), 21–30

H.C. Krueger, 'Post-war collapse and rehabilitation in Genoa, 1149–1162', in *Studi in onore di Gino Luzzatto*, vol. 1 (Milan, 1949), 117–28
A study of the financial crisis in Genoa after the Almeria campaign.

—— 'Genoese merchants, their partnerships and investments, 1155 to 1164', in *Studi in onore di A. Sapori*, vol. 1 (Milan, 1957), 257–72

—— 'Genoese merchants, their associations and investments, 1155 to 1230', in *Studi in onore di A. Fanfani*, vol. 1 (Milan, 1962), 415–26

—— 'Navi e proprietà navale a Genova. Seconda metà del sec. XII', *Atti della Società ligure di storia patria* n.s. 25 (1985)
A study of ships and shipowners in the second half of the twelfth century.

A.E. Laiou, 'Exchange and trade, seventh–twelfth centuries', in *eadem*, ed., *The Economic History of Byzantium* (Washington, DC, 2003), 697–770

R.-J. Lilie, *Handel und Politik zwischen dem byzantinischen Reich und den italienischen Kommunen Venedig, Pisa und Genua in der Epoche der Komnenen und der Angeloi (1081–1204)* (Amsterdam, 1984)
An important section is devoted to the Genoese and their places of trade in the Byzantine empire.

R.S. Lopez, *Storia delle colonie genovesi nel Mediterraneo* (Bologna, 1938; 2nd edn., Genoa, 1998)
A brilliant survey of Genoese expansion.

C. Manfroni, 'Le relazioni fra Genova, l'impero bizantino e i Turchi', *Atti della Società ligure di storia patria* 28 (1898), 575–856

The first survey dealing with Genoese politics in the Byzantine east.

H.L. Misbach, 'Genoese commerce and the alleged flow of gold to the east, 1154–1253', *Revue internationale d'histoire de la banque* 3 (1970), 68–87

B. Nelson, 'Blancardo (the Jew?) of Genoa and the restitution of usury in medieval Italy', in *Studi in onore di Gino Luzzatto*, vol. 1 (Milan, 1949), 96–116

S. Origone, *Bisanzio e Genova* (2nd edn., Genoa, 1997)
A study of political relations between Genoa and Byzantium.

G. Petti Balbi, *Caffaro e la cronachistica genovese* (Genoa, 1982)
A good analysis of the writings of the first Genoese chronicler.

G. Pistarino, *I Gin dell'Oltremare* (Genoa, 1988)
A volume of studies devoted to the Genoese east.

—— *Genovesi d'Oriente* (Genoa, 1990)
A second volume of studies devoted to the Genoese in the Orient.

—— *I Signori del mare* (Genoa, 1992)
A third volume of studies on Genoese expansion in the Orient.

A. Schaube, *Handelsgeschichte der romanischen Völker des Mittelmeergebietes bis zum Ende der Kreuzzüge* (Munich, 1906)

H. Sieveking, *Genueser Finanzwesen vom 12 bis 14 Jahrhundert* (Freiburg, 1898; repr. Osaka, 1974)
A classic work on Genoese taxation.

V. Slessarev, 'The pound value of Genoa's maritime trade in 1161', *Explorations in Economic History* 7 (1969–70), 95–111
An attempt to determine the volume of Genoa's trade in the middle of the twelfth century.

C. Verlinden, 'Le recrutement des esclaves à Gênes du milieu du XIIᵉ siècle jusque vers 1275', in *Fatti e idee di storia economica nei secoli XII–XX. Studi dedicati a Franco Borlandi* (Bologna, 1976), 37–57

V. Vitale, 'Vita e commercio nei notai genovesi dei secoli XII e XIII', *Atti della Società ligure di storia patria* 72 (1949)

## VENICE

See bibliography pp. 86–94.

## PISA

## HANDBOOKS, SURVEYS, PROSOPOGRAPHIES (alphabetical order)

G. Benvenuti, *Storia della Repubblica di Pisa* (4th edn., Pisa, 1982)

B. Casini, *Inventario dell'archivio del Comune di Pisa (secolo XI–1509)* (Livorno, 1960)

E. Cristiani, *Nobiltà e popolo nel Comune di Pisa. Dalle origini del podestariato alla signoria dei Donoratico* (Naples, 1962)

E. Grassini, *Biografie dei pisani illustri* (Pisa, 1838)

W. Heywood, *A History of Pisa, XI–XII Centuries* (Cambridge, 1921)

M. Luzzati, 'Note di metrologia pisana', *Bollettino storico pisano* 31–2 (1962–3), 191–219

F. Redi, *Pisa com'era: archeologia, urbanistica e strutture materiali (secoli V–XIV)* (Naples, 1991)

P. Tronci, *Memorie istoriche della città di Pisa* (Livorno, 1682)

C. Violante, *Economia, società, istituzioni a Pisa nel Medioevo* (Bari, 1980)

G. Volpe, *Studi sulle istituzioni comunali a Pisa. Città e contado, consoli e podestà (secoli XII–XIII)* (Pisa, 1902); 2nd edn. by C. Violante (Florence, 1970)


## PRIMARY SOURCES (chronological order)

### Charters

L.A. Muratori, ed., *Cronica di Pisa*, Rerum Italicarum Scriptores 15 (Milan, 1729)

F. dal Borgo, *Raccolta di scelti diplomi pisani*, 3 vols. (Pisa, 1765)

F. Bonaini, 'I diplomi pisani inediti col regesto di tutte le carte pisane che si trovano a stampa', *ASI* 6.2 (Florence, 1848)

—— *Statuti inediti della città di Pisa dal XII al XIV secolo*, 3 vols. (Florence, 1854–70)

G. Müller, *Documenti sulle relazioni delle città toscane coll'Oriente cristiano e coi Turchi fino all'anno 1531* (Florence, 1879)

N. Caturegli, *Regesto della Chiesa di Pisa*, Regesta Chartarum Italiae 24 (Rome, 1939)

B. Casini, 'Magistrature deliberanti del Comune di Pisa e leggi di appendice agli statuti', *Bollettino storico pisano* 24–5 (1955–6), 91–199

—— 'Gli atti pubblici del Comune di Pisa secondo un inventario della fine del Trecento', *Bollettino storico pisano* 28–9 (1959–60), 63–89

M. Tirelli Carli, *Carte dell'Archivio capitolare di Pisa*, vol. 4: *1101–1120* (Rome, 1969)

C. Violante, *Carte dell'Archivio capitolare di Pisa*, 4 vols. (Rome, 1971–6)

N. Caturegli, *Le carte arcivescovili pisane del secolo XIII*, vol. 1, *1201–1238*, Regesta Chartarum Italiae 37 (Rome, 1974)

M. D'Alessandro Nannipieri, *Carte dell'Archivio di Stato di Pisa*, vol. 1, *780–1070* (Rome, 1978)


### Narrative Sources

L.A. Muratori, ed., *Cronica varia pisana*, Rerum Italicarum Scriptores 15 (Milan, 1738)

F. Bonaini, 'R. Roncioni. Delle famiglie pisane', *ASI* 6.1 (Florence, 1848)

M. Lupo Gentile, ed., *Annales pisani di Bernardo Maragone*, Rerum Italicarum Scriptores 6.2 (2nd edn., Bologna, 1930)

O. Banti, ed., *Ranieri Sardo. Cronaca di Pisa*, Fonti per la storia d'Italia 99 (Rome, 1963)


### Notarial Deeds

R.S. Lopez, 'The unexplored wealth of the notarial archives in Pisa and Lucca', in *Mélanges d'histoire du Moyen Âge offerts à Louis Halphen* (Paris, 1951), 417–32

C. Otten-Froux, 'Documents inédits sur les Pisans en Romanie aux XIIIᵉ–XIVᵉ siè-cles', in M. Balard, A. Laiou and C. Otten-Froux, eds., *Les Italiens à Byzance* (Paris, 1987), 153–95


SECONDARY LITERATURE (alphabetical order)

D. Abulafia, 'Pisan commercial colonies and consulates in twelfth-century Sicily', *EHR* 93 (1978), 68–81
K.H. Allmendinger, 'Die Beziehungen zwischen der Kommune Pisa und Ägypten im hohen Mittelalter', *Vierteljahrschrift für Sozial- und Wirtschaftsgeschichte*, Beiheft 54 (Wiesbaden, 1967)
M. Balard, 'Génois et Pisans en Orient (fin du XIIIᵉ–début du XIVᵉ siècle)', in *Genova, Pisa e il Mediterraneo tra Due e Trecento. Per il VIIᵒ centenario della battaglia della Meloria. Atti della Società ligure di storia patria* 24.2 (1984), 179–209
—— 'I pisani in Oriente dalla guerra di Acri (1258) al 1406', *Bollettino storico pisano* 60 (1991), 1–16
O. Banti, ed., *Amalfi, Genova, Pisa e Venezia. Il commercio con Costantinopoli e il vicino Oriente nel secolo XII* (Pisa, 1998), 55–74
S. Borsari, 'I rapporti tra Pisa e gli stati di Romania nel Duecento', *RSI* 67 (1955), 477–92
—— 'Pisani a Bisanzio nel XII secolo', *Bollettino storico pisano* 60 (1991), 59–75
L. Cantini, *Storia del commercio e navigazione dei pisani*, 2 vols. (Florence, 1797–8; repr. Bologna, 1974)
M.L. Ceccarelli Lemut, *Medioevo pisano. Chiesa, famiglie, territorio* (Ospedaletto, 2005)
P. Classen, *Burgundio von Pisa. Richter, Gesandter, Übersetzer*, Sitzungsberichte der Heidelberger Akademie der Wissenschaften, phil.-hist. Klasse 4 (Heidelberg, 1974)
A. Dondaine, 'Hugues Ethérien et Léon Toscan', *Archives d'histoire doctrinale et littéraire du Moyen Âge* 27 (1952), 67–134
M.L. Favreau, 'Graf Heinrich von Champagne und die Pisaner im Königreich Jerusalem', *Bollettino storico pisano* 47 (1978), 97–120
G. Garzella, M.-L. Ceccarelli-Lemut and B. Casini, *Studi sugli strumenti di scambio a Pisa nel Medioevo* (Pisa, 1979)
L. Halphen, 'Le rôle des "Latins" dans l'histoire intérieure de Constantinople à la fin du XIIᵉ siècle', in *Mélanges Charles Diehl*, vol. 1 (Paris, 1930), 141–5
J. and B. Hamilton, *Hugh Eteriano. Contra Patarenos* (Leiden, 2004)
D. Haskins, 'Leo Tuscus', *EHR* 33 (1918), 492–6
W. Heinemeyer, 'Die Verträge zwischen dem oströmischen Reich und den italien-ischen Städten Genua, Pisa und Venedig vom 10 bis 12 Jahrhundert', *Archiv für Diplomatik* 3 (1957), 79–161
D. Herlihy, 'Una nuova notizia sulle origini della Curia del Mare in Pisa', *Bollettino storico pisano* 22–3 (1953–4), 222–7
—— 'Pisan coinage and the monetary history of Tuscany 1150–1250', in *Le zecche minori toscane fino al secolo XIV* (Pistoia, 1967), 169–92

R. Hiestand, 'L'arcivescovo Ubaldo e i pisani alla terza crociata alla luce di una nuova testimonianza', *Bolletino storico pisano* 57–8 (1988–9), 37–52

P. Kehr, 'Der angebliche Brief Paschals II an die Konsuln von Pisa und andere Pisaner Fälschungen', *Quellen und Forschungen aus italienischen Archiven und Bibliotheken* 6.2 (1904), 316–42

P. Lamma, *Comneni e Staufer. Ricerche sui rapporti fra Bisanzio e l'Occidente nel secolo XII*, 2 vols. (Rome, 1955–7)

L. Lenzi, *Le monete di Pisa* (Pisa, 1973)

A. Main, *I pisani alle prime crociate* (Livorno, 1893)

L. Naldini, 'La politica coloniale di Pisa nel Medioevo', *Bollettino storico pisano* 8 (1939), 64–87

C. Otten, 'Les Pisans en Orient de la première croisade à 1406', Thèse de IIIᵉ cycle, 2 vols., Université Paris 1 (1981)

C. Otten-Froux, 'Les Pisans en Egypte au Moyen Âge', *Praktika B' Diethnous Kypriologikou Synedriou* 2 (Nicosia, 1986), 127–43

V. Pacelli, 'Il contenuto economico della commenda nei documenti pisani e genovesi del secolo XII', *Bollettino storico pisano* 6 (1937), 7–41, 113–46

F. Panvini-Rosati, 'Note di numismatica pisana', *Rivista italiana di numismatica* 23 (1976), 209–19

P. Pierotti, *Pisa e Accon: l'insediamento pisano nella città crociata, il porto, il fondaco* (Pisa, 1987)

G. Rossetti, ed., *Pisa nei secoli XI e XII: formazione e caratteri di una classe di governo* (Pisa, 1979)

H. Rossi Sabatini, *L'espansione di Pisa nel Mediterraneo fino alla Meloria* (Florence, 1935)

A. Schaube, *Das Konsulat des Meeres in Pisa* (Leipzig, 1888)

D. Scorzi, *I pisani alla prima crociata* (Pisa, 1890)

M. Seidel, 'Dombau, Kreuzzugidee und Expansionspolitik. Zur Iconographie der pisaner Kathedralbaute', *Frühmittelalterliche Studien* 11 (1977), 340–69

M. Tangheroni, *Politica, commercio, agricoltura a Pisa nel Trecento,* Pubblicazioni dell'Istituto di storia della Facoltà di lettere dell'Università di Pisa (Pisa, 1973)

—— *Commercio e navigazione nel Medioevo* (Bari, 1996)

—— 'Pisa e la Romània', *Studi mediolatini e volgari* 47 (2001), 80–2

G. Vuillemin-Diem and M. Rashed, 'Burgundio de Pise', *Recherches de théologie et de philosophie médiévales* 64.1 (1997), 136–98

## BARCELONA

## HANDBOOKS, SURVEYS, PROSOPOGRAPHIES (alphabetical order)

Ll. Cases i Loscos, *Catàleg de protocols notarials de Barcelona* (Barcelona, 1990)

J. Oliveras Caminal, *Cartas reales (siglos XII–XV). Catálogo* (Barcelona, 1946)

F. Udina Martorell, *Guía del Archivo de la Corona de Aragon* (Madrid, 1986)

**PRIMARY SOURCES** (chronological order)

A. Capmany i de Montpalau, *Memorias históricas sobre la marina, comercio y artes de la antigua ciudad de Barcelona*, 4 vols. (Barcelona, 1779–92; repr. in 2 vols., Barcelona, 1961–3)
H. Finke, *Acta aragonensia*, 3 vols. (Berlin, 1908–22)
A. Rubio i Lluch, *Diplomatari de l'Orient català* (Barcelona, 1947)
G. Zurita, *Anales de la Corona de Aragon*, repr. A. Canellas Lopez, 9 vols. (Barcelona, 1967–86)
F. Soldevila, *Les quatre grans cròniques* (Barcelona, 1971)


**SECONDARY LITERATURE** (alphabetical order)

S. Bensch, 'Early Catalan contacts with Byzantium', in *Iberia and the Mediterranean World of the Middle Ages. Studies in honor of Robert I. Burns S.J.* (Leiden, New York, Cologne, 1995), vol. 1, 133–60
G. Feliu i Monfort, 'El comercio catalán con Oriente', *Revista de Historia Económica* 6.3 (1988), 689–707
M. Fernández Navarrete, 'Disertación histórica sobre la parte que tuvieron los Españoles en las guerras de Ultramar o de las Cruzadas', *Memorias de la Real Academia de Historia* 5 (1817), 37–190
M.T. Ferrer i Mallol and D. Duran i Duelt, 'Una ambaixada catalana a Constantinoble el 1176 i el matrimoni de la princesa Eudòxia', *Anuario de Estudios medievales* 30.2 (2000), 963–77
F. Giunta, *Aragonesi e Catalani nel Mediterraneo*, 2 vols. (Palermo, 1953–9)
E. Marcos Hierro, *Die byzantinisch-katalanischen Beziehungen in 12. und 13. Jahrhundert unter besonderer Berücksichtigung der Kronik Jakob I. von Katalonien-Aragon* (Munich, 1996)
—— 'Els catalans i l'imperi bizantí', in M.T. Ferrer i Mallol, ed., *Els catalans a la Mediterrània oriental a l'edat mitjana* (Barcelona, 2003), 23–77
Ll. Nicolau d'Olwer, *L'expansió de Catalunya en la Mediterrània oriental* (Barcelona, 1926; 3rd edn., Barcelona, 1974)

# 5

# The Venetian Chronicles and Archives as Sources for the History of Byzantium and the Crusades (992–1204)

## MICHAEL ANGOLD

VENICE IS ONE OF THE MAJOR REPOSITORIES of historical documentation for the Middle Ages. This is a concrete reflection of its splendid history, which may just possibly outshine both Byzantium and the crusades. The value of the Venetian sources for Byzantine and crusade history derives very largely from Venice's complicated relationship with both Byzantium and the crusades, which culminated in the Fourth Crusade and the temporary destruction of the Byzantine empire. This confirmed what had been in retrospect apparent since the First Crusade: that the histories of Venice, Byzantium and the crusades were interlinked. The Venetian sources illuminate this triangular relationship from a Venetian angle. But before 1204 they have much less to offer on the history of Byzantium or on the history of the crusades considered on their own. From the thirteenth century onwards it is a different matter. The Venetian sources become much richer. This was a reflection of Venice's enhanced position both in the old Byzantine empire and in the crusader states. The Venetians were able to build up a maritime empire which was a dominant feature of Mediterranean history down to the sixteenth century. In addition, Venice began to fulfil some of the functions formerly performed by Constantinople.[1] Before 1204 this had only been the remotest of possibilities.

---

[1] See A.E. Laiou, 'Venice as a centre of trade and of artistic production in the thirteenth century', in H. Belting, ed., *Il Medio Oriente e l'Occidente nell'arte del XIII secolo* (Bologna, 1982), 11–26.

*Proceedings of the British Academy* **132**, 59–94. © The British Academy 2007.

## SCHOLARLY APPROACHES TO RELATIONS BETWEEN VENICE AND BYZANTIUM

The rise to empire provided a theme of earlier histories of Venice. Particular attention is paid to the early history of Venice as it emerges from the Byzantine exarchate of Ravenna. Special emphasis is placed on emancipation from imperial authority, whether Byzantine or Carolingian. The period under consideration here from 992 to 1204 receives due attention. However, it is treated as a prelude to the creation of the Venetian *dominio* after 1204, rather than a period in its own right. J.J. Norwich has provided an excellent summation of the traditional approach to Venetian history.[2] It is based on a combination of the narrative sources and some official records, such as the treaties concluded with other powers. These were edited by T.L.F. Tafel and G.M. Thomas in three volumes published at Vienna in 1856 and 1857.[3] From the mid-twentieth century the documentary basis of Venetian history has been transformed by the publication of a whole series of new sources. A landmark was the edition in two volumes made by R. Morozzo della Rocca and A. Lombardo of *Documenti del commercio veneziano nei secolo XI–XIII* (Turin, 1940). This paved the way for a systematic publication of Venetian commercial documents, which provided detailed evidence of Venetian activities in Byzantium and the eastern Mediterranean from the early twelfth century. At the same time R. Cessi was editing the proceedings of the Great Council and the Senate. These have been calendered into French by F. Thiriet.[4] It has to be said that there is more or less nothing from before 1204.

These proceedings formed the foundation of Thiriet's *La Romanie vénitienne au Moyen Âge. Le développement et l'exploitation du domaine colonial vénitien (XIIe–XVe siècles)* (Paris, 1959). Nearly half a century later this remains the fundamental work on the Venetian empire. Thiriet was perhaps the first to begin the systematic exploitation of the wealth of new sources that was just starting to come on stream. The bulk of the book deals with the period after 1204. A short introduction along traditional lines traces the establishment of the Venetians in the Byzantine empire from the ninth and tenth centuries. In his *Byzantium and Venice: a study in diplomatic and cultural relations* (Cambridge, 1988) D.M. Nicol devotes substantially more space to the period before 1204. His treatment is dominated by the shadow

---

[2] J.J. Norwich, *A History of Venice* (London, 1982).

[3] Tafel and Thomas, *Urkunden*. There is a new edition of the treaties between Venice and Byzantium edited by M. Pozza and G. Ravegnani, *I trattati con Bisanzio, 992–1198* (Venice, 1993).

[4] R. Cessi, *Deliberazioni del Maggior Consiglio di Venezia*, 3 vols. (Bologna, 1931–50); F. Thiriet, *Délibérations des assemblées vénitiennes concernant la Romanie*, 2 vols. (Paris and The Hague, 1966–71).

of 1204. He pays due attention to the Venetian 'crusade' of 1122–5 which seems to prefigure subsequent events. He singles out Manuel I Komnenos's detention of Venetians in the Byzantine empire (1171) as marking 'a turning-point in relations between Byzantium and Venice'. It left a bitterness which to his mind led on to 1204. He has the support of Charles Brand, who argues that the return of the Venetians to Constantinople in the 1180s only made matters worse.[5] A rather different approach has been adopted by R.-J. Lilie in his *Handel und Politik zwischen dem byzantinischen Reich und den italienischen Kommunen Venedig, Pisa und Genua in der Epoche der Komnenen und der Angeloi (1081–1204)* (Amsterdam, 1984). His inclusion of Genoa and Pisa means that his canvass is rather broader than Nicol's, but it is all the same a work of political and diplomatic history. Lilie takes issue with those who see economic imperatives as the dominant issue determining the relations of Byzantium and the Italian republics. He does not believe that the increasing penetration of the Byzantine economy by the Italians from the early twelfth century led to its transformation. He disputes the notion that the market and commerce came to assume a preponderant role in the Byzantine economy. He agrees with the views set out by Michael Hendy in his *Studies on the Byzantine Monetary Economy ca.300–ca.1450* (Cambridge, 1985), where the contribution of the customs duties-cum-sales tax (known as *kommerkion*) to the state budget is deemed negligble by comparison with the proceeds of the land tax. Lilie sees the relations between Byzantium and Venice, or for that matter, between Byzantium and Pisa or Genoa, as determined by more obviously political and naval factors. To maintain its sea power Byzantium needed Italian support, which was equally necessary for Byzantine foreign policy. Lilie considers the period 1081–1204 on its own terms. His arguments are not overshadowed by the prospect of 1204. He is reluctant to accept that the fall of Byzantium in 1204 does emerge directly from the development of relations between Byzantium and Venice over the preceding hundred-and-twenty odd years. Instead, he argues for an equilibrium of interests, punctuated from time to time by crisis, normally brought on by the difficulties Byzantine emperors had in satisfying all the powers involved in a complicated foreign policy. So Manuel I Komnenos's decision to arrest Venetians in the Byzantine empire (1171) was taken in Lilie's opinion because of a conflict of interests in the Adriatic.

The main advocate for the importance of commercial relations in the development of Venice's relations with Byzantium has been Silvano Borsari, who over more than twenty years has produced a series of key studies, beginning with 'Il commercio veneziano nell'Impero bizantino nel XII secolo',

---

[5] C.M. Brand, *Byzantium Confronts the West, 1180–1204* (Cambridge, Mass., 1968), 195–206.

*Rivista storica italiana* 76 (1964), 982–1011 and culminating in *Venezia e Bisanzio nel XII. I rapporti economici* (Venice, 1988). Of particular import-ance is his 'Il crisobullo di Alessio I per Venezia', *Annali dell'Istituto italiano per gli studi storici* 2 (1970), 111–31, where he argues for the traditional dating of the chrysobull to May 1082. Borsari does not present an overall interpre-tation of Venice's role in the Byzantine empire. He is working in the tradition of G. Luzzatto, who was among the earliest scholars to exploit the wealth of Venice's commercial documentation.[6] Luzzatto helped to elucidate the nature of the contracts exchanged among Venetian merchants and financiers, and to establish the limitations of the documentation, while Borsari emphasises that the nature of its survival means that Venetian commercial documentation can only throw a patchy light on trading in the Byzantine empire. The papers of a single merchant or much more usually of a family were deposited with different Venetian monasteries. It means that you can follow the careers of a number of individual merchants, such as Romano Mairano, over longer or shorter periods. What do not survive from before 1204 are notarial ledgers, such as those that survive from Genoa, which give the activities of a clientèle over a set period of time. Borsari is wary of claiming too much, but he is able to use a series of case studies to follow the way that Venetian merchants developed their trading network within the Byzantine empire in the course of the twelfth century. Despite immersing himself in the commercial documen-tation he does not subscribe to economic imperative as the factor determin-ing the development of Byzantine relations with Venice. He never claims that there was any transformation of the Byzantine economy as a result of Italian activities, but he does produce evidence of Byzantine landowners selling off the produce of their estates to Venetian merchants. The inference is that this must have helped mobilise the agricultural potential of the Byzantine provinces. Borsari has also produced studies on the Venetian colonies after 1204,[7] but his work on the twelfth century approaches the period as a self-contained unit of importance in its own right and not simply as a prelude to empire.

The fundamental work on Komnenian foreign policy remains P. Lamma's *Comneni e Staufer. Ricerche sui rapporti fra Bisanzio e l'Occidente nel secolo XII*, 2 vols. (Rome, 1955–7), in which he gives due weight to the diplomatic and political relations between Byzantium and the Italian republics. In the wake of this book he contributed a study devoted to Venice and Byzantium.[8]

---

[6] Collected in his *Studi di storia economica veneziana* (Padua, 1954).

[7] S. Borsari, *Il dominio veneziano in Creta nel XIII secolo* (Naples, 1963); S. Borsari, *Studi sulle colonie veneziane in Romania nel XIII secolo* (Naples, 1966).

[8] P. Lamma, 'Venezia nel giudizio delle fonti bizantine dal X al XII secolo', *RSI* 74 (1962), 457–79.

Essentially a study of the Byzantine sources it broached another facet of Byzantine–Venetian relations: the creation of official images. The official Byzantine image of the Venetians became increasingly hostile over the twelfth century, as their presence became more intrusive. The Venetian image of Byzantium emerges from a series of studies by A. Pertusi which provided the basis for his 'Venezia e Bisanzio: 1000–1204', *Dumbarton Oaks Papers* 33 (1979), 1–22.[9] He takes as his starting-point the Venetian symbols of power, which derived initially from Byzantium. These became less and less appropriate with the rapid evolution of the Venetian constitution from the middle of the twelfth century, which saw the authority of the doge increasingly subordinated to a series of councils. By the late twelfth century on assuming office the doge had to make a *promissio* setting out his obligations to the *sapientes*, the judges, and the people. These constitutional changes were an important part of Venice's emergence as a fully autonomous political power. The argument is that these changes distanced Venice from Byzantium. The friction was something more than a matter of temporary disagreements, whether trade-related or a matter of diplomacy. Venice was emerging as a power in its own right rather than a client state. Byzantine resentment at Venetian insubordination was reciprocated. The famous charade where the Venetians dressed a negro in imperial vestments reflected their impatience with Byzantine pretensions.[10] While Manuel I Komnenos was remembered in the Frankish west as a great ruler who loved the Franks more than his own people, at Venice he appeared in a more sinister light. Though without any apparent foundation he was believed—even at the time of the Fourth Crusade—to have ordered the blinding of the Doge Enrico Dandolo.[11] The importance of Pertusi's work revolves around the way he underlines the significance of the changes in the relationship between Venice and Byzantium which occurred over the course of the twelfth century.

This does not exhaust the list of works devoted to Byzantine relations with Venice in the period 992–1204, but it is a representative sample of some of the most important work done to about the year 1990. Since then there has been something of a hiatus. This is perhaps best explained by the lack of new publications of source material on the period before 1204. However, Ch. Maltezou has done much to elucidate the topography of the Venetian quarter in Constantinople and the development in the years leading up to 1204 of

---

[9] A. Pertusi, '*Quedam regalia insignia*. Ricerche sulle insegne dei poteri dei dogi di Venezia nel Medioevo', *Studi veneziani* 7 (1965), 3–123; A. Pertusi, 'Venezia e Bisanzio nel secolo XI', in *La Venezia del Mille* (Florence, 1965), 117–60; A. Pertusi, 'Bisanzio e le insegne regali dei dogi di Venezia', *RSBN*, n.s. 2–3 (1965–6), 277–84.

[10] J.-L. Van Dieten, ed., Niketas Choniates, *Historia*, Corpus Fontium Historiae Byzantinae 11 (Berlin and New York, 1975), 86.

[11] T.F. Madden, *Enrico Dandolo and the Rise of Venice* (Baltimore, 2003), 64.

permanent Venetian settlement in Constantinople.[12] T.F. Madden's long-awaited book on Enrico Dandolo has recently appeared. It offers a new view of Venice's development in the twelfth century, where the main stress is on the relative independence of the Venetian church and on the far-reaching constitutional changes, which would eventually bring an oligarchy to power. On the Byzantine side Madden emphasises the non-confrontational stance adopted by the Venetian patriciate in the aftermath of the 1171 seizure. Patient diplomacy was the order of the day. Venice had little interest in turning a crusade against Byzantium in order to protect its interests.[13]

These studies lay out the shape of relations between Byzantium and Venice in the period from 992 to 1204. I have taken 992 as a starting-point because of the chrysobull granted to the Venetians by Basil II in that year.[14] It contained rather limited concessions reducing the tolls payable by Venetian ships as they passed through the Hellespont. This served as some reward for Venetian aid against Arab pirates in the Adriatic, but it pointed towards the growing need felt by Byzantium to harness Venetian naval power, which had recently become a significant factor. The alliance was renegotiated in 1081–2 in the face of the Norman threat to the Byzantine empire. The chrysobull issued by Alexios I Komnenos is by any standards a vital document.[15] It granted the Venetians freedom to trade in most of the ports of the Empire and exempted Venetians from customs duties and various other impositions. It was based on the assumption that the Venetians were 'true and faithful servants' of the Byzantine emperor; in other words that Venice was a client state of Byzantium, which had an exclusive call on the services of its fleet. The Venetians found these demands increasingly irksome, but it was quite impossible to tear up the chrysobull and begin again, because the privileges it granted opened up a world of new opportunities to the Venetians. Before 1082 Venetians had a prominent role to play in the carrying trade between Constantinople and Italy—not that this was on any great scale. Their participation in the internal trade of the Byzantine empire was still negligible. As the Venetians availed themselves of their privileged position, so they started to break into the internal trade of the Byzantine empire and to reconnoitre the possibilities of trade between Constantinople and Syria and Egypt. Trade between Italy and Byzantium was notoriously limited by the lack of capital

---

[12] C.A. Maltezou, 'Il quartiere veneziano'; C.A. Maltezou, 'Venetian *habitores, burgenses* and merchants in Constantinople and its hinterland (twelfth–thirteenth centuries)', in C. Mango and G. Dagron, eds., *Constantinople and its Hinterland*, (Aldershot, 1993), 233–41.

[13] T.F. Madden, *Enrico Dandolo and the Rise of Venice* (Baltimore, 2003). I have to thank the author for so generously and so readily sending me a copy of his new book.

[14] Tafel and Thomas, *Urkunden*, vol. 1, 36–9.

[15] Tafel and Thomas, *Urkunden*, vol. 1, 51–4.

in western hands. Venetians were able to build up capital after 1082 through their involvement in the trade of Byzantium and the eastern Mediterranean. It meant that Venetian prosperity depended more than ever on safeguarding its position in the Byzantine empire. From a Byzantine point of view the Venetian alliance was worth its inconveniences as long as the Normans of Sicily continued to be a threat to the Byzantine empire. From the mid-twelfth century this was less and less the case with obvious implications for Byzantine relations with Venice. For historians one of the major questions is whether the divergence of interests would inevitably lead to an attack upon Constantinople; whether it pointed the way to 1204.

It has become clear that the Venetian sources will illuminate the relations between Byzantium and Venice, while failing to provide material for the history of Byzantium for its own sake. Apart from treaties there are few Byzantine documents to be found in the Archivio di Stato at Venice. The Marciana Library, on the other hand, has one of the richest collections of Byzantine manuscripts. Their nucleus was the collection made by Cardinal Bessarion, who handed them over in 1468 to the safekeeping of Venice. For obvious reasons the contribution of the Marciana manuscripts to Byzantine history from 992 to 1204 will not be considered here. They represent—and were a product of—a quite different phase of Venice's relations with Byzantium.

The value of the Venetian sources for the period of Byzantine history that runs from 992 to 1204 depends very largely on how important Venice was to Byzantium. This is a problem which has received some attention in recent scholarship. Lilie has provided the clearest treatment. In economic terms Byzantium had relatively little need of the Venetians, but naval aid was another matter. Here the Byzantines had come to depend rather heavily on Venetian support. But even the economy may have functioned more effectively for the presence of Venetian merchants. This seems to be the lesson of Manuel I Komnenos's efforts at the end of his reign to normalise relations with the Venetians. Just because the Byzantine economy, like all economies until relatively recently, was overwhelmingly agrarian, it does not follow that trade was therefore of no consequence. Agrarian wealth has to be mobilised. Trade and the market have always been the most effective ways of doing this. The revenues accruing to the Byzantine state derived mainly from the agrarian sector, but the involvement of Venetian merchants in the trade in foodstuffs—largely to supply the appetite of Constantinople—can only have been beneficial. Even if we put aside for the present the question of 1204, it looks as though Byzantine relations with the Venetians constitute one of the dynamic elements of Byzantine history in the twelfth century. This is mostly a matter of the role that the Venetians came to assume in the wake of the concessions of 1082 in the internal trade of the Byzantine empire.

Down to the late eleventh century trade within the Byzantine empire had been closely regulated by the imperial government. It was done by government inspectors—the *kommerkiarioi*—established in provincial centres or through the guilds of Constantinople. Though never swept away the system of regulation ceased to function effectively, giving the Venetians and others a freer hand. It seems most unlikely that this was deliberate imperial policy. It was rather a consequence of the weakening of imperial control that was a feature of Byzantium in the eleventh century.[16] The Venetians were not the first foreigners to receive commercial privileges in the Byzantine empire. One has only to think of the Russians. But their privileges were granted as a way of ensuring a steady supply of the commodities provided by the Russian lands. Russian merchants made their way across the Black Sea to Constantinople, where they were granted quarters at St Mamas outside the city walls. Their trading was carefully supervised and they were not allowed to overwinter in Constantinople, but were required to return to Russia.[17] They did not infiltrate the trade of the Byzantine empire. This was the difference with the Venetians. It meant that, if the Venetians were not essential to the functioning of the Byzantine economy, they made a most valuable contribution which it was difficult for Byzantine emperors to ignore.

## NARRATIVE SOURCES FOR VENICE

The Venetian sources fall into three main groups. First, there are the narrative sources; then the diplomatic sources, and finally the commercial documents. The narrative and diplomatic sources have long been known; the commercial documents only relatively recently.

Venice does not boast a rich chronicle tradition in our period. There is a semi-official account of the early history of Venice which finishes in 1008. This is always ascribed to John the Deacon who features prominently in its closing pages.[18] There was, for whatever reason, nobody interested in continuing this work. Martin da Canal did not begin working on his *Estoires de Venise* until 1267. It was not an official history though he had official encouragement. It was also written in French rather than in Latin or Venetian. Martin da Canal makes it clear that he was addressing an audience beyond the confines of Venice.[19] It was left to the Doge Andrea Dandolo (1343–54)

---

[16] H. Antoniadis-Bibicou, *Les douanes à Byzance* (Paris, 1963), 145–55.
[17] S. Franklin and J. Shepard, *The Emergence of Rus 750–1200* (Harlow, 1996), 103–8, 117–21, 135–6.
[18] G. Monticolo, ed., *Giovanni Diacono*.
[19] A. Limentani, ed., *Martin da Canal*.

to produce an official history of Venice in the shape of his *Chronica per extensum descripta,* which took the story down to 1280.[20]

For the period under consideration there are some brief chronological entries—*Annales venetici breves*—that seem to have been collected around the beginning of the thirteenth century. More substantial is the anonymous *Historia ducum veneticorum*, which breaks off at the death of Doge Sebastiano Ziani in 1178, but there is a continuation in the shape of excerpts from the Giustiniani chronicle, which has not survived. This goes down to the death of Doge Pietro Ziani in 1229. It is clear that this chronicle emerged from circles close to the Ziani family, which was renowned as the richest in Venice and which supplied a succession of doges. If the form in which this chronicle has come down to us dates from *c.*1230, there is every likelihood that it was compiled over a much longer period of time, making use of previous annals to which the author refers. He noted for example at one point that he was basing his information on *Venetorum chronica*.[21] There is a good chance that the section down to the death of Sebastian Ziani was the work of a contemporary. The *Historia ducum veneticorum* has nothing on Byzantine history for its own sake but presents the Venetian side of events in the republic's dealings with Byzantium. It provides a detailed account of the 'crusade' of 1122–5.[22] Of particular interest is its insistence that it was only after the Venetian attack on the Aegean that John II banned the Venetians from the Empire. This makes sense because we know that the Venetians had continued to trade in the Byzantine empire despite the emperor's refusal to ratify Venetian privileges. Now as an act of retaliation against Venetian aggression he sought to sever all ties. According to the *Historia ducum veneticorum* John coupled this with secret messages to the Doge Domenico Michiel, suggesting that he send ambassadors to Constantinople to treat for peace. It was in other words a face-saving exercise. There is nothing in the Byzantine sources to corroborate this, but it is inherently likely. The next substantial entry in the *Historia ducum veneticorum* deals with the ramifications of Roger II of Sicily's attack on the Byzantine empire in 1147 at the time of the passage of the Second Crusade. Incidentally the crusade is totally ignored. It was not of interest to a Venetian chronicler. What at this point in his narrative he wanted to stress was that the Venetians had always been defenders of Byzantium. The phrase—*semper defensores Romanie*—is repeated on a number of occasions, as though a watchword of Venetian policy at this time. It made Manuel I Komnenos's decision to imprison the Venetians in the Byzantine empire in

---

[20] E. Pastorello, ed., *Andrea Dandolo.*
[21] H. Simonsfeld, ed., *Historia ducum veneticorum*, 75–6.
[22] *Historia ducum veneticorum*, 73–4.

March 1171 and impound their property all the more treacherous.[23] The *Historia ducum veneticorum* (p. 78) presents the Venetian case, which is competely at odds with that to be found in the Byzantine histories of John Kinnamos and Niketas Choniates. As the Venetian chronicler saw it, Manuel Komnenos deliberately lured the Venetians to the Byzantine empire, so that he could make an example of them. He invited 'the Venetians all to hasten to him and the lands of his empire as if to their own, as long as they brought plenty of money with them, because he proposed . . . that they alone should exploit Romania for trading purposes (*in mercationibus suis*)'. It is all too likely that Manuel I Komnenos made some such proposal at this juncture: he would not have offered the Venetians a monopoly of the trade of the Byzantine empire, but there may have been inducements to persuade Venetians to return to Constantinople. In 1168 the Doge Vitale Michiel had ordered all Venetians to return home to participate in a campaign in Dalmatia. Whatever the terms offered they were sufficiently favourable to attract Venetian interest. What the Venetian chronicler conceals is that once in Constantinople the Venetians breached their understanding with the Byzantine emperor and sacked the Genoese quarter. The *Historia ducum veneticorum* (pp. 79–80) then outlines the Venetian expedition despatched in 1172 as an act of retaliation. It failed. The Doge Vitale II Michiel was murdered on his return to Venice. In his place Sebastiano Ziani was elected unopposed. He was already an old man aged about seventy. There are details of his negotiations with the Byzantines, but at the time of his death in 1178 nothing definite had been secured. It did not matter so much because Sebastiano Ziani had done much to restore Venice's position and prestige. He concluded treaties with other powers: Sicily, Egypt, and the Magreb. His crowning achievement was the Peace of Venice of 1177. So important did the author of the *Historia ducum veneticorum* (pp. 82–9) consider this, that he included a document with the signatories of the peace. In retrospect, the Peace of Venice turns out to be a pivotal event, which saw Venice distancing itself from Byzantium. The Venetians were no longer *semper Romanie defensores*. The chronicler is not sufficiently aware of these shifts in Venice's position to be able to provide any sustained explanation of why it had ceased to perform this ancient function. The deceit of a Byzantine emperor was hardly the whole story or even the truth.

The *Historia ducum veneticorum* anticipated that series of private Venetian chronicles which are attested from the late thirteenth century. They cannot be dismissed as entirely worthless, but they have little concrete information on the period before 1204. They testify to a tradition of family chron-

---

[23] For the latest treatment of this incident, see Madden, *Enrico Dandolo*, 50–3.

icles, which compensated in part for the lack of official compilations. When one thinks of the official histories produced in the twelfth century—Caffaro at Genoa and Bernardo Maragone at Pisa—the lack of something similar in Venice is striking. It was not as though the patriotism which produced these chronicles was lacking in Venice.[24] However, the Venetians may have preferred to employ other means of articulating a sense of identity. At the centre of Venetian public life was the cult of St Mark. Hagiography may therefore have had a greater appeal than history as a way of defining themselves. The Venetian tradition of hagiography is far richer than its chronicle tradition. Some of the most valuable narratives were those of the translations of the relics of saints. As we shall see, the early Venetian chronicles have nothing on any Venetian participation in the First Crusade. We only learn about it from the contemporary *Translatio Sancti Nicolai*.[25] To judge from this narrative the acquisition of the relics of St Nicholas from Myra on the south coast of Asia Minor was of much greater importance than any help that the expedition may have given to the crusaders. Soon afterwards in 1110 the relics of St Stephen were acquired from Constantinople in a thoroughly underhand fashion and shipped to Venice. On the journey home a storm got up off Cape Malea. The passengers on board formed a confraternity to honour the saint, as a thank-offering to the saint for his protection. The Doge Ordelafo Falier gave the affair his approval and personally supervised the translation of the relics to the monastery of S. Giorgio Maggiore.[26]

Of greater historical importance is Cerbani Cerbani's *Translatio mirifici martyris Isidori a Chio insula in civitatem venetam (Jun. 1125)*.[27] This contemporary narrative is mixed up with an account of the Venetian 'crusade' of 1122–5. Cerbani had served at the Byzantine court under both Alexios I Komnenos and John II, but he decided to join up with the Venetian expedition. He was, however, refused permission to depart from Constantinople. He therefore left secretly and took ship across the Aegean, but was intercepted by the duke of Crete and taken to the island of Chios. There he prayed at the tomb of St Isidore that he would be released from captivity. Instead, he was taken back to Constantinople and condemned for disobeying the emperor.

[24] R.D. Face, 'Secular history in twelfth-century Italy: Caffaro of Genoa', *JMH* 6 (1980), 169–84; C. Wickham, 'The sense of the past in Italian communal narratives', in P. Magdalino, ed., *The Perception of the Past in Twelfth-century Europe* (London, 1992), 173–89, where it is stressed that other northern Italian cities, such as Milan and Piacenza do not produce official histories until the thirteenth century.

[25] *RHC Oc* 5 (Paris, 1895), 253–92.

[26] Fl. Cornelius (Corner), *Ecclesiae Venetae antiquis monumentis nunc etiam primum editis illustratae*, vol. 8 (Venice, 1729), 96–110. Cf. Andrea Dandolo, *Chronica per extensum descripta*, 227; S. Borsari, 'Per la storia del commercio', 105–8.

[27] *RHC Oc* 5 (Paris, 1895), 321–34.

He evades imprisonment and manages to get aboard a Greek ship, which is
driven by a storm to Chios, where once again he prays at the tomb of St
Isidore. He was able to make his way to Rhodes where he fell in with the
returning Venetian fleet, which proceeded to make its base at Chios. Cerbani
suggests that they should take St Isidore's relics back to Venice for safekeeping. Admittedly, this hagiographical narrative has little on Byzantine history
proper. However, it does reveal the dilemma of a Venetian in Byzantine
imperial service. The Venetian expedition forced Cerbani to make a choice
between his Byzantine and Venetian loyalties. He preferred the latter for three
reasons: his devotion to the Holy Sepulchre; the pressures placed upon him
by his compatriots; and the insolence of John II Komnenos, by which he presumably means his treatment of the Venetians in the Byzantine empire. It
reveals—it is true in just one case—how the division between Venetian and
Byzantine was hardening.

## DIPLOMATIC AND COMMERCIAL SOURCES

The Doge Andrea Dandolo not only produced an official history of Venice
down to 1280. He was also instrumental in putting into order Venice's treaties
with other powers. These were set out in the *Liber albus*, which dealt with
the Adriatic and points east and in the *Liber blancus* which dealt with Italy.
These already existed in some form or another, because Dandolo was responsible for a re-edition of the *Liber pactorum*, the original version of which is
to be dated, as L. Lanfranchi has argued, to the early thirteenth century.[28]
The documents preserved by the *Liber albus* contain the texts of most of the
treaties negotiated between Venice and Byzantium before 1204. They come in
the form of Latin translations of Greek originals. No Greek original of a
treaty between Venice and Byzantium survives before the 1277 chrysobull
that Michael VIII Palaiologos issued for Venice. The first chrysobull preserved in the original *Liber pactorum* is dated October 1148 and was granted
by Manuel I Komnenos to the Venetians. This is followed by Isaac II
Angelos's chrysobull of 1187 and a rescript of the same emperor of June
1189. Finally, there is the chrysobull of 1198 issued to the Venetians by
Alexios III Angelos. It comes as quite a surprise that earlier chrysobulls were
not included. It can only mean that there were no copies available when the
collection was being made. We only have the texts of Alexios I Komnenos's
chrysobull and its confirmation by his son John II in 1126 because they were
included in the chrysobulls of 1148 and 1187. This has caused problems

---

[28] L. Lanfranchi, *Famiglia Zusto*, 67.

because each has a slightly different text of Alexios's chrysobull. This is one of the reasons why there has been a debate as to the exact date of the chrysobull. It is complicated by Andrea Dandolo who in his *Chronica brevis* implies a date of 1084 and in his *Chronica per extensum descripta* a date of 1082. S. Borsari has given solid reasons for preferring the traditional date of 1082, not least that a document of 1083 shows the Doge Domenico Silvio bearing the title of *protosebastos* accorded to him in the treaty by Alexios I Komnenos.[29] The debate has otherwise hinged on Alexios's motives for conceding so much to the Venetians. The suggestion is that Alexios would have had little interest in making such concessions at a time when the Venetians had failed to prevent the conquest of Dyrrachion by the Normans. In fact, the Venetians remained Alexios's main hope of checking the Normans. They were still in a position to harry the Norman lines of communication.

The version contained in the 1148 chrysobull is usually considered authoritative. It is dated to May of the fifth indiction 6200 (i.e. AD 692). The year is obviously wrong. The fifth indiction, however, falls in 6590 (i.e. AD 1082). The version in the 1187 chrysobull is dated to May 6600 (i.e. AD 1092). But the indiction is still given as the fifth, whereas it should be the fifteenth. The Venetian copyist of the *Liber pactorum* is invariably correct in his use of the indiction, but is often hopelessly wrong about the Byzantine calendar year. Borsari's arguments by themselves provide a convincing case for the traditional date of 1082. The debate has moved on to the question of why the Venetian copyist should have got the year wrong. Thomas Madden suggests that it is tied up with converting Greek numerals into Roman numerals. He proposes that the copyist saw DXC (i.e. 590—the last three figures in the correct date of 6590) as CC (i.e. 200). David Jacoby has taken issue with this on the grounds that it is palaeographically unlikely. He prefers the idea that the Venetian copyist working in the early thirteenth century had got used to writing MCC (i.e. 1200) for the documents he was drawing up in Venice and absent mindedly added CC to 6000, which he wrote as a word not as a figure.

---

[29] S. Borsari, 'Il crisobullo di Alessio I per Venezia'. Very generously Peter Frankopan allowed me to see before publication his article 'Byzantine trade privileges to Venice in the eleventh century: the chrysobull of 1092', *JMH* 30 (2004), 135–60. He argues that 1092 provides a more plausible context for the grant of privileges to Venice on the part of Alexios I Komnenos, than does 1082. Specifically, Byzantium needed Venetian naval aid now that it was in a position to get to grips with Tzakas, the Turkish emir of Smyrna. Such a contention rests on a dismissal of Anna Komnene's information that her father made his grant to the Venetians in the context of his first war against the Normans. It is well known that Anna Komnene is often unreliable, but in this instance the arguments that she has misplaced her information are not compelling. Generally speaking, this attempt to reassign the chrysobull to the Venetians to the year 1092 means discarding on no very convincing grounds the evidence collected by Borsari which points to 1082 as the date when the privileges were first issued. On the other hand, Frankopan's suggestion that the privileges might well have been reissued in 1092 is something to take very seriously.

Unlikely as this sounds it is supported by the consistency with which the copyist made this mistake with other calendar dates.[30]

The Venetian dossier constitutes the most complete series of Byzantine treaties that has survived. The majority of the instruments date from after 1204. The treaties of 992, 1082, 1126, 1148, 1187, and 1198 are just a foretaste. They are also in a sense incomplete. There are no instructions to ambassadors, except for those of Enrico Dandolo to Enrico Navigaioso and Andrea Donà who negotiated the 1198 treaty.[31] It is therefore difficult to follow the complicated diplomacy that culminated in the signing of a treaty. It often lasted several years. No *praktikon* or survey of the Venetian quarter in Constantinople survives until 1148.[32] In the chrysobull of 1082 there is a reference to the *praktikon* through which property granted to the Venetians in Constantinople was to be handed over. It was drawn up by the imperial notary the *protanthypatos* George Makhetarios—a prosopographical snippet of the kind to be found in this documentation.[33] Much later on in 1189 arcades (*emboloi*) and quays (*skalai*) granted to Germans and Franks were handed over to the Venetians as part of the reparations they received for the losses they suffered in 1171. This was done through a *praktikon* drawn up by Constantine Petriotes in the presence of two imperial secretaries Constantine Pediadites and the *protonobelissimos* Niketas Balianites.[34] A still more serious loss are the *promissiones* of the Venetians, which first appear in the 1187 chrysobull.[35] These were the undertakings that the Venetians made in return for the privileges they received from the Byzantine empire.

As is well known, the treaties concluded between Byzantium and Venice took the form of an imperial chrysobull.[36] They were in other words notionally a unilateral concession—an act of benevolence on the part of the emperor. Underlying this was the assumption that Venice was a client of the Empire. The Venetians are compared in the prooimion of the 1082 chrysobull to friends and assistants (*amicis et ministris*).[37] Then more technically they are referred to as *rectis et veris dulis* of the Byzantine emperor.[38] That is

[30] T.F. Madden, 'The chrysobull of Alexius I Comnenus to the Venetians'; D. Jacoby, 'The chrysobull . . . a rejoinder'.

[31] H. Kretschmayr, *Geschichte von Venedig*, vol. 1 (Gotha, 1905), 473. Cf. Brand, *Byzantium Confronts the West*, 201–2; Madden, *Enrico Dandolo*, 114–15.

[32] Madden, *Enrico Dandolo*, 109–13.

[33] Madden, *Enrico Dandolo*, 54. Cf. A.P. Kazhdan, *Sotsial'nyi sostav gospodstvuiushchego klassa Vizantii XI–XII vv* (Moscow, 1974), 93, 107, 111, 120, 127, 137, 178, 192, 203, 212.

[34] Tafel and Thomas, *Urkunden*, vol. 1, 208. Cf. Kazhdan, *Sotsial'nyi sostav*, 51, 53, 95, 98, 105, 114, 115, 118, 119, 126, 128, 138, 149, 152, 153, 154, 166, 178, 179, 194, 210, 220.

[35] Tafel and Thomas, *Urkunden*, vol. 1, 196–201.

[36] F. Dölger and J. Karayannopoulos, *Byzantinische Urkundenlehre* (Munich, 1968), 94–100.

[37] Tafel and Thomas, *Urkunden*, vol. 1, 51.

[38] Tafel and Thomas, *Urkunden*, vol. 1, 53.

'true and trustworthy servants'. The chrysobull of 1126 assumed a return to this state of affairs after a brief rupture.[39] In the 1148 chrysobull the Venetians are referred to as 'most loyal to our Empire' (*fidelissimis Imperio nostro*).[40] The Venetians recognised an obligation of loyalty and service to the Empire and Romania, which they confirmed on oath. Manuel I Komnenos clearly thought that in 1171 the Venetians had failed to honour these obligations. Relations between the Venetians and the Byzantines were reviewed by the chrysobull of 1187 where it is stated that in recent times the Venetians had no longer been 'friends bound by treaty' (*federati amici*) nor numbered among Byzantium's 'favoured friends' (*amicis fautoribus*).[41] This was in contrast to an earlier time when 'they formed a single harmonious one-headed body with Byzantium' (*unum quoddam corpus unanime cum Romania effecti uno capite*).[42] The act of issuing this chrysobull, it was assumed, restored the previous state of affairs; it was as if 'an amputated limb had been rejoined to the body'.

It is clear that the exact status of the Venetians was a matter of concern to the Byzantine authorities. Byzantine foreign policy aimed to fix the exact degree of inferiority of the powers with which it had to deal. It was important because from that stemmed the mutual obligations created by the relationship. In theory, these ties were determined by imperial benevolence, but in practice—it could hardly be otherwise—they were a matter of negotiation. In 1082 client status suited the Venetians, though the overthrow of Doge Domenico Silvio who had negotiated the 1082 chrysobull suggests that there were those at Venice who were less than happy about the way it tied Venice more closely to Byzantium than had been the case for several centuries. Byzantium was unwilling to forgo the fiction of Venice's client status because this was inseparable from the latter's obligation to provide Byzantium with naval protection. But the traditional idea of Byzantine foreign policy and diplomacy as Machiavellian before the word has been called into question.[43] Byzantine foreign policy does not seem to have been based on carefully garnered intelligence, which identified Byzantine interests. Byzantine diplomacy was not the work of a carefully trained corps of diplomats. It was as often as not a matter of reacting to events. So the grant of the 1082 chrysobull was a desperate effort to retain Venetian support against the Normans. The implications of a grant of freedom from customs duties were only dimly

---

[39]  Tafel and Thomas, *Urkunden*, vol. 1, 96.
[40]  Tafel and Thomas, *Urkunden*, vol. 1, 123.
[41]  Tafel and Thomas, *Urkunden*, vol. 1, 179.
[42]  Tafel and Thomas, *Urkunden*, vol. 1, 180.
[43]  S. Franklin and J. Shepard, *Byzantine Diplomacy* (Cambridge, 1992), 41–71.

recognised. This chrysobull was renewed by successive Byzantine emperors under pressure of circumstances.

The Venetian dossier does however contain a warning against too extreme a revision of the traditional view of Byzantine diplomacy. It reveals both the flexibility and ingenuity that is inseparable from the proper conduct of a foreign policy and the expertise that one connects with skilled diplomats. The treaties themselves were crafted documents, often the product of the exchange of several embassies. The 1198 chrysobull has preserved the names of some of the Byzantine officials responsible for handling the complicated negotiations that led to its issue. The imperial secretary, the *protonobelissimos* John Kataphloros was initially despatched to Venice with a returning Venetian delegation to conclude preliminary negotiations, but failed to resolve some difficult points. So another Venetian embassy was sent to Constantinople, this time bringing back with them the imperial *akolouthos* John Nomikopoulos. The results were no more satisfactory. Yet another Venetian delegation left for Constantinople. On this occasion negotiations were in the hands of one of the most powerful figures at court, the logothete of the *dromos* Demetrios Tornikes.[44] The chrysobull that resulted was then taken to Venice by the imperial *protonotarios* Theodore Aulikalamos.[45]

Though chrysobulls purported to be an act of grace on the part of the Byzantine empire they were the product of careful negotiation. We do not have the instructions given to the Byzantine diplomats, but the care with which Venetian ambassadors to Constantinople were briefed may be a reflection of Byzantine practice. The negotiations that lay behind the issue of a chrysobull are most clearly revealed in the chrysobull of 1198. The Venetian ambassadors raised with the Byzantine emperor the question of the legal status of Venetians in the Byzantine empire—a matter still not settled in written form. The emperor had the position set out in the chrysobull, having made a number of concessions to the Venetians.[46] Something similar must have happened in 1148 when the Venetians outlined the difficulties they were confronting when trading in Crete and Cyprus.[47] This too was settled to the Venetians' satisfaction. Far from being rigid and doctrinaire Byzantine diplomacy was flexible and subtle. It was also designed to ensure that the exact obligations of the Venetians were set out. The first surviving Venetian *promissiones* date from February 1187. They were extensive and concentrated on the

---

[44] Tafel and Thomas, *Urkunden*, vol. 1, 249–50. Cf. Kazhdan, *Sotsial'nyi sostav*, 92, 105, 107, 115, 117, 127, 138, 149, 159, 164, 176, 179, 190, 205; *Oxford Dictionary of Byzantium*, s.vv. Kataphloron, Tornikios.

[45] Tafel and Thomas, *Urkunden*, vol. 1, 256.

[46] Tafel and Thomas, *Urkunden*, vol. 1, 273–6.

[47] Tafel and Thomas, *Urkunden*, vol. 1, 124.

provision of a naval force. It was even stipulated that the emperor would pay for galleys to be built at Venice.[48] It may be that the reason why earlier *promissiones* do not survive is because they were superseded by later undertakings and had become redundant. We can be fairly sure that in their broad outlines the *promissiones* of 1187 were similar to those made in 1082, in 1126 and in 1148.

The value of the series of treaties negotiated between Venice and Byzantium lies in the way it provides a case study of Byzantine diplomacy and the development of an area of foreign policy. It has to be studied in conjunction with Byzantine policy towards Genoa and Pisa, where at the end of the twelfth century there is not only a more complete documentation, but some of the key documents survive in the original, which is not the case for Venice.

The privileges granted to the Italians did not consist only of a reduction in—or in the case of the Venetians exemption from—the payment of customs duties along with a series of other port taxes. They were also granted property within Constantinople. The instrument of conveyance was the *praktikon*. This served as a title deed. It listed the properties in question, often the inhabitants, and any obligations to the state. It also contained a survey of the bounds of the properties. The chrysobull of 1082 lists properties along the Golden Horn granted to the Venetians.[49] These were then handed over by the grant of a *praktikon*, which is mentioned in a document of 1090.[50] This document has not survived. The first *praktikon* for the Venetian quarter in Constantinople is incorporated in the first chrysobull issued by Manuel I Komnenos for the Venetians in March 1148.[51] It contains a detailed survey of the Venetian quarter.[52] It comes in two sections. The first consists of the quarter as it existed at the start of Manuel Komnenos's reign. It is not clear that this was what Alexios I Komnenos had granted in the chrysobull of 1082, where it seems to have been more a question of individual properties rather than a whole area along the waterfront. The second deals with a block of property lying to the east of the original concession. This was a new grant made by Manuel Komnenos. The most valuable piece of property came in the form of the St Markianos wharf. It is specified that this was in the possession of one Chrysiobasilius, whose name indicates that he was Greek rather than

[48]  Tafel and Thomas, *Urkunden*, vol. 1, 196.
[49]  Tafel and Thomas, *Urkunden*, vol. 1, 52.
[50]  Tafel and Thomas, *Urkunden*, vol. 1, 56.
[51]  Tafel and Thomas, *Urkunden*, vol. 1, 109–13 *practico traditionis eorum* (i.e. properties) *corporalis*.
[52]  See S. Borsari, *Venezia e Bisanzio nel XII secolo*, 32–4 and esp. 34, n. 12, where he provides a fuller and more accurate text of the bounds of the Venetian quarter.

Venetian. There was no reason why the grant to the Venetians should have entailed his dispossession.

The value of a survey of this kind is that it provides an insight into the urban fabric of Constantinople, of a kind that is almost impossible to obtain otherwise. The core of the Venetian quarter was an *embolos* or arcade that ran parallel to the sea walls. Surrounding the Venetian quarter was property of one sort or another belonging to ecclesiastical institutions. Opening off were a number of small courtyards—the measurements of one are given as eight-and-a-half by seven-and-a-third *brachia*; that is roughly 50 feet by 45. There were workshops, for example three turning out candlesticks which belonged to a member of the Hikanatos family. There were two separate sets of money-changers' tables. In one there were nine tables and in another two belonging to the monastery of the Milion. There were two stalls (*stationes*) where bread was sold. There were small houses interspersed with some grander buildings often belonging to religious institutions. It was an area that was not completely built up. There were also empty spaces itemised.

The Venetians took over a working neighbourhood. Their presence must have produced some changes, but there was no effort made to replace the local inhabitants with Italian immigrants. For the townscape of twelfth-century Constantinople these *praktika* are invaluable. As Paul Magdalino has demonstrated,[53] the Venetian documents have to be taken in conjunction with Pisan and Genoese documents, which are a rather richer source. Among other things the Genoese archives have preserved two detailed inventories from 1192 and 1202 respectively of the so-called palace of Botaneiates in Constantinople, which had been granted to the Genoese. These allow a reconstruction of a Byzantine palace.[54] In one respect the Venetian documentation has something unique to offer. These are a series of contracts concluded from 1183 onwards when the Venetians began to return in numbers to their quarter in Constantinople. They have been preserved in the archives of the abbey of San Giorgio Maggiore, which was a major property-owner in Constantinople. They record the leases made by the abbey to a number of tenants, who were under an obligation to improve the property leased by building on it. Not all the lessees were Venetians. Some were Greeks, such as Ioannes 'de la Cretiky' who leased property in October 1195 from the prior of St Mark's in Constantinople, which was a dependency of San Giorgio Maggiore.[55] Occasionally, these leases include the bounds of the property

---

[53] P. Magdalino, 'The maritime neighbourhoods of Constantinople. Commercial and residential functions, sixth to twelfth centuries', *DOP* 54 (2000), 209–26.

[54] M.J. Angold, *The Byzantine Aristocracy IX to XIII Centuries*, BAR International Series 121 (Oxford, 1984), 254–66.

[55] L. Lanfranchi, ed., *S. Giorgio Maggiore*, vol. 3, no. 581, 399–401.

and provide some local landmarks, such as the stone wharf of St Nicholas,[56] which conceivably represents Venetian investment in the quarter. The tensions of the time are reflected in the frequent references in these leases to both imperial and Venetian violence.

These documents represent perhaps the most original contribution of the Venetian sources to the history of Byzantium—certainly of Constantinople—before 1204, even if we are only dealing in a handful of documents compared with the many hundreds of Venetian commercial documents edited by Morozzo della Rocca and Lombardo from before 1204. These allow us to reconstruct the development of Venetian trade in Byzantium and the eastern Mediterranean. Sadly, they tell us almost nothing about Byzantine history. These documents apparently reveal a closed world of Venetian merchants, who frequent the markets of the Byzantine empire, but who do business among themselves. Byzantines rarely appear in the documents. There are chance references to two Venetian businessmen buying up property at Halmyros in Thessaly—one of the main centres of Venetian trade at that time—from members of a local Greek family, the Pillari.[57] More revealing is a document of 1151 which shows Venetian merchants buying olive oil from the *archontes* of Sparta for despatch to Constantinople.[58] It stands to reason that the Venetians must have done business with Greeks. But why has this left almost no trace in the surviving record? A possible explanation is this: most of these transactions would have been recorded in Greek, but these would not have been of interest to a Venetian court and therefore not thought worth preserving. However, documents drawn up in Latin by Venetian notaries for Greeks have survived. Far and away the most important for Byzantine prosopography is a document of September 1111 drawn up in Constantinople by a Venetian notary. It was a quittance made out to a member of the Zusto family by Kalopetrus Xanthos, a *vestioprates* and imperial *vestarches*. He had engaged Enrico Zusto to transport silks to the Egyptian port of Damietta on a Venetian ship. For his part Enrico agreed to pay the Byzantine 125 *hyperpyra* of good gold for the silks within thirty days of his return. This he duly did.[59] The interest of the document resides in its revelation that the guild of the silk merchants (*vestiopratai*) was not only still in operation, but had retained its links to the imperial court. But this is its last mention in the sources. The advantages there were in using the services of a

---

[56] *Scala petrina S. Nicolai: S. Giorgio Maggiore*, vol. 3, no. 455, 232–3.
[57] *S. Giorgio Maggiore*, vol. 2, nos. 231–3, 463–70. The purchase was made *per cartula Grece scripta*, which of course does not survive.
[58] Lombardo and Morozzo della Rocca, *Nuovi documenti*, no. 11.
[59] Lanfranchi, *Famiglia Zusto*, no. 6, 23–4.

Venetian merchant for the export of silks may well be the explanation for its disappearance.[60] Venetian infiltration of Byzantium is further emphasised by the way the document was attested by a Venetian holding the relatively high title of *protonobelissimos* at the Byzantine court.[61] A different kind of infiltration emerges from a document of September 1188. By it Theodore 'de Calo Techaristo', a Greek inhabitant of Constantinople, promised to pay an annual rent of eighteen old *hyperpyra* for a term of nine years to the church of St Mark in Constantinople for house property in the Venetian quarter.[62] But infiltration never extended to the retail trade, which helps to explain the lack of Venetian involvement in the local economy.

The documentation is much better on the commodities in which Venetian merchants operating in the Byzantine empire trafficked. They were mostly foodstuffs, but a document from Smyrna shows that two Venetian brothers, Romano and Samuele Mairano, had in their possession gold, silver, copper, iron, lead and tin. In addition, they had male and female slaves as well as pearls.[63] Venetians to an extent grew rich on their trade in Byzantium. The companies they formed for trade there grew rapidly in value from a few *hyperpyra* to several thousand by the middle of the twelfth century. But this tells us little directly about the state of the Byzantine economy. The most original development was the way that Venetian merchants based mainly in Constantinople were able to build up a trading network that reached to Venice and southern Italy in one direction and to the crusader states and Egypt in another. They were infiltrating, but also developing on a much larger scale trading networks around the Aegean and eastern Mediterranean for which there is earlier evidence. By and large the Venetians were able to do this with little direct reference to the authorities in either Byzantium or the crusader states. The Venetian commercial documents are a capital source but not for Byzantine history.

## VENICE AND THE CRUSADER STATES

The value of the Venetian sources for Byzantine history depends upon an assessment of the importance and character of Veneto-Byzantine relations. A similar line can be taken when it comes to the history of the crusader states, which is distinct from crusader history. Contemporary chronicles have little

---

[60] See R.S. Lopez, 'The silk industry in the Byzantine empire', *Speculum* 20 (1945), 13–20; D. Simon, 'Die byzantinischen Seidenzünfte', *BZ* 68 (1975), 23–46; E. Frances, 'Alexis Comnène et les privilèges octroyés à Venise', *Byzantinoslavica* 29 (1968), 17–23.

[61] See F. Dölger, *Byzantinische Diplomatik* (Ettal, 1956), 26–33.

[62] Lombardo and Morozzo della Rocca, *Nuovi documenti*, no. 40.

[63] Morozzo della Rocca and Lombardo, *Documenti*, vol. 1, no. 131, pp. 130–1.

to say about the participation of the Venetians in the First Crusade, which contrasts with the way Genoese and Pisan chronicles laud the exploits of their compatriots. It is therefore normally assumed that the First Crusade was of little interest to Venice. A different story emerges, if you read between the lines of the narrative of the translation of the relics of St Nicholas, which is the major source for Venice's involvement in the First Crusade. If it is to be believed, the Venetian Doge Vitale I Michiel (1096–1101) not only took the cross but had a fleet of some 200 ships prepared. This would have been the largest naval expedition launched to support the crusaders. It reached Jaffa in June 1100, where a joint attack against Acre was planned with Godfrey de Bouillon, but this had to be abandoned on the latter's death. Instead, the Venetians helped conquer the less prestigious target of Haifa. It would seem that the Venetians had little to show for their efforts, which may explain why so much is made of the acquisition along the way at Myra of the relics of St Nicholas and of his uncle of the same name. The narrative records a blanket grant of privileges by Godfrey de Bouillon, but no such privileges have survived. There is even a question-mark hanging over the notion of a substantial Venetian involvement in the conquest of Haifa.

Currently Thomas Madden is challenging the accepted view of Venetian indifference to the crusade. He quite rightly points out that the old canard, 'Venetians first, Christians second' has no support in the sources.[64] However, compared to the Genoese and Pisans they contributed relatively little to the early crusades. Michel Balard has noted that despite this the Venetians did rather better than their rivals in terms of the privileges gained in the crusader states.[65] This can largely be explained by the way they exploited their central role in the 'crusade' of 1123.[66] The 'crusade' of 1123 is among the few episodes of twelfth-century history to which the contemporary Venetian chronicles devote a great deal of attention. Its importance for Venice was immediately apparent. It allowed the Venetians to establish themselves in the Holy Land on a par with the Pisans and the Genoese. The Venetians arrived in July 1123 and won a great victory over the Fatimid fleet off Askalon. They then made for the port of Acre, where they negotiated with the patriarch of Jerusalem Warmund (or Gormond), the king of Jerusalem Baldwin II having

---

[64] Madden, *Enrico Dandolo*, 241, n. 2. Cf. D.E. Queller and I.B. Katele, 'Venice and the conquest of the Kingdom of Jerusalem', *Studi veneziani* n.s. 12 (1986), 15–43.

[65] M. Balard, 'Communes italiennes, pouvoir et habitants des états francs de Syrie–Palestine au XIIᵉ siècle', in M. Shatzmiller, ed., *Crusaders and Muslims in Twelfth-century Syria* (Leiden, 1993), 47–8.

[66] J. Riley-Smith, 'The Venetian crusade of 1122–1124', in G. Airaldi and B.Z. Kedar, eds., *I communi italiani nel Regno crociato di Gerusalemme* (Genoa, 1986), 339–50, where it is argued that the Venetian expedition was part of a larger enterprise, which had the support of the First Lateran Council.

fallen into the hands of the Muslims. It was eventually decided that the Venetians should attack the port of Tyre, which was still in Muslim hands, and then possibly Askalon. In the event, it was only Tyre and its hinterland that fell. The Venetians were to receive a third part of any conquests made.

This was set out in the so-called *Pactum Warmundi*. It is one of the few Venetian documents of the time to survive in the original, as well as in copies in the *Liber albus* and the *Liber pactorum*.[67] As the price of their cooperation the Venetians required—in addition to the third part of any conquests—confirmation of their existing property and privileges in the crusader kingdom. These included the right to a church, a street, a market, a bath and a bakery in every city under the jurisdiction of the king of Jerusalem and of his barons. Such a concession may well be a reiteration of the grant originally made by Godfrey de Bouillon, but there are few signs that the Venetians ever availed themselves of this blanket provision. They were more concerned to secure confirmation of their rights and property at Acre which was their main centre of operations. There they already possessed a mill, a baker's and a bath-house and they had the privilege of using their own weights and measures. They were now granted additional property in their part of Acre along with confirmation of a grant made by Baldwin I in the town of Sidon. The *Pactum Warmundi* clarified the right the Venetians already enjoyed of using their own weights and measures. It was stipulated that they could use their own weights and measures for transactions among themselves or when selling to third parties, but when purchasing from a third party they had to use the royal weights and measures and to pay for the privilege. The inference is that Venetian merchants had to obtain goods for export on the royal markets. This raises the important problem of the Venetians' exact involvement in the economy of the Kingdom of Jerusalem and of the degree of control exercised over the Venetians by the kings of Jerusalem. J. Riley-Smith rejected the traditional view that unwise concessions by the first kings of Jerusalem meant that the Italians—and the Venetians in particular—enjoyed almost complete autonomy. He thought that the royal administration ensured not only that the Venetians were forced to make their purchases on the royal markets, but that they continued to exact payment of market taxes.[68] The *Pactum Warmundi* states that 'once the price has been given (*precio dato*)' the Venetians have the right to buy from other people using royal weights and measures. Riley-Smith translates *precio dato* as 'having paid the market tax'.

---

[67] Tafel and Thomas, *Urkunden*, vol. 1, 84–9; M. Pozza, 'Venezia e il Regno di Gerusalemme dagli svevi agli angioni', in *I communi italiani*, 353–72 (text: 373–9).

[68] J. Riley-Smith, 'Government in Latin Syria and the commercial privileges of foreign merchants', in D. Baker, ed., *Relations between East and West in the Middle Ages* (Edinburgh, 1973), 109–32.

M.-L. Favreau-Lilie objects that *precium* is never used in the sense of a tax.[69] In her opinion it was a matter of the price paid for the use of royal weights and measures. She must be correct because the next sentence categorically exempts with one exception the Venetians from all payments of taxes and dues. That exception was a tax on pilgrims, amounting to a third of the fare. Given the huge influx of pilgrims in the wake of the establishment of the Kingdom of Jerusalem this must have been a lucrative source of income and at this stage of much greater importance than any revenues derived from trade. On the other hand, in broad terms Riley-Smith is likely to be correct that the royal administration was not guilty of heedlessly granting away rights to the Italian mercantile states, such as Venice. It was careful to protect its most important source of revenue. This receives some support from a strange rider added to the stipulation about the payment of pilgrim taxes. The royal administration was to pay 300 bezants to the Venetians from the market revenues (*fonde*) of Tyre. In all probability this was a measure designed to encourage the Venetians to land pilgrims at Tyre once it was safely under Frankish control. Looked at in this light it would seem to be a way of ensuring that there was no infringement of the principle that all pilgrims paid tax to the king.

Another indication of the care taken by the twelfth-century kings to retain some degree of control over the Italians in their kingdom comes in the confirmation of the *Pactum Warmundi* drawn up for King Baldwin II in 1125.[70] It added that for the third part of Tyre and its hinterland the Venetians had to provide three knights service for the king. This established that the Venetians were not exempt from the feudal obligations that knit together crusader society. In 1138 Orlando Contarini was enfeoffed with the Venetian territories around Tyre, consisting of twenty-one villages and one third of a further fifty-one villages. He left no heirs and it is not possible to establish his successors. J. Prawer argued that the conquest of Tyre was the signal for Venetians to establish themselves on a permanent basis in the Holy Land.[71] The inference is that already in the twelfth century the Venetians constituted a powerful element of crusader society, integrated into both feudal and urban networks. M.-L. Favreau-Lilie takes issue with such an interpretation, which reads back into the twelfth century the conditions of the following century.[72] She convincingly shows that few Venetians were established in the Holy Land on a permanent basis in the twelfth century. The inhabitants

---

[69] M.-L.Favreau-Lilie, *Die Italiener im Heiligen Land vom ersten Kreuzzug bis zum Tode Heinrichs von Champagne (1098–1197)* (Amsterdam, 1989), 463.
[70] Tafel and Thomas, *Urkunden*, vol. 1, 90–4; Pozza, 'Venezia e il regno di Gerusalemme', 379–85.
[71] J. Prawer, *Crusader Institutions* (Oxford, 1980), 217–49.
[72] Favreau-Lilie, *Die Italiener*, 498–508.

of the Venetian quarter in Acre were mostly Frankish burgesses, over whom the Venetians had been granted jurisdiction by the *Pactum Warmundi*. The Venetians of Acre and Tyre were largely a floating population of merchants and their servants, sea captains and their crews. Some degree of continuity was provided by priests from Venice who were responsible for much of the day-to-day administration. It is not likely that Venetian trade in the Holy Land was of any great volume in the twelfth century. As we have seen in the case of the Byzantine empire, the Venetian commercial documents provide very little evidence of involvement with the local economy. It was more a matter of creating a trading network round the Aegean and eastern Mediterranean. A place such as Acre was a very useful stopping-off point on the trade route that linked Constantinople and the ports of the Nile delta. Contracts could be drawn up and debts settled. Ships could be built, fitted out or repaired in comparative safety. It is likely that Acre became more important after the Venetians were expelled from the Byzantine empire in 1171. Refugees from Constantinople made their way to Acre on a ship belonging to Romano Mairano.[73]

There does seem to have been more activity in the late 1170s, but this was temporary because the Venetians started to return in numbers from the mid-1180s to Constantinople. It may have been because their energies were devoted to re-establishing their trading network in the Byzantine empire that the Venetians did not react in the same way as Pisa and Genoa to the loss of the Kingdom of Jerusalem in 1187, even though Tyre, in which it had a special interest, was all that remained to the Franks. It was in Tyre that Conrad of Montferrat held out with the help of the Genoese and Pisans, whom he generously rewarded. However, the possibility that the Venetians would be displaced by their rivals forced them to act. A small expedition was despatched to the aid of the crusaders besieging Acre. In return, Conrad of Montferrat, then king of Jerusalem in his wife's name, confirmed the *Pactum Warmundi*.[74]

The Venetian sources do not have a great deal on the crusades and the crusader states for the period before 1187. The expedition of 1123 excepted the Venetians were not much involved in crusading activity. Though notionally they had a right to establish themselves in all the cities under the authority of the king of Jerusalem and of all his barons, they were mainly interested in Acre and Tyre. There is no sign that the Venetians were present in force in the crusader states before 1187. This is in direct contrast with the position in the thirteenth century, when the Venetians were much more deeply involved in the affairs of the Kingdom of Jerusalem. It was only from the early thirteenth century that the Venetians established themselves as a permanent pres-

[73] Tafel and Thomas, *Urkunden*, vol. 1, 168.
[74] Tafel and Thomas, *Urkunden*, vol. 1, 213–15.

ence in the crusader states. This was connected with the growing commercial importance of the Palestinian ports. It may also have something to do with the comparative weakness of royal power in the thirteenth century, which allowed the Italians greater freedom of action and gave them real political power in the Kingdom of Jerusalem, which they had not enjoyed in the twelfth century.[75]

## VENICE AND THE FOURTH CRUSADE

The Venetian sources shed light on Venetian activities in Byzantium and the crusader states. Their value for the history of Byzantium and the crusader states depends almost entirely on the impact made by the Venetians. In the case of the crusader states this was rather limited before 1204; in the case of Byzantium it was problematic. The best that can be said is that the commercial activities of the Venetians did not transform the Byzantine economy, but constituted a dynamic element. However, Venetian interests do not provide an adequate explanation of the outcome of the Fourth Crusade. On this Donald Queller[76] seems to be completely vindicated by recent work, notably by Thomas Madden[77] and by John Pryor, who skilfully argues that the composition of the crusader fleet only makes sense if Egypt was indeed the goal of the Fourth Crusade.[78] The diversion of the Fourth Crusade to Constantinople with the purpose of placing the young Alexios Angelos on the throne was espoused with most enthusiasm by the crusade leaders, Boniface of Montferrat to the fore. The Doge Enrico Dandolo was always far more reluctant. He is likely to have been persuaded by the practical difficulties of provisioning a great expedition.[79] Whatever the underlying reasons for the diversion of the Fourth Crusade its impact on Byzantine history was colossal. Venetian sources shed their own light on the enterprise, but they are far from satisfactory. They have surprisingly little to offer either on Byzantium or the crusade. This is in stark contrast to the amount of material

---

[75] Cf. M. Balard, 'Communes italiennes', 43–64.

[76] D.E. Queller and G.W. Day, 'Some arguments in defense of the Venetians on the Fourth Crusade', *American Historical Review* 81 (1976), 717–37; D.E. Queller and T.F. Madden, 'Some further arguments in defense of the Venetians on the Fourth Crusade', *Byz* 62 (1992), 433–73.

[77] Madden, *Enrico Dandolo*, 133–54.

[78] J.H. Pryor, 'The Venetian fleet for the Fourth Crusade and the diversion of the Fourth Crusade to Constantinople', in M. Bull and N. Housley, eds., *The Experience of Crusading*, vol. 1, *Western Approaches* (Cambridge, 2003). I have to thank John Pryor for making this available to me at a moment's notice.

[79] M.J. Angold, *The Fourth Crusade: event and context* (Harlow, 2003), 84–92. Cf. Madden, *Enrico Dandolo*, 147.

they contain for the establishment of a Venetian *dominio* after 1204 in former Byzantine territories.

The treaties concluded in April 1201 between Venice and the individual crusade leaders at least provide documentation of the basis for cooperation between the Venetians and the crusaders.[80] These initial treaties would then be supplemented by the agreement made between the Doge Enrico Dandolo and the crusade leaders in March 1204 for the partition of the Byzantine empire.[81] However, the Venetian archives preserve relatively little in comparison with the papal archives. This has suggested that the Venetians were careful to cover their tracks: an impression only reinforced by the lack of any substantial contemporary Venetian account of the Fourth Crusade. We have to wait until Martin da Canal for a sustained narrative of events from a Venetian chronicler. He was writing after 1267. As is well known, his account is a travesty. It has Innocent III openly supporting the restoration of the young Alexios to the throne of Constantinople. The pope was supposed to have ordered the crusaders to abandon their journey to Jerusalem and go to Constantinople instead.[82] At the very least, one might have expected a detailed contemporary account from a Venetian pen. But then we have already seen that Venice had not developed at this period any strong official chronicle tradition. There were plenty of short unofficial chronicles, but they are not very informative and it is not clear that they are contemporary with the events of the Fourth Crusade.[83] The Fourth Crusade was in any event something of an embarrassment for the Venetians. Enrico Dandolo will certainly have taken the expedition of 1123 as his model. In other words, if his main goal was the ports of Egypt, he had every intention of using the crusade to strengthen Venice's position, in the first instance in the Adriatic. The Venetians did not have any particular quarrel with the Byzantine government at the outset of the Fourth Crusade, though the Emperor Alexios III Angelos's negotiations with the Genoese, which culminated in the issue of a new chrysobull in October 1202, would have been worrying.[84] Some demonstration of Venetian seapower might have to be made, but not necessarily against Constantinople. The conquest of Constantinople then involved Venice in a whole series of uncertainties. It also meant a colossal effort to make good the opportunities that opened up. It was not until 1218 when peace was finally made with Genoa over Crete that the Venetians could see

---

[80] Tafel and Thomas, *Urkunden*, vol. 1, 358–73.
[81] Tafel and Thomas, *Urkunden*, vol. 1, 445–52.
[82] A. Limentani, ed., *Martin da Canal*, 44–67.
[83] A. Carile, *La cronachistica veneziana,* 172–209.
[84] F. Miklosich and I. Müller, *Acta et diplomata graeca medii aevi: sacra et profana, collecta et edita*; vol. 3, *Acta et diplomata res graecas italasque illustrantia* (Vienna, 1865; repr. Aalen, 1968), 49–58.

that the conquest of Constantinople might work to their long-term benefit. This had to be balanced against the rapid decay of Constantinople, which was a consequence of the establishment of the Latin empire. It produced a near collapse of Venetian trade at Constantinople.[85] Another impediment to a proper narrative of events was the breakdown of relations with the papacy, which blamed the Venetians for the diversion of the crusade to Zara and then to Constantinople. This was a very serious matter. Since the Peace of Venice in 1177 Venice had prided itself on being a loyal daughter of the papacy. It was an idea that was at the heart of the developing myth of Venice. Only after the death of Innocent III in 1216 did Venice's relations with the papacy begin to improve. It allowed Martin da Canal to present the conquest of Constantinople as an enterprise that had at the very least tacit papal approval. It took so long for even a semi-official view on Venice's role in the Fourth Crusade to emerge because far from being an event in which the Venetians could take undiluted pride it produced enormous complications. They were hardly guilty of a deliberate cover-up.[86]

The Venetian sources for both Byzantine and crusader history are much fuller from the thirteenth century. This is partly because record-keeping became more systematic. The disappearance of Alexios I Komnenos's 1082 chrysobull suggests that before 1204 the Venetians retained only what was of immediate importance, in other words, the latest confirmations of its privileges. The later Venetian sources are also stronger because of the development of a tradition of history-writing, which was lacking in the eleventh and twelfth centuries. It should not come as any great surprise that before 1204 the Venetian sources have disappointingly sparse material that directly illuminates Byzantine and crusader history. Their purpose—in so far as there was one—was quite different: to trace the emergence of Venice as an independent power.

---

[85] L.B. Robbert, 'Rialto businessmen and Constantinople, 1204–61', *DOP* 49 (1995), 43–58.
[86] A. Limentani, ed., *Martin da Canal*, 50. See Angold, *Fourth Crusade*, 151–62; Madden, *Enrico Dandolo*, 173–200; Thiriet, *Romanie vénitienne*, 74–88.

# VENICE: A BIBLIOGRAPHY
## MICHAEL ANGOLD AND MICHEL BALARD

## HANDBOOKS, SURVEYS, PROSOPOGRAPHIES

P. Braunstein and R. Delort, *Venise, portrait historique d'une cité* (Paris, 1971)
   A classic survey of the history of Venice and of Venetian expansion.
R. Cessi, *Storia della Repubblica di Venezia* (Florence, 1981)
   A classic study, though very brief on economic history.
L. Cracco-Ruggini, M. Pavan, G. Cracco and G. Ortalli, eds., *Storia di Venezia*, vol.
   1, *Origini—età ducale* (Rome, 1992)
G. Cracco and G. Ortalli, eds., *Storia di Venezia dalle origini all caduta della
   Serenissima*, vol. 2, *L'età del Comune* (Rome, 1995)
   The most recent general history of Venice.
F. Dölger, *Regesten der Kaiserurkunden des oströmischen Reiches*, 5 vols. (Munich and
   Berlin, 1924–65)
   Catalogue of Byzantine imperial charters.
H. Kretschmayer, *Geschichte von Venedig*, vol. 1 (Gotha, 1905)
   A classic history of Venice.
F.C. Lane, *Venice. A maritime republic* (Baltimore and London, 1973)
   A classic history of Venice.
G. Luzzatto, *Storia economica di Venezia dal XI al XVI secolo* (Venice, 1961)
   A brilliant synthesis of economic life in Venice.
G. Ortalli, 'Venezia dalle origini a Pietro II Orseolo', in P. Delogu, A. Guillou and G.
   Ortalli, *Longobardi e Bizantini*, in G. Galasso, ed., *Storia d'Italia*, UTET (Turin,
   1980), 339–438
A. Pertusi, *Venezia e il Levante*, 2 vols. (Florence, 1973)
   Proceedings of an important conference held in Venice in 1968.
S. Romanin, *Storia documentata di Venezia*, 10 vols. (2nd edn., Venice, 1912–20)
A. Tenenti and U. Tucci, eds., *Storia di Venezia*, vol. 12, *Il mare* (Rome, 1990)
F. Thiriet, *Histoire de Venise*, Que sais-je? no. 522 (4th edn., Paris, 1969)
   A very brief survey of Venetian history.
*Venezia dalla prima crociata alla conquista di Costantinopoli del 1204* (Florence, 1965)
*Storia della cultura veneta*. Vol. 1, *Dalle origini al Trecento* (Vicenza, 1973)

## PRIMARY SOURCES

### Chronicles

Andrea Dandolo, *Chronica brevis*
A short chronicle covering Venetian history from its origins to the death of Doge
Bartolomeo Gradenigo in 1342. It was written before Andrea Dandolo became doge
of Venice in 1343 and was intended for the procurators of St Mark. It tends towards
inaccuracy.

*Edition:*
E. Pastorello, ed., *Andrea Dandolo, Chronica brevis*, Rerum Italicarum Scriptores 12.1
   (Bologna, 1938), 1–327

Andrea Dandolo, *Chronica per extensum descripta*
An official history of Venice from its origins to 1280 written while Andrea Dandolo
was doge (1343–54) and completed at the end of 1352. Much of its value derives from
the use of official documents. He cites forty documents in full and calenders another
240. He provides the most detailed treatment of Venice's relations with Byzantium in
the twelfth century and had access to documentation that is now lost.

*Edition:*
E. Pastorello, ed., *Andrea Dandolo, Chronica per extensum descripta*, Rerum
   Italicarum Scriptores 12.1 (Bologna, 1938)

*Secondary Literature:*
G. Arnaldi, 'Andrea Dandolo Doge–Cronista', in A. Pertusi (ed.), *Aspetti della storiografia veneziana fino al secolo XVI*, Civiltà veneziana, Saggi 18 (Florence, 1970),
   127–268
*Dizionario biografico degli italiani* 32 (Rome, 1986), 432–40

*Annales venetici breves*
Covers the period from 1062 to 1195. A series of brief entries, some dealing with
Byzantium.

*Edition:*
H. Simonsfeld, ed., *Annales venetici breves*, MGHS 14 (Hanover, 1883), 69–72

*Chronicon altinate*
Covers the earliest period of Venetian history, but has additions in the shape of short
entries that go up to the reign of Alexios I Komnenos. There is a continuation which
then goes up to the Fourth Crusade. Not of much interest for the period under
consideration. The bulk is, however, a work of the twelfth century.

*Editions:*
H. Simonsfeld, *Chronicon venetum quod vulgo dicunt altinate*, MGHS 14 (Hanover,
   1883), 5–69
R. Cessi, *Origo civitatum Italiae seu Venetiarum (Chronicon altinate et Chronicon
   gradense)*, Fonti per la storia d'Italia, Scrittori, secoli XI–XII (Rome, 1933)
   Standard edition.

*Secondary Literature:*
G. Fasoli, 'I fondamenti della storiografia veneziana', in A. Pertusi, ed., *La storiografia veneziana fino al secolo XVI*, Civiltà veneziana, Saggi 18 (Florence, 1970),
   31–44; repr. in G. Fasoli, *Scritti di storia medievale* (Bologna, 1974)

John the Deacon, *Chronicle*
A semi-official history that covers the early history of Venice down to 1008. Detailed
on Venetian relations with Byzantium at the turn of the tenth century.

*Edition:*

G. Monticolo, ed., *Giovanni Diacono, Cronaca veneziana*, in *Cronache veneziane antichissime*, Fonti per la storia d'Italia, Scrittori, secoli X–XI (Rome, 1891), 57–171

*Secondary Literature:*

G. Fasoli, 'I fondamenti della storiografia veneziana', in A. Pertusi, *La storiografia veneziana fino al secolo XVI*, Civiltà veneziana, Saggi 18 (Florence, 1970), 11–31; repr. in G. Fasoli, *Scritti di storia medievale* (Bologna, 1974)

*Historia ducum veneticorum*

Covers the period from 1102 to the death in 1178 of Doge Sebastiano Ziani with a continuation to 1229. The likelihood is that it was composed in two stages because the continuation is clearly distinguished from the main body of the chronicle. The first part seems to have been written soon after 1204. It surveys Venetian relations with Byzantium down to 1178 from this vantage point. The continuation provides a detailed narrative of Byzantine political history from 1180 in order to explain Venice's involvement in the Fourth Crusade.

*Edition:*

H. Simonsfeld, ed., *Historia ducum veneticorum*, MGHS 14 (Hanover, 1883), 72–97

*Secondary Literature:*

A. Carile, *La cronachistica veneziana (secoli XIII–XVI) di fronte alla spartizione della Romania nel 1204*, Civiltà veneziana, Studi 25 (Florence, 1969)

G. Cracco, 'Il pensiero storico di fronte ai problemi del comune veneziano', in A. Pertusi, ed., *Aspetti della storiografia veneziana fino al secolo XVI*, Civiltà veneziana, Saggi 18 (Florence, 1970), 45–50

Martin da Canal, *Les estoires de Venise*

Covers in detail 1099–1275. A semi-official history of Venice, but written in French. Begun in 1267 and left unfinished in 1275 at the author's death. Had access to official documents. Takes as a starting-point for his detailed coverage the Venetian participation in the First Crusade. Much less interest shown in any Byzantine involvement. Long and erroneous account of the Fourth Crusade.

*Editions:*

F.L. Polidori, ed., *La Cronique des Veniciens de maistre Martin da Canal: Cronaca veneta del Maestro Martino da Canale dall'origine della città sino all'anno MCCLXXV*, with Italian translation by G. Galvani, *Archivio storico italiano*, ser. 1.8 (1845), 229–56, 268–798

A. Limentani, ed., *Martin da Canal, Les estoires de Venise. Cronaca veneziana in lingua francese dalle origini al 1275*, with Italian translation, Civiltà veneziana, Fonti e Testi 12, ser. 3.3 (Florence, 1972) Standard edition.

*Secondary Literature:*

G. Fasoli, 'La *Cronique des Veniciens* di Martino da Canale', *Studi medievali*, ser. 2.2 (1961), 42–74

A. Pertusi, 'Maistre Martino da Canal, interprete cortese delle crociate e dell'ambiente veneziano del secolo XIII', in *Venezia dalla prima crociata al conquista di Costantinopoli del 1204* (Florence, 1965), 103–35

## Marino Sanudo Torsello

An important chronicle which deals mainly with the Venetian 'Romania', but for the period after 1250.

*Editions:*

K. Hopf, ed., *Marino Sanudo Torsello, Istoria del regno di Romania*, in *Chroniques gréco-romanes inédites ou peu connues* (Berlin, 1873)

E. Papadopoulou, ed., Ἱστορία τῆς Ρωμανίας (Athens, 2000)

## Marino Sanudo the Younger

G. Monticolo, ed., *Marino Sanudo, Vitae ducum venetorum. Le vite dei dogi di Venezia*, Rerum Italicarum Scriptores 22.4 (Bologna, 1900)

## Documents

R. Cessi (ed.), *Documenti relativi alla storia di Venezia anteriori al Mille*, 2 vols. (Padua, 1942)

*Documenti del commercio veneziano nei secoli XI–XIII*

This ground-breaking collection of documents represents a selection of the commercial documents from a series of individual archives, which over the years were collected in the Archivio di Stato at Venice.

*Edition:*

R. Morozzo della Rocca and A. Lombardo, eds., *Documenti del commercio veneziano nei secoli XI–XIII*, Regesta Chartarum Italiae, 2 vols. (Turin, 1940)

*Nuovi documenti del commercio veneto dei secoli XI–XIII*

Additional commercial documents from the Archivio di Stato at Venice.

*Edition:*

A. Lombardo and R. Morozzo della Rocca, eds., *Nuovi documenti del commercio veneto dei secoli XI–XIII*, Deputazione di storia patria per le Venezie: Monumenti storici n.s. 7 (Venice, 1953)

*Secondary Literature:*

G. Migliardi O'Riordan and A. Schiavon, *Tipologie di documenti commerciali veneziani: nolo, mutuo, prestito a cambio marittimo, colleganza, atlante diplomatico* (Venice, 1988)

*Famiglia Zusto*

An example of a Venetian family archive, but this is exceptional for the number of early documents starting in 1083. It is also exceptional for the number of commercial documents it contains with details of trade to the eastern Mediterranean and Byzantium.

*Edition:*

L. Lanfranchi, ed., *Famiglia Zusto*, Fonti per la storia di Venezia. Sezione 4: Archivi privati (Venice, 1955)

*S. Giorgio Maggiore*
The archives of this monastery are rich in documents relating to the re-establishment of the Venetians at Constantinople in the late twelfth century.
*Edition:*
L. Lanfranchi, ed., *S. Giorgio Maggiore*, Fonti per la storia di Venezia. Sezione 2: Archivi ecclesiastici, Diocesi castellana, 3 vols. (Venice, 1968–86)

*S. Giovanni Evangelista di Torcello*
Despite the loss of some of the earliest documents the archives of the abbey of St John the Evangelist on the island of Torcello are rich in eleventh- and twelfth-century documents, a few of which relate to the Byzantine empire.
*Edition:*
L. Lanfranchi, ed., *S. Giovanni Evangelista di Torcello*, Fonti per la storia di Venezia. Sezione 2: Archivi ecclesiastici, Diocesi torcellana, (Venice, 1948)
*Secondary Literature:*
S. Borsari, 'Il commercio veneziano nell'Impero bizantino nel XII secolo', *RSI* 76 (1964), 982–1011
—— 'Per la storia del commercio veneziano col mondo bizantino nel XII secolo', *RSI* 88 (1976), 104–26
—— *Venezia e Bisanzio nel XII secolo. I rapporti economici*, Deputazione di storia patria per le Venezie, Misc. di Studi e Memorie 26 (Venice, 1988)

## Hagiography

*Translatio Isidori*
An account of the translation of the relics of St Isidore from Chios to Venice in 1125. It provides a vivid personal account by a Venetian in Byzantine service of the expedition against the Aegean islands carried out by the Venetians on their return from the 'crusade' of 1123.
*Edition:*
*Translatio Isidori: Cerbani Cerbani, clerici Veneti, Translatio mirifici martyris Isidori a Chio insula in civitatem venetam (Jun. 1125)*, RHC Oc 5 (1895), 321–34

*Translatio Sancti Nicolai*
Account of the translation of relics of St Nicholas and of his uncle of the same name which occurred in 1100 during the Venetian expedition to aid the crusaders. Without it there would be virtually no contemporary evidence that the Venetians had participated in the First Crusade.
*Edition:*
*Translatio Sancti Nicolai: Monachi anonymi littorensis, Historia de translatione Sanctorum magni Nicolai, terra marique miraculis gloriosi, eiusdem avunculi alterius Nicolai, Theodorique, martyri pretiosi, de civitate mirea in monasterium S. Nicolai de Littore Venetiarum, 6 Dec. 1100*, RHC Oc 5 (1895), 253–92

*Secondary Literature:*
A. Pertusi, 'Ai confini tra religione e politica: la contesa per la reliquie di San Nicola tra Bari, Venezia e Genova', *Quaderni medievali* 5 (1978), 6–58; repr. in A. Pertusi, *Saggi Veneto–Bizantini,* Civiltà veneziana, Saggi 37 (Florence, 1990)

D.E. Queller and E.B. Katele, 'Venice and the conquest of the Latin Kingdom of Jerusalem', *Studi veneziani* n.s. 12 (1986), 15–43

*Translatio Sancti Stephani*
Account of the theft of the relics of St Stephen from a church in Constantinople by the Venetians in 1110 and their translation to the monastery of St George at Venice. Interesting account of the creation of the confraternity.

*Edition:*
F. Cornelius (Corner), ed., *Translatio Sancti Stephani: De translatione Sancti protomartyris Stephani, Ecclesiae venetae et torcellanae illustratae* 7 (Venice, 1749), 96–110
No modern edition.

*Secondary Literature:*
S. Borsari, 'Per la storia del commercio veneziano col mondo bizantino nel XII secolo', *RSI* 88 (1976), 104–26


## Treaties

No systematic attempt was made to preserve Venice's treaties with foreign powers until the early thirteenth century, when the earliest version of the *Liber pactorum* was drawn up. As a result few early treaties survive in the original, the *Pactum Warmundi* being a notable exception. The Doge Andrea Dandolo may have been responsible for a second edition of the *Liber pactorum*. He certainly used it as the basis for the *Liber albus* and the *Liber blancus*, the former containing treaties with eastern powers and the latter those with western powers.

*Editions:*
M. Pozza, ed., *Gli atti originali della cancelleria veneziana,* 2 vols. (Venice, 1994–6)
M. Pozza and G. Ravegnani, ed., *I trattati con Bisanzio, 992–1198* (Venice, 1993)
New edition.
Review: D. Jacoby in *Mediterranean Historical Review* 9 (1994), 139–43
G.L.F. Tafel and G.M. Thomas, *Urkunden zur älteren Handels- und Staatsgeschichte der Republik Venedig mit besonderen Beziehungen auf Byzanz und die Levante,* Fontes Rerum Austriacarum, Abt.2: Diplomata 12–14, 3 vols. (Vienna, 1856–7)
Standard edition of the main Venetian charters and treaties with Byzantium.
M. Giordano and M. Pozza (ed.), *I trattati con Genova 1136–1251,* Pacta veneta (Venice, 2000)
A. Sopracasa (ed.), *I trattati con il regno armeno di Cilicia 1201–1333,* Pacta veneta (Venice, 2001)

*Secondary Literature:*
S. Borsari, 'Il crisobullo di Alessio I per Venezia', *Annali dell'Istituto italiano per gli studi storici* 2 (1969–70), 111–31

E. Francès, 'Alexis Comnène et les privilèges octroyés à Venise', *Byzantinoslavica* 29 (1968), 17–23

P. Frankopan, 'Byzantine trade privileges to Venice in the eleventh century: the chrysobull of 1092', *JMH* 30 (2004), 135–60

R. Gadolin Anitra, 'Alexius Comnenus and the Venetian trade privileges. A new interpretation', *Byz* 50 (1980), 439–46

D. Jacoby, 'The chrysobull of Alexius I Comnenus to the Venetians: the date and the debate: a rejoinder', *JMH* 28.2 (2002), 199–204

T.F. Madden, 'The chrysobull of Alexius I Comnenus to the Venetians: the date and the debate', *JMH* 28.1 (2002), 23–41

M.E. Martin, 'The chrysobull of Alexius I Comnenus to the Venetians and the early Venetian quarter in Constantinople', *Byzantinoslavica* 39 (1978), 19–23

A. Tuilier, 'La date exacte du chrysobulle d'Alexis Ier Comnène en faveur des Vénitiens et son contexte historique', *RSBN* 4 (1967), 27–48

O. Tůma, 'The dating of Alexius's chrysobull to the Venetians: 1082, 1084, or 1092?', *Byzantinoslavica* 42 (1981), 171–85

—— 'Some notes on the significance of the imperial chrysobull to the Venetians of 992', *Byz* 54 (1984), 358–66

## GENERAL SECONDARY LITERATURE

H. Antoniadis-Bibicou, 'Notes sur les relations de Byzance avec Venise. De la dépendance à l'autonomie et à l'alliance: un point de vue byzantin', *Thesaurismata* 1 (1962), 162–78

T. Bertelè, 'Moneta veneziana e moneta bizantina (secoli XII–XV)', in A. Pertusi, ed., *Venezia e il Levante fino al secolo XV*, vol. 1 (Florence 1973), 3–146

E. Besta, 'La cattura dei Veneziani in Oriente per ordine dell'imperatore Emanuele Comneno e le sue conseguenze nella politica interna ed esterna sul Comune di Venezia', *Antologia veneta* 1.1–2 (1900), 35–46, 111–23

H.E. Brown, 'The Venetians and the Venetian quarter in Constantinople to the close of the twelth century', *JHS* 40 (1920), 68–88

A. Carile, 'Partitio terrarum imperii Romanie', *Studi veneziani* 7 (1965), 125–305

A. Carile and G. Fedalto, *Le origini di Venezia* (Bologna, 1978)

R. Cessi, 'Da Roma a Bisanzio', in P. Marinotti, ed., *Storia di Venezia* (Venice, 1957), 179–401

—— 'Bizantinismo veneziano', *Archivio veneto*, ser. 5, 119 (1961), 3–22

—— *Venezia ducale*, vol. 1, *Duca e popolo* (Venice, 1963)

—— 'Venice to the eve of the Fourth Crusade', in *Cambridge Medieval History*, vol. 4.1 (1966), 250–74

—— *Venezia nel Duecento, tra Oriente e Occidente* (Venice, 1985)

G. Cracco, *Società e stato nel Medioevo veneziano (secoli XII–XIV)* (Florence, 1967)

—— *Un 'altro mondo'. Venezia nel Medioevo dal secolo XI al secolo XIV* (Turin, 1986)

E. Crouzet-Pavan, *Sopra le acque salse. Espaces, pouvoir et société à Venise à la fin du Moyen Âge*, 2 vols. (Rome, 1992)

—— *Venise triomphante. Les horizons d'un mythe* (Paris, 1999)

J. Danstrup, 'Manuel I's coup against Genoa and Venice in the light of Byzantine commercial policy', *CM* 10 (1949), 195–219

W. Dorigo, *Venezia. Origini* (Milan, 1983)

A. Grabar, 'Byzance et Venise', in *Venezia e l'Europa. Atti del XVIII Congresso internazionale di storia dell'arte (Venezia, 12–18 settembre 1955)* (Venice, 1956), 45–55

W. Heinemeyer, 'Die Verträge zwischen dem oströmischen Reiche und den italienischen Städten Genua, Pisa und Venedig von 10. bis 12. Jahrhundert', *Archiv für Diplomatik* 3 (1957), 79–161

W. Heyd, *Histoire du commerce du Levant au Moyen Âge*, 2 vols. (Leipzig, 1885–6, repr. Amsterdam 1967)
The first survey of Levantine trade, with an important section on the Venetians.

R. Heynen, *Zur Entstehung des Kapitalismus in Venedig* (Stuttgart, 1905)

J.-C. Hocquet, *Le sel et la fortune de Venise*, 2 vols. (Lille, 1978–9)

D. Jacoby, 'Silk in western Byzantium before the Fourth Crusade', *BZ* 84–85.2 (1991–2), 452–500

—— 'Italian privileges and trade in Byzantium before the Fourth Crusade: a reconsideration', *Anuario de Estudios Medievales* 24 (1994), 348–69

—— 'Dalla materia prima ai drappi fra Bisanzio, il Levante e Venezia: la prima fase dell'industria serica veneziana', in L. Molà, R.C. Mueller and C. Zanier, eds., *La seta in Italia dal Medioevo al Seicento* (Venice, 2000), 265–304

—— 'The Byzantine outsider in trade (c.900–c.1350)', in D.C. Smythe, ed., *Strangers to Themselves: the Byzantine outsider* (Aldershot, 2000), 129–47

—— 'Migrations familiales et stratégies commerciales vénitiennes aux XIIe et XIIIe siècles', in M. Balard and A. Ducellier, eds., *Migrations et diasporas dans la Méditerranée médiévale* (Paris, 2002), 355–73

R.-J. Lilie, *Handel und Politik zwischen dem byzantinischen Reich und den italienischen Kommunen Venedig, Pisa und Genua in der Epoche der Komnenen und der Angeloi (1081–1204)* (Amsterdam, 1984)
An important section is devoted to the Venetians and their places of trade in the Byzantine empire.

G. Luzzatto, 'Les activités économiques du patriciat vénitien du Xe au XIVe siècle', *Annales Economie, Sociétés, Civilisations* 1 (1937), 25–57

—— 'Capitale e lavoro nel commercio veneziano dei secoli XI e XII', in G. Luzzatto, ed., *Studi di storia economica veneziana* (Padua, 1954), 89–116

W.H. McNeal and R.L. Wolff, 'The Fourth Crusade', in K.M. Setton, ed., *A History of the Crusades*, vol. 2 (Philadelphia, 1962), 153–85

C. Maltezou, 'Il quartiere veneziano di Costantinopoli (scali marittimi)', *Thesaurismata* 15 (1978), 30–61

D. Neumann, 'Über die urkundlichen Quellen zur Geschichte der byzantinisch–venezianischen Beziehungen vornehmlich im Zeitalter der Komnenen', *BZ* 1 (1892), 366–78

D.M. Nicol, 'The Fourth Crusade and the Greek and Latin empires', in *Cambridge Medieval History*, vol. 4.1 (1966), 275–330

—— *Byzantium and Venice* (Cambridge, 1988)

M. Nystazopoulou-Pelekidis, 'Venise et la Mer Noire du XIe au XVe siècle', *Thesaurismata* 7 (1970), 15–51

A. Pertusi, 'Venezia e Bisanzio nel secolo XI', *La Venezia del Mille*, Storia della civiltà veneziana 10 (Florence, 1965), 117–60

—— 'Exuviae sacrae Constantinopolitanae. A proposito degli oggetti bizantini esistenti oggi nel Tesoro di San Marco', *Studi veneziani* n.s. 2 (1978), 251–5

—— 'Le profezie sulla presa di Costantinopoli (1204) nel cronista veneziano Marco (c. 1292) e le loro fonti bizantine (Pseudo Costantino Magno, Pseudo Daniele, Pseudo Leone il Saggio)', *Studi veneziani* n.s. 3 (1979), 13–46

—— 'Venezia e Bisanzio: 1000–1024', *DOP* 33 (1979), 1–22

G. Ravegnani, 'Il commercio veneziano nell'impero bizantino', in O. Banti, ed., *Amalfi, Genova, Pisa e Venezia. Il commercio con Costantinopoli e il vicino Oriente nel secolo XII* (Pisa, 1998), 55–74

Y. Renouard, *Les hommes d'affaires italiens du Moyen Âge* (Paris, 1968)

M. Roberti, 'Ricerche intorno alla colonia veneziana di Costantinopoli nel sec. XII', *Scritti storici in onore di C. Manfroni nel XL anno d'insegnamento* (Padua, 1925), 137–47

S. Runciman, 'L'intervento di Venezia dalla prima alla terza crociata', in *Venezia dalla prima crociata alla conquista di Costantinopoli del 1204* (Florence, 1965), 3–22

A. Schaube, *Handelsgeschichte der romanischen Völker des Mittelmeergebietes bis zum Ende der Kreuzzüge* (Munich, 1906)

P. Schreiner, 'Untersuchungen zu den Niederlassungen westlicher Kaufleute im byzantinischen Reich des 11. und 12. Jahrhunderte', *Byzantinische Forschungen* 7 (1979), 175–91

N.P. Sokolov, 'K voprosu o vzaimootnosheniiakh Vizantii i Venetsii v poslednie gody pravleniia Komninov (1171–1185)', *VV* 5 (1952), 139–51

F. Thiriet, *La Romanie vénitienne au Moyen Âge. Le développement et l'exploitation du domaine colonial vénitien (XIIᵉ–XVᵉ siècles)*, BEFAR 193 (Paris 1959, repr. 1975)

# 6

# The South Italian Sources

## VERA VON FALKENHAUSEN

IN 1025 SOUTHERN ITALY WAS POLITICALLY DIVIDED between the Byzantine empire, the Lombard principalities of Benevento, Capua and Salerno, and the duchies of Naples, Amalfi and Gaeta. The present regions of Apulia (including the Capitanata in the north), and Calabria belonged to the eastern Roman empire and so did the eastern part of Basilicata. During the last years of Basil II's reign, after a long period of anarchy, thanks to the efficient administration of the governor (*katepan*/κατεπάνω) Basil Boioannes (1017–28), the Byzantine territories in southern Italy were extended and fortified. It is, however, impossible to trace the exact boundaries.[1] The present region of Campania and the southern part of Latium were divided between the autonomous Lombard principalities of Benevento, Capua and Salerno, and the duchies of Naples, Amalfi and Gaeta, which were themselves independent of the Byzantine empire. The island of Sicily had been conquered by the Arabs during the ninth century, and in spite of several attempts at reconquest (964/965, 1025, 1038–1041), had never been recovered by Byzantium.

In the following pages I present the extant sources relevant to Byzantine prosopography, divided into separate sections according to the various political entities.

## 1. THE BYZANTINE PROVINCES

The Byzantine territories in southern Italy were originally organised into two and later three themes (*themata*): Longobardia (later Italia), Calabria and Lucania. With the creation of the katepanate of Italy during the reign of Nicephoros II Phocas (963–9) the position of the *katepan* of Italy (κατεπάνω Ἰταλίας), who had his residence in Bari, became predominant by comparison to that of the *strategoi* of the other provinces. Culturally and ethnically

---

[1] V. von Falkenhausen, 'Between two empires: Byzantine Italy in the reign of Basil II', in P. Magdalino, ed., *Byzantium in the Year 1000* (Leiden and Boston, 2003), 141–52.

*Proceedings of the British Academy* **132**, 95–121. © The British Academy 2007.

the population of the Byzantine territories was anything but homogeneous. The inhabitants of northern and central Apulia and of north-east Basilicata were for the most part Lombardised and Latin-speaking Roman Catholics, whereas those of southern Apulia, Calabria and southern Basilicata mostly spoke Greek and were Orthodox in religion. In fact, since the mid-eighth century Calabria had belonged to the ecclesiastical jurisdiction of the patriarch of Constantinople. Moreover, during the eleventh century Norman and French knights settled in Byzantine territories partly as imperial mercenaries, and partly as conquerors; the division between the two roles is not always easy to define.

While there is no doubt that in 1025 the above-mentioned areas belonged to the eastern Roman empire, it is far more difficult to establish when Byzantine domination in southern Italy came to an end. The Norman conquest of the Byzantine territories started in the early 1040s but proceeded slowly: in 1059 after the conquest of Reggio, capital of the theme of Calabria, Norman knights acclaimed Robert Guiscard their duke, a title which was immediately confirmed by Pope Nicholas II. Even earlier, in 1057/8, a Greek document written in Briatico in Calabria was annotated by the scribe with the words ὑπὸ τῶν Φράγγων, 'under the Franks'.[2] The Capitanata was conquered by the Normans in the early 1060s. Bari, the seat of the Byzantine governor, was not taken until 1071. After that date there was no longer any effective Byzantine authority in southern Italy, though in several towns, as for example in Barletta, Canne, Gallipoli, Molfetta, Rossano and Trani, the local Norman lords and their notaries sometimes dated private and public documents according to the reign of the Byzantine emperor.[3] Thus, in historical surveys and handbooks the end of Byzantine domination in southern Italy is generally given as the year 1071, a date which for reasons of convenience should be adopted here. Therefore, until 1071 we may in theory consider all the inhabitants of the Byzantine provinces as subjects of the eastern Roman empire and thus entitled to appear in a Byzantine prosopography.

The written sources from southern Italy for the period 1025–71 are certainly far more numerous and far richer than those for any other province of the Byzantine empire in the eleventh century. In addition to the narrative sources, around three hundred private and public documents (or fragments of documents) in Latin and Greek have survived, most of them published, but

---

[2] C. Rognoni, *Les actes privés grecs de l'Archivo Ducal de Medinaceli (Tolède)*, no. 7, p. 100.
[3] *Codice diplomatico barese*, vol. 7, nos. 1–4, pp. 3–9; vol. 8, nos. 19–33, pp. 39–56; vol. 10, nos. 1–5, pp. 3–9; vol. 32, nos. 3–4, pp. 52–5; Prologo, *Le carte*, nos. 23–30, pp. 67–77; Trinchera, *Syllabus*, no. 49, p. 65; no. 99, p. 131; Appendix 1, no. 1, p. 512.

some still unedited.[4] In almost every document no fewer than ten people are mentioned: those issuing the deed and some members of their family, the recipients, the notaries, the witnesses, the owners of the neighbouring properties and so on, which means that from the archival material the names of at least 3,000 Byzantine subjects can be compiled. Certainly, some of them are Byzantine officials, others have court titles, others again are priests, abbots or bishops, but most of them are not what one would call 'important people'; they are rather local inhabitants who happened to sell, to rent or to donate a house, a field or a vineyard to somebody by means of a contract which survived fortuitously in an ecclesiastical archive. In addition to their personal names the documents generally record those of their fathers and of other family members, the places where they lived at a certain date and the location of the property owned. Because all of them were Byzantine subjects, they will, I am afraid, give to the southern Italian provinces a disproportionate number of entries compared to those of other parts of the empire, from which only a few archival sources have survived.

To my knowledge, most of the surviving Latin documents of this period have been published. But there may be some unedited deeds from northern Apulia (especially from Lucera) in the archive of Santa Sofia in Benevento and in the archive of Montecassino. As for the known Greek documents, most are published; an edition of thirteen deeds of the Archivo Ducal Medinaceli (Toledo) has recently appeared.[5] Moreover, an edition of the Greek documents from the monastery of Santa Maria di Matina in Calabria (now in the Biblioteca Apostolica Vaticana) prepared years ago by André Guillou, should soon appear.[6] The quality of the various editions is not consistent. Those of the Latin documents, although dependent on their state of conservation, are normally quite accurate, but the editors have often misread the Greek subscriptions of some of the witnesses—or have not read them at all, so that they have to be checked against the originals. The edition of the medieval Greek documents once in the Archivio di Stato in Naples and those in the archives of the abbeys of Montecassino and Cava, published by Trinchera in 1865, is moderately accurate; Trinchera's transcriptions of the documents of Montecassino and Cava can easily be checked in the abbey

---

[4] In this context I consider as public documents the privileges and juridical documents of the Byzantine governors and other officers.

[5] The documents are published by Cristina Rognoni, *Les actes privés grecs de l'Archivo Ducal de Medinaceli (Tolède)*, nos. 1–10, pp. 62–114; nos. 25–7, pp. 189–207. Rognoni recently published short summaries of the private acts in Greek of the Archivio Medinaceli: Rognoni, 'Le fonds d'archives "Messine"'.

[6] The edition should appear as the sixth volume of the series *Corpus des actes grecs d'Italie du Sud et de Sicile. Recherches d'histoire et de géographie*, a series published by the Vatican Library.

archives, but the Neapolitan documents were destroyed during the Second World War and there are apparently no photographs. Gertrude Robinson's edition of the documents of the Greek monastery of St Anastasius and St Elias of Carbone in Basilicata is unreliable, but the originals are accessible in the Archivio Doria-Pamphilj in Rome. On the other hand, the more recent editions by André Guillou of various collections of Greek documents from Calabria are generally correct; furthermore, his readings can easily be checked, because he provides a photograph of every document.

The narrative sources are less difficult to deal with: the three versions of the *Annals of Bari*, the so-called *Lupus protospatharius,* the *Annales barenses* and the *Chronicon ignoti civis barensis,* provide names and dates of the higher Byzantine officials active in the katepanate of Italy and of members of the local aristocracy and clergy. The published texts of the three versions are not very reliable, but there is a better edition of *Lupus* and the *Annales* in the still unpublished Ph.D. thesis of William Churchill (University of Toronto), while no extant manuscript of the *Chronicon* is known. There is, however, no comparable historical text from any other Byzantine town in southern Italy. The *Cronica Trium Tabernarum*, probably composed in Calabria in Norman times, but preserved in a late and inaccurate transcription, quotes most of the names of Byzantine personalities in rather distorted forms.[7] Interesting information about the Byzantine government in southern Italy, its officials and their relations with Montecassino and the Lombard rulers is offered by the *Chronica monasterii casinensis,* which is available in the excellent edition by Hartmut Hoffmann in the MGH. For the last years of the Byzantine period we have available the various contemporary descriptions of the Norman conquest by William of Apulia, Amatus of Montecassino and Gaufredus Malaterra, while the so-called *Breve chronicon northmannicum* was proved to be a forgery by Pietro Polidori in the eighteenth century.[8]

There are few hagiographical sources concerning eleventh-century Byzantine Italy: one of the rare surviving texts is the Life of St Philaretos the Younger who was born into a Greek family in eastern Sicily in the 1030s; after the failure of the Byzantine campaign in Sicily (1041) he moved with his relatives to Calabria, where he became a monk.[9] The better known St Bartholomew the Younger, founder of the Calabrian monastery of S. Maria del Patir, may have been born during the Byzantine period, but he flourished and died in the Norman era (d. 1130). His Life was presumably written in the

---

[7] Caspar, 'Die Chronik von Tres Tabernae in Calabrien', 36–9.
[8] A. Jacob, 'Le breve chronicon northmannicum: un véritable faux de Pietro Polidori', *Quellen und Forschungen aus italienischen Archiven und Bibliotheken* 66 (1986), 378–92.
[9] BHG 235.

middle of the twelfth century.[10] The Latin Life of the holy monk St John of Matera,[11] and the *Translationes* of the relics of St Nicholas from Myra to Bari belong more or less to the same period.[12]

Finally, there are Greek manuscripts written in southern Italy, some with colophons which indicate not only the dates and the names of the scribes, but also those of the sponsors, or those of local bishops or of secular authorities. In their *Dated Greek Minuscule Manuscripts to the Year 1200* Kirsopp and Silva Lake collected most of the known dated manuscripts from southern Italy of our period, but more exist, and names of scribes and sponsors can be found also in manuscripts datable only on palaeographical criteria. Especially for southern Italy during the last twenty years, through the painstaking research of scholars like André Jacob and Santo Lucà, palaeographical methodology has been refined, and many manuscripts can be safely dated and attributed to Italian *scriptoria*. Unfortunately their various studies have not been collected, and so one has to check the individual articles through the bibliography of the *Byzantinische Zeitschrift*.

## 2. THE FORMER BYZANTINE TERRITORIES BETWEEN 1071 AND 1204

As noted earlier, the year 1071 is the conventional date for the end of Byzantine rule in southern Italy. Subsequently, at least until the third decade of the twelfth century, some documents from Apulia, Basilicata and Calabria give the names of former Byzantine, now Norman subjects, who continue to mention their former Byzantine positions and court titles or are even given new titles by the former rulers. In spite of continuous hostilities, from the beginning of the Norman conquest of Byzantine Italy, there were close connections at various levels between the eastern Roman empire and the conquerors. There were, for instance, dynastic marriages between the Hautevilles and the imperial family: in 1074, Constantine, the infant son of Michael VII, was betrothed to Olympias, a daughter of Robert Guiscard, whose name was changed to Helena in Constantinople;[13] in later years there were negotiations about a Byzantine bride for William II, but the marriage was not realised. In

---

[10] BHG 1513.
[11] BHL 4411–12.
[12] BHL 6179, 6180, 6182, 6190–3, BHG 1361b.
[13] V. von Falkenhausen, 'Olympias, eine normannische Prinzessin in Konstantinopel', in *Bisanzio e l'Italia. Raccolta di studi in memoria di Agostino Pertusi* (Milan, 1982), 56–72.

addition, many Norman knights and barons, dissatisfied with their feudal or
patrimonial allocation under Robert Guiscard and his successors, joined the
crusaders or left for Byzantium and entered the service of the Byzantine
emperor, at least for a certain period. Some of them stayed in the east and
were permanently integrated into the aristocracy of the eastern Roman
empire,[14] others, as for instance the *protosebastos* William of Grandmesnil,
returned to their Italian estates adorned with imperial titles;[15] finally, some
Norman knights, who remained in south Italy, were considered to be friends
of the Empire and awarded imperial titles: I think of Count Geoffrey,
*imperialis sebastos* Lord of Molfetta,[16] William, *gratia Dei cannensis comes
et imperialis protocuropalatus*,[17] and many others. All these people should
certainly be given entries in the Byzantine prosopography.

In his introductory lecture at our 2002 conference, however, Michael
Jeffreys proposed that all the people who lived up to the year 1204 in the territories which in 1025 belonged to the Byzantine empire should have an entry
in the Prosopography of the Byzantine World. As far as southern Italy is
concerned, I consider this idea unrealistic for several reasons. (1) For the
Norman and early Hohenstaufen period there are thousands of documents,
edited and unedited, from Apulia, Calabria and Basilicata with tens of thousands of names of people who never had anything to do with Byzantium.
Why should they appear in a Byzantine prosopography? (2) In the Norman
kingdom, provinces which had belonged to the Byzantine empire were united
with other states which were independent at the time of their conquest, as for
instance, Sicily, the principalities of Capua and Salerno, or the duchies of
Naples, Amalfi and Gaeta; after the Norman conquest many inhabitants of
these territories moved to other provinces within the boundaries of the new
state. Many Greeks from Calabria for various reasons moved to Sicily, as did
Salernitans to Calabria and Sicily. Thus, one would have to divide the population of the Norman kingdom rather arbitrarily into one group, which for
historical and geographical reasons would be incorporated into the PBW, and
another which would not. I am convinced that such a procedure would prove
quite impossible.

At the conference it was also said that at least all the Greek speakers
should be entered in the PBW. Once again, that idea is neither realistic, nor

---

[14] D. Nicol, 'Symbiosis and integration. Some Greco-Latin families in Byzantium in the 11th to
13th century', *Byzantinische Forschungen* 7 (1979), 113–35, reprinted in D. Nicol, *Studies in Late
Byzantine History and Prosopography* (London, 1986), III; J. Nesbitt, 'Some observations about
the Roger family', *Νέα ʿΡώμη* 1 (2004), 209–17.

[15] Trinchera, *Syllabus*, no. 83, p. 108; Burgarella and Guillou, *Castrovillari*, 66–71.

[16] *Codice diplomatico barese*, vol. 7, no. 4, pp. 8–9.

[17] *Codice diplomatico barese*, vol. 8, no. 33, p. 56.

convincing. (1) During the Middle Ages, there were many Byzantine subjects who did not speak Greek, and many Greek speakers who lived outside the borders of the Empire. I do not think that the fact that a person was Greek-speaking is a sufficient criterion for including him or her in the PBW. (2) In southern Italy during the Byzantine period most of the Greek speakers were concentrated in southern Apulia, southern Basilicata and Calabria, and in these provinces Greek continued to be used as the predominant administrative language until the end of the twelfth century. In fact, for most of the twelfth century private documents, many administrative, judical and baronial documents, and a great number of charters of the Norman rulers written in that area, or for recipients living there, were in Greek. But that does not necessarily mean that all of the people mentioned in these documents were Greek speakers. Certainly, we can assume that the notary who wrote the document was a Greek speaker, but we know very often that neither the author nor the recipients of the charters or documents were Greek speakers, and often it is impossible to decide whether the other people mentioned in the text are Greeks, Lombards, Normans or others; the ethnic origin of the various personal names is not a safe criterion, since a few years after the Norman conquest many Lombards and Greeks adopted names from the conquerors, especially those of the Hauteville family. Only the autograph Greek subscriptions, may safely be assumed to have been written by a Greek speaker. But how do we know that these subscriptions were really autographs? The elegant Greek signatures of the countess Adelasia and of Roger II were certainly not written by the Norman rulers themselves, but by some professional notary of their chancellery.[18]

In addition to what has been said, we should consider the case of Sicily, which during the eleventh century did not belong to the Byzantine empire. Under Islamic rule in the north-east of the island there existed a substantial Greek-speaking Christian minority who paid tribute to the Muslim rulers. The Greek/Arabic manuscript of the Gospel of St Luke (Paris BN, Supplément grec 911), copied in 1043 by the cleric Euphemios, has been attributed to a Sicilian scriptorium.[19] When, in the 1060s the Normans began to conquer Sicily, these local Christians collaborated to a certain extent with the invaders, whom they greeted as their liberators from the infidels. Many were rewarded by the conquerors, and some, such as the admiral Eugenios

---

[18] V. von Falkenhausen, 'I diplomi dei re normanni in lingua greca', in G. De Gregorio and O. Kresten, eds., *Documenti medievali greci e latini. Studi comparativi*, Incontri di studio 1 (Spoleto, 1998), 282–6.

[19] P. Géhin, 'Un manuscrit bilingue grec–arabe, BnF, Supplément grec 911 (année 1043)', in F. Déroche and F. Richard, eds., *Scribes et manuscrits du Moyen-Orient* (Paris, 1997), 162–75.

the Elder, received important positions within the Norman administration.[20] In the following years, numerous Greeks from Calabria, especially clerics and notaries, moved to Sicily to help reorganise the local administration and to re-establish Christianity among the local population. In fact during the first half of the twelfth century most Sicilian documents, private and public, were written in Greek.[21] For many years Greek was a kind of lingua franca of the Norman administration, but the people who used it were neither Byzantines nor normally connected with the Byzantine empire.

Nevertheless we cannot completely neglect the documents of the Norman period, for frequently they mention people who were in contact with the Byzantine empire. In this connection I have mentioned the Norman knights who were offered Byzantine titles for their services; but there were also Greek civil servants, who in one way or the other became involved with Constantinople, as for instance the *logothetes* Leo *protoproedros* (1086),[22] the admiral Christodoulos, chief of the Norman administration during the regency of the countess Adelasia and the first years of Roger II (1107–26), on whom Alexios I conferred the title of *protonobelissimos* in 1109,[23] and his contemporary Bonos, protonotary of Roger I, Adelasia and Roger II, who was awarded the same title before 1110.[24] Basil, *camerarius* of Roger II (1117–21) was *sebastos*,[25] Admiral George of Antioch (d. 1151), a former Byzantine subject from Syria who after having been employed at the Zirid court in Ifriqiyya fled to Sicily where he reorganised the central administration of the Norman kingdom for Roger II, held the Byzantine title of *panhypersebastos*.[26] Moreover, there were members of the local South Italian or Sicilian upper class who were sent by the Norman rulers as ambassadors to Constantinople such as Genesios Moschatos, a Greek from Stilo in Calabria (before 1098),[27] the so-called *Judex Tarentinus*, a judge of the royal court

---

[20] Ménager, *Amiratus*, 26–8.

[21] V. von Falkenhausen, 'The Greek presence in Norman Sicily: the contribution of archival material in Greek', in G.A. Loud and A. Metcalfe, eds., *The Society of Norman Sicily*, The Medieval Mediterranean 38 (Leiden, Boston, Cologne, 2002), 253–84.

[22] L.-R. Ménager, *Recueil des actes des ducs normands d'Italie* (1046–1127), vol. 1, *Les premiers ducs* (1046–1087), Società di storia patria per la Puglia. Documenti e monografie 45 (Bari, 1981), nos. 52–4, pp. 182, 184, 186.

[23] J. Johns, *Arabic Administration in Norman Sicily: the royal dīwān* (Cambridge, 2002), 69–74.

[24] K.A. Kehr, *Die Urkunden der normannisch-sicilischen Könige. Eine diplomatische Untersuchung* (Innsbruck, 1902), 413–15, no. 3; Houben, *Die Abtei Venosa*, no. 92, p. 328; Trinchera, *Syllabus*, no. 133, p. 172; Ménager, *Amiratus*, 40.

[25] Ménager, *Amiratus*, 187–9.

[26] A. Acconcia Longo, 'Gli epitaffi giambici per Giorgio di Antiochia, per la madre e per la moglie', *Quellen und Forschungen aus italienischen Archiven und Bibliotheken* 61 (1981), 40–6; F. Delle Donne, 'Giorgio d'Antiochia', *Dizionario biografico degli italiani* 55 (Roma, 2000), 347–50; Johns, *Arabic Administration*, 80–90, and *passim*.

[27] Mercati, Giannelli, Guillou, *Saint-Jean-Théristès*, no. 3, p. 55.

under William I,[28] or Henry Aristippus, the Latin archdeacon of Catania, who during his Byzantine embassy (1158–60) acquired Greek manuscripts which he translated into Latin.[29] Some of the Greek notaries who ran the Norman civil service were quite respectable intellectuals, poets or translators. The best-known name is that of Admiral Eugenios of Palermo (*c*.1130–after 1202),[30] but there are also the anonymous poets who wrote the epitaphs of the family of George of Antioch and the long poem by a civil servant exiled to Malta.[31] In addition there are ecclesiastical authors attached to the Norman court in one way or another. Neilos Doxapatres, presumably an exile from Byzantium, wrote his *Hierarchy of the Patriarchal Sees* (Τάξις τῶν πατριαρχικῶν θρόνων) in Palermo in 1142/3, a treatise which had a certain diffusion in the Byzantine empire, and was even translated into Armenian.[32] Philagathos Kerameus, a monk of the monastery of S. Maria del Patir near Rossano, was a well-known preacher who delivered sermons in the most important cathedrals of Norman Calabria and Sicily, occasionally even in the presence of the kings Roger II and William I. His homilies were widely copied in the Byzantine empire.[33]

As can be seen from the careers of men like Neilos Doxapatres and Philagathos Kerameus, the ecclesiastical aspect of the Norman kingdom presents a special problem in our context. During the Byzantine era the dioceses of Sicily, Calabria, southern Apulia and part of Basilicata depended on the jurisdiction of the patriarch of Constantinople. Bishops and metropolitans in these territories were Greek, as were most of the clergy and many monasteries. After the Norman conquest the ecclesiastical situation in south Italy changed dramatically. All the former Byzantine dioceses returned to Roman jurisdiction, but while in some dioceses the Greek bishops were replaced by Latin ones, in others, for instance Rossano, Crotone, Santa

[28] E. Aar, 'Gli studi storici in Terra d'Otranto', *Archivio storico italiano* n.s. 4.9 (1882), 253–5; E. Jamison, 'Judex Tarentinus. The career of *Judex Tarentinus magne curie magister justiciarius* and the emergence of the Sicilian *regalis magna curia* under William I and the regency of Margaret of Navarre, 1156–72', *Proceedings of the British Academy* 53 (1967), 290–344.
[29] E. Franceschini, 'Enrico Aristippo', *Dizionario biografico degli italiani* 4 (Rome, 1962), 201–6.
[30] E. Jamison, *Admiral Eugenius. His Life and His Work* (London, 1957); V. von Falkenhausen, 'Eugenio da Palermo', *Dizionario biografico degli italiani* 43 (Rome, 1993), 502–5; M. Gigante, *Eugenii panormitani versus iambici*, Istituto siciliano di studi bizantini e neoellenici. Testi 10 (Palermo, 1964).
[31] E. Th. Tsolakis, 'Ἄγνωστα ἔργα ἰταλοβυζαντινοῦ ποιητῆ τοῦ 12ου αἰῶνα', *Ἑλληνικά* 26 (1973), 46–66.
[32] V. von Falkenhausen, 'Nilo Doxapatres', *Dizionario biografico degli italiani* 41 (Rome, 1992), 610–13.
[33] The biographical note by L. Amelotti, 'Filagato da Cerami', *Dizionario biografico degli italiani* 47 (Rome, 1997), 564–5, is not entirely reliable.

Severina and Gerace, Greek bishops and metropolitans continued to be in charge, although under papal jurisdiction, until the thirteenth century. In Sicily, formerly Muslim, a new Latin (predominantly Norman or French) ecclesiastical hierarchy was installed, but in all the former Byzantine dioceses the lower clergy and most of the monks were of Greek origin and spoke, wrote and celebrated in Greek. Hundreds of names of Greek clerics, priests, monks, and even those of some Greek bishops are mentioned in the documents published by Trinchera, Cusa, Robinson, Pratesi, Guillou and Rognoni and in the still unedited documents of the Aldobrandini and Medinaceli archives. Should they be included in the Byzantine prosopography, although they did not officially belong to the patriarchate of Constantinople? Most of them no longer maintained a Byzantine connection, but for many of them Constantinople remained their spiritual centre. According to his Life, Bartholemew of Simeri, the founder and abbot of S. Maria del Patir, visited Constantinople where he acquired liturgical manuscripts and icons and was received by the Emperor Alexios I and his wife Irene; he also visited mount Athos.[34] His contemporary, the monk Luke, Greek bishop of Isola Capo Rizzuto, who after the Norman conquest was active for years as a missionary in Sicily, apparently also tried to travel to Constantinople, but for unknown reasons did not succeed.[35] In 1174 Paul, the Greek bishop-elect of Gallipoli, wrote a letter to the patriarch of Constantinople, Michael III Anchialos, asking for help with certain liturgical problems.[36] More widely known is the *grammatikos* Nicholas of Otranto, a gifted writer and learned theologian, who became abbot of the Greek monastery of S. Nicola di Casole close to Otranto (his monastic name was Nektarios), and who served as an interpreter to Benedict, legate of Innocent III to Constantinople in 1205–7, and to Cardinal Pelagius in 1214/15. Since he was born presumably during the late fifties of the twelfth century and died at Casole in 1235,[37] the greater part of his productive life was spent outside the chronological limits of the PBW.

## 3. THE LOMBARD PRINCIPALITIES

Since the second half of the tenth century the Lombard principalities, Benevento, Capua and Salerno, had been independent of the Byzantine

[34] BHG 235.

[35] BHG 2237.

[36] A. Jacob, 'La lettre partriarcale du typikon de Casole et l'évêque Paul de Gallipoli', *RSBN* n.s. 24 (1987), 143–63.

[37] J.M. Hoeck and R.J. Loenertz, *Nikolaos-Nektarios von Otranto, Abt von Casole. Beiträge zur Geschichte der ost-westlichen Beziehungen unter Innozenz III. und Friedrich II.*, Studia Patristica et Byzantina 11 (Ettal, 1965).

empire, but during the last years of Basil II, under the efficient katepanate of Basil Boioannes (1017–28), Byzantine authority was recognised by Capua and presumably by Salerno. Prince Pandulf IV (1016–49) presented the emperor with the golden key of Capua and accepted his overlordship, but very soon Byzantine influence diminished. I do not think there is any reason to include the population of the principality of Capua in the prosopography. In the territory of the principality of Capua there was, however, the monastery of Montecassino which, at least until the early twelfth century, was in contact with the Byzantine authorities in southern Italy and with the emperors (Constantine IX, Michel VII and Alexios I) themselves. Montecassino owned extensive property in Apulia which was regularly confirmed by the *katepans*; moreover, during the early Norman period, the abbots were involved in diplomatic activities between Rome and Constantinople.[38] During the years 1036–8 Basil, a Greek from Calabria and a protégé of Pandolf IV, was a much-hated abbot of Montecassino. In the same period, we find other Greek abbots in some smaller monasteries in this area which were sometimes, but not always, dependencies of Montecassino.[39] In fact from the second half of the tenth century many Greeks from Calabria and Sicily, fleeing from the Arab raids and invasions, left their homes to settle in the Lombard territories. Probably in 1034 (the date is not certain), Leo, *qui fuit ortus ex finibus Calabriae et nunc est Longobardus,* founded the church of St Nicholas, which was called later *de Graecis,* in his own house in Benevento.[40] Many of these Greeks, artisans, farmers, monks and priests, can be found in the principality of Salerno, that is, in the city itself, in the so-called Cilento, on the *costiera amalfitana* and in the Val di Diana. In these areas Greek communities and monasteries survived in a Lombard/Latin environment throughout the eleventh and twelfth centuries; they are well documented especially in the published and still unpublished acts of the archive of the abbey of the SS Trinità di Cava.[41] However, even though their ancestors were Byzantine, I do not think that we can consider these Greek-speaking inhabitants of Campania during the Lombard, then Norman, period to be Byzantines themselves.

Some members of the Lombard upper class had connections with Byzantium, especially during the period of the Norman conquest, when they desperately tried to get help against the invaders: in 1062, for instance, Gisulf

---

[38] V. von Falkenhausen, 'Montecassino e Bisanzio dal IX al XII secolo', in F. Avagliano and O. Pecere, eds., *L'età dell'abate Desiderio,* vol. 3.1, *Storia, arte e cultura. Atti del IV Convegno di studi sul Medioevo meridionale (Montecassino—Cassino, 4–8 ottobre 1987),* Miscellanea Cassinese 67 (Montecassino, 1992 [in fact 1995]), 87–107.

[39] von Falkenhausen, 'Montecassino e Bisanzio', 81–7.

[40] J. Mazzoleni, *Le pergamene della Società napoletana di storia patria,* vol. 1 (Naples, 1966), no. 23, pp. 75–8.

[41] *Codex diplomaticus cavensis, passim*; Cherubini, *Le pergamene, passim.*

II, prince of Salerno, together with Alfanus, who was later to become arch-bishop of the town, travelled to Constantinople, where they spent some time at the court of Constantine X. In addition to the political aim of the mission, Alfanus used the sojourn in Byzantium to translate Greek medical texts (Nemesios of Emesa) into Latin.[42] But some Salernitans stayed even longer in Constantinople and entered the service of the emperor. In a recent article, Paul Magdalino has identified the *protosebastos* Landulf Butrumile, who donated the Byzantine bronze doors to the cathedral of Salerno, with the homonymous *megas doux* and commander of the imperial navy between 1099 and 1108.[43]

## 4. THE DUCHY OF NAPLES

The Duchy of Naples is a special case. Although from the ninth century the dukes were elected locally without any Byzantine interference, up to the year 1139, when the duchy was conquered by Roger II, all the documents of Naples are dated according to the reigns of Byzantine emperors. Is that enough to consider all Neapolitans up to that date Byzantine subjects? Though the town was Latin in language and culture and Roman Catholic in religion, until the early twelfth century some Greek monasteries survived in the city and the presence of the Greek language and Greek culture was apparently stronger in Naples than in the other towns of Campania: during the tenth century especially, many Neapolitan witnesses signed their names in the Greek alphabet, though in the Latin language, a habit which continued even in the first half of the eleventh century though on a reduced level.[44] According to a document of 1041, all the nuns of the monastery of SS Peter and Marcellinus who were Greek or who knew how to write and read in Greek were to be buried in the monastery of St Sebastian.[45] As in other parts of Campania, during the tenth and eleventh centuries Greeks from Calabria moved to Naples and settled there, as for instance Peter Volicaci from Amantea.[46] These Greek immigrants, especially when they were clerics

[42] A. Lentini, 'Alfano di Salerno', *Dizionario biografico degli italiani* 2 (Rome, 1960), 253–7; P. Cherubini, 'Gisulfo II', *Dizionario biografico degli italiani* 56 (Rome, 2001), 644–8.

[43] P. Magdalino, 'Prosopography and Byzantine identity', in Averil Cameron, ed., *Fifty Years of Prosopography. The Later Roman Empire, Byzantium and beyond* (Oxford, 2003), 41–56.

[44] Capasso, *Monumenta*, vol. 2.1, no. 401, p. 251 (1025); nos. 419–20, pp. 264–5 (1028); no. 423, p. 266 (1030); no. 428, p. 269 (1031); no. 430, p. 270 (1031); no. 432, p. 271 (1031); no. 435, p. 273 (1032); no. 441, p. 276 (1033); no. 456, pp. 281–2 (1036); no. 483, p. 295 (1048); no. 489, pp. 296–7 (1058); no. 519, p. 312 (1074); no. 556, pp. 338–9 (1093).

[45] Capasso, *Monumenta*, vol. 2.1, no. 473, p. 290.

[46] Capasso, *Monumenta*, vol. 1, 276–7.

and monks, normally signed documents in the Greek alphabet and the Greek language.[47] Byzantine court titles were always rare among the Neapolitan aristocracy, but during the period of the Norman conquest the local dukes reinforced their relationship with Constantinople; Sergius VI (*c*.1077–1107) and John VI (*c*.1107–20) had both been awarded the title of *protosebastos*.[48] Most medieval Neapolitan documents were destroyed during the Second World War, but at the end of the nineteenth century Bartolomeo Capasso collected, studied and carefully presented all the known primary sources of Naples up to the year 1139. There is no equivalent scholarly work for the Norman period of the town.

## 5. THE DUCHY OF AMALFI

In the eleventh century the small duchy of Amalfi did not belong to the Byzantine empire. Its dukes belonged to the local dynasty which had been established by Sergius I in 958. During the years 1039–52 Amalfi was dominated by the Lombard principality of Salerno, and in 1073 the city-state surrendered to the Normans. Thereafter, except for a brief period of independence under the Duke Marinus (1096–1100), Amalfi was integrated into the Norman state. Nevertheless, more than any of the other independent southern Italian states, because of its commercial interests in the eastern Mediterranean Amalfi cultivated very strong relations with Byzantium which are visible at various levels. Some of the dukes were awarded Byzantine court titles. John II, who had lived on two occasions, each of several years, as an exile in Constantinople, was *patrikios* from 1030 and *anthypatos* and *vestes* from 1052, whereas Marinus, duke from 1096 to 1100, during the short period of the Amalfitan rebellion against the Normans, received the title of *sebastos*. Commercial relations between Amalfi and the Byzantine empire continued even after the Norman conquest, though on a reduced level. The Amalfitans possessed a quarter and at least one church in Constantinople, a church and a hospital in Antioch, and a monastery on mount Athos. In the Amalfitan documents up to the second half of the twelfth century, quite a number of private individuals are mentioned, probably merchants who had been awarded imperial titles or who are said to be living or travelling in the eastern Roman empire.[49] Some of them encouraged or commissioned Latin

---

[47] Capasso, *Monumenta*, vol. 2.1, no. 437, pp. 237–8 (1032); no. 406, p. 256 (1056, not 1026); nos. 414–414*, pp. 259–61 (1057 not 1027); no. 568, pp. 345–6 (1095); no. 608, pp. 368–9 (1113); no. 631*, p. 393 (1126).
[48] Capasso, *Monumenta*, vol. 2.2, nos. 20–5, pp. 58–73, 100–1.
[49] von Falkenhausen, 'Il commercio di Amalfi', 28–30.

translations of Greek hagiographical texts.[50] In particular the family *de comite Maurone* and its most important representative, Pantaleon, had a very intense and long-lasting political and cultural relationship with Byzantium. This is known not only from archival documents, but also from chronicles, such as that of Amatus of Montecassino, political and ecclesiastical treatises, hagiographical sources and works of art, like the bronze doors of the churches of Amalfi, Montecassino, Montesantangelo and San Paolo *fuori le mura* in Rome.[51] The archival material and the narrative sources from and for Amalfi up to 1100 have been carefully researched and presented by Ulrich Schwarz. As for the twelfth century, Bruno Figliuolo has done valuable research on the Amalfitans in the Latin Kingdom of Jerusalem and I myself have written about the relations between Amalfi and the Byzantine empire during the twelfth century. Further material may also still exist.[52]

## 6. THE DUCHY OF GAETA AND SOUTHERN LATIUM

Many archival documents for the medieval history of Gaeta have survived, but there is little evidence concerning relations between the duchy and Byzantium during the eleventh and twelfth centuries. In contrast to what is known from the tenth century when Gaeta was well connected with the eastern Roman empire, in our period apparently neither the duke nor members of the local aristocracy were awarded imperial titles; moreover, it seems that the merchants from Gaeta preferred commercial activities in the Tyrrhenian Sea to more ambitious and dangerous expeditions to the eastern Mediterranean. However, an undated letter written in Constantinople by Hilarios *sacerdos et monachus et magnae ecclesiae Novae Romae cubicularius* together with three other men (one of them, *Lupinus de Johanne de Lupino de Iusto comite,* an Amalfitan) to Bishop Leo (*c*.1049–72) has been published: in it they inform the ecclesiastical authorities that John, son of Peter *de domno Benedicto* from Gaeta had died in Constantinople leaving 35 *tetartera* to several churches in

---

[50] A. Hofmeister, 'Der Übersetzer Johannes und das Geschlecht der *comitis Mauronis* in Amalfi. Ein Beitrag zur Geschichte der byzantinisch–abendländischen Beziehungen besonders im 11. Jahrhundert', *Historische Vierteljahrsschrift* 27 (1932), 225–84, 493–508, 831–3; P. Chiesa, *Vita e morte di Giovanni Calabita e Giovanni l'Elemosiniere. Due testi 'amalfitani' inediti*, Quaderni Salernitani 1 (Cava dei Tirreni, 1995).

[51] G. Matthiae, *Le porte bronzee bizantine in Italia* (Rome, 1971).

[52] Figliuolo, 'Amalfi e il Levante', 610–20; von Falkenhausen, 'La chiesa amalfitana', 81–121; von Falkenhausen, 'Il commercio di Amalfi', 19–38.

his home town and to some relatives and friends.[53] Presumably John had died during a business trip to the eastern Mediterranean. Hence some merchants of Gaeta were apparently still active in Byzantium, maybe in joint ventures with colleagues from Amalfi.

Finally I think one should include in this survey the Greek abbey of Grottaferrata (about 18 km. south-east of Rome) which was founded in 1004 by Neilos of Rossano and still exists. Grottaferrata is situated outside the boundaries of the Byzantine empire, and the monastery never did belong to the jurisdiction of the patriarchal see of Constantinople, but was subject to the Holy See. Nevertheless during the eleventh and twelfth centuries the abbey flourished economically and was an active centre of Greek monastic culture. In addition to monastic property near Rome, Grottaferrata owned an important *metochion* at Rofrano south of Salerno, the possession of which was confirmed by Roger II in 1131.[54] Among the monks, who were normally of Calabrian or Sicilian origin, there were capable scribes, hagiographers and hymnographers, who continued to cultivate relations with the areas of Greek monasticism in southern Italy.[55] Given this cultural background, it is quite understandable that Pope Urban II in 1088 sent Abbot Nicholas of Grottaferrata on a diplomatic mission to Constantinople.[56]

In conclusion, the primary sources from post-Byzantine southern Italy provide substantial information about former subjects of the empire and about people who in one way or the other were connected with Byzantium during the period 1071–1204, but, as has already been said, in my judgement it is neither reasonable nor feasible, given the enormous quantity of archival documents, to include the entire population of the ex-Byzantine territories in the Prosopography of the Byzantine World.

---

[53] *Codex diplomaticus cajetanus*, vol. 2, no. 219, pp. 51–2; Skinner, *Family Power*, 283–4.

[54] E. Follieri, 'Il crisobullo di Ruggero II re di Sicilia per la badia di Grottaferrata (aprile 1131)', *Bollettino della badia greca di Grottaferrata* n.s. 42 (1988), 49–81, repr. in A. Acconcia Longo, L. Perria, A. Luzzi, eds., *Byzantina et Italograeca. Studi di filologia e di paleografia*, Storia e Letteratura 195 (Rome, 1997), 433–61.

[55] A. Acconcia Longo, 'Gli innografi di Grottaferrata', in *Atti del Congresso internazionale su S. Nilo di Rossano*, 317–28.

[56] Malaterra, *De rebus gestis*, 92.

# BIBLIOGRAPHY

## 1. THE BYZANTINE PROVINCES 1025–71[1]

### HANDBOOKS, SURVEYS, PROSOPOGRAPHIES (alphabetical order)

H. Enzensberger, 'Süditalien', in A. Haverkamp and H. Enzensberger, eds., *Italien im Mittelalter. Neuerscheinungen von 1959–1975*, Historische Zeitschrift, Sonderheft 7 (Munich, 1980)
Southern Italian bibliography for the years 1959 to 1975.

J. Gay, *L'Italie méridionale et l'empire byzantin depuis l'avènement de Basile I<sup>er</sup> jusqu'à la prise de Bari par les Normands (867–1071)*, École française de Rome (Paris, 1904)
Still valuable standard history of Byzantine domination in southern Italy.

W. Holtzmann and D. Girgensohn, eds., *Italia pontificia*, vols. 9–10 (Berlin, 1962 and Thur, 1975).
Summaries of pontifical documents for the southern Italian and Sicilian dioceses up to 1198.

J.-M. Martin, *La Pouille du VI<sup>e</sup> au XII<sup>e</sup> siècle*, Collection de l'École française de Rome 179 (Paris, 1993)
Excellent survey of the archival and narrative sources for Apulia.

V. von Falkenhausen, *La dominazione bizantina nell'Italia meridionale dal IX all'XI secolo* (Bari, 1978)
Useful especially for the prosopography of Byzantine officials in southern Italy.

### PRIMARY SOURCES

#### Documentary Sources in Greek (chronological order)

F. Trinchera, *Syllabus graecarum membranarum* (Naples, 1865), nos. 21–46, pp. 22–61
Twenty-five documents for the period from 1025–70. The edition is not perfect and most of the documents were destroyed during the Second World War.

G. Robinson, *History and Cartulary of the Greek Monastery of St Elias and St Anastasius of Carbone*, vol. 2.1, *Orientalia Christiana* 15.2 (1929), nos. 2–8, pp. 138–75
Seven documents for the period 1025–70. The edition is rather unreliable, but the documents are still extant and the readings can be checked.

A. Guillou, *Saint-Nicolas de Donnoso (1031–1060/1061)*, Corpus des actes grecs d'Italie du Sud et de Sicile. Recherches d'histoire et de géographie 1 (Vatican City, 1967)
Edition of four documents from the period 1025–70.

---

[1] This is the only part of the bibliography where I have tried to give a complete survey of the known sources, which would have been an impossible task for the other sections of the bibliography.

A. Guillou, *La Théotokos de Hagia-Agathè (Oppido) (1050–1064/1065)*, Corpus des actes grecs d'Italie du Sud et de Sicile. Recherches d'histoire et de géographie 5 (Vatican City, 1972)
Edition of forty-seven documents and fragments of documents from the period 1051–67.
—— *Le brébion de la métropole byzantine de Règion (vers 1050)*, Corpus des actes grecs d'Italie du Sud et de Sicile. Recherches d'histoire et de géographie 4 (Vatican City, 1974)
A long administrative document from about 1050 concerning the property of the church of Reggio di Calabria.
S.G. Mercati, C. Giannelli and A. Guillou, *Saint-Jean-Théristès (1054–1264)*, Corpus des actes grecs d'Italie du Sud et de Sicile. Recherches d'histoire et de géographie 5 (Vatican City, 1980), no. 1, pp. 31–42
One document from 1054. Guillou's editions are generally reliable, but can in any case be checked on the photographs included in the edition.
A. Guillou and C. Rognoni, 'Une nouvelle fondation monastique dans le thème de Calabre (1053–1054)', *BZ* 84/5 (1991/2), 423–9
Edition of a Greek document of 1053/4.
C. Rognoni, 'Le fonds d'archives "Messine" de l'Archivio de Medinaceli (Toledo). Regestes des actes privés grecs', *Byz* 72 (2002), 502–5
—— *Les actes privés grecs de l'Archivo Ducal de Medinaceli (Tolède)*, 1. *Les monastères de Saint-Pancrace de Briatico, de Saint-Philippe-de-Bojôannès et de Saint-Nicolas-des-Drosi (Calabre, XIᵉ–XIIᵉ siècles)* (Paris 2004), nos. 1–10, pp. 62–114, nos. 25–7, pp. 189–207
Thirteen unedited documents from Messina preserved in Toledo. The volume is accompanied by a CD with photographs of all the documents so that the published text can be checked.

## Documentary Sources in Latin (chronological order by archive)

P.M. Tropeano, ed., *Codice diplomatico verginiano*, vol. 1, 947–1102 (Montevergine, 1977), nos. 55, 69, pp. 210–13, 274–5.
Two documents (1051, 1067) from Ascoli Satriano.
G.B. Nitto de Rossi and F. Nitti di Vito, eds., *Codice diplomatico barese*, vol. 1 (Bari, 1897), nos. 13–26, pp. 21–46
Fourteen documents (1025–67) mostly from Bari.
F. Carabellese, ed., *Codice diplomatico barese*, vol. 3, (Bari, 1899), nos. 2–16, pp. 5–25
Fifteen documents (1033(?)–1071) from Terlizzi and Giovinazzo.
F. Nitti di Vito, ed., *Codice diplomatico barese*, vol. 4 (Bari, 1900), nos. 16–46, pp. 32–94; frag. 8, pp. 105–6
Thirty-two documents (1025–71) mostly from Bari.
—— ed., *Codice diplomatico barese*, vol. 8 (Bari, 1914), nos. 7–18, pp. 15–39
Twelve documents (1025–66) mostly from Canne and Barletta.
G. Beltrani, ed., *Codice diplomatico barese*, vol. 9 (Bari, 1923), nos. 2–3, pp. 3–6
Two documents (1063–4) from Trani.
G. Coniglio, ed., *Codice diplomatico pugliese*, vol. 20 (Bari, 1975), nos. 37–40, pp. 83–94

Four documents (1025–54) from Conversano.

J.-M. Martin, ed., *Codice diplomatico pugliese*, vol. 21 (Bari, 1976), nos. 3–15, pp. 83–108

Thirteen documents (1034–67) from Troia.

G.M. Monti, ed., *Codice diplomatico brindisino*, vol. 1 (Trani, 1940), nos. 3–5, pp. 6–10

Three documents (1033–60) from Oria and Monopoli.

M. Morcaldi, M. Schiani, S. De Stephano, eds., *Codex diplomaticus cavensis*, vol. 1 (Milan, Pisa, Naples, 1873), nos. 10, 11, 21, 22, 25, 126, 127, 143, pp. 11–12, 22–4, 28–9, 160–3, 183–5; vol. 5 (1878), nos. 793, 846, pp. 134, 219–21; vol. 6 (1884), nos. 911, 938, 1024, 1029, 1031, 1050, pp. 61, 99–101, 238–9, 248–51, 279–80; vol. 7 (1888), nos. 1078, 1130, 1180, 1186, 1192, pp. 34, 125, 202, 211, 218; vol. 8 (1893), nos. 1302, 1330, pp. 131, 183–5

Twenty-three documents, mostly from Bari, Lucera and Molfetta (1027–62). Very often, however, the editors have misinterpreted the dates.

S. Leone, G. Vitolo, *Codex diplomaticus cavensis*, vol. 9 (Badia di Cava, 1984), nos. 12, 30, pp. 35–8, 101–4

Two documents from Candela and Lucera (1066, 1067).

G. Beltrani, *Documenti longobardi e greci per la storia dell'Italia meridionale nel Medio Evo* (Rome, 1877), nos. 10–17, pp. 13–27

Eight documents (1025–71) from Trani. The edition is not very reliable.

A. Prologo, *Le carte che si conservano nello Archivio del capitolo metropolitano della città di Trani* (Barletta, 1877), nos. 9–16, pp. 38–55

A slightly better edition of the same documents.

L. Scarano, *Regesto delle pergamene del capitolo metropolitano e della curia arcivescovile di Trani dai longobardi agli angioini (845–1435)* (Bari, 1983), 17–83

Survey of the Trani documents from the Byzantine period.

A. Petrucci, ed., *Codice diplomatico del monastero benedettino di S. Maria di Tremiti (1005–1235)*, Fonti per la storia d'Italia 98, vol. 2 (Rome, 1960), nos. 1–81, pp. 3–244

Eighty-one documents from northern Apulia (1005–69). Most but not all the documents come from the Byzantine province.

F. Guerrieri, *Possedimenti temporali e spirituali dei benedettini di Cava nelle Puglie* (Trani, 1900), p. 191

One document of 1028 from Taranto. The Greek signatures of four Byzantine officials, which were not read by the editor, have been published by:

V. von Falkenhausen, 'Taranto in epoca bizantina', *Studi medievali*, ser. 3.9 (1968), 163.

T. Leccisotti, 'Le pergamene latine di Taranto nell'archivio di Montecassino', *Archivio storico pugliese* 14 (1961), 12

One document of 1061 from Taranto.

## Epigraphy

A. Guillou, *Recueil des inscriptions grecques médiévales d'Italie*, Collection de l'École française de Rome 222 (Rome, 1996)

A collection of medieval Greek inscriptions from Italy (photographs and editions with commentary). Many of them come from Byzantine and post-Byzantine southern Italy and Sicily.

## Sigillography

Greek lead seals of individuals active in our period in Byzantine and post-Byzantine southern Italy can be found in all collections of Byzantine seals and are published in all major sigillographic publications. There is a special Italian section in:

J. Nesbitt and N. Oikonomides, *Catalogue of Byzantine Seals at Dumbarton Oaks and in the Fogg Museum of Art*, vol. 1, *Italy, North of the Balkans, North of the Black Sea* (Washington, DC, 1991), 16–22

## Narrative Sources

(*a*) G.H. Pertz, ed., *Annales barenses*, MGHS 5 (Hanover, 1844), 51–6
Covering the years 605–1043.

(*b*) G.H. Pertz, ed., *Annales Lupi protospatharii*, MGHS 5 (Hanover, 1844), 52–63
Covering the years 855–1102.

(*c*) L.A. Muratori, ed., *Chronicon ignoti civis barensis sive Lupi protospatae cum notis C. Peregrini*, Rerum Italicarum Scriptores 5 (Milan, 1724), 147–56
Concerning the years 855–1118.
Three versions of the Annals of Bari. The editions are unsatisfactory. There is a better edition of (*a*) and (*b*) in the unpublished Ph.D. thesis of:

W.J. Churchill, 'The *Annales barenses* and the *Annales Lupi protospatharii*. Critical edition and commentary' (Ph.D. thesis, University of Toronto, Centre of Medieval Studies, 1979)

E. Caspar, 'Die Chronik von Tres Tabernae in Calabrien', *Quellen und Forschungen aus italienischen Archiven und Bibliotheken* 10 (1907), 1–56
Edition and commentary of a chronicle from the area of Catanzaro in Calabria during the Byzantine and early Norman period.

V. De Bartholomaeis, ed., *Amato di Montecassino, Storia de'Normanni volgarizzato in antico francese*, Fonti per la storia d'Italia 76 (Rome, 1935)
History of the Norman conquest of southern Italy, written in Latin around 1080, but preserved only in a fourteenth-century translation in Old French.

M. Mathieu, ed., *Guillaume de Pouille, La geste de Robert Guiscard. Édition, traduction, commentaire et introduction*, Istituto siciliano di studi bizantini e neoellenici. Testi e monumenti 4 (Palermo, 1961)
History of the Norman conquest of southern Italy, written in verse at the end of the eleventh century. Standard edition with a French translation.

E. Pontieri, ed., *Gaufredus Malaterra, De rebus gestis Rogerii Calabriae et Siciliae comitis et Roberti Guiscardi ducis fratris eius auctore Gaufredo Malaterra monacho benedictino*, Rerum Italicarum Scriptores 5.1 (2nd edn., Bologna, 1928)
History of the Norman conquest especially of Calabria and Sicily, up to the year 1099, written in Catania about 1100. The edition is not very reliable and should be used with the corrections of:

G. Resta, 'Per il testo di Malaterra e di altre cronache meridionali', *Liceo ginnasio 'T. Campanella' 1814–1964. Studi per il 150° anno* (Reggio Calabria, 1964), 399–456

H. Hoffmann, ed., *Chronica monasterii casinensis*, MGHS 34 (Hanover, 1980)
History of the monastery of Montecassino, from the foundation to the year 1138. Excellent edition with a short but efficient commentary.

**Hagiography**

U. Martino, ed., *Nilo, Vita di S. Filareto di Seminara* (Reggio Calabria, 1993)
Edition of the Greek text with an Italian translation.
G. Zaccagni, 'Il *Bios* di S. Bartolomeo da Simeri (BHG 235)', *RSBN* n.s. 33 (1996), 193–274
Edition of the Greek text (205–28) with an Italian translation and a short commentary (229–74).

**Manuscripts and Colophons**

K. Lake and S. Lake, *Dated Greek Minuscule Manuscripts to the Year 1200*, Monumenta Palaeographica Vetera, ser. 1 (Boston, Mass., 1934–45)
P. Canart and S. Lucà, eds., *Codici greci dell'Italia meridionale* (Rome, 2000)
Catalogue of the exhibition of Greek manuscripts at Grottaferrata (31 March–31 May 2000) with scholarly descriptions of eighty Greek manuscripts written in southern Italy and a useful bibliography.

## 2. THE FORMER BYZANTINE TERRITORIES, 1071–1204

## HANDBOOKS, SURVEYS, PROSOPOGRAPHIES

There are a great many historical surveys of Norman southern Italy. In addition to those cited in the first section I mention here only two:
D. Matthew, *The Norman Kingdom of Sicily* (Cambridge, 1992)
G.A. Loud and A. Metcalfe, eds., *The Society of Norman Italy* (Leiden, Boston, Cologne, 2002)
Recent volume of collected articles by various authors which gives an interesting introduction into the period.

L.-R. Ménager, *Amiratus-ἀμηρᾶς. L'émirat et les origines de l'amirauté (XIᵉ–XIIIᵉ siècles)* (Paris, 1960)
Prosopography of the Greek officials of the Norman administration.
—— 'Inventaire des familles normandes et franques emigrées en Italie méridionale et en Sicile (XIᵉ–XIIᵉ siècles)', in *Roberto il Guiscardo e il suo tempo. Atti delle prime giornate normanno-sveve, Bari, 28–29 maggio 1973* (Bari 1975, repr. 1991), 281–410
Prosopography of Norman families in southern Italy and Sicily.
H. Takayama, *The Administration of the Norman Kingdom of Sicily* (Leiden, New York, Cologne, 1993)
Valuable survey of the administration of the Norman kingdom providing useful biographical information about the various officials.

## PRIMARY SOURCES

### Documentary Sources in Greek (chronological order)

F. Trinchera, *Syllabus graecarum membranarum* (Naples, 1865), nos. 47–259, pp. 62–353
  Two hundred and twelve documents for the period 1071–1204. The edition is not perfect and most of the documents were destroyed during the Second World War.

S. Cusa, *Diplomi greci ed arabi di Sicilia* (Palermo, 1868, 1884).
  Edition of 150 Greek and Arabic documents from Sicily and southern Calabria (1092–1201).

G. Robinson, *History and Cartulary of the Greek Monastery of St Elias and St Anastasius of Carbone,* vol. 2.1, Orientalia Christiana 15.2 (1929), pp. 9–154; vol. 2.2, Orientalia Christiana 19.1 (1930), nos. 9–68, pp. 177–275
  Fifty-nine documents for the period from 1070 to 1204: the edition is rather unreliable, but the documents are still extant and the reading can be checked against the originals in the Archivio Doria-Pamphilj in Rome.

A. Guillou, *Les actes grecs de S. Maria di Messina,* Istituto siciliano di studi bizantini e neoellenici. Testi 8 (Palermo, 1963)
  Twenty documents from Calabria and Messina (1076–1201).

—— *Saint-Nicodème de Kellarana (1023/1024–1232),* Corpus des actes grecs d'Italie du Sud et de Sicile. Recherches d'histoire et de géographie 2 (Vatican City, 1968)
  Three documents for the period from 1070 to 1204.

S.G. Mercati, C. Giannelli, A. Guillou, *Saint-Jean-Théristès (1054–1264),* Corpus des actes grecs d'Italie du Sud et de Sicile. Recherches d'histoire et de géographie 5 (Vatican City, 1980), nos. 2–43, pp. 43–225
  Forty-two documents for the period 1070–1204. Guillou's editions are generally reliable, but can in any case be checked against the photographs included in the edition.

F. Burgarella and A. Guillou, *Castrovillari nei documenti greci del Medioevo* (Castrovillari, 2000)
  One document (1081).

C. Rognoni, *Les actes privés grecs de l'Archivo Ducal de Medinaceli (Tolède),* 1. *Les monastères de Saint-Pancrace de Briatico, de Saint-Philippe-de-Bojôannès et de Saint-Nicolas-des-Drosi (Calabre, XIᵉ–XIIᵉ siècles)* (Paris 2004), nos. 11–24, pp. 115–79, nos. 28–30, pp. 208–32
  Seventeen documents from 1062 to 1175. The volume is accompanied by a CD with photographs of all the documents so that the published text can be checked.

G. Breccia, *Nuovi contributi alla storia del Patir. Documenti del Vat. gr. 2605* (Rome, 2006), nos. 1–11, pp. 135–98, no. 16, pp. 222–34.
  Twelve Greek documents from 1109 to 1203, published on the basis of copies from the early eighteenth century: the originals are lost.

Other individual Greek documents, too numerous to list here, have been published in various places.

**Documentary Sources in Latin** (chronological order by archive)

*Codex diplomaticus Regni Siciliae*
The following volumes have been published to date, all with excellent commentaries:
H. Zielinski, *Tancredi et Willelmi III regum diplomata* (Cologne and Vienna, 1982)
Th. Kölzer, *Constantiae imperatricis et reginae Siciliae diplomata (1195–1198)* (Cologne and Vienna, 1983)
C. Brühl, *Rogerii II. regis diplomata latina* (Cologne and Vienna, 1987)
H. Enzensberger, *Guillelmi I. regis diplomata* (Cologne, Weimar, Vienna, 1996)
The charters of the Empress Constantia have been republished:
Th. Kölzer, *Die Urkunden der Kaiserin Konstanze*, MGH Diplomata regum et imperatorum Germaniae 11.3 (Hanover, 1990)

G.B. Nitto de Rossi and F. Nitti di Vito, eds., *Codice diplomatico barese*, vol. 1 (Bari, 1897), nos. 27–72, pp. 49–141
Forty-six documents (1073–1204) mostly from Bari.

F. Carabellese, ed., *Codice diplomatico barese*, vol. 3 (Bari, 1899), nos. 16–192, pp. 35–214
One hundred and seventy-eight documents (1074–1204) from Terlizzi and Giovinazzo.

F. Nitti di Vito, ed., *Codice diplomatico barese*, vol. 5 (Bari, 1902), nos. 1–164, pp. 4–281; frags. 1–24, pp. 285–304
One hundred and eighty-eight documents (1075–1194) mostly from Bari.

—— *Codice diplomatico barese*, vol. 6 (Bari, 1906), nos. 1–15, pp. 3–28
Fifteen documents (1195–1203).

F. Carabellese, ed., *Codice diplomatico barese*, vol. 7 (Bari, 1912), nos. 1–79, pp. 3–103
Seventy-nine documents (1076–1204) mostly from Molfetta.

F. Nitti di Vito, ed., *Codice diplomatico barese*, vol. 8 (Bari, 1914), nos. 19–192, pp. 39–247
One hundred and seventy-four documents (1072–1204) mostly from Canne and Barletta.

G. Beltrani, ed., *Codice diplomatico barese*, vol. 9 (Bari, 1923), nos. 6–78, pp. 7–88
Seventy-three documents (1073–1203) from Trani.

R. Filangieri di Candida, ed., *Codice diplomatico barese*, vol. 10 (Bari, 1927), nos. 1–47, pp. 3–70
Forty-seven documents (1074–1204) mostly from Barletta.

G. Coniglio, ed., *Codice diplomatico pugliese*, vol. 20 (Bari, 1975), nos. 37–40, pp. 83–94
Four documents (1025–54) from Conversano.

J.-M. Martin, ed., *Codice diplomatico pugliese*, vol. 21 (Bari, 1976), nos. 16–125, pp. 108–358
One hundred and ten documents (1080–1201) from Troia.

J.-M. Martin, ed., *Codice diplomatico pugliese*, vol. 32 (Bari, 1994), nos. 1–62, pp. 47–167
Sixty-two documents (1086–1203) from northern Apulia.

G.M. Monti, ed., *Codice diplomatico brindisino*, vol. 1 (Trani, 1940), nos. 6–39, pp. 13–68
Thirty-four documents mostly from Brindisi.

A. Prologo, *Le carte che si conservano nello Archivio del capitolo metropolitano della città di Trani* (Barletta, 1877), nos. 18–95, pp. 58–197
Seventy-eight documents from Trani (1072–1204).

F. Magistrale, *Le pergamene dell'Archivio arcivescovile di Taranto*, vols. 1–2 (1083–1258), (Galatina, 1999), nos. 1–12, pp. 3–48
Twelve documents (1083–1197) in Latin and Greek from Taranto.

A. Pratesi, *Carte latine di abbazie calabresi provenienti dall'Archivio Aldobrandini*, Studi e testi 197 (Vatican City, 1958) nos. 1–77, pp. 3–194
Edition of seventy-seven documents from Calabria (1065–1204).

H. Houben, *Die Abtei Venosa und das Mönchtum im normannisch-staufischen Süditalien*, Bibliothek des deutschen historischen Instituts in Rom 80 (Tübingen, 1995)
Edition of 176 seventeenth-century summaries of documents of the Norman period from the archive of the abbey of Venosa (Basilicata), with a useful introduction on monasticism in the Norman kingdom.

R. Pirri, *Sicilia sacra*, vols. 1–2 (Palermo 1733)
History of the church in Sicily with editions of many Latin documents.

C.A. Garufi, *I documenti inediti dell'epoca normanna in Sicilia*, Documenti per servire alla storia di Sicilia, ser. 1.18 (Palermo, 1899)
One hundred and eleven documents (1092–1194) from Sicily.

L.-R. Ménager, *Les actes latins de S. Maria di Messina (1103–1250)*, Istituto siciliano di studi bizantini e neoellenici. Testi 9 (Palermo, 1963)
Twelve documents mostly from Messina (1103–1200).

## Narrative Sources

E. D'Angelo, ed., *Falcone di Benevento, Chronicon beneventanum* (Florence, 1998)
Chronicle from 1102–40, written by the notary Falco from Benevento, hostile to the Normans.

C.A. Garufi, ed., *Romualdi Salernitani Chronicon,* in L.A. Muratori, Rerum Italicarum Scriptores 7 (2nd edn., Bologna, 1935)
Chronicle from Adam to 1178. For the Norman period the chronicle gives interesting and reliable information. Its author, archbishop of Salerno (1153–81), was an important and well-informed figure at the court of William I and William II.

G.B. Siragusa, ed., *(Hugo Falcandus), La historia o liber de regno Sicilie e la epistola ad Petrum, panormitane ecclesie thesaurarium*, Fonti per la storia d'Italia 22 (Rome, 1897)

## Hagiography

G. Schirò, ed., *Vita di S. Luca, vescovo di Isola Capo Rizzuto*, Istituto siciliano di studi bizantini e neoellenici. Testi 2 (Palermo, 1954)
Edition of the Greek Life of a learned monk from Calabria, who lived for years as a missonary in Sicily (late 11th/early 12th c.) and became bishop of Isola Capo Rizzuto in southern Calabria (d. 1114) = BHG 2237.

## 3. THE LOMBARD PRINCIPALITIES

## HANDBOOKS, SURVEYS, PROSOPOGRAPHIES (alphabetical order)

H. Bloch, *Montecassino in the Middle Ages* (Cambridge, Mass., 1986)
History of the abbey of Montecassino.

H. Dormeier, *Montecassino und die Laien im 11. und 12. Jahrhundert*, Schriften der
MGH 27 (Stuttgart, 1979)
Useful for the prosopography of the Lombard and Norman families connected
with Montecassino.

J.H. Drell, *Kinship and Conquest. Family strategies in the principality of Salerno during
the Norman period, 1077–1194* (Ithaca and London, 2002)
Helpful for the prosopography of the aristocracy of the principality of Salerno
during the Norman period. Useful bibliography.

P. Guillaume, *Essai historique sur l'abbaye de Cava d'après des documents inédits* (Cava
dei Tirreni, 1877)
History of the abbey of Cava with an appendix of editions of archival documents.

H. Taviani-Carozzi, *La principauté lombarde de Salerne (IX$^e$–XI$^e$)*, Collection de
l'École française de Rome 152 (Rome, 1991)
Useful survey of the history of the principality up to the Norman conquest in
1077.

## PRIMARY SOURCES

### Documentary Sources

It is absolutely impossible to indicate all the editions of documents concerning this
area for this period. I give those which seem to be most relevant.

M. Morcaldi, M. Schiani, S. De Stephano, eds., *Codex diplomaticus cavensis*, vol. 5
(Milan, Pisa, Naples, 1878) no. 759, p. 85 to S. Leone and G. Vitolo, eds., vol. 10
(1073–1080) (Badia di Cava, 1990)
Edition of documents mostly from the area of Salerno and its hinterland, but also
from other areas of Campania and from Apulia. In the archive of the abbey of
Cava there are thousands of documents from our period still unedited.

P. Cherubini, *Le pergamene di S. Nicola di Gallucanta (secc. IX–XII)* (Nocera
Inferiore, 1990)
Edition of ninety-five documents concerning a Greek monastery near Salerno
(1027–1151).

E. Gattola, *Historia abbatiae cassinensis per saeculorum seriem distributa* (Venice
1733)
—— *Ad historiam abbatiae cassinensis accessiones* (Venice, 1734).
Edition of documents relating to the history of Montecassino.

## 4. THE DUCHY OF NAPLES

### HANDBOOKS, SURVEYS, PROSOPOGRAPHIES

E. Pontieri, G. Cassandro, eds., *Storia di Napoli*, vol. 2.1–2 (Naples, 1969)
   Valuable history of Naples from late antiquity to the thirteenth century.
G. Pugliese Carratelli, ed., *Storia e civiltà della Campania. Il Medioevo* (Naples, 1992)
   Valuable survey of history and culture in medieval Campania.

### PRIMARY SOURCES

B. Capasso, *Monumenta ad neapolitanae ducatus historiam pertinentia*, vols. 1–2.2 (Naples, 1881–92)
   In these very valuable volumes Capasso collected all the medieval Neapolitan sources known to him: hagiography, epigraphy, charters of the dukes and private documents. Of the latter he gives precise summaries. Capasso's work is particularly precious, because most of the Neapolitan documents were destroyed in the Second World War.
R. Pilone, *L'antico inventario delle pergamene del monastero dei SS Severino e Sossio (Archivio di Stato di Napoli, Monasteri soppressi, vol. 1788)*, Fonti per la storia dell'Italia meridionale 48–51 (Rome, 1999)
   Fifteenth-century summaries of medieval Neapolitan documents. Most of them concern our period. Edition and presentation of the text are, however, quite sloppy.

## 5. AMALFI

### HANDBOOKS, SURVEYS, PROSOPOGRAPHIES

U. Schwarz, *Amalfi im frühen Mittelalter (9.–11. Jahrhundert). Untersuchungen zur Amalfitaner Überlieferung*, Bibliothek des Deutschen Historischen Instituts in Rom 49 (Tübingen, 1978)
   History of Amalfi to the year 1100 with an accurate survey of the primary sources.

The following three articles give useful information about the activities of Amalfitans in the eastern Mediterranean:
A. Figliuolo, 'Amalfi e il Levante nel Medioevo', in G. Airaldi and B.Z. Kedar, eds., *I comuni italiani nel Regno di Gerusalemme*, Collana storica di fonti e studi diretti da G. Pistarino 48 (Genoa, 1986), 573–664
V. von Falkenhausen, 'La chiesa amalfitana nei suoi rapporti con l'Impero bizantino (X–XI secolo)', with an appendix by L. Perria, *RSBN* n.s. 30 (1993), 81–121
—— 'Il commercio di Amalfi con Costantinopoli e il Levante nel secolo XII', in O. Banti, *Amalfi, Genova, Pisa e Venezia*, Società storica pisana. Biblioteca del *Bollettino storico pisano*. Collana storica 46 (Pisa, 1998), 19–38

## PRIMARY SOURCES

### Documentary Sources (chronological order)

M. Camera, *Memorie storico-diplomatiche dell'antica città e ducato di Amalfi*, 2 vols. (Salerno, 1876–81)
  Provides editions of medieval Amalfitan documents.
R. Filangieri di Candida, *Codice diplomatico amalfitano,* vol. 1 (Naples, 1917), vol. 2 (Trani, 1951)
  Edition of medieval Amalfitan documents.
U. Schwarz, 'Regesta amalfitana. Die älteren Urkunden Amalfis in ihrer Überlieferung', 1–3, *Quellen und Forschungen aus italienischen Archiven und Bibliotheken* 58 (1978), 1–132; 59 (1979), 1–157; 60 (1980), 1–156
  Summaries (and some editions) of all known Amalfitan documents, edited and unedited, up to the year 1100, with a useful commentary.
J. Mazzoleni and R. Orefice, *Il codice Perris. Cartulario amalfitano ( sec. X–XV )*, 2 vols., Centro di cultura e storia amalfitana. Fonti 1.1–2 (Amalfi, 1985–6)
  Edition of medieval Amalfitan documents.
V. Criscuolo, *Le pergamene dell'Archivio vescovile di Minori*, Centro di cultura e storia amalfitana. Fonti 5 (Amalfi, 1987)
  Edition of medieval Amalfitan documents.

### Narrative Sources

V. De Bartholomaeis, ed., *Amato di Montecassino, Storia de'Normanni volgarizzato in antico francese*, Fonti per la storia d'Italia 76 (Rome, 1935)
  History of the Norman conquest of southern Italy, written in Latin around 1080, but preserved only in a fourteenth-century translation in Old French.
*Chronicon amalfitanum*, in Schwarz, ed., *Amalfi im frühen Mittelalter*, 113–236
  Late and not very informative chronicle of Amalfi from the foundation of the town to the year 1081. Excellent edition and commentary.
*Chronicon archiepiscoporum amalfitanorum*
  Late and not very informative chronicle of the archbishops of Amalfi from the tenth to the sixteenth century.
*Editions:*
A.A. Pelliccia, *Raccolta di varie croniche, diari et altri opuscoli così italiani, come latini appartenenti alla storia del Regno di Napoli*, vol. 5 (Naples, 1782), 163–81
P. Pirri, *Il duomo di Amalfi e il chiostro del Paradiso* (Rome, 1941), 176–95
  Both editions are unreliable.
Commentary in Schwarz, *Amalfi im frühen Mittelalter*, 89–107.

## 6. GAETA AND SOUTHERN LATIUM

## HANDBOOKS, SURVEYS, PROSOPOGRAPHIES

*Atti del Congresso internazionale su S. Nilo di Rossano. 28 settembre–1 ottobre 1986* (Rossano-Grottaferrata, 1989)
This volume contains some interesting articles on the cultural history of Grottaferrata.

*Enciclopedia dei Papi*, vol. 2 (Rome, 2000), 135–350
This recent publication gives thorough biographies of the popes with ample bibliographies. The relevant popes are John XIX (1024–1032) to Innocent III (1198–1216).

M. Merores, *Gaeta im frühen Mittelalter (8. bis 12. Jahrhundert)* (Gotha, 1911)
Competently presented narrative history of Gaeta.

P. Skinner, *Family Power in Southern Italy. The duchy of Gaeta and its neighbours, 850–1139* (Cambridge, 1995).
The second part (pp. 149–303) deals with the eleventh and twelfth century. The volume has a useful bibliography.

## PRIMARY SOURCES

### Documentary Sources

*Codex diplomaticus cajetanus*, 2 vols. (Montecassino, 1887–91)
There are 226 documents relating to our period: vol. 1, no. 146, p. 284–vol. 2, no. 371, p. 330.

### Hagiography

G. Giovanelli, *S. Bartolomeo Juniore confondatore di Grottaferrata* (Badia greca di Grottaferrata, 1962)
Life of St Bartholemew, abbot of Grottaferrata (d. 1050) = BHG 233. The forthcoming edition by E. Paroli is expected in 2005.

S. Lucà, 'Graeco-Latina di Bartolomeo iuniore, egumeno di Grottaferrata (+ 1055 ca.)?', *Néa Ῥώμη* 1 (2004), 143–84
An excellent article about the religious activities of Abbot Bartholemew in Rome.

# 7

# Visitors from North-Western Europe to Byzantium. Vernacular Sources: Problems and Perspectives

## KRIJNIE CIGGAAR

> I have always wanted to travel to southern lands one day, for a man is thought
> to grow ignorant if he doesn't travel beyond this country of Iceland.
>
> (*Laxdaela Saga*)[1]

## NORTH-WESTERN EUROPE

A DEFINITION OF THE GEOGRAPHICAL TERM NORTH-WESTERN EUROPE is not
easy to give. Generally speaking the term north-western Europe covers the
British Isles, Iceland, Scandinavia and parts of the Continent, northern
France with Normandy, the northern part of Germany and the Low
Countries. In the context of this book this is, geographically speaking,
a wide-ranging area, which causes a number of problems for establishing a
bibliography dealing with visitors to Byzantium. As for the extent of the
population of this area, it was rather limited, especially in the Scandinavian
north. However, this does not mean that source material is also limited.

Migration within Europe took the northern peoples all over western
Europe. From the second half of the eleventh century onward, political and
ecclesiastical leaders and a varying proportion of the populations of
Scandinavia, of Anglo-Saxon and Anglo-Norman England, of Normandy
and of southern Italy were interrelated by family ties. They belonged to the
'Norman world', where features of daily life and, to some extent, language
skills, contributed to the feeling of living in a common culture. In this
'Norman ambience' news and other information could travel freely. Channels

---

Texts referred to are only accompanied by full bibliographical references in footnotes if they do
not feature in the bibliography of Scandinavian sources. This bibliography gives full details for
texts here cited in abbreviated form.

[1] *Laxdaela Saga*, tr. Magnusson and Pálsson, 225.

*Proceedings of the British Academy* **132**, 123–155. © The British Academy 2007.

of information were not the privilege of the ruling classes. Normans from all social backgrounds travelled and worked in foreign parts, including Byzantium. The term *Normannisches Lehngut* refers to topoi in literary texts where visitors to Byzantium sometimes play a role. Cultural exchange and access to information about the world of Byzantium was one of the outcomes of these contacts.[2]

## BYZANTINE TERRITORY AND THE HISTORICAL CONTEXT

For the inhabitants of north-western Europe the Byzantine empire was not an easily understood concept, not least because during the period under discussion they used the term Greece (*Grikkland*) for part of south-eastern Europe. They lived far away from Constantinople, the capital of the Byzantine empire, which had often, too often perhaps, a connotation of being an exotic city full of marvels where the inhabitants indulged in a grand life-style.

The expanding frontiers of the Byzantine empire during this period must have contributed to feelings of uncertainty as to the extent of its territory.

To understand the visits to Byzantium of the various peoples living in the area one has to realise what the historical context was like. The long distance between north-western Europe and the Byzantine empire prevented hostile relations and confrontations. When the Ottonians, the Saxon rulers of Germany in the second half of the tenth century, pretended to become the new rulers of Rome, some clashes with the Byzantines resulted, but on a limited scale. The conquest of southern Italy by Normans from Normandy had wider-ranging effects. Southern Italy had been part of the Byzantine empire. Norman invasions of Byzantine territory across the Adriatic were being organised. It is important to know when a specific visit to southern Italy took place, before the Norman conquest, when Bari was the capital of the Greek province, or after the Norman conquest, when Byzantine institutions and the use of Greek survived to some extent but when, politically speaking, the term Byzantine territory is no longer appropriate.[3]

Until the First Crusade hostilities between east and west were limited to the common frontier in Italy. When Antioch was taken by the crusaders in 1098 it was the Norman dynasty from southern Italy which established itself as the city's ruler. *De facto* Antioch was in Norman hands, *de iure* it was again a Byzantine city because the crusader rulers had sworn an oath of allegiance to the Byzantine emperor. In 1085 the Byzantines had lost the city to the

---

[2] de Vries, 'Normannisches Lehngut'; *Medieval Scandinavia, an Encyclopedia*, 453.
[3] See further Vera von Falkenhausen's chapter in this volume.

Turks. A certain familiarity in Norman and other western circles with the geography of the Byzantine empire is therefore very likely, although topographical names continued to create problems. Some of these names were known from earlier pilgrims, other names were familiar through biblical stories, in Latin or in the local vernaculars.

Before 1025 the history of the various northern peoples had differed greatly. The beginning of the eleventh century was not the start of travel to southern parts for the Scandinavians. Their recent Christianisation around the year 1000 stimulated pilgrimages to Jerusalem and other Holy Places and visits to the shrines of Constantinople. Northerners had long since gone to the east and to Constantinople to serve in the Greek army. There they joined the so-called Varangian Guard which was composed of Scandinavians and Russians and functioned as the emperor's bodyguard. The regiment was active all over the Byzantine empire, as far as southern Italy, Sicily and Syria. Many northerners from Scandinavia came as traders and combined the journey with a period of service in the Byzantine army.

The other peoples of north-western Europe had an even longer tradition of travelling to Jerusalem and visiting the sanctuaries of Constantinople with their prestigious relics of Christ's Passion. Their joining the Greek army, and more especially the Varangian Guard, is not surprising. They had heard about these possibilities in Byzantium and simply followed in the footsteps of the northerners. In the eleventh and twelfth centuries the Greek army attracted foreigners from all over the then known world. Some of these Norman military succeeded in establishing small realms of their own in Asia Minor.[4] When Constantinople was conquered in 1203 and 1204 people from western countries and from north-western Europe were involved in the hostilities. Some assisted the Greeks in defending Constantinople, others were part of the crusading army which stood before the walls of the city.

During the period under discussion Constantinople saw a mass immigration, such as she may never have seen before. Inhabitants from north-western Europe came to the city in hundreds and by the time of the crusades in thousands. Some visitors remained a short time, others remained for longer periods and became temporary or permanent residents. The latter eventually merged into the city's population leaving less and less trace of their identity. Reminiscences of their home countries, in linguistic practice and other aspects of life, are therefore worth 'excavating' and studying in the context of visits to Byzantium.

---

[4] J. Hoffmann, *Rudimente von Territorialstaaten im byzantinischen Reich (1071–1210)* (Munich, 1974).

## LINGUISTIC AND SOURCE PROBLEMS

Linguistic practice plays an important role in the search for visitors to Byzantium and in the bibliography which is the starting-point for a prosopography of visitors. Regardless of the exact definition of the extent of north-western Europe it is clear that we are dealing with a great variety of languages: Old Norse, Anglo-Saxon (Old English) and Middle English, Old German and Middle Flemish/Dutch. The use of these vernaculars in various sources did not always develop along the same lines or in the same historical period. The one linguistic factor which all these countries had in common was the use of Latin, the cement of western Christianity. For the Scandinavian north the use of Latin came along with its Christianisation and was rather limited. Therefore the use of the vernaculars was more predominant in source material in the Scandinavian north than in other parts of north-western Europe. A search of parallel sources in Latin may confirm data found in vernacular sources.

In the context of the Byzantine empire, sources in Greek and other languages have to be consulted as well. The great variety of languages in the west and in the north, where the Slavic world impinged on the life of the Scandinavians, necessitates a uniform system for the transliteration and orthography of personal and geographical names. In the various Scandinavian countries personal names had different spellings. Text editions and modern translations of these texts are often inconsistent in the spelling of these names. Cross-references have to solve the problem and one has to be conscious of this discrepancy when consulting an index. A few examples may suffice to explain the problem: Christine–Kristín, George–Girgir, Nicholas–Nikulás, Olaf–Olaeif(r), Sven–Svaein, Thorwald–Þorwald, not to mention their declensions in the original texts. That such names may be rendered in Greek characters is equally problematic and sometimes makes them unrecognisable.

A number of names of northern travellers to Byzantium have been preserved fragmentarily or in an incomplete and corrupted form. This goes for inscriptions in general and especially for rune stones, where the runic characters require an expert reading. The name of a person may occur on more than one rune stone, and in a different form. Runic inscriptions were not always ordered immediately after hearing of the death of a loved one in Byzantium or elsewhere in the east. Sometimes a remote relative came into possession of the heritage. In such cases the ordering of a rune stone to commemorate the deceased could take place some time later when the estate was finally settled. This does not make such inscriptions less reliable. When more references are brought together family names, mentioned on rune stones and in saga material, may be set in a wider context. The dating of runes, however, cannot always be given with precision. A dating like 'first half of the eleventh century', poses problems and requires ingenious interpretation, especially when more references to a specific person or family are available. With the help of the future prosopography names in runic inscriptions may possibly be 'restored' to their original form and to the right family setting.

A great variety of sources has to be consulted to find references to visitors to Byzantium. A complete bibliography for western Europe cannot be given. There is an enormous quantity of texts that refer to visitors, pilgrims, crusaders and others, who visited the Byzantine empire. Some of them are obscure and have not yet been exploited. This goes for texts in the various vernaculars and for texts written in Latin. A complete bibliography for visitors from north-western Europe is a desideratum but will be difficult to realise.

To find one's way to Byzantium in the sources of north-western Europe one should start with historical writing in Latin and literary texts in the vernaculars and in Latin since more than once Latin source material corroborates or complements the information given in vernacular sources. Sometimes parallel sources may cast doubt on the veracity of information and even repudiate it.

In the Scandinavian north, where historical texts in Latin are relatively scarce, historical events are described in sagas. These texts, mostly written in the vernaculars, are exemplary for the complexity of the material which has to be consulted. In these texts history and literature became osmotic. Oral traditions were strong in the north and saga texts more than once received a literary patina. One may presume that, where picturesque details may betray the fantasy of oral tradition or of a later redactor, the real names of travellers to Byzantium were preserved. Saga references to visits to Byzantium can sometimes be confirmed by consulting contemporary Latin sources produced in the north or elsewhere in Europe. Many sagas were written down in the thirteenth century. This goes also for sagas which relate visits to Byzantium. In 1046 Harald Hardrada became king of Norway after a long stay in Byzantium where he had served in the Greek army and had travelled all over the empire. Harald's service in Byzantium is confirmed by the eleventh-century Byzantine author Kekaumenos.[5] The written form of *King Harald's Saga* dates from the thirteenth century. Snorri Sturluson included the saga in his *Heimskringla*, a collection of royal biographies, written in the second half of the thirteenth century.

Harald was not the only member of a ruling family who served in the Greek army. Erik, brother of king Sigurd of Norway, did the same in the twelfth century. The impact of such journeys may have been considerable.

---

[5] *Cecaumeni Strategicon* 97 (Litavrin, 284; tr. Beck, 140–1); see also n.6 below.

Even if the stories were written down in later times, one should not neglect
the information they offer about the life and adventures of the main
characters. Anachronistic statements about life in Byzantium may tell their
own story.

A number of sagas have preserved old poetic material about the journey
to Byzantium and the beauty of its capital as seen by its visitors. An interesting example is the reference to Constantinople in *King Harald's Saga*
where the text says: 'The great prince saw ahead | the copper roofs of
Byzantium; | His swan-breasted ships swept | Towards the tall-towered city.'[6]

The Lives of saints and the miracles which they sometimes performed in
Byzantium are another line of research. The Constantinopolitan churches of
the communities from north-western Europe were sometimes the result of a
miracle which the saint had performed for his compatriots in Byzantium or
of special devotion to a particular saint. St Olaf, St Thorlac and St Augustine
of Canterbury were venerated by visitors to Byzantium. The sagas of the
bishops of Iceland, the *Biskupa sögur*, offer interesting material. The
*Heilagra Manna sögur*, the Lives of northern saints, have not yet been carefully studied. The Lives of other saints from north-western Europe mention
visits to Byzantium. The Life of King Edward of England for example, has
been preserved in several Latin versions and in more than one vernacular,
including Old Norse, where several historical layers have been detected.[7] Such
texts have to be searched for later local additions in the vernaculars and have
to be compared with the 'original' text. For Latin versions of saints' Lives,
one should realise that they have to be interpreted in the light of being the
'official and authorised ecclesiastical canon', and may betray the official
views on the sanctity of a saint. Legends about saints and about relics,
including their translation to the west, with or without permission, may contain interesting material. More material than the information known so far
may be found in the *Acta Sanctorum* (AASS) or in the Patrologia Latina.

Travel reports of pilgrims, anonymous or with the author's name, and of
individual crusaders hint at visits to shrines in Byzantium by individuals or
by groups. Many pilgrims from north-western Europe have left traces of such
visits, but only a few wrote a detailed report of their visit as did Joseph of
Canterbury.[8] From Scandinavia such reports are even fewer. Around the year
1150 a short list of relics in churches of Constantinople was compiled by an
anonymous author. On his way to Jerusalem Nicholas (Nikulás) Bergsson,
future abbot of the Benedictine monastery of Thingeyrar (Þingeyrar) in the

---

[6] *King Harald's Saga*, tr. Magnusson and Pálsson, 48.
[7] C. Fell, 'The Icelandic saga of Edward the Confessor: the hagiographic sources', *Anglo-Saxon
England* 1 (1972), 247–58.
[8] C.H. Haskins, 'A Canterbury monk at Constantinople', *EHR* 25 (1910), 293–5.

northern part of Iceland, visited various parts of the Byzantine empire. He described the visit in his *Leiðarvísir*. The journey of a group of Danish pilgrims and their visit to Constantinople is described in a Latin text called *De profectione Danorum in Terram Sanctam* where one finds an interesting description of an icon of the Virgin and some Greek *spolia*.

Collections of letters and of wills may contain interesting material. Encyclopaedic works, mostly written from the thirteenth century onwards, need to be consulted. Liturgical texts and service-books may contain references to the east which may be the result of earlier visits to Byzantium. So far these texts seem to remain unexploited.

We have already referred to the stones which men and women raised for relatives and friends who were to journey to Byzantium or who died during the voyage or their stay somewhere in the east. These stones with their inscriptions in runes are sources for information about visits to Byzantium and other places in the east. The interpretation of geographical names mentioned in these inscriptions may cause problems. Various categories of travellers, merchants, mercenaries and pilgrims were honoured with rune stones.

A search among the Byzantine seals of the Varangian Guard, the Corps of Interpreters and other Byzantine imperial services and of individual inhabitants of the Byzantine empire, may reveal names of people, groups and individuals, who came to Byzantium from north-western Europe. However, the rendering of their names in Greek characters or their adoption of Greek names make them sometimes 'unrecognisable' for the modern searcher.

Source-material which has been considered as fraudulent or not reliable may reveal itself as genuine if confirmed by references from other sources which are brought together in a prosopography.

Sources may be difficult to interpret in their historical, literary and intellectual setting. Linguistically and materially speaking the sources, their translations and secondary literature are sometimes difficult of access. This is especially the case for texts in Old Norse and secondary literature written in the vernaculars of the Scandinavian world.

Even in published form, saga material presents more problems than most other historical and literary texts from north-western Europe. Sagas are known in various versions. The *Saga of King Sigurd of Norway (Saga Sigurðar Jórsalafara)*, who visited Constantinople in 1111, has been preserved in more than one version. In the so-called *Morkinskinna* manuscript version the king is said to have thanked the Byzantine emperor in Greek for his generous gifts ('he held a speech in Greek').[9] Such a statement suggests

---

[9] Kalinke, 'Foreign language requirement', 858.

that the copyist or the redactor of the *Morkinskinna* manuscript thought it likely that the king could speak Greek or say a few words in this language for politeness' sake. Knowledge of Greek in saga material could be an indication of a journey to Byzantine lands.

Translations of sagas do not always make clear that the various versions of a saga may differ greatly. The English translation of the *Saga of King Sigurd* renders a version, less romantic as some scholars have it, which does not mention the Greek-speaking king. The existing translations of the *Kings' Sagas* (*Konungasögur*, life stories of the Scandinavian royalty) and the *Family Sagas* (*Íslendingasögur*, telling the story of Icelandic families), have to be compared with the other versions of the text. The translation itself has to be read carefully. Earlier translators and commentators, especially those who worked in the nineteenth century, were sometimes at loss when dealing with a visit to southern parts. Byzantine studies were at an infant stage and Byzantium was an unknown and exotic world to them, causing problems when translating personal names and geographical names. Byzantine institutions and features of daily life were sometimes *terra incognita* to them.

Geographical names in indices may help to detect visitors to Byzantium. Constantinople is rendered as Miklagarth, the church of Saint Sophia in Constantinople became Aegisif. Antioch becomes Anþekia, Laodikeia in Syria (until the First Crusade under Byzantine rule) occurs under the name Liz. Other geographical names like Grikkland (Greece), Syrland (Syria), Serkland (land of the Saracens) are used to designate the Byzantine empire and neighbouring areas, and may lead the interested reader to the tracks of northern visitors to the east. Thessalonike, Nicaea, Ephesus, Antioch occur in various forms and are not always easily recognisable. A complicating factor in the search for such names in source material is their declension and their absence in indices of text editions, in translations and in secondary works. This means that saga texts have to be read in their entirety which, although time-consuming, is an interesting and pleasant experience.

Not all the sagas have been published and/or translated. Texts which were not considered to be of great literary interest, have remained unpublished. One cannot exclude the possibility that unpublished saga material may hide interesting information about travellers to Byzantium.

The *Ordbog over det norrøne prosasprog* (*A Dictionary of Old Norse Prose*), now in progress at the Arnemagnean Institute in Copenhagen, does not include geographical names. The recently completed *Lexicographical Dictionary of Medieval Flemish/Dutch* gives only the vocabulary of manuscripts produced before 1300, and leaves out texts that were written earlier but only preserved in later manuscripts. Such works are of little use for the current subject. Dictionaries of Medieval Latin, covering certain areas of (north-western) Europe are in progress or have been stopped at an early stage, so that students cannot use them for girskir, Grikkland etc.

Other tools for detecting visitors to Byzantium, real or imaginary, need to be updated but may be helpful. This is the case for the surveys of proper names (personal names and geographical names) in the French *romans courtois* and in French epic material made by Flutre and Langlois. The more recent *Répertoire* of personal and geographical names in French epics by Moisan may confirm the presence of inhabitants of north-western Europe on Byzantine soil.[10] Like saga material, epics are a combination of fiction and facts and should be used carefully. French epics refer to Danes, English, Icelanders and others from north-western Europe as taking part in journeys to the east.

For the *Normannisches Lehngut*, recently called the 'anecdotal répertoire of Europe', one should also consult texts written in Normandy (Wace's *Brut*, for example) and in southern Italy.[11] For this specific material interdisciplinary research is needed. One has to keep in mind that runic inscriptions sometimes refer to Scandinavians in Byzantine service who died in the land of the Lombards. In such cases one has to 'reconstruct' the historical context, i.e. Byzantine or Norman, and look for confirmation in sources from the area.

Norman sources from the south refer sometimes to people who were sentenced by the pope to do penance and visit shrines on Byzantine or former Byzantine territory. In his *Chronicle*, written in Latin, Romuald of Salerno mentions the pope's verdict on the murderers of Thomas Becket. William de Tracy, Reginald fitzUrse, Hugh de Morville and Richard le Bret had to do penance in Jerusalem and spend the rest of their lives on the Black Mountain (near Antioch) with its concentration of eastern and western monasteries. Romuald, archbishop of Salerno (d. 1181) was related to the Norman ruling family in southern Italy and had ample occasion to obtain information. He had access to the papal court in Rome and may have been in touch with the rulers in Antioch. It is not known if the murderers actually set out for the east and lived near Antioch where Manuel Komnenos had strongly imposed himself as the legal ruler of the principality of Antioch.[12]

---

[10] Langlois, *Table des noms propres*; Flutre, *Table des noms propres*; Moisan, *Répertoire*.
[11] Kalinke in *Medieval Scandinavia, an Encyclopedia*, 453.
[12] Romuald of Salerno, *Chronicon*, MGHS 19 (Hanover, 1866), 439 (s.a. 1171).

## DEFINITION AND CATEGORIES OF VISITORS

The aforesaid brings us to the important question of who should be considered as visitors to the Byzantine empire. First of all we can consider as such the men and women who, according to the sources, returned to their homeland after a longer or shorter stay in Byzantium. A good example is the Icelander Bolli Bollason who came back to Iceland with eleven companions:

> ... Bolli brought with him a great deal of money and many treasures that princes and men of rank had given him. Bolli had such a taste for the ornate when he returned from his travels that he would not wear any clothes that were not made of scarlet cloth or gold-embroidered silk, and all his weapons were inlaid with gold. He was called Bolli the Proud ... He carried a lance in his hand, as is the custom in foreign lands ... the womenfolk paid no heed to anything but gazing at Bolli and his companions and all their finery ... Bolli's travels brought him great renown.[13]

Some people became residents of the Byzantine empire. Embassies sent to the west often consisted of a Greek envoy, accompanied by people whose roots were in the country to which the embassy was sent and who, thanks to their linguistic abilities and knowledge of the itinerary, functioned as interpreter and as guide for the journey, not only for embassies from Byzantium, but for westerners as well. The choice of such interpreters fell upon returning mercenaries or on those who had become residents and returned to Byzantium with the embassy. They could stay for a while in the west. The Norwegian Eindredi the Young was such a guide:

> During the summer Eindredi the Young came back from Constantinople where he had been employed as a mercenary for quite some time. He had plenty to tell people about it and they thought it great entertainment to ask him about those foreign parts.

Shortly afterwards he left the west and acted as a guide for Rognvald, earl of Orkney, when the latter went to Jerusalem. A conflict made the parties split up during the journey, and Eindredi went to Constantinople where eventually he met his former companion:

> When Earl Rognvald and his men reached Constantinople they were given a great reception by the Emperor and the Varangians. At that time Menelaus, whom we call Manula, was ruling Byzantium. He gave money freely to the Earl, and offered to hire them as mercenaries if they would agree to stay on. They spent the winter there enjoying the best of entertainment. Eindredi the Young was there, treated with honour by the Emperor, but having little to do

---

[13] *Laxdaela Saga*, tr. Magnusson and Pálsson, 236.

with Earl Rognvald and his men and trying to discredit them with other people.[14]

Problems arise in the case of those who, according to runic inscriptions, were planning a visit to the east and of whom we do not know if they actually set off.

The easiest category to deal with are the royal visitors. These visits are documented in Latin and in vernacular sources and have attracted attention from students. King Erik of Denmark, his wife Bothilde and their son Erik (later King Erik II) visited Constantinople and passed through Byzantine territory on their way to Jerusalem in 1103 but King Erik died on Cyprus, then part of Byzantium. Some years later King Sigurd of Norway came to the east where he visited the Byzantine capital in 1111. Royal visitors came with a large retinue. The names of the accompanying persons often remain unknown. Part of a royal visit comprised the exchange of gifts between the rulers and official receptions where the royal visitor could meet his former subjects who, unfortunately, remain anonymous.

Official embassies are sometimes documented in western and eastern sources. The Life and Saga of King Edward of England mention an embassy sent to Constantinople and Ephesus. The embassy was composed of a cleric, a monk and a knight, all three anonymous, but with an important mission. Their visit to Byzantine territory and meeting with the authorities, from whom they had to obtain permission to check the presence of the relics of the Seven Sleepers in Ephesus, may have left more reminiscences in Byzantium and in their own surroundings than the information known from the Life and Saga of King Edward.

We have already mentioned groups of people who joined the Varangian Guard. Some of them are referred to in rune stones, such as the companions of Ingvar, a Swedish leader. It is not unlikely that only the names of the leading members of such groups have been preserved. The impact of their visit and service in Byzantium, once back in their homeland, was probably more important than is suggested by the mention of just a few names.

Other groups arrived in Byzantium as refugees. An example is the large group of Anglo-Saxons who left England after the conquest by William of Normandy. The *Universal Chronicle* of Laon mentions only the names of a few nobles.[15] Many of these refugees have remained anonymous.

Pilgrims were another category of visitors. For safety reasons they often travelled in groups. More than once the names of the pilgrims remain

---

[14] *Orkneyinga Saga*, tr. Pálsson and Edwards, 156, 181.
[15] K. Ciggaar, 'L'émigration anglaise à Byzance après 1066. Un nouveau texte en latin sur les Varangues à Constantinople', *RÉB* 32 (1974), 301–42.

anonymous. At the end of the twelfth century a group of Danish pilgrims visited Constantinople. Their journey was recorded by a 'frater X [christianus] canonicus' under the name *De profectione Danorum in Terram Sanctam*.

For various reasons groups of travellers were joined by individual travellers such as merchants, pilgrims, guides, interpreters, envoys of lesser stature and people who, for various reasons, joined *en route*.

Nevertheless it seems very likely that, for various reasons, a number of individuals travelled to Byzantium on their own, without company, and stayed on in Constantinople for their own purposes. There were pilgrims who wanted to see the relics and the riches of Byzantium more at leisure and may have needed more time than the average pilgrim. Some *anonymi* have left interesting descriptions of Constantinople. The *Anonymus Mercati*, an anonymous English pilgrim around 1100, translated a Greek description of the city. From northern France came probably the *Anonymus tarragonensis*, who also left a description of Constantinople. Some individuals had intellectual interests, like the anonymous author of the *Guide du pèlerin de Saint-Jacques de Compostelle* (sometimes said to have been Aimery Picaud de Parthenay-le-Vieux), who mentions the library in the 'scola Grecorum' of Constantinople.[16] Another visitor has only left his first name, Johannes. This man, a certain Johannes *scholasticus*, may have come from the Rhineland. He says that he was an envoy to 'Gretia' in 1160. In Thessalonike he ordered a translation of the Life of Saint Demetrios from a *sacerdos* Bernhardus.[17] His name does not figure in texts that speak of embassies between the German rulers and the imperial court in Constantinople. He may have been one of the secretaries of an embassy whose names have not been preserved in official documents.

A special group of visitors were young people who, for various reasons, were adopted by the Byzantine emperor and had to be sent to the Constantinopolitan court for further education. They belonged to the ruling élite of western Europe. Another category of official visitors were those who were kept hostage in Constantinople. It is not easy to find their names in the sources.

Individuals sought temporary or permanent refuge in Byzantium. Thorbjorn Ongul, the murderer of the Icelander Grettir, came to

[16] K. Ciggaar, 'Une description de Constantinople traduite par un pèlerin anglais du XIIe siècle', *RÉB* 34 (1976), 211–67; K. Ciggaar, 'Une description de Constantinople dans le *Tarragonensis* 55', *RÉB* 53 (1995), 117–40; J. Vielliard, ed., *Le guide du pèlerin de Saint-Jacques de Compostelle* (Paris, 1984), 64–5.
[17] K. Ciggaar, 'Les villes de province byzantines et les échanges culturelles. Quelques traducteurs peu connus', in M. Balard and others, eds., *Byzance et le monde extérieur*, Byzantina Sorbonensia 21 (Paris, 2005), 83–95.

Constantinople to join the Varangian Guard. He was eventually killed in the east by a compatriot in revenge of the murder. The Princess Christine, a daughter of King Sigurd of Norway came to the east with her lover. In the *Saga of Magnús Erlingsson*, incorporated in the *Heimskringla*, a compilation of *Kings' Sagas*, one finds a reference to her departure to the east:

> With Kristín Kingsdaughter Erling had a daughter whose name was Ragnhild. She was married to Jón Thorbergsson. Kristín left Norway with a man named Grím Rusli. They journeyed to Miklagarth staying there for a while, and had some children together.[18]

It is not known if they ever returned to the north. Their 'familiarity' with the east through the visits of several relatives made them hide in Constantinople, the metropolis of twelfth-century Europe, where they may have thought they would find a safe haven, out of reach of those who sought revenge.

A special category of individual visitors are saints who made their presence in Byzantium known in dreams and visions. This was the case of King Olaf Tryggvason who disappeared during a sea-battle in the year 1000. According to the *Saga of Olaf Tryggvason* which was written at the end of the twelfth century, he ended his life in a monastery in Syria or Palestine. His armour was displayed in Antioch. Other northern saints worked miracles in Byzantium. Saint Olaf and Saint Thorlac assisted Scandinavian mercenaries.[19]

'Literary' visitors, interesting as they are, may enter a prosopography if clearly marked. Vernacular literatures in western Europe used the topos of visits to Byzantium to enhance the adventures of a hero and add to his prestige. North-western Europe was no exception. Such literary visits, in texts that were sometimes translated from Old French and which included the *Karlamagnus Saga*, express a new life-style: travel to Byzantium. Reference has already been made to the collections of proper names in Langlois, Flutre and Moisan. In Scandinavian literature such visits are more than once part of the so-called *Riddarasögur*.[20] A comparison between historical sources and literary texts may corroborate the actual visit of a 'fictional' hero. Such proof exists already for a number of heroes in saga literature.

Artists from the area are unfortunately likely to remain anonymous. Artefacts do not often bear names. Works of art may betray Byzantine influence but are no proof that the artist travelled to the east. Artists may have learned or perfected their craft in Byzantium or have followed Byzantine models. This may have been the case for the stone-carver on Gotland who is

[18] *Grettir's Saga*, tr. Fox and Pálsson, 175; *Heimskringla*, tr. Hollander, 812–13.
[19] Riant, *Expéditions*, 117; Ellis Davidson, *Viking Road*, 194–5.
[20] e.g. *Medieval Scandinavia, an Encyclopedia*, 497–8.

called 'Byzantios'.[21] Nevertheless names of artists who visited Byzantium and were inspired by its arts may emerge in future.

There is a difference between official visitors such as kings, princes, bishops, ambassadors and other envoys, and the multitude of nameless people. Official journeys to Byzantium are often recorded in official sources and in historical surveys like *Regesta*. The journeys of official visitors to the east may be referred to in letter collections which have been ignored so far. The already mentioned Johannes *scholasticus* was probably a lesser member of an official or unofficial embassy, whose existence may be confirmed in future. The majority of visitors did not leave a trace in source material. Their anonymity does not mean that their journey to Byzantium and their impressions had no effect on their life in later days, back in their homelands or in Byzantine lands.


## CONCLUSION

A search for visitors to Byzantium from north-western Europe may reveal interesting details of the life of many adventurers, pilgrims and merchants. Political and religious leaders of the eleventh and twelfth century had their own ambitions when they travelled to Constantinople. They all brought home great riches in cash and in the memories of adventures abroad. Some of them developed a taste for luxury. Some of them became great storytellers.

When relevant passages about the journey to Byzantium of saga heroes are brought together, their individual experiences may be compared with the adventures of others. This would enable students to study patterns of life among the northerners who went to Byzantium. One may then be able to detect features in their lives which were influenced by the contacts of these visitors with life in Byzantium, such as the imitation of Byzantine coins and the introduction of political institutions by some northern rulers. It is not to be excluded that *spolia* from north-western Europe, linguistic or other, may be detected in Byzantium.

---

[21] Cutler, 'The sculpture and sources of "Byzantios"'.

# BIBLIOGRAPHY[1]

## HANDBOOKS, SURVEYS, PROSOPOGRAPHIES

### Books[2]

T.M. Andersson, 'Kings' Sagas (*Konungasögur*)', in Clover and Lindow, *Old Norse–Icelandic Literature*, 197–238
   Introduction to the subject with extensive bibliography.

S. Blöndal, *The Varangians of Byzantium*, tr., rev. & rewritten by B.S. Benedikz (Cambridge, 1978): a revision of S. Blöndal, *Vaeringjasaga* (Reykjavik, 1954), in Icelandic.
   Gives rich information about Scandinavians who served in Byzantium. Selective index.

The *Byzantinische Zeitschrift* gives a bibliography of publications on Byzantium and the neighbouring world, including the north, in section III, *Politische Geschichte*, *b*. 7.–12. Jahrhundert, *c*. 13.–15. Jahrhundert. The bibliography from vol. 84 (1991) to vol. 94 (2001) is now available on CD-Rom. For Byzantine coins found in Scandinavia and Byzantine influence on northern coins there is a section called *Numismatik*. For current information consult the bibliography of the American Numismatic Society (see under 3).

K.N. Ciggaar, *Western Travellers to Constantinople. The west and Byzantium, 962–1204* (Leiden, New York and London, 1996), ch. 4, 'The northern countries', 102–28
   Discusses various sorts of contacts between Byzantium and Scandinavia.

C.J. Clover, 'Icelandic Family Sagas (*Íslendingasögur*)', in Clover and Lindow, *Old Norse–Icelandic Literature*, 239–315
   Introduction to the subject with extensive bibliography.

C.J. Clover and J. Lindow, eds., *Old Norse–Icelandic Literature: a critical guide*, Islandica 45 (Ithaca and London, 1985)
   Various chapters discuss the literary genres in Old Norse literature, with bibliographies.

H.R. Ellis Davidson, *The Viking Road to Byzantium* (Cambridge, 1976)
   General introduction to the subject, with bibliography. Selective index.

L. Flutre, *Table des noms propres avec toutes leurs variantes figurant dans les romans du Moyen Âge écrits en français ou en provençal et actuellement publiés ou analysés* (Poitiers, 1962)
   May be useful for personal, ethnic and geographical names, but needs updating. Terms such as *Danois, Islandais, Islaigne, Norois* etc. may lead to information in Old French sources.

---

[1] I am grateful to Andrea de Leeuw van Weenen, Het Koninklijk Penningkabinet (Leiden) and former colleagues, for help and information on some of the problems which showed up during the preparation of this bibliography.

[2] Short forms of titles are used after the first reference to a work and for edited volumes from which individual articles are cited.

M. Kalinke, 'Norse romance (*Riddarasögur*)', in Clover and Lindow, *Old Norse–Icelandic Literature*, 316–63
Introduction to the subject with extensive bibliography.

M.E. Kalinke and P.M. Mitchell, *Bibliography of Old Norse–Icelandic Romances*, Islandica 44 (Ithaca and London, 1985)

A.P. Kazhdan and others, eds., *The Oxford Dictionary of Byzantium*, 3 vols. (New York and Oxford, 1991)
Some articles on relations with Scandinavians, with bibliographical references.

*Kulturhistorisk leksikon for Nordisk Middelalder*, 22 vols. (Copenhagen and Malmö, 1956–82)
Interesting for articles on Byzantium or Byzantine influence, e.g. vol. 2 (1957), s.v. *Bysantinsk stilinflytelse* ('The influence of Byzantine style'), *Bysantinska mynt* ('Byzantine coinage'); vol. 14 (1969), s.v. *Reiser*.

E. Langlois, *Table des noms propres de toute nature compris dans les chansons de geste imprimées* (Paris, 1904)
Useful for personal, ethnic and geographical names (Ogier de Danemark, *Danois, Islandais, Nor(r)ois*, etc.); recently updated by Moisan, *Répertoire*.

*Medieval Scandinavia, an Encyclopedia*, Ph. Pulsiano and others, eds. (New York and London, 1993)
Useful for articles on sagas, runes, authors and other individuals. Gives good bibliographies. Unfortunately this encyclopaedia does not have articles on Byzantium, Constantinople, Greeks, the east or on the Varangian Guard.

A. Moisan, *Répertoire des noms propres de personnes et de lieux cités dans les chansons de geste* (Paris, 1986), 5 vols.
Useful for personal, ethnic and geographical names (*Danois, Islandais, Nor(r)ois*, etc.).

*Les pays du nord et Byzance (Scandinavie et Byzance)*, *Actes du Colloque d'Upsal 20–22 avril 1979*, R. Zeitler, ed. (Uppsala, 1981)
The various chapters deal with a range of aspects of the relations between Byzantium and Scandinavia, such as coin imitations, linguistics etc. Travellers, however, are hardly referred to.

O. Pritsak, *The Origin of Rus'*, vol. 1, *Old Scandinavian Sources other than the Sagas* (Cambridge, Mass., 1981), ch. 15, 'The Varangians at home and abroad', 385–8

P.E. Riant, *Expéditions et pèlerinages des Scandinaves en Terre Sainte au temps des croisades* (Paris, 1865); P.E. Riant, *Skandinavernes Korstog og Andagtsrejser til Palaestina* (Copenhagen, 1868), Danish edition
Gives rich information on northern travellers to the east. The book does not have an index. The *Table des matières* is useful.

M. Schlauch, *Romance in Iceland* (Princeton and New York, 1934; repr. New York, 1973), ch. 4, 'The road to the east', 69–94

G. Turville-Petre, *Origins of Icelandic Literature* (Oxford, 1953; repr. 1967, 1975)
General introduction to northern literature.

G. Vigfússon and F. York Powell, eds., *Corpus poeticum boreale. The poetry of the old northern tongue from the earliest times to the thirteenth century*, 2 vols. (Oxford, 1883)

Vol. 2 gives poems on kings who went to the east, corroborating information given in saga texts. The poems are published in their original form, most of them with an English translation.

J.P.A. van der Vin, *Travellers to Greece and Constantinople. Ancient monuments and old traditions in medieval travellers' tales*, 2 vols. (Leiden, 1980)
Refers to some Scandinavian travellers, with bibliographical references.

J. de Vries, *Altnordische Literaturgeschichte*, 2 vols. (Berlin, 1964, 1967)
Thorough introduction to medieval Scandinavian literature.

O. Widding, H. Bekker-Nielsen, L.K. Shook, 'Lives of the saints in Old Norse prose', *Mediaeval Studies* 25 (1963), 294–337
Lists the editions of the Lives of northern saints and the manuscripts used.

## Articles

K. Ciggaar, 'Réfugiés et employés occidentaux au XIᵉ siècle', in *Médiévales* 12 = E. Patlagean, ed., *Toutes les routes mènent à Byzance* (1987), 19–24
—— 'Denmark and Byzantium from 1184 to 1212. Queen Dagmar's cross, a chryso-bull of Alexius III and an "ultramarine" connection', *Mediaeval Scandinavia* 13 (2000), 118–42, with additional note by Andrea van Arkel-de Leeuw van Weenen, 142–3
Discusses the arrival of some Byzantine artefacts in the north and missions sent by the Byzantine emperor in which Scandinavians participated.

H. Damico, 'The voyage to Byzantium: the evidence of the sagas', *VV* 56 (81), (1995), 107–17
Literary analysis concerning Varangians travelling to the east.

R.M. Dawkins, 'The later history of the Varangian guard: some notes', *Journal of Roman Studies* 37 (1947), 39–46

M.E. Kalinke, 'The foreign language requirement in medieval Icelandic romance', *The Modern Language Review* 78 (1983), 850–61
Discusses the limited knowledge of Greek in the north and in northern sources.

E. Piltz, 'De la Scandinavie à Byzance', in *Médiévales* 12 = E. Patlagean, ed., *Toutes les routes mènent à Byzance* (1987), 11–18
Discussion of the itinerary of travellers to the south.

J. de Vries, 'Normannisches Lehngut in den isländischen Königssagas', in de Vries, *Kleine Schriften* (Berlin, 1965), 331–50

## PRIMARY SOURCES

### Geography, Pilgrimages

Anonymous, *De profectione Danorum in Terram Sanctam*
See Latin Sources, p. 142

The three following items are in some cases edited and studied by the same scholars, which can cause confusion:

Anonymous from Iceland (*c.* 1150), *List of Relics in Constantinople*
This list of relics has sometimes been attributed to Nicholas Bergsson. The text survives in an encyclopaedic compilation, consisting of a number of itineraries. The list of relics follows a statement that the (then) abbot of Thingeyrar had provided as information for a preceding itinerary to Jerusalem. According to this itinerary the abbot did not return via Constantinople. The textual tradition appears to be confused.

*Editions:*
(1) C.C. Rafn, *Antiquités russes d'après les monuments historiques des Islandais et des anciens Scandinaves* (Copenhagen, 1850–2), 416
(2) P.E. Riant, *Exuviae sacrae Constantinopolitanae*, 2 vols. (Geneva, 1877–8), 2. 213–16
(3) K. Kålund, ed., *Alfraeði íslenzk: islandsk encyklopaedisk litteratur*, vol. 1, Samfund til Udgivelse af Gammel Nordisk Litteratur 37 (Copenhagen, 1908), p. 25, l. 3 to p. 26, l. 17

*Translations:*
(1) Rafn, *Antiquités russes*, Latin tr.
(2) Riant, *Exuviae*, Latin tr.

Anonymous (the same as the preceding?)
Itinerary to Jerusalem, visit to some Greek islands.

*Editions:*
(1) E. Wertlauf, *Symbolae ad geographiam medii aevi ex monumentis islandicis* (Hauniae, 1821), 56–9
(2) Rafn, *Antiquités russes*, 417–20
(3) Kålund, *Alfraeði íslenzk*, p. 24, l. 17 to p. 31, l. 6 (a miscellany without headings)

*Translations:*
(1) Wertlauf, *Symbolae*, Latin tr.
(2) Rafn, *Antiquités russes*, Latin tr.
(3) van der Vin, *Travellers to Greece*, 522 (English tr. of the description of Constantinople)
(4) John Wilkinson, Joyce Hill and W.F. Ryan, *Jerusalem Pilgrimage, 1099–1185*, Hakluyt Society (London, 1988), 220–2

*Secondary Literature:*
B.E. Gelsinger, 'The Mediterranean voyage of a twelfth-century Icelander', *The Mariner's Mirror* 58 (1972), 155–65
J. Hill, 'From Rome to Jerusalem: an Icelandic itinerary of the mid-twelfth century', *Harvard Theological Review* 76 (1983), 175–203
B.Z. Kedar and C. Westergard-Nielsen, 'Icelanders in the crusader Kingdom of Jerusalem: a twelfth-century account', *Mediaeval Scandinavia* 11 (1978–9), 193–211
F.P. Magoun, 'The Rome of two northern pilgrims: Archbishop Sigeric of Canterbury and Abbot Nikolás of Munkaþverá', *Harvard Theological Review* 33 (1940), 267–89
—— 'The pilgrim-diary of Nikulás of Munkaþverá: the road to Rome', *Mediaeval Studies* 6 (1944), 314–54
Wilkinson and others, *Jerusalem Pilgrimage,* 18, 354

## Nicholas Bergsson, abbot of Thingeyrar, *Leiðarvīsir*

In the report given by him to the compiler of the encyclopaedia mentioned above, a short description of Constantinople is given, apparently inserted; it mainly concerns the church of Saint Sophia, although the abbot had probably not visited the Byzantine capital.

*Editions:*
(1) Wertlauf, *Symbolae*, 15–32
(2) Rafn, *Antiquités russes*, 407–15
(3) Kålund, *Alfraeði íslenzk*, p. 12, l. 26 to p. 26, l. 23

*Translations:*
(1) Wertlauf, *Symbolae*, Latin tr.
(2) Rafn, *Antiquités russes*, Latin tr.
(3) Kedar and Westergard-Nielsen, 'Icelanders in the crusader Kingdom of Jerusalem', 203–6
(4) Hill, 'From Rome to Jerusalem', 178–81 (partial translation into English)
(5) Wilkinson and others, *Jerusalem Pilgrimage*, 215–18 (partial translation into English)

*Secondary Literature:*
Gelsinger, 'The Mediterranean voyage', 155–65
Hill, 'From Rome to Jerusalem', 175–203
Kedar and Westergard-Nielsen, 'Icelanders in the crusader Kingdom of Jerusalem', 193–211
Magoun, 'The Rome of two northern pilgrims', 267–89
—— 'The pilgrim-diary of Nikulás of Munkaþverá', 314–54
*Medieval Scandinavia, an Encyclopedia*, 390–1
Wilkinson and others, *Jerusalem Pilgrimage*, 17–18, 353

## Hagiography

### *Biskupa sögur (Bishops' Sagas)*

Lives of Icelandic bishops from the eleventh century onwards.

*Editions:*
(1) J. Sigurðsson and G. Vigfússon, eds., 2 vols. (Copenhagen, 1858, 1878)
(2) G. Vigfússon and F. York Powell, eds., *Origines islandicae. A collection of the more important sagas and other narrative writings relating to the settlement and early history of Iceland*, 2 vols. (Oxford, 1905; repr. Millwood, 1976)
Not easy to find.
(3) J. Helgason, ed., *Biskupa sögur* (Copenhagen, 1938)

*Translations:*
(1) D. Leith, *Stories of the Bishops of Iceland* (London, 1895)
(2) G. Vigfússon and F. York Powell, in *Origines islandicae*

*Secondary Literature:*
*Medieval Scandinavia, an Encyclopedia*, 45–6

*Heilagra Manna sögur (Sagas of Holy Men)*

*Edition:*
C.R. Unger, ed., 2 vols. (Christiania, 1871)
No translation.

*Secondary Literature:*
*Medieval Scandinavia, an Encyclopedia,* s.v. Saints' Lives, 562–5
For the *Saga of Edward the Confessor,* see below, pp. 147–8.
For the *Saga of Olaf Tryggvason,* see below, pp. 151–2.
For the *Saga of Saint Thorlac,* see below, p. 154.

**Latin Sources**

Adam of Bremen, *Gesta hammaburgensis ecclesiae pontificum (The History of the Archbishops of Hamburg–Bremen)*

*Edition:*
R. Bruchner and W. Trillmich, eds., *Gesta hammaburgensis ecclesiae pontificum,* Ausgewählte Quellen zur deutschen Geschichte des Mittelalters 11 (Berlin, 1961)

*Translations:*
(1) German tr. in Bruchner and Trillmich
(2) Engl. tr., Fr. J. Tschan, Records of Civilization, Sources and Studies 53 (New York, 1959)
   Not easy to find.

Anonymous, *De profectione Danorum in Terram Sanctam (The Pilgrimage of Some Danes to the Holy Land)*

*Editions:*
(1) V.J. Langebek, ed., *Scriptores rerum danicarum,* vol. 5 (Copenhagen, 1783), 341–62
(2) M.Cl. Gertz, ed., *Scriptores minores historiae danicae Medii Aevi,* 2 vols. (Copenhagen, 1918–1920; repr. 1970), vol. 2, 443–92
No translation.

*Secondary Literature:*
*Medieval Scandinavia, an Encyclopedia,* 516–17

Anonymous, *Historia de antiquitate regum norwagiensium / Historia Norwegiae (History of the Ancient Kings of Norway)*
Brief history of the kings of Norway which ends halfway through the reign of Saint Olaf.

*Edition:*
G. Storm, ed., *Monumenta historica Norvegiae* (Oslo, 1880; repr. 1973), 69–124
   Not easy to find.

No translation (?)

*Secondary Literature:*
*Medieval Scandinavia, an Encyclopedia,* 284–5

*Diplomatarium islandicum (The Book of Official Icelandic Documents)*
(Reykjavik, 1857, etc.)
Still in progress and/or being supplemented. Not easy to find.

*Secondary Literature:*
*Medieval Scandinavia, an Encyclopedia*, 137–8

Saxo Grammaticus, *Gesta Danorum (History of the Danes)*
Book 12, for King Erik's visit to Constantinople; Book 16, for Danish *equites* who
served in the Byzantine army in the 1180s.

*Edition:*
J. Olrik, H. Raeder and F. Blatt, eds., *Saxo Grammaticus, Gesta Danorum*
    (Copenhagen, 1931–57)

*Translation:*
Eric Christiansen, *Saxo Grammaticus: Danorum regum heroumque Historia. Books
    X–XVI: the text of the first edition with translation and commentary*, 3 vols., BAR
    vols. 84, 118 (two parts) (Oxford, 1980–1)

*Secondary Literature:*
*Medieval Scandinavia, an Encyclopedia*, 566–9

Theodricus Monachus, *Historia de antiquitate regum norwagiensium
(History of the Ancient Kings of Norway)*
Brief history of the kings of Norway from Harald Hardrada to the death of King
Sigurd (1130).

*Edition:*
G. Storm, ed., *Monumenta historica Norvegiae* (Oslo, 1880; repr. 1973), 3–68
    Not easy to find.

*Secondary Literature:*
*Medieval Scandinavia, an Encyclopedia*, 643


**Poetry (Scaldic Poetry)**

*Editions:*
(1) Vigfússon and Powell, eds., *Corpus poeticum boreale*
(2) F. Jónsson, ed., *Den norsk-islandske skjaldedigtning*, 4 vols. (Copenhagen and
    Christiania, 1912–15; 2nd edn., Copenhagen, 1920–2), with Danish tr.

*Translations:*
(1) English tr. in Vigfússon and Powell, eds., *Corpus poeticum boreale*
(2) L.M. Hollander, *The Skalds: a selection of their poems*, with introductions and
    notes (Princeton, 1945; 2nd edn., Ann Arbor, 1968)
    Not easy to find.

*Secondary Literature:*
Roberta Frank, 'Scaldic poetry', in Clover and Lindow, eds., *Old Norse–Icelandic
    Literature*, 157–96
D. Whaley, *The Poetry of Arnórr jarlaskáld. An edition and study* (Turnhout, 1997)

Not easy to find. Arnórr benefited from the patronage of Harald Hardrada of Norway, Rognvald of Orkney and other rulers for whom he wrote poems on their adventures.

Introduction to the genre with bibliography:
*Medieval Scandinavia, an Encyclopedia*, 592–4

## Rune Stones, Runic Inscriptions

Blöndal, *Varangians of Byzantium*, 224–33
> Gives a considerable number of inscriptions of Scandinavians travelling to Greece and to the east, with English translations.

A. Goldschmidt and K. Weitzmann, *Die byzantinischen Elfenbeinskulpturen des X.–XIII. Jahrhunderts*, 2 vols. (Berlin, 1930–4)
> Vol. 1, p. 32–3, nos. 29a, b; vol. 2, pl. IX, 29a, b, gives a runic inscription on a Byzantine ivory representing the Virgin. The donors (?), Paulina and Rake, may have obtained the ivory in the east.

M.G. Larsson, 'Runklotter in Hagia Sofia', *Svenska Forstningsinstitut i Istanbul, Meddelanden* 13 (1988), 55–8, with 3 illus.
> Runic inscriptions in Saint Sophia, Constantinople; see also Svärdström, below.

M.G. Larsson, 'Nyfunna runor I Hagia Sofia', *Fornvännen* 84 (1989), 12–14, with illus.
> Runic inscriptions in Saint Sophia, Constantinople.

Pritsak, *The Origin of Rus'*, vol. 1, 374–84
> Gives a number of rune stones with English translations and corrects a few readings of Blöndal, *Varangians of Byzantium*.

E. Svärdström, 'Runorna i Hagia Sofia', *Fornvännen* 75 (1970), 247–9 (with Engl. summary)
> The names of Halfdan and Are were discovered in a runic inscription on a balustrade in Saint Sophia, Constantinople.

*Secondary Literature:*
*Lexikon des Mittelalters,* 9 vols. (Munich and Zurich, 1977–98), vol. 7, 1098–1101
> Fully documented encyclopaedia of the Middle Ages, with volume of indices.

*Medieval Scandinavia, an Encyclopedia*, 545–55

E.A. Melnikova, 'Scandinavian runic inscriptions as a source for the history of eastern Europe', in *Les pays du nord*, 169–73
> A short essay, without footnotes or bibliography.

## Sagas (a selection of sagas dealing with northerners going to Byzantium)

*1. Collections of sagas, which partly cover the same material as Snorri Sturluson's Heimskringla*

*Fagrskinna (Fair Parchment)*

*Edition:*
F. Jónsson, ed., *Fagrskinna* (Copenhagen, 1902–3)

*Translation:*
A. Finlay, *Fagrskinna, a Catalogue of the Kings of Norway. A translation with introduction and notes*, The Northern World 7 (Leiden, 2003)

*Secondary Literature:*
*Medieval Scandinavia, an Encyclopedia*, 177

## *Flateyjarbók (The Book of Flatey)*
Flatey is a small island off the west coast of Iceland.

*Editions:*
(1) G. Vigfússon and C.R. Unger, eds., *Flateyjarbók* (Christiania, 1860–8), 3 vols.
(2) F. Guðmunsson and S. Nordal, eds., *Flateyjarbók*, 4 vols. (Akraness, 1944–5) Based on previous edition of text, with a new introduction.

No translation of the complete text.

*Secondary Literature:*
*Medieval Scandinavia, an Encyclopedia*, 197–8

## *Morkinskinna (The Rotten Vellum)*
*Editions:*
(1) C.R. Unger, ed., *Morkinskinna* (Christiania, 1867)
(2) F. Jónsson, ed., *Morkinskinna* (Copenhagen, 1932)

No translation.

*Secondary Literature:*
*Medieval Scandinavia, an Encyclopedia*, 419–20

## *2. Snorri Sturluson, Heimskringla (The Circle of the World)*
*Editions:*
(1) F. Jónsson, ed., *Heimskringla*, 4 vols. (Copenhagen, 1893–1901)
(2) F. Jónsson, ed., *Heimskringla* (Copenhagen, 1911; repr. 1925)
(3) B. Aðalbjarnarson, ed., *Heimskringla,* 3 vols., Íslenzk fornrit 26–8 (Reykjavik, 1941, 1945, 1951)
   Important for visitors to Byzantium are *Haralds Saga Sigurðarsonar* (*Saga of Harald Sigurtharson*), *Magnússona Saga* (*Saga of the Sons of Magnús*), *Haraldssona Saga* (*Saga of the Sons of Harald*), *Hákonar Saga Herðibreiðs* (*Saga of Hákon the Broad-shouldered*) and the *Magnúss Saga Erlingssonar* (*Saga of Magnús Erlingsson*).

*Translations:*
(1) *Snorri Sturluson, Heimskringla*. Part one. *The Olaf Sagas*, in two volumes, translated by Samuel Laing, revised with an introduction and notes by Jacqueline Simpson, Everyman's Library (London and New York, 1914; rev. 1964, 1974) Various indices.
*Snorri Sturluson, Heimskringla*. Part two. *Sagas of the Norse Kings*, translated by Samuel Laing, revised with introduction and notes by Peter Foote, Everyman's Library (London and New York, 1930; rev. 1961; new rev. 1961; repr. 1975) Various indices.

(2) *Heimskringla, History of the Kings of Norway by Snorri Sturluson*, translated with introduction and notes by Lee M. Hollander (Austin, Texas, 1964, 1977)
The translation is made from the edition of B. Athalbjarnarson and gives a complete index. The translator gives a survey of earlier translations made by Scandinavians (pp. xxiv–xxv). Important for visitors to Byzantium are *Haralds Saga Sigurðarsonar* (*Saga of Harald Sigurtharson*, 577–663), for King Harald (Harald Hardradi) who as a young man spent a few years in Byzantium; *Magnússona Saga* (*Saga of the Sons of Magnús*, 688–714), for the pilgrimage of King Sigurd; *Haraldssona Saga* (*Saga of the Sons of Harald*, 736–67), for Earl Rognvald and Erling Skakki; *Hákonar Saga Herðibreiðs* (*Saga of Hákon the Broad-shouldered*, 768–88), for a miracle performed by Saint Olaf and the church which was erected for him in Constantinople, and the *Magnúss Saga Erlingssonar* (*Saga of Magnús Erlingsson*, 789–821), for the flight to Constantinople by the Princess Christine.

*Secondary Literature:*
*Medieval Scandinavia, an Encyclopedia*, 276–9

## Individual sagas of *Heimskringla*:

### *King Harald's Saga*
Describes the journey of Harald Hardrada, later king of Norway, to Byzantium where he and his companions, Halldor Snorrason, Ulf Ospaksson and others, took service in the Byzantine army.

*Translations:*
(1) Hollander, *The Skalds*, 577–663
(2) *King Harald's Saga. Harald Hardradi of Norway. From Snorri Sturluson's Heimskringla*, translated with an introduction by M. Magnusson and H. Pálsson (Harmondsworth, 1966)
Selective index of personal names.
(3) A miracle performed by Saint Olaf for the Varangians (from the manuscript *Hulda-Hrokkinskinna*) was translated by Christopher Sanders, in K. Ciggaar, 'Harald Hardrada: his expedition against the Pechenegs', *Balkan Studies* 21 (1980), 389–90; see also *Saint Olaf's Saga*, p. 151 below.
(4) Turville-Petre, *Origins*, 177–8

*Secondary Literature:*
S. Blöndal, 'The last exploits of Harold Sigurdsson in Greek service', *CM* 2 (1939), 1–26
—— *Varangians of Byzantium*, ch. 4, 'Haraldr Sigurðarson and his period as a Varangian in Constantinople, 1034–1043', 54–102
K. Ciggaar, 'Harald Hardrada: his expedition against the Pechenegs', *Balkan Studies* 21 (1980), 385–401
Comments on a battle in the Balkans where St Olaf performed a miracle.
J. Shepard, 'A note on Harold Hardraada: the date of his arrival at Byzantium', *JÖB* 22 (1973), 145–50
K. Skaare, 'Heimkehr eines Warägers', in *Dona Numismatica, Walther Hävernick zum 23. Januar 1965 dargebracht* (Hamburg, 1965), 99–111
Discusses coin imitations of Byzantine models by King Harold of Norway.

E.O.G. Turville-Petre, *Haraldr the Hard-ruler and his poets*, Dorothea Coke memorial
lecture (London, 1966)
Refers to Arnórr, Þjóðólfr, Bǫlverkr and Illugi Bryndoelaskáld, all court poets of
Harald some of whom, like the king himself in one of his poems, referred to
adventures in Byzantium; but Turville-Petre does not give translations of these
poems.

## Saga of the Sons of Magnús (Magnússona Saga)

Also called *Saga Sigurðar Jórsalafara*, for the pilgrimage of King Sigurd. This saga
has survived in the *Morkinskinna* manuscript in a more romantic version, see *Sigurðar
Jórsalafara, Saga of King Sigurd*, p. 153 below.

## 3. Individual Sagas

The Icelandic *Family Sagas* (the heroic *Fornaldar sögur*), such as *Grettirs Saga*,
*Laxdaela Saga* and *Njals Saga* are now available on CD-Rom, obtainable from
bookshops in Iceland.

### *Dámusta Saga (The Saga of Dámusti)[3]

The main character lives at the court of King Katalaktus of Grikkland. A love affair,
a murder and the appearance of the Virgin recall Harald Hardrada's journey to
Byzantium, as does the name Katalaktus for Michael IV (1034–41). The surname of
this emperor who 'changed' the value of money was not widely known.

*Editions:*
L.F. Tan-Haverhorst, *Þjalar Jóns Saga. Dámusta Saga* (Haarlem, 1939; Leiden thesis), vol. 1, 48–108

*Translations:*
Only into Swedish.

*Secondary Literature:*
Ciggaar, *Western Travellers*, ch. 4 'The northern countries', 117–18
Ellis Davidson, *Viking Road*, 274
Kalinke and Mitchell, *Bibliography*, 31–3
*Medieval Scandinavia, an Encyclopedia*, 119

## Saga of Edward the Confessor

*Edition:*
G. Vigfússon, ed., *Icelandic Sagas*, Rolls Series 88 (1887–94), vol. 1, 388–400

*Translation:*
G. Vigfússon, *Icelandic Sagas*, Rolls Series 88 (1887–94), vol. 3, 416–28

*Secondary Literature:*
C. Fell, 'The Icelandic Saga of Edward the Confessor: the hagiographic sources',
*Anglo-Saxon England* 1 (1972), 247–58

---

[3] An asterisk indicates sagas that are considered fictional. They deserve more attention from
scholars, as do a number of *Riddarasögur* not mentioned in this bibliography.

C. Fell, 'The Icelandic Saga of Edward the Confessor: its version of the Anglo-Saxon
  emigration to Byzantium', *Anglo-Saxon England* 3 (1974), 179–96
Widding and others, 'Lives of the saints', 308–9

## *Eiríks Saga viðfǫrla (The Saga of Eiríkr the Far-traveller)*

Erik, son of the king of Trondheim, goes to Constantinople (possibly before 1025),
where he is educated by the king of Constantinople (theology, geography, cosmology).
He converts to Christianity.

*Edition:*

H. Jensen, ed., *Eiríks Saga viðfǫrla*, Editiones Arnamagneanae, Series B, vol. 29
  (Copenhagen, 1983), with introduction in Danish.

No translation

*Secondary Literature:*
*Medieval Scandinavia, an Encyclopedia*, 160–1

## *Grettirs Saga (Grettir's Saga)*

Several northerners who went to work and live in Byzantium are described in this
saga, among them Harald Sigurtharson, later king of Norway, a certain Sigurd, a lady
called Spes, Thorbjorn the Traveller and Thorstein the Galleon.

*Editions:*
(1) R.C. Boer, ed., *Grettis Saga Ásmundarsonar*, Altnordische Saga Bibliothek 8
    (Halle, 1900)
(2) G. Jónsson, ed., *Grettis Saga Ásmundarsonar*, Íslenzk fornrit 7 (Reykjavik, 1936)

*Translations:*
(1) *Grettir's Saga*, English tr., E. Magnússon and William Morris (London, 1869)
(2) *Grettir's Saga*, English tr., G. Ainslie Hight (London, 1914)
(3) *Die Geschichte von dem starken Grettir, dem Geächteten*, German tr., Paul
    Herrmann, Thule 5 (Jena, 1922)
(4) *Grettir's Saga*, English tr., D. Fox and H. Pálsson (Toronto, 1974)
    Selective index of proper names.

*Secondary Literature:*
*Medieval Scandinavia, an Encyclopedia*, 241–3

## *King Harald's Saga,* see Snorri Sturluson, pp. 146–7 above.

## *Heimskringla,* see Snorri Sturluson, pp. 145–6 above.

## *Ingvars Saga (Saga of Ingvar the Wide-travelled)*

Swedish chieftain who goes to the south with a group of compatriots, some of whom
seem to be mentioned on rune stones.

*Edition:*
E. Olsen, ed., *Yngvars Saga* (Copenhagen, 1912)

*Translation:*
H. Pálsson and Paul Edwards, *Vikings in Russia: Yngvar's Saga and Eymund's Saga*
  (Edinburgh, 1989)

*Secondary Literature:*
Blöndal, *Varangians of Byzantium*, 228

Ciggaar, *Western Travellers*, ch. 4 'The northern countries', 127
Ellis Davidson, *Viking Road,* 87–8, 163–70, 277–8
Kalinke, 'Foreign language requirement', 858
*Medieval Scandinavia, an Encyclopedia*, 740–1

Karl Jónsson, see *Sverris Saga*, p. 154 below.

*Knýtlinga Saga ( The Saga of the Knýtlingar)*
The Knýtlingar were kings of Denmark from the tenth century until 1187. The saga
describes the pilgrimage to Jerusalem of King Erik of Denmark and his family, and
their visit to the Byzantine court.

*Editions:*
(1) Carl af Petersens and E. Olson, eds., *Sögur Danakonunga* (Copenhagen, 1919–25),
    27–294
(2) B. Guðnason, ed., *Danakonungasögur*, Íslenzk fornrit 35 (1982), 93–321
*Translation:*
*Die Geschichte von den Orkaden, Dänemark und der Jomsburg,* German tr. by W.
    Baetke, Thule 19 (Jena, 1924; repr. Düsseldorf, 1966)
*Secondary Literature:*
A. Fellman, *Voyage en Orient du roi Erik Ejegod et sa mort à Paphos* (Copenhagen, 1938)
*Medieval Scandinavia, an Encyclopedia*, 359–60
P.J. Riis, 'Where was Erik the Good buried?', *Mediaeval Scandinavia* 13 (2000),
    144–54

*\*Konraðs Saga ( The Saga of Konráðr, Son of an Emperor)*
One of the so-called *Riddarasögur*. Conrad, son of the emperor of Saxony (*Saxland*),
visits Constantinople to ask for the hand of the Greek emperor's daughter. Conrad,
who does not speak his language, is deceived by his foster-brother. Although this
saga is a romance, it may be a reminiscence of Conrad's visit to Constantinople during the Second Crusade where he met his sister-in-law, Bertha of Sulzbach, who had
married the Byzantine emperor Manuel Komnenos. It seems plausible that northern
interest in the saga was due to the presence of Icelanders and other Scandinavians in
Conrad's expedition army.

*Editions:*
(1) G. Cederschiöld, '*Konraðs Saga*', in *Fornsögur Suðrlanda* (Lund, 1884), 43–84
(2) J.M. Hunt, 'The major text of Konráðs Saga keisarasonar with a thesaurus of
    word forms', M. Phil. thesis, Univ. of London (London, 1972)
*Translations:*
(1) O. Zitzelsberger, English tr., '*Konráðs Saga*, keisarasonar', *Seminar for Germanic
    Philology, Yearbook* (1980), 38–67
(2) H. Gering, German tr. in G. Cederschiöld's edition, pp. cxxxix–cxlvii
*Secondary Literature:*
Kalinke, 'The foreign language requirement', 850–61
Kalinke, in Clover and Lindow, *Old Norse–Icelandic Literature, passim*
Kalinke and Mitchell, *Bibliography*, 75–7
*Medieval Scandinavia, an Encyclopedia*, 360–1

*Laxdaela Saga (The Saga of the Laxdaelir)*
Laxdaelir is a district of Norway. Tells the story of Bolli Bollason, one of the main
characters of the saga, and his journey to the east where he takes service in
Byzantium. He returns to Iceland with his companions.

*Edition:*
E.O. Sveinsson, ed., *Laxdaela Saga,* Íslenzk fornrit 5 (Reykjavik, 1934)

*Translations:*
(1) *Laxdaela Saga,* Engl. tr., M.A.C. Press (London, 1899)
(2) *Laxdaela Saga,* Engl. tr., R. Proctor (London, 1903)
(3) *Laxdaela Saga,* Engl. tr., T. Veblen (New York, 1925)
(4) *Laxdaela Saga,* Engl. tr., A.M. Arent (Washington, 1964)
(5) *Laxdaela Saga,* tr. with introd. by M. Magnusson and H. Pálsson
    (Harmondsworth, 1969, etc.)
    Selective index of proper names.

*Secondary Literature:*
Blöndal, *Varangians of Byzantium,* 206–8
*Medieval Scandinavia, an Encyclopedia,* 387–8

*Ljósvetninga Saga (The Saga of the Ljósavatn Family)*
Mentions the journey to Constantinople of Magnus konungsson and Þormóði.

*Edition:*
B. Sigfússon, ed., *Ljósvetninga Saga,* Íslenzk fornrit 10 (Reykjavik, 1940)

*Translations:*
(1) G. Vigfússon and F. York Powell, in *Origines islandicae. A collection of the
    more important sagas and other narrative writings relating to the settlement and
    early history of Iceland,* 2 vols. (Oxford, 1905; repr. Millwood, 1976), vol. 2,
    355–427
    Not easy to find.
(2) *Ljósvetninga Saga,* German tr., W. Ranisch, in *Fünf Geschichten aus dem östlichen
    Nordland,* Thule 11 (Jena, 1921), 131–227
    The index is a list of *Verdeutschte isländische Ortsnamen.*

*Secondary Literature:*
*Medieval Scandinavia, an Encyclopedia,* 393–4
de Vries, *Literaturgeschichte,* vol. 2, esp. 420–4

*Njals Saga (The Saga of Njáll)*
Some minor characters in the saga go to Byzantium. Kolskeg became leader of the
Varangian Guard and stayed in Byzantium for the rest of his life. Flosi Thordarson
went abroad and took the so-called Eastway, via Byzantium.

*Editions:*
(1) E.O. Sveinsson, ed., *Brennu-Njáls Saga,* Íslenzk fornrit 12 (Reykjavik, 1954)
(2) Robert Cook, ed., *Njal's Saga,* Penguin (London, 2001)

*Translations:*
(1) *Njal's Saga,* English tr., M. Magnusson and H. Pálsson, Penguin (Harmondsworth,
    1960, etc.)
    Selective index of personal names.

(2) *Die Geschichte vom weisen Njal*, German tr., A. Heusler (Düsseldorf and Cologne, 1963)

(3) *Njál's Saga*, English tr., C.F. Bayerschmidt and L.M. Hollander (Westport, USA, 1979)

(3) *Njál's Saga*, English tr., Robert Cook, Penguin (London, 2001)
   The index is not organised in the traditional way, but by character: see review in *Scandinavian Studies* 75 (2003), 450–1; a new series of translations in Penguin seems to be in progress.

*Secondary Literature:*
Blöndal, *Varangians of Byzantium*, 197
*Medieval Scandinavia, an Encyclopedia*, 432–4

*Oddr Snorrason*, see below, *Olafs Saga (Olaf I Tryggvason)*

*Olaf Haraldssons Saga (Saint)*, Olaf II, king of Norway (1015–28)
Performs a miracle during the reign of the Byzantine emperor Alexios I Komnenos. See also Snorri Sturluson, *Heimskringla*, pp. 145–6 above.

For the miracle:

*Editions:*
(1) P.A. Munch and C.R. Unger, eds., *Saga Olafs Konings ens Helga* (Chistiania, 1853), 242–3
(2) Vigfússon and Unger, *Flateyjarbók*, vol. 3, 380–1
(3) C.R. Unger, ed., *Olafs Saga hins Helga*, in *Heilagra Manna sögur*, vol. 2, 175–6
(4) O.A. Johnsen and J. Helgason, eds., *Den store Saga om Olav den hellige*, (Oslo, 1941), 633–5
(5) A. Heinrichs and others, eds., *Olaf's Saga Hins Helga*, Germanische Bibliothek, Reihe 4, Texte (Heidelberg, 1982), 212, 214

*Translations:*
(1) *Scripta historica Islandorum*, vol. 5, Latin tr. (Copenhagen, 1833), 147–9
(2) Heinrichs and others, *Olaf's Saga Hins Helga*, German tr., 213, 215

*Secondary Literature:*
Blöndal, *Varangians of Byzantium*, 185–6
K. Ciggaar, 'Flemish mercenaries in Byzantium. Their later history in an Old Norse miracle', *Byz* 51 (1981), 44–74, with additional note by Andrea van Arkel-de Leeuw van Weenen on the term *Blokumannaland*, 74–5
   During a battle in the Balkans St Olaf appears to Flemish mercenaries in the Byzantine army.
*Medieval Scandinavia, an Encyclopedia*, 445–6, 447–8
Widding and others, 'Lives of the saints', 327–8

For another miracle by Saint Olaf see Snorri Sturluson, *Heimskringla*, *Hákonar Saga Herðibreiðs (Saga of Hákon the Broad-shouldered)*, pp. 145–6 above.

*Olafs Saga (Saga of King Olaf I Tryggvason of Norway, 995–999/1000)*
Mentions a number of Scandinavians who went to the south. Miraculous appearances in Palestine and Syria. Oddr Snorrason, a monk in Thingeyrar, wrote this saga in Latin in the late twelfth century. He was convinced of the veracity of the stories told by recently returning pilgrims. This suggests that pilgrims from Iceland regularly

undertook the long journey to Jerusalem and passed more than once through Byzantine territory. Only the Old Norse version of the saga has been preserved.

*Editions:*
(1) F. Jónsson, ed., *Saga Óláfs Tryggvasonar af Oddr Snorrason munk*, 2 vols. (Copenhagen, 1932)
(2) O. Halldórsson, ed., *Ólafs Saga Tryggvasonar en mesta*, 2 vols. (Copenhagen, 1958–61)

*Translation:*
J. Sephton, *The Saga of King Olaf Tryggwason who reigned over Norway A.D. 995 to A.D. 1000* (London, 1895)

*Secondary Literature:*
Ellis Davidson, *Viking Road*, 255
*Medieval Scandinavia, an Encyclopedia*, 446–7, 448–9
Riant, *Expéditions*, 89, 116–17
Turville-Petre, *Origins of Icelandic Literature*, 83, 194–5

*Orkneyinga Saga (The Saga of the Orkney Islanders)*
Mentions King Harald of Norway, Rognvald Kali Kolsson (earl of Orkney), Eindredi the Young and others as journeying to and/or living in Byzantium.

*Editions:*
(1) S. Nordal, ed., *Orkneyinga Saga* (Copenhagen, 1915)
(2) F. Guðmundsson, ed., *Orkneyinga Saga*, Íslenzk fornrit 34 (Reykjavik, 1965)

*Translations:*
(1) *The Orkneyinga Saga*, English tr., J.A. Hjaltalín and G. Goudie, with introd. by J. Anderson (Edinburgh, 1873)
(2) *The Orkneyingers' Saga*, English tr., W. Dasent, Icelandic Sagas, Rolls Series 88, vol. 3 (London, 1894)
(3) *The Orkneyinga Saga,* Engl. tr., A.B. Taylor (Edinburgh, 1938)
(4) *Orkneyinga Saga. The History of the Earls of Orkney*, English tr., H. Pálsson and P. Edwards (London, 1978; Harmondsworth, 1981, etc.)
     Selective index of personal names and place names.

*Secondary Literature:*
Blöndal, *Varangians of Byzantium*, 155–6, 217
*Medieval Scandinavia, an Encyclopedia*, 456–7

*Qrvar-Odds Saga (*also spelled *Örvar-Odds Saga) (The Saga of Arrow-Oddr)*
The protagonist travels to the east, to Syria, then to part of Byzantium.

*Editions:*
(1) C.C. Rafn, ed., *Fornaldarsögur Norðlanda*, 3 vols. (Copenhagen, 1829–30), vol. 2
(2) R.C. Boer, ed., *Orvar-Odds Saga*, Groningen thesis (Leiden, 1888)
     Good index.
(3) R.C. Boer, ed., *Orvar-Odds Saga*, Altnordische Saga Bibliothek (Halle, 1892)
     Good index. This is another version of the text edited in 1888.
(4) G. Jónsson, ed., *Fornaldar sögur Norðurlanda*, 4 vols. (Reykjavik, 1954; repr. 1981), vol. 2

*Translation:*
P. Edwards and H. Pálsson, *Arrow-Odd: a medieval novel* (New York and London, 1970; repr. in *Seven Viking Romances*, Penguin (Harmondsworth, 1985), 25–137)
*Secondary Literature:*
*Medieval Scandinavia, an Encyclopedia*, 744
de Vries, *Literaturgeschichte*, esp. vol. 2, 483–7
I hope to come back to this text in the near future.

## Saga of King Sigurðar Jórsalafara (The Saga of Sigurd the Crusader)

The pilgrimage of Sigurðar Magnusson, King Sigurd I of Norway (1103–30) is commented upon in several contemporary and later sources. He visited Constantinople in 1111 and was officially received by the Byzantine emperor. His journey is confirmed by western and Arabic sources. (See also Snorri Sturluson, *Heimskringla, Saga of the Sons of Magnús*, p. 147 above.)

*Editions:*
(1) C.R. Unger, ed., *Saga Sigurðar Jórsalafara*, in *Morkinskinna* (Christiania, 1867), 156–98
(2) F. Jónsson, ed., *Saga Sigurðar Jórsalafara ok braeðra hans Eysteins ok Ólafs* (Copenhagen, 1932), 338–400

No translation: a translation of this version is a desideratum (see e.g. Ellis Davidson, 198, who refers to information on the hippodrome in Constantinople).

*Secondary Literature:*
Blöndal, *Varangians*, 136–40, 142, 156
Ellis Davidson, *Viking Road*, 158, 181, 198, 260–2, 271, 301
R.M. Dawkins, 'The visit of King Sigurd the Pilgrim to Constantinople', in *Eis mnemen S. Lamprou* (Athens, 1935), 55–62
M.E. Kalinke, 'Sigurðar Saga Jórsalafara. The fictionalization of facts in *Morkinskinna*', *Scandinavian Studies* 56 (1984), 152–67
    Discusses the visit of King Sigurd of Norway to Constantinople, stressing the romantic character of the version in *Morkinskinna*.
—— 'Foreign language requirement', esp. 858
*Medieval Scandinavia, an Encyclopedia*, see under *Heimskringla*
S. Runciman, *A History of the Crusades*, 3 vols. (Cambridge, 1951–4), vol. 2, 92–3, 485, 497

See also Collections of Sagas, *Morkinskinna*, p. 145 above.

## Sturlunga Saga (The Saga of the Sturlungar)

Mentions a Scandinavian called Sigurd the Greek who brought a Greek sword to Iceland.

*Editions:*
(1) G. Vigfússon, ed., *Sturlunga Saga*, 2 vols. (Oxford, 1878)
(2) K. Kålund, ed., *Sturlunga Saga*, 2 vols. (Copenhagen, 1906–11)
(3) K. Eldjarn and others, eds., *Sturlunga Saga* (Reykjavik, 1946)
*Translation:*
J. McGrew and R. George Thomas, *Sturlunga Saga*, 2 vols. (New York, 1970–4)

*Secondary Literature:*
Blöndal, *Varangians of Byzantium*, 101, 221–2
*Medieval Scandinavia, an Encyclopedia*, 616–18

*Sverris Saga (The Saga of King Sverri)* (sometimes attributed to Karl Jónsson)
A number of people who travelled to the east are mentioned in this saga, such as King Harald, Ulf and Hreidar.

*Edition:*
H. Indrebø, ed., *Sverris Saga* (Oslo, 1920)

*Translation:*
J. Sephton, *The Saga of King Sverri of Norway*, Engl. tr. (London, 1899)

*Secondary Literature:*
Blöndal, *Varangians of Byzantium*, 161, 218–20
*Medieval Scandinavia, an Encyclopedia*, 628–9

*Thorlaks Saga, Saint*
Miracle performed by the saint in the east.

*Edition:*
*Biskupa sögur*, vol. 1, 363–4

*Translation:*
English tr. by Chris Sanders, in A. van Arkel-De Leeuw van Weenen and K. Ciggaar, 'St. Thorlac's in Constantinople, built by a Flemish emperor', *Byz* 49 (1979), 432–3

*Secondary Literature:*
Andrea van Arkel-De Leeuw van Weenen and K. Ciggaar, 'St Thorlac's in Constantinople, built by a Flemish emperor', *Byz* 49 (1979), 428–46
*Medieval Scandinavia, an Encyclopedia*, 671
Widding and others, 'Lives of the saints', 336–7

*Yngvar Saga* see *Ingvars Saga*, pp. 148–9 above.


## SECONDARY LITERATURE OF A MORE GENERAL CHARACTER

### Books

*Byzantium and the North, Acta Byzantina Fennica, I. Papers presented at the symposium 'Byzantium and the North', at Valamo monastery 11th and 12th June, 1981* (Helsinki, 1985)
A variety of articles on various subjects; not easy to find.
M. Müller-Wille, ed., *Rom und Byzanz im Norden. Mission und Glaubenswechsel im Ostseeraum während des 8.–14. Jahrhunderts*, Band 1 (Mainz, 1997)
Contributions deal with religious topics.
*Varangian Problems. Scando Slavica, Supplementum 1, Report on the First international symposium on the theme 'The eastern connections of the Nordic peoples in the Viking period and Early Middle Ages* (Copenhagen, 1970)

Papers dealing with various aspects of the Varangians and their journey southward.

Else Ebel, ed., *Die Waräger. Ausgewählte Texte zu den Fahrten der Wikinger nach Vorderasien*. Mit Anmerkungen und Glossar (Tübingen, 1978)
Texts are given in the original vernaculars, with good indices.

## Articles

F. Amory, 'Things Greek and the *Riddarasögur*', *Speculum* 59 (1984), 509–23
L. Cansdale, 'Vikings by boat to Byzantium', in *Byzantium and the North*
Not easy to find.
A. Cutler, 'Garda, Källunge and the Byzantine tradition on Gotland', *The Art Bulletin* 51 (1969), 257–66; repr. in idem, *Byzantium, Italy and the North. Papers on cultural relations* (London, 2000)
—— 'Byzantine art and the north: meditations on the notion of influence', repr. in *Byzantium, Italy and the North*
—— 'The sculpture and sources of "Byzantios"', repr. in *Byzantium, Italy and the North*
H.-R. Toivanen, 'Constantinople as a mirror of architecture and notions', in *Byzantium and the North*
Not easy to find.

For the arts one could consult the bibliography of the *Byzantinische Zeitschrift*.

For coins and coin hoards one can consult the yearly edition of *Numismatic Literature* of the American Numismatic Society, New York, for the current year: www.amnumsoc.org./numlit/

# 8

# Slavonic Sources

## SIMON FRANKLIN

SLAVS ARE CONVENTIONALLY DIVIDED into three groups: west, south, and east. The west Slavs include Poles, Czech and Slovaks, south Slavs include Bulgarians and Serbs, while the early east Slav peoples are the linguistic ancestors of today's Russians, Ukrainians and Belarusians. From the end of the tenth century the divisions were also ecclesiastical, as south and east Slav rulers generally adopted for their countries the Byzantine version of Christianity, while west Slavs accepted its Roman version. Partly in consequence, and despite the fact that Slavonic scriptures were originally produced for west Slavs in Moravia in the mid-ninth century, the written culture of the west Slavs was substantially Latin, while written Slavonic was nurtured among east and south Slavs, among those who might be viewed as part of, in Dimitri Obolensky's capacious and influential term, the Byzantine Commonwealth, or as constituting what Riccardo Picchio has labelled *slavia orthodoxa*.[1] 'Slavonic' in the title of the present survey refers to the language of writing, not to the ethnicity or the location of the writer: 'sources in Slavonic', not 'sources by Slavs'. Hence coverage is restricted to south Slavs (Bulgaria and Serbia) and east Slavs (Rus).

However, even within *slavia orthodoxa* the production and survival of Slavonic written sources for the period 1025–1204 is uneven. Whether coincidentally or otherwise, the volume of production—or, more pertinently, the extent of survival—varies according to the political circumstances. Indeed, there appears to be an inverse relationship between the volume of original Slavonic writings and the degree of subordination to the Byzantine empire: native Slavonic sources proliferate in places and periods of Slav political autonomy, and diminish with political dependence on (and with varying degrees of cultural assimilation to) the Byzantine empire. Native Bulgarian Slavonic writings are reasonably represented in the First Bulgarian empire

---

[1] Dimitri Obolensky, *The Byzantine Commonwealth. Eastern Europe 500–1500* (London, 1971); Riccardo Picchio, 'Guidelines for a comparative study of the language question among the Slavs', in Riccardo Picchio and Harvey Goldblatt, eds., *Aspects of the Slavic Language Question*, vol. 1 (New Haven, Conn., 1984), 1–42.

*Proceedings of the British Academy* **132**, 157–181. © The British Academy 2007.

(roughly from the late ninth to the early eleventh century) and in the Second Bulgarian empire (whose independence was established in the 1180s and 1190s) but barely exist from the intervening century-and-three-quarters, when Bulgaria was part of the Byzantine empire. In Serbia the Golden Age of indigenous Slavonic written culture began only under the successors of Stefan Nemanja (d. 1199).[2] Thus the overwhelming majority of substantial native Slavonic sources (I do not here consider translations from Greek) from Serbia and Bulgaria fall neatly—or awkwardly—either side of the period relevant to the present study: either pre-1025 or post-1204.

Rus, by contrast, was never part of the Empire, nor was it an immediate neighbour of the Empire, not did it include areas of significant Greek-speaking or Greek-writing populations. Hellenisation was never an issue. The conventional date for the official conversion of the Rus to Christianity is 988, and native Slavonic sources from Rus proliferate precisely during the period of their relative scarcity in Bulgaria or Serbia.[3] Furthermore, even where south Slav sources do survive, they are prosopographically thin (by comparison with the east Slav sources). The densely inhabited genres and forms, such as seals and annalistic chronicles, are virtually absent from the extant written culture of Bulgaria and Serbia in this period, yet both are prominent in Rus. The present survey is therefore mainly—though not quite exclusively—concerned with sources from Rus. For a prosopographer whose principal interest is in the life of the Empire itself, this is, in a sense, unfortunate, in that the most copious Slavonic material derives from and deals principally with the Orthodox Slav area which was the most remote from and had the least intensive relations with the Empire. As we shall see, however, the very liminality of much of the material raises intriguing questions of definition, of marginality and of identity, of the shape and texture of our notions of the 'Byzantine'.

The problem can perhaps best be illustrated if we first present the sources in a sequence defined not by conventional text-book criteria such as genre or chronology, but by the nature or degree of their association with the Byzantine 'centre'. We start with prosopographical sources which are squarely and directly relevant to the Byzantine empire and the crusades,

---

[2] For historical outlines, see John V.A. Fine, Jr., *The Early Medieval Balkans: a critical survey from the sixth to the late twelfth century* (Ann Arbor, 1983); John V.A. Fine, Jr., *The Late Medieval Balkans: a critical survey from the late twelfth century to the Ottoman conquest* (Ann Arbor, 1987). On particular areas: Robert Browning, *Byzantium and Bulgaria. A comparative study across the early medieval frontier* (London, 1975); Paul Stephenson, *Byzantium's Balkan Frontier. A political study of the northern Balkans, 900–1204* (Cambridge, 2000).

[3] On Rus in this period, see Manfred Hellman, *Handbuch zur Geschichte Russlands*, 1.1: *Von der kiever Reichsbildung bis zum moskauer Zartum* (Stuttgart, 1981); Janet Martin, *Medieval Russia 980–1584* (Cambridge, 1995); Simon Franklin and Jonathan Shepard, *The Emergence of Rus 750–1200* (London, 1996).

whence we progress, via the somewhat more peripheral sources, towards those zones of uncertainty which blur the boundaries of the broader concept of a 'Byzantine world'. This sequence is also likely to represent an approximate order of priority for anybody wishing to trawl through the Slavonic sources in order to compile a prosopography of Byzantium and the crusades for the period from 1025 to 1204.

## 1. 'GREEK' BYZANTINE SOURCES IN SLAVONIC

The most narrowly 'Byzantine' of the Slavonic sources are those which were originally produced by 'Greeks' and in Greek, though they happen to survive only in Slavonic translation.[4] Such works are prosopographically straightforward. Edificatory, dogmatic or administrative in character, rather than narrative, they may be significant as evidence for the activities and opinions of their authors, but contain little information on anybody else. All but one of the texts are also very short. I place them first only because of the directness of their Byzantine connection, not because they contain great prosopographical riches. One of these texts—much the longest—was originally an internal Byzantine document written *for* 'Greeks'. The typikon of Patriarch Alexios Stoudites, created for his Constantinopolitan monastery of the Dormition of the Theotokos in 1034, was translated into Slavonic in the early 1070s for use in the Monastery of the Caves in Kiev. Usually, however, the authors were Byzantine churchmen writing for a Slav audience. Some wrote from Constantinople (e.g. a couple of letters from mid-twelfth-century patriarchs, Loukas Chrysoberges and Nicholas Mouzalon, on Rus ecclesiastical appointments). Others—the majority—held office in the Rus church and were writing for their local flock. Metropolitan Nikifor (i.e. Nikephoros) I (1104–21), for example, wrote a number of letters to Rus princes, including a detailed instruction of the duties of a ruler.[5] Bishop Manuel of Smolensk participated

---

[4] For references, see Translations, pp. 180–1 below. This survey does not include Slavonic translations of works which also survive in Greek. Such translations fill the overwhelming majority of medieval Slavonic manuscripts. They are important for the history of Slav culture and of the language, but they are of no independent prosopographic value. See e.g. Roland Marti, *Handschrift — Text — Textgruppe — Literatur. Untersuchungen zur inneren Gliederung der frühen Literatur aus dem ostslavischen Sprachbereich in den Handschriften des 11. bis 14. Jahrhunderts* (Wiesbaden, 1989); Francis J. Thomson, *The Reception of Byzantine Culture in Medieval Russia* (Aldershot, 1999).

[5] More generally on the writings of 'Greek' churchmen in Rus, see Gerhard Podskalsky, 'Der Beitrag der griechisch-stämmigen Metropoliten (Kiev), Bischöfe und Mönche zu altrussischen Originalliteratur (Theologie), 988–1281', *Cahiers du monde russe et soviétique* 24 (1983), 498–515; Anthony-Emil N. Tachiaos, 'The Greek metropolitans of Kievan Rus': an evaluation of their spiritual and cultural activity', *Harvard Ukrainian Studies* 12–13 (1988/9), 430–45.

in the issuing of a series of documents linked to the establishment of his bishopric in the mid-twelfth century, and we also have some of his responses to pastoral and disciplinary questions from the clergy.[6] An interesting aspect of these sources is that they can reflect the challenge posed to habitual Byzantine world-views in a non-habitual environment. They show Byzantine authors on the margins, having to cope with the practical problems of their own cultural liminality in a more direct and constructive way than the well-known contemporary genre of whingeing letters home to fellow Byzantines.[7]

No list of extant Slavonic writings by 'Greeks' could reasonably claim to be definitive, for 'Greeks' are not always easy to find or to define. Some 'Greeks' could write—or could order texts to be written—directly in Slavonic, and some Slavs could write—or could order texts to be written— in Greek, and the sources often provide inadequate information for anything more than the vaguest of biographical hypotheses. Several known figures may or may not be reckoned 'Greeks', and several anonymous writings may or may not be attributable to 'Greeks'. Should we, for example, include among writers the very poorly attested metropolitan Ioann I (1030s?) whom some identify as the author of the earliest offices to the Rus saints Boris and Gleb?[8] Or should we include among 'Greeks' a certain Feodosii (unless that should be 'Theodosios'), who was commissioned in the mid-twelfth century, by a monk at the Caves monastery in Kiev, to translate the epistle of Pope Leo I to Flavian, to which he wrote his own brief preface?[9] Or should we include the Olisei (unless that should be Elisaios, or Elisha), known from a cluster of birch-bark documents, apparently an icon-painter active in Novgorod at the turn of the thirteenth century, whose additional designation as 'Grechin' has been taken to mean 'the Greek', though the form was also assimilated into Slavonic as a name?[10] How do we assess the origins of 'Grigorii the

---

[6] Further on Manuel, see Simon Franklin, 'Who was the uncle of Theodore Prodromus?', *Byzantinoslavica* 45 (1984), 40–5, repr. in Franklin, *Byzantium—Rus—Russia. Studies in the translation of Christian culture* (Aldershot, 2002), no. VI (also cf. no. VII in the same collection).

[7] With regard to Bulgaria, for example, see the letters of Gregory Antiochos, or of Theophylakt of Ohrid: Alexander Kazhdan, with Simon Franklin, *Studies on Byzantine Literature of the Eleventh and Twelfth Centuries* (Cambridge, 1984), 219–20; Dimitri Obolensky, *Six Byzantine Portraits* (Oxford, 1988), 56–61; Margaret Mullett, *Theophylact of Ochrid. Reading the letters of a Byzantine archbishop*, Birmingham Byzantine and Ottoman Monographs 2 (Aldershot, 1997), 266–74.

[8] Gail Lenhoff, *The Martyred Princes Boris and Gleb: a socio-cultural study of the cult and the texts* (Columbus, Ohio, 1989), 56–65.

[9] See Gerhard Podskalsky, *Christentum und theologische Literatur in der Kiever Rus' (988–1237)* (Munich, 1982), 179–84.

[10] B.A. Kolchin, A.S. Khoroshev, V.L. Ianin, *Usad'ba novgorodskogo khudozhnika XII v.* (Moscow, 1981); cf. Aleksandr B. Strakhov, 'Filologicheskie nabliudeniia nad berestianymi gramotami: VI–IX', *Palaeoslavica* 3 (1995), 244–7; A. Gippius, 'K biografii Oliseia Grechina', in O.E. Etingof, ed., *Tserkov' Spasa na Nereditse: ot Vizantii k Rusi* (Moscow, 2005), 99–114.

Philosopher', apparently the author of some eleventh-century homilies?[11] Should we include the responses of Bishop Nifon of Novgorod (d. 1156) to questions posed by Kirik, a Novgorodian clergyman?[12] From about the mid-twelfth century the seals of bishops in Rus began to be inscribed in Slavonic rather than in Greek, but there is no clear evidence that the language of the inscription consistently correlates to the linguistic or geographical origins of the seal's issuer.[13] And what can we tell of the background of those graffitists who leave little more than their names scratched into the walls of churches?[14]

Thus if we seek to apply a narrow definition of 'Greek', as implying Greek-speakers originally from within the Empire, then a catalogue of Slavonic sources issued *by* Greeks covers the full spectrum of attributions from the relatively straightforward to the utterly speculative, with a substantial proportion of the sources allocated to the category of *dubia*. The position is similar with regard to sources *about* 'Greeks'.

## 2. SLAVONIC SOURCES EXPLICITLY ABOUT BYZANTIUM AND THE CRUSADERS

At the relatively straightforward end of the spectrum we have Rus pilgrim accounts both of Constantinople and of the Holy Land, by named authors: the pilgrimage of Daniil to the Holy Land (*c.*1105–8); and the account by Dobrynia Iadreikovich (future Archbishop Antonii of Novgorod) of his visit to the shrines of Constantinople in 1200.[15] As befits pilgrims, Daniil and Antonii were more interested in ancient places than in contemporary people, although Daniil's narrative is notable for its friendly attitude towards the Latin masters of Jerusalem. Briefer, though more problematic, is the only Slavonic text whose central theme combines both Byzantium and crusaders: the anonymous *Tale of the Capture of Tsargrad by the Franks* (i.e. an account of the capture of the city in 1204), which is clearly derived from an eye-witness account and which may have been composed as a separate work, but

---

[11] William R. Veder with Anatolij A. Turilov, *The Edificatory Prose of Kievan Rus'*, Harvard Library of Early Ukrainian Literature. English Translations 6 (Cambridge, Mass., 1994), xli–liii, 121–68; cf. Simon Franklin, 'Annotationes byzantino-russicae', *GENNADIOS: K 70-letiiu akademika V.V. Litavrina* (Moscow, 1999), 226–30, repr. in Franklin, *Byzantium — Rus — Russia*, no. IX.

[12] *Russkaia istoricheskaia biblioteka*, vol. 6 (St Petersburg, 1908), cols. 21–62 (including the responses attributed to Manuel of Smolensk).

[13] See Simon Franklin, 'Greek in Kievan Rus'', *DOP* 46 (1992), 69–81. repr. in Franklin, *Byzantium — Rus — Russia*, no. XII.

[14] See Epigraphic Sources, pp. 173–5 below.

[15] See Travel and Pilgrimage, pp. 178–9 below.

which only survives embedded in chronicles and other large-scale chrono-
graphic compilations. The *Tale* includes an account of diplomacy that is
favourable to Philip of Swabia, but again the main focus is more on places than
on people, on the details of the plundering of Hagia Sophia, for example.

In quite a different genre, we should probably include in this category the
famous sequence of Serbian 'Royal Lives': hagiographic biographies of successive Serbian rulers; or at least the beginnings of the sequence, which continues far beyond the relevant period. The most important of these are two
Lives of the founder of the dynasty, Stefan Nemanja (*c.*1167–96; d. 1199/
1200; also known by his monastic name of Simeon): one by his son and successor Stefan Nemanjic ('Stefan the First-crowned'; 1196–1227), one by a
second son Rastko, better known by his monastic name of Sava (d. 1235), the
key figure in the establishment of organised Serb monasticism both on Athos
(where, in 1198, with the permission of Alexios III, he founded the Hilandar
monastery) and in Serbia (as superior of the Studenica monastery). More
remote from direct contact with our period are two further Lives, written by
the monk Domentijan in the mid-thirteenth century: yet another biography
of Stefan Nemanja, and a very substantial Life of Sava himself.[16] A slighter
hagiographic text from Rus, which should probably be included in this section, is the *Life of Leontii of Rostov*. According to the story, Leontii was
appointed bishop of Rostov but was murdered by local pagans, probably in
the mid-1070s. The Life cannot be traced much before the mid-twelfth century,
so is of dubious documentary value. Nevertheless, one version of it opens
with the statement that Leontii was born and raised in Constantinople: that
he was, in other words, Leontios, a *bona fide* (in all senses) 'Greek'.[17]

## 3. SLAVONIC SOURCES WITH INCIDENTAL INFORMATION ON BYZANTIUM AND CRUSADERS

Although the texts described in this last section (works explicitly about
'Greeks') are prosopographically somewhat more rewarding than those in the
first section (works by 'Greeks' themselves), the cast of characters is still limited. For a more crowded stage we have to stray still further from the
Byzantine centre. By far the most voluminous and prosopographically popu-
lous sources are those which deal with local issues and events, where 'Greeks'

---

[16] Gerhard Podskalsky, *Theologische Literatur des Mittelalters in Bulgarien und Serbien
865–1459* (Munich, 2000), 356–76; see Hagiography, pp. 175–8 below.
[17] G.V. Semenchenko, 'Drevneishie redaktsii zhitiia Leontiia Rostovskogo', *Trudy Otdela
drevnerusskoi literatury* 42 (1989), 241–54.

figure sporadically, incidentally, unsystematically. First among such sources are the Rus chronicles.[18]

No Rus chronicle from the period survives as a complete and self-contained work in a contemporary manuscript. With the exception of a single defective manuscript of the *Novgorod First Chronicle*, all the pre-Mongol Rus chronicles survive only as parts of subsequent (fourteenth-century, fifteenth-century) compilations, from which the earlier texts can be extrapolated with varying degrees of precision. Thus several of the later compilations share an initial section, an extensive narrative from the sons of Noah to the second decade of the twelfth century. This common core is what has come to be known in English as the *Primary Chronicle*, put together in Kiev in something not too remote from its present form in the 1110s. The precursors and sources of the *Primary Chronicle* are less clear, for they have to be deduced mainly from internal evidence, but they include local written narratives from about the middle of the eleventh century, while its reconstruction of earlier history is based on a combination of oral record and translated Byzantine material. The continuations of the *Primary Chronicle* diverge according to region. The *Hypatian Chronicle* represents a southern and south-western tradition, in which the *Primary Chronicle* is followed by a detailed Kievan chronicle covering the twelfth century, and then by a Galician chronicle for the thirteenth century. The *Laurentian Chronicle* (named after the scribe of its earliest manuscript, dated 1377) represents a north-eastern tradition, in which the *Primary Chronicle* is followed by a rather more succinct chronicle focusing on Suzdal. Novgorod was also a centre of chronicle writing, at least from the late eleventh century.[19]

The chroniclers were not interested in Byzantium for its own sake. The compiler of the *Primary Chronicle* was unusual in combining narrative with a degree of interpretation and explanation, in apparently trying to convey not just the story but the point. Mostly, however, the chroniclers were—in the language of the conventional dichotomy—annalists rather than thematic historians. Their attention is fixed unwaveringly on the relentless year-by-year record of local and dynastic politics. Their narratives broadly reflect the extent to which the 'Greeks' impinged on political and cultural life in Rus: most frequently the comings and goings and occasional public activities of metropolitans and bishops, sometimes little flurries of diplomacy or conflict. The chronicles can also be useful sources for other peoples who had dealings both with Rus and with Byzantium. Both the *Primary Chronicle* and the twelfth-century Kievan chronicle give a fair amount of space to activities of

---

[18] See Chronicles, pp. 171–3 below.
[19] D.S. Lkhachev, *Russkie letopisi i ikh kul'turno-istoricheskoe znachenie* (Moscow, Leningrad, 1947), 173–288; V.K. Ziborov, *Russkoe letopisanie XI–XVIII vekov* (St Petersburg, 2002), 61–110.

steppe nomads (first Pechenegs, then Cumans [Polovtsians, Qipchaks]), for example, while the Kievan chronicle also includes quite detailed and regular reports on diplomatic relations with Hungary in the mid-twelfth century, which inevitably impinged on the Empire.[20]

Outside the chronicles the main narrative theme is hagiographic.[21] No hagiography is as prosopographically congested as the chronicles, but if we are hunting for names, then the text with the longest index is undoubtedly the *paterikon* of the Kievan Caves monastery, a substantial compilation of stories from the most prestigious of Rus monasteries, put together in the 1220s but going back to tales of the monastery's foundation in the mid-eleventh century. One of the monastery's founders, Feodosii, is the subject of a Life of his own, written by Nestor, a monk of the Caves: Feodosii is credited with organising the monastery as a 'proper' cenobitic community (through the Stoudite typikon), but he was also a fairly prominent public figure, and Nestor's biography of him is of some prosopographical value. Other Rus hagiographical texts are perhaps less significant for such purposes. The martyred princes Boris and Gleb died in 1015 and hence fall outside the chronological purview of the present project, although the literature on Boris and Gleb is not entirely irrelevant since it also contains some narrative of the growth of their cult, which involves people within the requisite period. At the opposite end, the late-twelfth-century subject of Efrem's *Life of Avraamii of Smolensk* is chronologically fit for inclusion, but the text contains little information on identifiable individuals, as does the very brief *Life of Leontii of Rostov*. And that more or less (more rather than less) exhausts the surviving store of Rus hagiography.

The Rus repertoire of narrative sources has been stable for a long time. Some sources are more thoroughly researched and published and indexed than others, but the group as a whole is stable. Epigraphic sources, by contrast, are a growth area (notably in Rus; less so in the south Slav areas):[22] graffiti on the walls of churches, seals, and the celebrated birch-bark documents that are continually being dug up in Novgorod and elsewhere—these are sources which increase year by year. And they are by nature a type of source in which names are common. Over the years we have become quite familiar not just with individual senders or recipients of birch-bark letters, but with whole families or with clusters of associates.[23] The graffiti contain as many names, but tell fewer stories and reveal fewer identities beyond the names themselves (the formula 'X wrote this' is as prevalent on the walls of

[20] V. Iu Franchuk, *Kievskaia letopis'* (Kiev, 1986).
[21] See Hagiography, pp. 175–8 below.
[22] See Epigraphic Sources, pp. 173–5 below.
[23] See, especially, Ianin, *Ia poslal tebe berestu . . .*

Rus churches as it is on public buildings or park benches in the twenty-first century). For the prosopographer of Rus, however, the two essential requirements must surely be: an index to the chronicles in one hand, and an index to the corpus of seals in the other hand. Seals are the chronicles' epigraphic complement, the *dramatis personae* with the narrative stripped away, people reduced to names alone, the purest of index-materials. Some 1,200 Rus seals from the relevant period have been published. Several of the earlier examples (and all the seals of metropolitans) are in fact inscribed in Greek, though this says more about the cultural context of their use than about the ethno-linguistic identity of their owners.

Like the chronicles, the seals mainly relate to people who were involved in local Rus political and administrative life; and similarly they can be of interest to the prosopographer of Byzantium and the crusades to the extent that the local stories and the wider stories intersect. Like the chronicles, therefore, the seals bring into focus the question of boundaries: what are the limits? Thus far our survey of sources has been arranged according to the degree of association with the Byzantine 'centre', starting with texts by or about 'core' Byzantines and moving outwards to the imperial and cultural periphery. The purpose has been to suggest an approximate order of significance with regard to the prosopography of Byzantium and the crusades. How far can one go while still remaining relevant to the theme? The question has two aspects. We have to decide, on the one hand, where to draw the line between sources, and on the other hand, where or how to draw the line between individuals within those sources. On the choice of sources I should simply declare an arbitrary—but, I hope, pragmatically justifiable—decision. Neither this survey nor the linked bibliography attempt to cover all extant Slavonic written sources of the period. I have already confessed to omitting Slavonic translations from Greek (i.e. the vast bulk of Slavonic written 'high' culture) where the Greek original survives, on the grounds that such texts are prosopographically irrelevant. But I have also omitted other categories of source: (i) almost all homiletic writing,[24] for it rarely conveys information on any individual except perhaps—in rare cases—its own named author; (ii) all hymnography and liturgical genres, for the same reason; (iii) large numbers of separate publications and studies of epigraphic materials (I have limited the bibliography to substantial collections); (iv) law codes, both ecclesiastical and secular; and (v) the rare specimens of what one might call 'literature' in something approaching a modern sense: a florid and witty *Petition* attributed to 'Daniil the Exile', or the highly poetic 'epic lament' known as the *Tale of*

---

[24] Except where the author is a known 'Greek': see above. Otherwise, see e.g. Simon Franklin, *Sermons and Rhetoric of Kievan Rus'*, Harvard Library of Early Ukrainian Literature. English Translations 5 (Cambrige, Mass., 1991).

*Igor's Campaign*, which is indeed well stocked with references to people, but which as a 'source' yields precedence to the narrative of the equivalent events in the *Hypatian Chronicle*. These sources offer diminishing or negligible prosopographical returns, and there is, I take it, a difference between the current survey for specific purposes and a complete account and bibliography of extant Slavonic writings. For fuller information on the omissions, interested readers can turn to the handbooks and reference works listed at the start of the bibliography.

The limitation of sources is pragmatic. The problem of the choice of individuals within those sources is more complex. The texts closest to the 'core' present no difficulty, for they are, in the prosopographical scales, relatively lightweight. The chronicles are much meatier, and a full prosopographical analysis of all chronicles and seals would be a very major undertaking. Here, then, is where we need to sort out the criteria of relevance. Where does 'Byzantineness' end? Thus far we have assumed a fairly narrow definition, imagining Byzantines as a restricted group whose members are quite clearly circumscribed both ethno-linguistically and geo-politically. In one perspective this is proper and appropriate. The authors of many of our Slavonic sources might well have shared such a perception: Byzantines were people whom Slav writers labelled as 'Greeks'. Yet viewed from other perspectives such simplicity is simplistic: at best unnecessarily restrictive, at worst, positively misleading.

The uncertainties are both factual and conceptual. The factual uncertainties are the most straightforward. They are standard problems of prosopography, by no means limited to the Slavonic sources. The authors of the sources were not interested in the requirements of modern prosopographers. Hence in many, many cases they neglected to provide even the most basic information that would enable us to identify a character as 'Greek' or 'non-Greek'. Place of birth, language of the home, place of education, employment . . .: as a rule the CV lacks precisely the categories of biographical fact that would be needed for ethno-linguistic or geo-political categorisation. Often there is inadequate evidence even for a tentative hypothesis and a decision to include or not to include somebody in a list of 'Greeks' would be arbitrary. Yet with regard to the Slavonic sources perhaps the factual uncertainties can to some extent be eased if we are prepared to accept a greater degree of conceptual flexibility, or at least to consider a range of alternative notions of what—or who—might legitimately be identified as Byzantine.

The ethno-linguistic and the geo-political criteria are not satisfactory either in themselves or in combination with each other. A purely ethno-linguistic definition of 'Greeks' is obviously untenable in this context: language is relevant to the culture of Empire, but Byzantine identity has little to do with ethnicity in any common current sense. There would be no justification—though it would lighten our task—in merely trawling through the

Slavonic sources for native Greek-speakers. Geo-political criteria—defining 'Greeks' as people within, or linked to, the Empire—appear more defensible, though (or because) somewhat nebulous. We can choose to regard, for example, all Serbs and Bulgarians as prosopographically Byzantine on the grounds that all or parts of their lands were at some time parts of the Empire, and we can retain the prosopographical boundaries even during periods of Serbian or Bulgarian independence regardless of whether any particular Serb or Bulgarian would have accepted such an identification. As a useful tool, proso-pography can, perhaps must, be more imperialist than Empire. Rus, however, was never part of the Empire. A straightforwardly imperial geo-political criterion for prosopographical Byzantineness would exclude all the Rus; and this, in turn, would allow us to ignore most of the largest and prosopograph-ically densest native Slavonic sources for the relevant period. The convenience of such a solution is attractive, but too crude. Rus was not part of the Empire but it—or parts of it—did enter into various levels of relationship with the Empire. For prosopographical purposes we need to decide which type of relationship we reckon significant, in what sequence of priority.

Two types of relationship are especially germane here. The first is defined by the principle of contiguity, the second by the principle of identity. A person merits inclusion in a Byzantine prosopography if he or she has some contact with Byzantium. Byzantineness (for prosopographical ends) is a kind of contagion, or infection: touch a Byzantine, speak to a Byzantine, receive a letter from a Byzantine, and you are infected with the bug of pro-sopographical relevance. War, diplomacy, pilgrimage, trade: the contexts for contacts are varied, and a prosopography should present information about individuals who played a direct personal role in specified areas of Byzantino-Slav relations.[25] The problem here, however, is that much still depends on speculative judgement. To this principle of contact we can oppose a principle of identity: inclusion or omission from the prosopo-graphy would, on this principle, depend on who somebody is rather than on who they have met. People included on grounds of identity are there as of right, not because of who they know.

The principle of identity might be applied to the Rus in at least two ways. First there is the issue of institutional identity. Rus was not subject to Byzantine secular institutions, but the church in Rus, established from the

---

[25] On personal contacts, see Ludolf Müller, 'Russen in Byzanz und Griechen im Rus'-Reich', *Bulletin d'information et coordination* 5 (1971), 96–118; Francis J. Thomson, 'Communications orales et écrites entre Grecs et Russes (IXᵉ–XIIIᵉ siècles): Russes à Byzance, Grecs en Russie: connaissance et méconnaissance de la langue de l'autre', in A. Dierkens and J.-M. Sansterre, eds., *Voyages et voyageurs à Byzance et en Occident du VIᵉ au XIᵉ siècle, Bruxelles 5–7 mai 1994* (Geneva, 2000), 113–63.

late tenth century, was part of the Byzantine ecclesiastical structure, as a metropolitanate within the patriarchate of Constantinople. Arguably, therefore, all Rus churchmen and churchwomen should be included automatically, regardless of their mother tongue or place of birth, because of their institutional subordination to Constantinople. Principles aside, there are also practical advantages in such an approach, since inclusivity here is probably simpler than selectivity. The total number of known churchmen (mainly from chronicles and seals) is not large, and it would be far easier—as well as being perfectly defensible—to include everybody than to spend significant time sifting through sources and interpretations in mostly doomed attempts to identify who was or was not (by other criteria) 'Greek'.

A second and more radical way of applying a principle of identity to the Rus is to set up cultural and confessional criteria: the Byzantine world is the Orthodox world, and all who would identify themselves as Orthodox should be included automatically. By this measure the prosopographical relevance of the Rus is determined not by specific personal dealings with Byzantium, nor through formal institutional affiliation with Byzantium, but through the acceptance and assimilation (albeit sometimes in partial or distorted or adapted form) of Byzantium's version of Christianity. Why draw a line between Empire and 'Commonwealth'? Why let political vicissitudes and contingencies split any part of *slavia orthodoxa*? Clearly this last solution, which implies that virtually everybody in the Slavonic sources should be included in the prosopography, is the most demanding of time and resources. Suddenly the potential list grows from a few dozen to perhaps a few thousand. The scope of prosopography with regard to the Rus, and the level of detail required in the analysis of, in particular, the chronicles, depends on the desired balance between these principles.

\* \* \*

Linguists and textual historians regularly bemoan the paucity and inadequacy—for the purposes of linguists and textual historians—of Slavonic source publications, but for prosopographical purposes there is quite enough to be getting on with. The major native sources for the period have been published and are, in differing degrees of amplitude, indexed. The *Primary Chronicle*, the Novgorod and Galician chronicles (but not the Suzdalian or— most importantly—the twelfth-century Kievan chronicles) have been translated into English, as have several of the major works of hagiography and exegesis, and a detailed edition and translation of Antonii's (i.e. Dobrynia Iadreikovich's) description of Constantinople is—at the time of writing— said to be in the final stages of preparation by George Majeska, who has produced exemplary annotated translations of later Russian descriptions of the city. Ongoing publications of epigraphic materials are kept reasonably up to date with new discoveries, and the publications of seals and of birch-bark documents are notable for the thoroughness of their indexes and for the prosopographical interest of the commentaries.

Reference guides to the sources exist across the full range. For the products of what might be called 'parchment literacy' we have Gerhard Podskalsky's excellent 1982 *Handbuch*, on writings from Rus, followed in 2000 by the same scholar's even more voluminous survey of writings from Bulgaria and Serbia. Systematic prosopography based on these sources is, however, patchy. At one extreme, a few prominent individuals have attracted their own modern biographers.[26] At the other extreme lies the only attempt at a comprehensive prosopography covering a substantive segment of the relevant period: the ambitious 1995 book by Jukka Korpela, which includes an annotated catalogue of about 1250 individuals (some 250 of whom are anonymous) mentioned in Rus sources down to 1125.[27] Between the extremes we have the normal range of genres which may be more or less helpful to the prosopographer. There are studies of dynastic relations, including Byzantino-Rus dynastic relations.[28] Political and institutional histories naturally deal with a lot of the most important sources, and on occasion they come close to a prosopographical arrangement. Thus O.M. Rapov's 1977 study of princely land-holdings is organised as a set of mini-biographies (uneven in their reliability),[29] and Martin Dimnik's remarkably detailed volumes on the ruling family of Chernigov are themselves rather like indexed chronicles.[30] A recent biographical dictionary of the dynasty—down to the sixteenth century—is of little practical value to the scholar since it lacks any direct references to sources.[31] V.L. Ianin's monograph on Novgorod governors is excellent in its niche.[32] Of more central interest to the Byzantine (according to a narrower definition) prosopographer is Andrzei Poppe's compilation of data on the metropolitans of Rhosia, published as an Appendix to Podskalsky's guide to

---

[26] See e.g. Obolensky, *Six Byzantine Portraits*; Hurwitz, *Prince Andrej Bogoljubskij*; D.G. Khrustalev, *Razyskaniia o Efreme Pereiaslavskom* (St Petersburg, 2002).

[27] Korpela, *Beiträge zur Bevölkerungsgeschichte und Prosopographie*; for problems with this work, see my review in *The Slavonic and East European Review* 75 (1997), 738–9.

[28] e.g. Alexander Kazhdan, 'Rus'-Byzantine princely marriages in the eleventh and twelfth centuries', *Harvard Ukrainian Studies* 12/13 (1988/9), 414–29.

[29] O.M. Rapov, *Kniazheskie vladeniia na Rusi v X-pervoi polovine XIII v.* (Moscow, 1977).

[30] Martin Dimnik, *The Dynasty of Chernigov 1054–1146* (Toronto, 1994), and the same author's *The Dynasty of Chernigov 1146–1246* (Cambridge, 2003).

[31] I.P. Ermolaev, *Riurikovichi. Biograficheskii slovar'* (Moscow, 2002). Cf., however, the detailed onomastic studies and tables in A.F Litvina and F.B. Uspenskii, *Vybor imeni u russkikh kniazei v X–XVI vv.* (Moscow, 2006).

[32] V.L. Ianin, *Novgorodskie posadniki* (2nd edn., Moscow, 2003).

the sources.[33] Biographical dictionaries of writers and painters vary in their thoroughness, from bare lists to annotated essays.[34]

In short, the Slavonic sources relevant to a prosopography of Byzantium and the crusades are far from being uncharted territory. They raise the kinds of problems of text and interpretation that will be familiar to anybody working with medieval material, and they require the prosopographer to make some decisions about the criteria of relevance, but in most cases fairly decent texts are available and in many cases those texts have already been subjected to a degree—sometimes a high degree—of prosopographical analysis.

# BIBLIOGRAPHY[1]

## HANDBOOKS, SOURCE SURVEYS, PROSOPOGRAPHIES

N.G. Berezhkov, *Khronologiia russkogo letopisaniia (Chronology of the Russian Chronicles)* (Moscow, 1963)
   Not a prosopography, but an essential tool for the prosopographer in sorting out who did what when in the chronicles, especially for the twelfth century.
Simon Franklin, *Writing, Society and Culture in Early Rus, c.950–1300* (Cambridge, 2002)
   Includes (pp. 16–82) survey of Rus written sources, with particular emphasis on the non-literary, non-parchment sources.
I.A. Kochetkov, ed., *Slovar' russkikh ikonopistsev XI–XVII vekov (Dictionary of Russian Icon Painters of the Eleventh to Seventeenth Centuries)* (Moscow, 2003)
   Comprehensive, with bibliographies, although this volume covers a much larger span of time and has no chronological index.
Jukka Korpela, *Beiträge zur Bevölkerungsgeschichte und Prosopographie der Kiever Rus' bis zum Tode von Vladimir Monomah*, Studia Historica Jyväskyläensia 54 (Jyväskylä, 1995)
   Attempt at a comprehensive Rus prosopography to 1125 (pp. 124–249), with over 1250 entries including nearly 230 *anonymi*. Good range of references; some uncritical readings of sources.
D.S. Likhachev, ed., *Slovar' knizhnikov i knizhnosti Drevnei Rusi. Vyp. 1 (XI–pervaia polovina XIV v.) (Dictionary of Early Rus Bookmen and Book Culture. Vol. 1, From the Eleventh to the First Half of the Fourteenth Century* (Leningrad, 1987)
   Reasonable coverage of Rus 'literary' sources; with bibliographies.

---

[33] In Podskalsky, *Christentum und theologische Literatur*, 282–301.
[34] See, especially, on writers: Likhachev, ed., *Slovar' knizhnikov i knizhnosti*; on painters: Kochetkov, ed., *Slovar' russkikh ikonopistsev XI–XVII vekov*.
[1] For the limits of the sources covered by this bibliography see above, pp. 165–7.

A.A. Medyntseva, *Gramotnost' v Drevnei Rusi. Po pamiatnikam epigrafiki X–pervoi poloviny XIII veka (Literacy in Early Rus. The epigraphic sources from the tenth to the first half of the thirteenth century)* (Moscow, 2000)
Both a survey and a corpus of some categories of source. Particularly detailed analyses of types of inscription which are not gathered in separate comprehensive editions (pot-graffiti, spindle whorls and other everyday objects, monumental inscriptions). No index.

Gerhard Podskalsky, *Christentum und theologische Literatur in der kiever Rus' (988–1237)* (Munich, 1982)
Standard comprehensive guide with copious bibliography. Updated version published in Russian: *Khristianstvo i bogoslovskaia literatura v Kievskoi Rusi (988–1237 gg.)* (St Petersburg, 1996).

—— *Theologische Literatur des Mittelalters in Bulgarien und Serbien 865–1459* (Munich, 2000)
Essential handbook. Even more voluminous than the same author's guide to Rus literature.

Ia.N. Shchapov, ed., *Pis'mennye pamiatniki istorii Drevnei Rusi. Letopisi. Povesti. Khozhdeniia. Poucheniia. Zhitiia. Poslaniia (Written Sources for the History of Early Rus: chronicles, tales, pilgrimages, sermons, Lives, epistles )* (St Petersburg, 2003)
Indexed and annotated guide to over 250 sources.

## PRIMARY SOURCES

### Chronicles

*Povest' vremennykh let (The Primary Chronicle)*[2]
Compiled in Kiev in the second decade of the twelfth century, and sometimes attributed to the monk Nestor. Survives only in later chronicle compilations, for which it constitutes a common core. The major narrative source for its period.

*Editions:*
(1) D.S. Likhachev and V.P. Adrianova-Peretts, eds., *Povest' vremennykh let*, 2 vols. (Moscow, Leningrad, 1950; 2nd edn. in one volume, with corrections and additions, St Petersburg, 1996)
Standard edition based on the Laurentian codex. Copious commentaries, thorough indexes; with modern Russian translation.
(2) O.V. Tvorogov, ed., in *Biblioteka literatury Drevnei Rusi (The Library of Early Rus Literature)* 1 (St Petersburg, 1997), 62–315

---

[2] A common cause of confusion arises from a mis-match between the conventional English and Russian titles. Strictly speaking, *Primary Chronicle* translates *Nachal'naia letopis'*, yet in Russian convention this is not in fact the name of the compilation of the 1110s (to which the name is applied in English) but of its main source, an earlier (and largely hypothetical) chronicle from the 1090s. Attempts to interpret the the title *Povest' vremennykh let* are themselves varied: sometimes *Tale of Bygone Years*, sometimes (assuming a slight emendation in the original) *Tale of Times and Years*, most likely (in my view) *Tale of the Years of Time*.

'Popular' edition, but based on the Hypatian codex. With modern Russian translation (facing pages) and commentaries (487–525) but no index.
(3) Donald Ostrowski, ed., *The 'Povĕst' vremennykh lĕt': an interlinear collation and paradosis*, 3 vols. (Cambridge, Mass., 2003)
Phrase by phrase, with all main variant versions.

*Translations:*
(1) Reinhold Trautmann, *Die altrussische Nestorchronik*, Slavisch-Baltische Quellen und Forschungen 6 (Leipzig, 1931)
(2) Samuel Hazard Cross and Olgerd P. Sherbowitz-Wetzor, *The Russian Primary Chronicle. Laurentian text* (3rd printing; Cambridge, Mass., 1973)
Useful English introduction, detailed commentaries and name index, though the translation itself is not fully reliable.

*Secondary Literature:*
D.S. Likhachov (Likhachev), *The Great Heritage. The classical literature of Old Rus* (Moscow, 1981), 44–135
Based on the introduction to the Likhachev/Adrianova-Peretts edition; very stilted translation from Russian, and now somewhat outmoded, but still the broadest substantial survey of the chronicle in English.
Donald Ostrowski, 'Principles of editing the *Povest' vremennykh let'*, *Palaeoslavica* 7 (1999), 5–25
Problems of presenting or determining the text.

*Ipat'evskaia letopis' (Hypatian Chronicle)*
Compilation which includes a version of the *Primary Chronicle* to 1117, followed by an ample Kiev-based chronicle to 1198, and then a Galician and Volynian chronicle to 1292.

*Edition:*
*Polnoe sobranie russkikh letopisei (Complete Collection of Russian Chronicles)* 2 (St Petersburg, 1908; repr. with new introduction and with added full name index, Moscow, 1998)
A.A. Shakhmatov's standard text, with apparatus.

*Translations:*
(1) George A. Perfecky, *The Hypatian Codex II: the Galician-Volynian chronicle. An annotated translation*, Harvard Series in Ukrainian Studies 16.2 (Munich, 1973)
From 1201 only. Name index. There is no English translation of the twelfth-century Kievan chronicle.
(2) Leonid Makhnovets', *Litopys rus'kyi* (Kiev, 1989)
Ukrainian translation of the entire compilation. Useful mainly for the extensively annotated name index (467–520) with far more thorough biographical notes than the indexes to the main editions either of the *Hypatian Chronicle* as such, or of the *Primary Chronicle*.

*Lavrent'evskaia letopis' (Laurentian Chronicle)*
Compilation which includes a version of the *Primary Chronicle*, followed by a somewhat more laconic Suzdal-based chronicle. Named after the scribe of its earliest manuscript dated 1377.

*Edition:*
*Polnoe sobranie russkikh letopisei (Complete Collection of Russian Chronicles)* 1
(Leningrad, 1926; repr. with new introduction, Moscow, 1997)
Standard text, with apparatus and indexes.

*Novgorodskaia pervaia letopis' (Novgorod First Chronicle)*
Mainly about Novgorod, though one of its sources was a Kievan compilation which
pre-dates the *Primary Chronicle*. Maintained under the supervision of Novgorod
bishops and archbishops. Includes an account of the fall of Constantinople in 1204
(see *Tale of the Taking of Tsargrad*)

*Edition:*
A.N. Nasonov, ed., *Novgorodskaia pervaia letopis' starshego i mladshego izvodov (The
Novgorod First Chronicle: the older and younger recensions)* (Moscow, Leningrad,
1950; repr. Riazan, 2001)
Standard edition, very thorough indexes.

*Translations:*
(1) Robert Mitchell and Neville Forbes, *The Chronicle of Novgorod 1016–1471*,
Camden Third Series 25 (London, 1914)
From the St Petersburg edition of 1888 based on the 'Older' recension but with
substantial passages from the 'Younger' recension (the 1950 edition prints the two
versions separately). Introductory articles on history (by C. Raymond Beazeley)
and the text (by A.A. Shakhmatov). Index.
(2) Joachim Dietze, *Die erste Novgoroder Chronik nach ihrer ältesten Redaktion
(Synodalhandschrift) 1016–1333/1352* (Munich, 1971)
Also reproduces the original text from Nasonov's edition, plus facsimile of the
manuscript from Savvaitov's edition of 1875. Introduction in German and English
(7–47). Full index (597–630). See review by Ludolf Müller in *Russia Mediaevalis* 2
(1975), 178–87.

*Secondary Literature:*
A.A. Gippius, 'K istorii slozheniia teksta Novgorodskoi pervoi letopisi' ('On the
history of the composition of the text of the Novgorod First Chronicle'),
*Novgorodskii istoricheskii sbornik* 6 (16) (1997), 3–72

## Epigraphic Sources

*Birch-bark Documents*
Regular discoveries in annual excavations, mainly in Novgorod, since first finds in
1951. Urban ephemera: debt-lists, domestic letters, business and commerce, juvenilia,
some literary fragments, etc.

*Editions:*
(1) A.V. Artsikhovskii *et al.*, eds. (since 1986 V.L. Ianin and A.A. Zalizniak; since 2004
plus A.A. Gippius), *Novgorodskie gramoty na bereste (Novgorod Documents on
Birch-Bark)* (Moscow, 1953–)
Eleven volumes to 2004. New finds are usually published annually in the journal
*Voprosy iazykoznaniia (Questions of Linguistics)*, then gathered every few years

into this series. Detailed commentaries, indexes, modern Russian translations. Also includes finds from Staraia Russa.

(2) A.A. Zalizniak, *Drevnenovgorodskii dialekt (The Early Novgorod Dialect)* (2nd edn., Moscow, 2004)

More convenient than (1) for some purposes, since a substantial part of the volume consists of publication of the documents in chronological groups.

*Secondary Literature:*

V.L. Ianin, *Ia poslal tebe berestu . . . (I Sent You a Birch-Bark . . .)* (3rd edn., Moscow, 1998)

## Bulgarian Slavonic Inscriptions

*Edition:*

Kazimir Popkonstantinov and Otto Kronsteiner, eds., *Altbulgarische Inschriften* 1, Die Slawischen Sprachen 34 (Salzburg, 1994)

Fullest collected edition. With German translations. The inscriptions in the second volume (1997) are all from a later period, with the exception of a ring and a seal of Tsar Kaloian (1197–1207) and a couple of other minor pieces.

## Colophons and Marginalia

Rare prosopographical source with first-person information.

*Edition:*

L.V. Stoliarova, *Svod zapisei pistsov, khudozhnikov i perepletchikov drevnerusskikh pergamennykh kodeksov XI–XIV vekov (Corpus of Annotations by Scribes, Artists and Binders of Rus Parchment Manuscripts, Eleventh–Fourteenth Centuries)* (Moscow, 2000)

In chronological sequence. Detailed annotation and commentary. Indexed.

## Graffiti

Quite large numbers from Rus churches. Mostly unidentifiable names and *anonymi*, but some inscriptions of prosopographical substance. Occasional Greek graffiti.

*Editions:*

(1) A.A. Medyntseva, *Drevnerusskie nadpisi Novgorodskogo Sofiiskogo sobora (Early Rus Inscriptions from St Sophia Cathedral in Novgorod)* (Moscow, 1978)

Several from old copies. Thorough linguistic analyses and index.

(2) S.A. Vysotskii, *Drevnerusskie nadpisi Sofii Kievskoi XI–XIV vv. (Early Rus Inscriptions of the Eleventh to Fourteenth Centuries from St Sophia in Kiev)* (Kiev, 1966)

—— *Srednevekovye nadpisi Sofii Kievskoi (po materialam XI–XVII vv.) (Medieval Inscriptions from St Sophia in Kiev: Eleventh- to Seventeenth-century Sources)* (Kiev, 1976)

—— *Kievskie graffiti X–XVII vv. (Kievan Graffiti of the Tenth to Seventeenth Centuries)* (Kiev, 1985)

A loosely linked trilogy by the pioneer of Early Rus graffito studies. Valuable corpus, but readings not always reliable and interpretation often speculative. Good reproductions, so the readings can be checked.

*Seals*

Seals of metropolitans of Rhosia in Greek; seals of princes (to *c.*1100) and bishops (to *c.*1150 also often in Greek, but subsequently in Slavonic.

*Edition:*

V.L. Ianin, *Aktovye pechati Drevnei Rusi X–XV vv. Tom l. Pechati X–nachala XIII v. (Early Rus Seals of the Tenth to Fifteenth Centuries. Vol. 1, Seals of the Tenth to Early Thirteenth Centuries)* (Moscow, 1970)

V.L. Ianin and P.G. Gaidukov, *Aktovye pechati Drevnei Rusi X–XV vv. Tom III. Pechati, zaregistrirovannye v 1970–1996 gg. (Early Rus Seals of the Tenth to Fifteenth Centuries. Vol. 3, Seals Recorded 1970–1996)* (Moscow, 1998)
Standard edition, extensive prosopographical commentaries and indexes.

## Hagiography

### Domentijan, *Life of Sava*

The only substantial biography of this key figure in Serbian literature and monasticism. Written *c.*1242–52 (hypotheses vary), a decade or two after Sava's death.

*Edition:*

Dj. Daničić, ed., *Život sv. Simeuna i sv. Save (Life of St Simeon and St Sava)* (Belgrade, 1865), 118–345

*Secondary Literature:*

Dimitri Obolensky, *Six Byzantine Portraits* (Oxford, 1988), 115–72

### Domentijan, *Life of Simeon* (=Stefan Nemanja)

Mid-thirteenth century; of little independent value.

*Edition:*

Dj. Daničić, ed., *Život sv. Simeuna i sv. Save (Life of St Simeon and St Sava)* (Belgrade, 1865), 12–117

### Efrem, *Zhitie Avraamiia Smolenskogo (Life of Avraamii of Smolensk)*

Probably mid-thirteenth-century account of controversial monk *c.*1150–1220. Prosopographically fairly thin.

*Editions:*

(1) S.P. Rozanov, *Zhitiia prepodobnogo Avraamiia Smolenskogo i sluzhby emu (Lives and Offices for the Venerable Avraamii of Smolensk)*, Pamiatniki drevnerusskoi literatury 1 (St Petersburg, 1912); repr. as *Die altrussischen hagiographischen Erzählungen und liturgischen Dichtungen über den Heiligen Avraamij von Smolensk*, Slavische Propyläen 15 (Munich, 1970)
Standard edition; introduction; index.

(2) *Biblioteka literatury Drevnei Rusi (Library of Early Rus Literature)* 5 (St Petersburg, 1997), 30–65
Edited by D.M. Bulanin; with parallel modern Russian translation.

*Translation:*
Paul Hollingsworth, *The Hagiography of Kievan Rus'*, Harvard Library of Early
Ukrainian Literature. English Translations 2 (Cambridge, Mass., 1992), 135–63
Index as part of general index for book. Introduction (lxix–lxxx).

*Kievo-pecherskii paterik (The Paterikon of the Kiev Caves Monastery)*
Compiled in the mid-1220s in the form of a correspondence between Simon, bishop
of Suzdal, and Polikarp, a monk of the Caves. Stories of prominent monks from the
mid-eleventh century onwards.

*Editions:*
(1) D. Abramovych, *Kyevo-pechers'kyi pateryk* (Kiev, 1930); repr. as *Das Paterikon des
kiever Höhlenklosters* (Munich, 1964)
With apparatus, brief notes, and index. From the 'Second Cassian' redaction of
1462: the fullest, but not the closest to the earliest. This redaction is also used for the
more accessible (but unindexed) text (with facing modern Russian translation) in
*Biblioteka literatury Drevnei Rusi (Library of Early Rus Literature)* 5 (St
Petersburg, 1997), 296–489
(2) L.A. Ol'shevskaia and S.N. Travnikov, *Drevnerusskie pateriki (Early Rus Paterika)*
(Moscow, 1999), 7–80
A version much closer to the 'basic' redaction. Also the most up-to-date textual
analysis (253–315), apparatus (351–83), commentary (386–424) and index, plus
modern Russian translation (109–85).

*Translations:*
(1) Dietrich Freydank, Gottfried Sturm, eds., *Das Väterbuch des Kiewer
Hohlenklosters* (Graz, 1989)
From Abramovych's text; tr. by Waldtraut Förster *et al.*
(2) Muriel Heppell, *The Paterik of the Kievan Caves Monastery*, Harvard Library of
Early Ukrainian Literature. English Translations 1 (Cambridge, Mass., 1989)
Based on Abramovych's edition. Introduction, bibliography, index.

Nestor, *Chtenie o sviatykh muchenikakh Borise i Glebe (Lesson on the Holy
Martyrs Boris and Gleb)*
The princes Boris and Gleb were murdered in 1015, but Nestor's *Lesson* includes an
account of early veneration and the origins of the cult, and hence is of some interest
for the period after 1025.

*Edition:*
D.I. Abramovich, *Zhitiia sviatykh muchenikov Borisa i Gleba i sluzhby im (Lives of the
Holy Martyrs Boris and Gleb, and Offices for them)* (Petrograd, 1916); repr. with
an introduction by Ludolf Müller as *Die altrussischen hagiographischen
Erzählungen und liturgischen Dichtungen über die heilige Boris und Gleb*, Slavische
Propyläen 14 (Munich, 1967)
The standard collection of works about Boris and Gleb. Index.

*Translation:*
Paul Hollingsworth, *The Hagiography of Kievan Rus'*, Harvard Library of Early
Ukrainian Literature. English Translations 2 (Cambridge, Mass., 1992), 3–32
Index as part of general index for book. Introduction (lxix–lxxx).

Nestor, *Zhitie Feodosiia Pecherskogo (Life of Feodosii of the Caves)*
Extensive account of Feodosii (d. 1074) by a near-contemporary. Some narrative about Feodosii's secular—as well as monastic—contemporaries.

*Edition:*
*Biblioteka literatury Drevnei Rusi (Library of Early Rus Literature)* 1 (St Petersburg, 1997), 252–433
Edited by O.V. Tvorogov; with parallel modern Russian translation; no index.

*Translation:*
Hollingsworth, *The Hagiography of Kievan Rus'*, 32–97
Index as part of general index for book. Introduction (lviii–lxviii).

*Secondary Literature:*
Gail Lenhoff, *The Martyred Princes Boris and Gleb: a socio-cultural study of the cult and the texts* (Columbus, Ohio, 1989)

Sava (Rastko), *Life of Simeon* (=Stefan Nemanja)
Life of Sava's father Stefan Nemanja (monastic name—Simeon), in the typikon of the Studenica monastery. Probably written *c.*1208.

*Edition:*
Vladimir Ćorović, ed., *Spisi sv. Save*, Zbornik za istoriju, jezik i književnost srpskog naroda, prvo odeljenje, spomenici na srpskom jeziku 17 (Belgrade, 1928), 151–5
Brief introduction and index.

*Translations:*
(1) Stanislaus Hafner, *Serbisches Mittelalter. Altserbische Herrscherbiographien. Band 1: Stefan Nemanja nach den Viten des hl. Sava und Stefans des Erstgekrönten*, Slavische Geschichtsschreiber 2 (Graz, Vienna, Cologne, 1962), 27–61, 131–47
Introduction, index, notes.
(2) Marvin Kantor, *Medieval Slavic Lives of Saints and Princes* (Ann Arbor, 1983), 255–304
Notes; no index. Facing photocopy of manuscript.

*Skazanie chudes sviatoiu strastoterptsu Khristovu Romana i Davida (Tale of the Miracles of the Holy Passion-Sufferers of Christ Roman and David)*
Roman and David are the secular names of Boris and Gleb (see under Nestor). The *Tale* is a compilation of the early twelfth century, appended to an anonymous account of the saints' murder in 1015.

*Edition:*
D.I. Abramovich, *Zhitiia sviatykh muchenikov Borisa i Gleba i sluzhby im (Lives of the Holy Martyrs Boris and Gleb, and Offices for them)* (Petrograd, 1916); repr. with an introduction by Ludolf Müller as *Die altrussischen hagiographischen Erzählungen und liturgischen Dichtungen über die heilige Boris und Gleb*, Slavische Propyläen 14 (Munich, 1967), 52–66

*Translation:*
Hollingsworth, *The Hagiography of Kievan Rus'*, 117–34

Stefan Nemanjic (Stefan the First-crowned), *Life of Simeon* (= Stefan
Nemanja)
Written *c.*1218, independently of Sava's earlier biography, and closer to contemporary
Byzantine hagiographical norms.

*Edition:*
Vladimir Ćorović, ed., 'Žitije Simeona Nemanje od Stevana Prvovenčanoga' ('Life of
   Simeon Nemanja by Stefan the First-Crowned'), *Svetosavski sbornik* 2 (Belgrade,
   1939), 1–76
   With introduction and name index.

*Translation:*
Stanislaus Hafner, *Serbisches Mittelalter. Altserbische Herrscherbiographien. Band 1:
   Stefan Nemanja nach den Viten des hl. Sava und Stefans des Erstgekrönten*,
   Slavische Geschichtsschreiber 2 (Graz, Vienna, Cologne, 1962), 65–129, 149–70
   Introduction, index, notes.

*Zhitie Leontiia Rostovskogo (Life of Leontii of Rostov)*
Brief account of late eleventh-century martyred bishop, perhaps from
Constantinople.

*Edition:*
G.V. Semenchenko, 'Drevneishie redaktsii zhitiia Leontiia Rostovskogo' ('The earliest
   redactions of the *Life of Leontii of Rostov*'), *Trudy Otdela drevnerusskoi literatury*
   42 (1989), 241–54


**Travel and Pilgrimage**

Antonii of Novgorod (Dobrynia Iadreikovich), *Kniga Palomnik (Pilgrim
Book)*
Visit to Constantinople in 1200 by a future archbishop of Novgorod (1212–20;
1225–8). A valuable description of the sites and relics of Constantinople on the eve
of the Fourth Crusade.

*Edition:*
Kh.M. Loparev, ed., 'Kniga palomnik. Skazaniie mest sviatykh vo Tsaregrade
   Antoniia arkhiepiskopa Novgorodskogo v 1200 godu' ('Pilgrim Book. An account
   of the Holy Places in Tsargrad in 1200, by Antonii, archbishop of Novgorod'),
   *Pravoslavnyi Palestinskii sbornik* 51 (1899)
   Still the standard edition. Substantial introductory study.

*Translation:*
(1) B. de Khitrowo, *Itinéraires russes en Orient* (Geneva, 1889), 85–111
   From an earlier edition than that of Loparev (by Savvaitov), based on one manuscript.
(2) Marcelle Ehrhard, 'Le livre du pèlerin d'Antoine de Novgorod', *Romania* 58
   (1932), 44–65
   Based on Loparev's edition.

*Secondary Literature:*
(1) Klaus Dieter. Seemann, *Die altrussische Wallfahrtsliteratur* (Munich, 1976), 213–21
(2) George Majeska, 'Russian pilgrims in Constantinople', *DOP* 56 (2002), 93–108

Daniil, hegumen, *Khozhdenie (Journey)*
Pilgrimage to the Holy Land *c.*1105–8, notable for its cordial attitude to King Baldwin I of Jerusalem.

*Edition:*
(1) M.V. Venevitinov, *Zhitie i khozhdenie Daniila, russkoi zemli igumena, 1106–1108 gg. (The Life and Journey of Daniil, Abbot of the Rus Land, 1106–1108* (St Petersburg, 1883–5); repr. as *Abt Daniil. Wallfahrtsbericht*, introd. by Klaus Dieter Seemann (Munich, 1970)
Very detailed indexes. Seemann's introduction to the 1970 reprint is substantial.
(2) *Biblioteka literatury Drevnei Rusi (Library of Early Rus Literature)* 4 (St Petersburg, 1997), 26–117
Edited by G.M. Prokhorov, with modern Russian translation (facing pages) and commentaries (584–99), but no index.

*Translations:*
(1) B. de Khitrowo, *Itinéraires russes en Orient* (Geneva, 1889), 3–83
(2) C.W. Wilson, *The Pilgrimage of the Russian Abbot Daniel in the Holy Land 1106–1107 A.D.*, Library of the Palestine Pilgrims' Text Society 4.3 (London, 1895)
Annotated, with appendices, no index. Based on Khitrowo's French version.

*Povest' o vziatii Tsar'grada friagami (Tale of the Capture of Tsargrad by the Franks)*
Account of the capture of Constantinople in 1204, preserved in the *Novgorod First Chronicle*. Clearly derived from an eye-witness report.

*Editions:*
(1) Sylvain Patri, 'La relation russe de la quatrième croisade', *Byz* 58 (1988), 461–501
Critical edition with textual introduction, commentaries and parallel French translation.
(2) *Biblioteka literatury Drevnei Rusi (Library of Early Rus Literature)* 5 (St Petersburg, 1997), 66–73
With parallel modern Russian translation. Brief commentaries (460–1).

*Translation:*
Jared Gordon, 'The Novgorod Account of the Fourth Crusade', *Byz* 43 (1973 [publ. 1974]), 297–311
English version 306–11 (Russian and French versions listed under 'Editions' above); cf. also the English version embedded in Mitchell and Forbes' translation of the *Novgorod First Chronicle*.

**Translations** (works originally in Greek but surviving only in Slavonic)

Alexios Stoudites, *Typikon*
Written in 1034 for Alexios's Monastery of the Dormition. Translated and adopted by Feodosii (d. 1074) for the Monastery of the Caves in Kiev, and hence a significant text for early Rus cenobitic monasticism.

*Edition:*
A.M. Pentkovskii, ed., *Tipikon patriarkha Aleksiia Studita v Vizantii i na Rusi (The Typikon of Patriarch Alexios Stoudites in Byzantium and Rus)* (Moscow, 2001)
The only complete edition (pp. 233–420); based on the fullest of the early manuscripts. Also a substantial introductory study (pp. 5–228), with a summary in English (pp. 423–8). No general index.

*Translation:*
D.M. Petras, *The Typicon of the Patriarch Alexis the Studite: Novgorod-St Sophia 1136* (Cleveland, 1991)
Annotated English translation of the liturgical prescriptions only, from an early but incomplete manuscript.

*Secondary Literature:*
Claire Farrimond, 'Tradition and originality in early Russian monasticism: the application of the Stoudite Rule at the Kievan Caves Monastery', unpublished Ph.D. Thesis (Cambridge, 2000)

Loukas Chrysoberges, patriarch, *Letter to Prince Andrei Bogoliubskii*
Late 1160s; refusing a request to establish a metropolitan see at Vladimir-on-the-Kliazma, and setting out some organisational principles for the hierarchy in Rus.

*Editions:*
(1) *Polnoe sobranie russkikh letopisei (Complete Collection of Russian Chronicles)* 9 (St Petersburg, 1862; repr.; Moscow, 1965), 223–9
The 'Nikon Chronicle'; late and not fully reliable.
(2) Makarii, metropolitan, *Istoriia russkoi tserkvi (History of the Russian Church)*, 3rd edn., vol. 3 (St Petersburg, 1888; repr. Düsseldorf, The Hague, 1968), 298–300
No critical apparatus.

*Translation:*
Ellen S. Hurwitz, *Prince Andrej Bogoljubskij: the man and the myth*, (Florence, 1980), 29–32
Extracts only.

*Secondary Literature:*
N.N. Voronin, 'Andrei Bogoliubskii i Luka Khrisoverg' ('Andrei Bogoliubskii and Loukas Chrysoberges'), *VV* 21 (1962), 29–50
Simon Franklin, 'Diplomacy and Ideology: Byzantium and the Russian church in the mid twelfth century', in Franklin, *Byzantium—Rus—Russia. Studies in the translation of Christian culture* (Aldershot, 2002), no. VIII

## Nicholas Mouzalon, patriarch of Constantinople, *Letter to Nifon of Novgorod*

A very short text, *c.*1147, supporting the bishop of Novgorod in his opposition to the Rus bishops' appointment of a local man as metropolitan of Rhosia without Byzantine participation.

*Edition:*

Makarii, metropolitan, *Istoriia russkoi tserkvi (History of the Russian Church)*, 3rd edn., vol. 3 (St Petersburg, 1888; repr. Düsseldorf, The Hague, 1968), 297
    No critical edition.

*Translation:*

Muriel Heppell, *The Paterik of the Kievan Caves Monastery*, Harvard Library of Early Ukrainian Literature, English Translations 1 (Cambridge, Mass., 1989), 223

*Secondary Literature:*

F.B. Poljakov, 'Zur Authentizität des Briefes vom Patriarchen Nikolaos IV. Muzalon an der Novgoroder Erzbischof Nifont', *Die Welt der Slawen* n.s. 12 (1988), 283–302

## Nikifor (=Nikephoros), metropolitan of Rhosia, *Letters,* etc.

Nikifor was metropolitan from 1104 until his death in 1121. His reasonably attributable writings consist of a homily for Quinquagesima, a Lenten epistle to Prince Vladimir Monomakh (prince of Kiev 1113–25) about the duties of a prince, another letter to the same prince warning against 'Latins', and another letter on the same subject to Prince Iaroslav Sviatopolkovich (prince of Vladimir-in-Volynia 1100–18).

*Editions:*

(1) Makarii, metropolitan, *Istoriia russkoi tserkvi (History of the Russian Church)*, 3rd edn., vol. 2 (St Petersburg, 1889; repr. Düsseldorf, The Hague, 1968), 349–52
    The homily for Quinquagesima.

(2) Albrecht Dölker, *Der Fastenbrief des Metropoliten Nikifor an den Fürsten Vladimir Monomach*, Skripten des slavischen Seminars der Universität Tübingen 25 (Tübingen, 1985)
    The Lenten epistle with variants from three manuscripts, plus German translation, linguistic notes and detailed commentary.

(3) N.V. Ponyrko, ed., *Epistoliarnoe nasledie Drevnei Rusi XI–XIII. Issledovaniia, teksty, perevody (The Epistolary Heritage of Early Rus, 11–13 c. Studies, texts, translations)* (St Petersburg, 1992), 59–93
    Standard edition of the three epistles, with variants from all manuscripts, brief commentaries, and translations into modern Russian.

# 9

# Georgian Sources

## STEPHEN H. RAPP Jr.

For [the Georgian monarch] made the sultan tributary to himself and the king of the Greeks like a member of his household; he overthrew the heathen, destroyed the barbarians, and made subjects of kings and slaves of rulers. The Arabs he put to flight, the Ishmaelites he plundered, and the Persians he ground to dust; their leaders he reduced to peasants. I shall explain succinctly: those who earlier were kings, judges, giants, heroes, long since renowned, valiant and strong, famous for various deeds—all these he so subjected that they were like animals by comparison.[1]

THE EVICTION OF THE MUSLIMS, the annihilation of the 'barbarians', the pacification of the Seljuk sultan and the Byzantine emperor: such is the bold assessment of Georgia's condition in the time of the crusades by the biographer of the Georgian King Davit' II (r. 1089–1125).[2] Though the anonymous twelfth-century writer has exaggerated Davit''s unprecedented accomplishments, under his patron the Georgian monarchy experienced its 'golden age', a period dominated by the establishment of a pan-Caucasian empire by the Georgian Bagratid house to which Davit' belonged.[3]

The contemporary relationship of Georgia and Byzantium was far more complicated than our passage suggests. Taken as a whole, Davit''s royal biography—and other contemporary Georgian sources—reflects the intensification of Georgia's connections to the Byzantine commonwealth, though it was and thereafter remained on the far eastern edge of that world.[4] The

---

[1] *The Life of Davit' II*, ch. 77, p. 206.10–18 Shanidze, 351–2 Qaukhch'ishvili, 342–3 tr. Thomson. For a less inflated perspective on the achievements under Davit''s great granddaughter T'amar, see *The Life of T'amar*, 123.20–124.5 Qaukhch'ishvili, 63–4 tr. Vivian. Full details of featured literature are supplied in the bibliography.

[2] For an overview of the connection of Georgia and the crusades, see Avalishvili, *Jvarosant'a droidan*.

[3] The Georgian Bagratids (Geo. Bagratuniani, Bagratoni) were a branch of the larger Bagratid (Arm. Bagratuni) family originating in the Armenian districts of southern Caucasia. For their early history, see Toumanoff, *Studies*.

[4] For the idea of commonwealth in this context, see Dimitri Obolensky, *The Byzantine Commonwealth: eastern Europe 500–1453* (New York and Washington, DC, 1971); and Garth Fowden, *Empire to Commonwealth: consequences of monotheism in late antiquity* (Princeton, 1993).

*Proceedings of the British Academy* **132**, 183–220. © The British Academy 2007.

alleged reduction of the emperor to a 'member of [Davit''s] household' represents the Georgians' own perception of their relationship to Byzantium. Georgia's vital contribution to—and not mere absorption into or passive membership of—the commonwealth signals that the Bagratid monarchs regarded their kingdom neither as subservient to Constantinople nor as some passive and peripheral member of the commonwealth.

Christian Georgia has traditionally been investigated as an extension of Byzantium. Though such an approach is not without its merits, Georgia was in many respects an unusual component of the commonwealth. The Georgian language belongs to an entirely different linguistic family from Greek, Slavic, Syriac, or Armenian. It is neither Indo-European nor Semitic; rather, it is the chief member of the southern Caucasian or K'art'velian (*k'art'veluri*) group. More significantly, Georgian social structure had more in common with the pre-Islamic Iranian world than the Byzantine. It was, of course, Georgia's Christian affiliation that enabled its attachment to the Byzantine *oikoumene*. Though later Bagratid-era traditions—appropriated from ones developed in Byzantium—credit the apostle Andrew and his companion Simon 'the Canaanite' with the introduction of Christianity to the Georgian lands,[5] the full-scale Christianisation of the Georgian territories commenced with the fourth-century conversion of Mirian III, king of the eastern Georgian district of K'art'li (Gk. Iberia). Significantly, this initial surge of Christianisation emanated from Syria, Palestine, Armenia, and eastern Anatolia, including Cappadocia. As I have argued elsewhere, we must be mindful not to inflate Christian Georgia's bonds to Byzantium, especially before the Bagratid 'golden age' of the eleventh to thirteenth century.[6] Although Mirian's fourth-century conversion had made possible an association with the Byzantine empire, close relations began to materialise only in the age of Herakleios,[7] and direct connections with Byzantium became an essential part of Georgian self-identity only under Bagratid rule, especially from the ninth and tenth century. In fact, prior to the consolidation of Bagratid power, the primary cultural and social orientation of eastern Georgia had not been to the west, towards Constantinople and everything it represented, but rather to the south, towards the Near Eastern world dominated by Iran.

---

[5] e.g. Francis Dvornik, *The Idea of Apostolicity in Byzantium and the Legend of the Apostle Andrew* (Cambridge, Mass., 1958), and Tamarati, *L'Église géorgienne*, 120–33. Cf. Vakhtang Licheli, 'St Andrew in Samtskhe—archaeological proof?', in T'amila Mgaloblishvili, ed., *Ancient Christianity in the Caucasus*, Iberica Caucasica 1 (Surrey, 1998), 25–37.

[6] e.g. Rapp, 'From *bumberazi* to *basileus*'.

[7] For the period, see Margit Bíró, 'Georgian sources on the Caucasian campaign of Heracleios', *Acta Orientalia Academiae Scientiarum Hungaricae* 35.1 (1981), 121–32.

The ancient Iranian heritage of Georgia and the whole of Caucasia resonates loudly in the earliest written Georgian historical sources which were composed in the initial years of the ninth century.[8] Significantly, Mirian's acceptance of the Christian God did not fundamentally alter this orientation and legacy. Even as the ninth century dawned, when the Bagratids first seized power in Georgia, local (Christian) writers unambiguously set their history within a Near Eastern matrix. Georgian society continued to be dominated by powerful aristocratic houses and their estates, a structure prevalent throughout the greater Iranian world and, as it had previously, local kingship was conceived and described in terms which shared a great deal with the Sasanid concept of the hero-king. This helps to explain why the twelfth-century biographer of the 'Byzantinising' monarch Davitʿ II would say in the passage quoted above that the heroes of old, i.e. the pre-Bagratid king-heroes, were 'like animals by comparison'. Early Bagratid attitudes toward this Iranian orientation and imagery are, regrettably, largely unknown. But when the Georgian Bagratids began to sponsor the writing of history in the eleventh century, their historians intentionally situated the Georgian experience within the framework of the Byzantine commonwealth and eastern Christendom. In other words, Bagratid historians, like their royal sponsors, deliberately substituted for Georgia's old southern orientation one that looked westward to Constantinople. This not only reflected the reality of unprecedented Georgian–Byzantine relations, especially through the conduit of the Georgian south-western districts and the growing presence of Georgian monks in Byzantine monasteries, but also the Bagratids' appropriation of select aspects of Byzantine power, culture, and society. Though Georgia always remained on the sidelines of the crusades, the vigour and zealousness of the crusaders also affected the Bagratids' emphasis of their Christian affiliation and the desirable connection of their realm and church to Christian Byzantium.

This background is essential for any investigation of the Georgian-language sources produced between the death of Basil II in 1025 and the sacking of Constantinople during the Fourth Crusade in 1204. This period overlaps almost exactly with the political apogee of the medieval Georgian monarchy. It was, among other things, a time of unprecedented literary output in terms of both translated and original Georgian literature. Though a Georgian script had been invented by Christians back in the early fifth century[9] and the first original Georgian literary works had been composed

---

[8] Rapp, 'From *bumberazi* to *basileus*', 'Imagining history at the crossroads' and *Studies in Medieval Georgian Historiography*.

[9] In English, see e.g. Thomas V. Gamkrelidze (Gamqrelidze), *Alphabetic Writing and the Old Georgian Script: a typology and provenience of alphabetic writing systems* (Delmar, NY, 1994).

about a hundred years later, precious few pre-Bagratid manuscripts have survived. Extant pre-Bagratid texts tend to be preserved in considerably later Bagratid-era copies. This circumstance, coupled with the Bagratid domination of the Georgian political scene for a millennium, has resulted in much of Georgian history and historiography having been projected through a Bagratid lens, a phenomenon which commenced in Bagratid times and has continued down to the present day. And since the Bagratids consciously linked themselves to Byzantine culture and society, their historiography has a pronounced Byzantine flavour.

Because Byzantinists as a whole are rather unfamiliar with sources written in Georgian, these are the primary focus here. Documents produced by and for Georgians in other languages, especially Greek (for instance, the various Greek texts from the Iveron monastery), have been excluded. First, the contemporary narrative historical sources and comment on their utility for prosopographical data will be described. A synopsis of other relevant contemporary Georgian-language sources follows, including hagiography, other varieties of ecclesiastical literature, colophons, charters and deeds, art, inscriptions, and graffiti. Finally, I shall briefly comment on the current state of historical scholarship in Georgian and specifically those scholarly researches which would be of primary interest to prosopographers.

## NARRATIVE HISTORICAL SOURCES

**Texts**

Though the Bagratids first seized power in the Georgian lands with the accession of Ashot I to the office of presiding prince in 813,[10] and although Ashot's kinsman Adarnase resuscitated Georgian royal authority in 888, the Georgian Bagratids did not immediately seek to commemorate their unprecedented accomplishments in writing. The oldest known Bagratid-era history

---

[10] Ashot's were not the first Bagratids to acquire a foothold in Georgia. An earlier presence in the eastern Georgian region of K'art'li has been traced to the second century BC. These Bagratids established themselves at Odzrq'e (mod. Odzrkhe) and flourished until the fifth century: Toumanoff, *Studies*, 202 and 316–17, for his association of these Bagratids with the *erist'avate* of Odzrq'e mentioned in pre-Bagratid texts, i.e. *The Life of the Kings*, 47 Qaukhch'ishvili and *The Life of Vakhtang*, 156, 185, and 189 Qaukhch'ishvili. Toumanoff equates these Bivritianis with Bagratids. However, it should be emphasised that neither text explicitly identifies them as one and the same, and it is not certain that either author understood the Bivritianis to be a branch of the larger Bagratid clan.

was produced in the eleventh century, less than two decades after King Bagrat III's creation of the first politically integrated Georgian enterprise in 1008.[11]

Written historical narratives are the single most important variety of Georgian source for prosopographical data. For the period from 1025 to 1204, Bagratid historiography underwent two distinct phases: first, long-view narratives commemorating the origin and early history of the Georgian Bagratid house; and second, royal biographies, each featuring a particular Bagratid monarch.

Adhering to a pattern established centuries before in the pre-Bagratid age, early Bagratid historians considered their works to be expressions, extensions, and justifications of royal authority. As a result, while these sources are exceptionally rich for the prosopography of the Georgian Bagratid family, they supply rather limited information about non-royal figures and even less about non-Georgians and non-élites. The anonymous, early-Bagratid text entitled *The Chronicle of K'art'li* is unique among extant Bagratid narrative histories in so far as it incorporates substantial information about local rulers who governed just before the rise of Bagratid power in Georgia. *The Chronicle of K'art'li*'s chief purpose is to describe the rule of the presiding princes and then kings of eastern and western Georgia (Ap'khazet'i; Rus. Abkhazia; Gk. Abasgia) from the 780s down to the death of Bagrat IV in 1072. It addresses, *inter alia*, the build-up to the eleventh-century political unification of Georgia by showing the burgeoning interaction and integration among the various Georgian peoples and regions. The text supplies limited prosopographical information for figures in the Byzantine empire, most noteworthy for emperors from Basil II (r. 976–1025) to Constantine IX Monomachos (r. 1042–55); for Maria 'of Alania' (a Georgian princess having an Alanian, or Ovsian, bloodline);[12] as well as for the rebellion of the two Nikephoroi in 1022 and several unnamed *mandatores* and *katepans*.[13] *The*

---

[11] It should be stressed that Georgian historiography was not invented under the Bagratid regime; rather its genesis belongs to the period c. 790–c. 800, if not earlier: Rapp, *Studies in Medieval Georgian Historiography*. In addition, with one exception, surviving medieval Georgian histories were written by and/or in support of the crown. Cf. the historical literature of neighbouring Armenia which was produced with the sponsorship of various aristocratic houses.

[12] Garland and Rapp, 'Mary "of Alania": woman and empress between two worlds'.

[13] Including Byzantine officials of the so-called 'theme of Iberia'. 'Iberia' here corresponds not to the eastern Georgian district of K'art'li but rather was used in this period for the Chalcedonian inhabitants of Caucasia. For the Iberian theme, see the publications of Viada Arutiunova-Fidanian, including her *Armiano-vizantiiskaia kontaktnaia zona (X–XI vv.): rezul'- taty vzaimodeistviia kul'tur (The Armeno-Byzantine Contact Zone (10th–11th Century))* (Moscow, 1994), Eng. summary, 233–5, and 'Some aspects of the military-administrative districts and of Byzantine administration in Armenia during the 11th century', *RÉA*, n.s. 20 (1986–7), 309–20. For Armenian and Armeno-Georgian/Chalcedonian ('Iberian') families in the Byzantine ruling élite of this period, see A.P. Kazhdan, *Armiane v sostave gospodstvuiushchego*

*Chronicle* also yields valuable evidence for the kings of the far eastern Georgian region of Kakhet'i, Alanian/Ovsian kings (e.g. Dorgholeli), Seljuk chieftains (e.g. Tughrul), and the Shaddādid lords of Ani in Armenia (e.g. Minchūihr).

Sumbat Davit'is-dze's *Life and Tale of the Bagratids* also belongs to this initial phase of Bagratid historiography and, in fact, was probably written a few decades before *The Chronicle of K'art'li*. Probably produced in 1030/1 or shortly thereafter,[14] Davit'is-dze's concise tract is nothing short of a declaration of Bagratid ideology, a work of carefully crafted propaganda yielding a narrow Bagratid perspective on Georgian history. Davit'is-dze's explicit objective is to substantiate, by means of a carefully manipulated biblical genealogy, the direct genetic connection of the Georgian Bagratids and the Old Testament King–Prophet David.[15] A primary implication of Davit'is-dze's genealogical fantasy is that the *Georgian* Bagratids comprise the nucleus of the Bagratid family. Consequently, the Armenian Bagratids are dismissed as a far less significant, collateral branch. In other words, the Georgian Bagratids were the 'real' Bagratids, and they alone represented the nucleus of the family. Thus, Davit'is-dze rewrote biblical history so as to buttress the Georgian Bagratids with a legitimacy that was as exceptional as it was uncontestable, both within and beyond the Caucasian isthmus. Though there are good reasons to think that the Bagratids and their supporters did not exert control over the content and imagery of *The Chronicle of K'art'li*, quite the opposite is true with respect to Sumbat Davit'is-dze's tract. With Davit'is-dze a distinctly Bagratid form of history-writing was born; this was a historiography with a pronounced political and ideological purpose which enhanced the ruling dynasty. The production and control of history became a necessary and indispensable political tool for articulating, justifying, sustaining, and enhancing Bagratid power.

In this light, it is hardly surprising that the prosopographical value of Davit'is-dze's work rests mainly in its information about the Georgian Bagratids. It is the most detailed source for the genealogy of the early Georgian Bagratids down to 1030. In addition, we encounter scattered

*klassa vizantiiskoi imperii v XI–XII vv.* (*Armenians in the Ruling Class of the Byzantine Empire in the 11th–12th Century*) (Erevan, 1975). See also the English summary, 'The Armenians in the Byzantine ruling class predominately in the ninth through twelfth centuries', in Thomas J. Samuelian and Michael E. Stone, eds., *Medieval Armenian Culture* (Chico, CA, 1982), 439–51.
[14] Arakhamia, the most recent editor of the Georgian text, prefers a date in or around the 1050s.
[15] This is the first instance in Georgian literature of a genealogy for a specific *family*, royal or non-royal. Note also that Sumbat's Bagratid genealogy is traced through a different son of Noah from the genealogy of the K'art'velian *people* described in the *c.* 800 *Life of the Kings*. See also Martin-Hisard, 'L'aristocratie géorgienne et son passé'.

references to eleventh-century Byzantine figures, including the emperors from Basil II to Romanos III Argyros (r. 1028–1034) and a number of Byzantine officials, some of them explicitly named, including John (Iovane) the *parakoimomenos* and Valang the *chartularios*, and others left unnamed, including a *katepan* of the east and some anonymous *mandatores*. Finally, Davit'is-dze offers brief, yet valuable, information on the insurrection of 1022 as well as narratives of the armed conflicts pitting Georgians against Byzantines in western Georgia.[16]

The second stage of Bagratid historical literature to 1204 is dominated by royal biographies. There are three principal examples of this genre, all of which were composed by anonymous historians: the aforementioned twelfth-century *Life of King of Kings Davit' II* and two thirteenth-century sources concerned chiefly with the reign of Davit''s great-granddaughter Queen T'amar (1184–1213), *The Histories and Eulogies of the Crowned* and *The Life of the Monarch of Monarchs T'amar*. What is particularly striking about these biographies is the conspicuous application of Byzantine imperial imagery, the regular incorporation of biblical quotations and allusions, the direct comparison of the Bagratid monarchs with Hellenic, Hellenistic, Roman, Byzantine, and Judeo-Christian celebrities, and their obvious adaptation of hagiographical structures and conventions. These Bagratid biographies emphasise that the Georgian monarch—*mep'e*[17]—had been specially placed on the throne by God and had been divinely charged with the defence of Christianity. It is clear that the Georgian kings and queens were directly employing the Eusebian theory's vision of monotheistic kingship for the first time since the Georgian monarchy's initial Christianisation back in the fourth century. King Davit' II, also called Aghmashenebeli, 'the Builder', is credited with convening the first all-Georgian ecclesiastical council in imitation of Constantine 'the Great'.[18] The Bagratids adopted a customised version of the *labarum* as their royal crest; contemporary Georgian histories allude to this symbol and crude images were integrated into coins and border markers, several of which are extant.[19]

---

[16] Some of this information was also incorporated into the slightly later *Chronicle of K'art'li*.

[17] The Georgian language lacks a formal grammatical gender. *Mep'e* was thus applied to male and female monarchs. Ruling queens (and queen-consorts) were also called *dedop'ali*, a conflation of the words *deda* ('mother') and *up'ali* ('lord, ruler').

[18] Davit' Aghmashenebeli actually convened at least two all-Georgian church councils, the most famous of which is that held at the neighbouring Ruisi and Urbnisi cathedrals in 1103. The acts of the 1103 council are extant. It should be noted that there is substantial variation in the ordinals assigned to the Georgian Bagratids owing to the numerous branches of the family. Davit' Aghmashenebeli has been variously called Davit' II, III, and IV; scholars in the Georgian Republic favour Davit' IV.

[19] Rapp, 'Coinage of T'amar'.

As with sources for the earlier phase of Bagratid historiography, these three royal biographies salute and commemorate the Bagratid house. Among their primary functions is the underscoring of the incomparable Davidic legitimacy of the Bagratid monarchs. Because Byzantine-inspired royal imagery is applied to an unprecedented degree in these sources, we might expect a goldmine of prosopographical data for the Byzantine empire itself. This is, unfortunately, not the case. We certainly find frequent mention of Byzantium in these narratives, but references to particular Byzantines are curiously scarce. One such instance occurs in *The Life of Davit'* where we encounter 'Grigol, son of Bakuriani',[20] that is to say, the famous Byzantine general of mixed Georgian and Armenian extraction, Gregory Pakourianos.[21] Of special significance for Byzantine studies is *The Life of T'amar*'s concise account of the blood-relationship of the Georgian Bagratids and the Komneni and, moreover, the refuge of Alexios Komnenos, grandson of Andronikos, at the Georgian court and Alexios's subsequent capture of Trebizond with the backing of the Georgian army.[22] Our three Bagratid royal biographies often emphasise marriage ties to foreign dynasties including those of Byzantium. Thus, King Davit' II sent his daughter Kata to Constantinople while he arranged the marriage of another daughter, T'amar, to the Muslim ruler of Sharvān in eastern Caucasia. Moreover, the famous Queen T'amar, not to be confused with Davit''s daughter, herself was married successively to the Rus'ian prince Iurii Bogoliubskii, son of Andrei Bogoliubskii of Rostov-Suzdal, and then to Davit' Soslani, an Alanian (Ovsian) aristocrat having a Bagratid pedigree.

A particular value of these biographies is their detailed information about the expanding Georgian administration and the holders of specific offices. *The Histories and Eulogies of the Crowned* is particularly rich in this regard. For example, its anonymous writer draws a textual map of the reach of T'amar's authority:

> And in these times the *erist'avi*s [i.e., regional governors/generals] were: Baram Vardanis-dze—*erist'avi* of the Suans [mod. Svans]; Kakhaberi Kakhaberis-dze—*erist'avi* of Racha and T'akueri; and Ot'agho Sharvashis-dze—*erist'avi* of Ts'khumi [mod. Sokhumi/Sukhumi]; Amanelis-dze—[*erist'avi* of Arguet'i]; and the *erist'avi* of Odishi, Bediani. [And the *erist'avi*s] of Likht'-ameri [were]: the *erist'avi* of K'art'li—Rati Surameli; and the *erist'avi* of Kakhet'i—Bakurqma Dzaganis-dze; and the *erist'avi* of Heret'i—Asat', son of Grigoli. . . and the *erist'avi* of Samts'khe and the *spasalari* [i.e. general] . . . Bots'o Jaqeli . . .[23]

---

[20] *Life of Davit'*, 157.9–158.1 Shanidze, 318 Qaukhch'ishvili.

[21] See n. 13 on the use of 'Iberian' to denote the Chalcedonian inhabitants of Caucasia.

[22] *The Life of T'amar*, 142–3 Qaukhch'ishvili, 86–7, tr. Vivian.

[23] *Histories and Eulogies*, 33.20–34.7 Qaukhch'ishvili.

The pan-Caucasian empire of the Georgian Bagratids was built upon the back of the army, and it is not surprising that we should find frequent references to military officials in this passage and elsewhere in the royal biographies of this period. Among the *amirspasalari*s (commanders-in-chief) are many references to the Armenian Mq'argrdzeli (modern orthography: Mkhargrdzeli, var. Mxargrdzeli) house, in their native tongue known as the Zak'areans/Zakarids. Sargis Mq'argrdzeli served as Queen T'amar's *amirspasalari*; after him his son Zak'aria held the post while Zak'aria's younger brother, Ivane, not only was the *msakhurt'-ukhuts'esi*, the chief of the secretaries,[24] but also a convert to Georgian Orthodoxy. From a religious perspective, Bagratid royal biographies supply indispensable data about prominent bishops and chief prelates of the Georgian church, including the archbishop of K'ut'at'isi, Antoni Saghiris-dze, and some Georgian clerics and monks, like Nik'olaoz Gulaberis-dze, who were active beyond the borders of Georgia, especially in Jerusalem, Syria, and Byzantium. These biographies draw attention to royal donations bestowed upon Georgian monks and monasteries abroad. In addition, beginning with the reign of Davit' II, we routinely encounter the *mtsignobart'-ukhuts'esi chqondideli*, a post combining one of the highest secular positions with that of the important bishopric of Chqondidi in western Georgia.

Though the structure, flavour, and royal imagery of the Bagratid biographies are overwhelmingly Byzantine in inspiration, there is also prosopographical information for rulers and other notable figures in greater Caucasia and the northern part of the Near East. We find several allusions to chieftains of the nomadic Cuman-Qipchaqs, thousands of whom had been resettled by royal invitation in northern Caucasia starting in or about 1118.[25] Even more prominent are references to Muslim élites. Rulers of the Seljuks, the Sultanate of Rūm, the *atabeg*s of Gandza and Adarbadagan (cf. Azerbaijan), the Sharvānshāhs, the sultans of Ardebil, and others are often encountered in our texts. Thus, while the Bagratids drew most strongly upon Byzantine and Judaeo-Christian traditions for their carefully constructed royal image, and while the Georgian Orthodox church looked to Byzantium as never before,

---

[24] For this and other offices of the period, see Allen, *History of the Georgian People*, ch. 23, 'Court and administration', 257–65 and esp. the list, 258–60.

[25] Golden, 'Cumanica I: the Qipčaqs in Georgia', who enumerates four periods of relations of the nomads with the Caucasian realms, the second of which is 'the "Seljuq" or "Seljuq-Qipčaq" period (mid-eleventh to thirteenth century) witness[ing] the Turkicization of Azarbāijān (an ethno-linguistic change of enormous importance) and the destruction of Armenian statehood. The latter process had already been significantly advanced by Byzantium. Curiously, the Georgian state, although submerged at one point by the Oğuz-Seljuk tide, struggled back and, with the aid of yet other Turkic nomads, the Qipčaqs, embarked on a brief period of "empire", creating in the process a pan-Transcaucasian monarchy.'

the relatively large number of Muslim individuals recorded in these royal biographies demonstrates that Bagratid Georgia had not been severed from the Islamic Near East but that it remained an integral part of it. The fact that Georgian coinage of this period typically features Arabic inscriptions is another indication of Georgia's position on the overlapping edges of the Byzantine and Islamic commonwealths.

One other contemporary Georgian history should be mentioned. *The History of the Five Reigns*, sometimes called *The Chronicle of the Era of Giorgi Lasha*, is a concise source occupying some seven pages in the standard printed edition. Compiled in the second half of the thirteenth century, this text has come down to us in a single manuscript.[26] It joins highly condensed biographies of the Bagratid monarchs from Demetre I (r. 1125–54) to Giorgi IV Lasha (r. 1213–23). In these the usual references to the Georgian Bagratids are met. Though reflecting the pattern of Bagratid royal biographies, these notices are quite short and may be abbreviations of more elaborate narratives which are no longer extant.

### Principal Manuscripts, Printed Editions, and Translations

Over the past century, Georgian historical scholarship has flourished in many areas, perhaps none more than in the realm of critical editions. The historiographical sources surveyed above—*The Chronicle of K'art'li*, the ideologically charged tract of Sumbat Davit'is-dze, the two separate *Lives* of Davit' and T'amar, the anonymous *Histories and Eulogies*, and the brief *History of the Five Reigns*—have come down to us exclusively within the medieval historical corpus known as *K'art'lis ts'khovreba* (variant transliteration: *K'art'lis c'xovreba*), in English sometimes called *The Life of Georgia*, the 'Georgian Chronicles', or even the 'Georgian Royal Annals'.[27] The origin, evolution, and individual components of *K'art'lis ts'khovreba* have been hotly debated; my research has revealed thirteen distinct medieval texts which were composed between the early ninth and fourteenth century.[28]

---

[26] i.e. the Anaseuli MS of *K'art'lis ts'khovreba* (for which see further below) deriving from the late fifteenth century. A defective version is incorporated into the C/c hybrid redaction, and excerpts of *The History of the Five Reigns* were used in a later, Vakhtangiseuli, *History of Demetre and Davit' III*. The absence of this text in the vast majority of surviving MSS of *K'art'lis ts'khovreba* suggests that it was not accepted as canonical by a great many contemporary scribes.

[27] For an overview of *K'art'lis ts'khovreba*, see Lort'k'ip'anidze, *Ra aris k'art'lis ts'khovreba?* and Javakhishvili's older *Dzveli k'art'uli saistorio mtserloba*. In English, see Toumanoff, 'Medieval Georgian historical literature' and Rapp, *Studies in Medieval Georgian Historiography* and 'Imagining history at the crossroads'.

[28] e.g. Rapp, *Studies in Medieval Georgian Historiography*, introduction.

The greatest complication to the study of *K'art'lis ts'khovreba* is the corpus' rather late manuscript tradition. The autograph manuscript(s) and early copies are not extant. *K'art'lis ts'khovreba*'s oldest surviving redaction is actually an abbreviated but carefully adapted version in Armenian copied at some point between 1274 and 1311. This adaptation is known in Armenian as the *Patmut'iwn Vrats'*, *The History of the Georgians*. The oldest surviving Georgian-language manuscript, the Anaseuli (A) redaction, was created sometime between 1479 and 1495. Anaseuli is defective, however; the oldest complete variant to come down to us, the Mariamiseuli (M) manuscript, was produced in the 1630s or 1640s. Owing to their importance, both of these Georgian manuscripts have been published separately in their entirety: the Anaseuli manuscript was edited and published by Simon Qaukhch'ishvili (Qauxch'ishvili) in 1942, and the Mariamiseuli by Ek'vt'ime T'aqaïshvili in 1906. There are two other early Georgian variants which have not been published independently: the early and incomplete folios of the Chalashviliseuli (C/c) redaction of the sixteenth century and the so-called Mts'khet'ian (Q) version copied in 1697, though copied from an original known to have existed in 1546. It should be noted that the vast majority of the Georgian-language variants of the corpus are now housed in the Korneli Kekelidze Institute of Manuscripts in T'bilisi, the capital of the Republic of Georgia.

The majority of the surviving redactions of *K'art'lis ts'khovreba* constitute the so-called Vakhtangiseuli recension. Vakhtangiseuli—literally '[reflecting the editorial project ordered] by [King] Vakhtang [VI]'—manuscripts reflect the editorial changes made by a commission of scholars appointed by the Bagratid King Vakhtang VI (r. 1711–14, 1719–23) in the early eighteenth century. Though drawing upon older, pre-Vakhtangiseuli manuscripts, this early modern recension offers no new information for the period from 1025 to 1204. The famous Georgian edition and accompanying French translation of *K'art'lis ts'khovreba* by Marie-Félicité Brosset published from 1849 onwards is based upon these very late Vakhtangiseuli documents.[29] Therefore, so far as medieval history is concerned, Brosset is useful not so much for its edition and translation but for the introduction and commentary.

All of the historical texts discussed so far have been published in excellent critical editions. The standard critical edition of the entire corpus of *K'art'lis ts'khovreba* was published in two volumes under the supervision of Simon Qaukhch'ishvili in the 1950s, the first having been republished with a new English commentary in 1998. Appended to both of Qaukhch'ishvili's volumes are indices which include individuals, though, unfortunately, these are

---

[29] *Histoire de la Géorgie*, ed. and French tr. Brosset, vol. 1, *Histoire ancienne, jusqu'en 1469 de J.-C.* For the Vakhtangiseuli recension, see especially Grigolia, *Akhali k'art'lis ts'khovreba*.

interspersed with toponyms and ethnonyms. Only one early manuscript, the seventeenth-century Mts'khet'ian redaction, has been discovered since the appearance of Qaukhch'ishvili's edition.[30] The importance of the Mts'khet'ian variant has necessitated the re-edition of some of the constituent texts. So far only two texts for the period under review here have been updated: the history of Sumbat Davit'is-dze re-edited by Goneli Arakhamia and *The Life of Davit' II* magnificently re-edited by Mzek'ala Shanidze. These are to be given precedence over Qaukhch'ishvili's older edition.[31]

Though the texts discussed above are, quite obviously, best used in the original, we are fortunate to have scholarly English translations of some of them.[32] As part of his translation and commentary on the medieval Armenian adaptation of *K'art'lis ts'khovreba*, Robert W. Thomson furnished translations of the corresponding Georgian texts as reconstructed by Qaukhch'ishvili in the two volumes just cited. It should be stressed that Thomson did not translate all of the medieval components of the Georgian-language *K'art'lis ts'khovreba*, but only those incorporated into the medieval Armenian adaptation. Thomson's translations of *The Chronicle of K'art'li* (his 'Book of K'art'li') and *Life of Davit' II* are superb, though it should be noted that his English rendering of the latter is unfortunately not based upon Shanidze's improved text. Of the remaining histories for our period, only the history of Sumbat Davit'is-dze and *The Life of T'amar* have been translated into English in their entirety.[33] Select passages of the other two texts—*The Histories and Eulogies* and *The History of the Five Reigns*—have been translated; these appear in Katherine Vivian's *The Georgian Chronicle: the period of Giorgi Lasha*.[34]

## BEYOND HISTORIOGRAPHY:
## OTHER PROSOPOGRAPHICAL SOURCES

A number of other contemporary Georgian sources yield additional data. Perhaps the most significant alternate category consists of hagiographical literature. Biographies of holy women and men constitute the earliest known

[30] Klimiashvili, 'Novyi spisok'.

[31] In 2001 *The Life of T'amar* was edited anew by K'adagidze under the title *The Chronicle of the Age of Queen T'amar* (*T'amar mep'is droindeli matiane*). It should be noted that this text does not appear in the Mts'khet'ian variant of *K'art'lis ts'khovreba*.

[32] Russian translations are common; translations in other languages are sometimes available (see the bibliography for detailed information).

[33] See Vivian, *Georgian Chronicle* and Rapp, *Studies in Medieval Georgian Historiography*, respectively.

[34] But Vivian's translation must be used cautiously; see the bibliography below.

form of original Georgian literature. The oldest of these, *The Martyrdom of Shushaniki*, was written towards the end of the fifth century. The nature of extant texts suggests that Lives were the most popular form of original Georgian literature until the tenth century. As we have seen, the hagiographical model was adopted by royal historians in the period from 1025 to 1204 for their accounts of Bagratid monarchs like Davit' II and T'amar. As compared to earlier times, relatively few hagiographies were produced during the Bagratid 'golden age', a curious situation which may be explained by the fact that the Bagratids jealously guarded, so far as possible, a special connection to the sacred. Ultimately, the Georgian Bagratids wished to limit their saintly competition—and to monopolise political power in the present day—while appropriating the requisite sacred symbols and imagery.[35]

There are, however, two extensive, original Georgian hagiographies of the period. Both are associated with the substantial Georgian presence at the Iveron monastery on mount Athos and were produced outside Georgia, beyond immediate Bagratid control.[36] The first, *The Life of Iovane and Ep't'wme*, barely intersects our period. Writing around the year 1045, its author, the famous Georgian Athonite Giorgi Mt'atsmi[n]deli (George 'the Athonite/Hagorite'),[37] devotes the lion's share of his attention to the last half of the tenth century and especially to the foundation of Iveron, the monastery 'of the Iberians/Georgians'. Of greater relevance is *The Life of Giorgi Mt'atsmideli*, composed *c.* 1070 by his pupil Giorgi Mts'ire (George 'the Lesser/Little'). These two Lives provide valuable information about Georgian–Byzantine/eastern Christian relations. As with all major sources of original Georgian hagiography, excellent critical versions of these saintly biographies have been published in the essential corpus *Dzveli k'art'uli agiograp'iuli literaturis dzeglebi* (*Monuments of Old Georgian Hagiographical Literature*) edited by the renowned scholar Ilia Abuladze. The one serious drawback to Abuladze's published edition is the lack of an index. For the *Life of Iovane and Ep't'wme*, however, the index of proper names found in the French translation by Bernadette Martin-Hisard will prove most beneficial. It should also be said that a few excerpts of these two hagiographical texts were published in David Marshall Lang's *Lives and Legends of the Georgian Saints*. This concise sourcebook is also indexed, but Lang translated the

---

[35] Among other things, the Bagratids applied textual imagery which had previously been restricted to holy men and women, e.g. the concepts *brtsqinvale* ('resplendent, brilliant') and *sharavandedi* ('corona, aureole of the Sun', and perhaps 'halo'): Rapp, 'Imagining history at the crossroads', 658–62.

[36] For Georgians on Mt Athos, see the collected essays of Metreveli, *Narkvevebi at'onis kulturul-saganmanat'leblo keris istoriidan.*

[37] *Mt'atsmideli* in Old Georgian, *mt'atsmindeli* according to the modern orthography.

various texts with a general audience in mind and greatly abbreviated the texts without notation.

The eleventh, twelfth, and thirteenth centuries witnessed vibrant literary undertakings on the part of Georgian ecclesiastics both in the Caucasus region and throughout the Byzantine commonwealth. This literary efflorescence was fuelled first and foremost by the translation of various Greek ecclesiastical texts into Georgian. A relatively large number of these translated texts have come down to us, and some of these survive in contemporary and even autograph manuscripts. The sources relating to church canon and structure are gathered in the third volume of I. Dolidze's valuable *K'art'uli samart'lis dzeglebi* (*Monuments of Georgian Law*) which, *inter alia*, includes the prosopographically rich acts of the 1103 synod of Ruisi-Urbnisi. Among the Georgian literary celebrities of the time are the aforementioned Athonite monks Ep't'wme (Euthymios) and Giorgi Mt'atsmi[n]deli, Ep'rem Mts'ire, Arsen Iqalt'oeli ('of/from Iqalt'o'), and Ioane Petritsi[38] (John Petritsi), a student of John Italos and Michael Psellos. The literary endeavours of these men are catalogued chronologically in the seminal study by Korneli Kekelidze, *K'art'uli literaturis istoria* (*A History of Georgian Literature*), a German-language adaptation of which was published by Michel Tarchnishvili in 1955.[39]

Compared to earlier periods of Georgian history, ours is abundant in manuscripts. Other contemporary texts survive in later copies. A great many of the particular texts, especially translations from the Greek, have yet to be edited and published. The vast majority of surviving Georgian-language manuscripts is now housed in the Kekelidze Institute of Manuscripts in T'bilisi, and we are fortunate that the collection's thousands of manuscripts have been well catalogued in the series *K'art'ul khelnatsert'a aghtseriloba* (*Description of Georgian Manuscripts*).[40] A typical description entails not only the physical condition of the manuscript but also its constituent texts, information about scribes and patronage, and also the texts of colophons. Colophons might prove to be a goldmine of prosopographical data for our period; unfortunately, they are scattered throughout the manuscript catalogues and have not been collated and published separately.[41] Other

---

[38] Marr, 'Ioann Petritsskii, gruzinskii neoplatonik'.

[39] *Geschichte der kirchlichen georgischen Literatur*. See now Khintibidze, *Georgian-Byzantine Literary Contacts*.

[40] For an overview in English, see the Institute's website: *http://georgianmanuscripts.caucasus. net/en/institute.asp*

[41] Consider, for instance, the illuminated Alaverdi Gospels originally copied in 1054 at Kalipos near Antioch. Its colophons name several individuals, including (but by no means limited to) the scribe/illustrator Swmeon, his parents, children, and spiritual teachers, another scribe Iovane

substantial collections of Georgian manuscripts can be found in St Petersburg, at St Catherine's on mount Sinai, Jerusalem,[42] Oxford, London, Cambridge, Bloomington (Indiana, USA), and elsewhere. The more extensive of these collections have been catalogued. The collection on mount Sinai may turn out to be especially important for prosopography as a cache of medieval Georgian manuscripts was discovered there after a fire in 1975, and the contents of these manuscripts are just starting to see the light of day. A trilingual catalogue of the new Georgian Sinai documents is currently in press.[43]

We possess a number of Georgian charters and deeds from the eleventh to the thirteenth century. These have been assembled in *K'art'uli istoriuli sabut'ebi IX–XIII ss.* (*Georgian Historical Documents, 9th–13th Century*), edited by T'. Enuk'idze, V. Silogava, and N. Shoshiashvili. This volume, which appeared in 1984, supplies introductions to the documents, an extensive index, and photographs of manuscripts. Documents numbered two to twenty fall within our time-frame and furnish prosopographical information on the Georgian Bagratid family, a wide array of Georgian ecclesiastics from *katholikoi* to priests, some noblemen, and occasional references to Byzantines, especially emperors. There are personal letters but the most common variety of sources are royal decrees concerning possessions and rights of monasteries, especially the lavra of Shio-Mghwme (modern orthography: Shio-Mghvime) not far from Tp'ilisi[44] and Mts'khet'a (variant transliteration: Mc'xet'a).

There are yet other Georgian sources which yield limited prospographical data. Georgian art, including paintings in and inscriptions on churches and monasteries, has received considerable scholarly attention. Artistic sources have been described and investigated in a variety of books and articles. Particularly important in English are the publications of Wachtang Djobadze and, most recently, those of Antony Eastmond, particularly his *Royal Imagery in Medieval Georgia*. There are a number of donor portraits in Georgian churches of the period. For example, the *c.*1200 portraits of the K'olagiri cave monastery in the Garesja (variants: Gareja, Gareji) desert of

---

Dvali, the Antiochene patriarch, the Byzantine emperor Constantine IX Monomachos, and the Georgian king, '*novelissimos* of all the east', Bagrat IV (his visit to Constantinople is mentioned): *K'art'ul khelnatsert'a aghtseriloba: qop'ili saeklesio muzeumis (A) kolek'ts'iisa (Description of Georgian Manuscripts: collection of the former Ecclesiastical Museum (A))*, vol. 2.1 (T'bilisi, 1986), 210–16, esp. 212–16.

[42] See e.g. Metreveli, *Masalebi ierusalemis k'art'uli koloniis istoriisat'vis*.

[43] The 'new' documents are summarised by Alek'sidze, 'The new recensions of the "Conversion of Georgia" and the "Lives of the 13 Syrian Fathers"', esp. 409–14.

[44] Tp'ilisi is the Old Georgian form; T'bilisi is the modern form (cf. Russian Tiflis). I use the Old Georgian form when referring to medieval Georgia or medieval Georgian texts.

south-eastern Georgia have recently been investigated by Zaza Skhirtladze.[45] Skhirtladze and a number of other scholars have also been collecting and publishing the extensive graffiti, many of them carved by pilgrims, in the monasteries scattered throughout Garesja. Valeri Silogava's catalogue of such inscriptions from the ninth to the thirteenth century is representative of the content of these materials, but certain of his readings have been contested by other specialists.[46] Indeed, there are numerous stone inscriptions for our period and they have been published in many books and articles since the nineteenth century. One recent compendium, also by Silogava, catalogues and publishes inscriptions from the Georgian region of Samts'khe–Javakhet'i not far from Byzantine Anatolia. These inscriptions, which specify a number of royal, ecclesiastical, and aristocratic individuals, have been photographed and translated into English.[47] Yet another booklet by Silogava features the late twelfth-century inscriptions at Bet'ania near T'bilisi and incorporates English renderings.[48] There are contemporary inscriptions in other languages, especially Armenian[49] and Greek. For the latter, the corpus of Greek inscriptions, *Sak'art'velos berdznuli tsartserebis korpusi* (*Corpus of Greek Inscriptions in Georgia*) by T'inat'in Qaukhch'ishvili is particularly useful. Its two volumes, devoted to Greek inscriptions of the pre-modern period found in western and eastern Georgia respectively, contain summaries in German.[50] For the Bagratid monarchs of the 'golden age', numismatic evidence is also valuable. The primary catalogues of medieval Georgian coinage are E. Pakhomov, *Monety Gruzii* and D.G. Kapanadze, *Gruzinskaia numizmatika* (both in Russian). David Marshall Lang's *Studies in the Numismatic History of Georgia in Transcaucasia* provides a sound overview in English.[51]

---

[45] Skhirtladze, *Istoriul pirt'a portretebi garejis mravalmt'is k'olagiris monastershi*, with extensive English summary.

[46] Silogava, ed., *Tsartserebi garejis mravaltsqarodan*. Far more precise is Kldiashvili and Skhirtladze, eds., *Garejis epigrap'ikuli dzeglebi*.

[47] Silogava, ed., *Samts'khe-javakhet'is istoriuli muzeumis k'art'uli epigrap'ikuli dzeglebi*.

[48] Silogava, ed., *Bet'aniis tsartserebi*.

[49] e.g. Muradian, ed., *Armianskaia epigrafika Gruzii*.

[50] See also the important series in Georgian, *Dzveli k'art'uli tsqaroebi bizantiis shesakheb* (*Old Georgian Sources on Byzantium*), the first volume of which was edited by S. Qaukhch'ishvili and published in T'bilisi in 1974.

[51] There are yet other lines of evidence. For our period inscriptions incorporated into enamels refer to royal figures in western and eastern Georgia as well as Byzantium. See the trilingual (Georgian, English, Russian) catalogue by Khuskivadze, *Shua saukuneebis tikhruli minank'ari*. By the end of the thirteenth century, secular epic literature in the Iranian style also became popular in Georgia, e.g. the *Vep'khistqaosani* (*Knight in the Panther's Skin*) by Shot'a Rust'aveli. For a somewhat dated overview, see Blake, 'Georgian secular literature' and now Rayfield, *The Literature of Georgia*, 63–86.

## POSTSCRIPT: THE STATE OF GEORGIAN SCHOLARSHIP

Because of the nature of PBW, this essay has concentrated on contemporary sources and the relevant published editions. But it should be emphasised that these editions do not exist in a scholarly vacuum. The Georgians have an extensive and sophisticated scholarship, especially for their pre-modern history. Because the vast majority of this scholarship is in Georgian, it is inaccessible to a western audience. In imperial Russian and Soviet times, some investigations were published wholly in Russian and almost all scholarly researches in Georgian were supplemented with Russian summaries of varying length and quality. For better and worse, those days have vanished. While some post-Soviet studies have summaries in western languages, a great many of them are entirely in Georgian.

Space does not permit a survey of all the relevant scholarly literature written in Georgian: there are literally thousands of articles and monographs which might prove useful to the project. In Georgian the second volume of Ivane Javakhishvili's *K'art'veli eris istoria* (*A History of the Georgian People*) remains vital.[52] An investigation of the eleventh and twelfth centuries originally published in Russian by Mariam Lort'k'ip'anidze has been translated into English, but the translation lacks the original footnotes and documentation.[53] Specialised researches in Georgian devoted to our period are far too numerous to mention here.

In English, W.E.D. Allen's *A History of the Georgian People* and the various publications of David Marshall Lang are rather general and dated for the eleventh to thirteenth century. For an overview of medieval Georgian literature, one might begin with the relevant chapters of Donald Rayfield's *The Literature of Georgia: a history*, originally published by Oxford University Press. Eastmond's study of contemporary Georgian art gives numerous historical insights and these might be supplemented with Cyril Toumanoff's 'Armenia and Georgia' published in *The Cambridge Medieval History* and his 'Caucasia and Byzantine studies' appearing in the journal *Traditio*. Many aspects of the history of the Georgian church have been well researched, but there is not a single, comprehensive, up-to-date scholarly investigation available in any language. On this topic we must still rely on Michel Tamarati's *L'Église géorgienne* published back in 1910.[54]

---

[52] Reprinted in his *T'khzulebani*, vol. 2.

[53] Lort'k'ip'anidze, *Georgia in the XI–XII Centuries*.

[54] For the period up to the eleventh century, see now Martin-Hisard, 'Christianisme et Église dans le monde géorgien'. The recent survey by Anania Jap'aridze, *Sak'art'velos samots'ik'ulo eklesiis istoria* (*History of the Georgian Apostolic Church*), 4 vols. (T'bilisi, 1996), represents the official view of the Georgian Orthodox church.

It is fitting to end with three recent works which are absolutely essential for Georgian prosopographical research. The first is a Georgian-language guide, *K'art'uli paleograp'ia* (*Georgian Palaeography*) published in T'bilisi in 1997 by Korneli Danelia and Zurab Sarjveladze. Although limited in its utility for prosopographical data directly, this book is a brilliant introduction to Georgian palaeography and joins together a wealth of information about Old Georgian texts, manuscripts, and language. Its first chapter, 'Old Georgian inscriptions', reproduces inscriptions from the fifth to the thirteenth century.

Of greater direct relevance is Cyril Toumanoff's magisterial *Les dynasties de la Caucasie chrétienne* published in Rome in 1990. In excess of five hundred pages, this hefty tome presents detailed genealogical charts and tables for Georgian, Armenian, and Caucasian aristocracy and royalty from ancient times down to the nineteenth century. Though numerous genealogical studies are available in Georgian and Armenian, none surpasses Toumanoff's marvellous achievement.[55]

An indispensible complement to Toumanoff's *Dynasties* is a detailed catalogue of Georgian individuals who lived between the eleventh and seventeenth century. The first two volumes of *Pirt'a anotirebuli lek'sikoni* (*Annotated Dictionary of Individuals*) appeared in 1991 and 1993 under the collective editorship of D. Kldiashvili, M. Surguladze, E. Ts'agareishvili and G. Jandieri. Encompassing surnames beginning with the letters 'A' to 'L' so far, this essential research guide furnishes dates and references in major contemporary sources. Unfortunately, there is no chronological listing of these individuals. So far as the Byzantine commonwealth is concerned, these volumes are perhaps unmatched among modern studies and researches for their prosopographical relevance. Though the other volumes of this series have been completed, they remain unpublished because of the grave economic situation in the Georgian Republic.

# BIBLIOGRAPHY

## TRANSLITERATION

The system of Georgian transliteration employed here is a modification of that used by the Library of Congress (LOC), USA. Other systems sometimes render Georgian *kh* as *x*; similarly *ts*—*c*; *gh*—*ğ*; *ch*—*č*; *sh*—*š*; and *zh*—*ž*. It

---

[55] In Georgian, two recent genealogical guides should also be mentioned: Lort'k'ip'anidze and R. Metreveli, eds., *Sak'art'velos mep'eebi*, and R. Metreveli, ed., *Sak'art'velos kat'alikos-patriark'ebi*.

should be noted that Georgian *j* is normally rendered *dzh* in Russian; thus Javakhishvili is transliterated in Russian as Dzhavakhishvili. Three scripts (*asomt'avruli*, *nuskhuri*, and *mkhedruli*) have been used to write Georgian since the end of the fourth/start of the fifth century AD. *Mkhedruli* has been employed since just before the Bagratid 'golden age' and a variant of it is still used today. None of the Georgian scripts distinguishes between 'capital' and 'small' letters, e.g. proper nouns are not capitalised and the first word of a sentence is not capitalised. See also Howard I. Aronson, 'Transliterating Georgian', *Annual of the Society for the Study of Caucasia* 4–5 (1992–3), 77–84.

### Asomt'avruli

| a | b | g | d | e | v | z | ē | t' | i | k | l | m |
|---|---|---|---|---|---|---|---|---|---|---|---|---|
| **n** | **y** | **o** | **p** | **zh** | **r** | **s** | **t** | **w** | **u** | **p'** | **k'** | **gh** |
| **q** | **sh** | **ch'** | **ts'** | **dz** | **ts** | **ch** | **kh** | **q'** | **j** | **h** | **ō** | |

### Nuskhuri

| a | b | g | d | e | v | z | ē | t' | i | k | l | m |
|---|---|---|---|---|---|---|---|---|---|---|---|---|
| **n** | **y** | **o** | **p** | **zh** | **r** | **s** | **t** | **w** | **u** | **p'** | **k'** | **gh** |
| **q** | **sh** | **ch'** | **ts'** | **dz** | **ts** | **ch** | **kh** | **q'** | **j** | **h** | **ō** | — |

### Mkhedruli

| a | b | g | d | e | v | z | ē | t' | i | k | l | m |
|---|---|---|---|---|---|---|---|---|---|---|---|---|
| **n** | **y** | **o** | **p** | **zh** | **r** | **s** | **t** | **w** | **u** | **p'** | **k'** | **gh** |
| **q** | **sh** | **ch'** | **ts'** | **dz** | **ts** | **ch** | **kh** | **q'** | **j** | **h** | **ō** | |

## HANDBOOKS, SURVEYS, PROSOPOGRAPHIES

### Surveys

W.E.D. Allen, *A History of the Georgian People: from the beginning down to the Russian conquest in the nineteenth century* (London, 1932, repr. 1971)
  Eloquent but dated overview. Weakened by its dependence upon the later 'Vakhtangiseuli' edition of *K'art'lis ts'khovreba* as published by Brosset.

Ivane Javakhishvili, *K'art'veli eris istoria* (*History of the Georgian People*), 3 vols.; reprinted in his *T'khzulebani* (*Collected Works*), vols. 1–3 (T'bilisi, 1979, 1983, and 1982 respectively)
  Originally published from 1908, Javakhishvili's *magnum opus* remains vital though, unfortunately, is available only in Georgian. These volumes address Georgian history down to the fourteenth century.

David Marshall Lang, *The Georgians* (New York and Washington, DC, 1966)
  Overview of Georgian history and culture for a general audience.

—— *Landmarks in Georgian Literature: an inaugural lecture delivered on 2 November 1965* (London, 1966)
  Succinct, 35-page introduction to the literature of Georgia.

David Marshall Lang and Charles Burney, *The Peoples of the Hills: ancient Ararat and Caucasus* (New York and Washington, DC, 1972)
  Scholarly consideration of the ancient and early medieval history of the Near East, eastern Anatolia, and Caucasia.

Mariam Lort'k'ip'anidze (Lordkipanidze), *Essays on Georgian History* (T'bilisi, 1994)
  Three essays on Georgia in the fourth to tenth centuries, Georgia in the eleventh and twelfth centuries, and Ap'khazet'i/Abkhazia.

Donald Rayfield, *The Literature of Georgia: a history* (Oxford, 1994)
  Patchy coverage of medieval historiography; better for literature produced in early modern times and later.

Kalistrat Salia, *History of the Georgian Nation*, tr. Katharine Vivian (2nd edn., Paris, 1983)
  Lengthy study though largely undocumented and sometimes unabashedly patriotic.

Ronald Grigor Suny, *The Making of the Georgian Nation* (rev. edn., Bloomington, Ind., 1994)
  Survey of Georgian history emphasising the eighteenth–twentieth century.

Akaki Surguladze, *K'art'uli kulturis istoriis narkvevebi*, vol. 1 (T'bilisi, 1989); English summary, 'Review of the history of Georgian culture', 478–500
  Overview of Georgian culture from prehistory down to the eighteenth century.

Michel Tamarati, *L'Église géorgienne des origines jusqu'à nos jours* (Rome, 1910)
  Comprehensive survey of Georgian ecclesiastical history down to the early twentieth century.

## Maps

Robert H. Hewsen, *Armenia: a historical atlas* (Chicago, 2001)
  Excellent atlas that, despite its title, encompasses the whole of Caucasia, including the various Georgian lands.
Ivane Javakhishvili, *Sak'art'velos istoriuli ruka* (*Historical Map of Georgia*) (T'bilisi, 1923)
  Detailed large-format map, reprinted in 1991.
Zurab Tatashidze, *et al.*, eds., *Bagrationi Vakhushti, Sak'art'velos atlasi* (*Atlas of Georgia*) (T'bilisi, 1997)
  Large-format reprinting of Vakhushti's detailed maps of Georgia and Caucasia originally produced in the mid-eighteenth century.


## Dictionaries and Linguistic aids

Ilia Abuladze, ed., *Dzveli k'art'uli enis lek'sikoni* (*Lexicon of the Old Georgian Language*) (T'bilisi, 1973)
  Essential dictionary of Old Georgian.
Howard I. Aronson, *Georgian: a reading grammar* (corrected edn., Columbus, Ohio, 1990)
  Though geared towards linguists, Aronson's grammar remains the best choice for English speakers.
Soso Chanturia and Shorena Sulamanidze, eds., *English–Georgian and Georgian–English Dictionary = Inglisur–k'art'uli da k'art'ul–inglisuri lek'sikoni* (K'ut'aisi, 1998)
  Basic two-way dictionary; many lacunae.
E. Cherkesi, ed., *Georgian–English Dictionary* (Oxford, 1950)
  Though less ambitious than Harrell *et al.*, Cherkesi is useful for reading Old Georgian and older scholarly literature.
Davit' Ch'ubinashvili, ed., *K'art'ul–rusuli lek'sikoni* (*Georgian–Russian Dictionary*) (2nd edn., T'bilisi, 1984)
  Reprinting of a detailed Georgian–Russian dictionary first published in St Petersburg in 1887.
S.J. Harrell, Maia Koupounia, Maia Tsitsishivili, and Ketevan Gabounia, eds., *Georgian–English Dictionary* (Springfield, Virginia, 2002)
  With over 28,000 headwords, this new dictionary is especially useful for reading modern Georgian.
Alice C. Harris, ed., *The Indigenous Languages of the Caucasus*, vol. 1, *The Kartvelian Languages* (Delmar, NY, 1991)
  Includes J. Neville Birdsall's 'Georgian paleography' (87–128) and Heinz Fähnrich's 'Old Georgian' (131–217).
George Hewitt, *Georgian: a learner's grammar* (London and New York, 1996)
  Useful supplement to Aronson's grammar.
Zurab Sarjveladze, ed., *Dzveli k'art'uli enis lek'sikoni* (*Lexicon of the Old Georgian Language*) (T'bilisi, 1995)
  Supplements Abuladze's Old Georgian dictionary (see above).

Zurab Sarjveladze, *Dzveli k'art'uli ena* (*Old Georgian Language*) (T'bilisi, 1997)
Grammar of the Old Georgian language with basic dictionary (pp. 385–578).
Kita Tschenkeli, ed., *Georgisch–Deutsches Wörterbuch*, 3 vols. (Zurich, 1965–74)
Widely regarded as the most comprehensive Georgian dictionary in any western
language.

## Prosopographical and Genealogical aids

Darejan Kldiashvili *et al.*, *Pirt'a anotirebuli lek'sikoni: XI–XVI ss. k'art'uli istoriuli
sabut'ebis mikhedvit'* (*Annotated Dictionary of Individuals according to Georgian
Historical Documents of the 11th–16th Century*), 3 vols. published (T'bilisi, 1991,
1993, 2004); French introduction, vol. 1, 26–40
Unsurpassed prosopographical guide to individuals living between the eleventh
and sixteenth century. Published volumes cover A–O; vol. 3 is newly available; the
remaining volumes have been completed but remain unpublished.
Mariam Lort'k'ip'anidze and Roin Metreveli, eds., *Sak'art'velos mep'eebi* (*Kings of
Georgia*) (T'bilisi, 2000)
Relative chronology of the monarchs of the various Georgian regions from antiqu-
ity to the Russian conquest of the nineteenth century.
Roin Metreveli, ed., *Sak'art'velos kat'alikos-patriark'ebi* (*Kat'alikos-Patriarchs of
Georgia*) (T'bilisi, 2000)
Relative chronology of the supreme prelates of K'art'li/Georgia from the fourth
century to the present.
Cyril Toumanoff, *Les dynasties de la Caucasie chrétienne de l'antiquité jusqu'au XIX^e
siècle: tables généalogiques et chronologiques* (Rome, 1990); revision of his *Manuel
de généalogie et de chronologie pour l'histoire de la Caucasie chrétienne* (Rome,
1976)
Premier genealogical catalogue of the various dynasties of Caucasia; especially
rich for Georgia and Armenia.

## Handbooks and Guides

Korneli Danelia and Zurab Sarjveladze, *K'art'uli paleograp'ia* (*Georgian
Palaeography*) (T'bilisi, 1997)
Essential handbook for Georgian palaeography and literature.
Ivane Javakhishvili, *Dzveli k'art'uli saistorio mtserloba* (*V–XVIII ss.*) (*Old Georgian
Historical Writing, 5th–18th Century*), repr. in his *T'khzulebani* (*Collected Works*),
vol. 8 (T'bilisi, 1977)
Somewhat dated yet essential guide to medieval Georgian historical literature.
Korneli Kekelidze, *K'art'uli literaturis istoria* (*History of Georgian Literature*), vol. 1,
*Dzveli mtserloba* (*Ancient Writing*) (T'bilisi, 1960)
Standard guide to medieval Georgian literature. Printed in several editions includ-
ing a German adaptation by Mich[a]el Tarchnishvili, *Geschichte der kirchlichen
georgischen Literatur*, Studi e Testi 185 (Vatican City, 1955).

Bernard Outtier, 'Langue et littérature géorgiennes', in Micheline Albert, Robert Beylot, René-G. Coquin, Bernard Outtier and Charles Renoux, eds., *Christianismes orientaux: introduction à l'étude des langues et des littératures* (Paris, 1993), 261–96 Concise but detailed guide to the Georgian language and literature.

## Select Catalogues

### *T'bilisi/Kekelidze Institute of Manuscripts*
An English summary of the Institute's holdings is available on the Internet at: *http:georgianmanuscripts.caucasus.net/en/institute.asp*

*K'art'ul khelnatsert'a aghtseriloba: qop'ili k'art'velt'a shoris tsera-kit'khvis gamovrts'-elebeli sazogadoebis (S) kolek'ts'iisa* (*Description of Georgian Manuscripts: the collection of the former Society for the Propagation of Literacy among the Georgians (S)*), vols. 1–7 (T'bilisi, 1959–73)
The various catalogues of manuscripts housed in the Georgian Republic include accession numbers, physical descriptions, and overviews of contents. Important colophons are also reproduced. Many of these volumes are indexed.

*K'art'ul khelnatsert'a aghtseriloba: qop'ili saeklesio muzeumis (A) kolek'ts'iisa* (*Description of Georgian Manuscripts: the collection of the former Ecclesiastical Museum (A)*), 5 vols. (T'bilisi, 1954–86)

*Sak'art'velos sakhelmtsip'o muzeumis k'art'ul khelnatsert'a aghtseriloba: muzeumis khelnatsert'a akhali (Q) kolek'ts'ia* (*Description of the Georgian Manuscripts of the Georgian State Museum: Museum manuscripts, new collection (Q)*), vols. 1–2 (T'bilisi, 1957 and 1958)

*Sak'art'velos sakhelmtsip'o muzeumis k'art'ul khelnatsert'a aghtseriloba: sak'art'velos saistorio da saet'nograp'io sazogadoebis qop'ili muzeumis khelnatserebi (H kolek'ts'ia)* (*Description of the Georgian Manuscripts of the Georgian State Museum: manuscripts of the former museum of the Georgian Historical and Ethnographic Society, H collection*) (T'bilisi, 1946–51)

### *T'bilisi/Central State Historical Archive, P'ondi/fond 1446*
V. Kacharava, Sh. Ch'khetia, D. Marjgaladze and S. Lekishvili, eds., *Tsentral'nyi gosudarstvennyi istoricheskii arkhiv: putevoditel'* (*Handbook of the Central State Historical Archive*) (2nd edn., T'bilisi, 1976)
Korneli Kekelidze, ed., *Ts'entraluri sakhelmtsip'o saistorio ark'ivi: k'art'ul khelnatsert'a kolek'ts'iis aghtseriloba* (*Central State Historical Archive: description of the collection's Georgian manuscripts*), 2 vols. (T'bilisi, 1949 and 1950)

### *K'ut'aisi/K'ut'aisi State Historical–Ethnographic Museum*
E. Nikoladze, ed. (*K'ut'aisis sakhelmtsip'o istoriul-et'nograp'iuli muzeumis*) *khelnatsert'a aghtseriloba* (*Description of Manuscripts*), vol. 2 (T'bilisi, 1964)

*Svanet'i*
Valeri Silogava, ed., *Svanet'is tserilobit'i dzeglebi* (*Written Monuments of Svanet'i*), vol. 1, *Istoriuli sabut'ebi da sult'a matianeebi* (*Historical Documents and Synodika*) (T'bilisi, 1986)
With photographs of several manuscripts.

*Jerusalem/Library of the Greek Patriarchate*
Robert P. Blake, ed., *Catalogue des manuscrits géorgiens de la Bibliothèque patriarcale grecque à Jérusalem* (Paris, 1924)
N.Ia. Marr, ed., with Elene Metreveli, *Ierusalimis berdznuli sapatriark'o tsignsats'avis k'art'uli khelnatserebis mokle aghtseriloba* (*Short Description of the Georgian Manuscripts in the Library of the Greek Patriarchate of Jerusalem*) (T'bilisi, 1955)

*Mt Sinai/Library of St Catherine's Monastery*
*K'art'ul khelnatsert'a aghtseriloba: sinuri kolek'ts'ia* (*Description of Georgian Manuscripts: Sinai collection*), vols. 1–3 (T'bilisi, 1978–87)
Gérard Garitte, *Catalogue des manuscrits géorgiens littéraires du Mont Sinaï*, CSCO, vol. 165, subsidia 9 (Louvain, 1956)
N.Ia. Marr, *Opisanie gruzinskikh rukopisei sinaiskago monastyria* (*Description of the Georgian Manuscripts of the Sinai Monastery*) (Moscow and Leningrad, 1940)

*Mt Athos/Iveron Library*
Oliver Wardrop, 'Georgian manuscripts at the Iberian monastery on mount Athos', *Journal of Theological Studies* 12 (1911), 593–607

*St Petersburg/Oriental Institute*
R.R. Orbeli, *Gruzinskie rukopisi Instituta Vostokovedeniia* (*Georgian Manuscripts of the Oriental Institute*), vol. 1 (Moscow and Leningrad, 1956)
Includes photographs of several manuscripts.

*Oxford/Bodleian Library, Wardrop Collection*
David Barrett, *Catalogue of the Wardrop Collection and of Other Georgian Books and Manuscripts in the Bodleian Library* (Oxford, 1973)
Splendid catalogue of the extensive Georgian holdings of the Wardrop Collection. Well indexed.

*London/British Library*
David Marshall Lang, *Catalogue of Georgian and Other Caucasian Printed Books in the British Museum* (London, 1962)
Splendid catalogue of the Georgian holdings of the British Library. Well indexed.

*Cambridge/Cambridge University Library*
Robert P. Blake, 'Catalogue of the Georgian manuscripts in the Cambridge University Library', *Harvard Theological Review* 25.3 (1932), 207–24

*European Repositories (overview)*
Ilia Tabaghua, ed., *Sak'art'velo evropis ark'ivebis da tsignsats'avebshi*, 3 vols. (T'bilisi, 1982–7); French summary, 'La Géorgie dans les archives et dans les bibliothèques de l'Europe'
Extensive review of materials in European repositories related to Georgian studies.

## PRIMARY SOURCES

The eleventh to thirteenth century was a particularly vibrant period for Georgian literary production. Works listed here are of special importance for prosopographical research.

### K‘art‘lis ts‘khovreba (K‘art‘lis c‘xovreba) and its constituent texts (11th–13th c.)

*K‘art‘lis ts‘khovreba*, literally 'The Life of K‘art‘li/Georgia', known informally as 'The Georgian Royal Annals' and 'Georgian Chronicles'. With very few exceptions, extant pre-modern historical works in Georgian have come down to us exclusively within this corpus. Its medieval section consists of as many as thirteen distinct texts composed between *c.* 800 and the fourteenth century. Scholarly literature devoted to *K‘art‘lis ts‘khovreba* is voluminous, but in English see Toumanoff, 'Medieval Georgian historical literature' and Rapp, 'Imagining history at the crossroads' and *Studies in Medieval Georgian Historiography* (full references below under 'Selected Studies', pp. 216–20).

*Standard critical Georgian edition (entire corpus)*
Though originally published in the 1950s, Qaukhch‘ishvili's edition remains the superior edition for the whole of *K‘art‘lis ts‘khovreba*. It is indexed and incorporates a detailed apparatus. Since its publication, only one old ('pre-Vakhtangiseuli') manuscript, the so-called Mts‘khet‘ian (Q) redaction of 1697, has been discovered; a few individual component texts have been re-edited with Q (see below, e.g., *The Life of Davit‘ II*). Qaukhch‘ishvili's two volumes are commonly abbreviated $K‘Ts‘^1$ and $K‘Ts‘^2$ respectively.

Simon Qaukhch‘ishvili, ed., *K‘art‘lis ts‘khovreba*, vols. 1 and 2 (T‘bilisi, 1955 and 1959). The first volume was reprinted as Stephen H. Rapp Jr., general ed. and intro., *K‘art‘lis c‘xovreba: the Georgian Royal Annals and their medieval Armenian adaptation*, vol. 1 (Delmar, NY, 1998)

*Translations:*
Robert W. Thomson, tr. and comm., *Rewriting Caucasian History: the medieval Armenian adaptation of the Georgian Chronicles, the original Georgian texts and the Armenian adaptation* (Oxford, 1996)
Georgian texts are translated below the double line. Thomson's splendid translations are preferable to those in other western languages. For the Georgian text, the translator relied entirely on the edition of Qaukhch‘ishvili. Thomson has translated only those texts appearing in the medieval Armenian adaptation; thus the two biographies of Queen T‘amar and *The History of the Five Reigns* are not included.
Katharine Vivian, *The Georgian Chronicle: the period of Giorgi Lasha* (Amsterdam, 1991)
Though based on Qaukhch‘ishvili's standard critical edition, Vivian's translations are incomplete and sometimes stray from the literal meaning. Evidently targeting a popular audience, in several instances Vivian skips lines and entire

paragraphs of Georgian text without comment; in at least one case (in *The Histories and Eulogies of the Sovereigns*), Vivian has resequenced the text as it has come down to us.

Gertrud Pätsch, *Das Leben Kartlis, Eine Chronik aus Georgien 300–1200* (Leipzig, 1985)
Not seen; rarely cited.

*Editions of individual Georgian manuscripts*
Anaseuli (A) redaction of 1479–95: Simon Qaukhch'ishvili, ed., *K'art'lis ts'khovreba: ana dedop'liseuli nuskha* (*K'art'lis ts'khovreba: the Queen Anna copy*) (T'bilisi, 1942)
Mariamiseuli (M) redaction of 1633–45/6: Ek'vt'ime T'aqaïshvili, ed., *K'art'lis ts'khovreba: mariam dedop'lis varianti* (*K'art'lis ts'khovreba: the Queen Mariam variant*) (Tp'ilisi, 1906)

*Medieval Armenian adaptation of K'art'lis ts'khovreba (Patmut'iwn Vrats')*
The Armenian adaptation (*Arm. Adapt.*), an abbreviated but faithful edition of *K'art'lis ts'khovreba*, is the most immediate witness to the medieval provenance of the corpus. The adaptation's oldest surviving manuscript derives from 1274–1311, while the oldest extant Georgian manuscript—the Anaseuli (A) redaction—was produced at the end of the fifteenth century. The adaptation is sometimes attributed to a certain Juansher, hence 'Juansher's Chronicle', but this attribution is erroneous.

Ilia Abuladze, ed. and Georgian tr., *K'art'lis ts'khovrebis dzveli somxuri t'argmani* (*The Old Armenian Translation of K'art'lis ts'khovreba*) (T'bilisi, 1953), reprinted as Stephen H. Rapp Jr., general ed. and intro., *K'art'lis c'xovreba: the Georgian Royal Annals and their medieval Armenian adaptation*, vol. 2 (Delmar, NY, 1998)
Abuladze's edition supersedes that of A. T'iroyean, ed., *Hamarot patmut'iwn Vrats'* (Venice, 1884).

*Translation:*
Robert W. Thomson, tr. and comm., *Rewriting Caucasian History: the medieval Armenian adaptation of the Georgian Chronicles, the original Georgian texts and the Armenian adaptation* (Oxford, 1996)
The Armenian adaptation is translated above the double line. Thomson's translation is based upon earlier manuscripts which are much preferrable to those serving as the basis of the now-outdated French rendering by Marie-Félicité Brosset, *Additions et éclaircissements à l'histoire de la Géorgie* (St Petersburg, 1851), 1–61.

*Early modern 'Vakhtangiseuli' Georgian edition*
This later edition of the corpus was produced by the order of Vakhtang VI (r. 1711–14, 1719–23). Though it is of enormous value for the understanding of ancient and medieval history in the eighteenth century, pre-Vakhtangiseuli redactions (see above) are far superior for the earlier periods. Brosset's edition includes a full French translation.

Marie-Félicité Brosset, ed. and French tr., *Histoire de la Géorgie depuis l'antiquité jusqu'au XIXᵉ siècle*, vol. 1, *Histoire ancienne, jusqu'en 1469 de J.-C.* (St Petersburg, 1849)

Individual component texts of *K'art'lis ts'khovreba*, 11th–13th c.

| Historical text | Date of origin | Qaukhch'ishvili critical ed., *K'art'lis ts'khovreba* | Published English translations |
| --- | --- | --- | --- |
| Sumbat Davit'is-dze, *History and Tale of the Bagratids* | *c.*1030 | vol. 1.372–86* | Rapp, *Studies in Medieval Georgian Historiography*, ch. 6 |
| *Chronicle of K'art'li* | 11th century | vol. 1.249–317 | Thomson, *RCH*, 255–308** |
| *Life of Davit' II* | 12th century | vol. 1.318–64* | Thomson, *RCH*, 308–53 |
| *Histories and Eulogies* | 13th century | vol. 2.1–114 | excerpts in Vivian, *GC*, 107–42*** |
| *Life of T'amar* | 13th century | vol. 2.115–50**** | Vivian, *GC*, 55–96 |
| *History of the Five Reigns* | 13th century | vol. 1.365–71 | excerpts in Vivian, *GC*, 49–54 |

*Texts re-edited with the Mts'khet'ian variant of *K'art'lis ts'khovreba* discovered after the completion of Qaukhch'ishvili's edition.
**Thomson, *RCH* = Robert W. Thomson's *Rewriting Caucasian History* (with parallel translation of the medieval Georgian variant (bottom of page) and medieval Armenian adaptation (top of page)).
***Vivian, *GC* = Katharine Vivian's *The Georgian Chronicle: the period of Giorgi Lasha*.
****New edition by Marine K'adagidze, *T'amar mep'is droindeli matiane*.

### Sumbat Davit'is-dze, *Life and Tale of the Bagratids* (*c.*1030)

Though Davit'is-dze's tract commences with a biblical stemma, his coverage of Georgian history begins in the sixth century and continues to *c.*1030. Narrowly focused on the Georgian Bagratid house, it is particularly reliable starting from the eighth century.

*Editions and Translations:*
Goneli Arakhamia, ed., *Ts'khorebay da utsqebay bagratoniant'a* (T'bilisi, 1990)
English tr. of this ed. in Stephen H. Rapp Jr., *Studies in Medieval Georgian Historiography: early texts and Eurasian contexts*, CSCO, vol. 601, subsidia 113 (Louvain, 2003), ch. 6

*Older Georgian Editions:*
Qaukhch'ishvili, ed., *K'Ts'*[1], 372–86
Ek'vt'ime T'aqaïshvili, ed., in his *Sami istoriuli khronika* (*Three Historical Chronicles*) (Tp'ilisi, 1890), 41–79
T'aqaïshvili, ed. and comm., *Sumbat davit'is dzis k'ronika tao-klarjet'is bagrationt'a shesakheb* (*Sumbat Davit'is-dze's Chronicle on the Bagratids of Tao-Klarjet'i*) (T'bilisi, 1949)

*Russian Translation:*
Mariam Lort'k'ip'anidze (Lordkipanidze) (T'bilisi, 1979)

### Anonymous, *Chronicle of K'art'li*, (second half of 11th c.)

Addresses the period just after Arch'il II (d. 785/6) to Bagrat IV (r. 1027–72). Essential for the early Bagratid period and unique among extant Georgian histories in its treatment of both pre-Bagratid and Bagratid rulers. Though writing in the early Bagratid era, its anonymous author employed pre-Bagratid sources.

*Editions and Translations:*
*Matiane k'art'lisay, K'Ts'*[1], 249–317; tr. Thomson, 255–308 ('Book of K'art'li')

*Additional English Translation:*
Arrian Tchanturia, *The Georgian Chronicle: Matiane kartlisa*, Roin Metreveli, intro. and comm. (T'bilisi, 1996)

*Russian Translations:*
Mariam Lort'k'ip'anidze (Lordkipanidze), *Matiane kartlisa* (T'bilisi, 1976)
G.V. Tsulaia, *Letopis' Kartli* (T'bilisi, 1982)

## Anonymous, *Life of King of Kings Davit'*

Perhaps written by the king's famous contemporary, the monk Arsen Beri/?Iqalt'oeli (12th c., after 1125). First of the Bagratid-era royal biographies. Eloquent text dedicated to the reign of Davit' II (IV) Aghmashenebeli ('the Builder' or 'the Rebuilder', r. 1089–1125) is the first in Georgian historiography to exhibit a deep familiarity with Byzantine literary models and conventions.

*Editions and Translations:*
Mzek'ala Shanidze, ed., *Ts'khorebay mep'et'-mep'isa davit'isi* (T'bilisi, 1992)
Older Georgian ed. in Qaukhch'ishvili, *K'Ts'*[1], 318–64
English tr. of Qaukhch'ishvili's older ed. by Thomson, 308–53
> For a table relating the page correspondences between Shanidze, Qaukhch'ishvili, and Thomson, see Rapp, ed., *Arm. Adapt.*, 18–23.

*Other printed versions include:*
Brosset, ed., 236–63, and French tr., 345–81

*German Translation:*
M. Tsereteli, 'Das Leben des Köenige Dawith (Dawith II, 1089–1125)', *Bedi Kartlisa* 2–3 (1957), 45–73

## Anonymous ('The First Historian of T'amar'), *Histories and Eulogies of the Crowned* (13th c.)

Addresses the reigns of Giorgi III (1156–84) and his daughter T'amar (1184–1213). This text is not found in the Anaseuli (A) redaction, the oldest surviving Georgian manuscript of *K'art'lis ts'khovreba*, but is incorporated into other early pre-Vakhtangiseuli variants. Contains the most elaborate description of the basis of royal legitimacy in Bagratid Georgia and demonstrates a fusion of Georgian, Byzantine/Christian, and Islamic (especially Turko-Iranian) models of kingship.

*Editions and Translations:*
Qaukhch'ishvili, ed., *Istoriani da azmani sharavandedt'ani, K'Ts'*[2], 1–114

*Russian Translation:*
Korneli Kekelidze, 'Istoriia i voskhvalenia ventsenostsev', repr. in his *Etiudebi dzveli k'art'uli literaturis istoriidan (Studies in the History of Old Georgian Literature)*, vol. 12 (T'bilisi, 1973), 164–232

*English Translation:*
Scattered excerpts in Vivian, 107–42
> From a scholarly perspective, this is the most problematic of Vivian's translations. Only a small part of the overall text has been translated; elided passages/para-

graphs/pages have not always been indicated; some sub-titles not appearing in the manuscripts have been added without comment; transliterations sometimes do not match the Georgian text; Qaukhch'ishvili's paragraph breaks have sometimes been reworked; and in one especially troublesome instance, Vivian has resequenced the text (first on p. 123, sentence beginning 'The wretched Russian' represents an unacknowledged jump in Qaukhch'ishvili's text from page 55.2 to 61.3. Later on the same page, the paragraph starting 'The army mustered . . .' skips back to Qaukhch'ishvili, 58.3).

## Anonymous ('The Second Historian of T'amar') *Life of Monarch of Monarchs T'amar* (13th c.)

Sometimes erroneously ascribed to Basil Ezosmodzghuari. Features the reigns of Giorgi III and especially his daughter T'amar. This text has reached us in a defective condition, its second part having been lost and replaced in some later manuscripts with excerpts from the *Histories and Eulogies of the Crowned* (see above). As a consequence, this *Life of T'amar* may not have been originally incorporated into *K'art'lis ts'khovreba*.

*Editions and Translations:*
Qaukhch'ishvili, ed., *Ts'khovreba mep'et'-mep'isa t'amarisi*, *K'Ts'*², 115–50
English tr. of Qaukhch'ishvili's ed., Vivian, 55–96
   Vivian's translation of this text is more-or-less complete (with only a few small phrases and passages missing), though she has incorporated some 'interpolated' materials from later sources without comment.

*Russian Translation:*
V.D. Dondua, tr. and M.M. Berdzenishvili, comm., *Zhizn' Tsaritsy Tsarits Tamar* (T'bilisi, 1985); English summary, 70–1

For a new edition of the Georgian text, see Marine K'adagidze, ed., *T'amar mep'is droindeli matiane ('ts'khovreba mep'et' mep'isa t'amarisi')* (T'bilisi, 2001).

## Anonymous, *History of the Five Reigns* (13th c.)

Describes reigns from Demetre I (1125–54) through T'amar's son Giorgi IV Lasha (1213–23). This work is not properly a chronicle, though some dates in the Georgian era (*k'oronikon*) are furnished.

*Editions and Translations:*
Qaukhch'ishvili, ed., *Lasha giorgis-droindeli mematiane (Chronicle of the Time of Lasha Giorgi)*, *K'Ts'*¹, 365–71

*Earlier Georgian Edition:*
Ivane Javakhishvili, *Lasha-giorgis-droindeli mematiane (Chronicon anonymum tempore regis Lasha-Georgii scriptum)* (Tp'ilisi, 1927)

Partial English tr. of the accounts of Demetre I, Davit' III, Giorgi III, and Giorgi IV Lasha (one paragraph) by Vivian, 49–54.

**Lives**

*Critical Editions of Georgian Hagiography* (11th–13th c.):
Ilia Abuladze, ed., *Dzveli k'art'uli agiograp'iuli literaturis dzeglebi* (*Monuments of Old Georgian Hagiographical Literature*), vols. 1–3 (T'bilisi, 1963/4, 1967, and 1971)
Contains the standard critical editions of medieval Georgian hagiographies and supersedes all previous ones, including Mik'ael Sabinin, ed., *Sak'art'ūēlos samot'khe* (*Georgia's Paradise*) (St Petersburg, 1882). Abuladze's editions are splendid, complete with variant readings, though these three volumes are not indexed.
David Marshall Lang, *Lives and Legends of the Georgian Saints*, rev. edn. (Crestwood, NY, 1976)
Short excerpts of several prominent Lives. This short volume has a skeletal index, though it should be noted that Lang often skips sentences and paragraphs within a given text without any indication. His translations are geared for a general audience and sometimes lack scholarly precision.

Giorgi Mt'atsmi[n]deli (1009–65), *Life of Iovane and Ep't'wme* (11th c.)

Ilia Abuladze, ed., *Ts'khorebay iovanesi da ep't'wmesi*, in *Dzveli k'art'uli agiograp'iuli literaturis dzeglebi* (*Monuments of Old Georgian Hagiographical Literature*), vol. 2, 38–100

*Partial English Translation:*
Lang, *Lives and Legends*, 155–65

*French Translation:*
Bernadette Martin-Hisard, 'La vie de Jean et Euthyme et le statut du monastère des Ibéres de l'Athos', *RÉB* 49 (1991), 67–142

*Modern Latin Translation:*
Peeters, 'Histoires monastiques géorgiennes', *Analecta Bollandiana* 36–7 (1917–18), 8–68

Giorgi Mts'ire (d. after 1083), *Life of Giorgi Mt'atsmideli* (second half of 11th c.)

Ilia Abuladze, ed., *Ts'khorebay giorgi mt'atsmidelisay*, in *Dzveli k'art'uli agiograp'iuli literaturis dzeglebi* (*Monuments of Old Georgian Hagiographical Literature*), vol. 2, 101–207

*Partial English Translation:*
Lang, *Lives and Legends*, 165–8
Wachtang Z. Djobadze, *Materials for the Study of Georgian Monasteries in the Western Environs of Antioch on the Orontes*, CSCO, vol. 372, subsidia 48 (Louvain, 1976), 50–9

*Modern Latin Translation:*
Paul Peeters, 'Histoires monastiques géorgiennes', *Analecta Bollandiana* 36–7 (1917–18), 69–159

## Metaphrases

Ilia Abuladze, ed., *Dzveli k'art'uli agiograp'iuli literaturis dzeglebi* (*Monuments of Old Georgian Hagiographical Literature*), vol. 3
Metaphrastic redactions of older texts deriving from the eleventh–thirteenth century.

Nargiza Goguadze, ed., *Dzveli metap'rasuli krebulebi* (*Old Metaphrastic Collections*) (T'bilisi, 1986); French summary, 546–8
Not seen.

## Ecclesiastical Documents

Ilia Abuladze, ed., *Dzveli k'art'uli agiograp'iuli literaturis dzeglebi* (*Monuments of Old Georgian Hagiographical Literature*), vol. 4 (T'bilisi, 1968)
Features synaxaria of the eleventh–eighteenth century, including the Lives of Ek'vt'ime Mt'atsmideli and Prokhore 'the K'art'velian'. Splendid critical edition.

I. Dolidze, ed., *K'art'uli samart'lis dzeglebi* (*Monuments of Georgian Law*), vol. 3, *Saeklesio sakanonmdeblo dzeglebi (XI–XIX ss.)* (*Ecclesiastical Legislation, 11th–19th Century*) (T'bilisi, 1970)
Various ecclesiastical documents with variant readings, including the acts of the 1103 Ruisi-Urbnisi synod (#6, 106–27). Indexed.

T'ina Enuk'idze, ed., *Tbet'is sult'a matiane* (T'bilisi, 1977); English summary, 'The Tbet'i synodal records', 54–8
Prosopographically rich document, whose oldest layer belongs to the twelfth to thirteenth century. With detailed index and reproduction of select manuscript leaves.

## Secular Legal Documents

I. Dolidze, ed., *K'art'uli samart'lis dzeglebi* (*Monuments of Georgian Law*), vol. 2, *Saero sakanonmdeblo dzeglebi (X–XIX ss.)* (*Popular/Secular Legislation, 10th–19th Century*) (T'bilisi, 1965)
Documents #3–#13 pertain to the period 1025–1204. Extensive index.

### Testament of King Davit' II

Andro Gogoladze, ed., *Davit' aghmasheneblis anderdzi shiomghvimisadme (istoriul-tsqarot'mts'odneobit'i gamokvleva)* (*Davit' Aghmashenebeli's Will to Shio-Mghwme*) (T'bilisi, 2001), text 168–79, German summary, 186–91

*Older Edition with Russian Translation:*

T'. Zhordania, ed. and tr., *Zaveshchanie Tsaria Davida Vozobnoviteliia, dannoe Shio-mgvimskoi lavre v 1123 g.* (*The Will of King Davit' 'the Builder', presented to the Shio-Mghwme Lavra in 1123*) (Tiflis, 1895)
Limited prosopographical information, especially for clerics.

## Charters and Other Documents

S.S. Kakabadze, tr., *Gruzinskie dokumenty IX–XV vv. v sobranii leningradskogo otde-
    leniia Instituta vostokovedeniia AN SSSR* (*Georgian Documents of the 9th–15th
    Century in the Collection of the Leningrad Branch of the Oriental Institute of the
    USSR Academy of Sciences*) (Moscow, 1982)
    Russian translation of and commentary on important legal documents from the
    period.

T'. Enuk'idze, V. Silogava, and N. Shoshiashvili, eds., *K'art'uli istoriuli sabut'ebi
    IX–XIII ss.* (*Georgian Historical Documents, 9th–13th Century*) (T'bilisi, 1984)
    Good Georgian edition with indices and numerous photographs of documents.

T'. Zhordania, ed., *K'ronikebi da skhva masala sak'art'velos istoriisa da mtserlobisa*
    (*Chronicles and Other Materials on Georgian History and Literature*), vol. 1
    (Tp'ilisi, 1893)
    Includes numerous documents unpublished elsewhere. Rare in western libraries.

## Epic Literature

Shot'a Rust'aveli, *Knight/Man in the Panther's Skin* (?12th/13th c.)
Most renowned literary figure in Georgia. Rust'aveli's *floruit* is uncertain, though he is
normally associated with the reign of Queen T'amar (1184–1213). His epic poem combines Georgian, Turko-Iranian, Christian, Muslim, Byzantine, and even Neoplatonic
imagery.

*Editions and Translations:*
Many Georgian editions, though A. Baramidze, Korneli Kekelidze, and Akaki
    Shanidze, eds., *Vep'khistqaosani*, (T'bilisi, 1957) is perhaps the most scholarly.

*English Translations:*
Venera Urushadze, with intro. by David Marshall Lang, *Shota Rustaveli, The Knight
    in the Panther's Skin* (T'bilisi, 1986)

Marjory Scott Wardrop, *The Man in the Panther's Skin* (T'bilisi, 1966, repr. of
    London, 1912)
    With an extensive index of transliterated Georgian terminology.

## Anthology

Ivane Lolashvili, ed., *Dzveli k'art'uli literaturis dzeglebi* (*Monuments of Old Georgian
    Literature*), (T'bilisi, 1978)
    Handy anthology of non-historiographical works of medieval Georgian literature
    produced between the fifth and thirteenth century. Among the featured texts are
    works by Giorgi Mt'atsmi[n]deli, Giorgi Mts'ire, Arsen Iqalt'oeli, Ep'rem Mts'ire,
    Ezra Mt'atsmideli, Ioane Petritsi, Ioane Shavt'eli, Arsen Gulmaisimisdze, and
    Ch'akhrukhadze. Geared towards a popular audience, this volume contains use-
    ful, but short, biographies of the writers (pp. 619–41) and an index of 'rare and
    archaic' terminology.

## Art

A. Alpago-Novello, V. Beridze, J. Lafontaine-Dosogne, *et al.*, *Art and Architecture in Medieval Georgia*, Publications d'histoire de l'art et d'archéologie de l'Université catholique de Louvain, vol. 21 (Louvain, 1980)

Shalva Amiranashvili, *Georgian Metalwork from Antiquity to the 18th Century* (London and New York, 1971)

Vaxtang (Vakhtang) Beridze, Gaiané Alibegashvili, Aneli Volskaja and Leila Xuskivadze, *The Treasures of Georgia*, tr. Bruce Penman (London, 1984)

Antony Eastmond, *Royal Imagery in Medieval Georgia* (University Park, PA, 1998)
Recent, comprehensive study of the few surviving artistic representations of medieval Bagratid monarchs; up-to-date bibliography.

Leila Khuskivadze, ed., *Medieval Cloisonné Enamels at [the] Georgian State Museum of Fine Arts (Shua saukuneebis tikhruli minank'ari sak'art'velos khelovnebis sakhelmtsip'o muzeumshi)* (T'bilisi, 1984)
In English and Georgian.

Rusudan Mepisaschwili and Wachtang Zinzadse. *Die Kunst des alten Georgien* (Leipzig, 1977)

Ori Z. Soltes, ed., *National Treasures of Georgia* (London, 1999)
Catalogue for an aborted exhibition of Georgian antiquities with essays written by several Georgian and non-Georgian scholars. Some of the essays, e.g., Rapp, 'Medieval Christian Georgia' (pp. 84–96), were apparently subjected to patriotic editing. The end of the first sentence of Rapp's essay originally read 'thus inaugurated the official sanction and support of the Christian Church in the domains of P'arnavaz', i.e., in eastern Georgia, not 'in Transcaucasia' (!), as published.

## Coinage

T'. Abramishvili, *Sak'art'velos sakhelmtsip'o muzeumis bizantiuri monetebi (Byzantine Coinage of the Georgian State Museum)* (T'bilisi, 1989); Russian summary, 'Vizantiiskie monety gosudarstvennogo muzeia Gruzii', 72.

D.G. Kapanadze, *Gruzinskaia numizmatika (Georgian Numismatics)* (T'bilisi, 1955)
Along with Pakhomov, one of the standard catalogues of Georgian coinage.

David Marshall Lang, 'Coins of Georgia in Transcaucasia acquired by the American Numismatic Society: 1953–1965', *American Numismatic Society Museum Notes* 12 (1966), 223–32

—— 'Notes on Caucasian numismatics (part 1)', *The Numismatic Chronicle*, 6th ser. 17 (1957), 137–46

—— *Studies in the Numismatic History of Georgia in Transcaucasia*, Numismatic Notes and Monographs, vol. 130 (New York, 1955)
Detailed survey of the Georgian coins in the collection of the museum of the American Numismatic Society.

E.A. Pakhomov, *Monety Gruzii (The Money of Georgia)* (repr. T'bilisi, 1970)
An unpublished English translation of this volume by H. Bartlett Wells is available at the museum of the American Numismatic Society, New York.

Stephen H. Rapp, Jr., 'The coinage of T'amar, sovereign of Georgia in Caucasia: a pre-
liminary study in the numismatic inscriptions of twelfth- and thirteenth-century
Georgian royal coinage', *Le Muséon* 106.3–4 (1993), 309–30
Supplements Lang's study of coinage in the collection of the American
Numismatic Society.

### Inscriptions

P.M. Muradian, ed., *Armianskaia epigrafika Gruzii: Kartli i Kakheti* (*Armenian
Inscriptions of Georgia: K'art'li and Kakhet'i*) (Erevan, 1985)
Valeri Silogava, ed., *Bet'aniis tsartserebi* (T'bilisi, 1994); English summary, 'The
inscriptions of Betania', 61–3
Darejan Kldiashvili and Zaza Skhirtladze, eds., *Garejis epigrap'ikuli dzeglebi*, vol. 1,
*Tsm. davit'is lavra, udabnos monasteri (XI–XVIII ss.)* (T'bilisi, 1999); English
translation of preface, 'The inscriptions of Gareja and the history of their
research', 43–72
Excellent initial volume of a series featuring the inscriptions of the monasteries of
the Garesja desert. This first instalment addresses the inscriptions of the Lavra of
St David of the Udabno monastery dating to the eleventh to eighteenth century.
T'inat'in Qaukhch'ishvili, ed., *Sak'art'velos berdznuli tsartserebis korpusi*, 3 vols.
(T'bilisi, 1999–2000); German summaries, 'Korpus der griechischen Inscriften
in Georgien'
Comprehensive corpus of the Greek inscriptions found on Georgian territory.
Valeri Silogava, ed., *Tsartserebi garejos mravaltsqarodan (IX–XIII ss.): paleograp'iuli
da tsqarot'mts'odneobit'i gamokvleva* (T'bilisi, 1999); English summary, 'Old
Georgian inscriptions-graffiti from the rock-cut complex Mravaltskaro of Gareji:
research in paleography and source studies', 281–3
Presentation of graffiti from the Davit' Garesja (var. Gareja, Gareji) monastic
complex in south-eastern Georgia; hastily published before the appearance of a
competing study.
—— ed., *Samts'khe-javakhet'is istoriuli muzeumis k'art'uli epigrap'ikuli dzeglebi*,
(Akhalts'ikhe, 2000); English summary and translations of inscriptions,
'Georgian epigraphic monuments of the Samtskhe-Javakhetey Historical
Museum', 123–38
Presents several Georgian inscriptions from the districts of Samts'khe and
Javakhet'i which bordered Byzantine Anatolia.

### SELECTED STUDIES

The flagship scholarly journal of the historical and cultural branches of K'art'velol-
ogy (Georgian Studies) outside the former USSR is *Georgica* published by Friedrich-
Schiller-Universität in Jena in association with T'bilisi State University (T'SU). T'SU's
Institute of Classical Philology, Byzantine, and Modern Greek Studies also publishes
*Caucasica: The Journal of Caucasian Studies*; many of its articles are in English and
Russian. Despite their importance, these journals are absent from all but the largest

research libraries outside the Republic of Georgia. In the past, *Bedi Kartlisa* and its successor *Revue des études géorgiennes et caucasiennes* filled this role more visibly. In Georgian, numerous articles have appeared in the various series of *Mats'ne* (*Herald*) and *Mravalt'avi* (*Polycephalon*), both published under the aegis of the Georgian Academy of Sciences. The small, bilingual (Georgian and English) bulletin *The Kartvelologist* (Geo. *K'art'velologi*) is also helpful. The sporadic *Annual of the Society for the Study of Caucasia* is, like its parent organisation, now defunct.

Alek'sandre Abdaladze, *Amierkavkasiis politikur ert'eult'a urt'iert'oba IX–XI saukuneebshi* (*Inter-relation of the Political Formation of Transcaucasia in the 9th–11th Century*) (T'bilisi, 1988); Russian summary, 'Vzaimootnosheniia politicheskikh obrazovanii Zakavkaz'ia v IX–XI vekakh', 278–81

G. Akop'ashvili, *P'eodaluri urt'iert'obis istoriidan XI–XII ss sak'art'veloshi* (*History of Feudal Relations in Georgia, 11th–12th Century*) (T'bilisi, 1984)

A. Alek'sidze (Alexidze), 'Martha-Maria: a striking figure in the cultural history of Georgia and Byzantium', in Marianna Koromila, ed., *The Greeks in the Black Sea* (Athens, 1991), 204–12

A. Alek'sidze, and Sh. Burjanadze, *Masalebi sak'art'velos istoriuli geograp'iisa da toponomikisat'vis* (*Materials for Georgian Historical Geography and Toponyms*), vol. 1, 'X–XVII ss-is istoriuli dokumentebis mikhedvit'' (*According to Historical Documents of the 10th–17th Century*) (T'bilisi, 1964)

Zaza Alek'sidze (Alexidze) 'The new recensions of the "Conversion of Georgia" and the "Lives of the 13 Syrian Fathers" recently discovered on Mt. Sinai', in *Il Caucaso: Cerniera fra culture dal Mediterraneo alla Persia (secoli IV–XI)*, Settimane di Studio del Centro italiano di studi sull'alto Medioevo, vol. 43.1 (Spoleto, 1996), 409–26

Ilia Ant'elava, *XI–XV saukuneebis sak'art'velos sots'ialur-politikuri istoriis sakit'khebi* (*Questions on the Socio-political History of Georgia, 11th–15th Century*) (T'bilisi, 1980); Russian summary, 'Voprosy sotsial'no-politicheskoi istorii Gruzii XI–XV vv.', 238–9

—— *Sak'art'velos ts'entraluri da adgilobrivi mmart'veloba XI–XIII ss.* (*Central and Local Administration of Georgia, 11th–13th Century*) (T'bilisi, 1983); Russian summary, 'Tsentral'noe i mestnoe upravlenie Gruzii v XI–XIII vv', 229–30

—— *XI–XIV ss. k'art'uli saistorio tsqaroebi* (*Georgian Historical Sources, 11th–14th Century*) (T'bilisi, 1988); Russian summary, 'Gruzinskie istoricheskie istochniki XI–XIV vv.', 157–9

Zurab Avalishvili (Avalichvili, Avalov), *Jvarosant'a droidan: ot'khi saistorio narkvevi* (*From the Time of the Crusades: four historical studies*) (Paris, 1929; repr. T'bilisi, 1989)

Shot'a Badridze, *Sak'art'velos urt'iert'obebi bizantiasa da dasavlet'evropist'an (X–XIII ss.)* (*Georgia's Relations with Byzantium and Western Europe, 10th–13th Century*) (T'bilisi, 1984); Russian summary, 'Vzaimootnosheniia Gruzii s Vizantiei i Zapadnoi Evropoi', 176–8

Guram Bedoshvili, *K'art'uli toponimt'a ganmartebit'-etimologiuri lek'sikoni* (T'bilisi, 2002); English summary, 'Dictionary of Georgian geographical names', 570–3

Mamisa Berdzenishvili, 'Sak'art'velos sakhelmtsip'os sazghvarebi XIII saukunis damdegs' ('The state borders of Georgia at the start of the 13th century'), in *Sak'art'velo rust'avelis khanashi* (*Georgia in the Time of Rust'aveli*) (T'bilisi, 1966),

52–65; Russian summary, 'Granitsy gruzinskogo gosudarstva v nachale XIII veka', 296–7

—— *Sak'art'velo XI–XII saukuneebshi* (*Georgia in the 11th–12th Century*) (T'bilisi, 1970)

—— *Met'ert'mete saukunis k'art'uli saistorio tsqaroebi sak'art'velos sots'ialurekonomikuri istoriis shesakheb* (*Georgian Historical Sources of the 11th Century on Georgia's Socio-economic History*) (T'bilisi, 1979); Russian summary, 'Gruzinskie istochniki XI veka o sotsial'no-ekonomicheskoi istorii Gruzii', 117–23

N. Berdzenishvili, *Gzebi rust'avelis epok'is sak'art'veloshi* (*Roads in Georgia in the Epoch of Rust'aveli*) (T'bilisi, 1966)

Robert P. Blake, 'Georgian secular literature: epic, romantic, and lyric (1100–1800)', *Harvard Studies and Notes in Philology and Literature* 15 (1933), 25–48

Antony Eastmond, 'Gender and orientalism in Georgia in the age of Queen Tamar', in Liz James, ed., *Women, Men, and Eunuchs: gender in Byzantium* (London and New York, 1997), 100–18

—— 'Art and identity in the thirteenth-century Caucasus', *UCLA Near East Center Colloquium Series* (Los Angeles, 2000), 3–40

—— '"Local" saints, art, and regional identity in the Orthodox world after the Fourth Crusade', *Speculum* 78 (2003), 707–49

Lynda Garland and Stephen H. Rapp Jr., 'Mary "of Alania": woman and empress between two worlds', in L. Garland, ed., *Byzantine Women: varieties of experience* (Aldershot, UK, 2006), 89–121

Peter B. Golden, 'Cumanica I: the Qipčaqs in Georgia', *Archivum Eurasiae Medii Aevi* 4 (1984), 45–87

—— 'The Turkic peoples and Caucasia', in Ronald Grigor Suny, ed., *Transcaucasia, Nationalism, and Social Change: essays in the history of Armenia, Azerbaijan, and Georgia*, (rev. edn., Ann Arbor, 1996), 45–67

Konstantine Grigolia, *Akhali k'art'lis ts'khovreba* (*The New K'art'lis ts'khovreba*) (T'bilisi, 1954)

Ivane Javakhishvili (Dzhavakhishvili, Dzhavakhov), *K'art'uli samart'lis istoria* (*Georgian Legal History*), 2 vols., repr. in his *T'khzulebani* (*Collected Works*), vols. 6–7 (T'bilisi, 1982 and 1984)

—— *Sak'art'velos ekonomikuri istoria* (*Economic History of Georgia*), 2 vols., repr. in his *T'khzulebani* (*Collected Works*), vols. 4–5 (T'bilisi, 1996 and 1986 respectively)

—— *T'khzulebani* (*Collected Works*), 12 vols. (T'bilisi, 1979–98)

Elguja Khint'ibidze, *Afonskaia gruzinskaia literaturnaia shkola* (T'bilisi, 1982); English summary, 'Georgian literary school on Mt. Athos', 129–37

—— *Georgian–Byzantine Literary Contacts* (Amsterdam, 1996)

A.E. Klimiashvili, 'Novyi spisok 'Kartlis Tskhovreba' 1697 goda' ('A new redaction of *K'art'lis ts'khovreba* dated 1697'), *Soobshcheniia Akademii Nauk Gruzinskoi SSR* = *Sak'art'velos ssr mec'nierebat'a akademiis moambe* 24.3 (1960), 371–6

V. Kopaliani, *Sak'art'velosa da bizantiis politikuri urt'iert'oba 970–1070 tslebshi* (*Political Relations of Georgia and Byzantium, 970–1070*) (T'bilisi, 1969); Russian summary, 'Gruzino-vizantiiskie politicheskoe vzaimootnosheniia v 970–1070 gg.', 310–20

Jacques Lefort, Nicolas Oikonomidès, Denise Papachryssanthou with Hélène Métrévéli, eds., *Actes d'Iviron*, vol. 1, 'Des origines au milieu du XIe siècle' (Paris, 1985)

B. Lominadze, 'Sakhelmtsip'osa da eklesiis urt'iert'oba VIII–XII saukuneebis sak'art'veloshi' ('Georgian church–state relations, 8th–12th century'), in *Sak'art'velo rust'avelis khanashi (Georgia in the Time of Rust'aveli)* (T'bilisi, 1966), 66–92; Russian summary, 'Vzaimootnosheniia mezhdu tserkov'iu i gosudarstvom v Gruzii XIII–XII vv.', 297–9

Mariam Lort'k'ip'anidze (Lortkipanidze), 'Iz istorii vizantiisko-gruzinskikh vzaimootnoshenii (70-e gody XI v.)' ('From the history of Byzantine–Georgian relations (70s of the 11th century)'), *VV* 40 (1979), 92–5

—— *Georgia in the 11th–12th Centuries*, ed. George B. Hewitt (T'bilisi, 1987)

Guram Mamulia, *Patronqmoba* (T'bilisi, 1987); Russian summary, 'Gruzinskii vassalitet', 193, and French summary, 'La vassalité géorgienne', 194

N.Ia. Marr, 'Ioann Petritsskii, gruzinskii neoplatonik XI–XII veka' ('Ioane Petritsi, a Georgian Neoplatonist of the 11th–12th century'), *Zapiski vostochnago Otdeleniia imperatorskago russkago arkheologicheskago Obshchestva* 19.2–3 (1909), 53–113

Bernadette Martin-Hisard, 'Du T'ao-K'lardzheti à l'Athos: moines géorgiens et réalites sociopolitiques (IXe–XIe siècles)', *Bedi Kartlisa* 41 (1983), 34–46

—— 'L'aristocratie géorgienne et son passé: tradition épique et références bibliques (VIIe–XIe siècles)', *Bedi Kartlisa* 42 (1984), 13–34

—— 'Le biens d'un monastère géorgien (IXe–XIIIe siècle): le témoignage des acts du monastère Saint-Shio de Mghvime', in V. Kravari, J. Lefort and C. Morrisson, eds., *Hommes et richesses dans l'empire byzantin*, vol. 2 (Paris, 1991), 113–52

—— 'Christianisme et Église dans le monde géorgien', in J.-M. Mayeur, C. and L. Pietri, A. Vauchez and M. Venard, eds., *Histoire du christianisme des origines à nos jours*, vol. 4 (Paris, 1993), 549–603

Levan Menabde, *Dzveli k'art'uli mtserlobis kerebi*, 2 vols. (T'bilisi, 1962–80); English summary of vol. 2, 'Seats of ancient Georgian literature abroad', 433–43; English summary of vol. 1: *Centres of Ancient Georgian Culture* (T'bilisi, 1968)

Shot'a Meskhia, *Didgorskaia bitva (The Battle of Didgori (1122 AD))* (T'bilisi, 1974)

Elene Metreveli, *Masalebi ierusalemis k'art'uli koloniis istoriisat'vis (XI–XVII ss.)* (*Materials for the History of the Georgian Colony in Jerusalem*) (T'bilisi, 1962)

—— *Narkvevebi at'onis kulturul-saganmanat'leblo keris istoriidan (Studies on the History of the Cultural-educational Center of Athos)* (T'bilisi, 1996)

Roin Metreveli, *Davit' aghmashenebeli = David the Builder*, tr. Givi Daushvili (T'bilisi, 1990)

—— ed., *Davit' aghmashenebeli: statiebis krebuli (Davit' Aghmashenebeli: collection of essays)* (T'bilisi, 1990)

—— *Mep'e t'amari* (T'bilisi, 1991); English summary, 'Queen Tamar', 354–74

—— *Foreign Policy of Georgia in the Middle Ages (12th Century)*, tr. V.D. Amiranashvili (T'bilisi, 1997)

Vladimir Minorsky, *Studies in Caucasian History* (London, 1953)

—— *A History of Sharvan and Darband in the 10th–11th Centuries* (Cambridge, 1958)

M.P. Murguliia and V.P. Shusharin, *Polovtsy, Gruziia, Rus' i Vengriia v XII–XIII vekakh (The Polovtsy, Georgia, Rus', and Hungary)* (Moscow, 1998)

Davit' Muskhelishvili, *Sak'art'velos istoriuli geograp'iis dzirit'adi sakit'khebi* (*Fundamental Questions on the Historical Geography of Georgia*), 2 vols. (T'bilisi, 1977 and 1980); Russian summaries, 'Osnovye voprosy istoricheskoi geografii Gruzii', 230–5 and 245–51 respectively

T'engiz Papuashvili, *Rant'a da kakht'a samep'o ( VIII–XI ss.)* (*Kingdom of the Ranians and Kakhet'ians, 8th–11th Century*) (T'bilisi, 1982)

Stephen H. Rapp Jr., 'Imagining history at the crossroads: Persia, Byzantium, and the architects of the written Georgian past', 2 vols., Ph.D. dissertation, University of Michigan (Ann Arbor, 1997)

—— 'From *bumberazi* to *basileus*: writing cultural synthesis and dynastic change in medieval Georgia (K'art'li)', in Antony Eastmond, ed., *Eastern Approaches to Byzantium* (Aldershot, 2001), 101–16

—— *Studies in Medieval Georgian Historiography: early texts and Eurasian contexts*, CSCO, vol. 601, subsidia 113 (Louvain, 2003)

J.M. Rogers, 'The Mxargrdzelis between east and west', *Bedi Kartlisa* 34 (1976), 315–26

Akaki Shanidze (Chanidzé), 'Le Grand Domestique de l'Occident, Gregorii Bakurianis-dze, et le monastère géorgien fondé par lui en Bulgarie', *Bedi Kartlisa* 28 (1971), 133–66

Jemal Step'nadze, *Sak'art'velo XII saukunesa da XIII saukunis pirvel meot'khedshi* (*Georgia in the 12th Century and in the First Quarter of the 13th Century*) (T'bilisi, 1985); Russian summary, 'Gruziia v XII v. i pervoi chetverti XIII v.', 188–9

Zaza Skhirtladze, *Istoriul pirt'a portretebi garejis mravalmt'is k'olagiris monastershi* (T'bilisi, 2000); English summary, 'Historical figures at Kolagiri Monastery in the Gareja desert', 108–24

Giorgi Tcheishvili (Cheishvili), 'Georgian perceptions of Byzantium in the eleventh and twelfth centuries', in Antony Eastmond, ed., *Eastern Approaches to Byzantium* (Aldershot, 2001), 199–209

Cyril Toumanoff, 'On the relationship between the founder of the empire of Trebizond and the Georgian Queen Thamar', *Speculum* 15 (1940), 299–312

—— 'Medieval Georgian historical literature (VII[th]–XV[th] centuries)', *Traditio* 1 (1943), 139–82

—— 'Caucasia and Byzantine studies', *Traditio* 12 (1956), 409–25

—— 'Armenia and Georgia', in *Cambridge Medieval History*, vol. 4.1 (Cambridge, 1966), 593–637

# 10

# Armenian Sources

## TIM GREENWOOD

THE STRATEGIC SIGNIFICANCE OF HISTORIC ARMENIA has long been recognised. Straddling the borders of neighbouring powers—whether Rome and Persia or Byzantium and the caliphate—it linked the Anatolian and Iranian plateaux and afforded access into the steppe world to the north and Mesopotamia and the Jazira to the south. All of these routes could be utilised or blocked in Armenia. It possessed that ideal combination of remote mountainous terrain and accessible river valleys which could be exploited for either defensive or offensive warfare as the situation required. Unsurprisingly, this landscape was studded with fortresses and other strongpoints. There was one further strategic consideration, namely the long-standing tradition of Armenian service in the military forces of one or other of the neighbouring powers.

In the course of the eleventh century, historic Armenia underwent dramatic political upheaval, as the Armenian kingdoms of Vaspurakan (in 1021), Ani (1045) and Kars (1064) were absorbed by the Byzantine empire. This Byzantine occupation proved short-lived; Ani fell to the Seljuks in 1064 and after Mantzikert (1071), the Empire was excluded for good from historic Armenia. Thereafter only the small kingdoms of Loṙi-Tashir north of Lake Sevan and Bałk' in eastern Siwnik' remained, along with shadowy Armenian lords in Vaspurakan and Taron. However historic Armenia represents only one of the centres of Armenian settlement in this period. During the second half of the eleventh century, a patchwork of independent and quasi-independent Armenian principalities emerged in Cilicia and northern Syria. Squeezed once again between rival powers, some proved short-lived but others, through a combination of military ability, judicious alignment and good fortune, became more permanent features of that fractured and fluid political landscape. The latter is attested most strikingly by the Rubenid dynasty whose rise to prominence after the death of Gogh Vasil in 1112 culminated in the coronation of Leo in January 1198 or 1199. Intriguingly the above description of historic Armenia largely suits Lesser or Cilician Armenia as well. It too straddled a frontier zone, affording access into the Anatolian plateau and northern Syria, although admittedly along different corridors; it too combined natural and man-made defences with good communications; and it too contained reserves of experienced soldiers.

This strategic significance, and the long-standing engagement of Armenians in the service of neighbouring powers, whether Sasanian, Byzantine, Seljuk or Latin, has prompted scholars of the Near East in the medieval period to consult Armenian historical sources. There was a well-established Armenian tradition of writing history which continued in this period, both in respect of historic Armenia and, increasingly, Cilician Armenia. The majority of these works do not possess an exclusively Armenian focus, commenting regularly upon non-Armenian matters. For scholars faced with meagre or contentious historical traditions in their own fields, these histories have afforded an important, different perspective. There has, however, been something of a tendency to 'cherry-pick' Armenian historical texts for information relevant to the specific research interest and to ignore the remainder of the work. Armenian histories tend to be much more than simple vehicles for the preservation of bare factual information. They are frequently complex compilations which need to be handled with care and exploited only after careful textual scrutiny. This does not mean that Armenian histories necessarily lack accuracy, nor that they have no part to play in a prosopographical exercise—in fact quite the reverse. It is simply that they have their own strengths and shortcomings and these need to be identified and acknowledged before historians of the medieval Near East can begin to utilise them.

The study of Armenian history as a scholarly discipline continues to adhere to a fairly rigid profile, according to which priority has been afforded to those periods in which there was an independent kingdom of Armenia. One of the consequences of this approach is that those sources relating to periods when there was no kingdom of Armenia have not been studied in anything like the same detail as those sources which do consider Armenian kingship. Unfortunately the sources relevant for the period 1025–1204 fall largely within such a gap. These histories have not been subjected to repeated textual criticism and evaluation and do not currently inhabit an active theatre of academic dispute or controversy. In the short term at least, it is hard to see any dramatic upswing in scholarly interest. This relative dearth of source criticism means that it remains very difficult to assess the merits of one Armenian source over another where they are found to contradict, and equally hard to assess the Armenian evidence against Greek, Arabic or Latin sources. Is it the case for example that non-Armenian sources have traditionally been preferred simply because they have been more thoroughly studied or available in translation rather than because they necessarily contain a more reliable account? An invaluable, though secondary function of the Prosopography of the Byzantine World (PBW) project is that it will identify parallel accounts, not simply within the Armenian historical tradition but also across different historical traditions hitherto separated from one another by linguistic barriers. In relation to at least one of the Armenian sources, namely the *Chronicle* of Smbat Sparapet, this may prove to be extremely valuable as this text seems to draw upon both Byzantine and Latin sources. It repeats a prediction of Peter the Hermit in relation to the First Crusade 'whose full history and the names of the princes are recorded by the Frank historians, *i Frang patmagirk'n'*.[1] Dédéyan has suggested that Smbat had found this prediction in William of Tyre's *History* and argued that he exploited works by Niketas Choniates and George Akropolites as well.[2] This text may bridge several separate historical traditions and serves as an important reminder that Armenian historical sources should not be treated as if they were somehow sealed from non-Armenian influences.

If the Byzantine empire is defined in geographical rather than institutional terms, all of the Armenian historical works covering the period need to be taken into consideration. The temporary Byzantine occupation of Vaspurakan and Ani in the eleventh century justifies interest in historic Armenia under successive, non-Byzantine regimes down to 1204. Likewise, the Armenian, Latin, Turkic, Fatimid and Ayyubid polities in Cilicia and Syria developed in regions which had been within the boundaries of the Byzantine empire in 1025. All of the Armenian sources bar one report events in both historic Armenia and Cilician Armenia, although there is an understandable stress upon one or other region, depending upon where the author of the work was based and the materials at his disposal. The one exception is the late-thirteenth-century *History of Siwnik'*, compiled by Step'anos Orbelean, since the primary focus of this work is the sequence of kings and bishops of Siwnik', a region to the east of the kingdoms of Vaspurakan and Ani which was never incorporated within the borders of the Empire. However since this source records the actions of many of the leading figures in the Caucasus during this period, it has been included in the survey.

The Armenian sources may be divided into two categories: firstly, historical compositions, and secondly, other sources which include prosopographical data, including colophons, inscriptions, charters, letter collections and contemporary, non-historical texts which indicate the intellectual concerns and interests of well-known Armenian scholars.

---

[1] Smbat Sparapet, *Chronicle*, 100.
[2] Dédéyan, *La chronique attribuée au Connétable Smbat*, 30.

## HISTORICAL COMPOSITIONS

Table 1 gives a simple guide to the current state of scholarship in respect of each of the Armenian historical texts. The bibliography follows the same sequence. Although the table is mostly self-explanatory, the fourth column headed Mss. states the total number of manuscripts for each text, including complete and partial copies, as reflected in the catalogues of six major collections of Armenian manuscripts: the Matenadaran in Erevan, the monastery of St James in Jerusalem, the Armenian Catholic Mkhit'arist monastery on the island of San Lazarro in Venice, the Mkhit'arist Library in Vienna, the Bibliothèque nationale in Paris, the British Library in London and the Bodleian Library in Oxford.[3] These figures represent the minimum number of manuscripts as there are other collections which have not been consulted. This column also highlights individual manuscripts of particular significance. The next column identifies the standard edition or editions, the date of publication and, in square brackets, the total number of manuscripts consulted in the course of preparation of that edition. The final column gives the number of pages of text which contain potentially relevant information.

Several observations may be made. Aristakēs' *History* is the only extant source from the eleventh century. We know of one other eleventh-century Armenian history which is now lost, that composed by Yovhannēs Taronets'i, focused upon the history of the Bagratuni family, and written in two parts, the first from Adam until the coronation of Ashot I Bagratuni in August 884 and the second from Ashot until *c*.1050. Six works belong to the twelfth century and at least one more, by Yovhannēs Sarkavag (d. 1129) is lost. Of the six, the *Continuation of T'ovma* is extremely brief, the surviving fragments of the *History* of Mkhit'ar Anets'i are largely irrelevant, covering events which date almost exclusively to the period before 1020, and the *Chronicle* of Michael the Syrian is strictly not an Armenian text, being composed in Syriac. However I have chosen to include it because there are two separate Armenian translations—or more accurately adaptations—of this work, completed in 1246 and 1248; these comprise the earliest witnesses of this work. The two recensions adopt different chronologies; substantively they are very close. Later Armenian historical texts exploited this work, usually without acknowledgement. Indeed there is an argument that this work

---

[3] Full references appear in the bibliography. 'Mat.' identifies the manuscript as belonging to Matenadaran, Erevan; 'Jer.' indicates the Monastery of St James in Jerusalem; 'Ven.' identifies the collection of the Armenian Catholic Mkhit'arist monastery in Venice, founded by Mkhit'ar of Sebasteia in 1717 on the island of San Lazarro; and 'Vien.' indicates the Mkhit'arist monastery in Vienna, founded in 1810 after a group of monks had broken away from Venice in 1773 and settled in Vienna.

**Table 1.** Armenian Sources

| | Source | Scope | Date | Mss. | Edition(s) | Translation(s) | Pages |
|---|---|---|---|---|---|---|---|
| 1. | Aristakēs Lastivertts'i | 1000–1072 | Before 1080 | 25+ Mat.2865 Jer. 341 | Yuzbashyan 1963 [9] | Canard 1973 | 105/124 |
| 2. | Continuator of T'ovma Artsruni | 1020– after 1121 | After 1121 | 1 | Patkanean 1887 | Thomson 1985 | 15/326 |
| 3A. | Matthew of Edessa | 951–1129 | c.1129 | 39+ Mat.6686 Vien.574 | Anonymous 1869; [3] Mlk'-Adam. 1898 [9] | Dulaurier 1858; Dostourian 1993 | 400/465 |
| 3B. | Gregory the Priest | 1136–1162 | c.1162 | ? | Ibid. | Ibid. | 83/83 |
| 4. | Samuēl Anets'i | Adam– c.1180 | c.1180 | 66+ Ven.873 Jer.3397 Mat.3613 | Tēr-Mik'elean 1893 [13] | Zohrab/Mai 1818; Brosset 1876 | 42/160 |
| 5. | Mkhit'ar Anets'i [Fragments] | Paroyr Haykazean– Third Crusade | c.1193 | 1 Mat.2678 | Margaryan 1983 | None | |
| 6. | Michael the Syrian [in translation] | Adam–1195 | 1246 and 1248 | 76+ Jer.32 Mat.5904 | Jerusalem 1870 [2]; Jerusalem 1871 [1] | Langlois 1868 | 141/532 and 142/526 |
| 7. | Kirakos Gandzakets'i | St Grigor– 1266 | Before 1271 | 53+ | Melik'-Awhanjanyan 1961 [47] | Brosset 1870 Bedrosian 1986 | 98/399 |
| 8. | Vardan Arewelts'i | Creation– 1267 | Before 1271 | 25+ Ven.877 Ven.879 | Emin 1861 [2]; Alishan 1862 [2] | Thomson 1989 | 46/164 |
| 9. | Smbat Sparapet | 951–1274 | Before 1276 | 9+ Ven.875 | Shahnazareants' 1859 [2]; Agĕlean 1956 [1] | Der Nersessian 1959 Dédéyan 1980 | 196/255 |
| 10. | Mkhit'ar Ayrivanets'i | Creation– 1289 | After 1297? | 8+ Mat.582 Mat.1723 | Patkanov 1867 [2] | Brosset 1869 | 9/84 |
| 11. | Step'anos Orbelean | Sisak–1299 | 1299 | 32+ (15+ only ch.66) | Emin 1861 [2] | Brosset 1864 | 45/363 |

inspired a revival in Armenian historical writing in the second half of the thirteenth century. The remaining five texts were all compiled after 1204 but have been included because they contain material not found in earlier sources; again there is at least one work, by Vanakan Vardapet, which has been lost. As we shall see, these later texts are far from being independent of the earlier works.

Taking the editions and the manuscripts together, the obvious conclusion is that almost all of these texts lack modern editions. Setting aside concerns about accuracy, the very age of these editions may prove to be something of a stumbling-block, with access outside specialist collections a serious problem. Fortunately the Leiden Armenian Database includes four of the eleven texts—Aristakēs, Tʻovma Artsruni, Kirakos Gandzaketsʻi and Vardan Areweltsʻi—whilst the Digital Library of Classical Armenian Literature has five—the same four, plus Mkhitʻar Anetsʻi.[4] Of the editions, in my view, only the 1961 edition of Kirakos Gandzaketsʻi by Melikʻ-Awhanjanyan comes close to being critical in the sense that he consulted almost all of the relevant manuscripts, setting aside five fragments found in the Matenadaran collection. The other texts all lack critical editions. Perhaps most surprising is the recent edition of Aristakēs by Yuzbashyan, which is commonly cited as being critical. Whilst he drew upon the oldest extant copy of the text, Mat.2865, he was unable to consult the important collections outside the Soviet Union, including those in Jerusalem, Vienna and Venice. Thus despite the fact that Jer.341 was copied in 1599 in Bitlis, making it the second oldest manuscript to contain this text, it was not apparently utilised by Yuzbashyan. The oldest manuscript of Matthew of Edessa appears to be Mat.6686, dated 1582, although I do not know whether this was consulted for the 1898 edition. Since there are at least thirty-nine manuscripts containing this text, Dostourian's statement that the number of extant manuscripts is not large is misleading.[5] Reputedly, this text survives in more than one recension but much work clearly remains to be done. The two independent Armenian recensions of Michael the Syrian's *Chronicle* also require extensive work. Jer.32 is unquestionably the earliest, being dated 1273 and containing marginalia referring to none other than Vardan Areweltsʻi, who was closely involved in both translations. Mat.2152 and Mat.5904 also bear thirteenth-century attributions whilst Mat.9309 is dated 1397 and was copied in

---

[4] See http://www/let.leidenuniv.nl/vtw/Weitenberg/projects_weitenberg.html for the Leiden Armenian Database ('LAD') and http://sunsite.berkeley.edu/~aua for the Digital Library of Classical Armenian Literature ('DLCAL'). Both databases contain a mixture of scanned and manually entered texts, with varying degrees of precision and hence reliability. In order to consult LAD, please contact Professor Jos Weitenberg (weitenberg@rullet.leidenuniv.nl).

[5] Dostourian, *Armenia and the Crusades*, xi.

Jerusalem. There are at least two separate Armenian continuations of Michael's *Chronicle*, one brief, the other rather more substantial and extending down to 1229. Alishan's edition of Vardan Arewelts'i's *Historical Compilation* drew upon only two manuscripts but their close proximity to the date of composition of the text suggests that there would be little to gain from a detailed investigation of all the other manuscripts. Ven.877 was commissioned by Step'anos Orbelean (d. 1304) whilst Ven.879 is dated 1307. Whilst these are not autographs, they were copied within a generation. The one glaringly deficient edition is that of Samuēl Anets'i. This is significant not least because the text had several continuators. The oldest extant manuscript is Ven.873, copied in 1206 at the monastery of Sanahin. Mat.3613, dating from the thirteenth century, was copied in the monastery of Hoṙomos, just to the north of Ani by one Mkhit'ar Anets'i; his relationship to the historian of the same name is unclear. Jer.3397 appears to contain completely new material for the years 1181 and 1189. Fortunately these passages have been quoted in full in Boṙarian's excellent catalogue entry.[6] Quite evidently this edition is the least satisfactory. But having pinpointed all of these problems, the next question must be—do these deficiencies adversely affect a prosopographical exercise? The answer must be 'Unlikely, and even if they do, there is almost nothing that can be done about it.'

There is again a wide range in the quality of the translations and the commentaries which sometimes accompany them, varying from excellent, as in the case of Professor Thomson's two contributions, to average, as in the case of Dostourian, whose commentary does little more than identify parallel accounts without any attempt at assessment or comparative analysis. Canard and Dédéyan supplied commentaries to their respective translations of Aristakēs and Smbat Sparapet, giving parallel references but again tended to shy away from making any assessment as to the relative worth of the respective texts. It is worth noting that Canard's French translation of Aristakēs follows Yuzbashyan's Russian translation in omitting long sections of theological discourse and speculation. This is not particularly helpful for scholars interested in contemporary Armenian perceptions of, and explanations for, the Turkic invasions, although it will not have any effect upon a prosopography. Neither Der Nersessian nor Dédéyan translated the whole of Smbat Sparapet's *Chronicle*, picking up after 1159 and 1165 respectively. Although their decision not to translate those passages which were lifted from Matthew of Edessa's *History* and Gregory's continuation can be justified on the grounds that they are unoriginal, it does prevent the non-Armenian specialist from comparing Smbat's version with the original and

---

[6] Boṙarian, *Mayr ts'uts'ak*, vol. 10, 288–91.

thereby studying the criteria by which Smbat selected or rejected material for his composition. It also ignores several passages which are not found in either Matthew or Gregory's *History*s. Are these interpolations from parallel texts or are they in fact present in one or more of the manuscripts that have yet to be consulted? Direct access to the earlier part is currently afforded only through Langlois' translated excerpts from an older, inferior edition, and Dulaurier's translated excerpts in the *Recueil des historiens des croisades*. I found this volume to be dangerously deficient with regard to Samuēl Anets'i.[7] It seems that not only was the text lopped to conform to the set chronological parameters; it was also filleted, with all the material deemed irrelevant being excised. This meant that a good deal of information that would be considered relevant, particularly for PBW, was omitted. This has prompted me to be wary of the translations in this compilation and I have avoided citing them when alternatives exist. Finally it is worth noting that several translations appear only in rare nineteenth-century Russian publications and have yet to be reprinted or otherwise reproduced.

As noted previously, there is a dearth of close textual scrutiny and source criticism for the majority of these texts. The bibliography identifies what little relevant secondary literature exists beyond the short commentaries and footnotes which accompany some but not all of the translations. The majority of the articles tend to be descriptive and short rather than analytical or comparative. The overriding impression is that whilst many of these texts benefited from scholarly attention in the second half of the nineteenth century, the initial interest did not act as a spur to further textual scrutiny, either at an individual level or by way of comparison. Unsurprisingly therefore, there has been almost no comparative work between the Armenian histories and contemporary non-Armenian sources, whether Byzantine, Arabic or Latin—and thus it is hard to see how historians have selected one account over another when they contradict one another. To give one example, in relation to the origin of the Rubenid dynasty, Matthew of Edessa does not specify whether it was Constantine or his father the eponymous Rubēn who was one of the soldiers of King Gagik II Bagratuni; Vardan Arewelts'i and Smbat Sparapet describe him as one of the nobles of Gagik; the Armenian adaptations of Michael the Syrian state that Rubēn was descended from both royal Armenian lines, the Bagratuni and Artsruni.[8] Not only is there contradiction; there must be doubt as to whether there was any link at all between the Rubenids and these dynasties.

[7] *RHC* 1, 445–68.

[8] Matthew of Edessa, *History*, 312; Vardan Arewelts'i, *Historical Compilation*, 111; Smbat Sparapet, *Chronicle*, 112; Michael the Syrian (1870), 417; Michael the Syrian (1871), 411.

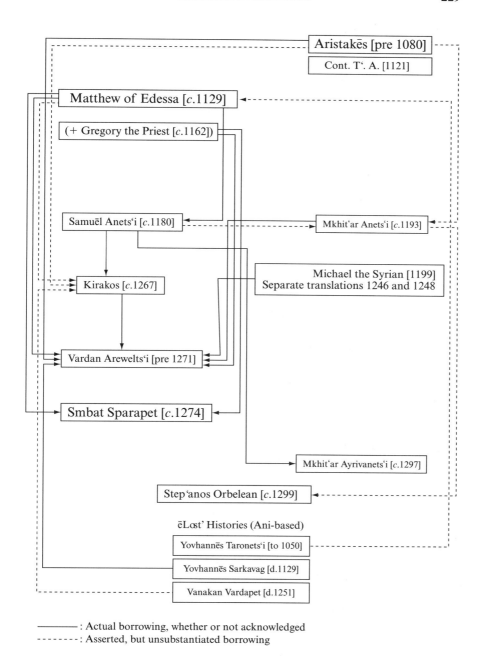

**Figure 1.** An impression of the links between the Armenian sources and their relative prosopographical values

Although this dearth of textual analysis cannot be remedied quickly, I have attempted to represent the relationships between the Armenian sources in the form of a simple diagram (Fig. 1). The hatched lines reflect connections that are asserted in the later text but which remain, to my mind, unsubstantiated. The solid lines reflect actual borrowings, whether or not acknowledged. The font size reflects my current thinking on the relative importance of these texts for the prosopography. The value of this exercise is undermined by the very obvious fact that we do not have all the pieces. In addition to the three 'lost' histories cited at the bottom of Figure 1, each of which seems to have originated from Ani or a monastery nearby, very little relevant material can be recovered of Mkhit'ar Anets'i's work. If nothing else, this diagram illustrates how closely the majority of the Armenian historical texts are related to one another. This is a very narrow, conservative historical tradition, one in which authors exploited older histories, many of which survive. The original title of Vardan Arewelts'i's composition, literally *Historical Compilation*, is a very accurate reflection of his work, drawing upon a very broad range of earlier Armenian historical works, themselves largely extant. From a practical perspective, once the original source for a particular episode has been identified, it should be relatively straightforward to cite the later works which quote the same episode. This exercise will also highlight fresh detail preserved in the thirteenth-century histories.

Looking at the Armenian historical sources for this period, two distinct groups may be discerned. It is clear from their identical start date (951) that there is a direct relationship between the *History* of Matthew of Edessa and, to a slightly lesser extent his continuator, Gregory the Priest, and the composition of Smbat Sparapet—indeed so close is their relationship that as we have seen, neither Der Nersessian nor Dédéyan thought it worth translating the overlapping section. It seems more than simply coincidental that these three authors all had a Syrian or Cilician provenance: Matthew was resident in Edessa, Gregory his continuator in K'esun and Smbat served his brother King Het'um I. They seem to form one distinct 'group' of Armenian historians whose works reflect an interest in contemporary history. Excluding Step'anos Orbelean's *History of Siwnik'*, all the other Armenian histories, both known and lost, seem to have originated in the region of Ani. These histories too reveal a broad uniformity in their understanding of what a historical composition should comprise. With one exception, each author began with Adam, Creation or Paroyr Haykazean, the first, mythic king of Armenia, and each author extended his work in strict chronological sequence down to the present day. Only Kirakos differs in this respect, beginning instead with the conversion of Armenia to Christianity. Whilst the conventions of historical writing appear to have allowed the writer to cover recent history, this is placed in each work in the context of world history stretching back to the beginning of time. Why should this be?

Although such a question is incapable of a complete answer, the surviving prefaces are very revealing. Samuēl Anets'i states, 'Let us apply ourselves to both these ones for their assistance, I mean Eusebios and Movsēs Khorenats'i. And having begun from Adam, let us reach to Noah and from there as far as Abraham and from there to the birth of Christ and then according to the *K'ronikon*, through the lineages, let us finish at the present, omitting what is superfluous, including what is important.'[9] In other words, Samuēl went back to Eusebios' *Chronicle* and not his *Ecclesiastical History*.[10] In fact, it is clear from Brosset's work that Samuēl strove to organise his work on similar principles to those in Eusebios. The insistence on chronological precision, even when this generates two notices of the same event under different dates, then begins to make sense. Samuēl's model for the writing of history was therefore the *Chronicle* of Eusebios. This work was composed in two parts. The first part, commonly called the *Chronographia*, consists of short passages excerpted from pre-existing sources which record the different chronological systems employed by different peoples of the ancient world and lists of their kings. This survives only in Armenian translation and, according to Karst, was translated directly from Greek.[11] The second part, the *Chronological Canons*, comprises parallel columns of lists of kings synchronised with each other, together with brief notices inserted at the appropriate year mentioning important persons and events. These were translated into Latin by Jerome and extended down to 378 but also exist in Armenian translation, perhaps via an intermediate version in Syriac. Neither part can have been translated into Armenian before the first decades of the fifth century, as the Armenian script was not devised until around AD 400. However both parts existed in Armenian translation by the last quarter of the seventh century, judging from the contents of the so-called *Anonymous Chronicle*, sometimes attributed to Anania Shirakats'i.[12] Although the date of translation is unknown, it is very tempting to associate it with Armenian activity in Jerusalem, particularly since a lectionary detailing liturgical rites in Jerusalem

[9] Samuēl Anets'i, *Chronicle*, 3.

[10] J. Aucher, ed., *Eusebii Pamphili caesariensis episcopi, Chronicum bipartitum*, 2 vols. (Venice, 1818); J. Zohrab, ed., A. Mai, tr., *Eusebii Pamphili caesariensis episcopi, Chronicum libri duo*, Scriptorum Veterum Nova Collectio 8 (Rome, 1833), 1–406; repr. PG 19, 99–598; J. Karst, ed., *Die Chronik des Eusebius aus dem armenischen übersetzt*, Die griechischen christlichen Schriftsteller der ersten drei Jahrhunderte 20 (Leipzig, 1911).

[11] Karst, *Die Chronik*, XXXVIII–XLIII.

[12] B. Sargisean, *Ananun Zhamanakagrut'iwn* (Venice, 1904); A.G. Abrahamyan, *Anania Shirakats'u matenagrut'yunĕ* (Erevan, 1944), 357–99.

at the very beginning of the fifth century survives only via its Armenian translation.[13]

Nor was Samuēl the only Armenian historian to adopt this approach. Mkhit'ar Anets'i acknowledged his debt to Eusebios by beginning his list of sources with his '*History of the Church* and the *K'ronikon*'.[14] Kirakos refers to 'the great Eusebios who left two books, the *K'rovnikon*, begun from the first man Adam . . . up to the coming of Christ and to here, the leaders and kings of several peoples. And the *History of the Church*, beginning at the shining of the sun of righteousness, the times of kings and the preaching of the holy apostles, which of them did what and to which region each of them went and how they were martyred. And the action and courage of holy bishops and notable men and advancing up until the days of the pious Constantine and there he ended.'[15] Vardan's text refers to Eusebios in the context of an Old Testament chronological calculation.[16] The debt of Mkhit'ar Ayrivanets'i to Eusebios is even more obvious, since he inserted marginal ten-year divisions, though whether this is a direct borrowing or an indirect one through Samuēl Anets'i and/or Michael the Syrian is unclear. Nor were these references to Eusebios simply copied verbatim by successive authors, for each citation is different. The first Armenian historian to base his whole work upon the demands of chronological precision was Step'anos Taronets'i just after the year AD 1000.[17] Although I cannot expand upon this subject here, it is my view that this text reflects the author's millenarianism, his conviction that the Second Coming would coincide with the year 1000. The key point to note however is that his *History* attests the link between Eusebios, chronology and the writing of history. In the absence of any secular sponsor—which was certainly the case in historic Armenia during the period—I believe that clerics justified their continuing interest in the writing of history on the basis that the correct calculation of time was an appropriate exercise for them, as Eusebios had demonstrated in antiquity. The one exception appears to be Kirakos. Why did he start with St Gregory the Illuminator, credited with the conversion of Armenia at the start of the fourth century? Although speculative, it seems significant that in his preface, quoted above, he cited Eusebios' other work, his *Ecclesiastical History* with such approval. That work ended with Constantine, the exact contemporary

---

[13] A. Renoux, *Le codex arménien Jérusalem* 121, 2 vols., PO 163 (35.1) and 168 (36.2) (Brepols, 1969, 1971); Ch. Renoux, *Le lectionnaire de Jérusalem en Arménie: Le Čašoc'. Introduction et liste de manuscrits*, PO 200 (44.4) (Turnhout, 1989).

[14] Mkhit'ar Anets'i, *History*, 73.18–19.

[15] Kirakos, *History*, 5.1–11.

[16] Vardan Arewelts'i, *Historical Compilation*, 20.

[17] S. Malkhazean, *Step'anos Taronets'woy Patmut'iwn Tiezerakan* (St Petersburg, 1885). I am currently engaged in producing a new translation of, and commentary upon, this text.

of St Grigor. Thus, however imperfectly, it is at least possible that Kirakos tried to write history along the lines established by Eusebios in his *Ecclesiastical History*. Whether or not one is persuaded by the above, it is clear that the historical tradition, at least in historic Armenia, was extraordinarily conservative.

The relative strengths of these Armenian historical sources for prosopography are set out in the bibliography. All of them have a contribution to make. Three works however deserve particular attention. Aristakēs' *History* is a key source, being the only extant eleventh-century source and hence a near-contemporary record. Since the work is devised around the imperial succession and summarises the character and achievements of successive emperors and empresses, it is possible that Aristakēs exploited a Greek source. The presence of an indiction date in the text—almost unprecedented in an Armenian source—supports this contention.[18] Aristakēs supplies a detailed impression of the short-lived Byzantine administration in Ani and Vaspurakan, specifying a large number of names, titles and offices, including those awarded to Armenians. By contrast, although those passages detailing Seljuk raids are dated precisely and specify their targets, named individuals are rare. These passages seek to record and understand the fate of the inhabitants of those towns which were captured. They are generally described as laments and seem to be prose analogues to the twelfth-century elegies written by Nersēs Shnorhali on the fall of Edessa in 1144 and by the *katholikos* Grigor Tłay on the fall of Jerusalem in 1187; neither mentions a single individual by name.[19] In my view, it is very striking that the Seljuk attacks are presented in terms of the devastation of urban centres rather than the destruction of noble families and their territories. The explanation for this is not obvious. It may reflect a significant change in Armenian society during the decades of relative peace after 990, specifically a deliberate demilitarisation under Byzantine direction and the promotion of an urban culture in which Armenians participated. Alternatively, it may be drawing upon a familiar Old Testament precedent, the capture of Jerusalem by the Babylonians and the subsequent exile of God's people.[20] The circumstances in which such laments were produced is also unclear but they may have been intended to commemorate the fate of these centres in a liturgical context, functioning as collective martyrdoms and celebrated by former inhabitants of those centres now in exile. Although its individual detail is not extensive,

[18] Aristakēs, *History*, 103: 'And this occurred in five hundred and six of our era, in which it was Roman diktion ten.'
[19] See bibliography, Laments, p. 252 below.
[20] 2 Kings 24, 25; Jeremiah 21–52; Lamentations.

Aristakēs has a significant contribution to make to prosopography and should be tackled at an early stage.

Important as it is, even Aristakēs' *History* is overshadowed by the *History* of Matthew of Edessa. In my opinion, this is the single most important Armenian source for the project. The lack of a scholarly edition and commentary is therefore all the more frustrating. The work is divided into three parts: the first covering the period 400–500 Armenian Era (AD 951–1051), the second covering the fifty years between 1051 and 1101 and the third covering the last thirty years. As has been noted above, the underlying sources employed by Matthew are opaque. However the opening section of the second part records Matthew's own views on his composition. By his own testimony, Matthew had collected and collated historical writings about the three nations, the Armenians, Turks and Romans as well as 'patriarchs and various other inquiries of peoples and kings'.[21] This is an accurate reflection of Book 1. Its end date, 1051, coincides with the conclusion of Yovhannēs Taronets'i's lost *History of the Bagratunik'*. It is tempting to envisage that Matthew may have had access to this. Intriguingly his text contains several documents, including a letter from the Emperor John Tzimiskes to Ashot III Bagratuni in 974.[22] Whilst it is hard to envisage circumstances in which he could have viewed the original letter, it does seem possible, even likely, that Yovhannēs would have had access to such records eighty years before. There is clearly a good deal of other material being exploited as well, not least a cluster of notices about Edessa after 1031. The course of Book 2 marks a change of focus away from historic Armenia and Sebasteia and towards Mesopotamia, northern Syria and Antioch. Book 3 accelerates this trend, to the extent that there is barely a single reference to Byzantine, Seljuk or historic Armenian affairs, although Davit' king of Georgia suddenly, and surprisingly, appears at the very end of the *History* and Georgians also feature in the final entries in the *Continuation*, specifically in relation to the cities of Ani and Duin. In my opinion, Matthew's history originally concluded with the two notices under the year 577 (1128/29). The final notice is dated eight years later and is focused upon events around K'esun involving 'our prince Baldwin', the lord of K'esun.[23] It seems to me that Gregory the Priest and not Matthew was responsible for this notice; his link is with K'esun rather than Edessa and he included a long funeral oration composed for Baldwin. This reattribution produces a gap of eight years between the end of Matthew's *History* and the start of the *Continuation* rather than between the penultimate and final notices in the original text.

[21] Matthew of Edessa, *History*, 133–4.
[22] Matthew of Edessa, *History*, 23–33.
[23] Matthew of Edessa, *History*, 464.

The third key Armenian historical source for this project is the *History* of Smbat Sparapet, specifically those notices covering the period after 1165. The work is already well known for preserving a full list of those lords who attended the coronation of Leo in Tarsos but it contains a mass of other relevant information which will both overlap and complement that found in non-Armenian sources.

## OTHER ARMENIAN SOURCES

Moving away from the complexities of the Armenian historical compositions, let us consider briefly four other categories of evidence: colophons, inscriptions, charters and contemporary, non-historical texts, including correspondence, biblical commentaries and other scholarly treatises generally.

Two major collections of relevant Armenian colophons have been published, by Yovsēpʻean and, more recently (1988), Matʻevosyan. Matʻevosyan included 253 colophons from this period, of which 194 are specifically dated. Sixty-three, approximately one-fifth, date from the eleventh century and one hundred and ninety, approximately four-fifths, were produced in the twelfth century. This total, 253, is a minimum figure and should be expected to rise. Matʻevosyan reproduced some but not all of the colophons previously published by Yovsēpʻean. Volumes 10 and 11 of Bołarian's Jerusalem catalogue and volumes 4–8 of the Venice catalogue have been published since 1988. Matʻevosyan was unable to consult the full catalogues of those manuscripts preserved in Vienna, the Bodleian Library in Oxford or the Bibliothèque nationale in Paris. However the Department of Comparative Linguistics in Leiden plans to issue a simple CD-ROM database of colophons, including a great number of unpublished examples contributed by Matʻevosyan himself, and this should provide a more complete, and accessible, collection.

The potential contribution of these colophons is significant. They usually specify the scribe, the date, the place of composition and the sponsor. Several known historical figures are identified as the sponsors. Indeed the relatively large number of translations associated with Grigor Vkayasēr, *katholikos* between 1065 and 1105, not only implies that some part of his personal library has been preserved; their colophons also allow us to date his travels in the Near East more precisely.[24] Equally the colophons reveal the existence of

---

[24] Matʻevosyan, *Hayeren dzeṙagreri hishatakaranner*, no. 168, describes how, 'in the one thousand one hundred and second year of the coming of our God and Lord, Jesus Christ, and in the five hundred and sixtieth year of our own era, and in the seventeenth year of the reign of the tyrant Alēks', Grigor arrived at the holy mountain 'which is called Black' and undertook translation work 'in the thirty-sixth year of my holding office'.

a number of active communities scattered across the Near East. The evidence is often surprising. Thus, for example, a collection of hagiographical material commemorating the martyrdoms of Saints Evdok'sia, Maŕinos, Ŕomel and Makaros was translated from Greek into Armenian in 1092 in the Armenian *mayrk'ałak'* or capital of Melitene, some thirty-five years after the sack of the city in 1057.[25] Or again, a Gospel dated 1099 and copied by one Aharovn/Aaron not only contains—or purports to contain—a contemporary sketch of the First Crusade, including the fall of Antioch and the capture of Jerusalem; it also records that it was finished in the *mayrk'ałak'* of Ałek'sandr, at the monastery of Yovhannēs/John the Evangelist.[26] This supplies unique evidence for the existence of an Armenian monastic community in Alexandria. Several sources record significant Armenian settlement in Egypt in the last quarter of the eleventh century in general terms but the location of this settlement is harder to pinpoint.

Potentially therefore Armenian colophons have a significant contribution to make to this project. I say potentially because the vast majority have yet to be translated. Without a published translation, any reference would be limited to the Armenian edition and I suspect that this would be of little value to all but a handful of scholars. However a brief survey has shown that many of these colophons are short and almost all of them are straightforward.

The epigraphic material is at a similar stage of research. To date, some 151 potentially relevant inscriptions have been identified. This figure includes five inscriptions from Cilicia, four of which are incomplete. Twenty-six, about one-sixth, date from the eleventh century, with the remaining five-sixths, 125 in total, carved in the twelfth century. Thus there is a broad correlation in the distribution of both colophons and inscriptions across the period, with approximately eighty per cent of the material dating from the twelfth and early thirteenth centuries. There is a very obvious downturn in the number of inscriptions after 1060 and this lasts until approximately 1150; thereafter they become far more numerous and distributed across a greater number of locations, although the number of sites remains relatively small. By way of example, the key monasteries of Sanahin and Hałbat account for no fewer that 31 of the inscriptions.

As with the colophons, the inscriptions range in length from no more than a few words to several sentences. The majority tend to mark the foundation, expansion or repair of a church or monastic complex or a particular bequest to a religious community, usually in return for prayers and services

---

[25] Mat'evosyan, *Hayeren dzeŕagreri hishatakaranner*, no. 136.
[26] Mat'evosyan, *Hayeren dzeŕagreri hishatakaranner*, no. 140.

for the soul of the sponsor and sometimes his immediate family. Since the sponsor is usually known from another source, the inscriptions allow titles, offices and other details associated with him to be compared. Moreover there are a few inscriptions which had a very different purpose. The western façade of the cathedral in Ani bears a public inscription in Armenian dating from the period of the short-lived Byzantine administration.[27] It records that the *magistros* and *katepan* of the east, Bagarat Vkhats'i, reduced the taxes due on certain commercial transactions 'through the charity of the holy autocrator, King Constantine Duk'; both the original duty and the reduced figure are given. This inscription therefore supplies unique information about the Byzantine approach to the government of Ani immediately before its fall in 1064. Whilst few inscriptions are as useful as this, it illustrates their potential. Again, however, very few have been translated.

In contrast to the numerous colophons and inscriptions, only two charters are relevant to this project. Both date from 1201 and were produced in the chancellery of King Leo I in 1201. One confirmed certain privileges to Genoese traders whilst the second accorded privileges to Venetians. These were published by Langlois as long ago as 1863 but do not seem to be well known.

This introduction has sought to focus upon those sources which have the greatest prosopographical value and has not attempted to encompass the totality of Armenian scholarly activity and endeavour across the period. Many of the key figures in the Armenian intellectual tradition, such as Grigor Magistros, Nersēs of Lambron and Nersēs Shnorhali, are mentioned in the historical sources and will therefore generate prosopographical entries. These entries will require at least a basic knowledge of their scholarly output.[28] Frustratingly almost none of the ninety-six letters of Grigor Magistros have been translated and this pivotal figure for the study of mid-eleventh-century Armenian and Byzantine politics, administration and scholarship remains, for the moment, tantalisingly out of reach.[29] The correspondence of Nersēs of Lambron has yet to be translated. Yet, with the exception of

---

[27] Mahé, 'Ani sous Constantin X', 407.

[28] An impression of scholarly output, and the present state of research, may be obtained from Thomson's invaluable *Bibliography*. A brief survey of this indicates that there are at least twenty-nine Armenian scholars from this period. The vast majority are mentioned in the historical compositions.

[29] The letters of Grigor Magistros were edited and published almost a century ago but, to my knowledge, only three have been translated. In May 2003, Professor T.M. van Lint addressed a conference in Oxford at which he suggested that a new edition and full translation and commentary on this important collection was now long overdue.

these letter collections, my impression is that these contemporary scholarly non-historical works will not have a significant contribution to make to prosopography.


## CONCLUSION

In the context of prosopography, the Armenian sources appear manageable. All of the Armenian historical works have been edited and translated, although these publications vary greatly in quality. In addition to recording Armenian history, collectively these sources supply useful and occasionally unique information about eleventh-century Byzantine history and the plethora of successor states which emerged on former imperial territory after 1071, whether Seljuk, Fatimid, Latin, Ayyubid or Armenian. The *History*s attributed to Aristakēs, Matthew of Edessa and Smbat Sparapet should be given priority but the contribution of the other sources, including colophons and inscriptions, should not be ignored.


## TRANSCRIPTION OF ARMENIAN

In order to assist the reader in the pronunciation of Armenian words, the system prescribed in *Revue des études arméniennes* has not been employed. The ' after a consonant indicates the aspirated form. The final letter was developed in the time of the crusades to assist the writing of foreign words, including Ֆրանգ , 'Frank' and Ֆրիր , 'frère'.

| a | b | g | d | e | z | ē | ě | t' | zh | i | l |
|---|---|---|---|---|---|---|---|---|---|---|---|
| ա | բ | գ | դ | ե | զ | է | ը | թ | ժ | ի | լ |

| kh | ts | k | h | dz | ł | ch | m | y | n | sh | o |
|---|---|---|---|---|---|---|---|---|---|---|---|
| խ | ծ | կ | հ | ձ | ղ | ճ | մ | յ | ն | շ | ո |

| ch' | p | j | ṙ | s | v | t | r | ts' | w | p' | k' |
|---|---|---|---|---|---|---|---|---|---|---|---|
| չ | պ | ջ | ռ | ս | վ | տ | ր | ց | ւ | փ | ք |

| aw | f |
|---|---|
| օ | ֆ |

# BIBLIOGRAPHY

## HANDBOOKS, SURVEYS, PROSOPOGRAPHIES

H. Achaṙyan, *Hayots' andzannuneri baṙaran (Dictionary of Armenian Names)*, 5 vols. (Erevan, 1942–62; repr. Beirut, 1972)

Principal Armenian prosopographical resource, listing all textual references to named individuals across Armenian literature down to 1500; each entry numbered, the list of names being organised chronologically; very brief biographical details; restricted to Armenians and Armenian texts only.

M. Amouroux-Mourad. *Le comté d'Édesse 1098–1150* (Paris, 1988)

H.S. Anasyan, *Haykakan matenagitut'yun (Armenian Literature)*, 2 vols. (Erevan, 1959, 1976)

S.B. Dadoyan, *The Fatimid Armenians*, Islamic History and Civilization, Studies and Texts 18 (Leiden, 1997)

G. Dédéyan, *Les Arméniens entre Grecs, Musulmans et Croisés. Étude sur les pouvoirs arméniens dans le Proche-Orient méditerranéen (1068–1150)*, 2 vols., Bibliothèque arménologique de la Fondation Calouste Gulbenkian (Lisbonne, 2003)

Long-anticipated work on the emergence of a patchwork of Armenian principalities and settlements in Cilicia and northern Syria. Volume 1 is titled 'Aux origins de l'état cilicien: Philarète et les premiers Roubeniens; volume 2 is titled 'De l'Euphrate au Nil: le reseau diasporique'.

——— 'L'œcuménisme de Grigor III et de Nersēs Šnorhali', *RÉA* 23 (1992), 237–52

R.W. Thomson, *A Bibliography of Classical Armenian Literature to 1500 AD* (Turnhout, 1995)

Essential reference work; comprehensive guide to primary sources and all associated secondary literature down to 1992.

———'The crusaders through Armenian eyes', in A.E. Laiou and R.P. Mottahedeh, eds., *The Crusades from the Perspective of Byzantium and the Muslim World* (Washington, DC, 2001), 71–82

## Catalogues

N. Bołarian, *Mayr ts'uts'ak dzeṙagrats' Srbots' Yakobeants' (Grand Catalogue of St. James Manuscripts)*, 11 vols. (Jerusalem, 1966–95)

Excellent catalogue with full descriptions of the collection housed in the monastery of St James in Jerusalem, the largest outside the Matenadaran.

S. Chemchemean, *Mayr ts'uts'ak hayerēn dzeṙagrats' Matenadaranin Mkhit'areants' i Venetik (Grand Catalogue of the Armenian Manuscripts of the Mkhit'arist Library in Venice)*, vols. 4–8 (Venice, 1993–8)

Excellent modern catalogue providing full description of re-numbered manuscripts in the San Lazarro monastery in Venice, the second largest collection outside the Matenadaran.

F.C. Conybeare, *A Catalogue of the Armenian Manuscripts in the British Museum* (London, 1913)

O. Eganyan, A. Zayt'unyan, P. Ant'abyan, *Ts'uts'ak dzeṙagrats' Mashtots'i anvan Matenadarani (Catalogue of Manuscripts of the Mashtots' Matenadaran)*, 2 vols. (Erevan, 1965, 1970)
Brief descriptions of the manuscripts of the largest collection; a new catalogue was begun several years ago but only the first volume, covering some four hundred manuscripts, has been published; other volumes prepared but awaiting publication.

R. Kévorkian, A. Tēr-Stepanian, *Catalogue des manuscripts arméniens de la Bibliothèque nationale de France* (Paris, 1998)
Excellent modern catalogue providing full descriptions.

B. Sargisean, *Mayr ts'uts'ak hayerēn dzeṙagrats' Matenadaranin Mkhit'areants' i Venetik (Grand Catalogue of the Armenian Manuscripts of the Mkhit'arist Library in Venice)*, vols. 1 and 2 (Venice, 1914, 1924)

B. Sargisean and G. Sargsean, *Mayr ts'uts'ak hayerēn dzeṙagrats' Matenadaranin Mkhit'areants' i Venetik (Grand Catalogue of the Armenian Manuscripts of the Mkhit'arist Library in Venice)*, vol. 3 (Venice, 1966)

Y. Tashean, *Ts'uts'ak hayerēn dzeṙagrats' Matenadaranin Mkhit'areants' i Vienna (Catalog der armenischen Handschriften in der Mechitaristen-Bibliothek zu Wien)*, vol. 1 (Vienna, 1895); H. Oskean, vol. 2 (Vienna, 1963); O Sek'ulean, vol. 3 (Vienna, 1983)


## PRIMARY SOURCES

### Histories and Chronicles

Aristakēs Lastivertts'i, *History*
Covers 1000–72; records expansion of Byzantine control over Armenia, the Seljuk attacks and the Mantzikert campaign; arranged by imperial reign; written before 1080; 105/122 pages relevant; used by Vardan Arewelts'i and allegedly by Mkhit'ar Anets'i and Kirakos Gandzakets'i; reveals close knowledge of places and events in western Armenia and imperial Byzantine history.

*Edition:*
K.N. Yuzbashyan, ed., *Patmut'iwn Aristakisi Lastivertts'woy (History of Aristakēs Lastivertts'i)* (Erevan, 1963). For digital versions, see both Leiden Armenian Database (http://www/let.leidenuniv.nl/vtw/Weitenberg/projects_weitenberg.html) and Digital Library of Classical Armenian Literature (http://sunsite.berkeley.edu/~aua) Standard edition but not critical, being based upon only 9 of 25+ mss.; separate indices of personal names and places and peoples.

*Translations:*
(1) M. Canard and H. Berbérian, *Aristakès de Lastivert, Récit des malheurs de la nation arménienne. Traduction française avec introduction et commentaire*, Bibliothèque de *Byzantion* 5 (Brussels, 1973)
Standard translation; reasonably reliable but omits long passages of theological discourse interpreting present circumstances; includes introduction and commentary by way of notes; combined index.

(2) K.N. Yuzbashyan, *Povestvovanie vardapeta Aristakesa Lastivertts'i (Narrative of vardapet Aristakes Lastivertts'i)* (Moscow, 1968)
Also incomplete, omitting the same passages of theological discourse.
(3) V. Gevorgyan, *Aristakes Lastivertts'i Patmut'yun* (Erevan, 1971)

*Secondary Literature:*
G.A. Manukyan, *Aristakes Lastivertts'i matenagrut'yan banasirakan k'nnut'yun (Philological Study)* (Erevan, 1977)

## Continuator of T'ovma Artsruni, *History of the House of Artsrunik'*
Covers 1020–after 1121; a disjointed narrative but important because it is focused upon events in Vaspurakan (southern Armenia); describes the departure of King Sennek'erim to the Byzantine empire *c.*1021, Seljuk raids, the rule of *protocuropalates* Abdlmseh at the beginning of the twelfth century and his two successors, Aluz and Khedenik; written perhaps one generation after the death of Abdlmseh in 1121; 15 pages; not exploited in subsequent historiographical tradition.

*Edition:*
K'. Patkanean, ed., *T'ovmayi vardapeti Artsrunwoy Patmut'iwn tann Artsruneats' (History of the House of Artsrunik' of vardapet T'ovma Artsruni)* (St Petersburg, 1887; repr. Tiflis, 1917; repr. Delmar, NY, 1991), 305–18. For digital versions, see http://www/let.leidenuniv.nl/vtw/Weitenberg/projects_weitenberg.html http://sun site.berkeley.edu/~aua
Standard edition, based upon the one surviving ms.; single index.

*Translations:*
(1) R.W. Thomson, *Thomas Artsruni History of the House of the Artsrunik'. Translation and commentary* (Detroit, MI, 1985), 368–83
Introduction and complete, accurate translation with brief notes; single index.
(2) V. Vardanyan, *T'ovma Artsruni ew Ananum, Patmut'yun Artsrunyats' tan (T'ovma Artsruni and Anonymous, History of the House of Artsrunik')* (Erevan, 1978; repr. 1985)

## Matthew of Edessa/Matt'ēos Uṙhayets'i, *History*
Covers 951–1129; arranged in three unequal books; Book 1 covers the period 951–1051 and records the history and demise of the Armenian kingdoms of Vaspurakan and Ani and their interaction with the Byzantine empire, although there is also a cluster of notices reporting affairs in Edessa after 1031; Book 2 records the period 1051–1101 and marks a change in focus, away from historic Armenia and towards northern Syria and Antioch; Book 3, reporting events from the period 1101–29, accelerates this trend, to the extent that there is barely a mention of events beyond these geographical limits; written *c.*1129 (*contra* the traditional date of 1136). 400/465 pages relevant; used by Samuēl Anets'i, Vardan Arewelts'i, Smbat Sparapet and allegedly by Kirakos Gandzakets'i; a principal source, although its own sources remain unidentified and much of its content still awaits scholarly assessment.

## Continuator Gregory the Priest/Grigor Erēts'
Continues from the end of Matthew's composition, 1136–62; focus shifts way from Edessa and towards K'esun, including a long funeral elegy for count Baldwin; written *c.*1162; 83 pages; intriguing information about Georgian princes and their ambitions

in Armenia and Ani, implying that Gregory had access to a very different set of contacts and sources; a short but important work.

*Editions:*
(1) Anonymous, *Patmut'iwn Matt'ēosi Uṙhayets'woy (History of Matthew of Edessa)* (Jerusalem, 1869)
Based on three mss.; brief index, not infallible.
(2) M. Melik'-Adamean and N. Tēr-Mik'ayēlean, eds., *Patmut'iwn Uṙhayets'woy (History of Matthew of Edessa)* (Vaḷarshapat, 1898)—not seen
Based upon the earlier edition and a further six mss.; however the work survives in at least 39 mss., and it is known that it exists in more than one recension, although this has yet to be properly explored; the number of mss. containing Gregory's *Continuation* is unknown.

*Translations:*
(1) E. Dulaurier, *Chronique de Matthieu d'Édesse (962–1136) avec la continuation de Grégoire le Prêtre jusqu'en 1162* (Paris, 1858)—not seen
(2) H. Bart'ikean, *Zhamanakagrut'yun (Chronicle)* (Erevan, 1973)
Introduction, translation and commentary—not seen.
(3) A. Dostourian, *Armenia and the Crusades, 10th to 12th Centuries: The Chronicle of Matthew of Edessa. Translation, commentary and introduction* (Lanham, MI, 1993)
Based upon 1898 edition; adequate but not infallible translation; the introduction and commentary are of limited value and require careful handling; single index.

*Secondary Literature:*
H. Achaṙean, 'Matt'ēos Uṙhayets'i', *Handēs Amsoreay* 67 (1953), 350–4
K. Kostanean, *Matt'ēos Uṙhayets'i'* (Vaḷarshapat, 1899)
Ṙ.I. Mat'evosyan, 'Matt'ēos Uṙhayets'u "Patmut'ean" tarēnt'erts'umnerē Bagratunineri veraberyal (Concerning the "History" of Matthew of Edessa as a source for the Bagratid period)', *Patmabanasirakan Handēs* 117 (1987/2), 120–5
H. Pērperēan, 'Bnagrakan k'ani mē srbagrut'iwnner Matt'ēos Uṙhayets'i "Zhamanakagrut'ean" mēj ew Ch'mshkiki koḷmē Ashot Oḷormatsi uḷḷuats' namakin verjabanē (Several textual anomalies in the "Chronicle" of Matthew of Edessa and postscript on corrections to the letter from Tzmisces to Ashot the Merciful)', *Sion* (1950), 54–7 and 87–9

## Samuēl Anets'i/Samuel of Ani, *Compilation/Chronicle/Chronology*

Covers Adam to *c.*1179; arranged in two parts; part 1 runs from Adam to the birth of Christ and part 2 extends from there to 1179; closely modelled upon Eusebios' *Chronological Canons*, with several columns of figures calibrating, in the relevant section, Olympiads, years from the birth of Christ, regnal years of Byzantine emperors, years of princes, kings and *katholikoi* of Armenia and years of the Armenian Era, in that order; brief marginal entries but also longer digressions which interrupt the columns, recording, for example, the fall of Ani in 1124; written *c.*1180 but several different continuations whose scope and significance has yet to be fully established; 42/160 pages relevant; extensive overlap with Books 1 and 2 of Matthew of Edessa but not, it seems, Book 3 or Gregory's continuation, perhaps implying the use of common sources rather than a direct relationship—thus Samuel's harsh portrait of Alexios I Komnenos is not found in Matthew's work; exploited by Kirakos Gandzakets'i and

Mkhit'ar Ayrivanets'i; considers events in both historic Armenia and northern Syria/Cilicia, in particular late twelfth-century Rubenid history; of limited prosopographical value.

*Editions:*

A. Tēr-Mik'elean, ed., *Hawak'munk' i grots' patmagrats' (Compilation of Historical Writings)* (Ejmiatsin, 1893)

Based on 13 mss. but 66+ mss. survive; not set out in tabular form and so difficult to interpret; brief notes but no index. A new edition presently being prepared in Armenia.

*Translations:*

(1) J. Zohrab, ed., A. Mai, tr., *Samuelis presbyteri aniensis, temporum usque ad suam aetatem ratio e libris historicorum* in *Eusebi Pamphili Chronicorum canonum* (Milan, 1818), 1–80; repr. PG 19, 599–742

Full Latin translation of both parts down to 1179; organised in tabular form with brief notes; single index.

(2) M.F. Brosset, 'Samouel d'Ani, Tables chronologiques', in *Collection d' historiens arméniens*, vol. 2 (St Petersburg, 1876), 339–483

Translates only part 2, but includes continuation after 1179 down to 1358; no index.

*Secondary Literature:*

G.V. Abgaryan, 'Kornak Sparapeti avandut'yunĕ Samvel Anets'u "Zhamanakagrut'yunum" (The legend of Kornak Sparapet in the "Chronicle" of Samuel Anets'i)', *Lraber* (1964/1), 80–4

M. Brosset, 'Samouel d'Ani: revue générale de sa chronologie', *Bulletin de l'Académie des Sciences de St. Pétersbourg* 18 (1873), 402–42

K.A. Mat'evosyan, 'Samuel Anets'u "Zhamanakagrut'yan" avartman t'vakanĕ ew patviratun (The date and the sponsor of the "Chronicle" of Samuel Anets'i)', *Patmabanasirakan Handēs* 134 (1992/1), 156–62

## Mkhit'ar Anets'i, *History/Chronicle*

Originally covered period from the legendary Paroyr down to the expulsion of the Franks from Jerusalem in 1187 but only fragments survive, extending for the most part down to the death of the Bagratid King Gagik I in 1020; arranged in three parts; part 1 covered the period from Paroyr to the death of Yovhannēs-Smbat, son of Gagik I, in 1041; part 2 ran to the ordination of Lord Barsel; part 3 extended to the capture of Jerusalem; exploited by Vardan Arewelts'i and perhaps by Step'anos Orbelean; with the exception of occasional notices, and its list of *katholikoi*, reaching to the end of the thirteenth century, the published text is not relevant to PBW.

*Edition:*

H.G. Margaryan, ed., *Mkhit'ar Anets'i. Matean ashkharhavēp handisaranats' (Mkhit'ar Anets'i Manuscript of historical scenes)* (Erevan, 1983). For digital version, see http://sunsite.berkeley.edu/~aua

Introduction and commentary on the surviving fragments, cited in full; single index.

*Translation:*

None.

*Secondary Literature:*

D. Kouymjian, 'Mkhit'ar of Ani on the rise of the Seljuks', *RÉA* 6 (1969), 331–53

—— 'The Mxit'ar of Ani fragment', *International Journal of Middle East Studies* 4 (1973), 465–75

## Michael the Syrian, *Chronicle*

Two separate Armenian versions of this Syriac work exist, both of which are adaptations of the text rather than simple translations or abridgements and hence have an independent value; both start with Adam and extend beyond the original conclusion in 1196, one, briefly, to 1226 (1870—ironically the longer version) and the other, in more detail, to 1229 (1871—the shorter version); both versions include notices on imperial Byzantine history down to Andronikos I Komnenos, the Seljuk attacks and settlement, the emergence of Armenian principalities in Cilicia and northern Syria, with particular attention upon the Rubenids, the Kingdom of Jerusalem and other crusader states, the campaigns of Ṣalāḥ al-Dīn/Saladin, the capture of Jerusalem and other cities and the power struggle within his family after his death; the sequence of events is almost identical in both but the specific dates applied to these events are entirely independent of one another; initially the chronology found in the 1871 edition is more accurate but the position later reverses, with dates from the 1870 edition found to be more accurate; traditionally the first version has been dated 1246 and attributed jointly to Ishoh the Priest and *vardapet* Vardan Arewelts'i, whilst the second has been dated 1248 and attributed to Vardan alone; however this interpretation is hard to square with either edition; 141/532 pages of 1870 edition and 142/526 pages of 1871 edition relevant; relationships to previous Armenian texts presently unclear; direct influence upon the histories of Vardan Arewelts'i, Smbat Sparapet, Mkhit'ar Ayrivanets'i and perhaps Step'anos Orbelean; in the light of independence from original Syriac work, of some importance.

*Editions:*

(1) Anonymous, *Tearn Mikhayēli Patriark'i Asorwoy Zhamanakagrut'iwn (Chronicle of Lord Michael, Syrian Patriarch)* (Jerusalem, 1870)

Based on 2 mss.; no introduction or index; comprises an unfortunate conflation of material from both recensions, as the footnote at 511 indicates; the distribution of the surviving 76+ mss. between the two recensions remains unclear.

(2) Anonymous, *Zhamanakagrut'iwn ew yałags k'ahanayut'ean tearn Mikhayēli Asorwots' Patriark'i (Chronicle and Concerning the Priesthood of Lord Michael, Patriarch of the Syrians)* (Jerusalem, 1871)

Based on 1 ms.; introduction and single index.

*Translations:*

(1) V. Langlois, *Chronique de Michel le Grand, patriarche des syriens jacobites, traduite pour la première fois sur la version arménienne du prêtre Ischôk* (Venice, 1868), 281–361

A translation of the recension upon which the 1870 edition of the text was largely based; as noted above, additional passages from the other recension, published in 1871, were interpolated into the 1870 edition, creating a hybrid; hence this translation is currently the only published witness to the exact form of one of the recensions; no index.

(2) E. Dulaurier, 'Extrait de la Chronique de Michel Syrien, traduit de l'arménien', in *RHC Documents arméniens. Tome prémier* (Paris, 1869), 309–409
A partial translation derived from the recension upon which the 1871 edition of the text was based; differences revealed through comparison with Langlois' translation will therefore be significant.

*Secondary Literature:*
F. Haase, 'Die armenische Rezension der syrischen Chronik Michaels des Großen', *Oriens Christianus* n.s. 5 (1915), 60–82, 271–84
A.B. Schmidt, 'Die zweifache armenische Rezension der syrischen Chronik Michaels des Großen', *Le Muséon* 109 (1996), 299–319

## Kirakos Gandzakets'i, *History of Armenia*

Covers period from the time of St Grigor the Illuminator at the start of the fourth century down to 1266; records history and demise of Bagratuni kingdom, the sequence of *katholikoi* and their achievements, with brief inserts on Byzantine and Seljuk history; several other discrete passages, recording, for example, the line of bishops of Hałbat, notable Armenian scholars, including Mkhit'ar Gosh, the confession of faith by Nersēs Shnorhali dated 1165/6 and the dominant position achieved by Zak'aria and Ivanē in historic Armenia at the end of the twelfth century; few notices of significance for the period between 1070 and 1140 and little on Cilicia or northern Syria before the coronation of Rubenid prince Leo (Levon/Lewon) II as King Leo I in 1198 or 1199, although the Second Crusade features briefly; arranged into sixty-five chapters but these divisions unevenly distributed across the work; thus chapter 1, devised around the sequence of *katholikoi* of Armenia, extends from St Grigor down to the death of Grigor VI Apirat in 1203 and runs to some 111 pages; episodic and disorganised, reflecting its composite nature; written in 1266, or very shortly after, and in any event before 1271; 112/399 pages relevant; extensive borrowings of material, though not specific dates from the *History* of Samuel Anets'i, as well as the lost works by Yovhannēs Sarkawag and Vanakan Vardapet; relationship to Aristakēs and Matthew of Edessa unproven; exploited by Vardan Arewelts'i; of limited prosopographical value, at least up to the third quarter of the twelfth century, although it is worth recalling that it supplies much important information about thirteenth-century conditions, and in particular Armenian responses to, and interaction with, the Mongols.

*Edition:*
K.A. Melik'-Awhanjanyan, ed., *Kirakos Gandzakets'i Patmut'yun Hayots' (History of Armenia)* (Erevan, 1961). For digital version, see either
http://www.let.leidenuniv. nl/vtw/Weitenberg/projects_weitenberg.html or
http://sunsite.berkeley.edu/~aua
Critical edition, with comprehensive introduction and single index.

*Translations:*
(1) M. Brosset, *Deux historiens arméniens. Kiracos de Gantzac, XIIIᵉ s. Histoire d'Arménie; Oukhtanès d'Ourha, Xᵉ s. Histoire en trois parties* (St Petersburg, 1870), 1–194
Full annotated translation; no index.
(2) A.A. Khanlarjan, *Kirakos Gandzakets'i Istoriia Armenii* (Moscow, 1976)—not seen

(3) V.D. Aṙakʻelyan, *Kirakos Gandzaketsʻi Hayotsʻ Patmutʻyun* (Erevan, 1982)—not seen

(4) R. Bedrosian, *Kirakos Gandzaketsʻiʻs History of the Armenians* (New York, 1986) Adequate, though not infallible translation which omits passages of theological discourse; marginal references to the pages of Melikʻ-Awhanjanyanʻs edition supplied by Bedrosian confusing, as they relate to the preceding rather than subsequent passages and therefore seem to be wrong by a factor of 1; very short introduction; no index.

*Secondary Literature:*

V.D. Aṙakʻelyan, 'Bnagrakan uḷḷumner Kirakos Gandzaketsʻu "Patmutʻyun hayotsʻ"' erkum (Textual corrections to the "History of Armenia" of Kirakos Gandzaketsʻi)', *Patmabanasirakan Handēs* 45 (1969/2), 63–74

V.D. Aṙakʻelyan, 'Kirakos Gandzaketsʻi', *Patmabanasirakan Handēs* 56 (1972/1), 48–62

Z. Arzoumanian, 'Kirakos Ganjakecʻi and his *History of Armenia*', in T.J. Samuelian and M.E. Stone, eds., *Medieval Armenian Culture* (Chico, CA, 1984), 262–71

H.H. Oskean, 'Kirakos Gandzaketsʻi', *Handēs Amsoreay* 36 (1922), 89–94, 214–21

## Vardan Areweltsʻi/Vardan Vardapet, *History/Historical Compilation/Chronicle*

Covers period from Creation down to 1267; extremely condensed history which combined extracts from Aristakēs, the lost *History* of Yovhannēs Sarkawag, Matthew of Edessa, Mkhitʻar Anetsʻi, the Armenian translation of Michael the Syrian, the lost work of Vanakan Vardapet and Kirakos Gandzaketsʻi, sometimes conflating separate accounts to create a new, composite version; significant overlap with earlier works; however an important source for early Seljuk and Ghaznavid history, derived from Mkhitʻar Anetsʻiʻs lost *History*, who in turn exploited a Persian source written before 1148; elsewhere Vardan records that Mkhitʻar translated a Persian *zič* or astronomical almanac in 1187, supporting the contention of a Persian original—hence the presence of Hijri dates, the relative accuracy in the rendering of Muslim titles and the extensive use of Arabic and Persian words; also new material about local affairs in Ani and the rise of the Shaddādids, and for events more generally in historic Armenia, Loṙi and Duin, perhaps from Yovhannēs Sarkavag; these alternate with reports focused upon Cilician Armenia derived from known sources; with rare exceptions, twelfth-century Byzantium is not in Vardanʻs field of vision; completed 1267; 46/164 pages; for Vardan, Armenians, whether in historic Armenia or Cilicia, remain centrestage; with the exception of those new notices referred to above, a compilation and conflation of earlier extant works and thus of limited value.

*Editions:*

(1) J.-B. Emin, ed., *Hawakʻumn Patmutʻean. Vseoschaia istoriia Vardana velikogo* (Moscow, 1861)
   Based on two manuscripts, one undated, the other copied in 1514 from an earlier example dated 1425.

(2) Ł. Alishan, *Hawakʻumn Patmutʻean Hayotsʻ (Compilation of Armenian History)* (Venice, 1862; repr. Delmar, NY, 1991 with introduction by R.W. Thomson). See also digital versions, at
   http://www/let.leidenuniv.nl/vtw/Weitenberg/projects_ weitenberg.html or
   http://sunsite.berkeley.edu/~aua

Based on Venice 877 (formerly San Lazarro ms. 516), dated 1301 and owned by Step'anos Orbelean, who died in 1304, and Venice 879 (formerly San Lazarro ms. 1244), dated 1307 but containing the text only down to 1236—the point reached by Vardan in 1265 when his manuscript was stolen by bandits and recovered eighteen months later in a market in Tiflis. Although this edition cannot be described as critical, it should be treated as supplying an accurate version of the work since the two manuscripts consulted were copied within a generation of the completion of the work.

*Translation:*
R.W. Thomson, 'The Historical Compilation of Vardan Arewelc'i', *DOP* 43 (1989), 125–226
  Valuable introduction and complete, accurate translation, accompanied by useful notes; no index.

*Secondary Literature:*
P'.P'. Ant'abyan, 'Vardan Arewelts'i', *Patmabanasirakan Handēs* 59 (1972/4), 59–66
P'.P'. Ant'abyan, 'Vardan Arewelts'u "Patmut'yan" ałbyurnerě (The sources for the "History" of Vardan Arewelts'i)', *Banber Matenadarani* 14 (1984), 78–105
P'.P'. Ant'abyan, *Vardan Arewelts'i. Kyank'n u gortsunēut'yuně (His Life and Works)*, 2 vols. (Erevan, 1987, 1989)
M. Brosset, 'Analyse critique de l'Histoire de Vardan', *Mémoires de l'Académie impériale des Sciences de St. Pétersbourg*, 7ᵉ Série, Tome 4, no. 9 (St Petersburg, 1862), 1–30
J. Muyldermans, 'Une source de l'Histoire Universelle de Vardan l'historien', *Shinarar* 2/20 (1957), 13
R.W. Thomson, 'Vardan's Historical Compilation and its sources', *Le Muséon* 100 (1987), 343–52
G.B. T'osunyan, 'Vardan Arewelts'u "Havak'umn patmut'ean" erkě (The "Historical Compilation" of Vardan Arewelts'i)', *Banber Erevani Hamalsarani* (1993/2), 172–5

## Smbat Sparapet/Smbat the Constable, *Chronicle*

Covers 951–1274; at least two recensions, one of which is preserved in a single manuscript, Venice 875 (old 1308); both appear to derive from a single archetype now lost rather than having a direct relationship to one another; a significant proportion of the work is based upon the *History* of Matthew of Edessa and his Continuator, Gregory the Priest, although several additional passages have been inserted, notably into Gregory's continuation, recording the death of prince Het'um of Lambron, the death of John II Komnenos, the fall of Edessa in 1144 and the triumphal entry of Manuel I Komnenos into Antioch in 1159; diverse sources for the latter part of this work have been suggested, including William of Tyre, Niketas Choniates, George Akropolites, the Armenian adaptation of Michael the Syrian (though which recension is unclear) and Kirakos Gandzakets'i; a complex, composite work drawing upon both Armenian and non-Armenian sources and thus exceptional in Armenian historiography; the recension in Ven. 875 has preserved a considerable amount of detail from the latter part which is missing from the other recension; it supplies a detailed record of events in Cilicia after 1159, with a particular focus upon the rise of the Rubenids; thus for example, it supplies a list of the princes and clerics and their districts under Rubenid suzerainty at the time of coronation of King Leo I (January 1198 or 1199); however

historic Armenia has not disappeared from view, as the account of the fall of
Karin/Erzurum in 1201 to Rukn al-Dīn attests; composed before 1276; 196/255 pages
relevant if one includes the overlap with Matthew of Edessa; otherwise 34/255; indicates an on-going engagement with, and knowledge of, the Byzantine empire; an
important source of information for prosopography, particularly in relation to Cilicia
and northern Syria, including Antioch, during the second half of the twelfth century.

*Editions:*
(1) O. Yovhannēseants', ed., *Smbatay Sparapeti ełbawr Het'moy aṙajnay ark'ayi
    Hayots' Patmut'iwn (History of Smbat Sparapet Brother of King Het'um Previous
    King of Armenia)* (Moscow, 1856)
    First edition, based on a single ms. from Ejmiatsin; opens with notice dated 951;
    final entry dated 1274; also includes a short, intriguing continuation down to 1331;
    brief introduction; no commentary or index.
(2) K. Shahnazareants', ed., *Smbatay Sparapeti Patmut'iwn* (Paris, 1859)—not seen
    Based upon the earlier edition and a second ms. from Ejmiatsin.
(3) S. Agĕlean, *Smpatay Sparapeti Taregirk' (Chronicle of Smbat Sparapet)* (Venice,
    1956)
    Not critical, being based exclusively upon Venice 875, the only ms. identified thus
    far which preserves the second recension; little engagement with the earlier edi-
    tions; single index.

*Translations:*
(1) V. Langlois, 'Extraite de la chronique de Sempad, seigneur de Baboron,
    Connétable d'Armène; suivie de celle de son continuateur', *Mémoires de
    l'Académie impériale des Sciences de St. Pétersbourg*, 7ᵉ Série, Tome 4, no. 6 (St
    Petersburg, 1862)
    Brief introduction; single long annotated extract translated from the second edi-
    tion of Shahnazareants', although aware of the Moscow edition, covering the
    period 1091–1331; no index.
(2) E. Dulaurier, *RHC. Documents arméniens. Tome prémier* (Paris, 1869), 610–72
    Translated extract, prepared on basis of copy of best ms. in Ejmiatsin and the two
    published editions; covers period 1098–1331; no separate index, references being
    merged into general indices for the whole volume.
(3) S. Der Nersessian, 'The Armenian Chronicle of the Constable Smpad or of the
    "Royal Historian"', *DOP* 13 (1959), 143–68
    Introduction, textual analysis and annotated translated passages from Agĕlean's
    edition, beginning with Manuel Komnenos' entry into Antioch in 1159; limited to
    'those passages which are not restricted to the local history of Cilicia'; omits all
    the passages derived from Matthew of Edessa and those inserted into that text; no
    index.
(4) G. Dédéyan, *La chronique attribuée au Connétable Smbat. Introduction, traduction
    et notes* (Paris, 1980)
    Introduction, textual analysis and annotated translated passages from Agĕlean's
    edition, also beginning at 1159 but comprehensive thereafter; divisions inserted by
    Dédéyan and not found in any edition of the text; separate indices of names and
    places.
(5) A.G. Galstyan, *Smbat Sparapet, Letopis* (Erevan, 1974)—not seen

*Secondary Literature:*

L.H. Babayan, 'Smbat Sparapetĕ ew "Taregrk'i" hełinaki harts'ĕ (Smbat Sparapet and the problem of authorship of the "Chronicle")', *Patmabanasirakan Handēs* 72 (1976/1), 243–54

G. Dédéyan, 'Les listes "féodales" du pseudo-Smbat', *Cahiers de civilisation médiévale* 32 (1989), 25–42

A. Suk'iasyan, 'Smbat Sparapetĕ orpes patmich', awrensget ev awrensgir (Smbat Sparapet as annalist, lawyer and legislator)', *Banber Erevani Hamalsarani* (1974/1) 100–9

N. Tsovakan (= N. Bołarian), 'Smbat Sparapeti "Taregirk'ĕ" (The "Chronicle" of Smbat Sparapet)', *Sion* (1960), 304–5

## Mkhit'ar Ayrivanets'i, *Chronicle/History*

Covers period from Creation to 1289; divided into three parts; part 1 tells of the six days of Creation; part 2 records history from Adam to the birth of Christ; part 3 covers the period since Christ down to 1289; extremely abbreviated, with 6,487 years crammed into 69 pages of text; marginal Armenian Era dates at ten-year intervals, although specific entries may also be dated; chronologically suspect; exploited Samuel Anets'i, the Armenian adaptation of Michael the Syrian (though which recension is unknown); occasional additional information and focus remains broad, with Cilicia, historic Armenia, Byzantium and Georgia all featuring, albeit intermittently; written 1289; 9/84 pages relevant; of very little prosopographical significance.

*Editions:*

(1) N. Emin, ed., *Mkhit'aray Ayrivanets'woy Patmut'iwn hayots' (History of Armenia of Mkhit'ar Ayrivanets'i)* (Moscow, 1860)

No introduction; text, prepared on basis of single ms.; brief notes; no index.

(2) K'. Patkanov, ed., *Mkhit'aray Ayrivanets'woy Patmut'iwn zhamanakagrakan (Chronological History of Mkhit'ar Ayrivanets'i)* (St Petersburg, 1867)

No introduction, notes or index; prepared on basis of a more complete ms. whilst also acknowledging the earlier edition.

*Translation:*

M. Brosset, 'Histoire chronologique par Mkhithar d'Aïrivank', *Mémoires de l'Académie impériale des Sciences de St. Pétersbourg*, 7ᵉ Série, Tome 13, no. 5 (St Petersburg, 1869), Préface and 1–110

*Secondary Literature:*

M. Brosset, 'Études sur l'Histoire arménienne Mkhithar d'Aïravank', *Bulletin de l'Académie impériale de St Pétersbourg* 8 (1865), 391–410

E. Harut'yunyan, *Mkhit'ar Ayrivanets'i. Kyank'n u stełtsagortsut'yunĕ (Life and Output)* (Erevan, 1985)

G. Yovsēp'eants', 'Mkhit'ar Ayrivanets'i. Noragiwt ardzanagrut'iwn ew erker (Mkhit'ar Ayrivanets'i. A newly found inscription)', *Sion* (1930), 395–7; (1931), 18–21, 50–2, 118–120, 148–150, 184–7, 214–16, 237–9, 277–9

—— 'Nor ałbiwr Mkhit'ar Ayrivanets'u masin (Concerning a new source of Mkhit'ar Ayrivanets'i)', *Ejmiatsin* (1945/5), 17–21

Step'anos Orbelean/Orpelean, *History of the Province of Siwnik'*
Covers period from eponymous Sisak down to 1299; focus largely upon the sequence
of princes, kings and bishops of Siwnik' and their actions, with external matters and
outsiders (apart from Armenians, Georgians and Ałuank') intruding only occasionally and then through relationship to Siwnik'—thus the fall of Jerusalem in 1187 is
noted only because a Siwni bishop happened to be visiting and was martyred; used
works by Armenian historians, unspecified, with the notable exception of Mkhit'ar
Anets'i who may be one of the sources used by Step'anos for his extended account
of Orbelean history, beginning in 1049; also drew upon the works of Petros bishop of
Siwnik', correspondence and documents involving princes and bishops of Siwnik'
preserved in the patriarchal residence at T'atev, and inscriptions from T'atev,
Noravank' and other sites; almost no information about Cilicia, northern Syria or the
Byzantine world; the separate Orbelean family history in ch. 66 records events in
twelfth-century historic Armenia and Georgia and their interaction with Seljuk and
other Muslim polities—brief but significant; completed in 1299; 45/363 pages relevant; in the light of its different focus and twelfth-century records relating to historic
Armenia, of some prosopographical importance.

*Editions:*
(1) K. Shahnazareants', ed., *Patmut'iwn nahangin Sisakan arareal Step'annosi Orbēlean
    ark'episkoposi Siwneats' (History of the Province of Siwnik' produced by Step'anos
    Orbelean, Archbishop of Siwnik')* (Paris, 1860; repr. Tiflis, 1910)
    First edition, based on a single ms.; single index.
(2) N. Emin, ed., *Step'annosi Siwneats' episkoposi Patmut'iwn tann Sisakan* (Moscow,
    1861)
    Based upon single ms., with variants from earlier edition noted; no index.

*Translations:*
(1) M. Brosset, *Histoire de la Siounie par Stéphannos Orbélian* (St Petersburg, 1864)
    Complete translation, made on basis of both existing printed editions, with anno-
    tations; chapter divisions located in same places but numbered differently, being
    ahead by a factor of 1; no index.
(2) A.A. Abrahamyan, *Step'anos Orbelyan Syunik'i Patmut'yun* (Erevan, 1986)—not
    seen

*Secondary Literature:*
A.A. Abrahamyan, 'Bnagragitakan ditarkumner Step'anos Orbelyani patmakan
    erkum (Textological observations on Step'anos Orbelean's historical writing)',
    *Patmabanasirakan Handēs* 110 (1985/3), 55–67
Z. Avetik'yan, 'Step'anos Ark'episkopos Orbelyan', *Ejmiatsin* (1980/9), 47–55;
    (1980/10), 22–30
T. Hakobyan and S. Melik'-Bakhshyan, *Step'anos Orbelyan* (Erevan, 1960)

## Colophons

*Editions:*
G. Yovsēp'ean, ed., *Yishatakarank' dzeṙagrats' (Colophons of Manuscripts)* (Antelias,
    1951)
A.S. Mat'evosyan, *Hayeren dzeṙagreri hishatakaranner 5–12 dd (Colophons of
    Armenian Manuscripts Fifth–Twelfth Centuries)* (Erevan, 1988)

K.A. Matʻevosyan, ʻAnium Zakʻaryanneri hastatman zhamanakn ĕst norahayt hishatakarani (The date of the Zakarians' settlement in Ani according to a newly discovered colophon)', *Patmabanasirakan Handēs* 147 (1997/1), 280–3

*Translations:*
P. Peeters, ʻUne témoignagae autographe sur le siège d'Antioche par les croisés en 1098', in *Miscellanea historica in honorem Alberti de Meyer*, vol. 1, Recueil de travaux d'histoire de l'Université de Louvain, 3rd ser. 22 (Louvain, 1946), repr. in *Recherches d'histoire et de philologie orientales*, Subsidia Hagiographica 27 (Brussels, 1951), vol. 2, 164–80

## Inscriptions

*Editions:*
Ł. Alishan, *Ayrarat* (Venice, 1890)
—— *Shirak tełagrutʻiwn patkeratsʻoytsʻ (Shirak. Illustrated Topography)* (Venice, 1881)
—— *Sissouan ou L'Arméno-Cilicie* (Venice, 1899)
K.Y. Basmajean, *Hayerēn ardzanagrutʻiwnkʻ Anwoy, Bagnayr ew Marmashinu (Armenian Inscriptions of Ani, Bagnayr and Marmashēn)* (Paris, 1931)
M. Gevorgeantsʻ, *Hamaṙot tełagrutʻiwn hnutʻeantsʻ Metsin Shiraka ev mayrakʻałakʻin Anwoy (Brief Topography of the Antiquities of Greater Shirak and the Capital Ani)* (Alexandropol, 1903)
S. Jalaleantsʻ, *Chanaparhordutʻiwn i Metsn Hayastan (Travels in Greater Armenia)*, 2 vols. (Tiflis, 1842–58)
K. Kostaneantsʻ, *Vimakan Taregir. Tsʻutsʻak zhołovatsoy ardzanagrutʻeantsʻ Hayotsʻ (Chronicle in Stone. A catalogue of a selection of Armenian inscriptions)* (St Petersburg, 1913)
H.A. Orbeli, ed., *Divan hay vimagrutʻyan (Corpus inscriptionum armenicarum)*, 7 vols. (Erevan, 1966–99)
N. Sargisean, *Tełagrutʻiwnkʻ i Pʻokʻr ew i Mets Hays (Topography of Greater and Lesser Armenia)* (Venice, 1864)
G. Yovsēpʻean, *Grchʻutʻean aruestĕ hin hayotsʻ mēj. Kartēz hay hnagrutʻean (The Art of Writing among the Ancient Armenians. Album of Armenian palaeography)* (Vałarshapat, 1913)

*Translations:*
J.-P. Mahé, ʻAni sous Constantin X, d'après une inscription de 1060', in *Mélanges Gilbert Dagron*, Travaux et Mémoires 14 (2002), 403–14
—— ʻLes inscriptions de Hoṙomos', *Monuments Piot* 81 (2002), 147–214
G. Uluhogian, ʻLes églises d'Ani d'après le témoinage des inscriptions', *RÉA* 23 (1992), 237–52

## Charters

*Edition:*
V. Langlois, *Le trésor des chartres d'Arménie ou cartulaire de la chancellerie royale des Roupéniens* (Venice, 1863), 105–12: documents 1 and 2

## Letter Collections

*Editions:*

Grigor    kat'ołikosi    Tłay    koch'ets'eloy,    Namakani;    Teaŕn    Nersēsi
Lambronats'woy ... t'ułt' ew chaŕk' (Letters of Katholikos Grigor Tłay and Letter
and Homilies of Lord Nersēs Lambronats'i (Venice, 1838)

Grigor Tłay ew s. Nersēs Lambronats'i. Namakani Grigori kat'ołikosi . . . ew N.
Lambronats'woy Atenabanut'iwn T'ułt' aŕ Lewon t'agawor, Nerboł i Hambardzumn
K'ristosi ew i Galust Hogwoyn Srboy (Grigor Tłay and St Nersēs Lambronats'i.
Letters of Katholikos Grigor ... and Oration of N. Lambronats'i Letter to King
Lewon, Eulogy to the Ascension of Christ and the Coming of the Holy Spirit)
(Venice, 1865)

'T'ułt' Nersisi Ark'episkopi Kilikets'wots' Tarsoni pataskhani yOskann argelakan chgnawori i metsn Antiok (Letter of Nersēs, archbishop of Tarsos in Cilicia, in reply to
Oskan, a monk imprisoned in Antioch the Great)', Chŕak'al (1859) 1, 3–11; 2, 37–44

'Pataskhani Oskan argelakan chgnawori i metsn Antiok (Reply of Oskan, a monk
imprisoned in Antioch the Great)', in Khurhrdatsut'iwn srbazn pataragi
(Commentary on the Divine Liturgy) (Jerusalem, 1842)

K'. Kostaneants', ed., Grigor Magistrosi t'ułt'erĕ (Letters of Grigor Magistros)
(Alexandropol, 1910)

*Translations:*

E. Gjandschezian, 'Ein Brief des Gregor Magistros an den Patriarchen Petros',
Zeitschrift für armenischen Philologie 2 (1903/4), 75–80 = letter no. 5 of Kostaneants'

——— 'Ein Brief des Gregor Magistros an den Emir Ibrahim', Zeitschrift für
armenischen Philologie 2 (1903/4), 234–63 = letter no. 70 of Kostaneants'

A.K. Sanjian and A. Terian, 'An enigmatic letter of Gregory Magistros', Journal of
the Society for Armenian Studies 2 (1985–6), 85–95 = letter no. 12 of Kostaneants'

## Laments

### Nersēs Shnorhali

*Critical Edition:*
M. Mkrtch'yan, ed., Ołb Edesioy (Erevan, 1973)

*Translations:*
(1) E. Dulaurier, 'Elégie sur la prise d'Édesse', in RHC 1, 223–68
(2) I. Kéchichian, Nersēs Šnorhali. La complainte d'Édesse, Bibliotheca Armeniaca.
   Textus et Studia 3 (Venice, 1984)
(3) T.M. van Lint, 'Lament on Edessa by Nersēs Šnorhali', in K. Ciggaar and H. Teule,
   eds., East and West in the Crusader States. Context, contacts, confrontations,
   Orientalia Lovaniensia Analecta 92 (Leuven, 1999), 49–105

*Secondary Literature:*
T.M. van Lint, 'Seeking meaning in catastrophe: Nersēs Šnorhali's Lament on Edessa',
   in Ciggaar and Teule, eds., East and West (Leuven, 1999), 29–47

### Grigor Tłay

*Edition and Translation:*
E. Dulaurier, 'Elégie sur la prise de Jérusalem', in RHC 1, 269–307

# 11

# Syriac Historiographical Sources

WITOLD WITAKOWSKI

SYRIAC HISTORIOGRAPHY HAS ONLY THREE WORKS which provide historical, including prosopographical, information for the period in question. These are the chronicles (in chronological order) by Michael the Elder (Syr. Mika'el Rabo, (*Mīkhā'ēl Rabbā*; hereafter MR), an anonymous Edessene (*The Chronicle to the Year 1234*; hereafter *X1234*) and John Gregory BarEbroyo (Yōḥannān Grēghoryōs Bar'Ebhrāyā; hereafter BE), also known in Arabic as Abu'l Faraj ('Father of what is pleasant').[1]

Generally the Syriac chronicles can be regarded as less important than Greek sources for mainstream Byzantine history, and even less for Byzantine prosopography. This is due to the fact that for most of the period 1025–1204 the area inhabited by the Syrians, the members of the Syrian Orthodox (i.e. Jacobite) church to which all the three authors here examined belong, was not directly adjacent to the Byzantine empire. Thus Byzantium did not loom large within the geographical horizon of our historians, who were consequently less interested in its affairs. The prosopographical contribution of the chronicles for the period in question is not as rich as it is for the pre-Islamic period, during which the Syrians lived within the Roman/Byzantine empire so that historiographical narrative of their affairs was naturally also a narrative of Byzantine affairs. As a result, for the period 1025–1204 the Syriac chronicles—and there is hardly any other kind of Syriac source that contains relevant material—recede from the position of being primary sources. This does not mean, of course, that they can be ignored. One should be aware, however, that we do not learn much from them about the most important events of Byzantine history and the people involved in them, who often belonged to court circles or the army. An example is provided by the story of

---

[1] In what follows the spelling of Syriac names with a so-called 'patronymic' ('so-called' because it does not always provide the name of the bearer's father) is normalised so that the 'patronymic' is combined with the preceding 'Bar' ('son of') but begins with a capital letter. 'Patronymics' and names with no corresponding counterparts in English are spelt according to a simplified post-classical Western Syriac pronunciation; at first occurrence they are accompanied by transcription according to classical Syriac rules in parentheses, as is the case here. Obsolete Latinised forms such as 'Bar Hebraeus' or 'Barhebraeus' are avoided.

*Proceedings of the British Academy* **132**, 253–282. © The British Academy 2007.

the 1204 Crusade and the conquest of Constantinople as told by the author of the *X1234*.[2] For this event of such tremendous importance no names of Greeks are given, making an interesting contrast to the mention of the sultan of Ikonion (with whom the crusaders reached an agreement concerning their passage to Syria), whose full name and patronymic are provided: Rukn al-Dīn, the son of Kilic Arslan.[3] However, although the central events of Byzantine history are only sporadically reported, at least the names of the emperors are provided, usually on the occasion of one succeeding the other.

The Syriac chroniclers were not only less interested in Byzantine affairs for this period but also less well informed about details of the events of Byzantine history which they did in fact narrate. Unfortunately the missing details include the names of the people who took part in the events described. Moreover the dates provided are not always reliable.

These deficiencies are, however, balanced by much more abundant information, including prosopographical, concerning individuals who had contacts with the Empire, be it Syrians, Armenians, Arabs, Turks, or crusaders. Generally the Syriac chronicles are more interested in events in the Byzantine eastern border provinces, close to the Syriac-speaking area. This is especially true for the early years of the period in question during which Byzantine governors controlled territories inhabited by Syrians (such as Melitene), before the Turkish conquests removed those areas from Byzantine political control. Thus for the subsequent period the Turkish rulers take the place once held in the chronicles by the Byzantine governors. As an example we might name the passage of the *X1234*, which provides names of Turkish emirs, who became governors of territories and cities captured from Byzantium.[4]

Historical facts are reported if they take place within the Syriac historians' geographical horizon, as for instance the information given by the author of the *X1234* about the expedition of Emperor John (II Komnenos) to Cilicia and his death.[5] Another example may be the account of Kassianos, a Byzantine governor in Anatolia, who went over to the Danishmendid emir Ghazi and in return was given a position in the service of the emir.[6] However, there is hardly any mention of the affairs of the empire on its northern borders,[7] let alone of the people involved in them.

---

[2] *X1234*, vol. 2, § 502, 214–15/tr. 160–1.
[3] *X1234*, vol. 2, § 502, 214/tr. 161.
[4] *X1234*, vol. 2, § 240, 50–1/tr. 36–7.
[5] *X1234*, vol. 2, § 399, 107–9/tr. 81–6.
[6] MR 610 central col./tr. vol. 3, 227; BE *Chronography* 289/tr. 255.
[7] Occasionally pieces of information on events in that area can be found, such as an account of the Cumans in MR, which is an excerpt from the *Chronicle* of Basil BarShumno (BarŠumnā): MR 600–1, central col./tr. vol. 3, 207. The author of the *X1234*, who also knew Basil's work, does not however mention the Cumans.

Byzantine civil governors or ecclesiastical hierarchs are most often named if they had contacts with Syrians, or, respectively, with the Jacobite hierarchs, as was the case, for example, with Nikephoros, the Greek Orthodox metropolitan of Melitene, who opposed the Jacobite patriarch John (VIII) BarAbdun's (Bar'Abhdun) warm reception in Constantinople.[8] In such cases the Syriac chronicles are definitely very valuable, since such persons would probably not be mentioned by non-Syriac sources.

In addition one must point to the fact that the Syriac sources have a bias: some measure of grudge, if not hostility, against the Greeks is present, especially in Michael the Elder's work. This is, however, hardly a circumstance that diminishes their source value. By studying the Syriac sources one sees Byzantine history from a different perspective.

## MICHAEL THE ELDER

Michael the Elder (MR) is known to western scholars under the name Michael the Syrian due to the fact that the first (and so far the only) editor of his *Chronicle*, Jean-Baptiste Chabot, gave him this name (Michel le Syrien), most probably following the title of the edition of the Armenian version by Édouard Dulaurier, published first (fragments only) in the *Journal asiatique* (1848–9) and later in 1869 in the *Recueil des historiens des croisades*.[9] Even if such a name makes sense when used in Armenian sources[10] it has no justification in Syriac. In fact our chronicler is never so named in the Syriac sources. There he is referred to by the name Mika'el Rabo. 'Rabo' means in Syriac both 'great' and 'elder'. Our historian was certainly one of the more important patriarchs of the Syrian Orthodox church (1166–99), but it seems that he is called Rabo in later sources (BarEbroyo)[11] to distinguish him from his namesake and nephew, Michael (II) Zeoro (Zə'ōrā), i.e. 'the Little', or 'the Younger, Junior'. The latter was the anti-patriarch (1199–1215), opposed to Patriarch Athanasios IX Slibo Qroho (Ṣəlībhā Qərāḥā; 1199–1207) and, after the latter's death, his successor.

MR was born in 1126/7 in Melitene, a son of Elias who was a priest and a physician. As a young man MR became a monk, and after some time, at the age of thirty, abbot of the BarSawmo (BarṢawmā) monastery (between

---

[8] MR 562–3/tr. vol. 3, 140–1.

[9] Dulaurier, *Extrait de la Chronique de Michel le Syrien*.

[10] However, V. Langlois, another translator of the Armenian version of MR's work, did not call him by this name: Langlois, *Chronique de Michel le Grand*.

[11] *Gregorii Barhebraei Chronicon ecclesiasticum*, vol. 1, cols. 535–6, 617–18.

Melitene and Samosata). He was offered the episcopacy of Amida in 1165, but did not accept it, whereas in the next year he was elected patriarch by a synod convened in the monastery of Pesqin (Pəsqīn), and was consecrated on 18 October 1166 in the monastery of BarSawmo.

As the patriarch elect, Michael announced that he would accept the pontificate if the bishops promised more strict observance of the canons (there had been cases of simony among the bishops, changes of diocese and other irregularities). Soon after his enthronement he passed twenty-nine disciplinary canons. These reform efforts, followed by the deposition of some corrupt bishops, caused dissension, which in 1175 even led to MR's temporary imprisonment by the emir of Mosul, Sayf al-Dīn.

A more serious problem was the schism in 1180, when his former pupil and godson Theodore BarWahbun (BarWahbūn) was elected—by some bishops opposed to MR—as an anti-patriarch. MR promptly deposed Theodore and shut him up in the monastery of BarSawmo, but some of the monks helped him to escape, whereupon he went first to Damascus and Jerusalem in order to bring his cause before the Muslim authorities (Ṣalāḥ al-Dīn, Saladin) and, when this did not succeed, he went to Cilicia where he was recognised as the patriarch of the Jacobites in the kingdom of Armenia. The schism lasted until Theodore's death in 1193.

Much of his pontificate MR spent travelling from place to place as required by the administration of the church. When not travelling he resided in Mardin or, most often, in his previous monastery, that of BarSawmo. His relations with the monks were, however, not good. Serious conflicts occurred in 1171 and 1176.

As the head of his church MR maintained good relations with the ecclesiastical and secular authorities of his time. In 1169 he was approached by Emperor Manuel I Komnenos who invited him to Constantinople for talks concerning church unity. MR refused to go in person but did send delegates. Another meeting on the question of union took place in 1172, with the Greek Orthodox representative Theorianos.[12] Michael's delegate was then Theodore BarWahbun.[13]

MR had good relations with the crusaders. While still abbot of BarSawmo monastery he participated, together with Patriarch Athanasios VIII, in the consecration of a Latin church in Antioch; later, in 1168, when he had already become patriarch, he was received with honours by Amaury (Amalric) of Nesle, the Latin patriarch of Jerusalem, and later by Aimery of

[12] The Greek acts of this meeting are extant, PG 133, 114ff.
[13] MR tr. vol. 3, 334–6 (there is a lacuna in the Syriac text; Chabot's translation is provided on the basis of the text in BE's *Chron. eccl.* vol. I, cols. 549–60).

Limoges, the Latin patriarch of Antioch.[14] In 1178/9 he paid a visit to the king of Jerusalem, Baldwin IV, in Akko (Acre). He was invited to participate in the Third Lateran Council (1187, against the Albigenses), but did not attend it. He did nonetheless write a treatise on the topic which was to be discussed at the Council.

He supported the patriarch of the Coptic church against a schismatic by writing a polemical work. He maintained equally good relations with the Armenian ecclesiastics, *katholikos* Nerses IV Shnorhali (1166–73), and his successor Gregory IV Degha, after the affair of Theodore BarWahbun. In 1198 (or 1199) MR participated in the coronation of King Levon I.

In his contacts with the Muslim authorities he was, often due to his personal courage and deftness, able to avert dangers that threatened the church. In 1181 he visited the Seljuk sultan Kilic Arslan II.[15] During the visit he held a religious discussion with a Muslim philosopher Kamāl al-Dīn.

MR died on 7 November 1199 in the monastery of BarSawmo, where he was also buried.[16]

MR spoke Syriac, Armenian and Arabic. He took an interest in manuscripts and libraries; he himself copied books, some of which are preserved.[17] His intellectual/literary production[18] can be divided into the following groups:

Canon law: *29 Canons*[19] which he passed soon after his installation, a treatise[20] and decretals concerning church administration, e.g. that on the handing over of the diocese of Mardin to the authority of the *maphrian*.[21]

Liturgy: MR revised the Syrian Orthodox pontifical,[22] and the rite of ordination (e.g. ms. Vaticanus Syr. 51); composed an *Anaphora*, the prayers of which are arranged to form an acrostich of the Syriac alphabet; he also wrote prayers called *sedrē*, which are inserted in the books of offices.

---

[14]  MR tr. vol. 3, 332 (BE's *Chron. eccl.* vol. I, col. 545).

[15]  MR 725–6/tr. vol. 3, 390–1.

[16]  The monastery is today in ruins, Honigmann, *Le couvent de Barsauma*, 3–5.

[17]  F. Nau, 'Sur quelques autographes de Michel le Syrien patriarche d'Antioche de 1166 à 1199', *Revue de l'Orient chrétien* 19 (1914), 378–97.

[18]  Tisserant, 'Michel le Syrien', 1714–17.

[19]  These are included by BarEbroyo in his *Nomocanon: Nomocanone di Bar-Hebreo*, Italian tr. by G. Ricciotti, Sacra Congregazione per le Chiese orientali: Codificazione canonica orientale: Fonti 3: Disciplina antiochena (Siri) (Vatican, 1931).

[20]  Text in A. Vööbus, ed., *The Synodicon in the West Syrian Tradition*, vol. 2, CSCO vol. 375, SS 163 (Louvain, 1976), 167ff.; tr. in the *Versio* volume, CSCO vol. 376, SS 164, 179ff; see also A. Vööbus, 'Discovery of a treatise about the ecclesiastical administration ascribed to Michael the Syrian: a unique document in the literary genre of canon law', *Church History* 47 (1978), 23–6.

[21]  The title of the metropolitan of the eastern dioceses (on the territory of the former Sasanid kingdom) of the Syrian Orthodox church, second only to the patriarch. The decree is quoted in *X1234*, vol. 2, 331–3/tr. 247–8.

[22]  J.-M. Vosté, 'Les textes bibliques dans le pontifical de Michel le Grand (1166–1199)', *Biblica* 27 (1946), 107–12.

Hagiography and biography: he made a revision of the *Life of Mar Abhay* (*Abhḥay*), the legendary bishop of Nicaea at the end of the sixth century, in fact a composition of the iconoclast period defending the cult of relics;[23] wrote panegyrical homilies on John of Mardin (unpublished)[24] and on Mar BarSawmo;[25] a poem celebrating a young Christian woman whom the Arabs of Mosul tried to force to accept Islam; a (lost) panegyric on his friend, the metropolitan of Amida, Dionysius BarSalibi (BarṢalībī; d. 1171).

Theology: a miaphysite creed, the result of his contacts with ecclesiastics of other churches;[26] a dogmatic statement written in 1180 at the request of the Coptic patriarch Marqus III ibn Zurʿa, directed against Marqus Ibn al-Qanbar, a Coptic priest and reformer with Messalian inclinations, being a refutation of his views except those on the necessity of confession before the communion, since this was the usage of the Syrian Orthodox church;[27] the *Treatise against the Albigenses* (a result of his being invited to the Third Lateran Council; written in 1178, now lost); instructions for Theodore BarWahbun (1172) for his talks in Constantinople on the union;[28] letters to the Armenian *katholikos* Nerses IV Shnorhali.

But MR's most highly valued work today is his comprehensive *Chronicle* (Syr. *Makhtəbhānūth zabhnē*). It is a developed universal chronicle, i.e. beginning with the Creation (and ending with the year 1195/6), and containing historiographical material of a narrative character. The work is divided into twenty-one books, each containing several chapters. The material is laid out in three columns providing respectively a record of church history, secular history and *varia* (which often include copies of documents relevant to the events described in other columns, or longer quotations from other writers). With this arrangement in columns MR modified the pattern established by the *Chronicle* of Eusebios of Caesarea,[29] increasing the *spatium historicum* to three columns and reducing the *fila regnorum* to 'footnotes', i.e. placing them at the bottom of the manuscript page. This change had become necessary due to the abundance of historiographical material.

---

[23] P. Bedjan, ed., *Acta martyrum et sanctorum syriace*, vol. 6 (Paris, 1896; repr. Hildesheim, 1968), 557–615.

[24] A. Vööbus, 'Die Entdeckung des Panegyrikus des Patriarchen Mīkaʾēl über Jōḥannān von Mardē', *Oriens Christianus* 55 (1971), 204–9.

[25] A. Vööbus, 'Discovery of a panegyric by Michael Syrus', in *Mélanges Antoine Guillaumont: contributions à l'étude des christianismes orientaux*, Cahiers d'Orientalisme 20 (Geneva, 1988), 271–85 (text in facsimile, no tr.).

[26] The creed, addressed to the Emperor Manuel Komnenos in 1169, is known only from translations into Greek and Arabic, Graf, 'Michael der Grosse', 266.

[27] Graf, 'Michael der Grosse', 266–7.

[28] The beginning is preserved in the *X1234*, vol. 2, 311–14/tr. 233–4.

[29] Cf. W. Witakowski, 'The *Chronicle* of Eusebius; its type and continuation in Syriac historiography', *Aram Periodical* 11–12 (1999–2000), 419–37.

MR made use of several earlier historiographical works, which he frequently quoted verbatim. For earlier epochs his work is a conscientious compilation based partly on known and partly on unknown (i.e. not preserved) sources. These are,[30] up to Constantine, Eusebios of Caesarea (both the *Chronicle* and *Church History*), Annianos, Andronikos; for the years 325–431, the *Church Histories* of Socrates and Theodoret; for 431–565, the *Church History* of Pseudo-Zachariah the Rhetor; for 325–582, the *Church History* of John of Asia; from Justinian to Herakleios, the *Chronicle* of Guria (lost); for 565–82, that of Cyrus (Qūrā) of Batnae/Serug (lost); for 325–726 the *Chronicle* of Jacob of Edessa (partly lost); and for later periods historiographical works which are all lost, i.e. those of John the Stylite of Litarba to 726, Dionysios of Tel-Mahre for the period 582–842, Ignatios of Melitene for 325–1118, Basil BarShumno (BarŠumnā)[31] of Edessa for the period 1118–43, and finally John (Iwannīs) of Kaishoum (d. 1134) and Dionysios BarSalibi (d. 1171) for the period practically contemporary with MR. The last three books (19–21) are based on MR's own observations as patriarch.

He names all these sources, but it is not certain whether he used all of them directly. In addition to being mentioned in the main text, they were also enumerated in the preface, but since the first folio or perhaps two are lost, this list is also gone. It can be restored on the basis of the preface in the Armenian version (Chabot used this for his translation),[32] and that of the Arabic version.[33] MR also had at his disposal numerous documents, letters, acts of councils, canons, etc., which he frequently quoted in long fragments or in full. His sources also include an Arabic work, now lost, for the years 1107–19, which was also known to Ibn al-Athīr (d. 1233). Book 14, which contains an account of the history and customs of the Turks, is most probably based on Muslim sources.

Michael added seven appendices to the *Chronicle*, containing (1) a list of the priestly succession starting from the Jewish high priests and continuing with the patriarchs of the four main sees (Rome, Alexandria, Ephesus/Constantinople and Antioch), (2) lists of secular rulers of various peoples from Adam through the Roman emperors to the caliphs and the crusader kings, (3) a sketch of the history of the Arameans, (4) an annotated list of the patriarchs of the Syrian Orthodox church from Severos of Antioch (512–18) up to MR himself, together with a list of the bishops consecrated by every

---

[30] According to J.-B. Chabot's analysis, *Chronique de Michel*, vol. 1, pp. XXIV–XXXVII. A more thorough analysis of Michael's sources is badly needed.

[31] The name, known only from consonantal spelling, can also be pronounced BarShumono (BarŠummānā).

[32] Chabot's tr., vol. 1, 1–2.

[33] Meissner, 'Eine syrische Liste'.

Syrian Orthodox patriarch, starting from Kyriakos (792) again up to MR (it contains about 950 names, mostly otherwise unknown), (5) a list of the same bishops, this time arranged by their dioceses, (6) a sketch of the history of Armenia. The last of the appendices contains (7) a list of the *katholikoi* of the Church of the East from Akakios (484) to John V (1000).

The *Chronicle* is regarded as the greatest achievement of Syriac historiography in general. It is an extremely valuable source—in its compilatory part for its preservation of fragments of other Syriac historiographical works which would otherwise have been totally lost, and in its original part for the history of the twelfth century, the epoch of the crusades, due to its being partly an eye-witness narrative, as Michael had often participated himself in the events he describes.

The *Chronicle* was used by Gregory BarEbroyo in the thirteenth century, for whose historiographical works it was the main source.

The Syriac original of the *Chronicle* was discovered in 1887 (the Armenian version was known earlier) by the Syrian Catholic patriarch Ignatius Ephrem Rahmani in a manuscript of 1598 in Edessa, which is the only one known, and of which Rahmani had a copy made in 1887. Another copy was made for J.-B. Chabot, in 1899, and it is this (imperfect) copy which was used by Chabot for the edition, which is in facsimile. He published it in several instalments from 1899 to 1910 (introduction and index in 1924), along with a French translation.

Besides the Syriac original there are two Armenian translations: a longer one from 1246 attributed to Vardan Arewelts'i (d. 1271) and his Syrian collaborator Ishoh (Išōh), and a shorter one from 1248 attributed to Vardan Arewelts'i alone. Both differ in many respects from the Syriac original, presenting partly an abbreviated text of MR, but also having additional passages of historical interest for Armenian readers.[34]

In 1759 an Arabic translation, very close to the Syriac original, was made by the Syrian Orthodox metropolitan of Damascus, Ḥannā aṣ-Ṣadadī ibn ʿĪsā. It must have been done on the basis of the Edessene manuscript as it has the same lacunae. The Arabic version is written in Karshuni, i.e. in the Arabic language but in Syriac characters.[35]

In addition to the narration of the events in which Michael the Elder took part himself, the *Chronicle* is also characterised by making the succession of the Byzantine emperors the principle of chapter division in the earlier part of

---

[34] Schmidt, 'Die zweifache armenische Rezension', 302, mentions that about forty manuscripts of the two are known, but this is an underestimate: on number of manuscripts and the attributions to Vardan Arewelts'i, see Tim Greenwood in this volume, pp. 224–5, 226–7, 244–5.

[35] Graf, 'Michael der Grosse', 267.

the period dealt with here.[36] It is true that the Arab or Turkish rulers are regularly mentioned here too, but the Byzantine emperors are usually named first. For the latter part, dealing with the author's lifetime and personal observations, he had much more material to hand than for the previous period and consequently keeping to the rule of starting a new chapter with a new reign would have made the chapters too long.

Michael has a rather negative attitude towards the Byzantines. He often narrates events which show their hostility towards the Syrians, such as the persecution of the anti-Chalcedonians, both Jacobites and Armenians, in 1061.[37] Frequently he uses derogatory speech when talking about the Greeks ('the cruel Greeks' *Yawnayē ḥarmē*; 'evil' *Yawnayē bīšē*; 'always intent on evil things' *'ammīnay lə-bhīšāthā*).[38]

## THE CHRONICLE TO THE YEAR 1234

This chronicle is anonymous. It is possible that the name of the author was provided in the colophon, but since the unique manuscript is mutilated at the end nothing more can be said. As can be established from the text itself, the author may have been an ecclesiastic at Edessa. In any case he was a native of the region of northern Mesopotamia, and belonged to the Syrian Orthodox church. Only twice does he say anything about himself. He mentions that he was present in Jerusalem at the time when the city was captured by Ṣalāḥ al-Dīn (Saladin) in 1187.[39] In another place he says that in 1189 he accompanied *maphrian* Gregory I[40] on the latter's travel to Takrit, Sinjar and other eastern districts of the Syrian Orthodox church.[41]

One can surmise that he was born not long after 1150 and died not long after 1237. It is generally believed that the anonymous author was a native of Edessa, as the history of this city looms large in his work. J.-B. Chabot suggested,[42] however, that this may be due to the fact that the material on Edessa most probably comes from one of his sources, the *Chronicle* of Basil BarShumno, the metropolitan of Edessa (not preserved). Therefore it is possible, in Chabot's view, that the anonymous chronicler wrote his work in the

---

[36] Up to Book 15, chapter 7: Emperor Alexios (I Komnenos, 1081–1118) (MR 583/tr. vol. 3, 178).

[37] MR 576/tr. vol. 3, 166–7 (both columns).

[38] MR 606, outer col., 4 from the bottom/tr. 222; 608 outer col. 1/tr. 225; 608 outer col., 6–5 from the bottom/tr. 226.

[39] *X1234*, vol. 2, 200/tr. 150.

[40] Michael the Elder's nephew Jacob, *maphrian* in the years 1189–1214. For the title *maphrian*, see above, n. 21.

[41] *X1234*, vol. 2, 318/tr. 238.

[42] In the preface to the edition of the second part of the *X1234*, p. I.

monastery of BarSawmo (the monastery from which MR hailed), where he could use the library (he quotes archival documents). He may have been a monk there.[43] But, as J.-M. Fiey observes,[44] the information on events in Edessa is continued beyond the year 1171 when Basil died, and seems to be the account of an eye witness.[45] This does not exclude the possibility that the work was written, at least partly, in the BarSawmo monastery.

The *Chronicle* was not his only work. He mentions that he wrote at least one other work, a biography of Athanasios, the metropolitan of Edessa (1171–92), which has not survived. The anonymous chronicler says: 'We wrote extensively in other books about the difficulties which accumulated against him, and made known those who had instigated them and were causes of all the wrong things.'[46]

The *X1234* is, like Michael the Elder's, a developed universal chronicle, which starts from the Creation and goes up to—as the conventional title shows—the year 1234. It does not necessarily mean that it was written or finished in that year. For example, the author writes about the governor of Sinjar, Malik al-Ašraf 'of blessed memory',[47] but the latter died on 17 August 1237.

The *Chronicle* is preserved in a unique manuscript copied at the end of the fourteenth century. At the beginning of the twentieth century (the time from which we have information about it) the manuscript was in the private possession of one Boutros Fehim in Constantinople.[48] The manuscript is mutilated and several folios are missing. It was discovered and in part also published by Ignatius Ephrem Rahmani, the patriarch of the Syrian Catholic church, in 1904–11, fragments of this part subsequently being translated into French by François Nau (published in *Revue de l'Orient chrétien* in the years 1907–8). The full text was published by Jean-Baptiste Chabot in the CSCO series in 1916 (the second part) and 1920 (the first part). Chabot also translated the first part into Latin (1937), whereas the translation of the second part (into French) was provided by Albert Abouna, and appeared in 1974. In 1933 A.S. Tritton published an English translation of the section relating to the First and Second Crusades.

The *Chronicle* contains two parts (not identical with the parts of the standard edition): the secular (the entire vol. 1 and vol. 2 up to p. 241/tr. 181) and the ecclesiastical (*Kəthābhā də-šarbē ʿedhtānāyē*,[49] vol. 2, pp. 242–350/

---

[43] Chabot's preface to the edition of the *X1234*, part 2, p. II.
[44] In the introduction to the translation of the second part, p. VIII.
[45] e.g. vol. 2, 171–2/tr. 128 (§ 452b, churches in Edessa), 192–3/tr. 144–5 (§ 475, trouble-makers at Edessa), 223/tr. 167 (§ 515, the Edessenes' prayers for rain).
[46] *X1234*, vol. 2, 324/tr. 242.
[47] *X1234*, vol. 2, § 518, 229, 19–20 (*šāwē lə-dukhrānā ṭābhā*)/tr. 172.
[48] Chabot, *Mes chroniques*, 12.
[49] *X1234*, vol. 2, 17, 19/tr. 12; 22/tr. 15.

tr. p. 182–end). The latter part is shorter and in the manuscript it begins, after a lacuna, from the reign of the Emperor Justinian (527–65). We know however that the author started it much earlier, as he says that he treated ecclesiastical and civil history together only up to the Emperor Constantine.[50] The ecclesiastical part is continued up to 1207, where again the manuscript breaks off. It was written before the secular part, as we know from the fact that it is quoted in the latter.[51] However, in the manuscript (and the edition) it is placed after the secular. The author may have planned to stop in 1203–4: this can be inferred from two notes to that effect.[52] It seems, however, that a couple of decades later he changed his mind and continued his work to 1234 or perhaps beyond that date (the end of the secular part is also lost). It is, however, also possible that after these notes the *Chronicle* was continued by somebody else.[53]

The anonymous chronicler names some of his sources in his introduction (the *Chronicles* of Eusebios, of Andronikos and of Jacob of Edessa), some he does not name (the Bible, the *Cave of Treasures*). For the earlier periods one can identify the *Church History* of Eusebios and those of Socrates Scholastikos, John of Asia (6th c.), Pseudo-Zachariah the Rhetor (6th c.), and Dionysios of Tel-Mahre (d. 845). The latter's work has not been preserved and in fact the *X1234* (along with the *Chronicle* of MR) is the best source by which Dionysius's work can be recovered.[54]

It is rather surprising that our anonymous chronicler did not use MR's *Chronicle*, which he apparently did not know. On the other hand he did use many of the sources MR used, as well as some of documents written by him, such as for instance Michael's letter to Theodore BarWahbun,[55] or the patriarch's decree of 1195, bringing the diocese of Mardin under the sway of the *maphrian* rather than that of the patriarch.[56]

For the late period, at least from 1144,[57] he used the (lost) *History of Edessa* by Basil BarShumno, the metropolitan of Edessa (d. 1171), but, on his own testimony, he abbreviated it.[58]

Since in some cases he gives dates according to Hijra, it seems that he also used Muslim Arabic sources,[59] as well, probably, as an Armenian source

---

[50] *X1234*, vol. 1, 137/tr. 109.
[51] e.g. vol. 1, 152/tr. 120; 313/tr. 244, etc. (Fiey, introd., IX, n. 23).
[52] *X1234*, vol. 2, 213–14/tr. 160 (secular part), 340/tr. 253 (ecclesiastical).
[53] As L.I. Conrad believes, 'Syriac perspectives', 34–5.
[54] Cf. the quotations in part 2, 18/tr. 13 (§ 206), 20/tr. 14 (§ 208).
[55] *X1234*, vol. 2, 312–14/tr. 233–4.
[56] *X1234*, vol. 2, 331–3/tr. 247–8.
[57] *X1234*, vol. 2, 120/tr. 90.
[58] *X1234*, vol. 2, 309, 22–4: 'What we have written above about the Edessenes we have copied from the writing of the late metropolitan Basil, abbreviating in many cases.' (French tr., 231).
[59] Between the years AD 812 and 846 (= 197–232 Hij.); Fiey's introd., X.

(or sources?), since in one place he uses the Armenian form of the name of Jacob, namely Agōb (and not Yaʿqōbh) Arslān.[60]

Some scholars have considered our chronicler to be biased against the Franks.[61] This opinion was dismissed by J.M. Fiey,[62] who showed that the anonymous chronicler was rather objective, both in appreciating some Muslim rulers, and in pointing to the crusaders' excesses (e.g. the pillaging of the monastery of BarSawmo by Joscelin in 1148). His sympathies were nevertheless with the crusaders, as he twice calls them 'the blessed Franks'.[63]

The source value of *X1234* is considerable since it preserves source material which is not known from elsewhere, as well as the author's own observations. However in places where his text can be compared with the other chronicles, it is shorter due to the fact that he abbreviated his sources more than the other historians. Such is the case, for instance, in the account of the capture of Constantinople by the Latins in 1204,[64] which is shorter than that of BarEbroyo,[65] although both seem to have used the same source.

Of the three chronicles presented here this one has been studied least, and consequently there are many unsolved or only tentatively solved problems in it (the sources, the author's sympathies). It definitely deserves a more systematic study.


## JOHN GREGORY BAREBROYO


BarEbroyo (BE) is the author of two historiographical works in Syriac and one in Arabic. He is also known for many other works covering practically all the scholarly knowledge of the period. He is regarded as the greatest Syriac polymath of his time or perhaps the greatest Syriac scholar *tout court*.

John BarEbroyo was born in Melitene in 1225/6, the son of a physician Aaron. His 'patronymic', mistakenly Latinised as *BarHebraeus*, misled generations of scholars into believing that he was of Jewish descent (*BarʿEbhrāyā*—Syr. 'the son of a Hebrew'). Only recently has it become clear that the name refers to his (or rather his family's) origins in the village of ʿEbro (class. Syr. *ʿEbhrā*) near Melitene.[66] The Arabic form of his name is Ibn al-ʿIbrī, and he is also called Abu'l Faraj ('Father of what is pleasant').

---

[60] *X1234*, vol. 2, 159.8/tr. 120, Fiey's introd., XI.
[61] Cf. René Grousset, *L'histoire des croisades et du royaume de Jérusalem*, vol. 2 (Paris, 1935), 866–7.
[62] Fiey, 'Chrétiens syriaques entre croisés et mongols', 328–33.
[63] *Phrangāyē bǝrīkhē*, *X1234*, vol. 2, 113.7/tr. 85; 139.10/tr. 104.
[64] See above, n. 2.
[65] BE, secular part, 415–16/tr. Budge 357–9.
[66] Cf. Fathi-Chelhod, 'L'origine du nom Bar ʿEbroyo'.

He received a thorough education, which, in addition to languages (Syriac, Arabic and Greek), included theology, philosophy, and medicine, the latter under the direction of his father. In 1244 the family moved to Antioch, then in the hands of the crusaders, where BarEbroyo continued his studies. At the age of about seventeen he became a monk, but soon moved to Tripolis (also under the crusaders' domination) for further studies, in rhetoric and medicine, under an East Syrian ('Nestorian') teacher named Jacob. Soon, however, he was summoned by Patriarch Ignatios II and ordained bishop of Gubos (near Melitene), being then only twenty years old. It is believed that he assumed the name Gregory on that occasion, John being his baptismal name. Next year he was transferred to the nearby see of Laqabin and in 1253 to Aleppo; after a temporary recall by Patriarch John BarMadani (BarMa'dānī), due to BE's supporting another candidate for the patriarchal throne, he was reconfirmed there in 1258.

He probably played an important part in the election of the next patriarch, Ignatios III (1264), whereupon he was raised by the latter to the position of *maphrian*. Due to political unrest he was consecrated at Sis in Armenia (Cilicia), and was not able to assume the maphrianate at Takrit until 1266. He was well received by the Christians, both the Syrian Orthodox and those belonging to the Church of the East, as well as by the Muslims. His office demanded much travelling. He not only visited the dioceses within the maphrianate, but also Armenia (Cilicia) and Baghdad, where he maintained friendly relations with the East Syrian ecclesiastics. In 1282 he went to Tabriz in Persia to vow allegiance to the new Mongol ruler Aḥmad, and was reconfirmed in his office. In the later period of his pontificate he often spent longer spells at Maragha (Persian Azerbaijan), where the Mongol court was based, but where many Christians of various confessions also lived. He died there on 30 July 1286, and was buried in the Mar Mattay monastery near Mosul. His burial was attended by Christians of all denominations, showing their appreciation of BE's truly ecumenical outlook.[67]

Most of the information about his life comes from his *Autobiography*,[68] which was posthumously continued by his brother BarSawmo. There is in

---

[67] Compare what he wrote in the *Book of the Dove* (A. Wensinck, tr., *Bar Hebraeus' Book of the Dove together with some chapters from his Ethicon* (Leiden, 1919), 60, quoted by H.G.B. Teule, '*It is not right to call ourselves Orthodox and the others heretics*: ecumenical attitudes in the Jacobite church in the time of the Crusaders', in Krijnie Ciggaar and Herman Teule, eds., *East and West in the Crusader States. Context, contacts, confrontations*, Acts of the Congress held at Hernen Castle in May 1997, vol. 2, Orientalia Lovaniensia Analecta 92 (Leuven, 1999), 22: 'Thus I discovered that all Christian peoples, notwithstanding their differences, are in concord with each other.'

[68] In *Chronicon ecclesiasticum*, vol. 3, cols. 431–86.

addition a rhymed biography composed by his disciple Gabriel of Barṭellē.[69]

BE was a genuine intellectual and prolific author. He left over thirty works in such different areas as theology (e.g. *Lamp of the Sanctuary*,[70] a *summa theologiae* in twelve books), exegesis (*The Storehouse of Mysteries*, an extensive commentary on the Bible),[71] canon law (*The Book of Directions*, i.e. the *Nomocanon*),[72] ethics (*Ethikon*),[73] logic (*Book of the Pupils of the Eyes*, unpubl.), philosophy and physics (*The Wisdom of Wisdoms*, an unpublished encyclopaedic work covering the whole Aristotelian corpus; translations of the works of Ibn Sīnā (Avicenna) into Syriac), medicine (several books, including translations from Greek: Dioscorides, *De materia medica*), grammar (*The Book of Rays*),[74] astronomy (*Ascent of the Mind*),[75] and historiography. Nor was entertaining literature alien to him, as he collected a volume of *Laughable Stories*.[76]

Most of his works were written in Syriac, some in Arabic. He may not have been an original thinker, but his erudition over the whole scientific gamut of the epoch is most impressive. He enriched the Syriac intellectual tradition by introducing into it material from Greek and Muslim scholarship. It is mainly due to his scholarly output that the whole period of the twelfth and thirteenth centuries is called the 'Syriac Renaissance'.

In the field of historiography BE is known for his *Chronography* (*Makhtəbūth zabhnē*), a universal chronicle. It is the last work of Syriac classical historiography, after which the Syrians did not venture to write universal history any more. As the last chronicle of this type it was often copied and

---

[69] Cf. Sauma, 'Commentary on the "Biography" of Bar Hebraeus'.

[70] In PO, vols. 22, 24, 27, 30, 31, 35, 40, 41, 43 (1930–86).

[71] J. Göttsberger, *Barhebraeus und seine Scholien zur Heiligen Schrift*, Biblische Studien 4–5 (Freiburg im Breisgau, 1900); M. Sprengling and W.C. Graham, eds., Barhebraeus' *Scholia on the Old Testament, part I: Genesis–II Samuel* (Chicago, 1931); Assad Sauma, *Gregory Bar-Hebraeus's Commentary on the Book of Kings from his Storehouse of Mysteries: a critical edn. with an English trans., introduction and notes* (Uppsala, 2003); W.E.W. Carr, tr. and ed., *Gregory Abu'l Faraj commonly called Bar-Hebraeus, Commentary on the Gospels from the Horreum Mysteriorum* (London and New York, 1925).

[72] See above, n. 19.

[73] H.G.B. Teule, ed. and tr., Gregory Barhebraeus' *Ethicon (Memra I)*, CSCO 534–5, SS 218–19 (Louvain, 1993).

[74] Axel Moberg, ed., *Le livre des splendeurs: la grande grammaire de Grégoire Barhebraeus*, (Lund, 1922); A. Moberg, tr., *Buch der Strahlen: die grössere Grammatik des Barhebräus* (Leipzig, 1913).

[75] F. Nau, ed. and French tr., *Le livre de l'ascension de l'esprit sur la forme du ciel et de la terre: cours d'astronomie rédigé en 1279 par Grégoire Aboulfarag, dit Bar-Hebraeus*, Bibliothèque de l'École des hautes études; sciences philologiques et historiques, 121 fasc. (Paris, 1900). These works are listed in *Chronicon ecclesiasticum*, vol. 3, cols. 475–82. For further literature, see Fiey, 'Esquisse d'une bibliographie de Bar Hébraeus (+ 1286)'.

[76] E.A.W. Budge, ed. and tr., *The Laughable Stories, collected by Mar Gregory Bar Hebraeus* (London, 1897).

consequently—contrary to the case with all other Syriac historiographical works—it is preserved in more than one manuscript.

As the material that BE collected for this work was quite bulky, he divided it into two parts, secular and ecclesiastical, but, abandoning the arrangement of the other two chronicles described above, he seems to have published the two parts separately. In any case the two are sometimes transmitted in separate manuscripts.[77]

The secular part (known from its first edition of 1789 as *Chronicon syriacum*, or from the title of its English translation as *Chronography*) is a universal chronicle covering the period from the Creation until BE's own time. After his death it was continued by an anonymous writer (probably his brother BarSawmo) up to the year 1297. It is divided into eleven parts called 'successions' or 'dynasties' (*yubbālē*) by which BE encapsulates the idea of world empires originating from the prophecies of the *Book of Daniel*, but developed and brought up to date: he includes as the eleventh empire that of the Huns, i.e. the Mongols. Within the era of the Arabs he deals with the history of the early crusades, inluding the capture of Constantinople by the Franks.[78]

The ecclesiastical part (*Chronicon ecclesiasticum*) is itself divided into two parts of which the first contains the succession of incumbents of the Jewish and Christian sacerdotal office as it was understood in Christian chronography. Consequently it begins with Aaron, the Old Testament high priest, and continues with the line of the Jewish high priests up to Caiaphas and Annas of the New Testament epoch; after them the *sacerdocium* was taken over by the church, of which Peter was the first 'high priest'. The hierarchs dealt with turn out, however, to be merely the patriarchs of Antioch, and from Severos of Antioch on, those of the Syrian Orthodox church, which is of course in accordance with the vision of church history as conceived by an ecclesiastic of that church. The second part is a chronicle of the ecclesiastical affairs of the east (i.e of Christianity in Mesopotamia and Persia). It starts with the apostles Thomas, Addai and Mari, and continues with the *katholikoi* of the Church of the East, but from the sixth century onwards (from Aḥūdh'emmeh) with the succession of the Syrian Orthodox *maphrians* up to BE himself. What is important, however, is that material concerning the hierarchs of the Church of the East is included, a rare phenomenon in West Syriac (Jacobite) historiography, showing BE's irenic and ecumenical attitude.

This part was also continued after BE's death, first by his brother, BarSawmo, and later on up to the year 1496 by an anonymous hand.[79]

---

[77] For a list of the manuscripts, see Baumstark, *Geschichte der syrischen Literatur*, 318, n. 6.
[78] The secular part, 415–16/tr. 357–9.
[79] There is also a further continuation up to 1582, which, however, remains unpublished: Brock, 'Syriac historical writing', 21.

In dividing his historiographical work into two parts (like the author of *X1234*) BE gave up the model of the Eusebian chronicle with its column construction, which had still been preserved by his predecessor, Michael the Elder.[80]

The latter's *Chronicle* was BE's main source for the period up to the last years of the twelfth century, but MR's material is abbreviated and arranged in a different way. The secular chronicle also includes material based on other sources. The work is of course fully original for the period after MR's work came to an end. Although the account of many events in this section, for which he was an eye witness, is BE's own contribution, he also used written sources—documents in Syriac, Arabic and Persian, to which he had access in the Ilkhans' library in Maragha.

For the ecclesiastical part of the *Chronicle*, the sources were—in addition to MR's work—documents of the Syrian Orthodox church, and, as far as the Church of the East is concerned, the *Book of the Tower* (*Liber turris*), a history of the East Syrian *katholikoi*, written in Arabic by Mari ibn Sulaiman.[81]

The secular part of the *Chronicle* was first edited and translated into Latin in 1789 by Paul Jakob Bruns and Georg Wilhelm Kirsch, but neither the edition nor the translation was satisfactory. In 1890 another and better edition of the Syriac text was published, anonymously, by Paul Bedjan. E.A.W. Budge's publication of 1932 provides a facsimile edition of a manuscript in the Bodleian Library, Oxford, but his English translation is based on the text edited by Bedjan.[82] The ecclesiastical part has been edited and translated (into Latin) only once, in 1872–7, by J.B. Abbeloos and Th.J. Lamy.

At the request of some Muslim friends, in 1285 BE wrote an 'abridgement' of his Syriac secular chronicle in Arabic, entitled *An Abbreviated History of the Dynasties* (*Ta'rīkh mukhtaṣar al-duwal*). However this is not a simple abbreviation of his Syriac work, as the title may suggest, but one that has been adjusted to the needs of his Muslim readers, *inter alia* by replacing the material taken from MR with Arabic Muslim sources, e.g. the *Chronicle* of 'Izz al-Dīn ibn al-Athīr of Mosul (d. 1233).[83] The *Abbreviated History* became known to western scholars before BE's Syriac historiographical works, as it was published, with a Latin translation, as early as 1663 in Oxford by Edward Pococke.

[80] See above, n. 29.
[81] Maris, Amri et Slibae, *De patriarchis Nestorianorum commentaria,* ex codicibus vaticanis edidit [ac latine reddidit] Henricus Gismondi, *pars prior: Maris textus arabicus* (Rome, 1899) [Arabic]; *Maris versio latina* (Rome, 1899); *pars altera: Amri et Slibae textus* (Rome, 1896) [Arabic], *Amri et Slibae textus versio latina* (Rome, 1897).
[82] The Bodleian Library manuscript is imperfect.
[83] As has been shown by Teule, 'The crusaders in Barhebraeus', 47.

Although BE's historiographical works have been known to scholars for quite a long time, and have often been used as sources for historical research into the history of the Near East, no systematic monograph on any of them has ever been produced. Such a study or studies remains an overdue desideratum.

As far as the extent of coverage of Byzantine history is concerned, the most comprehensive chronicles are those of MR and the secular chronicle of BE. The latter has of course also the advantage of covering the epoch after MR's work came to an end. BE's ecclesiastical part is the least informative for our purpose, as its focus is mainly on the internal affairs of the Syrian Orthodox church. The *X1234* occupies an intermediate position between the BE's ecclesiastical part on the one hand and his secular and MR's work on the other. The work of the Patriarch Michael is of course very valuable because of its author's direct involvement in the politics of his time, a privilege that the other two chroniclers did not possess. MR's account of his pontificate is abbreviated by BE (in his *Ecclesiastical Chronicle*), but much is lost, for example the name of the Emperor Manuel, who corresponded with MR, does not even occur in BE. However these two, MR and BE, have each their own individual virtues, a fact which, incidentally, makes a study of their respective sources an urgent desideratum.

# BIBLIOGRAPHY

## BIBLIOGRAPHIES

Eberhard Nestle, *Brevis linguae syriacae grammatica, litteratura, chrestomathia* (Paris, 1881)
Carl Brockelmann, *Syrische Grammatik mit Paradigmen, Literatur, Chrestomathie und Glossar* (10th edn., Leipzig, 1965), 150–84
    These two contain a short but comprehensive list of the essential older literature.
Cyril Moss, *Catalogue of Syriac Printed Books and Related Literature in the British Museum* (London, 1962)
    Covers the period up to 1959.
S.P. Brock, *Syriac Studies: a classified bibliography:*
    [1] 1960–70, *Parole de l'Orient* 4 (1973), 393–465
    [2] 1971–80, *Parole de l'Orient* 10 (1981–2), 291–412
    [3] 1981–5, *Parole de l'Orient* 14 (1987), 289–360
    [4] 1986–90, *Parole de l'Orient* 17 (1992), 211–301
    [5] 1991–5, *Parole de l'Orient* 23 (1998), 211–301
    Items 1–4 are collected in a separate publication:

Sebastian P. Brock, *Syriac Studies: a classified bibliography (1960–1990)* (Kaslik, Lebanon, 1996)

## GENERAL LITERATURE QUOTED IN ABBREVIATED FORM

Barsoum 2003
Ignatius Aphram I. Barsoum, *The Scattered Pearls: a history of Syriac literature and sciences*, tr. and ed. Matti Moosa (2nd edn., Piscataway, NJ, 2003)
A translation of a monograph written in Arabic by the patriarch of the Syrian Orthodox church (1933–57). Using the results of western scholarship, Barsoum combines them with his own studies of Syriac literature, extending his work to the beginning of the 20th c. However, as far as our historians are concerned, he provides little new material.

Baumstark 1922
Anton Baumstark, *Geschichte der syrischen Literatur: mit Ausschluß der christlich-palästinensischen Texte* (Bonn, 1922)
The best monograph so far on the history of Syriac literature; in addition to bibliographical references (which require updating) it provides information on the extant manuscripts.

Brock 1979–80
Sebastian Brock, 'Syriac historical writing: a survey of the main c[=s]ources', *Journal of the Iraqi Academy, Syriac Corporation* 5 (1979–80), 1–30
The basic short account of Syriac historiography.

Brock 1997
Sebastian Brock, *A Brief Outline of Syriac Literature*, Mōrān 'Eth'ō Series 9 (Baker Hill, Kottayam, Kerala, 1997)
English translations of fragments of many items of Syriac literature.

Chabot 1921
J.-B. Chabot, 'La littérature historique des Syriens', *Revue historique* 137 (année 46) (1921), 74–80
An early brief account of Syriac historiography.

Chabot 1934
J.-B. Chabot, *Littérature syriaque*, Bibliothèque catholique des sciences religieuses: Littératures chrétiennes de l'Orient (Paris, 1934)
A monograph on the history of Syriac literature: still useful.

Chabot 1947
J.-B. Chabot, *Mes chroniques* (Louvain, 1947)
An account of the discovery of the Syriac manuscripts of the *Chr.* of MR and *X1234* and of the circumstances of their publication.

Conrad 1991
Lawrence I. Conrad, 'Syriac perspectives on Bilâd al-Shâm during the Abbasid period', in Muhammad Adnan al-Bakhit and Robert Schick, eds., *Bilâd al-Shâm during the Abbasid Period (132 A.H./750 A.D.–451 A.H./1059 A.D.). Proceedings of the Fifth international conference on the history of Bilâd al-Shâm, 7–11 Sha'ban 1410 A.H./4–8 March 1990* (Amman, 1991), English and French section, 1–44
Includes presentation of historiographical sources.

Duval 1907

Rubens Duval, *La littérature syriaque*, Bibliothèque de l'enseignement de l'histoire ecclésiastique: anciennes littératures chrétiennes 2 (3rd edn., Paris, 1907)

An early monograph on the history of Syriac literature arranged in chapters covering the genres; historiography, pp. 177–215.

Haase 1925

Felix Haase, *Altchristliche Kirchengeschichte nach orientalischen Quellen* (Leipzig, 1925)

Includes presentation of the sources, pp. 6–24.

Kawerau 1960

Peter Kawerau, *Die Jakobitische Kirche im Zeitalter der syrischen Renaissance: Idee und Wirklichkeit*, Berliner byzantinistische Arbeiten 3 (1st edn., Berlin, 1955; 2nd supplemented edn., 1960)

A general presentation of the sources, i.e. all the three chronicles dealt with here.

Nagel 1990

Peter Nagel, 'Grundzüge syrischer Geschichtsschreibung', in Friedhelm Winkelmann and Wolfram Brandes, eds., *Quellen zur Geschichte des frühen Byzanz (4.–9. Jahrhundert): Bestand und Probleme*, Berliner byzantinistische Arbeiten 55 (Berlin, 1990), 245–59

A more up-to-date account of Syriac historiography.

Ortiz de Urbina 1965

Ignatius Ortiz de Urbina, *Patrologia syriaca* (2nd edn., corrected and supplemented, Rome, 1965)

An account of Syriac religious literature, including historiography of the post-patristic period.

Segal 1962

J.B. Segal, 'Syriac chronicles as source material for the history of Islamic peoples', in B. Lewis and P.M. Holt, eds., *Historians of the Middle East* (London, 1962), 246–58

A short account of the Syriac historiographical works relevant to Segal's topic.

Witakowski 1987

Witold Witakowski, *The Syriac Chronicle of Pseudo-Dionysius of Tel-Maḥrē: a study in the history of historiography*, Acta Universitatis Upsaliensis, Studia Semitica Upsaliensia 7 (Uppsala, 1987)

Includes a sketch of Syriac chronicle-writing.

Witakowski 2001

Witold Witakowski, 'Interpreting the past: Syriac historical writing', in *At the Turn of the Third Millennium: the Syrian Orthodox witness*, The Hidden Pearl: the Syrian Orthodox church and its ancient Aramaic heritage 3 (Rome, 2001), 167–8, 185–94

A general account of Syriac historiography.

Wright 1894

William Wright, *A Short History of Syriac Literature* (Amsterdam, 1966 = London, 1894)

The classic monograph on the history of Syriac literature.

Yousif 2002

Ephrem-Isa Yousif, *Les chroniqueurs syriaques* (Paris, 2002)

Provides short introductions and French translations of fragments of the chronicles in question.

Rev.: Amir Harrak, *Hugoye: Journal of Syriac Studies* 6.2 (2003), http://syrcom. cua.edu/hugoye

## GENERAL LITERATURE ON ALL THREE CHRONICLES

R.A. Guseĭnov, 'Posledstviia srazheniia pri Mantsikerte (1071 g.) dlia Zakavkaz'ia', *VV* 29 (1968–9), 148–52
Consequences of the battle of Mantzikert for the Caucasian region on the basis of the late Syriac chronicles.

——'Iz istorii otnoshenii Vizantii s Sel'dzhukami', *Palestinskii Sbornik* n.s. 23 (= 86) (1971), 156–67
Syriac sources (MR, *X1234*, BE) on the history of Byzantine relations with the Seljuks, mainly on the battles of Mantzikert and Myriokephalon.

——'Siriiskiie istochniki po istorii Vizantii XI–XII vv.', *VV* 33 (1972), 120–8
Syriac sources (MR, *X1234*, BE) on 11th- and 12th-century Byzantium.

Anneliese Lüders, *Die Kreuzzüge im Urteil syrischer und armenischer Quellen*, Berliner byzantinistische Arbeiten 29 (Berlin, 1964)
A thorough study based on MR's *Chronicle*, BE's *Secular Chronicle*, his *Ta'rīkh* and the Armenian *Chronicle* of Matthew of Edessa.
Rev.: R.W. Thomson, *Journal of Theological Studies* n.s. 16 (1965), 232–3
Rev.: Peter Kawerau, *Zeitschrift für Kirchengeschichte* 76 (1965), 170–1
Rev.: Stephanou Pelopidas, *Orientalia Christiana Periodica* 31 (1965), 215–16
Rev.: E. V[oordeckers], *Byz* 34 (1964), 312–13
Rev.: J. Assfalg, *BZ* 58 (1965), 121–2

A. Rücker., 'Aus der Geschichte der jakobitischen Kirche von Edessa in der Zeit der Kreuzfahrer', *Oriens Christianus* 32 (1935), 124–39
Using all three Syriac chronicles and the Armenian *Chronicle* of Matthew of Edessa.

## THE LATE SYRIAC CHRONICLES

### Michael the Elder

*Editions and Translations:*

J.-B. Chabot, ed. and tr., *Chronique de Michel le Syrien, patriarche jacobite d'Antioche (1166–1199)*, 4 vols. (Paris, 1899–1924; repr. Brussels, 1963 with the Syriac text in vol. 4)
Edition of the Syriac text in a facsimile of the unique manuscript, together with a French translation, and valuable notes and introduction, providing the best account so far of the sources.
Rev. of vol. 1, fasc. 1: J. Parisot, *Revue de l'Orient chrétien* 5 (1900), 322–5
Rev. of vol. 1, fasc. 1: F. Nau, *Revue de l'Orient chrétien* 5 (1900), 328–9
Rev. of vol. 1, fasc. 2: J. Parisot, *Revue de l'Orient chrétien* 5 (1900), 660–2
Rev. of vol. 1: A. Baumstark, *Oriens Christianus* 1 (1901), 187–91

Rev. of vol. 1, fasc. 1–2 (1899–1900); vol. 2, fasc. 1 (1901): Rubens Duval, *Journal asiatique* 9.20 (1902), 326–34
Rev. of vol. 2, fasc. 2 (1904): Rubens Duval, *Journal asiatique* 10.1 (1903), 576–8
Rev. of vol. 2, fasc. 3 (1904): Rubens Duval, *Journal asiatique* 10.4 1904), 177–84
Rev. of vol. 3, fasc. 1 (1905): Rubens Duval, *Journal asiatique* 10.5 (1905), 557–8
Rev. of vol. 3, fasc. 2 (1906): Rubens Duval, *Journal asiatique* 10.9 (1907), 353–6

*The Armenian Versions:*
See Tim Greenwood in this volume, pp. 244–5.

*An Arabic Translation:*
Yuhanna Ibrahim, ed., *The General Chronicle of Michael the Syrian, Patriarch of Antioch*, vols. 1–3, translated into Arabic by Mar Gregorios Saliba Shamoun, metropolitan of Mosul, edited and introduced by Yuhanna Ibrahim, metropolitan of Aleppo (Aleppo, 1996)
In Arabic; not seen.

*Secondary Literature:*
Barsoum 2003, 445–8
Baumstark 1922, 298–300
Brock 1979–80, 15–17
Brock 1997, 268–70
Chabot 1921, 78
Chabot 1934, 125–7
Chabot 1947, 2–10
Conrad 1991, 1–44
Duval 1907, 196–8, 401
Haase 1925, 21–2
Kawerau 1960, 4–6
Nagel 1990, 257
Ortiz de Urbina 1965, 221
Segal 1962, 255–6
Witakowski 1987, 83–5
Witakowski 2001, 189–90
Wright 1894, 250–3
Yousif 2002, 123–204

J. Aßfalg, 'Michael I', in W. Jens, ed., *Kindlers neues Literatur Lexikon* 11 (1990), 630–1
An encyclopaedia article.
Abdulmesih BarAbrahem, 'Patriarch Michael the Great: beyond his world chronicle', *Journal of Assyrian Academic Studies* 12.2 (1998), 33–45
Reflections in response to D. Weltecke's paper of 1997, on the basis of the Arabic translation, *The General Chronicle of Michael the Syrian* (Aleppo, 1996).
J.-B. Chabot, 'La chronique de Michel le Syrien', *Académie des inscriptions et belles lettres: comptes rendus des séances de l'année* 1899, ser. 4, vol. 27, 476–84
An early account of the *Chronicle*.

J.-B. Chabot, 'Les évêques jacobites du VIII^e au XIII^e siècle d'après la chronique de Michel le Syrien', *Revue de l'Orient chrétien* 4 (1899), 444–51, 491–511; 5 (1900), 605–36; 6 (1901), 189–220
Pre-publication of the lists of bishops from Appendices 4 and 5 of MR's *Chr.*

—— 'Échos des croisades', *Académie des inscriptions et belles lettres: comptes rendus des séances de l'année* 1938, 448–61
Pages 455–61 deal with MR's evidence on the date of the death of Aimery, the Latin patriarch of Antioch.

W. de Vries, 'Michael I der Syrer', *Lexikon für Theologie und Kirche* 7 (1962), col. 401
A short encyclopaedia article.

E. von Dobschütz, 'Die Chronik Michael des Syrers (Nachtrag zu Nr. XV, S. 364–392)', *Zeitschrift für wissenschaftliche Theologie* 41 (1898), 456–9
MR's perspective when relating historical facts, different from that of Byzantine chroniclers.

R.Y. Ebied and M.J.L. Young, 'Extracts in Arabic from a chronicle erroneously attributed to Jacob of Edessa', *Orientalia Lovaniensia Periodica* 4 (1973), 177–96
Actually from the Arabic translation of MR's *Chr.*

Siegmund Fraenkel, 'Zu Michael Syrus', in idem, 'Bemerkungen zu syrischen Texten, 1.', *Zeitschrift der deutschen morgenländischen Gesellschaft* 56 (1902), 98–9
A few emendations to the Syriac text of the *Chr.*

Stephen Gero, 'The relation of Michael the Syrian, Bar Hebraeus, and the Armenian epitome', in idem, *Byzantine Iconoclasm during the Reign of Leo III*, CSCO Subsidia 41 (Louvain, 1973), 205–9
The relation between these sources in their accounts of the Emperor Leo and Caliph Yazid's iconoclasm.

——'The resurgence of Byzantine iconoclasm in the ninth century according to a Syriac source', *Speculum* 51 (1976), 1–5
Based on MR's *Chr.*

Georg Graf, 'Michael der Grosse', in idem, *Geschichte der christlichen arabischen Literatur, zweiter Band: Die Schriftsteller bis zur Mitte des 15. Jahrhunderts*, Studi e Testi 133 (Vatican City, 1947), 265–7
An account of the Arabic translations of MR's works.

I. Guidi, 'La cronica siriaca di Michele I', *Giornale della Società asiatica italiana* 3 (1889), 167–9
Announces the finding of the Syriac manuscript of MR's *Chr.* by E. Rahmani.

R.A. Guseìnov, '"Khronika" Mikhaila Siriìtsa', *Palestinskiì sbornik* 68 (= n.s. 5) (1960), 85–105
A general account of MR's *Chronicle*.

Felix Haase, 'Die armenische Rezension der syrischen Chronik Michaels des Großen', *Oriens Christianus* 2.5 (1915), 60–82, 271–84
The Armenian version is not a literary translation but rather a reworking of the Syriac original, some parts of the latter being removed, others abbreviated, whereas sections concerning Armenian church history are added.

Wolfgang Hage, 'Michael der Syrer (1126/27–1199)', *Theologische Realenzyklopädie* 22 (1992), 710–12
An encyclopaedia article.

Ernst Honigmann, *Le couvent de Barṣaumā et le patriarcat jacobite d'Antioche et de Syrie*, CSCO 146, Subsidia 7 (Louvain, 1954)

History of the monastery of MR, and of the geographical spread of the Syrian Orthodox church written largely on the basis of MR's *Chronicle*.

P. Kawerau, 'Barbarossas Tod nach 'Imād ad-Dīn und Michael Syrus', *Oriens Christianus* 48 (1964), 135–42

Quotes MR's short but informative account of the emperor's death.

Krikor H. Maksoudian, 'Michael the Syrian', *Dictionary of the Middle Ages* 8 (1987), 305–6

An encyclopaedia article.

Bruno Meissner, 'Eine syrische Liste antiochenischer Patriarchen', *Wiener Zeitschrift für die Kunde des Morgenlandes* 8 (1894), 295–317

Appended to the Arabic version of MR's *Chronicle*.

Michael G. Morony, 'Michael the Syrian as a source for economic history', *Hugoye: Journal of Syriac Studies* 3.2 (July 2000), http://syrcom.cua.edu/hugoye

The economic information in MR's *Chr.* concerns agricultural production, livestock, the labour force, commerce, etc. The author argues for a comparison between MR's material and other sources.

F. Nau, 'Notice sur un manuscrit de l'*Histoire de Michel le Grand*, patriarche d'Antioche 1126–1199', *Journal asiatique* 9.8 (1896), 523–7

A few remarks on the sources of the *Chr.* on the basis of a Karshuni manuscript.

——'Lettre du R.P. Constantin Bacha sur un nouveau manuscrit carchouni de la chronique de Michel le Syrien et sur Théodore Abou-Kurra', *Revue de l'Orient chrétien* 11 (1906), 102–4

Announces the existence of the third Karshuni manuscript of MR's *Chr.* in Jerusalem.

Ignace Ephrem Rahmani, 'Lettre de S.B. Mgr Rahmani au sujet de la publication de la chronique de Michel', [éd. par] F.N.[au], *Revue de l'Orient chrétien* 10 (1905), 435–8

Criticises J.-B. Chabot's edition of MR's *Chr.*, the unique manuscript of which was discovered in 1888 by Rahmani.

Andrea B. Schmidt, 'Die zweifache armenische Rezension der syrischen Chronik Michaels des Großen', *Le Muséon* 109 (1996), 299–319

Analyses the two Armenian translations of MR's *Chr.*, and provides a concordance of the contents of the two by comparison with the Syriac text.

——'Syrische Tradition in armenischer Adaption: die armenische Rezeption des Geschichtswerks von Michael Syrus und der antichalcedonische Judenbrief an Kaiser Markianos', in René Lavenant, ed., *Symposium Syriacum VII, Uppsala University, Department of Asian and African Languages 11–14 August 1996*, Orientalia Christiana Analecta 256 (Rome, 1998), 359–71

On the reception of MR's *Chr.* in Armenia, analysed in detail using the example of the anti-Chalcedonian propagandistic *Letter of the Jews to the Emperor Marcian*.

H. Suermann, 'The Turks in Michael the Syrian', *The Harp* 5 (1992), 39–51

Deals with the origin, migration, religion and customs of the Turks, on the basis of the fourteenth book of the *Chr.*

Erwand Ter-Minassiantz, *Die armenische Kirche in ihren Beziehungen zu den syrischen Kirchen bis zum Ende des 13. Jahrhunderts, nach den armenischen und syrischen*

*Quellen,* Texte und Untersuchungen zur Geschichte der altchristlichen Literatur
36.4, neue Folge 11.4 (Leipzig, 1904)
Includes a chapter on MR and his relations with the Armenian church,
pp. 122–36.

E. Tisserant, 'Michel le Syrien', *Dictionnaire de théologie catholique* 10.2 (1929), 1711–19
An encyclopaedia article.

Jürgen Tubach, 'Michel Syrus', *Biographisch-bibliographisches Kirchenlexikon* 5 (1993),
1467–71
An encyclopaedia article.

Jan J. van Ginkel, 'Making history: Michael the Syrian and his sixth-century sources',
in René Lavenant, ed., *Symposium syriacum VII, Uppsala University, Department
of Asian and African Languages, 11–14 August 1996*, Orientalia Christiana
Analecta 256 (Rome, 1998), 351–8
The paper shows how MR used his sources taking the example of John of Asia's
*Church History*, of which about 75% was left out. Only what was 'relevant' in
MR's view was taken over.

—— 'Michael the Syrian and his sources: reflections on the methodology of Michael
the Great as a historiographer and its implications for modern historians', *Journal
of the Canadian Society for Syriac Studies* 6 (2006), 53–60
Methodological warning against drawing conclusions about the views of the historians whose works were used by MR: he arranged the material taken from these
sources according to his own ideas.

Dorothea Weltecke, 'The world chronicle by Patriarch Michael the Great (1126–1199):
some reflections', *Journal of Assyrian Academic Studies* 11.2 (1997), 6–29
A general account of MR's work, subsequently developed in her 2003 monograph.

——'Originality and function of formal structures in the chronicle of Michael the
Great', *Hugoye: Journal of Syriac Studies* 3.2 (July 2000),
http://syrcom.cua.edu/hugoye
Argues that the formal layout (in tables) of MR's *Chr.* is an essential part of the
work; there are, however, doubts as to whether the arrangement of the material as
known from Chabot's facsimile edition is the original one.

——*Die 'Beschreibung der Zeiten' von Mōr Michael dem Großen (1126–1199): eine
Studie zu ihrem historischen und historiographiegeschichtlichen Kontext*, CSCO 594,
Subsidia 110 (Louvain, 2003)
A thorough monograph on MR and his work, dealing with research on MR so far,
MR's epoch and his life, his historiographical methods, the *Chronicle*'s tabular
layout, and the author's vision of history.

Witold Witakowski, 'Michael I der Syrer', *Lexikon für Theologie und Kirche* 7 (1998),
401
A short encyclopaedia article.

——'Michael the Elder (the Syrian)', *Aram* (Stockhom) 7 (1998), 28–34
A general account of MR's life and literary output.

### The Chronicle to the Year 1234

*Editions:*

Ignatius Ephraem Rahmani, ed., *Chronicon civile et ecclesiasticum anonymi auctoris
ex unico codice edesseno* (Scharfeh, 1904, 1911)
The first and second instalment of the first edition of the *X1234*, planned to be
complete, but never actually completed.
Rev.: F. Nau, *Revue de l'Orient chrétien* 10 (1905), 439–40

J.-B. Chabot, ed., *Anonymi auctoris Chronicon ad annum Christi 1234 pertinens*, vol. 1. *Praemissum est Chronicon anonymum ad A.D. 819 pertinens*, curante Aphram Barsaum, CSCO 81, SS 3.14 [= 36] (Paris, 1920)
    The standard edition of the *X1234*, part 1.
——*Anonymi auctoris Chronicon ad annum Christi 1234 pertinens*, vol. 2, CSCO 82, SS 3.15 [= 37] (Paris, 1916)
    The standard edition of the *X1234*, part 2.

*Translations:*

F. Nau, tr., 'Traduction de la chronique syriaque anonyme éditée par Sa Béatitude Mgr Raḥmani patriarche des Syriens catholiques', *Revue de l'Orient chrétien* 12 (1907), 429–40; 13 (1908), 90–9, 321–8, 436–43
    A French translation of extracts of the part published by I.E. Rahmani (from Creation to the death of the Emperor Anastasius).
J.-B. Chabot, tr., *Chronicon anonymum ad annum Christi 1234 pertinens*, vol. 1, CSCO 109, SS 3.14 [= 56] (Louvain, 1937)
    A Latin translation of the first part of Chabot's edition.
Albert Abouna, tr., and J.-M. Fiey, introduction and notes, *Anonymi auctoris Chronicon ad A.C. 1234 pertinens*, CSCO 354, SS 154 (Louvain, 1974)
    A French translation of the second part of Chabot's edition.
A.S. Tritton, tr., and H.A.R. Gibb, notes, 'The First and Second Crusades from an anonymous Syriac chronicle', *Journal of the Royal Asiatic Society* (1933), 69–101, 273–305
    An English translation of the part relevant to the crusades.

*Secondary Literature:*

Barsoum 2003, 454–5
Baumstark 1922, 302
Brock 1979–80, 17–18
Chabot 1921, 78–9
Chabot 1934, 129–30
Chabot 1947, 10–12
Conrad 1991, 12–13, 34–5
Nagel 1990, 257–8
Ortiz de Urbina 1965, 212
Segal 1962, 254–5
Witakowski 1987, 85
Witakowski 2001, 190
Yousif 2002, 205–37

Claude Cahen, 'Some new editions of oriental sources about Syria in the time of the crusades', in B.Z. Kedar, H.E. Mayer, R.C. Small, eds., *Outremer: Studies in the History of the Crusading Kingdom of Jerusalem presented to Joshua Prawer* (Jerusalem, 1982), 323–31
    Concludes that there must have been two authors of the *X1234*, one living in 1187 and the other in 1139, but this conclusion is based on a printing error in J.-M. Fiey's introduction to the French translation of the second part of the *X1234* by A. Abouna (p. VII) where 1139 is printed instead of 1189.

*Witold Witakowski*

J.-B. Chabot, 'Un épisode inédit de l'histoire des croisades (le siège de Birta, 1145)',
  *L'Académie des inscriptions et belles-lettres: comptes rendus des séances de l'année
  1917*, 77–84
  The siege of Birtha on the Euphrates by Zengi, after his conquest of Edessa, as
  recorded in the *X1234*.
—— 'Édesse pendant la première croisade', *Académie des inscriptions et belles-lettres:
  comptes rendus des séances de l'année 1918*, 431–42
  Based on the history of Edessa by Basil BarShumno, as transmitted in the *X1234*.
—— 'Un épisode de l'histoire des croisades', in *Mélanges offerts à M. Gustave
  Schlumberger . . . à l'occasion du quatre-vingtième anniversaire de sa naissance
  (17 octobre 1924)* (Paris, 1924), 169–79
  A French translation of the account of the conquest of Edessa by Zengi in 1144,
  according to the *X1234*, taken by its author from the work of Basil BarShumno.
Muriél Debié, 'Record keeping and chronicle writing in Antioch and Edessa', *Aram
  Periodical* 11–12 (1999–2000), 409–17
  Points to the use of material in local archives, *inter alia* by the author of the
  *X1234*.
Jean-Maurice Fiey, 'Chrétiens syriaques entre croisés et mongols', in *Symposium
  Syriacum 1972, célebré dans les jours 26–31 octobre 1972 à l'Institut pontifical
  oriental de Rome: rapports et communications*, Orientalia Christiana Analecta 197
  (Rome, 1974), 327–41
  Argues for impartiality and even sympathy towards the crusaders by the author of
  *X1234*.
R.A. Guseìnov, 'Siriìskiì anonim 1234 g. o Vizantii i ìo sosedìakh', *Antichnaìa
  drevnost' i sredniye veka* 10 (1973), 146–50
  A general account of the *X1234* as a source for the history of Byzantium.
N.V. Pigulevskaìa, *Vizantiìa i Iran na rubezhe VI i VII vekov*, Trudy Instituta
  Vostokovedeniìa Akademii Nauk SSSR 46 (Moscow, 1946)
  Pages 252–89 have a Russian translation of an extract from *X1234*, concerning
  sixth–seventh century relations between Byzantium (from Maurice to Herakleios)
  and Persia, including the Arab conquests.

## The Chronicles of Barebroyo

The Secular

*Editions and Translations:*

P.J. Bruns and G.W. Kirsch, eds., *Bar-Hebraei Chronicon syriacum e codicibus
  bodleianis descriptum* (Leipzig, 1789)
  An early edition, not very reliable.
P.J. Bruns and G.W. Kirsch, trs., *Gregorii Abulpharagii sive Bar-Hebraei Chronicon
  syriacum e codicibus bodleianis* (Leipzig, 1789)
  A Latin translation of the previous item.
Paul Bedjan, ed., *Kəthābhā də-makhtəbhānūth zabhnē də-sīm lə-mār(y) Grīghoryos
  Bar 'Ebhrāyā = Gregorii Barhebraei Chronicon syriacum e codd. mss. emendatum
  ac punctis vocalibus adnotationibusque locupletatum* (Paris, 1890)
  The best edition of the chronicle so far; the Syriac text is vocalised by the editor.

E.A.W. Budge, ed. and tr., *The Chronography of Gregory Abū'l-Faraj 1225–1286, the Son of Aaron, the Hebrew Physician, known as Bar Hebraeus, being the first part of his Political History of the World*, vol. 1, English translation; vol. 2, facsimiles of the Syriac texts in the Bodleian MS. Hunt No 62 (London, 1932; repr. Amsterdam, 1976)

The Syriac text is published in a facsimile edition of a manuscript in the Bodleian Library; the translation is based on Bedjan's edition.

Rev.: Ernst Honigmann, 'Zur Chronographie des Bar Hebraeus', *Orientalistische Literaturzeitung* 37 (1934), 273–83

Provides corrections (esp. of the toponyms) important for the understanding of BE's text.

*The Arabic Version:*

Edward Pococke, ed. and tr., *Historia compendiosa dynastiarum authore Gregorio Abul-Farajio malatiensi medico, historiam complectens universalem a mundo condito, usque ad tempora authoris res orientalium accurantissime describens*, 2 vols. (Oxford, 1663)

An early edition and Latin translation of BE's Arabic *Abbreviated History*.

M. Georg Lorenz Bauer, tr., *Gregorius Abulfaradsch, Kurze Geschichte der Dynastien oder Auszug der allgemeinen Weltgeschichte besonders der Geschichte der Chalifen und Mongolen*, 2 vols. (Leipzig, 1783, 1785)

A German translation of Pococke's Arabic text, with notes.

Anṭūn Ṣālḥānī, ed., *Ta'rīkh mukhtaṣar al-duwal* (Beirut, 1890, repr. 1958, 1983)

A good edition of BE's Arabic *Chronicle*.

Isḥāq Armalet, tr., *Ta'rīkh al-zamān* (Beirut, 1986)

An Arabic translation of the secular part of BE, from E.A.W. Budge's English translation, starting with the Abbasid period.

*Modern Translations:*

Şerafeddin Yaltkaya, *Ebülferec Ibnülibri, Tarihi muhtasarüddüvel*, Türk Tarihi Kaynakları 1 (Istanbul, 1941)

A Turkish translation of some fragments of BE's *Ta'rīkh mukhtaṣar al-duwal* concerning Turkish history, translated from A. Ṣālḥānī's text.

Ömer Riza Doğrul, *Gregory Abû'l Farac (Bar Hebraeus), Abû'l Farac Tarihi, Cilt I*, Türk Tarih Kurumu Yayınlarından, 2nd ser. no. 11a (Ankara, 1945)

A Turkish translation of the secular part of BE's *Chr.* made from E.A.W. Budge's English translation.

## The Ecclesiastical

*Editions and Translation:*

J.B. Abbeloos and T.J. Lamy, ed. and tr., *Gregorii Barhebraei Chronicon ecclesiasticum quod e codice Musei Britannici descriptum conjuncta opera ediderunt, latinitate donarunt, annotationibusque theologicis, historicis, geographicis et archaeologicis illustrarunt*, vol. 1 (Louvain, 1872), vol. 2 (Paris and Louvain, 1874), vol. 3 (Paris and Louvain, 1877)

Edition and Latin translation.

Julius Yeshu', ed., *Grigorios Bar'Ebhrāyā, Makhtabhzabhno d-eqlesyasṭiqi* [*Ecclesiastical Chronicle*], (Glane, Holland, 1987)
Syriac text only; not seen.

*Secondary Literature:*

Barsoum 2003, 463–81
Baumstark 1922, 312–20
Brock 1979–80, 19–20
Brock 1997, 276–7
Chabot 1921, 79–80
Chabot 1934, 131–7
Conrad 1991, 14–17
Duval 1907, 198–200
Haase 1925, 22–3
Kawerau 1960, 7–12
Nagel 1990, 258–9
Ortiz de Urbina 1965, 221–3
Segal 1962, 256–8
Witakowski 1987, 85–7
Witakowski 2001, 190–1
Wright 1894, 265–81
Yousif 2002, 239–76

Friedrich Wilhelm Bautz, 'Bar Hebräus', *Biographisch-bibliographisches Kirchenlexikon* 1 (1975), 370–1
An encyclopaedia article.

Ludger Bernhard, 'Die Legitimität des lateinischen Kaiserreiches von Konstantinopel in jakobitischer Sicht', *Jahrbuch der österreichischen byzantinischen Gesellschaft* 16 (1967), 133–8
BE in his *Ta'rīkh* writes that in 1204 Constantinople was 're-captured' by the Franks, an expression which is explained by his belief that 'the Romans were Franks'.

Sebastian Brock, 'Gregor ibn al-'Ibrī', *Lexikon für Theologie und Kirche* 3 (4th edn., 1995), 1001–2
An encyclopaedia article.

Hayat El-Eid Bualwan, 'Syriac historical writing in the thirteenth century: the histories of Ibn al-'Ibrī (Bar Hebraeus Abū l-Faraǧ)', *Parole de l'Orient* 26 (2001), 145–58
A general account of BE's Arabic *al-mukhtaṣar ta'rīkh*.

J.-B., Chabot, 'Échos des croisades', *Académie des inscriptions et belles lettres: comptes rendus des séances de l'année 1938*, 448–61
BE's *Chr. eccl.* does not confirm some western data on Patriarch Ignatios II's conversion to Catholicism (pp. 448–55).

Lawrence I. Conrad, 'On the Arabic chronicle of Bar Hebraeus: his aims and audience', *Parole de l'Orient* 19 (1994), 319–78
An important study of the *Ta'rīkh*; on the basis of a detailed comparison (pp. 341–78) of the material of the first book of the Syriac secular *Chronicle* and the Arabic *Ta'rīkh*, the author argues that the latter was also written for a Christian audience and not for Muslims.

Jean Fathi-Chelhod, 'L'origine du nom Bar 'Ebroyo: une vieille histoire d'homonymes', *Hugoye: Journal of Syriac Studies* 4.1 (2001), http://syrcom.cua. edu/hugoye
Shows that the long western tradition of interpreting the name BarEbroyo (Bar'Ebhrāyā) as 'the son of a Hebrew' is wrong; it points to the origins of BE's family from the village of 'Ebro ('Ebhrā).

Jean-Maurice Fiey, 'Esquisse d'une bibliographie de Bar Hébraeus (+ 1286)', *Parole de l'Orient* 13 (1986), 279–312
An extensive bibliography of BE containing both the western and Arabic works; BE's historiographical works, pp. 299–304.

Stephen Gero, 'The relation of Michael the Syrian, Bar Hebraeus, and the Armenian epitome', in S. Gero, *Byzantine Iconoclasm during the reign of Leo III*, CSCO Subs. 41 (Louvain, 1973), 205–9
The relationship between these sources in their accounts of the Emperor Leo and Caliph Yazid's iconoclasm.

Wolfgang Hage, 'Gregor Barhebräus (1225/26–1286)', *Theologische Realenzyklopädie* 14 (1985), 158–64
An encyclopaedia article.

——'Gregory Bar-Hebraya, the Syrian Orthodox scholar and Maphrian of the East, in W. Hage, *Syriac Christianity in the East*, Mōrān 'Eth'ō Series 1 (Baker Hill, Kottayam, Kerala, 1988), 80–93
A general account of BE's life and work.

Edouard R. Hambye, 'Bar 'Ebroyo and the Byzantine empire', in René Lavenant, ed., *V Symposium syriacum 1988, Katholieke Universiteit, Leuven, 29–31 août 1988*, Orientalia Christiana Analecta 236 (Rome, 1990), 403–8
A short account of BE's mentions of Byzantium on the basis of both the Syriac *Chronicle* and the Arabic *Ta'rīkh*, the latter being more informative than the former.

E. Herman, 'Barhébraeus', *Dictionnaire d'histoire et de géographie ecclésiastiques* 6 (1932), 792–4
An encyclopaedia article.

George Lane, 'An account of Gregory Bar Hebraeus Abu al-Faraj and his relations with the Mongols of Persia', *Hugoye: Journal of Syriac Studies* 2.2 (July 1999), http://syrcom.cua.edu/hugoye
Presents BE's biography with emphasis on his contacts with and attitude towards the Mongols.

F. Nau, 'Bar Hebraeus', *Dictionnaire de théologie catholique* 2.1 (1910), 401–5
An encyclopaedia article.

Theodor Nöldeke, 'Barhebraeus', in Theodor Nöldeke, *Orientalische Skizzen* (Berlin, 1892), 251–73
A sketch of BE's life; a little information on his works as well.

——'Barhebraeus', in Theodor Nöldeke, *Sketches from Eastern History*, translated by John Sutherland Black (London, 1892), 236–56
An English translation of the previous item.

Linda Rose, 'Bar Hebraeus', *Dictionary of the Middle Ages* 2 (1983), 108
An encyclopaedia article.

Assad Sauma, 'Commentary on the "Biography" of Bar Hebraeus', *Aram* (Stockholm) 7 (1998), 35–68
A summary of BE's biography by Gabriel of Barṭellē (d. 1300).

J.B. Segal, 'Ibn al-'Ibrī', *The Encyclopaedia of Islam, new edition* 3 (1971), 804–5
An encyclopaedia article.

N.I. Serikov, 'O putiakh proniknoveniia vizantiiskoi dukhovnoi kul'tury na musul'manskii Vostok: Grigorii Ioann Abu-l-Faradzh Ibn-al-'Ibri (Bar Ebrei) i vizantiiskaia istoriograficheskaia traditsiia', *VV* 45 (1984), 230–41
In BE's *Ta'rīkh* connections with Byzantine historiography can be observed as well as a tendency to assimilate the Christian vision of history to that of Muslim readers.

Hidemi Takahashi, 'Simeon of Qal'a Rumaita, Patriarch Philoxenus Nemrod and Bar 'Ebroyo', *Hugoye: Journal of Syriac Studies* 4.1 (January 2001), http://syrcom.cua.edu/hugoye
BE's contacts with the priest–physician Simon BarYeshu', who was an important figure at the Ilkhanid court in the 1260s and to whom BE dedicated two of his works.

Herman G.B. Teule, 'The crusades in Barhebraeus' Syriac and Arabic secular chronicles: a different approach', in Krijnie Ciggaar, Adelbert Davids, and Herman Teule, eds., *East and West in the Crusader States. Context, contacts, confrontations. Acts of the Congress held at Hernen Castle in May 1993*, Orientalia Lovaniensia Analecta 75 (Louvain, 1996), 39–49
BE used different sources for his secular Syriac *Chronicle* (MR's *Chr.*) and for the *Ta'rīkh* for the period of the crusades (*Kāmil fi'l-ta'rīkh* by Ibn al-Athīr).

——'Ebn al-'Ebrī', *Encyclopaedia Iranica* 8, fasc. 1 (1997), 13–15
An encyclopaedia article.

——'Gregory Barhebraeus and his time: the Syrian Renaissance', *Journal of the Canadian Society for Syriac Studies* 3 (2003), 21–43
Presents a general intellectual portrait of BE, partly in connection with his historiographical output; BE's knowledge of languages other than Syriac (these included Persian), Christian and Muslim sources and their use.

Susanne Regina Todt, 'Die syrische und die arabische Weltgeschichte des Bar Hebraeus: ein Vergleich', *Der Islam* 65 (1988), 60–80
Shows differences between BE's Syriac and Arabic historiographical works: he omits in the *Ta'rīkh* events that have a meaning only for Christian readers, uses different dating systems and mentions different physicians in each.

Witold Witakowski, 'L'horizon géographique de l'historiographie syriaque: aperçu préliminaire', in Arnaud Sérandour, ed., *Des Sumériens aux Romains d'Orient: la perception géographique du monde: espaces et territoires au Proche-Orient ancien: Actes de la table ronde du 16 novembre 1996 organisée par l'URA 1062 Études sémitiques*, Antiquités sémitiques 11 (Paris, 1997), 199–209
BE's secular *Chronicle*, its material on the division of the world between the sons of Noah (*Diamerismos*), and its arrangement in eleven 'dynastic' periods: pp. 206–9.

——'The *Ecclesiastical Chronicle* of Gregory Bar'Ebroyo', *Journal of the Canadian Society for Syriac Studies* 6 (2006), 61–81
A general account of the ecclesiastical part of BE's chronicle, dealing with its structure, contents, sources and vision of history.

Īwāṣ Zakkā, 'Ibn al-'Ibrī (1226–1286)', *Journal of the Iraqi Academy, Syriac Corporation* 5 (1979–80), 5–43
Not seen.

Joseph Zolinski, *Zur Chronographie des Gregorius Abulpharagius*, Inaugural-Dissertation, Heidelberg (Breslau, 1894)
Chronological (Eusebian) tables derived from BE's Bible commentary, *The Storehouse of Mysteries*.

# 12

# Sources in Arabic

## CAROLE HILLENBRAND

'In the last thirty years prosopographical studies have significantly enlarged the understanding of Islamic medieval societies.' (Manuela Marin)[1]

AFTER A BRIEF INTRODUCTION, this overview will focus on three major areas: a discussion of medieval Arabic (and, to a lesser extent, Persian) narrative sources which deal with the period 1025–1204, a survey of medieval Islamic prosopographical material, including biographical and autobiographical literature, and an analysis of the current state of research on Islamic prosopography. This overview will also mention certain ancillary sources, such as inscriptions, which are a useful prosopographical tool. The bibliography which follows this essay provides comments, sometimes detailed, on certain individual authors and works which will be of special value to the Prosopography of the Byzantine World project. These comments will not be recapitulated here. Instead, an attempt will be made to give a background analysis of the historiography of the period under investigation.

## INTRODUCTION

### The Geographical and Historical Background

In the eleventh century, the Muslim world lay on the eastern and southern flanks of the Byzantine empire. The 'House of Islam' controlled the sinews of Byzantine trade and its fleets dominated the Mediterranean. The Muslim world was effectively boundless, immeasurably richer than Byzantium. Moreover, since the seventh century and for almost the whole of the eleventh, Muslims held sway in Jerusalem and the Holy Land.

The days of a Muslim world, ruled by a single theocratic state, were long since past. From the ninth century onwards smaller political entities governed

---

[1] M. Marin, 'Biography and prosopography in Arabic–Islamic medieval culture. Introductory remarks', in M. Marin, ed., *Medieval Prosopography. History and collective biography. Special issue. Arab-Islamic Medieval culture* 23 (2002), 12.

*Proceedings of the British Academy* **132**, 283–340. © The British Academy 2007.

the vast areas of the 'House of Islam', stretching from Spain to northern India. Since the death of the Prophet Muḥammad in 632, major religious splits had appeared amongst Muslims who disagreed about who should govern the Muslim world. The majority came to believe that legitimate rule had lain initially with the line of four so-called Rightly Guided caliphs (*khalīfa* = 'successor') who had been appointed after 632. This majority group eventually received the title of Sunnis. A minority, itself gradually divided into several groups, held that legitimate rule in Islam should be vested in the Prophet's family and descendants through his daughter Fāṭima and her husband ʿAlī, Muḥammad's cousin. This minority within the Muslim community came to be known as Shiʿites (the name was derived from the phrase *shīʿat ʿAlī*, 'the party of ʿAlī').

By the eleventh century, the Sunni caliphate, since 750 established within the Abbasid dynasty at Baghdad, held no temporal power. However, the caliph still acted as a legal and religious figurehead, although even this role of his was challenged by the existence of a second caliph, the Ismāʿīlī[2] Shiʿite ruler of the Fatimid empire in Egypt. Despite political and religious fragmentation, however, the Muslim world, with its lingua franca, Arabic, remained united by common cultural norms and aims, and scholars could travel freely within it in search of knowledge in the great centres of learning in Baghdad, Damascus, Cairo, Jerusalem and elsewhere.

## *The Fatimid Empire (909–1171)*

The Shiʿite Ismāʿīlī Fatimid caliphs (named Fatimids after the Prophet's daughter) had ruled Egypt since 969. In its time, their empire had included North Africa (conquered in 909) and southern Syria, and for a while in the 1050s it even threatened Baghdad itself. The Fatimids had also taken Sicily. Despite their religious persuasion and their overall missionary aim to topple the Sunni Abbasid caliph at Baghdad and to convert the whole Muslim world to their beliefs, the Fatimid caliphs—with the notorious exception of the Caliph al-Ḥākim (ruled 996–1021)—had been generally tolerant to their own Sunni Muslim subjects and to Christians and Jews within their territories.

Most of the eleventh century saw the long reign of al-Mustanṣir (1036–94). By his death the Fatimid caliphate had passed its peak and begun to fall prey to internal instability and weak rule. The twelfth century saw the further decline of the Fatimid state, as it became the object of the predatory eyes of both the Franks and the Muslim commanders, Nūr al-Dīn and

---

[2] A group of Shiʿites, also known as 'Seveners', who believed that legitimate succession within Islamic government was vested in a line of seven *imāms* (charismatic rulers who were infallible in matters of doctrine).

Saladin. The latter finally put an end to the dynasty in 1171 and returned the former Fatimid territories to Sunni Islam.

## The Buyids of Iran and Iraq (945–1055)

To the east, in Iraq and Iran, a group of mercenaries from the remote province of Daylam near the Caspian Sea had conquered Baghdad in 945, now ruled Iraq and western Iran and were in control of the weakened Abbasid caliphate. In Baghdad the Buyids espoused Twelver Shi'ism,[3] but they kept the Sunni Abbasid caliph *in situ* and presided over a flourishing Arabo-Persian culture.

## The New Power in the East: the Seljuk Empire (1030–1194)

Unlike the Fatimids, the Seljuk sultans were newcomers. They led their fellow-Turkish nomads from Central Asia into the Islamic world, took Baghdad in 1055, ousting the Buyids, and by the 1050s had created an empire stretching from Syria and Palestine to Central Asia. Like other medieval military warlords who had seized power in the eastern Islamic world, the Seljuks used Perso-Islamic government structures and they formed an alliance with the existing Persian bureaucratic élite. After 1092 the unity of the Seljuk empire was fragmented into smaller family polities but the dynasty continued in weakened form for another century.

## The Seljuk Successor-states of the Twelfth Century

In the breakup of the Seljuk empire into smaller principalities after 1092, Seljuk princelings and their military commanders who had been appointed as provincial governors in the cities of Syria and Palestine took power for themselves. The same process occurred in Anatolia with the emergence of a number of petty Seljuk successor states, such as the Danishmendids and the Artukids, who modelled their government structures, such as they were, on the Seljuk pattern from further east. Central Anatolia, however, was to see the appearance of an altogether more formidable political entity, the state normally known as the Seljuks of Rūm, which was to have close ties with its Byzantine neighbour. In time, the Rūm Seljuks extended their control over most of Anatolia, as evidenced by their networks of caravanserais, some of which serviced the trade that funnelled slaves from southern Russia to Egypt and the Levant.

---

[3] A branch of Shi'ites, also known as Imāmīs, who held that legitimate succession within Islamic government was vested in a line of twelve *imāms*.

The rivalries between the various Seljuk successor-states, such as the Danishmendids and the Artukids, helped to delay the development of a unified Muslim power in Anatolia whose obvious goal would be the capture of Constantinople and the extirpation of Byzantium. But this process did not, of course, begin, until the fourteenth century.

### The Scope of this Enquiry

Given the daunting vastness of the medieval Muslim world, stretching from Spain to India, this survey, and its accompanying bibliography, cannot hope to be comprehensive. What is given here can be called only the tip of an enormous iceberg. Even within the geographical limitations which have necessarily been imposed on the available medieval Islamic historiographical material, the task of selecting what to omit proved difficult. However, the sources chosen and the discussion of them will, it is hoped, show the richness and diversity of Muslim source material in the period 1025–1204.

A deliberate decision has been taken to restrict the discussion to the areas traditionally regarded as the heartlands of medieval Islam, the areas long Islamicised—namely Egypt, Greater Syria, Iraq and Iran. Anatolia, newly conquered in part by the Seljuk Turks in this period, will be given brief mention but, as a newly conquered, frontier territory, it had still to make an important contribution to Muslim culture. The historiographical contributions of Spain and India will not be covered, nor will the historiographical traditions of North Africa under the Berber Almoravid and Almohad dynasties. These areas, often regarded by scholars of the Islamic world as 'peripheral', should rightly be the subject of a separate study, as recent scholarship testifies, notably the meticulous book on Arabic administration in Sicily by Johns,[4] who has contributed the next chapter in this volume. On the other hand, this overview will give brief mention of some of the works of Christian historians who lived in Egypt, Syria and Iraq under Muslim rule and wrote in Arabic.

Whilst it remains true that the major patterns of Islamic historiography were set in the high Abbasid period and that Arabic remained the major vehicle for such writings until Ottoman times, the picture was already becoming more nuanced and Persian historical works cannot be ignored.[5] By the eleventh century, with the divisive impact of the Turkish invasions and the sponsorship of Persian culture by Seljuk sultans, New Persian began to rival

---

[4] J. Johns, *Arabic Administration in Norman Sicily. The royal dīwān* (Cambridge, 2002).
[5] See J. Meisami, *Persian Historiography* (Edinburgh, 1999). New Persian became the medium of choice for both poetry and prose in Seljuk lands, causing the formation of a linguistic division in the field of *adab* (*belles-lettres*) between the Persian-speaking world of Iran, northern India and Central Asia, and the areas further to the west where Arabic still held sway.

Arabic as a court language and literary vehicle in the eastern Islamic world. Hence some at least of the most important historical works in Persian will also be discussed here when appropriate; these clearly point to the emergence of a second historiographical tradition. These two traditions were not, however, hermetically sealed. Whilst it it true that Arabic writers from the Fertile Crescent rarely knew Persian, ethnically Persian scholars, both those living in Iran and those, such as Saladin's adviser, 'Imād al-Dīn al-Iṣfahānī, who moved from Iran to Syria and Egypt, were at home in both languages and could draw on earlier sources written in both.

The selection of primary sources for inclusion in the bibliography was a difficult task. The first choice was made on the basis of geography and sources from countries neighbouring Byzantium were prioritised. Others were selected for their prosopographical interest. Even with the virtual exclusion of sources from Spain, North Africa and Central Asia, the richness and diversity of Islamic historiography are daunting.

Unsurprisingly, medieval Islamic sources, like their western Christian counterparts, deal with rulers and élites rather than ordinary people, cities rather than the countryside, with men rather than women and children, with political and military events rather than with social and economic trends. Like their counterparts in Europe or Byzantium, medieval Muslim writers of history aimed not only at narrating events; they wished to point a moral. They saw in the overarching sweep of history the inexorable and ineluctable will of God whose purpose was the eventual victory of Islam.

## MEDIEVAL ARABIC AND PERSIAN NARRATIVE SOURCES

### General Characteristics

Unfortunately, raw material comprising documents in archives, charters and the like, which forms such an important resource for western medieval history, is almost entirely lacking in the Islamic world.[6] Our knowledge of the medieval Islamic world therefore comes mainly from chronicles, as well as religious and legal works.

There is no doubt that the written narrative historical texts of this period—as distinct from the numerous other types of sources—are the most valuable resource for the Prosopography of the Byzantine World (PBW) project within the period 1025–1204, although it should be stressed that this timescale fits the rhythms of Byzantine, and not Islamic, history. In the

---

[6] Sicily is exceptional in its documentary record: see Ch. 13.

Middle East the period 1055–1250 would offer a more useful framework. During this time, some Muslim historians continued to write overarching works embracing the whole *umma*, God's worldwide community of Muslims. Others became more focused and wrote about their own locality or a particular dynasty ruling in one specific part of the Islamic world. With this increased regionalisation came pride in one's own area and the desire to vaunt it over other Muslim regions. Preoccupation with one's own city or territory also brought introversion; indeed, Muslim historians in Spain and North Africa showed little interest in the historiography of the eastern Islamic world and the same tendency happened in reverse. The Persian-speaking region, especially, as already mentioned, with the gradual demise of Arabic as the major vehicle for the writing of history in eastern Iran and Central Asia in the twelfth century, was, not surprisingly, largely interested in itself.[7] That solipsistic emphasis helps to explain why the language of choice for these historical accounts was increasingly Persian. It is interesting to note that only one chronicle in Arabic, the *Akhbār al-dawla al-Saljūqiyya* (*The Accounts of the Seljuk State*) of al-Husaynī, is known from the early thirteenth century in this area. By then, the split between the Arabic and Persian-speaking parts of the Islamic world was becoming more pronounced. Even religious and legal works were often written in Persian.

The works of medieval Islamic history and literature were written by religious scholars and high-ranking government officials, the latter being often of a pronounced 'secular' bent. Although there are many unasked and unanswered questions in this material about prosopographical issues, these sources speak, often in great detail, about the individuals who have shaped medieval Muslim society, and there is a strong anecdotal aspect to their accounts.

By the eleventh century historical writing was a well-established part of Islamic scholarship. However, the earlier practice of presenting the reader with a selected number of different accounts of the same event, without adjudicating between them, and with each account given authenticity by a chain of transmitters, had largely disappeared. Instead, the chronicler chose what he wanted from a variety of sources and presented his own synthesis of them. It was uncommon for him to stray from the annalistic mode, let alone to seek to discern a pattern in events or to meditate on broad historical processes. But for him, as already noted, the sequence of events, however random they might seem, unfolded according to the sovereign will of God.

It was still the practice in the period under discussion to copy excerpts, often lengthy, from earlier sources, with or without attribution. This practice enabled writers to build on the work of their predecessors, before they

---

[7] C. Cahen, 'Réflexions sur la connaissance du monde musulman par les historiens', in *Les peuples musulmans dans l'histoire médiévale* (Damascus, 1977), 4–5.

embarked on their own new account of the historic present in which they themselves lived. Copying or adapting the work of earlier authors meant that histories now lost were preserved, in extracts at least, in the writings of later scholars. A notable example of the value of such a process is the oft-quoted chronicle of the thirteenth-century Shi'ite historian of Aleppo, Ibn Abī Ṭayyi'. This lost work, a valuable corrective, for example, to the laudatory accounts of Saladin found in other works, can be pieced together, at least in part, from the extensive quotations of it found in later authors such as Abū Shāma, al-'Aynī and others. It is precisely for this reason that much later sources, which might otherwise be ruled out of court because they were written so long after the events that they describe, can sometimes be of crucial value.

As well as the genealogies and family histories of caliphs, sultans and governors, Muslim narrative souces frequently give lists of administrators and government ministers who have held office, which offices they held, often with precise dates. Power networks can thus be constructed. Such information is usually given at the end of a ruler's period in power, either through death or removal from office.

### Historiographical Genres: City Chronicles, Universal Histories and Dynastic Histories

An important genre of Muslim historical writing in the period is the city chronicle. The history of important cities, such as Aleppo and Damascus, was recorded by chroniclers who would draw for their material on previous local histories, oral accounts and administrative documents. Ibn al-Qalānisī, for example, composed the local history of Damascus which covers much of the twelfth century. A city chronicler, such as he, often provides detailed information not found elsewhere. However, the focus of such a work is narrow, fixated as it is on local preoccupations and ignoring the wider significance of some of the events it records.

A more panoramic perspective is given by the genre of historical writing known as the *Universal History*. Embracing the history of the world (or rather the world of Islam) from the Creation until the author's own time, this genre can deal with territories as far-flung as Spain to the west and Central Asia in the east. However, the Muslim heartlands—Egypt, Palestine, Syria and Iraq—usually receive more extended coverage. The most valuable source in this genre for the PBW is the *Universal History* of Ibn al-Athīr (d. 1233).

Another kind of Muslim historical work was the dynastic history. Ibn al-Athīr wrote a second work in this genre, a highly laudatory account of the Zengid dynasty founded in Mosul by the conqueror of Edessa, Zengi. Other chroniclers, Ibn Wāṣil and al-'Asqalānī, performed the same services for the Ayyubids, the family dynasty of Saladin, and in distant Central Asia, the *Akhbār al-dawla al-Saljūqiyya* (*The Accounts of the Seljuk State*) of al-Ḥusaynī, is a very useful source in the same genre.

## The Limitations of Medieval Islamic Historical Narrative Sources

Byzantium occupied a time-honoured place in the medieval Muslim consciousness. It had always been there, since the very beginning of Islam. It was the familiar 'other', a long-standing neighbour. References to it float in and out of the Muslim chronicles but they occasion little comment and apparently required no explanation. It had always been the Christian rival and enemy on the Muslim doorstep. In the eleventh century Byzantium attracted attention when it came into contact or conflict with Muslims, notably in Syria and Anatolia, and in its relations with the Buyids, the Fatimids and the Franks.

As for the new and alien Christian presence, that of the Franks from the end of the eleventh century onwards, a presence, moreover, right in the heart of Muslim territory, in Syria and Palestine, they are mentioned in Islamic writings with much greater frequency than the Byzantines, but in a rather blinkered way, at least in the twelfth century. The Muslims did not, it seems, fully understand the wider social, political and religious context from which the Franks came and within which they operated. Moreover, the ideological divide, as will be shown below, allows the Franks to be given only rare prosopographical treatment in the Muslim sources.

Within the Muslim world itself, it is also important to note the ideological differences which underly the corpus of medieval Islamic historiographical material in this period. The great Syrian and Iraqi chroniclers of the thirteenth century, such as Ibn al-Athīr and Sibṭ b. al-Jawzī, for example, on whom one must rely for much of the period 1025–1204, were Sunni Muslims, working within the orbit of the Abbasid caliphate and for masters who drew their authority from that caliphate. Their testimony, when they choose to speak of the Ismā'īlīs at all, on the activities of both the rival Ismā'īlī Shi'ite Fatimid caliphate in Egypt and its offshoot, the Assassins of Iran, and later Syria, is flawed and patently hostile. It must also be admitted that even in modern scholarship in both the west and the Middle East greater weight is given to the Sunni historiographical tradition and little attention is paid to the Ismā'īlīs or other Shi'ite evidence.

This leads to the more general question of what exactly is 'Islamic historiography'. What this grandiose term, with its potentially vast horizons, actually means in the period under discussion is 'Sunni Arab historiography'.

The frequent marginalisation of Shi'ite historiography in general works on Islamic history or thought is here, unfortunately, imposed not by choice but by the lack of extant material. So the complete picture cannot be given for the period 1025–1204 and indeed, it is true to say that in the bibliography of primary sources that follows this essay the medieval writers mentioned are Sunni, unless there is an explicit statement to the contrary.

## Fatimid Sources

Work on the Fatimids has proliferated in recent years but the results do not always receive the attention they deserve. This is particularly significant in the study of Fatimid–Byzantine relations and Fatimid involvement in the history of the Franks in the first half of the twelfth century. But the Fatimid caliphate (ruled 909–1171), it must be remembered, was a major Mediterranean power, and it did attempt to oust its Sunni rival institution in Baghdad, so it is not surprising that it generated a new historiography of its own. Unfortunately, many of the achievements of Fatimid historiography have been lost to us.[8]

However, some fragments and extensive quotations from Fatimid sources have been preserved in the works of the Mamluk era (1250–1517). The oeuvre of al-Maqrīzī (d. 1442), the great Muslim historian of Egypt, is a particularly valuable resource in this respect. His evidence constitutes the main source for the history of Egypt for the period of the project. For the much-neglected Fatimid history of the twelfth century, for example, al-Maqrīzī draws on the lost history of Ibn al-Ma'mūn (d. 1192). Despite the long gap between his own time and that of the early Fatimids, al-Maqrīzī quotes such early Fatimid sources as al-Musabbiḥī (d. 1030) and he adopts a comprehensive and systematic approach to them. Mamluk historians are all the more important, since works written about the Fatimids in the Ayyubid period (1174–1250) have also been lost. In the work of the Egyptian scholar Ibn al-Furāt (d. 1405), we also find many extracts from lost sources. Nevertheless, it is impossible to discern how much these later Sunni writers, by their selections and omissions of quotations from lost Fatimid sources, may have 'doctored' them for their own purposes.

## Christian Arabic Sources

A good number of texts written in Arabic by Christians—Melkites and Copts—have survived. There had long been a robust and extensive Christian

[8] For a comprehensive overview of Fatimid sources, see P.E. Walker, *Exploring an Islamic Empire: Fatimid history and its sources* (London, 2002).

historiographical tradition written in Arabic; in addition to those Middle Eastern Christians who wrote in Armenian, Greek or Syriac, some chose to write in Arabic. Although the Jacobites continued writing in Syriac until the thirteenth century, some of their number, notably Bar Hebraeus (called in Arabic Ibn al-'Ibrī), also composed works in Arabic.[9]

The Christian Arab viewpoint is a valuable supplement and even corrective to the approaches followed in the Muslim chronicles. The *Naẓm al-jawhar* (*String of Jewels*), the chronicle of Saʿīd b. Baṭrīq, known also as Eutychios (d. 940), the Melkite patriarch of Alexandria from 933–40, was continued in a *Dhayl (Appendix)* by another Melkite historian, Yaḥyā al-Anṭākī (John of Antioch; d. 1066). Christian Arab sources, such as the *Dhayl*, help to fill the gap in early Fatimid historiography. It is a useful resource for Arab–Byzantine relations. On the other hand, Christian Arab historians who opted to write in Arabic exposed themselves to being understood in their writings by their Muslim overlords; one may assume therefore that they had come to terms to some extent with their Muslim governors and that they exercised caution in their accounts of non-ecclesiastical matters inside the 'House of Islam'. It should also be stressed that the boundaries between Christian and Muslim historical writings were permeable and that both sides unashamedly copied material from each other.

The better-known Coptic writer, Jirjīs al-Makīn Ibn al-'Amīd (d. 1273), is less useful for the period 1025–1204. His chronicle on the Ayyubids begins in 1205 and thus is outside our period; it should, however, be consulted for its valuable information on the thirteenth century in Egypt and elsewhere. al-Makīn also composed a work entitled *al-Majmūʿ al-mubārak (The Blessed Collection)*, a *Universal History* from the Creation until the year 1260. This short work received much, perhaps unwarranted, attention, given its highly derivative nature, in western Europe because of its early translation into Latin.

### Eleventh-century Sources

It is worth mentioning that at the very beginning of the period 1025–1204 we find the work of Miskawayh (d. 1030), a very important Muslim historian who in his work entitled *Tajārib al-umam (The Experiences of Nations)* adopted an ethical and philosophical approach to history.[10] He used his own judgement in assessing the information in front of him and he used the first

---

[9] See the contribution by Witold Witakowski in this volume.
[10] See the discussion in C. Robinson, *Islamic Historiography* (Cambridge, 2003), 100.

person in his narrative. Some have seen in his wider vision of historical processes a precursor of the work of the more famous Ibn Khaldūn (d. 1406).

Buyid historiography was also dominated by a prominent Sabian family[11]—doctors, men of letters and administrators—and in particular by Hilāl al-Ṣābi', who converted to Islam, and his son Ghars al-Ni'ma. The historical works of both these men are now lost but fortunately they were quoted by later writers from the Baghdad historiographical 'school', such as Ibn al-Jawzī (d. 1200) and especially his maternal grandson, Sibṭ b. al-Jawzī (d. 1256), who uses the work of Ghars al-Ni'ma in detail for his account of the years 1055–76.[12]

Mention should also be made of the little-known Kurdish Muslim dynasties who ruled on the eastern borders of Byzantium, in Armenia and Transcaucasia, the Shaddādids of Ganja (951–1075) and the Shaddādids of Ani (1064–1198). The pioneeering work on these dynasties is that of Minorsky entitled *Studies in Caucasian History*. In it, Minorsky draws on an anonymous Arabic source from the area, probably written around 1075.[13]

### Twelfth- and Thirteenth-century Sources

The twelfth century yields disappointingly little in the way of extant narrative sources. However, the situation improves dramatically in the thirteenth century where there is a vast wealth of such material, from Iraq, Syria and Egypt, providing extremely rich documentation. As already mentioned, the practice of copying predecessors' works, helped to preserve the lost contributions of eleventh- and twelfth-century chroniclers.

Pride of place amongst the medieval Muslim historians writing about the period 1025–1204 must go to Ibn al-Athīr (d. 1233). This chronicler shows the true instincts of the historian in his *al-Kāmil fi'l ta'rīkh* (*The Complete in History*), with his breadth of vision and masterly synthesis of sources. The work of Sibṭ b. al-Jawzī (d. 1256), the *Mir'āt al-zamān* (*The Mirror of the Time*) is a rich resource for the history of the twelfth and thirteenth centuries in Syria.

---

[11] The Sabians (*Ṣābi'ūn*) are mentioned in the Quran as possessing a religion revealed by God, but their identity is controversial. The name has been attached to at least three communities: the Manichaeans, the Elchasaites of southern Iraq (an ancient Jewish–Christian sect) and the Sabians of Harran who followed an ancient Semitic polytheistic religion, with a strongly Hellenised upper class. For a detailed discussion of this issue, see F. de Blois, s.v. Ṣābi', in *Encyclopaedia of Islam* (2nd edn.), vol. 8, 672–5.
[12] See C. Cahen, 'The historiography of the Seljuqid period', in B. Lewis and P.M. Holt, eds., *Historians of the Middle East* (London, 1962), 61.
[13] (Cambridge, 1953), 3–5.

## ISLAMIC PROSOPOGRAPHICAL WORKS

There is a wealth of extant medieval Muslim prosopographical literature relating to the period 1025–1204. After a discussion of general characteristics of this kind of material, the genres—biographical dictionaries, biographies and autobiographies—will be analysed. The possible value and interest to Byzantine prosopographical studies will then be highlighted.

### The Format and Content of Medieval Islamic Prosopographical Sources

Generally speaking, an independent biographical work devoted to one individual person is called a *sīra*; a biographical entry inserted into a collection of biographies is called a *tarjama*. There is, however, some overlap between these two terms.[14] The major sources of biographical material in the medieval Islamic world were the *ṭabaqāt* (generation) books; these were biographical works classified according to death dates. Other biographical books were ordered alphabetically. A typical notice in a biographical dictionary reads rather like an entry in a medieval 'Who's Who?' It includes the dates of birth and death, if known, of the subject, the person's names, titles, genealogy, education, the scholars with whom the person studied, the offices he held, the titles of the book he wrote, and in some cases, anecdotal material about the person. Some entries are short but others cover several pages. Although they often contain nuggets of unexpected and valuable information, they are formulaic in their structure and phrasing and they can be somewhat discouraging to use.

Biographical dictionaries that step outside the narrow remit of the *ṭabaqāt* literature appeared at a later date. In their works, al-Khaṭīb al-Baghdādī (d. 1071), focusing on Baghdad, and Ibn al-'Asākir (d. 1176), writing about Damascus, aimed at quantity and comprehensiveness, wanting to give a complete record of élites living in or connected with a specific place. Such works were also written by Shi'ites and other 'sectarian' groups. Yet other biographical works were compiled on a regional basis, covering Spain to Central Asia. The genre of biographical dictionary reached its apogee with a flood of such works in the Mamluk period (1250–1500). Amongst these are the great biographical works of the writers who lived in the thirteenth and fourteenth centuries, such as Ibn Khallikān, Ibn al-'Adīm, al-Maqrīzī, al-Ṣafadī and others.

---

[14] R.S. Humphreys, *Islamic History. A framework for inquiry* (Princeton, 1991), 190–1; D.F. Reynolds, ed., *Interpreting the Self. Autobiography in the Arabic literary tradition* (Berkeley, Los Angeles and London, 2001), 42–3.

Who deserved mention in biographical dictionaries? At first, the genre focused on obituaries of religious lawyers who belonged to one of the four main Sunni *madhhab*s (*madhhab* literally means 'way' but it is usually translated as 'legal school').[15] As is sometimes forgotten in the west, Islam had no established 'church' and it was these men who shaped religious orthodoxy. However, by the period under discussion here the genre of biographical dictionaries had broadened to include administrators, Sufis (Muslim mystics), doctors, poets and other specific groups. Nevertheless, the *'ulamā'* (the religious scholars of Islam, for want of a more precise definition),[16] are the group which figure most prominently in medieval Muslim biographical dictionaries. It is they too who compiled these works. The major criterion for inclusion was scholarship or religious piety, although this is not explicitly stated. For a writer such as Ibn Khallikān, however, his selection (and his dictionary contains 855 entries) was dictated by the yardstick of fame itself and his is the first general biographical dictionary. As he himself wrote: 'I have not restricted myself to any given group, like the *'ulamā'*, kings, princes, viziers or poets. On the contrary, I have mentioned everybody who was famous.'[17] Some of the Muslim leaders against the Franks are given an entry in at least one biographical dictionary. Delving in the hundreds of pages of such works the reader is even rewarded occasionally by the discovery of a short biography of famous Franks, such as Baldwin I or Reynald of Châtillon.

These works provide rich prosopographical information. They shed light on the dealings of religious notables with each other and also on how they interacted with the rest of society. They show typical career paths for scholars and they shed light on the nature of religious institutions, such as the *madrasa* (a religious college devoted to the study of the jurisprudence of a particular legal 'school'),[18] and on urban social élites and structures. In addition to information on religious scholars, these biographical collections provide a mine of information on urban élites, governors, administrators, merchants and women.[19] Such sources have enabled scholars to begin to write

[15] There had been other 'legal schools' in early Islam but by the eleventh century the number had become fixed as four among the Sunnis. All four *madhhab*s had their own books of *fiqh* (jurisprudence), based on the four sources of the *Sharī'a* (Islamic revealed law)—the Quran, the *ḥadīth* (the canonical sayings of the Prophet), *ijmā'* (consensus) and *qiyās* (analogy). These legal schools did not differ on matters of fundamental belief but on their interpretations of praxis. These differences could often be on matters of minute detail.

[16] For problems of defining this group in medieval Islamic society, cf. Humphreys, *Islamic History*, 187.

[17] Ibn Khallikān, *Wafayāt al-a'yān*, ed. I. Abbas (Beirut, 1968–72), vol. 1, 20.

[18] Legal scholars belonging to a particular *madhhab* would learn about its version of Islamic law in a *madrasa*, sitting at the feet of a master whose words they would write down and memorise.

[19] See Robinson, *Islamic Historiography*, 71.

social and cultural history and to address themes, such as the transmission and circulation of knowledge, the movement of books and scholars, and onomastic and genealogical issues.[20]

Biographical dictionaries have, however, clear limitations. They are aimed at depicting the religious and scholarly achievements of medieval Muslim society but their value as documents that record other aspects of that society is sporadic. For political and social history, they can only ever be a supplementary source to be used alongside chronicles and other writings.

Except for occasional entries about saints and mystics, nobody anonymous could be included in the biographical dictionaries. Moreover, the exact registering of an individual's names was of paramount importance. These names are composite. In addition to the person's forename *(ism)* received at birth and selected from a rather small repertoire, other names were given, including the *nisba* (to denote place of birth or residence), the *kunya* (the personal name which indicates someone as the 'father' or 'mother' of so and so—for example, 'Abū Muḥammad' = 'father of Muḥammad') and the *laqabs* (honorific titles). Some dictionaries are organised according to *ism*, others prefer to use a person's *kunya*, whilst yet others identify their subjects by their *nisba*. Clearly, then, one must be in possession of quite a range of information, if one wishes to track down a given individual. The complete, or even a partial, set of names reveals much about a person's life, travels and career.

In general, Islamic prosopographical studies suffer from many problems: the daunting amount of works to be tackled and the relative lack of researchers working as a team on this material. These works are still a largely unexploited source for modern scholars. This is perhaps not surprising, since only one of them, the work of Ibn Khallikān, has been fully translated into a European language. The rest of this corpus of material remains difficult of access to scholars who cannot read Arabic, for it is translated piecemeal and only in small fragments or, much more frequently, untranslated. A good number of the editions of these works still lack an index, a deficiency which, given their great length, makes them very difficult for anyone to use. A major desideratum is a computerised corpus of all persons mentioned in each of the important biographical dictionaries.

It is important to stress within the context of this Byzantine and crusader prosopographical project that the very material on the Islamic side—these biographical dictionaries—which ought to be of great help, is hard to use as an inter-disciplinary tool. The genre of biographical writing in the medieval Islamic world developed as an indigenous entity, the natural result of a soci-

---

[20] See, for example, the works of Pouzet and Morray mentioned in the bibliography of secondary sources.

ety's desire to record the achievements of its religious, scholarly élites. The classical models of Greece and Rome do not seem to have exerted any influence from outside, nor is there any obvious parallel to the penetrating observations about Byzantine rulers from the pen of Michael Psellos.

The avowed aim of the PBW of identifying individuals from Byzantium mentioned in non-Greek sources will be extremely hard to achieve on the basis of using Arabic and Persian prosopographical works in this period or any other. Mention of Byzantine persons in medieval Islamic sources is extremely rare and difficult to find. Literally hundreds of pages of medieval biographical works will yield only a few, or no, such references. The situation is slightly better in the case of the Franks, whose leaders are mentioned very occasionally. When such references do occur, it is difficult to decide why such a nugget has been included—is it there by chance because the Muslim compiler had access to a source which mentioned a specific Byzantine or Frankish individual or has the short biographical notice been chosen for a purpose?

## RECENT SCHOLARLY APPROACHES TO
## ISLAMIC PROSOPOGRAPHY

### The Western Contribution

The French scholar, Cahen, was not certain of the value of what he rather sweepingly described as 'all these bulky dictionaries', remarking that they were full of people 'of little significance'.[21] Fortunately, this rather harsh judgement, whilst true up to a point in the case of certain works in this genre, is certainly not now the view of scholars who are keen to tap the biographical dictionaries for all kinds of data. Much of this information is incidental from the standpoint of the compiler. But when such snippets are used with imagination and care, they have already produced interesting results.

Byzantinists will be interested to learn of recent approaches and achievements in the burgeoning field of research on Islamic prosopography. Perhaps ironically, the two main areas where there has been significant interest in this field are Spain and eastern Iran, far removed from the central Islamic lands which border Byzantium. For some time now, Spanish scholars, under the influence and inspiration of Manuela Marin, have been doing pioneering prosopographical research focused on Muslim Spain. In addition to her own considerable output in this area, Marin recently edited a special issue of the

---

[21] C. Cahen, 'Editing Arabic chronicles: a few suggestions', in *Les peuples musulmans dans l'histoire médiévale* (Damascus, 1977), 34.

journal *Medieval Prosopography* devoted to Arab–Islamic medieval culture. The emphasis in this volume (seven out of eleven articles) is heavily on material from Spain, where the study of medieval Muslim prosopography has been flourishing for some time and is clearly well ahead of comparable work in the central and eastern Islamic lands.

For the area of eastern Iran, the work of Bulliet has been notably adventurous in the field of medieval Islamic prosopographical studies. In his book *The Patricians of Nishapur*[22] he collected data from a single city to draw a picture of how power was concentrated in the hands of a few families over a period of generations. For this research he leant on three summarised versions of two Persian biographical dictionaries which deal with the notables of this city betweeen the middle of the tenth century and the middle of the twelfth. Basing himself on this material, he has assembled useful data on the role of the ʿulamāʾ in an important centre of religious learning in eastern Iran. In a later work, *Conversion to Islam in the Medieval Period: an essay in quantitative history*,[23] Bulliet suggested a controversial but thought-provoking method for gauging the rate of conversion to Islam in different parts of the Muslim world. Here again he used material from biographical dictionaries and in particular he interpreted the evidence of naming patterns for a person who is converted and takes a Muslim name. Most recently, he has turned his attention to the role and education of women in the pre-Mongol period, again using data from biographical dictionaries, in both Persian and Arabic.[24]

But this field is only in its infancy in the case of the central Islamic lands. Humphreys argues with reference to Mamluk studies, which lie outside the remit of this present essay, that only the barest beginnings of a prosopographical approach to Mamluk administration can be found in recent scholarship.[25] Models of good practice are rare and Humphreys singles out for praise the work of Petry on Mamluk bureaucrats which is based on data derived from two fifteenth-century biographical dictionaries. The contributions of Pouzet, Ephrat, Cohen, and Morray should also be singled out for praise.[26]

## The Contribution of Modern Scholarship in the Middle East

For this book, bearing in mind a probable readership of Byzantinists and western medievalists and the aims and nature of the PBW project, an editor-

---

[22] (Cambridge, Mass., 1972).
[23] (Cambridge, Mass., 1979).
[24] R.W. Bulliet, 'Élite women in the pre-Mongol period', in G. Nashat and L. Beck, eds., *Women in Iran from the Rise of Islam to 1800* (Urbana and Chicago, 2003), 68–79.
[25] Humphreys, *Islamic History*, 183.
[26] For details, see the bibliography of secondary sources.

ial decision has been taken in this chapter to focus, in the secondary literature listed in the bibliography, on work done in European languages. This has meant the exclusion of a massive corpus of scholarly books and articles written in Arabic, Persian and Turkish on the period 1025–1204. There is also relevant research done in Hebrew. These works, almost always untranslated, remain out of the reach of all but a few western scholars. There is no room here even to mention the thousands of such books and articles.

It is important, however, to emphasise that every year, in the major publishing houses of Cairo, Beirut, Damascus, Riyadh, Tehran, Istanbul and elsewhere, scholarly monographs regularly appear, as do serious journals with articles relevant to the subjects discussed in this overview. These works have included topics such as the relationship between the Arabs and Byzantium, social and cultural studies of the eleventh to the thirteenth centuries, and biographies of major figures like Saladin. These books, many of which are based on doctoral theses, are, as in the west, of varying quality.

The contribution of scholars from the Middle East to the pressing task of editing and publishing primary sources is quite simply indispensable. It is not only that they have produced new and improved editions of key texts, such as those of Ibn Khallikān and Ibn al-Athīr, which were first published in the nineteenth century by orientalist scholars. They have also edited—and this is a continuing process—many crucial works which have long been available only in manuscript form. Such editions include the history of al-Nuwayrī and the multi-volume biographical dictionary of al-Ṣafadī. In this essential work of editing core texts, the contribution of Ihsan Abbas has been outstanding. Major remaining desiderata for publication include a proper and full edition of the histories of Sibṭ b. al-Jawzī and of al-ʿAynī, whose works contain important excerpts from lost sources, and the completion of the editing work begun on Ibn al-Furāt.

## BIOGRAPHICAL AND AUTOBIOGRAPHICAL LITERATURE

As already mentioned, the term *sīra* was used to denote a full-length biography. Apart from the central importance of the *Biography of the Prophet*, this kind of biographical work came relatively late in medieval Arabic historical writing. Indeed, in the period 1025–1204, such works are still rare.[27] Within the Persian tradition there is a similar absence of writing in this genre, although the Sufis did occasionally produce works focusing on the head

[27] The chapter, entitled 'Islamic biographical literature', by H.A.R. Gibb in the work edited by Lewis and Holt (n. 12) is devoted entirely to a discussion of medieval Arabic biographical dictionaries: *Historians of the Middle East*, 54–8.

(*shaykh*) of a particular religious order. An example of this kind of writing is a work devoted to a famous mystic, Abū Saʿīd b. Abi'l Khayr (d. 1048–9), and his miraculous powers.[28]

Those medieval Muslim biographical accounts that do exist are couched in stylised narrative form and are exemplary in character. Such material can appear, therefore, as rather tedious and repetitive, full of clichéd phrases, which are transferred from one famous person to another. Moreover, medieval Muslim biographies almost always speak of the virtues of the famous person about whom they are writing, suppressing his faults since they are not worthy of emulation. It is worth recalling that panegyric was a principal mode of medieval Islamic poetry.

Who was accorded the honour of a biography? Predictably, the men whose lives are recorded in medieval biographical accounts belonged to specific groups and categories. Mostly they were religious scholars and mystics, and sometimes governors, military commanders and rulers. How could it be otherwise, since the lives of the rest of society were not considered a worthy model for the whole community? The modern reader looks in vain in a medieval Muslim biography for a full account of the life of a famous person. There is no attempt to depict an entire life from the cradle to the grave, warts and all. There is little interest shown in physical appearance or even psychological motivation. Whether they are full-blown narratives or short obituaries, medieval Muslim biographical accounts are very stereotyped, opaque and hard to read. In their concern to demonstrate God's will for the world and the inevitable triumph of Islam, these sources exploit rhetorical devices, poetry, speeches and Quranic quotations to the full.

During the period under discussion the few important full biographies were not written for caliphs but rather for two usurping military warlords, Nūr al-Dīn and Saladin, Muslim heroes in the *jihād* against the Franks. Indeed, Saladin's two biographers, Ibn Shaddād and ʿImād al-Dīn, use their works to justify his seizure of power and they focus on glorifying his reputation as a valiant warrior in the Holy War and as a pious Sunni ruler. However, the work of ʿImād al-Dīn, *The Syrian Lightning*, crosses two genres, the biography and the autobiography. Indeed, the book is both a biography of Saladin and an autobiography of the author himself, proud to show his own close relationship with his master.[29] As for Nūr al-Dīn, he is accorded a biography, together with Saladin, by Abū Shāma (d. 1267), in his panegyrical

---

[28] For details, see A.K.S. Lambton, 'Persian biographical literature', in Lewis and Holt, *Historians of the Middle East*, 148–9.

[29] B. Lewis, 'First-person narrative in the Middle East', in M. Kramer, ed., *Middle Eastern Lives. The practice of biography and self-narrative* (Syracuse, 1991), 25.

work, *The Book of the Two Gardens*. In this carefully constructed book, the author devotes attention to Nūr al-Dīn but clearly brings his work to a climax with his even more glowing description of Saladin.

## Autobiographies

It was once thought that autobiographies in medieval Islamic literature were very few and far between. Recent scholarship, and especially the excellent book edited by Reynolds,[30] has somewhat modified this viewpoint. This volume, completed by a team of scholars, provides an annotated guide to Arabic autobiographical writings from the ninth to the nineteenth centuries; it covers non-extant works and short autobiographical extracts preserved by later authors. Full autobiographies, however, for the period 1025–1204, number only six. Of these, the *Kitāb al-I'tibār* (*The Book of Instruction by Example*) of Usāma b. Munqidh (d. 1188), his so-called *Memoirs*, has been known for a long time in the west. Attitudes to this material have been refined and sharpened over the years; recent scholarship has focused on the didactic nature of the work. The other two autobiographies from the central lands of the Islamic world in this period are written by religious scholars. The 'spiritual autobiography' of the famous theologian and mystic, al-Ghazālī (d. 1111), entitled *Deliverer from Error,* is also well known in the west, whereas the unusual autobiography of the Fatimid missionary, al-Mu'ayyad fi'l Dīn al-Shīrāzī, *The Biography of al-Mu'ayyad fi'l Dīn al-Shīrāzī the Chief Missionary*, has remained neglected until recently. This latter work contains the author's own speeches and sermons and gives lively accounts of court intrigues.

In a sense, travel writings are clearly autobiographical but their focus is deliberately circumscribed. Such accounts abound in the medieval Islamic world and they will not be discussed here.

## ANCILLARY SOURCES

## Documents

Archival documents from the Islamic Middle Ages are much rarer than in Europe. They certainly existed, as testified by the mention of them in chronicles, encyclopaedias and administrative manuals. Some archives have survived

[30] Reynolds, *Interpreting the Self* (n. 14).

in mosques, shrines, synagogues or monasteries. Was this dearth of archival material caused by the lack of institutions known in the west or by recurring invasions?

The Genizah archives have been described elsewhere in this volume,[31] so they will not be discussed here. Other decrees and diplomas from Islamic chancelleries have survived, such as those in the monastery of St Catherine in Sinai. Letters and diplomas dating from the Fatimid period are assembled in a volume collected by Jamal al-Din El-Shayyal, entitled *Majmū'at al-wathā'iq al-fāṭimiyya* (*Anthology of Fatimid Documents*).[32] In Iran, Afshar and Tahir have recently edited a very important collection of administrative archival documents from the late Seljuk period, *Mukhṭārāt min al-rasā'il* (*Selections from the Epistles*), mostly in Persian but some in Arabic; they were found in the southern city of Yazd and hence escaped destruction in the Mongol invasions. These are a valuable resource for the names and networks of administrative élites in the second half of the twelfth century in Iran.[33] This corpus deserves to be studied in depth. Palestine and Syria yield disappointingly few documents. The large collection (a thousand or so documents) from the Haram al-Sharif in Jerusalem postdates the period of this volume.

### *Mirrors for Princes*

This genre flourished in the eleventh and twelfth centuries and offers a useful adjunct for the modern scholar seeking to shed light on the ethos of medieval Islamic government and courtly life. Such works, written in Arabic and Persian, and occasionally even Turkish, trace their origins to the ancient Near East (for example, the *Khudaynāma* of Sasanian Iran) and India (for example, the *Pančatantra*), but they were thoroughly assimilated into Islamic society and have developed accordingly. This didactic genre uses the device of historical anecdotes about famous people to point a moral, but these have been carefully chosen with that aim in mind. As historical evidence they should be treated with caution. It is difficult to tell to what extent theory was applied in reality.

---

[31] See the discussions of Jeremy Johns (on Sicily) and Nicholas de Lange and Joshua Holo (on Jewish sources).
[32] Vol. 1 (Cairo, 1958).
[33] (Tehran, 2000).

**Epigraphy and Coins**

*General*

Inscriptions and coins present invaluable information about medieval people and their public face. In one sense, their evidence is hard to judge because it involves stereotyped titulature, and the rhythms of such artefacts are not necessarily those of chronological history. However, the titles rulers gave themselves or which were bestowed on them are often revealing. Changes in titulature often reflect political events. Above all, surviving coins and inscriptions, especially when they are dated, are genuinely contemporary documents and not, as in much medieval historiography, the fruit of retrospective reflections and interpretations of later generations of scholars.

*Epigraphy*

In contrast to its dearth of archival material, the Muslim world possesses astoundingly rich extant epigraphic evidence—on buildings, tombstones and all kinds of artefacts. Such inscriptions chart the realities of political power, recording the titulature and achievements of individual rulers. They often give precise dates of death and assist in the construction of genealogies—thanks to their formulae for the rendering of names—thus acting as an adjunct to the evidence of written sources and often reinforcing them. They also shed light on the establishments of religious endowments (*waqf*s).

The *Corpus inscriptionum arabicarum*, confined to Egypt, the Levant and Anatolia, is organised country by country and it focuses on monuments. The *Répertoire chronologique d'épigraphie arabe* gives all inscriptions, both on buildings and objects, according to the actual or approximate year. Each inscription is given in Arabic transcription and French translation.

*Coins*

Coins are the most reliable source for establishing a dated sequence of rulers (often governors as well as caliphs or sultans) across the entire Islamic world. They are also a prosopographical resource of the first importance, thanks to the Islamic custom of always rendering a name by more than one element, and thereby avoiding ambiguity. There is virtually no figural representation. The striking of coins was the prerogative of the ruler; they give his titles, his names, the place of the mint, and the date of the striking of the coin. On the other side of the coin are Quranic quotations. These can often be related to specific religious or political concerns.

## EDITIONS AND TRANSLATIONS

Until relatively recently, the period under discussion in this volume was less well served with editions of texts than those of the high Abbasid period of Arabic historical writing in the ninth and tenth centuries. Nowadays, later medieval Islamic historical—and in particular Mamluk studies—are thriving, and new, high-quality editions of relevant texts are appearing regularly.

However, given the large number of publishing houses in the Middle East, it is not easy to keep abreast of all the new editions or the latest volumes of ongoing publications which appear each year (although the Internet is an increasing help in this matter).

Existing translations vary in quality. Building on the efforts of numerous scholars, such as de Sacy, Quatremère, de Slane and Blochet, the French corporate enterprise, known as the *Recueil des historiens des croisades* (*RHC*), was published towards the end of the nineteenth century. Five out of the sixteen volumes were devoted to Arabic sources, edited and translated into French. A couple of generations later, the French scholar, Cahen, attacked the *Recueil* very vigorously,[34] rightly criticising both the choice of texts made and the quality of the translations, and discoursing on the harm caused by the *Recueil*. This material should therefore be used with some care. But for all its faults, it has been of cardinal importance in presenting the story of the crusades from the Muslim side and thus acting as a counterweight to the understandably though regrettably Eurocentric tendencies of crusader studies in the west.

Fortunately, a good number of the texts in the *Recueil* have been re-edited since that time and better translations of many of the texts have been published.[35] It is, however, important that as many relevant texts as possible should be translated. It is unfortunate that so many scholars, somewhat cravenly, choose to retranslate texts that have already been translated, often more than once, rather than boldly to embark on the more useful but more difficult task of bringing a new text to the attention of a wider audience that does not know Arabic.

[34] C. Cahen, 'Editing Arabic chronicles', 30, n. 1.
[35] See the bibliography for details.

# BIBLIOGRAPHY

## HANDBOOKS, SURVEYS, PROSOPOGRAPHIES

### Handbooks and Guides

C. Brockelmann, *Geschichte der arabischen Litteratur* (Weimar, 1898–1902; 2nd edn., Leiden, 1945–9); 3 supplementary vols. (Leiden, 1937–42)
  Still a starting-point for information about manuscripts and editions of key sources, although the work has been much criticised. However, many new manuscripts and editions of texts have appeared since its publication.
C. Cahen, *Introduction à l'histoire du monde musulman médiéval: VIIIᵉ–Xvᵉ siècle* (Paris, 1983); a revision of J. Sauvaget and C. Cahen, *Introduction à l'histoire de l'Orient musulman* (Paris 1961); trans. as *Introduction to the History of the Muslim East: a bibliographical guide* (Berkeley, 1965)
  Despite its date of publication, still a useful entrée into the subject.
*Encyclopaedia Iranica,* ed. E.Yarshater (London and Boston, 1982–)
  A very substantial ongoing enterprise with contributions from scholars from Iran and the west.
*Encyclopaedia of Islam,* 1st edn., 4 vols. and *Supplement* (Leiden, 1938); 2nd edn., 11 vols. (Leiden, 1954–2002)
  The most important reference work for Islamic history.
W. Hinz, *Islamische Masse und Gewichte* (Leiden, 1955)
  The best work on Islamic weights and measures.
R.S. Humphreys, *Islamic History. A framework for inquiry* (Princeton, 1991)
  An invaluable bibliographical resource, which also discusses approaches to medieval Islamic history in a thought-provoking manner. Chapter 8, which concerns the role of religious scholars in Islamic society, deals with medieval biographical dictionaries and prosopographical issues.
I.K. Poonawala, *Bibliography of Ismaili Literature* (Malibu, 1977)
  A very informative work for research on the various groups (including the Fatimids and the Assassins) which comprise the world's Ismāʿīlī Muslims. It is organised according to sub-groups and then according to authors.
F. Sezgin, *Geschichte des arabischen Schrifttums,* 9 vols. (Leiden, 1967–)
  This massive, ongoing venture aims at replacing Brockelmann's classic work. So far the volumes have only just recently reached the period of the project.
C.A. Storey, *Persian Literature, a bio-bibliographical survey*, 3 vols. (London, 1927–84)
  Volume 1.2 on history and biography is especially relevant.

### Chronology and Genealogy

C.E. Bosworth, *The New Islamic Dynasties* (Edinburgh, 1996); an updated and fuller edition of his earlier work, *The Islamic Dynasties: a chronological and genealogical handbook* (Edinburgh, 1967)
  A very useful research tool. The first edition has been translated into Russian and Persian. There is also a Turkish edition, based on the first edition but expanded to

include some lesser-known Turkish dynasties from the eleventh century onwards: *Islâm devletleri tarihi*, ed. E. Merçil and M. Ipşirli (Istanbul, 1980).

T.W. Haig, *Comparative Tables of Muhammadan and Christian Dates* (London, 1932)

S. Lane-Poole, *The Mohammedan Dynasties: chronological and genealogical tables with historical introductions* (London, 1893; repr. Beirut, 1966); revised Turkish edition and translation, H. Edhem, *Duval-i islamiyyah* (Istanbul, 1927)

F. Wüstenfeld, *Genealogische Tabellen der arabischen Stämme und Familien*, 2 vols. (Göttingen, 1852–3)

F. Wüstenfeld and E. Mahler, *Vergleichungstabellen der muhammadenischen und christlichen Zeitrechnung* (Leipzig, 1854); 3rd edn., rev. J. Mayr and B. Spuler (Wiesbaden, 1961)
Gives conversion tables for Hijri and Christian dates.

E. von Zambaur, *Manuel de généalogie et de chronologie pour l'histoire de l'Islam* (Hanover, 1927; repr. Bad Pyrmont, 1955)


## Maps

G. Cornu, *Atlas du monde arabo-islamique à l'époque classique IX$^e$–X$^e$ siècles* (Leiden, 1985)

H. Kennedy, *An Historical Atlas of Islam* (Leiden, 2002)

*Tübinger Atlas des vorderen Orients* (Wiesbaden, 1977–84)


## Dictionaries and Other Linguistic Tools

G.L.M. Clauson, *An Etymological Dictionary of Pre-Thirteenth Century Turkish* (Oxford, 1972)
Difficult to use, because the author organises his entries according to reconstructed Turkish roots, but still the best resource for the earliest extant texts in Turkish.

R.J. Dozy, *Supplément aux dictionnaires arabes* (Leiden 1881; repr. 1927 and 1960; also repr. Beirut, 1968)
The most useful Arabic dictionary for the period of the project, although it bases its findings primarily on evidence from Spain and North Africa.

J. Fück, *'Arabiya. Recherches sur l'histoire de la langue et du style arabe,* French tr., C. Denizeau (Paris, 1955)

G. Graf, *Die Sprachgebrauch der ältesten christlich-arabischen Litteratur. Ein Beitrag zur Geschichte des vulgär-arabisch* (Leipzig, 1905)

M.T. Houtsma, *Ein türkisch–arabisches Glossar* (Leiden, 1894)

E.W. Lane, *An Arabic–English Lexicon*, 8 vols. (London, 1863–93; repr. Beirut, 1980)
A vast resource, based on data from medieval Arabic dictionaries. It was unfinished, so the last eight letters of the Arabic alphabet are presented only in fragmentary fashion.

F. Steingass, *A Comprehensive Persian–English Dictionary* (London, n.d)
The standard dictionary of classical Persian. It is often also helpful in elucidating meanings of obscure Arabic words in the late medieval period.

M. Ullmann, ed., *Wörterbuch der klassischen arabischen Sprache* (Wiesbaden, 1957–)
A very ambitious and comprehensive but slow-moving enterprise. It began where

Lane had stopped in his *Lexicon*—with the letter *kāf.* The entries are based on texts up to AD 1500.

F. Wehr, *A Dictionary of Modern Written Arabic* (Ithaca, 1961; revised and expanded, Wiesbaden, 1979)
Despite its title, this work is useful for the Arabic of the later medieval period.

## Select List of Catalogues

I. Afshar, *Bibliographie des catalogues des manuscripts persans* (Tehran, 1337/1958)

W. Ahlwardt, *Verzeichnis der arabischen Handschriften der königlichen Bibliothek zu Berlin*, 10 vols. (Berlin, 1887–99)
A remarkable early achievement in surveying Islamic manuscripts.

A.J. Arberry, *The Chester Beatty Library: a handlist of the Arabic manuscripts,* 6 vols. (Dublin 1955–64)

A.S. Atiya, *The Arabic Manuscripts of Mount Sinai* (Baltimore, 1955)

C.F. Baker and M.R.P. Polliack, *Arabic and Judeo-Arabic Manuscripts in the Cambridge Genizah Collections* (Cambridge, 2001)

C. Cahen, 'Les chroniques arabes concernant la Syrie, l'Égypte, et la Mésopotamie de la conquête arabe à la conquête ottomane dans les bibliothèques d'Istanbul', *RÉI* 10 (1936), 333–62

M. de Slane, *Catalogue des manuscrits arabes* (Paris, 1883)

R.J.W. Jefferson and E.C.D. Hunter. *Published Material from the Genizah Collections. A bibliography 1980–1997* (Cambridge, 2004)

G. Khan, *Arabic Legal and Administrative Documents in the Cambridge Genizah Collections* (Cambridge, 1993)

A. Munzavi, *Fihrist-i nuskhahā-yi khaṭṭi-i fārsī ( Index of Manuscripts in Persian Script)*, 6 vols. (Tehran, 1969–)

W. Pertsch, *Verzeichnis der persischen Handschriften der königlichen Bibliothek zu Berlin*, 10 vols. (Berlin, 1888)

—— *Verzeichnis der türkischen Handschriften der königlichen Bibliothek zu Berlin* (Berlin, 1889)
The two works by Pertsch were models in the same way as the work of Ahlwardt.

C. Rieu, *Supplement to the Catalogue of the Arabic Manuscripts in the British Museum* (London, 1894)

F. Sezgin, *Beiträge zur Erschliessung der arabischen Handschriften in Istanbul und Anatolien*, 4 vols. (Frankfurt am Main, 1986)
A useful tool giving a description of some of the lamentably little-known riches of the Turkish libraries.

Türkiye Cumhuriyeti Kultur ve Turizm Bakanliği, Kütübhaneler Genel Müdürlügü, *Türkiye yazmaları toplu katalogu ( The Collected Catalogue of Turkish Manuscripts)*, 11 vols. (several publishers, 1979–)

G. Vajda, *Répertoire des catalogues et inventaires de manuscripts arabes* (Paris, 1949)

## Select List of Historical Surveys

*General Histories of the Islamic World*

E. Ashtor, *A Social and Economic History of the Near East in the Middle Ages* (London, 1976)

M.G.S. Hodgson, *The Venture of Islam*, 3 vols. (Chicago, 1974)

H. Kennedy, *The Prophet and the Age of the Caliphates: the Islamic Near East from the sixth to the eleventh century* (London and New York, 1986)
For the timeframe of the PBW project, this book is particularly helpful in its unusually detailed coverage of the eleventh century.

*Studies of Particular Areas of the Islamic World*

*(i) Syria and Palestine*

T. Bianquis, *Damas et la Syrie sous la domination fatimide 359–468/969–1076* (Damascus, 1986)

M. Canard, *Histoire de la dynastie des H'amdanides de Jazira et de Syrie*, vol. 1 (Paris, 1953)

A.-M. Eddé, *La principauté ayyoubide d'Alep (579/1183–658/1260)* (Stuttgart, 1999)
An exemplary study, based on a wide array of Arabic sources.

M. Gil, *A History of Palestine, 634–1099* (Cambridge, 1992)
Contains a great quantity of useful information but is somewhat dense to read.

R.S. Humphreys, *From Saladin to the Mongols* (Albany, NY, 1977)
The classic work on the Ayyubid family dynasty.

J.-M. Mouton, *Damas et sa principauté sous les Saljoukides et les Bourides 468–549/1076–1154* (Cairo, 1994)

A. Sevim, *Süriye-Filistin Selçuklu devleti tarihi (The History of the Syrian-Palestinian Seljuq State)* (Ankara, 1989)

M. Yared-Riachi, *La politique extérieure de la principauté de Damas 468–549AH/1076–1154* (Damascus, 1997)

S. Zakkar, *The Emirate of Aleppo 1004–1094* (Beirut, 1971)

*(ii) Egypt*

M. Barrucand, ed., *L'Égypte fatimide, son art et son histoire. Actes du colloque de Paris (May 1998)* (Paris, 1999)

*The Cambridge History of Egypt*, ed. C.F. Petry, 2 vols. (Cambridge, 1998)
A fine volume of corporate scholarship.

F. Daftary, *The Ismāʿīlīs: their history and doctrines* (Cambridge, 1990)

S.D. Goitein, *A Mediterranean Society: the Jewish communities of the Arab world as portrayed in the documents of the Cairo Geniza*, 4 vols. (Berkeley, 1967–93)

H. Halm, *Die Kalifen von Kairo. Die Fatimiden in Ägypten 973–1074* (Munich, 2003)

Y. Lev, *State and Society in Fatimid Egypt* (Leiden, 1991)

J. Mann, *The Jews in Egypt and in Palestine under the Fatimid Caliphs: a contribution to their political and communal history based chiefly on Geniza material hitherto unpublished*, ed. S.D. Goitein, 2 vols. (New York, 1970)

A. Raymond, *Le Caire* (Paris, 1993)

A.F. Sayyid, *Les Fatimides en Égypte* (Cairo, 1992)

S.J. Staffa, *Conquest and Fusion: the social evolution of Cairo, A.D. 642–1850* (Leiden, 1977)

S. Stern, *Fatimid Decrees* (London, 1964)

F. Wüstenfeld, *Geschichte der Fatimiden-Chalifen. Nach arabischen Quellen* (Göttingen, 1881)

*(iii) Iraq and Iran*

C.E. Bosworth, 'The political and dynastic history of the Iranian world (AD 1000–1217)', in J.A. Boyle, ed., *The Cambridge History of Iran*, vol. 5, *The Saljuq and Mongol Periods* (Cambridge, 1968), 1–202

H. Busse, *Chalif und Grosskönig. Die Buyiden im Iraq (945–1055)* (Beirut, 1969)

C. Cahen, 'The Turkish invasion: the Selchükids', in K.M. Setton and M.W. Baldwin, eds., *A History of the Crusades* (Madison, Milwaukee and London, 1969), 135–76

H. Horst, *Die Staatsverwaltung der Grossseljuqen und Ḫorazmshahs (1038–1231). Eine Untersuchung nach Urkundenformularen der Zeit* (Wiesbaden, 1964)

C.L. Klausner, *The Seljuk Vezirate. A study of civil administration, 1055–1194* (Cambridge, Mass., 1973)

A.K.S. Lambton, 'The internal structure of the Saljuq empire', in J.A. Boyle, ed., *The Cambridge History of Iran*, vol. 5, *The Saljuq and Mongol Periods* (Cambridge, 1968), 203–82

B. Lewis, *The Assassins. A radical sect in Islam* (London, 1967)

R. Mottahadeh, *Loyalty and Leadership in an Early Islamic Society* (Princeton, 1980)

M. Hodgson, *The Order of Assassins* (The Hague, 1955)
The classic work on this important topic.

*(iv) Turkey*

C. Cahen, *Pre-Ottoman Turkey*, trans. J. Jones-Williams (London, 1968); new revised French edn., *La Turquie pré-ottomane* (Istanbul and Paris, 1988); new tr., P.M. Holt, *The Formation of Turkey* (London, 2001)
Cahen updated the French revised edition which he provided with fuller annotation. He himself criticised the somewhat hurried 1968 edition.

I. Kafesoğlu, *A History of the Seljuks*, ed. and tr. G. Leiser (Carbondale and Edwardsville, 1988)
A study by one of the best, if not the best, of the Turkish historians who worked on the pre-Ottoman period in Anatolia.

M.F. Köprülü, *The Seljuks of Anatolia. Their history and culture according to local Muslim sources*, ed. and tr. by G. Leiser (Salt Lake City, 1992)
—— *Islam in Anatolia after the Turkish Invasion (Prolegomena)*, ed. and tr. G. Leiser (Salt Lake City, 1993)

A. Sevim, and E. Merçil, *Selçuklu devletleri tarihi (The History of the Seljuq States)* (Ankara, 1995)

O. Turan, *Doğu Anadolu Türk devletleri Tarihi (The History of Eastern Anatolian Turkish States)* (Istanbul, 1973)

*(v) Byzantium: Muslim viewpoints*

N.M. El-Cheikh, 'Byzantium through the Islamic prism from the twelfth to the thirteenth century', in A.E. Laiou and R. Mottahedeh, eds., *The Crusades from the Perspective of Byzantium and the Muslim World* (Washington, DC, 2001), 53–70
—— 'Byzantium viewed by the Arabs', unpublished Ph.D. thesis (Harvard, 1992)

W. Felix, *Byzanz und die islamische Welt im frühen 11. Jahrhundert* (Vienna, 1981)

M. Marin, 'Constantinopla en los geografos arabes', *Erytheia* 9.1 (1988), 49–60
—— 'Rūm in the works of three Spanish Muslim geographers', *Graeco-Arabica* 3 (1984), 109–17

*(vi) The Crusades: Islamic aspects*

L. Atrache, *Die Politik der Ayyubiden* (Münster, 1996)
C. Cahen, *La Syrie du nord à l'époque des croisades et la principauté franque d'Antioche* (Paris, 1940)
C. Hillenbrand, *The Crusades: Islamic perspectives* (Edinburgh, 1999)
P.M. Holt, *The Age of the Crusades* (London, 1986)
M.A. Köhler, *Allianzen und Verträge zwischen frankischen und islamischen Herrschern im Vorderen Orient* (Berlin and New York, 1991)
A. Nasrallah, *The Enemy Perceived: Christian and Muslim views of each other during the crusades* (New York, 1980)
E. Sivan, *L'Islam et la croisade* (Paris, 1968)
W.B. Stevenson, *The Crusaders in the East* (Cambridge, 1907)

*(vii) Christian Arabic sources*

J. Assfalg, 'Nichtislamische religiöse Litteratur in arabischer Sprache; christliche Litteratur', in H. Gätje, ed., *Grundriss der arabischen Philologie*, vol. 2 (Wiesbaden, 1987), 384–92.
G. Graf, *Geschichte der christlichen arabischen Litteratur* (Vatican City, 1947)
J. Nasrallah, *Histoire du mouvement littéraire dans l'Église melchite du V<sup>e</sup> au XX<sup>e</sup> siècle* (Louvain, 1988)
G. Troupeau, *Études sur le christianisme arabe au Moyen Âge* (London, 1995)

## PRIMARY SOURCES

Sources are arranged in chronological order according to the death date of the author.

### Histories: Select Muslim Primary Sources in Arabic

al-Musabbiḥī, 'Izz al-Mulk (d. 1030), *Akhbār Miṣr (Accounts of Egypt)*
An Egyptian chronicler who served in the Fatimid administration. A prolific writer, but almost all his works are no longer extant (perhaps destroyed during the more militant phase of the reign of al-Ḥākim). Generally regarded as a Sunni who worked for the Ismāʿīlī Fatimids, it has recently been suggested by Daftary that al-Musabbiḥī may have been an Ismāʿīlī himself.

Only the fortieth chapter of his vast history of Fatimid Egypt has survived, preserved in a single Escorial manuscript—this covers a few months of the year 414/1023–4 and most of the year 415/1024–5. al-Musabbiḥī wrote on an annalistic basis but he sub-divided each year into months. At the end of each year he assembled obituaries of those who had died in that year. This short extant part of an enormous and detailed work, reputed to have been written in forty volumes, demonstrates the serious loss to Fatimid historiography of the rest of the chronicle.

*Edition:*

A.F. Sayyid and T. Bianquis, *al-Musabbiḥī. al-juz' al-arba'ūn min Akhbār Miṣr (The Fortieth Part of the Accounts of Egypt)*, 2 vols. (Cairo, 1978)

*Secondary Literature:*

T. Bianquis, *Damas et la Syrie sous la domination fatimide* (Damascus, 1989), vol. 2, 393–4

——'al-Musabbiḥī', in *Encyclopaedia of Islam* (2nd edn.), vol. 7, 650–2

F. Daftary, *Ismaili Literature* (London, 2004), 23

## Miskawayh, Abū 'Alī (d. 1030), *Tajārib al-umam (The Experiences of Nations)*

A very important writer, a rare combination of historian and philosopher as well as bureaucrat and librarian. He often wrote in the first person and he could criticise his sources.

His *Universal History* covers the period from the Flood to the year 980. It is mentioned here, although it is outside the period of the PBW project, because of its unusual methodology and viewpoints.

*Partial Edition:*

L. Caetani (Leiden, 1909–17), 2 vols.

*Partial Edition and Translation:*

H.F. Amedroz and D.S. Margoliouth, *The Eclipse of the Abbasid Caliphate: original chronicles of the fourth century* (Oxford, 1920–1)

*Secondary Literature:*

M. Arkoun, *Contribution à l'humanisme arabe au iv<sup>e</sup>/x<sup>e</sup> siècle: Miskawayh, philosophe et historien* (Paris, 1970, 1982)

J. Kraemer, *Humanism in the Renaissance of Islam: the cultural revival during the Buyid age* (Leiden, 1993)

## Ibn al-Qalānisī, Abū Ya'lā (d. 1160), *Dhayl ta'rīkh Dimashq (Supplement to the History of Damascus)*

This is an extremely important source. The early part of the work, which begins in 363/973, contains extracts from the non-extant history of Baghdad by Hilāl al-Ṣābi'. The work of Ibn al-Qalānisī himself gives an account of events from 1056–1160. The work is particularly valuable for the 12th c. in Syria and its entries are of increasing length from the year 497/1103–4 onwards. The chronicle gives a very lively account of political and social events from the viewpoint of Damascus and extends its remit to include narratives about central Syria, Palestine and, occasionally, beyond, to Cairo and Baghdad. It is the oldest extant Arabic source for the events of the First and Second Crusades and it contains an eye-witness account of the siege of Damascus in 1148. It is a rigidly annalistic chronicle and the author deals with episodes which occur over two years in two parts, one in each year.

The opening pages of the work are missing. The first part of the work is based on earlier sources and especially Hilāl al-Ṣābi'. In the second part of the work, the author, who lived until his nineties, draws on eye-witness accounts, as well as archival material to which he had access in his administrative career (he was twice mayor of Damascus, the last period being in 548/1153). The work reveals a strong sense of regional pride.

*Editions:*
The text has two good editions:
1. H.F. Amedroz (Leiden, 1908)
2. S. Zakkar (Damascus, 1983)

*Translations:*
There are two good partial translations of this work:
1. H.A.R. Gibb, *The Damascus Chronicle of the Crusades* (London, 1932; 1967)
   This translation omits all passages to do with internal Damascene affairs.
2. R. Le Tourneau, *Damas de 1075 à 1154* (Damascus, 1952)
   This translation for the years 1075 to 1154 covers all the narratives within this period, including those omitted by Gibb.

*Secondary Literature:*
H.A.R. Gibb, *The Damascus Chronicle*, introduction, 7–14
C. Cahen, 'Note d'historiographie syrienne. La première partie de l'histoire d'Ibn al-Qalānisī', in G. Makdisi, ed., *Arabic and Islamic Studies in Honor of Hamilton A.R. Gibb* (Cambridge, Mass., 1965), 156–68
F. Gabrieli, 'The Arabic historiography of the crusades', in Lewis and Holt, eds., *Historians of the Middle East*, 102–3

## al-ʿAẓīmī, Muḥammad b. ʿAlī (born 1090 and died after 1161), *Taʾrīkh (History)*

A still rather neglected chronicler. Only one of his two known works is extant—a world history until 538/1143–4. The work contains laconic but important accounts, seen from the viewpoint of Aleppo, about events in the late 11th c. and the first half of the 12th c., and includes occasional references to Anatolia; it is interesting on the period immediately preceding the coming of the Franks.

*Editions:*
1. C. Cahen, 'La chronique abrégée d'al-ʿAẓīmī', *Journal asiatique* 230 (1938), 335–448
   Cahen begins his edition with the entry of the nomadic Turks into Syria. He includes the years 455/1063 to 538/1143–4.
2. I. Zaʿrur, *Taʾrīkh Ḥalab (The History of Aleppo)* (Damascus, 1984)

*Secondary Literature:*
C. Cahen, *La Syrie du nord à l'époque des croisades* (Paris, 1940), 42–3
Cahen's edition of the text, 354–6

## Ibn al-Azraq al-Fāriqī, Aḥmad b. Yūsuf (d. after 572/1176–7), *Taʾrīkh Mayyāfāriqīn wa-Āmid (The History of Mayyāfāriqīn and Āmid)*

The author was employed in the service of Temurtash, the second Artukid ruler of Mayyafariqin, and he held various administrative offices in that city. He also visited Tiflis and worked for a while for the Georgian king, Dimitri. This town chronicle contains valuable information for the 12th c. on the Turcoman Artukid dynasty which ruled Mayyafariqin and Mardin. Despite its local focus, it has a surprisingly wide coverage, with excurses on the Fatimids and the Almohads, and a few references to Byzantium. Its structure is annalistic, but the text presents at times a disordered narrative, uneven and unco-ordinated, with very inaccurate dating. Nevertheless, it is a useful source for events in northern Syria and the Jazira in the period 1100–50 and was used extensively by later chroniclers.

*Editions:*
1. B.A.L. ʿAwad, *Taʾrīkh al-Fāriqī (The History of al-Fāriqī)* (Cairo, 1959)
   A good edition covering the years 347/958 to 502/1108–9.
2. A. Savran, 'A critical edition of the Artukid section in Taʾrīkh Mayyāfāriqīn wa-Āmid', unpublished Ph.D. thesis (St Andrews, 1975)
   Covers the period of the first three Artukid rulers—498/1104–5 to 572/1176–7.

*Edition and Translation:*
C. Hillenbrand, *A Muslim Principality in Crusader Times* (Leiden, 1990)
This is an edition and translation of the events of the years 498/1104–5 to 549/1154.

*Secondary Literature:*
H.F. Amedroz, 'The Marwānid dynasty at Mayyāfāriqīn in the tenth and eleventh centuries A.D.', *JRAS* (1903), 123–54
C. Hillenbrand, 'Marwānids', in *Encyclopaedia of Islam* (2nd edn.), vol. 7, 626–7
———*A Muslim Principality*, 5–14

Ibn al-Jawzī, ʿAbd al-Raḥmān (d. 1200), *al-Muntaẓam fī taʾrīkh al-mulūk waʾl-umam (Systematic Arrangement in the History of Kings and Nations)*
A Baghdad Ḥanbalite scholar, preacher and prolific writer. The *Muntaẓam* is a chronicle which in many ways resembles a biographical dictionary; it provides obituaries, mostly of scholars, under each year. These often occupy much more space than that given to political events. The chronicle is a rich source for the history of the caliphate, covering the years 971 to 1179, but it is less wide-ranging in its focus than the history written by his grandson, Sibṭ b. al-Jawzī.

*Editions:*
1. F. Krenkow (Hyderabad, 1938–40)
2. M.A. Ata and others (Beirut, 1992–3)
   This is a better edition.

*Secondary Literature:*
H. Laoust, 'Ibn al-Djawzī', in *Encyclopaedia of Islam* (2nd edn.), vol. 3, 751–2

ʿImād al-Dīn al-Iṣfahānī, Muḥammad (d. 1201) *Kitāb al-Fatḥ al-qussī fiʾl fatḥ al-qudsī (The Book of Eloquent Rhetoric in the Conquest of Jerusalem)*
This famous Persian scholar, poet and historian worked for the Seljuks, before moving to Syria where he was in the service first of Nūr al-Dīn and then Saladin, for whom he acted as scribe and close adviser.

This important work begins with Saladin's conquest of Jerusalem in 1187 and ends with his death in 1193. It follows an annalistic arrangement.

*Editions:*
1. C. Landberg (Leiden, 1888)
2. M.M. Subh (Cairo, *c.*1975)

*Translation:*
H. Massé, *Conquête de la Syrie et de la Palestine par Saladin* (Paris, 1972)

'Imād al-Dīn al-Iṣfahānī, *Nuṣrat al-fatra (Help for Lassitude)*
The earliest extant history of the Seljuks completed in 1183 for Saladin. The work is
based on the lost Persian memoirs of the 12th-c. Seljuk vizier, Anūshirwān b. Khālid
(died in the 1130s).
It is still only in unpublished manuscript form (Bibliothèque nationale, Paris, ms.
arabe 2145). The work was summarised by al-Bundārī (see below) who removed some
at least of the verbal conceits of the original text. The title is a pun on the word *fatra*
which means both lassitude and a period of time.

*Secondary Literature:*
D. Little, 'Historiography', in *The Cambridge History of Egypt* (Cambridge, 1998),
vol. 1, 416–17
D.S. Richards, ''Imād al-Dīn al-Iṣfahānī: administrator, littérateur and historian', in
M. Shatzmiller, ed., *Crusaders and Muslims in Twelfth-century Syria* (Leiden,
1993), 133–46
L. Richter-Bernburg, 'Observations on 'Imād al-Dīn al-Iṣfahānī's al-Fatḥ al-Qussī
fi'l-fatḥ al-Qudsī', in W. al-Qadi, ed., *Studia Arabica and Islamica. Festschrift for
Ihsan 'Abbas* (Beirut, 1981), 373–9
—— 'Funken aus dem kalten Flint: 'Imād al-Dīn al-Kātib al-Iṣfahānī (I–II)', *Welt des
Orients* 20–1 (1989–90), 121–66; 22 (1991), 105–41
—— *Der syrische Blitz. Saladins Sekretär zwischen Selbstdarstellung und
Geschichtsschreibung* (Beirut, 1998), 176–89

Ibn Ẓāfir al-Azdī, Jamāl al-Dīn (d. 1216 or 1226), *Kitāb al-Duwal
al-munqaṭi'a (The Book of Discontinued Dynasties)*
The most important section of this work concerns the Fatimids. The author, based in
Egypt and a scribe in the chancery of the early Ayyubids, writes his chronicle
according to dynasty. Most of the work remains unpublished.

*Edition:*
A. Ferré (Cairo, 1972)
Fatimid section.

*Secondary Literature:*
C. Cahen, 'Quelques chroniques anciennes relatives aux derniers Fatimides', *BIFAO*
38 (1937), 2ff.

Ibn al-Ṭuwayr, Abū Muḥammad (d. 1220), *Nuzhat al-muqlatayn fī akhbār
al-dawlatayn (The Entertainment of the Eyes in the Accounts of the Two
Dynasties)*
This work by an Egyptian high official is an account of the Fatimid and Ayyubid
dynasties in Saladin's time. A useful source for Ibn al-Furāt, al-Maqrīzī, Ibn
Taghribirdī and other Mamluk historians and for general institutions.

*Edition:*
A.F. Sayyid (Beirut and Stuttgart, 1992).

*Secondary Literature:*
C. Cahen, 'Quelques chroniques anciennes relatives aux derniers Fatimides', *BIFAO*
38 (1937), 10–14,16, n.1

al-Ḥusaynī, Ṣadr al-Dīn (d. ?1220s), *Akhbār al-dawla al-Saljūqiyya (The Accounts of the Seljuk State)*, also called *Zubdat al-tawārīkh (The Cream of Histories)*

There is scholarly debate over the authorship of this work or indeed its real title. al-Ḥusaynī is still cited tentatively as its author in scholarly literature, in the absence of any clear alternatives.

This dynastic history of the Seljuks from the extreme east of the Islamic world is a rather under-used work. It is full of valuable information gleaned from a wide variety of sources. It covers the history of the Seljuks from their semi-legendary origins until the end of the dynasty in 1193. The text continues thereafter until 622/1225 but this last section is likely to have been added by another author. This chronicle, drawing on lost works, from the Baghdad historiographical 'school' of late Buyid and early Seljuk times, and others, is especially useful for the history of the 11th c., so depleted of surviving sources.

*Edition:*
M. Iqbal (Lahore, 1933; repr. Beirut, 1984)
    A poor edition with many dubious readings of this difficult text.

*Unpublished Translation:*
Q. Ayaz, 'An unexploited source for the history of the Saljuqs: a translation and critical commentary', unpublished Ph.D. thesis (Edinburgh, 1985)

*Secondary Literature:*
C. Cahen, 'Historiography of the Seljuqid period', in Lewis and Holt, eds., *Historians of the Middle East*, 69–72

al-Bundārī, Fatḥ b. ʿAlī (d. after 1226), *Zubdat al-nuṣra wa nukhbat al-ʿuṣra (The Choicest Part of Help and the Pick of the Age)*

Little is known about this Arabic chronicler, who originated in Iran but moved to Syria. He probably worked for an Ayyubid ruler of Syria, al-Muʿaẓẓam ʿĪsā, to whom he dedicated this dynastic history of the Seljuks, begun in 1226. The work, which is an accurate summary of the *Nuṣrat al-fatra*, aims to prune down and simplify the ornate style of his predecessor, ʿImād al-Dīn al-Iṣfahānī.

*Edition:*
M.T. Houtsma, *Recueil de textes relatifs à l'histoire des Seljoucides*, vol. 2 (Leiden, 1889)

al-Bundārī, *Sanā al-barq al-shāmī (The Radiance of the Syrian Lightning)*

An abridgement of the work entitled *al-Barq al-shāmī* of ʿImād al-Dīn al-Iṣfahānī: see below under Autobiographies, p. 334.

*Editions:*
1. R Şeşen (Beirut, 1971)
2. F. al-Nabarawi (Cairo, 1979)

Ibn al-Athīr, ʿIzz al-Dīn ʿAlī (d. 1233), *al-Kāmil fi'l ta'rīkh (The Complete in History)*

This is a *Universal History* and the key Arabic chronicle for the period 1024–1204. For his time, its author has the instincts of a true historian. The work covers world history from the Creation until 628/1230–1. Its geographical scope is unusually wide, embracing the Muslim world from Spain to Central Asia, but information is fullest on the central lands of Egypt, Syria and Iraq. It is arranged annalistically but not too mechanistically so and the author gives excurses on various important topics, such as the rise of the Turks or the Assassins in a more overarching way. He is capable of interpreting events as well as recording them. He makes a synthesis of the data from his sources, although he rarely cites their names. Occasionally he devotes his attention to Byzantine matters; he includes, for example, a report on the events of 1204.

*Edition:*
1. C.J. Tornberg, 12 vols. (Leiden and Uppsala, 1851–76; corrected repr., 13 vols., Beirut, 1965–7)
   The classic edition. Vol. 13 of the reprint contains only indices.

*Edition and Translation:*
*RHC: historiens orientaux,* vol. 1 (Paris, 1872), 189–714 (covers the activities of the Franks during the years 491/1098 to 585/1189–90); vol. 2 (Paris, 1887), 3–180 (covers the activities of the Franks during the years 585/1189–90 to 628/1230–1)
   The edition is unreliable, as usual with the *Recueil.* Mistakes of translation are therefore inevitable; moreover, the translation sometimes reads like a paraphrase.

*Translation:*
D.S. Richards, *The Annals of the Seljuq Turks* (London, 2002)
   Translates a crucial section of this work, which concerns the history of the Seljuk Turks from 420/1029 to 490/1096–7. This translation is reliable and scholarly and should be used, wherever possible, in preference to the French translation of comparable passages in the *Recueil des historiens des croisades.*

*Secondary Literature:*
D.S. Richards, *Annals,* 1–8
—— 'Ibn al-Athīr and the later parts of the *Kāmil*: a study of aims and methods', in D.O. Morgan, ed., *Medieval Historical Writing in the Christian and Islamic Worlds* (London, 1982), 76–108

Ibn al-Athīr (d. 1233), *Ta'rīkh al-bāhir fi'l-dawlat al-atābakiyya (The Brilliant History about the Atabeg State)*
This is a full but highly partisan dynastic history of the Zengids. The author reveals on occasion a bias against Saladin and his family. The work was written as an exemplary history, a kind of *Mirror for Princes,* for al-Qāhir b. Nūr al-Dīn Arslān (d. 615/1218).

*Edition and Translation:*
*RHC: historiens orientaux,* vol. 2, 5–375
   Here erroneously called *Ta'rīkh al-dawlat al-atābakiyya mulūk al-Mawṣil (The History of the Atabeg State, the Princes of Mosul).* After a lengthy panegyrical introduction, the work covers the years 477/1084–5 to 608/1211–12.

*Edition:*
A.A. Tulaymat, *al-Ta'rīkh al-bāhir fi'l dawlat al-atābakiyya (The Brilliant History about the Atabeg State)* (Cairo, 1963)
   This reliable edition covers the years 521/1127 to 608/1211–12. The title given here is the one mentioned by the author himself in his *Universal History,* discussed above.

*Secondary Literature:*
D.S. Richards, 'Ibn al-Athīr and the later parts of the *Kāmil*', 78–9, 85

Sibṭ b. al-Jawzī, Yūsuf Qizoğlu (d. 1256), *Mi'rāt al-zamān fī ta'rīkh al-a'yān* *(The Mirror of the Time in the History of Famous Men)*
This Ayyubid historian was the grandson of the famous Baghdad Ḥanbalite scholar Ibn al-Jawzī on his mother's side. At the beginning of the 13th c. he moved from Baghdad to Damascus and worked for a number of Ayyubid rulers there. His immense *Universal History*, modelled on the work of his grandfather, the *Kitāb al-Muntaẓam*, is a very important text. It begins with the Creation and stops in the year of the author's death. Important events are recorded for each year, and are then followed by short obituary notices of notables who have died in that year. Until the beginning of the 13th c., the work conforms to the model of a universal chronicle with a comprehensive approach to the Islamic world. Its coverage of events in the 13th c. is focused on Damascus and is an invaluable source, drawn on by many subsequent Syrian chroniclers.

This source is particularly valuable for the 11th c. since it cites, at length but uncritically, sources such as the lost history of the Baghdad historian, Hilāl al-Ṣābi', and the work of his son Ghars al-Ni'ma. For example, the *Mir'āt* contains a very full description of the battle of Mantzikert.

*Editions:*
The editions of this text are at best only mediocre.
1. A. Sevim (Ankara, 1968)
   Partial edition. It selects events about the Seljuks and concerns the years 448/1056–7 to 480/1087–8.
2. J.R. Jewett (Chicago, 1907)
   This facsimile edition covers the years 495/1101 to 654/1256. Jewett used a faulty manuscript and its pages are badly arranged.
3. Printed edition of the Jewett text, editor unidentified, 1 vol. in 2 parts (Hyderabad, Deccan, 1951–2)

*Edition and Translation:*
*RHC: historiens orientaux*, vol. 3, 517–70
   Extracts concerning the Franks from the year 490/1097 to 532/1137–8.

*Secondary Literature:*
M. Ahmad and M. Hilmy, 'Some notes on Arabic historiography during the Zengid and Ayyubid periods', in Lewis and Holt, eds., *Historians of the Middle East*, 91–2
C. Cahen, 'Editing Arabic chronicles: a few suggestions', in *Les peuples musulmans dans l'histoire médiévale* (Damascus, 1977), 11–36
—— 'The historiography of the Seljuqid period', in Lewis and Holt, eds., *Historians of the Middle* East, 60–1

Ibn al-'Adīm, Kamāl al-Dīn (d. 1262), *Zubdat al-ḥalab fī ta'rīkh Ḥalab* *(The Cream of the Milk in the History of Aleppo)*
A concise local history of Aleppo written by a member of an élite family in the city who served in various important positions there, including scribe, judge, and chief minister to two Ayyubid rulers. The chronicle gives a clear exposition of events from the viewpoint of Aleppo, often without citing the author's sources. The work is a

chronicle of Aleppo from the early Islamic period until 1243 and is organised according to dynasty and ruler or governor.

*Editions:*
1. S. Dahan, 3 vols. (Damascus, 1951–68)
2. S. Zakkar (Damascus, 1997)

*Translations:*
1. *RHC: historiens orientaux,* vol. 3, 577–690
   The extracts translated cover the years 1097–1146.
2. E. Blochet, *ROL* (1896–8)
   Blochet translates extracts from the chronicle. The poor quality of his translation has always been criticised.

*Secondary Literature:*
S. Dahan, in Lewis and Holt, eds., *Historians of the Middle East,* 111–13

Ibn Muyassar, Tāj al-Dīn (d. 1278), *Akhbār Miṣr (The Accounts of Egypt)*
The Egyptian continuator of al-Musabbiḥī (d. 1030). This is the most important work on the late Fatimids, containing much original information.

*Editions:*
1. H. Massé (Cairo, 1919)
   This covers the years 1047–1158, with a lacuna for the years 502/1108–9 to 514/1120–1. Fortunately, the later chronicler, al-Nuwayrī, borrows from the work of Ibn Muyassar and fills these missing years.
2. A.F. Sayyid (Cairo, 1981)
   Here other lost sections have been partially reconstructed from later quotations.

*Translation:*
*RHC: historiens orientaux*, vol. 3, 461–73

*Secondary Literature:*
C. Cahen, 'Quelques chroniques anciennes relatives aux derniers Fatimides', *BIFAO* 38 (1937), 1–27

Ibn Wāṣil, Jamāl al-Dīn (d. 1298), *Mufarrij al-kurūb fī akhbār Banī Ayyūb (The Dispeller of Anxieties about the Accounts of the Ayyūbid Family)*
The key source for the Ayyubid period (1171–1250). It is untranslated and still relatively unexploited. Despite the existence of four good manuscripts of this text, it was unfortunately left out of the *Recueil des historiens des croisades*. The author was educated in Syria but was sometimes resident in Egypt where he had access to the Ayyubid and Mamluk courts. The work, covering Egypt and Syria in Zengid and Ayyubid times, begins with Saladin's father, Ayyūb, and his brother Shīrkūh, and then it goes further back to give an account of the Zengids. However, the work is primarily an idealised dynastic history of the Ayyubids until 645/1247–8. For earlier periods it leans on previous histories, such as the works of Abū Shāma and Ibn al-Athīr; for his own time his work is invaluable.

*Edition:*
J. al-Shayyal, vols. 1–3 (Cairo, 1953–60); S.A.F. Ashur and H. Rabie, vols. 4–5 (Cairo, 1972)
   Good clear editions.

*Secondary Literature:*
R.S. Humphreys, *From Saladin to the Mongols: the Ayyubids of Damascus, 1193–1260* (Albany, 1977)
C. Cahen, *La Syrie du nord* (Paris, 1940), 70

Ibn Wāṣil, Jamāl al-Dīn, *Ta'rīkh al-Ṣāliḥī (The Ṣāliḥī History)*
An abridged general history of the Islamic world from the age of the Prophet to the year 637/1240. It is dedicated to the Ayyubid ruler, al-Malik al-Ṣāliḥ Najm al-Dīn. Still only in manuscript.

Abu'l Fidā', Ismā'īl (d. 1331), *al-Mukhtaṣar fī akhbār al-bashar (The Abridged Work on the Accounts of Mankind)*
This chronicle, written by an Ayyubid prince of Hama in Syria, a chronicler, geographer and man of letters, covers the history of the Islamic world from the rise of Islam until 1329. This compilation is heavily dependent on Ibn al-Athīr but is a useful summary of events. The work has been known in the west for a long time and was translated into Latin as early as 1754. Because of this, it was always the first port of call for historians to use, until the publication of the work of Ibn al-Athīr.

*Editions:*
1. J.J. Reiske and J.G.C. Adler, *Annales moslemici* (Leipzig, 1754 and Copenhagen, 1789–94)
2. The first complete text was edited in Istanbul, 2 vols. (1869–70)
3. 4 vols., editor unidentified (Cairo, 1914)

*Edition and Translation:*
*RHC: historiens orientaux*, vol. 1, 1–165
This translation covers the years 485/1092–3 to 702/1302–3.

al-Nuwayrī, Shihāb al-Dīn (d. 1333), *Nihāyat al-arab fī funūn al-adab (The Attaining of the Goal in the Arts of Culture)*
An Egyptian administrator and encyclopaedist, who wrote a vast and ambitious work of nine thousand pages in thirty-one volumes. The last of the five sections of the work concerns history; it is arranged chronologically, beginning with the Creation and reaching the year 1331. It is very focused and well-structured and not slavishly wedded to the annalistic format. The Fatimid volume has been published and is a very important source, containing extracts from a number of lost sources.

*Edition:*
Volumes 1–25 and 28 have been published, edited by various scholars (Cairo, 1923–92). The Fatimid period is covered in vol. 28, ed. M.M. Amin, M. Hilmi and M. Ahmad (Cairo, 1992).

*Secondary Literature:*
D. Little, 'Historiography', in *The Cambridge History of Egypt* (Cambridge, 1998), vol. 1, 430
M. Chapoutot-Remadi, 'al-Nuwayrī', in *Encyclopaedia of Islam* (2nd edn.), vol. 8, 156–60

Ibn al-Dawādārī, Sayf al-Dīn (d. after 1335), *Kanz al-durar wa jāmiʿ al-ghurar (The Treasure of Pearls and the Collection of Shining Objects)*
A bureaucrat from a Mamluk family in Egypt, Ibn al-Dawādārī wrote an annalistic *Universal History* up to the year 1335. The *Kanz al-durar* is an abridgement of an even longer chronicle. The section on the Fatimids has valuable information in it.

*Editions:*
Part 6, entitled *al-Durra al-māḍiya fī akhbār al-dawla al-fāṭimiyya (The Past Pearl in the Accounts of the Fatimid State)*, ed. S. al-Munajjid, *Die Chronik des Ibn ad-Dawadari* (Cairo, 1961)
Part 7, entitled *al-Durr al-maṭlūb fī akhbār mulūk Banī Ayyūb (The Desired Pearls in the Accounts of the Princes of the Ayyubid Family)* ed. S.A.F. Ashur (Cairo, 1972)

*Secondary Literature:*
B. Lewis, 'Ibn al-Dawādārī', in *Encyclopaedia of Islam* (2nd edn.), vol. 3, 744
D. Little, 'Historiography', in *The Cambridge History of Egypt* (Cambridge, 1998), vol. 1, 424–5

Ibn Kathīr, ʿImād al-Dīn (d. 1373), *al-Bidāya waʾl nihāya fiʾl taʾrīkh (The Beginning and the End in History)*
This is a universal 'salvation' history written from the Creation to his own time and, unusually, beyond that, to include predictions about the end of the world. The work is focused on Damascus and includes valuable information on that city.

*Editions:*
14 vols. (Cairo, 1932–9; repr. Beirut, 1932–77)

*Secondary Literature:*
H. Laoust, 'Ibn Katīr historien', *Arabica* 2 (1955), 42–88

Ibn al-Furāt, Nāṣir al-Dīn Muḥammad (d. 1405), *Taʾrīkh al-duwal waʾl mulūk (The History of States and Kings)*
An Egyptian chronicler who wrote this enormous *Universal History* in draft. He then revised and completed twenty volumes which deal with the twelfth, thirteenth and fourteenth centuries. The work begins in 501/1107–8. This is an important source because it draws on lost chronicles, such as the history of Aleppo by the Shiʿite historian, Ibn Abī Ṭayyiʾ (d. *c.* 630/1232). The majority of the extant volumes concern the twelfth and thirteenth centuries.

*Manuscript:*
The major manuscript of the text is in the Österreichische Nationalbibliothek, Vienna, MS. A.F. 118 (Flügel 814, II).

*Editions:*
H. al-Shamma, vol. 4, pts. 1–2 (Basra, 1967–9)
    For the period of the project, only this volume has been edited, covering the years 563/1167 to 615/1218.

The Vienna manuscript has been the subject of several doctoral theses, which have involved critical editions of varying quality, but these remain unpublished. The best is:

M.F. Elshayyal, 'A critical edition of volume II of *Taʾrīkh al-duwal waʾl-mulūk* by Muḥammad b. ʿAbd al-Raḥīm b. ʿAlī Ibn al-Furāt', unpublished Ph.D. thesis (Edinburgh, 1986)

This includes an edition of vol. 2, which covers the years 522/1128 to 543/1148–9 and gives a summary of major events.

*Secondary Literature:*
U. and M.C. Lyons, *Ayyubids, Mamlukes and Crusaders* (Cambridge, 1971), vol. 2, vii–xi
C. Cahen, 'Ibn al-Furāt', in *Encyclopaedia of Islam* (2nd edn.), vol. 3, 768–9

al-Maqrīzī, Taqī al-Dīn (d. 1442), *Itti'āẓ al-ḥunafā' bi-akhbār al-a'imma al-fāṭimiyyīn al-khulafā' (Warning of the Pious about the News of the Fatimid Imam Caliphs)*
Perhaps the most important and versatile of the Mamluk polymaths, al-Maqrīzī wrote on a wide range of historical topics, focusing on Egypt. This chronicle, which preserves material from such lost sources as al-Musabbiḥī, Ibn al-Ma'mūn and Ibn al-Ṭuwayr, is the only separate history of the Fatimids composed by a Sunni writer. It remains untranslated.

*Edition:*
J. al-Shayyal, vol. 1 (Cairo, 1967)
M.H.M. Ahmad, vols. 2–3 (Cairo, 1971–3)
*Secondary Literature:*
D. Little, 'Historiography of the Ayyūbid and Mamlūk epochs', in *The Cambridge History of Egypt* (Cambridge, 1998), 436–7

al-Maqrīzī, *Kitāb al-Sulūk li-ma'rifat duwal al-mulūk (The Book of Access to the Knowledge of the Dynasties of Kings)*
This chronicle, which covers the history of the Ayyubids and the Mamluks, is a useful source for the project. It gives the history of Egypt from the accession of Saladin in 1169 until 1440–1.

*Editions:*
M.M. Ziyada and S.A.F. Ashur, 4 vols. (Cairo, 1934–73)
This is a good edition.

*Translations:*
1. E. Quatremère, *Histoire des sultans mamlouks de l'Égypte* (Paris, 1837–45)
   Quatremère's translation, which covers the Mamluk period and is therefore outside the remit of the project, is still worth studying because of its many valuable footnotes about earlier dynasties.
2. E. Blochet, *Histoire d'Égypte de Makrizi* (Paris, 1908)
   As usual, a translation to be treated with caution.
3. R.J.C. Broadhurst, *History of the Ayyubid Sultans* (Boston, 1980)
   A competent translation.

*Secondary Literature:*
D. Little, 'Historiography', in *The Cambridge History of Egypt* (Cambridge, 1998), vol. 1, 437

al-'Aynī, Badr al-Dīn (d. 1451), *'Iqd al-jumān fī ta'rīkh ahl al-zamān (The Necklace of Pearls in the History of the People of the Time)*
This major chronicle, written by a high-ranking Egyptian official, has still not yet been fully edited and evaluated. It is a vast, encyclopaedic work with quotations from

lost sources, such as Ibn Abī Ṭayyi' and others. The parts of the text that deal with the period of the project have not yet been edited and the translated excerpts in the *Recueil des historiens des croisades* lie outside the chosen timeframe. The edition of all this manuscript is a major desideratum.

*Secondary Literature:*
M. Quatremère, *Histoire des sultans mamlouks de l'Égypte* (Paris, 1837), 219–28

Ibn Taghribirdī, Abu'l Maḥāsin Yūsuf (d. 1470), *al-Nujūm al-ẓāhira fī mulūk Miṣr wa'l-Qāhira (The Brilliant Stars in the Kings of Egypt and Cairo)*
A general history of Egypt from the Arab conquest to 1467.

*Edition:*
Editor unidentified, 16 vols. (Cairo, 1929–72)

*Edition and Translation:*
RHC: historiens orientaux, vol. 3, 481–509
The translated extracts deal with the years 491/1098 to 552/1157.

*Secondary Literature:*
R.S. Humphreys, *Islamic Historiography*, 137–47
A. Darrag, 'La vie d'Abu'l-Maḥāsin Ibn Tagrībirdī et son oeuvre', *AI* 11 (1972), 163–81
W. Popper, 'Abu'l-Maḥāsin', in *Encyclopaedia of Islam* (2nd edn.), vol. 1, 138

al-ʿAsqalānī, Aḥmad b. Ibrāhīm (d. 1471), *Shifāʾ al-qulūb fī manāqib Banī Ayyūb (The Cure of the Hearts in the Glorious Deeds of the Ayyūbid Family)*
This is a dynastic history of the Ayyubids, organised on biographical lines. This scholar should not be confused with the more famous Ibn Ḥajar al-ʿAsqalānī. There is controversy over the authorship of this work.

*Manuscript:*
BM. Ms. Add. 7311

*Edition:*
Editor unidentified (Baghdad, 1978)

## Histories: Select Muslim Primary Sources in Persian

Nīshāpūrī, Ẓahīr al-Dīn (d. c.1186–7), *Saljūqnāma (The Book of the Seljuks)*
Little is known about Nīshāpūrī but he was probably employed as a tutor to a Seljuk prince or princes in the 1140s. His chronicle is the *Urtext* for most of the subsequent histories of the Seljuks written in Persian. It is a dynastic history of the Seljuks, completed sometime before 1186. The text is simple and lively with interesting depictions of the Seljuk sultans.

*Editions:*
1. I. Afshar (Tehran, 1954)
   In this edition Afshar wrongly published as the original *Saljūqnāma* of Nīshāpūrī a recension of the history of the Seljuks by Nīshāpūrī produced by a later Persian author, Qāshānī (early 14th c.). The edition is poorly produced.

2. A.H. Morton, *The Saljūqnāma of Ẓahīr al-Dīn Nīshāpūrī* (Chippenham, 2004)
This recent edition is based on the unique manuscript in the library of the Royal Asiatic Society in London. The edition is very good, with a meticulous scholarly apparatus. It is clear from this edition that the original version of the text was much less full and flowery than the version of it produced by Qāshānī. A more famous contemporary of Qāshānī, Rashīd al-Dīn (d. 1318), in the Seljuk sections of his *Universal History* (see p. 324 below) also draws on the history of Nīshāpūrī.

*Translation:*
The recension of Nīshāpūrī made by Rashīd al-Dīn was translated by K.A. Luther with an introduction by C.E. Bosworth as *The History of the Seljuq Turks, from the Jāmi' al-tawārīkh (an Ilkhānid adaptation of Ẓahīr al-Dīn Nīshāpūrī)* (London, 2001).

*Secondary Literature:*
J. Meisami, *Persian Historiography to the End of the Twelfth Century* (Edinburgh, 1999), 229–34
A.H. Morton, edition, 1–63

Rāwandī, Muḥammad b. 'Alī (d. early 13th c.), *Rāḥat al-ṣudūr wa-āyat al-surūr dar ta'rīkh-i āl-i Saljūq (The Ease for Breasts and the Marvel of Joy in the History of the Seljuk Family)*
Rāwandī was a Persian scholar, calligrapher and gilder from Rāwand near Kāshān. After the demise of the Seljuk dynasty in Iran at the end of the 12th c., he dedicated his work to the Seljuk sultan of Anatolia, Kay-Khusraw I. This work is a dynastic history of the Seljuks, with strong *Mirror for Princes* overtones, written in rhetorical style. The narrative is interspersed with proverbs and quotations from Arabic and Persian poetry and prose. The work's historical information is derived from the chronicle of Nīshāpūrī.

*Edition:*
M. Iqbal (London, 1921; repr. Tehran, 1985)
A reasonable edition.

*Secondary Literature:*
E.G. Browne, 'Account of a rare, if not unique, manuscript history of the Seljuqs', *JRAS* (1902), 567–610, 849–87
J. Meisami, *Persian Historiography* (Edinburgh, 1999), 237–56
C. Schefer, *Nouveaux mélanges orientaux* (Paris, 1886), 3–47

Ibn Bībī, al-Ḥusayn b. Muḥammad (d. after 1285), *al-Awāmir al-'Alā'iyya fi'l umūr al-'Alā'iyya ('Alā'id Commands about 'Alā'id Matters)*
Ibn Bībī was an important official working for the Seljuks of Rūm (Anatolia). The work was completed in 1281. It is a detailed memoir of the period 1190 to 1280 in Seljuk Anatolia, written in an ornate rhetorical style. The abstruse title may be interpreted as follows: the author was asked to write the work by 'Alā' al-Dīn Juwaynī and its subject was to be the achievements of the sultan, 'Alā' al-Dīn Kayqubād I, whose reign was the apogee of Seljuk rule in Anatolia.

*Edition:*
M.T. Houtsma, *Histoire des Seldjoucides d'Asie Mineure d'après Ibn Bībī; recueil de texts relatifs à l'histoire des Seldjoucides*, vol. 3 (Leiden, 1902)

*Translation:*
H.W. Duda, *Die Seltschukengeschichte des Ibn Bībī* (Copenhagen, 1959)
   A good German translation.

Rashīd al-Dīn, Faḍl Allāh (d. 1318), *Jāmiʿ al-tawārīkh (The Compendium of Histories)*
This famous doctor, scholar and government minister was a convert to Islam from Judaism. He served the Mongol ruler of Iran, Abaqa (ruled 1265–82), but he achieved his highest office in the reign of Ghazan (after 1298). His *Universal History* extends from the Creation until his own time. Though known principally in its Persian versions, it also existed early in an Arabic form.

*Edition:*
A. Ateş (Ankara, 1960; repr. Tehran, 1983)
   This edition covers the Ghaznavid and Seljuk periods.

Ḥamd Allāh, al-Mustawfī al-Qazwīnī (d. after 1339–40), *Taʾrīkh-i guzīda (The Choice History)*
Persian Shiʿite scholar and contemporary of the more famous Rashīd al-Dīn. This concise work, describing the history of the Islamic world until his own time, was completed in 730/1330.

*Edition:*
E.G. Browne and R.A. Nicholson (Leiden and London, 1911–14)

*Translation:*
C. Defrémery, 'Histoire des Seldjoukides', *Journal asiatique* (April–May 1848), 417–62; (September 1848), 259–79; (October 1848), 334–70
   A very useful translation of the Seljuk sections of the text.


**Histories: Select Christian Primary Sources in Arabic**

al-Anṭākī, Yaḥyā b. Saʿīd (John of Antioch) (d. 1066), *Taʾrīkh al-Anṭākī (The History of al-Anṭākī)*
A doctor at the Fatimid court, this Melkite chronicler was the continuator of the work entitled *Naẓm al-jawhar (String of Jewels)* written by his relative, the patriarch of Alexandria, Saʿīd b. Baṭrīq (Eutychios) (d. 940). al-Anṭākī continued this work until 1034, where the extant parts of the work stop, but it probably went even further. Forced to leave Egypt at the time of the persecutions of the Fatimid caliph al-Ḥākim, al-Anṭākī moved to Byzantine Antioch in 405/1014–15. His chronicle is a valuable source for Arab–Byzantine relations; in it he draws on his own experiences, non-Arabic Christian writings, as well as a variety of Muslim sources, such as Thābit b. Sinān, al-Musabbiḥī and other chronicles, now lost. The chronicle is arranged chronologically according to caliphs.

*Editions:*
1. L. Cheikho, B. Carra de Vaux and H. Zayyat, CSCO Scriptores arabici 3.7 (Paris, 1909)
2. U.A. Tadmuri (Tripoli, 1990)

*Secondary Literature:*
M. Canard, 'al-Anṭākī', *Encyclopaedia of Islam* (2nd edn.), vol. 1, 516
G. Graf, *Geschichte der christlichen arabischen Litteratur* (Vatican, 1957), vol. 2, 49–51

al-Makīn, Ibn al-ʿAmīd Jirjīs (d. 1273), *al-Majmūʿ al-mubārak (The Blessed Collection)*
A Coptic bureaucrat who was in the service of the Ayyubids in Egypt. He wrote a suc-cinct *Universal History* in Arabic from the Creation until the accession of Sultan Baybars in 1260. This work was known early in Europe through its edition by Erpenius in 1625. It was translated very early into European languages and influenced the scholarship of early orientalist scholars as a result. It was a largely derivative work until the lifetime of the author. The Islamic section of the work until 1238 seems, according to Cahen, to be copied from the *Taʾrīkh al-Ṣāliḥī* of Ibn Wāṣil or from a common source.

*Edition and Translation:*
T. Erpenius, *Historia saracenica* (Leiden, 1625), with a Latin translation by J. Golius
    This edition stopped at the year 512/1117–18.

*Secondary Literature:*
C. Cahen, 'al-Makīn', in *Encyclopaedia of Islam* (2nd edn.), vol. 6, 143–4
—— 'al-Makīn Ibn al-ʿAmīd et l'historiographie musulmane: un cas d'interpénétra-tion confessionnelle', *Orientalia hispanica, sive Studia F.M. Pareja octgenario dicata*, vol. 1.1 (Leiden, 1974), 158–67

al-Makīn, *Akhbār al-Ayyūbiyyīn (Accounts of the Ayyūbids)*
A chronicle of events in the Ayyubid period, beginning in 1205 and ending with the accession of the Mamluk sultan, Baybars, in 1260.

*Edition:*
C. Cahen, 'La "chronique des Ayyoubides" d'al-Makīn b. al-ʿAmīd', *BÉO* 15 (1958), 127–77
    Contains a very useful summary of the events covered in the chronicle (pp. 116–26).

*Translation:*
A.-M. Eddé and F. Micheau, *Chronique des Ayyoubides* (Paris, 1994)

Bar Hebraeus, Abu'l Faraj, known in Arabic as Ibn al-ʿIbrī (d. 1286),
*Taʾrīkh mukhtaṣar al-duwal (An Abbreviated History of the Dynasties)*
See Witold Witakowski in this volume under John Gregory BarEbroyo.

## Select Biographical Dictionaries

The choice of biographical dictionaries made in this section is intended to show the rich diversity of this genre in the medieval Islamic tradition, but it is by no means com-prehensive. Examples have been taken over a wide chronological framework and from the different social groups covered by this important corpus of works. Entries are arranged chronologically according to the death-date of the author.

al-'Abbādī, Abū 'Āṣim Muḥammad (d. 1066), *Ṭabaqāt al-fuqahā'*
*al-Shāfi'iyya (The Generations of Shāfi'ite Jurisprudents)*
A legal scholar from Harat who wrote a biographical dictionary devoted to his
predecessors in the Shāfi'ite *madhhab* ('legal school').
*Edition:*
G. Vitestam (Leiden, 1964)

al-Khaṭīb al-Baghdādī, Abū Bakr (d. 1071), *Ta'rīkh Baghdād (The History*
*of Baghdad)*
An Iraqi religious scholar, preacher and historian of Baghdad. He is famous princi-
pally for his massive, fourteen-volume biographical encyclopaedia known as the
*Ta'rīkh Baghdād*, completed in 1070. It is the first biographical dictionary of a wider
scope, though it still focuses especially on scholars of *ḥadīth* (the 'sayings' of the
Prophet Muḥammad). It contains 7,831 entries; these record the lives of famous men
(and thirty women) involved in the social and cultural life of Baghdad.
*Edition:*
Editor unidentified (Cairo, 1931; repr. Beirut, 1968)

*Edition and Translation:*
G. Salomon, *L'introduction topographique à l'histoire de Baghdad* (Paris, 1904)
A partial edition and translation which deals with the introduction on the topog-
raphy of Baghdad.

*Secondary Literature:*
R.W. Bulliet, 'Women and the urban religious élite in the pre-Mongol period', in
G. Nashat and L. Beck, eds., *Women in Iran from the Rise of Islam to 1800*
(Urbana and Chicago, 2003), 68–79
R. Sellheim, 'al-Khaṭīb al-Baghdādī', *Encyclopaedia of Islam* (2nd edn.), vol. 4,
1111–12

Abū Isḥāq al-Shīrāzī (d. 1083), *Ṭabaqāt al-fuqahā' (The Generations of*
*Legists)*
This work, written around 1060, records, regardless of their particular school of law,
all the jurists, whose opinion could be sought in order for a consensus to be reached.
Later works of this kind would be confined to jurists of one particular 'school' only.
*Edition:*
Editor unidentified (Baghdad, 1937)

al-Sam'ānī, 'Abd al-Karīm (d. 1166), *al-Ansāb (Genealogies)*
A religious scholar from Marw in the eastern province of Khurasan. This is a massive
biographical dictionary of scholars of *ḥadīth* (the 'sayings' of the Prophet
Muḥammad). Its 5,348 entries are arranged alphabetically according to *nisba* (a person's name based on place of origin or residence). The work provides advice on how
to pronounce names and their derivations, as well as the names of teachers and their
pupils.
*Edition:*
D. Margoliouth (Leiden and London, 1912)

*Facsimiles:*
1. A. al-Muʿallimi and others, 13 vols. (Hyderabad, 1952–82)
2. A.U. al-Barudi (Beirut, 1998)

## Ibn al-ʿAsākir, Thiqat al-Dīn (d. 1176), *Taʾrīkh madīnat Dimashq (The History of the City of Damascus)*

A famous historian of Damascus who belonged to an important family of Shāfiʿite scholars from that city. This grandiose prosopographical work, arranged alphabetically, records all the important people who lived in or visited Damascus and a number of other cities in Syria. It has a valuable introduction, which gives the historical topography of the city. The most recent publication of this enormous work is ongoing.

*Editions:*
1. A. Badran and A. Ubayd, 7 vols. (Damascus, 1911–32)
   This edition is abridged.
2. S. al-Munajjid, vol. 1, pt. 2 (Damascus, 1954)
3. Complete edition, edited by several scholars (Damascus, 1951–)

Cf. also A. Badran, *Tahdhīb taʾrīkh Dimashq (The Pruned Version of the History of Damascus)* (Damascus, 1911–32)
   This is a rearrangement of the *Tarʾīkh madīnat Dimashq* up to the letter ʿayn. It is an unsatisfactory effort.

*Translation:*
N. Elisséeff, *La description de Damas d'Ibn ʿAsâkir* (Damascus, 1959)
This is a translation of the section edited by Munajjid.

*Secondary Literature:*
R.S. Humphreys, *Islamic History. A framework for inquiry* (Princeton, 1991), 238–9

## Yāqūt al-Rūmī al-Ḥamawī, Shihāb al-Dīn (d. 1229), *Muʿjam al-udabāʾ (The Dictionary of Men of Letters)*

A traveller and prolific writer. Born in Byzantine territory, he was taken as a slave to Baghdad as a small boy. His master, a merchant, saw to it that he received a thorough Islamic education and he travelled widely on his master's business.

Not all this colossal work has survived, but its most recent editior, Ihsan Abbas, restored thirty-two entries that were not in the first edition by Margoliouth. It is, as its title suggests, concerned with the writers—poets, lexicographers and other kinds of scholars—whom the author met.

*Editions:*
1. D. Margoliouth, 7 vols. (Cairo, 1907–27)
2. A.F. Rifāʿī, 20 vols. (Cairo, 1936–8)
   A poor edition.
3. I. Abbas, 7 vols. (Beirut, 1993)

*Secondary Literature:*
C. Gilliot, 'Yāḳūt al-Rūmī', *Encyclopaedia of Islam* (2nd edn.), vol. 11, 264–6
   A very fine and full treatment of this author's work with full bibliographical details.

Ibn al-'Adīm (d. 1262), *Bughyat al-ṭalab fī ta'rīkh Ḥalab (The Desired Object of Seeking in the History of Aleppo)*
For details of this author, see the entry under Histories, p. 317.

In this monumental work (even though only a quarter of it has survived), Ibn al-'Adīm vaunts his own city by a full biographical coverage of its great personalities. Anyone who lived there or visited the city or its surrounding areas in any historical period may qualify for inclusion in his work. However, if the entry deals with a traveller to Aleppo, his inclusion in the dictionary must be justified.

The dictionary is organised in alphabetical order. The typical biographical entry follows a generally predictable plan; it includes the name of the subject, a summary of that person's links with Aleppo, an assessment of his qualities and the most important parts of his career. After some illustrative anecdotes, the date and details of his death are provided. The author draws on an unusually wide range of sources, both oral and written, extant and lost.

*Editions:*
1. A. Sevim (Ankara, 1976)
    Partial.
2. F. Sezgin, 11 vols. (Frankfurt, 1986–90)

*Facsimile Edition:*
S. Zakkar, 11 vols. (Damascus, 1988)

*Translations:*
1. *RHC: historiens orientaux*, vol. 3, 695–732
    These extracts cover the biographies of five Muslim rulers of Syria in the twelfth century.
2. B. Lewis, 'Three biographies from Kamāl al-Dīn', in O. Turan, ed., *Fuad Köprülü Armağanı*, (Istanbul, 1953), 325–44
    These three biographies throw light on the history of the Syrian Assassins: two of the entries chosen concern their alleged victims, Janāḥ al-Dawla, the ruler of Ḥimṣ, and Khalaf b. Mulā'ib, the governor of Afāmiya. The other biography is that of the Assassin leader in Syria himself, Rashīd al-Dīn Sinān.

*Secondary Literature:*
D. Morray, *An Ayyubid Notable and his World. Ibn al-'Adīm and Aleppo as portrayed in his Biographical Dictionary of people associated with the city* (Leiden, 1994)
    A remarkably thorough and learned study of this very important biographical work.
——'Egypt and Aleppo in Ibn al-'Adīm's *Bughyat al-ṭalab fī ta'rīkh Ḥalab*', in H. Kennedy, ed., *The Historiography of Islamic Egypt (c.950–1800)* (Leiden, 2001), 13–22

Abū Shāma, 'Abd al-Raḥmān (d. 1267), *Tarājim rijāl al-qarnayn al-sādis wa'l sābi' (Biographical Notices of the Men of the Sixth and Seventh Centuries)*
A Syrian scholar from Damascus. The work gives, as its title suggests, biographical notices of important local people in the sixth and seventh centuries of the Muslim era (i.e. the twelfth and thirteenth centuries of the Christian calendar).

*Edition:*
M. al-Kawthari (Cairo, 1947; Beirut, 1984)

Ibn Abī Uṣaybiʿa, Muwaffaq al-Dīn (d. 1270), ʿ*Uyūn al-anbāʾ fī ṭabaqāt al-aṭibbāʾ* *(Choice News about the Generations of Doctors)*
A Syrian doctor who lived and practised in Damascus. His biographical work on classical and Muslim physicians contains 380 entries, arranged according to area and generation.

*Editions:*
1. A. Müller, 2 vols. (Cairo, 1882–4)
2. N. Rida (Beirut, 1965)

*Secondary Literature:*
A-M. Eddé, 'Les médecins dans la société syrienne du VIIᵉ/XIIIᵉ siècle', *AI* 29 (1995), 91–109

Ibn Khallikān, Aḥmad b. Muḥammad (d. 1282), *Kitāb Wafāyāt al-aʿyān wa anbāʾ abnāʾ al-zamān* *(The Book of the Deaths of the Famous and Information about the Sons of the Time)*
Ibn Khallikān had a very varied public life in different cities of the Near East, reaching the rank of Chief Judge. His is the best known of the medieval Islamic biographical dictionaries outside the Middle East, because of its English translation by de Slane in the nineteenth century. It is arranged in alphabetical order, according to the person's *ism* (personal name), and it contains only the biographies of those whose death dates he could find out for sure. It is a very useful source indeed for the period of the project, especially for the twelfth and thirteenth centuries. It is often witty and is intended to entertain, with frequent use of poems and lively anecdotes. It is much wider in scope than the other biographical dictionaries which precede it and it includes anyone who had excelled in almost all spheres of public life, such as scholars, princes, commanders, ministers, poets and women. It omits the lives of the Abbasid caliphs, on the grounds that they are sufficiently well covered in other sources, but it does provide biographies of the 'heretical' Fatimid caliphs of Egypt.

*Editions:*
1. E. Wüstenfeld (Göttingen, 1835–43)
2. Baron W.M. de Slane (Paris, 1838–42)
   Not a complete edition.
3. M. Muhyi al-Dīn, 2 vols. (Cairo, 1299/1881–2)
4. I. Abbas, 8 vols. (Beirut 1968–72; repr. Beirut, 1997)
   The best edition.

*Translations:*
1. Baron W.M. de Slane, *Ibn Khallikan's Biographical Dictionary,* 4 vols. (Paris, 1843–71; repr. Beirut, 1970)
2. *RHC: historiens orientaux,* vol. 3, 379–430
   The biographies of Ibn Shaddād, the biographer of Saladin, and of Saladin himself are translated here.

al-Ṣafadī, Khalīl b. Aybak (d. 1363), *Kitāb al-Wāfī' bi'l-wafayāt (The Supplement to the Necrologies)*
This scholar came from a Turkish family in Ṣafad and worked in the Mamluk administration. This is the fullest of the medieval biographical dictionaries. It purportedly once contained over 140,000 entries. It is now published in over thirty volumes with more than 5,000 entries. They are arranged alphabetically, except that the work gives precedence to the name Muḥammad. It aims to continue and build on the dictionary of Ibn Khallikān. Its contents can be gleaned from Gabrieli's summary. It is a rich source on Fatimid Egypt.

*Edition:*
Hellmut Ritter and others, eds., *Das biographische Lexikon des Ṣalāhaddīn Ḫalīl ibn Aibak aṣ-Ṣafadī*, Bibliotheca Islamica 6a–zc, 29 vols. (all published by various houses in Istanbul and Beirut on commission from a succession of publishers in Berlin, Leipzig, Stuttgart, and Wiesbaden, 1931–2004)
Standard critical edition.

*Secondary Literature:*
G. Gabrieli, 'Indice alfabetico di tutte le biografie contenute nel *Wafi bi'l wafayat*', *Rendiconti dell'Accademia nazionale dei Lincei, classe di scienze morali, storiche e filologiche* 22 (1913), 547–77, 581–629; 23 (1914), 191–208, 217–65; 24 (1915), 551–615; 25 (1916), 341–98

al-Subkī, Tāj al-Dīn (d. *c.*1369/70), *Ṭabaqāt al-shāfiʿiyya (The Generations of the Shāfiʿites)*
A Syrian preacher and religious scholar from Damascus. This is a collection of biographies of Shāfiʿite jurists. It exists in three versions, the 'largest', the 'middle-sized' and the 'smallest'. It gives a thorough intellectual history of the Shāfiʿite *madhhab* ('legal school').

*Edition (of the 'largest' (al-kubrā)) version:*
1. 6 vols. (Cairo, 1908)
   A bad edition.
2. M.M. al-Tanahi and M.A. al-Hilw, 10 vols. (Cairo, 1964–76)

*Secondary Literature:*
H. Halm, *Die Ausbreitung der šafiʿitischen Rechtsschule von den Anfängen bis zum 8./14. Jahrhundert* (Wiesbaden, 1974)

Ibn Rajab, Zayn al-Dīn (d. 1392), *Kitāb al-Dhayl ʿalā ṭabaqāt al-ḥanābila (The Book of the Appendix to the Generations of Ḥanbalites)*
A Ḥanbalite legist from Damascus. This is a biographical work restricted to the Ḥanbalite *madhhab* ('legal school').

*Edition:*
H. Laoust and S. Dahhan, vol. 1 (Damascus, 1951)
   This covers the years 460/1067 to 540/1145.

al-Maqrīzī, Taqī al-Dīn (d. 1442), *Kitāb al-Taʾrīkh al-kabīr al-muqaffā li-miṣr (The Great History Limited to Egypt)*
For details of this author, see the entry under Histories, p. 321.

Only partly extant but a most valuable and extensive prosopographical resource. It was originally planned in eighty volumes but only sixteen were completed by the author. It includes a wide range of biographies and is especially important for its some four hundred entries on famous people connected to the Fatimid state, including the caliphs. It also has the odd biographical notice of a prominent Frank, such as Baldwin I of Jerusalem.

*Edition:*
M. al-Ya'lawi, 8 vols. (Beirut, 1991)

*Translation:*
E. Quatremère, 'Mémoires historiques sur la dynastie des Khalifes Fatimites', *Journal asiatique* (1836), 97–142
Partial French translation.

Ibn al-'Imād, 'Abd al-Ḥayy (d. 1679), *Shadharāt al-dhahab fī akhbār man dhahab (Fragments of Gold in the Accounts of Those who have Passed on)*
A Syrian scholar of the Ḥanbalite *madhhab* ('legal school'). His comprehensive biographical dictionary was completed in 1670. Despite its late date of composition, it is very useful because of its encyclopaedic scope. It is arranged annalistically and covers the first Islamic millennium (the years 1/622 to 1000/1591–2).

*Editions:*
1. (Cairo, 1284/1867–8)
2. A. and M. al-Arna'ut, 11 vols. (Beirut, 1986)

**Biographies in Arabic**

Ibn Shaddād, Bahā' al-Dīn (d. 1239), *al-Nawāḍir al-sulṭāniyya wa'l maḥāsin al-yūsufiyya (The Sultanal Rarities and the Josephal Virtues)*
A contemporary of Saladin who travelled and worked with him from 1188 until Saladin's death in 1193. The title of his biography of Saladin refers to the fact that the name Yūsuf (Joseph), a figure famed for his beauty in the Quran, was also one of Saladin's names. The work begins with a laudatory section extolling Saladin's virtues. The middle part of the book is a narrative of Saladin's activities in the *jihād*, drawn largely from the work of another companion of Saladin, 'Imād al-Dīn al-Iṣfahānī. The last section, however, recounts Ibn Shaddād's own personal views of his master and he writes movingly of Saladin's death.

With this work, medieval Arabic biographical writing as a genre is properly launched.

*Edition:*
J. El-Shayyal (Cairo, 1964)

*Edition and Translation:*
RHC: historiens orientaux, vol. 3, 3–370

*Translations:*
1. C.R. Conder and C.W. Wilson, *The Life of Saladin* (London, 1897; repr. New York, 1971)
Richards rightly suggests that this translation is too dependent on the French translation in the *Recueil*.

2. D.S. Richards, *The Rare and Excellent History of Saladin* (Aldershot, 2001)
This recent reliable translation draws on a Berlin manuscript which was not used by El-Shayyal in his edition.

*Secondary Literature:*
D.S. Richards, 'A consideration of two sources for the life of Saladin', *JSS* 25 (1980), 46–65
—— Introduction to his translation, 1–9

Abū Shāma, 'Abd al-Raḥmān (d. 1267), *Kitāb al-Rawḍatayn fī akhbār al-dawlatayn (The Book of the Two Gardens in the Accounts of the Two States)*
See also his entry under Biographical Dictionaries, p. 328.
This work deals in a laudatory way with the 'Two Gardens', the reigns of Nūr al-Dīn and Saladin. It is carefully structured. It draws on a number of lost sources and makes ample use of poetry and official correspondence, including many extracts from the letters of Saladin's companion and adviser, the Qāḍī al-Fāḍil.

*Editions:*
1. 2 vols. (Cairo, 1871–5)
2. M.H.M. Ahmad and M.M. Ziyada, 2 vols. (Cairo, 1956–62)

*Edition and Translation:*
*RHC: historiens orientaux,* vol. 4, 3–522; vol. 5, 3–206

*Translation:*
E.P. Goergens in *Arabische Quellenbeiträge zur Geschichte Ṣalāḥ-ad-Dīns, vol. 1: Zur Geschichte Salahadins* (Berlin, 1879; repr. Hildesheim, 1975)
Partial translation, covering the second half of the book, which deals with the life of Saladin, and then takes the narrative up to the early years of the thirteenth century.

*Secondary Literature:*
P.M. Holt, 'Saladin and his admirers; a biographical reassessment', *BSOAS* 46 (1983), 235–9

## Autobiographies

al-Mu'ayyad fi'l-Dīn al-Shīrāzī, Hibat Allāh (d. 1078), *Sīrat al-Mu'ayyad fi'l-Dīn dā'ī al-du'āt (The Biography of al-Mu'ayyad fi'l Dīn the Chief Missionary)*
An important Persian Ismā'īlī missionary and scholar, he moved to Cairo and became deeply involved in the politics of his time, serving as envoy and negotiator for the Fatimid caliph al-Mustanṣir in his attempts to take Baghdad in the 1050s. These events and other parts of his life are recounted in his autobiography.

*Edition:*
M.K. Husayn (Cairo, 1949)

*Secondary Literature:*
V. Klemm, *Memoirs of a Mission. The Islamic scholar, statesman and poet al-Mu'ayyad fi'l-Dīn al-Shīrāzī* (London, 2003)

I.K. Poonawala, *Biobibliography of Ismāʿīlī Literature* (Malibu, 1977), 103–9

al-Ghazālī, Abū Hamid, Muḥammad (d. 1111), *al-Munqidh min al-ḍalāl (The Deliverer from Error)*
al-Ghazālī was probably the most famous medieval Muslim scholar. This short work, written towards the end of his life, is his 'autobiography'; in it he bares his soul and charts his spiritual journey as a model for the whole community to follow. His search for 'certain truth' leads him to the mystical path of the Sufis. Known early in the west, the work has enjoyed great popularity and has been often translated into European languages.

*Edition and Translation:*
F. Jabre, *al-Munqiḍ min aḍalāl (Erreur et déliverance)* (Beirut, 1959)

*Translations:*
1. W.M. Watt, *The Faith and Practice of al-Ghazali* (London, 1953)
   This sometimes reads more like a paraphrase than an exact translation.
2. R.J. McCarthy, *Freedom and Fulfilment: an annotated translation* (Boston, 1980)
   A faithful, literal translation.

*Secondary Literature:*
C. Hillenbrand, 'al-Ghazali', in M. Jolly, ed., *Encyclopedia of Life Writing*, vol. 1 (London and Chicago, 2001), 374–5
W.M. Watt, *Muslim Intellectual: a study of al-Ghazali* (Edinburgh, 1963)

Usāma, b. Murshid b. ʿAlī, generally known as Usāma b. Munqidh (d. 1188) *Kitāb al-Iʿtibār (The Book of Instruction (by Example))*
An Arab aristocrat, warrior and scholar, born in 1095, who came from Shayzar in northern Syria and whose autobiographical memoirs record his experiences, in war and peace, during his rich and long life. His aim in these memoirs is both to entertain and instruct, and the stories are often exaggerated and stereotypical, with a clear didactic aim. However, the work is a precious account of social relations between upper-class Muslims and Franks in the twelfth century.

*Editions:*
1. P.K. Hitti (Princeton, 1930)
2. Q. al-Samarra'i (Riyadh, 1987)
3. H. Zayd (Beirut, 1988)

*Translations:*
1. H. Derenbourg, *Ousama Ibn Mounkidh, un emir syrien au premier siècle des croisades* (Paris, 1889)
2. G.R. Potter, *The Autobiography of Ousama* (London, 1929)
3. P.K Hitti, *Memoirs of an Arab-Syrian Gentleman* (New York, 1929; repr. Beirut, 1964 and Princeton, 1987)
4. A. Miquel, *Des enseignements de la vie* (Paris, 1983)
5. H. Preisser, *Die Erlebnisse des syrischen Ritters Usāma ibn Munqidh* (Munich, 1985)

*Secondary Literature:*
C. Hillenbrand, *The Crusades: Islamic perspectives* (Edinburgh, 1999), 259–62
A. Miquel, *Ousâma. Un prince syrien face aux croisés* (Paris, 1986)
D.W. Morray, *The Genius of Usāmah ibn Munqidh: aspects of the Kitāb al-Iʿtibār* (Durham, 1987)

'Imād al-Dīn al-Iṣfahānī, Muḥammad (d. 1201), *al-Barq al-shāmī (The Syrian Lightning)*
This famous Persian scholar, poet and historian worked for the Seljuks, before moving to Syria where he was in the service first of Nūr al-Dīn and then Saladin, for whom he acted as scribe and close adviser.

This is a detailed autobiographical account of the author's service under Nūr al-Dīn and Saladin, written in a very difficult, highly ornate rhymed prose. It covers the years 1166 to 1193 and draws on the author's own personal knowledge, as well as official chancellery documents. Most of the seven volumes are lost; there are two surviving parts which deal with Saladin's campaigns—part 3 (covering the years 1177–9) and part 5 (covering the years 1182–3).

*Editions:*
M. al-Hiyari (Amman, 1987)

*Partial Edition and Translation:*
L. Richter-Bernburg, *Der syrische Blitz. Saladins Sekretär zwischen Selbstdarstellung und Geschichtsschreibung* (Beirut, 1998)
The edition and translation cover the year 573/1177–8.

'Abd al-Laṭīf al-Baghdādī, Muwaffaq al-Dīn (d. 1231), *Kitāb al-Ifāda wa'l i'tibār fi'l umūr al-mushāhada wa'l ḥawādith al-mu'āyana bi-arḍ Miṣr (The Book of Benefit and Instruction about Matters Which Have Been Witnessed and Events Which Have Been Seen with the Eye in the Land of Egypt)*
An Iraqi doctor who travelled widely and lived in Egypt for some years. As its title suggests, this work records things seen and experienced personally by the author. It is a short but valuable description of Egypt. The work seems to have been part of a larger history but only excerpts of it have survived.

*Edition:*
Editor unidentified (Cairo, date uncertain, 1869?)

*Edition and Translation:*
RHC: *historiens orientaux*, vol. 3, 435–9
A very short extract.

*Translations:*
1. S. de Sacy, *Relation de l'Égypte* (Paris, 1910)
2. K.H. Zand and J.A. and I. Videan, *The Eastern Key* (Cairo and London, 1964)

*Secondary Literature:*
C. Cahen, "Abdallatīf al-Baghdādī, portraitiste et historien de son temps', *BÉO* 23 (1970), 101–28
G. Makdisi, *The Rise of Colleges* (Edinburgh, 1981), 84–8
This is a very useful discussion of the educational career of this scholar, with translated excerpts.
S.M. Stern, "Abd al-Laṭīf al-Baghdādī', *Encyclopaedia of Islam* (2nd edn.), vol. 1, 74
S. Toorawa, 'The educational background of 'Abd al-Latif al-Baghdadi', *Muslim Educational Quarterly* 13.3 (1996), 35–53

**Biographies in Persian**

Ibn al-Munawwar, Muḥammad (d. ?early 12th c.?), *Asrār al-tawḥīd fī*
*maqāmāt al-Shaykh Abū Saʿīd (The Secrets of Oneness in the (Mystical)*
*Stages of the Shaykh Abū Saʿīd)*
This scholar, a descendant of Abū Saʿīd b. Abi'l Khayr (d. 1048–9), wrote a hagiographical biography of this famous mystic between 1179 and 1192. The cousin of Ibn
al-Munawwar, Jamāl al-Dīn Abū Rawḥ b. Abī Saʿīd had also written a similar work
on the same subject.

*Edition:*
1. V. Zhukowski (St Petersburg, 1899)
2. D. Safa (Tehran, 1953)

*Translation:*
M. Achena, *Les étapes mystiques du Shaykh Abū Saʿīd* (Paris, 1974)

*Secondary Literature:*
G. Böwering, 'Abū Saʿīd Abi'l Ḳayr', *Encyclopaedia Iranica*, vol. 1. fasc. 4, 377–80
H. Ritter, *Das Meer der Seele* (Leiden, 1955)


**Major Collections of Translated Texts**

*Recueil des historiens des croisades: historiens orientaux*, vols. 1–5 (Paris, 1872–1906)
    This collection of Arabic texts and French translations contains long excerpts
    from major medieval Arabic chronicles from Syrian, Egyptian and Iraqi histori-
    ans of the twelfth, thirteenth and fourteenth centuries. Information on Byzantine
    affairs occurs from time to time but its appearance is rather sparse and unpre-
    dictable. It is fuller when Byzantium involves itself in Syria against the Muslims or
    Franks, or in eastern Anatolia against the Seljuk Turks and other Turcoman
    dynasties in that border area. The erratic quality of the Arabic editions in the
    *Recueil* is also mirrored in some of the French translations.
F. Gabrieli, *Arab Historians of the Crusades* (London, 1969)
    This volume contains extracts from important primary Arabic texts which were
    translated by Gabrieli into Italian and thereafter translated from Italian into
    English by Costello. Inevitably the passages sometimes read more like para-
    phrases than translations and seem distant from the original Arabic. There is lit-
    tle on Byzantium in this selection of texts.
B. Lewis, *Islam from the Prophet Muhammad to the Capture of Constantinople*, 2 vols.
    (New York, 1974)
    Contains a few extracts from the period of the project.
A.-M. Eddé, and F. Micheau, *L'Orient au temps des croisades* (Paris, 2002)
    This very useful book contains a good number of extracts from hitherto
    untranslated texts.
D.F. Reynolds, ed., *Interpreting the Self. Autobiography in the Arabic literary tradition*
    (Berkeley, 2000)
    This is a useful and interesting volume. Part 2 contains translations from medieval
    Arabic autobiographies, including the works of Mu'ayyad al-Shīrāzī and ʿImād al-
    Dīn al-Iṣfahānī. See especially the annotated guide to Arabic autobiography; the
    part relevant to the period 1025–1204 is pp. 259–66.

**Select Bibliography on Material Culture**

This corpus of material is very important indeed for any prosopographical or onomastic study, since it contains vital, often dated, visual evidence on the names and titles
of rulers and prominent people.

*Monumental Inscriptions*
The following entries are intended as an entrée into the vast bibliography on this subject. The work of Max van Berchem towers over the field; for full details of his
remarkable scholarly output, see the introduction by A. Louca in M. van Berchem,
*Opera minora*, vol. 1 (Geneva, 1978), xviii–xxxvi.

E. Combe, J. Sauvaget and G. Wiet, eds., *Répertoire chronologique d'épigraphie arabe*
(Cairo, 1935–9)
Volumes 6–10 are relevant to the period 1025–1204. For each inscription the
Arabic text is given (but not its Quranic quotations, if it contains any) together
with a French translation.
M. Sharon, ed., *Corpus inscriptionum arabicarum Palestiniae*, vol. 1 (Leiden, 1997)
N. Elisséeff, 'Les monuments de Nūr al-Dīn', *BÉO* 12 (1949–51), 5–43
—— 'La titulature de Nūr al-Dīn d'après ses inscriptions', *BÉO* 14 (1952–4), 155–96
M. van Berchem, *Matériaux pour un Corpus inscriptionum arabicarum. Première partie,
Égypte* (Paris, 1894–1903)
—— *Matériaux pour un Corpus inscriptionum arabicarum. Deuxième partie, Syrie du
nord* (Cairo, 1909)
—— *Matériaux pour un Corpus inscriptionum arabicarum. Troisième partie, Asie
Mineure* (Cairo, 1910, 1917)
—— *Matériaux pour un Corpus inscriptionum arabicarum. Deuxième partie, Syrie du
sud. Jérusalem (III. Planches)* (Cairo, 1920)
—— *Matériaux pour un Corpus inscriptionum arabicarum. Deuxième partie, Jérusalem
(I. Ville)* (Cairo, 1922–3)
—— *Matériaux pour un Corpus inscriptionum arabicarum. Deuxième partie. Jérusalem
(II. Haram)* (Cairo, 1927)
—— *Matériaux pour un Corpus inscriptionum arabicarum. Deuxième partie. Syrie du
sud. Jérusalem (Index)* (Cairo, 1949)
M. van Berchem and E. Fatio, *Voyage en Syrie* (Cairo, 1913–15)

*Coins*

M. Bates, *Islamic Coins* (New York, 1982)
N. Elisséeff, *Nūr al-Dīn. Un grand prince musulman de Syrie au temps des croisades*
(Damascus, 1967), vol. 3, 812–23
I. Ghalib, *Catalogue des monnaies turcomanes* (Constantinople, 1894)
G. Hennequin, *Catalogue des monnaies musulmanes de la Bibliothèque nationale: Asie
pré-mongole: les Saljuqs et leurs successeurs* (Paris, 1985)
S. Lane-Poole, *Catalogue of Oriental Coins in the British Museum. 3. The Coins of the
Turkman Houses of Saljook, Urtuk, Zenge, etc.* (London, 1877)
N. Lowick, 'The religious, the royal and the popular in the figural coinage of the
Jazira', in J. Raby, ed., *The Art of Syria and the Jazira* (Oxford, 1985), 159–74
H. Mitchell Brown, 'Some reflections on the figured coinage of the Artuqids and the
Zengids', in D. Koyuymjian, ed., *Studies in Honor of George Miles* (Beirut, 1974),
353–8

W.E. Spengler and W.S. Sayles, *Turkoman Figural Bronze Coins and their Iconography* (Lodi, 1996)

## SELECT STUDIES

### Select Items on the Historiography of the Eleventh and Twelfth Centuries

M. Ahmad and M. Hilmy, 'Some notes on Arabic historiography during the Zengid and Ayyubid periods (521/1127–648/1250)', in Lewis and Holt, eds., *Historians of the Middle East*, 79–97

C. Cahen 'Quelques chroniques anciennes relatives aux derniers Fatimides', *BIFAO* 37 (1937), 1–27

—— 'The historiography of the Seljuqid period', in Lewis and Holt, eds., *Historians of the Middle East*, 59–78

—— 'Reflexions sur la connaissance du monde par les historiens', *Folia Orientalia* 12 (1970), 41–9; repr. in C. Cahen, *Les peuples musulmans dans l'histoire mediévale* (Damascus, 1977), 1–10
An unjustly neglected article on the intellectual horizons of medieval Islamic historians.

—— 'Some new editions of oriental sources about Syria in the time of the crusades', in *Outremer Studies in the History of the Crusading Kingdom of Jerusalem* (Jerusalem, 1982), 323–31

E. Daniel, 'Historiography', in *Encyclopaedia Iranica*, vol. 12, fasc. 4, 340–8
Excellent coverage of Persian historiography.

A.M. Eddé, 'Sources arabes des XIIᵉ et XIIIᵉ siècles d'après le dictionnaire biographique d'Ibn al-'Adīm *(Bughyat al-ṭalab fī ta'rīkh Ḥalab)*', *Itinéraires d'Orient. Hommages à Claude Cahen, Res Orientales* 6 (1994), 293–308

F. Gabrieli, 'The Arabic historiography of the crusades', in Lewis and Holt, eds., *Historians of the Middle East*, 98–107

H.A.R. Gibb, 'al-Barq al-shāmī, the history of Saladin by the Kātib 'Imād al-Dīn al-Iṣfahānī', *WZKM* 52 (1953), 93–115

C. Hillenbrand, 'Some medieval Islamic approaches to source material', *Oriens* 27–8 (1981), 197–225

—— 'Some reflections on Seljuq historiography', in A. Eastmond, ed., *Eastern Approaches to Byzantium* (Aldershot, 2001), 73–88

H. Kennedy, ed., *The Historiography of Islamic Egypt, c. 950–1800* (Leiden, 2000)

B. Lewis and P.M. Holt, eds., *Historians of the Middle East* (London, 1962)

D.P. Little, *History and Historiography of the Mamluks* (London, 1986)

—— 'Historiography of the Ayyubid and Mamluk epochs', in C.F. Petry, ed., *The Cambridge History of Egypt: Islamic Egypt 640–1517* (Cambridge, 1998), 412–44

M.C. Lyons and D.E.P. Jackson, *Saladin: the politics of the Holy War* (Cambridge, 1982)

J.S. Meisami, *Persian Historiography to the End of the Twelfth Century* (Edinburgh, 1999)

F. Micheau, 'Croisades et croisés vus par les historiens arabes chrétiens d'Égypte', *Itinéraires d'Orient. Hommages à Claude Cahen, Res Orientales* 6 (1994), 169–85

D.S. Richards, 'Ibn al-Athir and the later parts of the *Kāmil*', in D.O. Morgan, ed., *Medieval Historical Writings in the Christian and Islamic Worlds* (London, 1982), 76–108

L. Richter-Bernburg, 'Funken aus dem alten Flint: 'Imād al-Dīn al-Kātib al-Iṣfahānī', *Die Welt des Orients* 20–1 (1990), 121–66; 22 (1991), 15–41

—— *Der syrische Blitz: Saladins Sekretär zwischen Selbstdarstellung und Geschichtsschreibung* (Beirut, 1998)

C.F. Robinson, *Islamic Historiography* (Cambridge, 2003)
Part 1, chapter 4 (pp. 55–79) provides a very helpful discussion of biography, prosopography and chronography.

F. Rosenthal, *A History of Muslim Historiography* (Leiden, 1968)
This book is not what it seems. It considers the role of historical writing within medieval Islamic culture. However, its bibliographical information is invaluable.

A.F. Sayyid, 'Lumières nouvelles sur quelques sources de l'histoire fatimide en Egypte', *AI* 13 (1977), 1–41

## Prosopography and Biography

A. Abd al-Raziq, 'Le vizirat et les vizirs d'Égypte au temps des Mamluks', *AI* 16 (1980), 183–239

J. Ahola, 'The community of scholars: an analysis of the biographical data from the *Ta'rīkh-Baghdād*', unpubl. Ph.D. thesis (St Andrews, 2005)

P. Auchterlonie, *Arabic Biographical Dictionaries: a summary guide and bibliography* (Durham, 1987)

—— 'Historians and the Arabic biographical dictionary: some new approaches', in R.G. Hoyland and P.F. Kennedy, eds., *Islamic Reflections, Arabic Musings. Studies in honour of Alan Jones* (Oxford, 2004), 186–201
A helpful overview of recent scholarly approaches to Arabic biographical dictionaries.

M.L. Avila. *La sociedad hispanomusulmana al final del califato: aproximación a un estudio demográfico* (Madrid, 1985)

M. Benaboud, 'The value of biographical dictionaries for studying al-Andalus during the period of the Taifa states', in C. Vazquez de Benito and M.A. Manzano Rodríguez, eds., *Actas XVI Congreso UEAI* (Salamanca, 1995), 57–71

R. Bulliet, 'A quantitative approach to medieval Muslim biographical dictionaries', *JESHO* 13 (1970), 195–211

—— *The Patricians of Nishapur: a study in medieval Islamic social history* (Cambridge, Mass., 1972)
A prosopographical survey of the religious scholars in Nishapur in eastern Iran, based on two biographical dictionaries.

—— *Conversion to Islam in the Medieval Period: an essay in quantitative history* (Cambridge, Mass., 1979)
A pioneering study, using biographical dictionaries to chart the process of conversion to Islam.

—— 'Women and the urban religious élite in the pre-Mongol period', in G. Nashat and L. Beck, eds., *Women in Iran from the Rise of Islam to 1800* (Urbana and Chicago, 2003), 68–79

L. Caetani and G. Gabrieli, *Onomasticon arabicum, ossia repertorio alfabetico dei nomi di persona e di luogo contenuti nelle principali opere storiche* (Rome, 1915)
A tentative beginning to the task of assembling and analysing Arabic proper names.

H.J. Cohen, 'The economic background and the secular occupations of Muslim jurisprudents and traditionists in the classical period of Islam', *JESHO* 13 (1970), 17–61

D. Ephrat, *A Learned Society in a Period of Transition: the Sunni 'ulamā' of eleventh-century Baghdad* (Albany, 2000)

H.E. Fähndrich, 'The *Wafāyāt al-a'yān* of Ibn Khallikān: a new approach', *JAOS* 93 (1973), 432–45

H.A.R. Gibb, 'Islamic biographical literature', in Lewis and Holt, eds., *Historians of the Middle East*, 54–8

C. Gilliot, 'Prosopography in Islam: an essay of classification, *Medieval Prosopography* 23 (2002), 19–54

—— 'Ṭabaqāt', in *Encyclopaedia of Islam* (2nd edn.), vol. 10, 7–10

R.J.H. Gottheil, 'A distinguished family of Fatimid cadis', *JAOS* 27 (1906), 217–96

I. Hafsi, 'Recherches sur le genre "ṭabaqāt" dans la littérature arabe', *Arabica* 23 (1976), 227–65; 24 (1977), 1–41, 150–86
Explains how biographical dictionaries are organised and the kinds of topic covered.

H. Halm, *Die Ausbreitung der šāfi'itischen Rechtsschule von den Anfängen bis zum 8/14. Jahrhundert* (Wiesbaden, 1974)

R.S. Humphreys, 'Banū Munqidh', in *Encyclopaedia of Islam* (2nd edn.), vol. 7, 577–80
A study of the family of the famous memoir-writer Usāma b. Munqidh who lived through much of the twelfth century.

F. Justi, *Iranisches Namenbuch* (Hildesheim, 1963)

U.R. Kahhala, *Mu'jam al-mu'allifin (The Compendium of Writers)*, 15 vols. (Damascus, 1957–61)
Concise entries in alphabetical order on all Arabic writers, both medieval and modern, together with their works. Knows Arabic biographical literature very well.

T. Khalidi, 'Islamic biographical dictionaries: a preliminary assessment', *Muslim World* 63 (1973), 53–65

A.K.S. Lambton, 'Persian biographical literature', in Lewis and Holt, eds., *Historians of the Middle East*, 141–51

M. Marin, and others, eds., *Estudios onomástico-biográficos de al-Andalus,* 12 vols. (Madrid, 1988–2003)
An impressively thorough, regional approach to Muslim prosopography.

—— 'Anthroponymy and society: the occupational *laqab* of Andalusian *'ulamā'*", in J. Lüdtke, ed., *Romania Arabica. Festschrift für Reinhold Kontzi* (Tübingen, 1996), 271–9

—— 'Biographical dictionaries and social history of al-Andalus: trade and scholarship'. *Scripta Mediterranea* 19–20 (1998–9), 239–57

B. Martel-Thoumian, *Les civils et l'administration dans l'état militaire mamluk, IX^e–XV^e siècle* (Damascus, 1991)

J.A. Mojaddedi, *The Biographical Tradition in Sufism: the ṭabaqāt genre from al-Sulamī to Jāmī* (London, 2001)

D. Morray, *An Ayyubid Notable and his World. Ibn al-ʿAdīm and Aleppo as portrayed in his Biographical Dictionary of people associated with the city* (Leiden, 1994)

—— 'Egypt and Syria in Ibn al-ʿAdīm's *Bughyat al-ṭalab fī taʾrīkh Ḥalab*', in Kennedy, ed., *The Historiography of Islamic Egypt*, 13–22

C.F. Petry, *The Civilian Élite of Cairo in the Later Middle Ages* (Princeton, 1981)
A model study from a later period of Islamic history. It analyses data about Mamluk bureaucrats from two fifteenth-century biographical dictionaries.

L. Pouzet, *Damas au VIIᵉ–XIIIᵉ siècles: vie et structure religieuses d'une métropole islamique* (Beirut, 1998)

—— 'Remarques sur l'autobiographie dans le monde arabo-musulman au Moyen Âge', in U. Vermeulen and D. de Smet, eds., *Philosophy and Arts in the Islamic World* (Louvain, 1998), 97–106

W. al-Qadi, 'Biographical dictionaries: inner structure and cultural significance', in G.N. Atiyeh, ed., *The Book in the Islamic World: the written word and communication in the Middle East* (Albany, 1995), 93–122

D.F. Reynolds, ed., *Interpreting the Self. Autobiography in the Arabic literary tradition* (Berkeley, 2000)
Contains a very useful guide to autobiography in the Arab world. For works written in the period of the project, see pp. 259–66.

R. Roded, *Women in Islamic Biographical Collections: from Ibn Saʿd to Who's Who* (Boulder, 1994)

F. Rosenthal, 'Die arabische Autobiographie', *Studia Arabica* 1 (1937), 1–40

—— *The Technique and Approach of Muslim Scholarship* (Rome, 1947)

A. Schauer, *Muslime und Franken. Ethnische, soziale und religiöse Gruppen im Kitāb al-Iʿtibar des Usāma ibn Munqid* (Berlin, 2000)

A. Schimmel, *Islamic Names* (Edinburgh, 1989)

J. Sublet, ed., *Cahiers d'onomastique arabe* (Paris, 1979, 1981, 1985, 1989, 1993–)
This pioneering venture, begun in the days when computers were not as advanced as now, is still ongoing.

—— *Le voile du nom: essai sur le nom propre arabe* (Paris, 1991)

D. Urvoy, *Le monde des ulemas andalous du v/xi au vii/xiii siècle: étude sociologique* (Geneva, 1978)
A study of the Muslim religious élites in medieval Spain.

J. Vallve Bermejo, 'La literature biográfica árabe y la toponimia de al-Andalus', in C. Vazquez de Benito and M.A. Manzano Rodríguez, eds., *Actas XVI Congreso UEAI* (Salamanca, 1995), 531–8

M.J.L. Young, 'Arabic biographical writing', in M.J.L. Young, J.D. Latham, R.B. Serjeant, eds., *The Cambridge History of Arabic Literature: religion, learning and science in the Abbasid period* (Cambridge, 1990), 168–87

# 13

# Arabic Sources for Sicily

JEREMY JOHNS

THE FOLLOWING BRIEF INTRODUCTION TO THE HISTORY OF SICILY 1025–1204 concentrates upon the less well-known and more complicated periods—the last years of Islamic Sicily, and the passage from Norman rule to the reign of the future Emperor Frederick II—and passes swiftly over the politically uncomplicated reign of the Norman kings, dwelling only upon the fate of the Muslims of Sicily under Christian rule and the unique corpus of Arabic documentary sources from Norman Sicily.

## THE KALBID DYNASTY (948–1052/3)

Byzantine Sicily was conquered by Arab and Berber forces sent by the Aghlabid emirs of Ifriqiyya (central North Africa, from Tripolitania to central Algeria) during the ninth and early tenth centuries. After the Fatimid caliphs ousted the Aghlabid dynasty in 909, the island was ruled by governors appointed by the Fatimids until the latter migrated to Egypt in 969–73. The Fatimids entrusted Ifriqiyya to the Berber Zirid dynasty (972–1148), and Sicily to the Arab Kalbid dynasty (948–1052/3). Although the Kalbid governor theoretically owed allegiance directly to the Fatimid caliph, the Zirid emir often acted as if he were the ruler of the island.

The Kalbids continued to prosecute the Holy War (*jihād*) in Calabria and, when attacked, in eastern Sicily. Nonetheless, under their rule, the island was transformed from a frontier province organised for war into a relatively peaceful centre of Islamic civilisation. The arts of peace were cultivated at and around the Kalbid court in Palermo, where Quranic and grammatical studies and poetry were especially favoured. Beyond Palermo and its hinterland, only the west and centre of Sicily, where the greatest number of Ifriqiyyans had settled, was profoundly arabicised and islamised, the north and east of the island largely retained its Greek cultural orientation, especially the cities, towns and strongholds of the Ionian coast.

During the first half of the eleventh century, Islamic Sicily was riven by deep social divisions within the Muslim community—between the descendants of original colonists and newcomers, between Arabs and Berbers. Such unrest first became endemic and then developed into civil war. The Kalbid governor Aḥmad ibn Abi'l-Futūḥ Yūsuf, known as al-Akḥal, 'the Dark' (1019–38) was challenged by one of his brothers, who appealed successfully to the Zirid emir for support. Al-Akḥal countered by appealing to the Byzantine emperor Michael IV (1034–41). Constantine Opos, the *katepan* (governor) of Italy, crossed to Sicily and helped al-Akḥal to defeat a Zirid expedition in 1037. After the assassination of his ally, al-Akḥal, in 1038, Michael IV launched a major expedition, led by George Maniakes and intended to reconquer Sicily. Most of the strongholds of the east coast were taken, including the old Byzantine capital of Syracuse, before Maniakes was recalled to Constantinople in 1040. The expedition rapidly collapsed and, by 1042, all that Maniakes had won had been lost.

The Muslims of Sicily united around a brother of al-Akḥal, al-Ḥasan b. Abi'l-Futūḥ, who took—or was awarded by the Fatimid caliph—the title Ṣamṣām al-Dawla, 'Sword of the State'. Ṣamṣām al-Dawla is a shadowy figure, whose career can only be reconstructed with difficulty. A careful reading of the Arabic sources, apparently confirmed by two letters from the Cairo Genizah,[1] indicates that he may have ruled for more than a decade, until 1052–3, when he was expelled by the elders of Palermo.


## THE END OF ISLAMIC RULE (1052/3–1072)

Ṣamṣām al-Dawla was the last Kalbid governor of Sicily and, on his fall, unitary Kalbid rule fragmented into a kaleidoscope of rival petty principalities. When Ibn al-Thumna, the ruler of Syracuse, was defeated by Ibn al-Ḥawwās, lord of Castrogiovanni (Enna), in 1060, he sought mercenary support from the leaders of the Normans, who were rapidly gaining control of southern Italy. Following two preliminary raids, Robert Guiscard, duke of Apulia, and his younger brother, Roger de Hauteville, count of Calabria, crossed to Sicily in May 1061 with a mercenary force in support of Ibn al-Thumna. After the latter was murdered by the Muslim commander of Entella in the summer of 1062, the Norman brothers pursued the conquest of Sicily.

In 1062, the new Zirid emir, Tamīm ibn al-Muʿizz (1062–1108) dispatched two of his sons, Ayyūb and ʿAlī, at the head of a relief expedition to the island. Ayyūb landed at Palermo and soon established himself as master of the west, while ʿAlī based himself at Agrigento, in order to support Ibn al-Ḥawwās against the Norman threat to Castrogiovanni. A joint force of Sicilian and Ifriqiyyan troops was heavily defeated at Cerami in June 1063.

---

[1] See further below and Ch. 14.

In the mid 1060s, Ayyūb withdrew from Palermo to Agrigento. The affection shown for him by the citizens excited the jealousy of Ibn al-Ḥawwās, who ordered them to expel Ayyūb and, when they refused, attacked. Ibn al-Ḥawwās was killed in the fighting, and Ayyūb proclaimed ruler. Subsequently, Ayyūb returned to Palermo, where fighting broke out between his men and the citizens. The Arabic sources blame this conflict for the decision of Ayyūb and ʿAlī to abandon the island in the year 461 AH (31 October 1068–19 October 1069). But, if that date is correct, the immediate threat to the capital posed by the Norman victory at Misilmeri, in the spring or summer of 1068, is likely to have contributed to their decision.

Events in Palermo during the period between the withdrawal of Ayyūb and the Norman conquest of the city are particularly obscure. The Latin sources report only that the surrender of the capital to the Normans in January 1072 was negotiated by its leading citizens. It is therefore possible that, after the flight of Ayyūb, the city was governed by a council drawn from its most prominent men. However, it seems that, for at least some of this period, Ibn al-Baʿbāʾ, a Muslim merchant who figures largely in the letters of the Cairo Genizah,[2] became the last ruler of Islamic Palermo. His fate is uncertain, but he may have escaped to Alexandria before the Norman siege closed around the city in July or August 1071.[3]

## NORMAN SICILY (1072–1189)

After the surrender of Islamic Palermo to Duke Robert and Count Roger in January 1072, the west of the island soon fell to the Normans, but the mountainous east held out far longer against their advance, and Noto, the last Islamic stronghold, surrendered only in 1091. Roger held the island as count of Sicily from his elder brother, Robert Guiscard, the duke of Apulia (1057–85), and then from Robert's son, Duke Roger Borsa (1085–1111). On Roger I's death in 1101, his infant son, Simon, ruled as count under the regency of his mother, Adelaide, until his death in 1105. He was succeeded by his nine year-old brother, also named Roger—Roger II—who ruled as count of Sicily with Adelaide until he came of age at the end of 1111. By then, his overlord, Duke Roger Borsa, had died and been succeeded by his son, William. After William's death in 1127, Roger II of Sicily assumed the

---

[2] See above, n. 1.
[3] This account of the career of Ṣamṣām al-Dawla and of the last years of Islamic Sicily differs significantly from the reconstruction of events given by Amari and by Gil (see below: Amari, *Storia*, vol. 2, 478–90; Gil, 'Sicily and its Jews', 546–62) and summarises the conclusions of a forthcoming study by the present author.

title of duke of Apulia. Then, on Christmas Day 1130, Roger II had himself crowned king of Sicily by the anti-Pope Anacletus II (1130–8). For the next sixty years years, King Roger II (1130–54), his son William I (1154–1166), and his grandson William II (1166–1189) ruled the Norman kingdom of Sicily and presided over a period of greater peace and prosperity than the island had known since antiquity.

## THE END OF NORMAN RULE (1189–94)

When William II died in November 1189, he left no legitimate male heir, and the succession to the kingdom was contested by three candidates. The weakest was Roger, count of Andria, who had the support of the nobility but no claim to royal blood to match that of the rival Sicilian candidate, Tancred of Lecce, the illegitimate son of Roger II's eldest son, Roger, duke of Apulia (d. 1148). Tancred also had the populace of Palermo on his side, and commanded the support of the all-important palace faction. Early in 1190, he was crowned king of Sicily in Palermo. The third candidate was Constance, the only child of Roger II to survive William II. In 1184, she had married Henry, son and heir of Frederick Barbarossa, the Hohenstaufen emperor of Germany (1152–90). The mainland barons who supported Roger of Andria rose in rebellion against Tancred and, in May 1190, a German army invaded the kingdom, but Tancred succeeded in preventing his enemies from uniting against him: Roger of Andria was captured and executed, and the German army withdrew. After the death of Barbarossa in June 1190, Henry and Constance crossed the Alps and, in April 1191, were crowned emperor and empress in Rome by Pope Celestine III (1191–8). Henry promptly invaded the kingdom and encountered little opposition as he advanced, through Capua, Aversa and Salerno, to besiege Naples. There he halted and, threatened by Pope Celestine's support for Henry the Lion, his Welf rival for the imperial throne, turned back in August 1191, leaving the Empress Constance in Salerno and only weak imperial garrisons to secure his conquests. Constance fell into Tancred's hands and, at Gravina in June 1192, Celestine and Tancred came to an agreement. But Celestine persuaded Tancred to release Constance into his custody and, on the road to Rome, she was seized by imperial troops and restored to Henry.

Henry VI was prevented by the Welf opposition from resuming his campaign against Sicily throughout 1192 and, early in 1193, Tancred set the seal on a potentially important alliance with the Byzantine emperor Isaac Angelos (1185–95) by marrying his elder son, Roger duke of Apulia, to Isaac's daughter Irene. But Roger died before the end of the year, and Tancred followed him to the grave in February 1194.

## HENRY VI AND THE MINORITY OF FREDERICK II (1194–1208)

Henry VI landed unopposed at Naples in August 1194 and, having encountered little significant resistance in Sicily, entered Palermo on 20 November. On Christmas Day, he was crowned king of Sicily in Palermo cathedral. Tancred's widow, Sibylla, and her three daughters were confined in the convent of Hohenburg in Alsace; the Byzantine Princess Irene was married to Henry's brother, Philip of Swabia; and Tancred's son, the young King William III was made to disappear. On the day after Henry's coronation in Palermo, Constance gave birth to his son, the future Emperor Frederick II, at Jesi near Ancona.

Early in 1195, Henry VI crossed to the mainland and marched north to secure the succession for the young Frederick, and to prepare for the crusade made opportune by the palace coup of Alexios Angelos (1195–1203). Constance, who was sent to Palermo to represent the German emperor, spent 1195–6 energetically seeking to reclaim the privileges of the Sicilian king that Tancred had ceded to the Pope. In March 1197, Henry returned to Sicily, where he survived a conspiracy that seems to have been suppressed with exemplary ferocity, before dying of dysentery on 28 September.

The young Frederick had already been elected as both successor to the German crown and king of the Romans, but the death of his father undid these careful preparations for the permanent union between the German empire and the kingdom of Sicily. On 8 May 1198, Henry's brother, Philip of Swabia, was formally elected king in Germany, while Constance had Frederick brought to Palermo, where he was crowned king of Sicily on 17 May. The late emperor's seneschal, Markwald of Anweiler, recognised Philip and, claiming that Henry's will had granted him the custody of Frederick and the kingdom of Sicily, threatened to invade. Constance fought hard to secure her son's rights and succeeded in gaining the support of the new Pope Innocent III (1198–1216), who published his grant of the Sicilian kingdom to Constance and Frederick on 19 November 1198. But, when Constance herself died on 28 November, Pope Innocent assumed control of the kingdom as its feudal overlord. In Sicily, both the palace faction and the clergy prepared to resist Innocent's claims, and the Pope was reduced to negotiating an agreement with Markwald. The latter reached Trapani in October 1199 and immediately began to defy papal authority. Innocent countered by allying himself with Sibylla's son-in-law, Walter of Brienne, and supporting his rule in southern Italy from 1201 to 1205. This apparent betrayal of the young Frederick, persuaded the palace faction in Palermo to join with Markwald, who gained control of Frederick in November 1201. Markwald had obtained effective authority over much of Sicily, and was about to take Messina and cross to the mainland, when he died after surgery in September 1202.

In Sicily, Markwald was replaced by another German, William Capparone, who seized control of the palace and the young Frederick, and assumed the title of Defender of the King and Grand Captain of Sicily. William was a mere usurper, for Philip of Swabia had appointed Conrad of Uerslingen as Markwald's successor as custodian of Sicily, and Pope Innocent restored his old enemy, Walter of Palear, as chancellor of the Kingdom, and appointed Cardinal Gerhard Allocingola to act as his legate to Sicily. The most faithful of Markwald's German allies, Dipold of Acerra, finally defeated and killed Walter of Brienne in June 1205. Walter's death opened the way for an agreement between the Pope and much of the nobility of the kingdom and, in the same year, Philip of Swabia and Innocent began negotiations. Dipold and his German associates, including William Capparone, were reconciled to Innocent, and Frederick was restored to the care of the papal legate. This unsteady balance of power in Sicily continued until 26 December 1208 when Frederick reached his majority and succeeded to the kingdom of Sicily, and when Pope Innocent gave up the regency. The reign of Frederick lies beyond the scope of this volume.

## MUSLIMS IN CHRISTIAN SICILY

After the Norman conquest of Sicily in the late eleventh century, the majority of the population of the island, especially in the west and centre, remained Muslim and Arabic-speaking throughout the twelfth century. The Muslims of Sicily were incorporated under Norman rule according to an adaptation of the Islamic law and practice whereby communities of Christians and Jews were incorporated into the Islamic state. Thus, Muslim communities that surrendered to the Normans were permitted to retain freedom for their persons and property and to follow their own customs, laws and religious practices, and were afforded protected status (*dhimma*) by the Norman ruler, on the condition that they paid the *jizya*, a tax levied upon each Muslim household that was part tribute, part penal religious charge. Throughout the twelfth century, Muslims probably constituted the majority of the population in Palermo and the other cities and towns of the west and centre of the island, including Trapani, Agrigento, Corleone and Sciacca, while sizeable Muslim minorities survived in Catania, Syracuse and other eastern towns. In the countryside, a vast area of inland western Sicily, where Muslim settlement was heaviest, was annexed to the de Hauteville demesne and farmed as a Muslim reservation, from which Latin settlers and the Latin church was largely excluded until the mid 1170s.

But the protected status in law of the Muslims of Sicily was effective only when and where the Norman ruler was able to enforce it. In practice, whenever and wherever his authority failed, the growing numbers of Latin immigrants from the mainland took the opportunity to drive the Muslims from their houses and their lands, and to massacre them. Such pogroms occurred during the minority and early rule of Count Roger II (1105–11), during the baronial rebellion against William I in 1161–2, and—most disastrously—on the death of William II in November 1189. As news of the king's death spread through the city, the Latin citizens began to massacre the Muslims of Palermo, and to loot their property. The Muslims sought to escape by fleeing to the hills of the Muslim reservation, where resistance to persecution gradually hardened into open rebellion. For much of the half century from 1189 until 1246, inland western Sicily was controlled by an independent rebel Islamic state, ruled by its own leaders, from a chain of hill-top castles, where they minted their own coins bearing the Islamic profession of faith, and from where they sought to obtain the assistance of the Muslim rulers of the Mediterranean and beyond. It was largely the support of Muslim rebels that permitted Markwald of Anweiler to seize control of Sicily in 1201 and the Emperor Frederick II was obliged to launch two concerted campaigns against the Musim rebels, in 1221–3 and again in 1245–6, before warfare, massacre, compulsory transportation to the mainland, forced conversion, and immigration effectively destroyed the Muslim community of Sicily.

## THE ARABIC SOURCES FOR SICILY:
## THE DOCUMENTARY MATERIAL

The Arabic sources for Sicily 1025–1204 may be divided into two: literary sources (including histories, geographies and travelogues, anthologies of poetry, and biographical dictionaries); and documentary sources (including Arabic and bilingual documents issued by the Norman administration of the island, private documents prepared for the Muslims of Sicily, Judaeo-Arabic letters relating to Sicily from the Cairo Genizah, and inscriptions). The Arabic literary sources for Sicily are not significantly different from those for the rest of the Islamic world, discussed by Carole Hillenbrand in the preceding chapter, and require no special comment here. However, the survival of a substantial corpus of Arabic documents from Christian Sicily is an important exception to the general rule that Arabic administrative documents do not survive before the later medieval period, and thus requires a few words of explanation.

During the conquest of the island, the Norman leaders seem to have systematically preserved some written records of the Islamic administration and to have made use of the officials of the Islamic administration to keep records of the subsequent division of lands and populations amongst their followers.

At this early stage, rather than issuing documents that described the boundaries of a piece of land to be granted, it was easier to list the names of the heads of household that inhabited it, and to grant them with all their property. Thus, from as early as 1093, Count Roger I issued Arabic and bilingual (Arabic–Greek) registers (*jarā'id*, sing. *jarīda*) of the populations granted to the Latin churches that he founded in Sicily, such as Palermo cathedral or the abbey of St Agatha at Catania, or to his barons, such as Roger Forestal or Julian of Labourzi. The young Roger II and the regent Adelaide also issued bilingual Arabic–Greek decrees, addressed to their Arabic- and Greek-speaking officials. But, within a generation or so of the conquest, as the pre-conquest officials employed by the Norman regime came to the end of their careers and were increasingly replaced by Greek administrators, Arabic gradually ceased to be a language in which documents were issued by the central administration. For a period of twenty years from 1111 to 1130, no Arabic document has survived, and none is known to have been issued.

After his coronation on Christmas Day 1130, Roger II and his leading ministers, especially George of Antioch, a probably Cilician Armenian who had been trained in Byzantine Syria, and had subsequently defected first to Zirid Ifriqiyya and then to Norman Sicily, set about creating the Sicilian monarchy *de novo* by importing wholesale the essential accoutrements and symbols of kingship from Byzantium, the courts of the Islamic Mediterranean, and the Latin west. Among the imports from Fatimid Cairo, which George of Antioch had visited many times as Roger's ambassador and where he cultivated close friendships with leading officials amongst the Cilician Armenian diaspora, were scribes, diplomatic forms and practices, and bureaucratic structures drawn from the Fatimid administration. Immediately after Roger's coronation, his reformed Arabic administration (*dīwān*) began to issue a series of Arabic and bilingual documents which continued until the reign of Constance and which Frederick II attempted, unsuccessfully, to revive. The primary purpose of royal *dīwān* was not administrative efficiency but the projection of the image of the multicultural Norman monarchy. None of the internal records of the royal *dīwān* are preserved, but only the Arabic and bilingual documents that it issued to baronial and—especially—ecclesiastical beneficiaries. Most are grants of lands, men and other privileges from the royal demesne, including registers (*jarā'id*) of the names of the men and descriptions of the boundaries of the lands (*ḥudūd*) granted. With the exception of one or two documents that were preserved in private family archives, most were preserved by the Christian churches of the island.

The ecclesiastical archives of Sicily also preserved most of the private Arabic documents prepared according to Islamic law and practice for Muslims under Norman rule. Some were transferred to ecclesiastical archives when the property to which they relate passed to the church, others were apparently acquired and retained in complete ignorance of their content but in the hope that they might be used by the church to support a future claim to property or rights. The majority relate to property transactions, and reflect the forms and organisation of comparable documents from the medieval Islamic world, such as the Arabic papyri from Egypt and the Arabic documents from the Cairo Genizah.

The value of the Judaeo-Arabic letters of Jewish traders preserved in the Cairo Genizah is discussed in Chapter 14 of this volume. Here it is necessary to stress only that they are of especial importance for the history of Islamic Sicily. Given the relative paucity of narrative sources for the history of the island, and the absolute absence of other documentary records before the Norman conquest, the 138 Genizah letters relating to Islamic Sicily constitute a unique source not just for the social history of the Jewish community of the island, but also for the commercial, economic and social history of Islamic Sicily as a whole—they even throw light into some of the more obscure corners of the island's political history. The Genizah correspondence relating to Sicily ceases circa 1070 and only resumes in 1123. This gap of approximately half a century could reflect nothing more significant than the chance survival of the Genizah materials. However, it is unlikely to be mere coincidence that the Sicilian letters stop on the eve of the Norman conquest of Palermo and resume at almost precisely the moment when there is the earliest evidence of direct contact between Roger II and the Fatimid caliph al-Ḥāfiẓ bi'llāh. It is therefore tempting to suggest that the Norman conquest of Palermo interrupted the trade of the Genizah merchants with Ifrīqiyya and Egypt, and that, fifty years later, the rapprochement between the Normans and the Fatimids reopened the ports of Sicily to the Genizah merchants.

# BIBLIOGRAPHY

## HANDBOOKS, SURVEYS, PROSOPOGRAPHIES

M. Amari, ed., *Biblioteca arabo-sicula, ossia raccolta di testi arabici che toccano la geografia, la storia, le biografie e la bibliografia della Sicilia*, 1 vol. and 2 appendices (Leipzig, 1857–87; repr. Baghdad, Maktabat al-muthannā, n.d., missing 2nd appendix); 2nd edn. rev. U. Rizzitano and others, 2 vols., Accademia nazionale di scienze lettere e arti di Palermo (Palermo, 1988); Italian trans. M. Amari, *Biblioteca arabo-sicula, ossia raccolta di testi arabici che toccano la geografia, la storia, la biografia e la bibliografia della Sicilia. Raccolti e tradotti in italiano*, 2 vols. and appendix (Turin, 1880–9; various reprints, e.g. Edizioni Dafni, Palermo, 1982); 2nd edn. rev. U. Rizzitano and others, 3 vols., Accademia nazionale di scienze lettere e arti di Palermo, (Palermo, 1997–8)

Indispensable and immensely convenient compendium of extracts from Arabic primary sources (not documents) relating to Sicily, Italy and the crusading activities of Sicilians. Includes: geographers and travellers (al-Idrīsī, Ibn Jubayr, Yāqūt, etc.); historians (Ibn al-Athīr; Ibn ʿIdhārī al-Marrākushī, Ibn Khaldūn, etc.); poets and anthologists (Ibn Ḥamdīs, ʿImād al-Dīn al-Iṣfahānī, etc.); and biographers (Ibn Khallikān, al-Dhahabī, al-Ṣafadī, etc.). Brief biographical and bibliographical notes on sources (trans., 1st edn., vol. 1, xxii–lxxxiii; 2nd edn., vol. 1, xix–lxxxviii). New edition (very rare outside Italy) corrects many of Amari's misreadings and mistranslations, and updates bibliography, but infuriatingly does not introduce sources or versions unknown to Amari. Good indices to 1st edn., but those of 2nd edn. (text and trans.) are poor and unreliable. (Only those sources unknown to Amari and of particular importance for this volume are listed individually below under Primary Sources.)

M. Amari, *Storia dei musulmani di Sicilia*, 2nd edn. rev. C.A. Nallino, 3 vols. (Catania, 1933–9; various reprints, most recently Edumond Le Monnier, Milan, 2002)
Inevitably out of date but still indispensable introduction to the history of the Muslims of Sicily from the first Arab raids to the late thirteenth century. (The first edition—Florence, 1854–72—lacking Nallino's revision, is of purely historiographical interest.) Complements *Biblioteca arabo-sicula*. Vol. 1 from rise of Islam to conquest of Syracuse in 878; vol. 2, 875–1060; vol. 3, 1060–1265. Useful analytical table of primary sources (vol. 1, 37–104) is preferable to notes on sources in *Biblioteca arabo-sicula*. Good indices to all three volumes at end of vol. 3 (separate index of personal names).

E. Besta and others, eds., *Centenario della nascita di Michele Amari: scritti di filologia e storia araba; di geografia, storia, diritto della Sicilia medievale; studi bizantini e giudaici relativi all'Italia meridionale nel Medio Evo; documenti sulle relazioni fra gli stati italiani ed il Levante*, 2 vols. (Palermo, 1910)
First concerted attempt to celebrate and update Amari's achievement. Includes extracts relating to Sicily of Arabic primary sources unknown to Amari.

*Testimonianze degli arabi in Italia (Roma, 10 dicembre 1987)* Giornata di studio, Fondazione Leone Caetani, Accademia nazionale dei Lincei (Rome, 1988)

B. Scarcia Amoretti, ed., *Del nuovo sulla Sicilia musulmana (Roma, 3 maggio 1993)*, Giornata di studio, Fondazione Leone Caetani, Accademia nazionale dei Lincei (Rome, 1995)

*La Sicile à l'époque islamique. Questions de méthode et renouvellement récent des problématiques*, Mélanges de l'École française de Rome. Moyen Âge 116.1 (Rome, 2004)
Acts of three recent conferences bringing study of Islamic Sicily more or less up to date. Include further newly discovered Arabic primary sources and/or important bibliography.

G. Caracausi, *Dizionario onomastico della Sicilia. Repertorio storico-etimologico di nomi di famiglia e di luogo. Repertorio storico-etimologico di nomi di famiglia e di luogo*, Centro di studi filologici e linguistici siciliani, Lessici siciliani 7, 2 vols. (Palermo, 1993)
Etymological and historical dictionary of Sicilian personal names (and toponyms). May be used together with G. Caracausi, *Lessico greco della Sicilia e dell'Italia meridionale (secoli X–XIV)*, Centro di studi filologici e linguistici sicil-

iani, Lessici siciliani 6 (Palermo, 1990)—to which there is regrettably no Arabic equivalent—to search for first occurrence of Sicilian personal names, including many derived from Arabic. (See below for other onomastic studies.)

## PRIMARY SOURCES

### Literary Sources

Only those sources unknown to Amari and of particular importance for this volume are listed individually below (see above under Amari, *Biblioteca arabo-sicula*).

al-Ḥimyarī, *Kitāb Rawḍ al-miʿṭār fī khabar al-aqṭār (The Scented Garden of Information about Foreign Lands)*
Historical and geographical dictionary compiled by Andalusian scholar Abū ʿAbd Allāh Muḥammad ibn ʿAbd al-Munʿim al-Ḥimyarī (d. 1326/7). Sole source for naval battle between Sicilian Muslims and Byzantines off Pantelleria, c. 1050. Biography of Sicilian Muslim jurist the *imām* Abū ʿAbd Allāh Muḥammad ibn ʿAlī al-Māzarī (d. 1141). Important source for career of Muḥammad ibn ʿAbbād, leader of Muslim rebels of Sicily against Frederick II. Remarkable accounts of Palermo and Rome.
*Editions:*
I. ʿAbbās, ed., *Kitāb Rawḍ al-miʿṭār fī khabar al-aqṭār. A Geographical Dictionary* (Beirut, 1975)
    Standard critical edition.
*Translations:*
A. De Simone, *La descrizione dell'Italia nel Rawḍ al-miʿṭār di al-Ḥimyarī*, Quaderni de Corso «al-Imām al-Māzarī» 7 (Mazara del Vallo, 1984)
    Accurate translation of entries relating to Italy and Sicily, with excellent introduction and notes. Virtually unobtainable outside Sicily.

Ibn Qalāqis, *al-Zahr al-bāsim waʾl-ʿarf al-nāsim fī madīḥ al-ajall Abiʾl-Qāsim (Smiling Flowers and Redolent Perfume in Praise of the Sublime Abuʾl-Qāsim)*
Remarkable autobiographical *roman à lettres* describing visit of Abuʾl-Futūḥ Naṣr ibn ʿAbd Allāh ibn Qalāqis al-Lakhmī al-Iskandarī (b. 1137, d. 1172), the versatile Alexandrian poet, to Sicily in 1168–9, under patronage of hereditary leader of the Muslims of Sicily, Abuʾl-Qāsim Muḥammad ibn Ḥammūd (*fl.* 1162–85). Important source for Norman court during minority of William II and regency of Margaret of Navarre, for the life of Abuʾl-Qāsim and his circle, and for the condition of Sicilian Muslims under Norman rule.
*Editions:*
ʿAbd al-ʿAzīz ibn Nāṣir al-Māniʿ, ed., *al-Zahr al-bāsim waʾl-ʿarf al-nāsim fī madīḥ al-ajall Abiʾl-Qāsim* (Riyāḍ, 1984)
    Adequate, uncritical edition with minimal apparatus.
*Translations:*
A. De Simone, *Splendori e misteri di Sicilia in un'opera di Ibn Qalāqis* (Messina, 1996)
    Generally reliable Italian translation of whole work with useful introduction and notes. Index.

*Secondary Literature:*
A. De Simone, 'Ibn Qalāqis in Sicilia', in B. Scarcia Amoretti and L. Rostagno, eds., *Yād-Nāma in memoria di Alessandro Bausani*, 2 vols. (Rome, 1991), vol. 2, 323–44
—— 'Una ricostruzione del viaggio in Sicilia di Ibn Qalāqis sulla base dell'*az-Zahr al-bāsim*', in *Arabi e Normanni in Sicilia. Atti del Convegno internazionale euro-arabo (Agrigento, 22–25 febbraio 1992)* (Agrigento, 1993), 109–25
—— '*Al-Zahr al-bāsim* di Ibn Qalāqis e le vicende dei musulmani nella Sicilia normanna', in B. Scarcia Amoretti, ed., *Del nuovo sulla Sicilia musulmana (Roma, 3 maggio 1993)*, Giornata di studio, Fondazione Leone Caetani, Accademia nazionale dei Lincei (Rome, 1995), 99–152
J. Johns, *Arabic Administration in Norman Sicily: the royal dīwān* (Cambridge, 2002), 35, 133, 212, 233–4, 235–6, 237, 239–41
With her introduction to the translation, De Simone's three studies provide a comprehensive account of Ibn Qalāqis's visit to Sicily (with a few additional notes by Johns).

## Ibn Qalāqis, *Dīwān (Collected Poems)*
Poems dedicated to many of the leading Muslim rulers and ministers of his day, including the Ayyubid sultan Ṣalāḥ al-Dīn (Saladin, 1169–93), the Almohad caliph 'Abd al-Mu'min ibn 'Alī (1130–63), and the last Fatimid caliph al-'Aḍid li-dīn Allāh (1160–71). Dedicatees include: Sicilian regent Margaret and young King William II; their Muslim eunuch chamberlain and familiar, Richard; the hereditary leader of the Muslim community of Sicily, Abu'l-Qāsim ibn Ḥammūd; his rival al-Ṣadīd Hibat Allāh ibn al-Ḥusrī (*fl.* 1167–9); and other members of the Sicilian Muslim élite.

*Editions:*
Sihām 'Abd al-Wahhāb Furayḥ, ed., *Dīwān Ibn Qalāqis* (Kuwayt, 1988)
Adequate edition. Uncritical. Minimal apparatus (unreliable).

*Translations:*
Many of the most important poems dedicated to Sicilian subjects are either reproduced in the *Zahr al-bāsim* and translated by De Simone in *Splendori e misteri di Sicilia* or translated in her articles (see above).

*Secondary Literature:*
Johns, *Arabic Administration*, 233–4
Discussion of ode dedicated to eunuch Richard.

## Ibn Qalāqis, *Tarassul (Letters)*
Includes letters to at least three Sicilians: Ghārāt ibn Jawshan, a royal familiar, Ibn Fātiḥ—neither of whom are otherwise known—and al-Ṣadīd Hibat Allāh ibn al-Ḥusrī (see above).

*Editions:*
'Abd al-'Azīz ibn Nāṣir al-Māni', ed., *Tarassul Ibn Qalāqis al-Iskandarī* (Riyāḍ, 1984)
Adequate, uncritical edition with minimal apparatus.

Ibn al-Qaṭṭāʿ, *al-Durra al-khaṭīra waʾl-mukhtār min shuʿarāʾ al-jazīra* (*The Precious Pearl, or The Anthology of the Poets of the Island*) Anthology of one hundred and seventy Sicilian poets made by leading Sicilian scholar, Abuʾl-Qāsim ʿAlī ibn Jaʿfar ibn ʿAlī Ibn al-Qaṭṭāʿ (b. Sicily 1041, d. Egypt 1121), who migrated to Cairo after Norman conquest.

*Editions:*

B. al-Bakkūsh, ed., *al-Durra al-khaṭīra fī shuʿarāʾ al-jazīra: jazīrat Ṣiqillīya* (Beirut, 1995)

al-Qāḍī ʿIyāḍ, *Tartīb al-madārik* (*The Descent of Reason*) Biographical dictionary devoted to jurists belonging to the Mālikite school by al-Qāḍī Abuʾl-Faḍl ʿIyāḍ ibn Mūsā ibn ʿIyāḍ al-Yaḥṣubī (d. 1149). Contains twenty-nine lives of Muslim jurists linked to Sicily, eighteen from the eleventh and twelfth centuries.

*Editions:*

E. Griffini, 'Nuovi testi arabo-siculi: I. Estratti dal «Tartîb al-madârik» del qâdî ʿIyâḍ', in Besta, ed., *Centenario della nascita di Michele Amari*, vol. 1, 365–84 Edition of extracts relevant to Sicily.

al-Maqrīzī, *Kitāb al-Taʾrīkh al-kabīr al-muqaffā li-miṣr* (*The Great History Limited to Egypt*) Biographical dictionary of Muslims of Egypt by late medieval polymath Aḥmad ibn ʿAlī al-Maqrīzī (b. 1358, d. 1442). In addition to the notices of Sicilians extracted by Amari, *Biblioteca arabo-sicula*, see the unique life of King Roger II's vizier, George of Antioch, b. *c.*1061, d. 1151 (vol. 3, 18–20).

*Editions:*

Muḥammad al-Yaʿlāwī, ed., *Kitāb al-Muqaffā al-kabīr*, 8 vols. (Beirut, 1991)

*Secondary Literature:*

Johns, *Arabic Administration*, 80–90, 261–4, 282–3, 326–8 Translation and analysis of life of George of Antioch.

al-Ṣafadī, *Kitab al-Wāfī biʾl-wafayāt* (*The Supplement to the Necrologies*) Massive biographical dictionary, intended to supplement that of Ibn Khallikān, by punctilious Syrian scholar, Ṣalāḥ al-Dīn Khalīl ibn Aybak al-Ṣafadī, (b. 1297, d. 1363). To the extracts on Sicilian subjects—Roger II, George of Antioch, the poet Ibn Ḥamdīs, the scholar Ibn Ẓafar, etc.—published by Amari, *Biblioteca arabo-sicula*, much could now be added, including the important account of flight to and reception by Roger I of Muḥammad ibn ʿAbd Allāh, great-grandson of Idrīs II al-ʿĀlī (Ḥammūdid prince of Málaga, 1043–6, 1054–5), and father of the geographer al-Idrīsī (vol. 8, 324–6).

*Editions:*

Hellmut Ritter and others, eds., *Das biographische Lexikon des Ṣalāḥaddīn Ḫalīl ibn Aibak aṣ-Ṣafadī*, Bibliotheca Islamica 6a–zc, 29 vols. (all published by various houses in Istanbul and Beirut on commission from a succession of publishers in Berlin, Leipzig, Stuttgart, and Wiesbaden, 1931–2004) Standard critical edition.

Aḥmad al-Arnāʾuṭ and Turkī Muṣṭafā, eds., *Kitāb al-Wāfī bi-l-wafayāt*, 29 vols. (Beirut, 2000) Uncritical facsimile edition.

*Secondary Literature:*
A. Amara, and A. Nef, 'Al-Idrīsī et les Ḥammūdides de Sicile: nouvelles données
   biographiques sur l'auteur du *Livre de Roger*', *Arabica* 48 (2001), 121–7
   Presents newly discovered information from al-Ṣafadī concerning Ḥammūdids in
   Sicily (but see also Johns, *Arabic Administration*, 236, n. 101).

## Arabic and Bilingual Documents from Norman Sicily

Approximately eighty Arabic and bilingual documents (Arabic–Greek and Arabic–
Latin) are known from Norman and Hohenstaufen Sicily before 1204, and
constitute an important source for the economic and social history of the Muslims
of Norman Sicily, and for the prosopography of the ruling élite of all three
communities—Arab, Greek and Latin. Of the forty-six issued by the Norman *dīwān*
or Arabic administration, thirty-three survive as originals, and thirteen are known
from official translations into Latin or Sicilian or are lost but are mentioned in other
documents. The originals include grants of lands, men and other privileges and
rights from the demesne of the Norman ruling family. Fifteen are registers (*jarā'id*,
sing. *jarīda*), listing hundreds of names of heads of households granted to feuda-
tories by the Norman rulers. Most of the individuals recorded in the registers appear
only once, and cannot be linked to any other family or individual. The majority
are Muslims, but some Arab Christians are included. Of the private documents,
eighteen are original documents written in Arabic or containing substantial Arabic
text, or translations of Arabic originals; the remainder are Greek or Latin documents with one or more Arabic signatures. Most are deeds of sale of property,
but the following are also represented: exchange of irrigation rights; exchange of
houses; contracts of sea-exchange (*cambium maritimum*); re-commendation of
Muslim villeins to a Christian lord; letters patent; donations to ecclesiastical institutions. Most of the documents are published, but an important group from the
archive of the archimandra of San Salvatore di Messina (the institution responsible for the administration of the Greek church in Norman Sicily) relating to the
Greek monastery of San Giorgio di Triocala, remain unedited. Only the Greek and
Latin texts are published of two original bilingual documents: an Arabic–Greek
decree of William II and the regent Margaret dated November 1166 concerning
the archdeaconry of Messina; and a Latin–Arabic decree of Constance, dated
November 1198, concerning the governing of Malta. A catalogue of Arabic and
bilingual documents issued by the Arabic administration (*dīwān*) and a provisional
catalogue of private documents—neither more than substantially complete—are
published in Johns, *Arabic Administration*, 301–25. A new edition of the whole
corpus is in preparation by the present author, with Vera von Falkenhausen, Nadia
Jamil, Alex Metcalfe, and others.

*Editions and Translations:*
S. Cusa, ed., *I diplomi greci ed arabi di Sicilia pubblicati nel testo originale, tradotti ed
   illustrati*, 2 vols., 1 only published in 2 parts (Palermo, 1868–82; repr. Cologne and
   Vienna, 1982)
   Uncritical edition of most of the corpus. Commentary and translation never
   published. A major achievement, despite many errors and complete lack of
   scholarly apparatus. Useful chronological summary of documents. Indices poor
   and incomplete.

G. Trovato, *Sopravvivenze arabe in Sicilia* (Monreale, 1949; repr. in F.G. Arezzo, *Sicilia. Miscellanea di studi storici, giuridici ed economici sulla Sicilia, glossario di voci siciliane derivate dal greco, latino, arabo, spagnuolo, francese, tedesco, etc.*, Palermo, 1950)

Unreliable, unscholarly Italian translations of many of the Arabic documents published in Cusa, *Diplomi*.

The most important editions and translations of individual documents since publication of Cusa's *Diplomi* are cited below in the chronological order of the date of the documents.

G. La Mantia, *Il primo documento in carta (Contessa Adelaide, 1109) esistente in Sicilia e rimasto sinora sconosciuto* (Palermo, 1908)

March 1109. Bilingual decree of Adelaide and young Roger II in favour of San Filippo di Fragalà, with Italian trans. Cusa, *Diplomi*, no. 23, 402–3. Johns, *Arabic Administration*, 302, no. 7.

A. Guillou, *Les actes grecs de S. Maria di Messina: enquête sur les populations grecques d'Italie du sud et de Sicile (XIᵉ–XIVᵉ s.)*, Istituto siciliano di studi bizantini e neoellenici (Palermo, 1963), no. 3, 51–5

May 1111. Arabic–Greek register (*jarīda*) confirming grant (by Roger I) of eight families and their lands to the knight Julian, with French trans. (In the Arabic, for *Ḥalīq* read *Juliyan*.) Not in Cusa, *Diplomi*. Johns, *Arabic Administration*, 302, no. 8.

J. Johns, 'Arabic contracts of sea-exchange from Norman Sicily', in P. Xuereb, ed., *Karissime Gotifride. Historical essays presented to Godfrey Wettinger on his seventieth birthday* (Malta, 1999), 55–78

Circa 1130 to circa 1160. Rough drafts of three Arabic contracts of sea-exchange in which a Latin investor, Ser Ghulyalim (William) lends various sums in silver pounds to Sicilian Muslims to be repaid in gold *tarì* (Sicilian quarter-dinars). Critical edition of Arabic text, English translation, commentary and analysis. Cusa, *Diplomi*, 502–4, no. 90 (transcription of *recto* only). Johns, *Arabic Administration*, 317–18, no. 8.

L.-R. Ménager, *Amiratus—'Αμηρᾶς. L'émirat et les origines de l'amirauté (XIᵉ–XIIIᵉ siècles)* (Paris, 1960), Appendix 2, no. 24, 200–2

February 1133. Chancery copy of Greek donation (*sigillion*), incorporating Arabic boundary description, of donation of land and men granted by Rainald Avenal to Bishop John of Lipari-Patti. French translation. Cusa, *Diplomi*, no. 45, 515–17. Johns, *Arabic Administration*, 303–4, no. 12.

M.E. Gálvez, 'Noticia sobre los documentos árabes de Sicilia del Archivo Ducal de Medinaceli', in Scarcia Amoretti, ed., *Del nuovo sulla Sicilia normanna*, 167–82

November 1141. Renewal by Roger II of register (*jarīda*) of Muslims held by San Giorgio di Triocala. Defective and unreliable edition and Spanish translation. Not in Cusa. Johns, *Arabic Administration*, 305, no. 18.

H. Grégoire, 'Diplômes de Mazara (Sicile)', *Annuaire de l'Institut de philologie et d'histoire orientales de l'université de Bruxelles* (1932–3), 79–107

November 1145. Renewal of Greek donation (*sigillion*), with Arabic *jarīda* issued by Roger II to San Michele Arcangelo di Mazara. Diplomatic status uncertain; probably a thirteenth-century forgery. Not in Cusa, *Diplomi*. Johns, *Arabic Administration*, 302–3, no. 9 and 308, no. 27.

J. Johns and A. Metcalfe, 'The mystery at Chùrchuro: conspiracy or incompetence in twelfth-century Sicily?', *BSOAS* 62 (1999), 226–59
December 1149. Chancery copy of Arabic privilege of Roger II granting lands and men to Greek monastery of San Nicolò di Chùrchuro. June 1154. Second chancery copy of same privilege, granting same men but—mistakenly—different lands. Cusa, *Diplomi*, 28–30, no. 89 and 34–6, no. 93. Johns, *Arabic Administration*, 308, nos. 28–9 and 309–10, no. 33. See also J. Johns, 'Arabic "June" (*bruṭuyūn*) and "July" (*isṭiriyūn*) in Norman Sicily', *BSOAS* 64 (2001), 98–100, for interesting example of Greek influence upon Sicilian Arabic.

S. Simonsohn, *The Jews in Sicily. Volume 1: 383—1300* (Leiden, New York and Cologne, 1997), pp. 418–21, no. 185
January 1161. Greek–Arabic deed of sale recording purchase from royal administration (*dīwān*), by Jew Ya'qūb ibn Ṣāliḥ of an estate near Palermo. Greek text and English trans. of Arabic (after Cusa, *Diplomi*, 622–6, no. 101). Johns, *Arabic Administration*, 310–11, no. 35.

H. Enzensberger, *Guillelmi I regis diplomata*, Codex diplomaticus Regni Siciliae: 1st ser., Diplomata regum et principum e gente Normannorum, vol. 3 (Cologne, Weimar and Vienna, 1996), 85–7, no. 32
September 1164. Greek–Arabic privilege in which William I grants land to Santa Maria la Gadera, near Polizzi. Disastrous edition of Greek, and inadequate edition of Arabic. Cusa, *Diplomi*, 650–2, no. 49 (wrongly assigned to Roger II). Johns, *Arabic Administration*, 311, no. 36.

L.-R. Ménager, *Amiratus—Ἀμηρᾶς*, 215–24
October 1172. Greek–Arabic record of a boundary inquest, critical edition of Greek and Arabic texts with French translation. Cusa, *Diplomi*, no. 119, 80–3. Johns, *Arabic Administration*, 312, no. 39.

J. Johns, 'The boys from Mezzoiuso: Muslim *jizya*-payers in Christian Sicily', in R. Hoyland and P. Kennedy, eds., *Islamic Reflections, Arabic Musings: studies in honour of Professor Alan Jones* (Oxford, 2003), 243–56. (English version of J. Johns, 'Sulla condizione dei musulmani di Corleone sotto il dominio normanno nel XII° secolo', in *Byzantino-Sicula IV: Atti del I Congresso internazionale di archeologia della Sicilia bizantina* (Palermo, 2002), 275–94)
August 1177–9. Copy of a contract in which three Arab Muslim brothers acknowledge themselves to be *rijāl al-jarā'id* ('men of the registers') belonging to San Giovanni degli Eremiti, and agree to return to their lands, from which they had fled, and to obey their lord, the Abbot Donatus, paying the *jizya* ('poll-tax') and *qānūn* ('land-tax'). Critical edition, English translation, commentary and analysis. Cusa, *Diplomi*, 111–12, no. 129 (with many crucial errors). Johns, *Arabic Administration*, 320, no. 16.

J. Wansbrough, 'A Judaeo-Arabic document from Sicily', *BSOAS* 30 (1967), 305–13
Christmas 1187. Judaeo-Arabic letter patent recording the agreement between the Jewish community of Syracuse and the bishop of Cefalù regarding the lease of a piece of land belonging to the priory of Santa Lucia of Syracuse which adjoined the Jewish cemetery. Critical edition, English translation, commentary and analysis. Cusa, Diplomi, 495–6, no. 156. Johns, *Arabic Administration*, 322–3, no. 25.

*Secondary Literature:*

L. Genuardi, 'I defetari normanni', in E. Besta, *Centenario della nascita di Michele Amari*, vol. 1, 159–64

> Unreliable, but historiographically interesting, discussion of the Sicilian registers (*jarāʾid*).

D. Clementi, 'Notes on Norman Sicilian surveys', in V.H. Galbraith, ed., *The Making of Domesday Book* (Oxford, 1961), 55–8

> Historiographically interesting attempt to compare Sicilian registers (*jarāʾid*) of lands and men to Domesday Book.

A. D'Emilia, 'Diplomi arabi siciliani di compravendita del secolo VI Egira e loro raffronto con documenti egiziani dei secoli III–V Egira', *Annali dell'Istituto universitario orientale di Napoli* 14 (1964), 83–109

> Important study demonstrating the close parallels between Sicilian Arabic deeds of sale and comparable documents from Islamic Egypt.

A. Noth, 'I documenti arabi di Ruggero II', in C. Brühl, *Diplomi e cancelleria di Ruggero II* (Palermo, 1983), 189–222 (rev. Italian version of A. Noth, 'Die arabis-chen Dokumente Roger II', in C. Brühl, *Urkunden und Kanzlei König Rogers II von Sizilien*, Studien zu den normannisch-staufischen Herrscherkunden Siziliens, vol. 1 [Cologne and Vienna, 1978], 217–61)

> Important preliminary study of the Arabic and bilingual documents of Roger II preparatory to the edition of the documents themselves, which Noth was regrettably unable to complete before his untimely death. Firmly relocates the Arabic administration of Norman Sicily in an Islamic context.

J. Wansbrough, 'Diplomatica siciliana', *BSOAS* 47 (1984), 10–21

> Generally slight review, with occasional startling insights.

G. Caracausi, 'I documenti medievali siciliani in lingua araba', in G. Brincat, ed., *Incontri siculo-maltese. Atti del II Convegno su Malta–Sicilia: contiguità e continuità linguistica e culturale (Malta, 4–6 aprile, 1986)* (Malta, 1986), 13–26

> Rich study of the language of Sicilian Arabic documents from the perspective of a classical philologist.

A. De Simone, 'I diplomi arabi di Sicilia', in *Testimonianze degli arabi in Italia*, 57–75

> Important and useful general overview of Sicilian Arabic documents.

O.R. Constable, 'Cross-cultural contacts: sales of land between Christians and Muslims in 12th-century Palermo', *Studia Islamica* 85 (1997), 67–83

> Potentially interesting attempt to use Sicilian Arabic deeds of sale as a source for status of Muslim community of Palermo under Norman rule. Marred by errors of detail (often Cusa's) and by general unfamiliarity with Sicilian context.

J. Johns, *Arabic Administration* (Cambridge, 2002)

> Comprehensive study of the Arabic and bilingual documents issued by the Norman administration (*dīwān*).

A. Metcalfe, *Muslims and Christians in Norman Sicily. Arabic speakers and the end of Islam* (London and New York, 2003)

> Important study of Sicilian Arabic language and its uses in Norman Sicily.

*Secondary Literature (Onomastics of Sicilian Arabic Documents):*

In the absence of a definitive study of all the Sicilian Arabic documents, especially of the registers of men (*jarāʾid*), the following studies constitute an important source for the prosopography of the communities that they describe.

A. De Simone, 'L'*Onomasticon arabicum* e gli antroponomi arabo-greco nei *Diplomi di S. Cusa*', *Atti dell'Accademia di scienze lettere e arti di Palermo*, 4th ser., 35 (1975–6), 261–6

—— *Spoglio antroponomico delle giaride (ǧarā'id) arabo-greche dei Diplomi editi da Salvatore Cusa* (Rome, 1979)

—— 'Gli antroponimi arabo-greci ed il vocalismo dell'arabo di Sicilia', in *Onomastica e trasmissione del sapere nell'Islam medievale*, Studi orientali, vol. 12 (Rome, 1992), 59–90

—— 'La *kunyah* negli antroponimi arabi di Sicilia tra metafora e ambiguità', in *Studi linguistici offerti a Girolamo Caracausi* (Palermo, 1992), 77–98

G. Caracausi, 'Onomastica araba in Sicilia', *Zeitschrift für romanische Philologie* 109 (1993), 348–80

A. Nef, 'Anthroponymie et *jarā'id* de Sicile: une approche renouvelée de la structure sociale des communautés arabo-musulmanes de l'île sous les normandes', in M. Bourin and others, eds., *L'anthroponymie: document de l'histoire sociale des mondes méditerranéens médiévaux. Actes du colloque international organisé par l'École française de Rome avec le concours du GDR 955 du C.N.R.S. «Genèse médiévale de l'anthroponymie moderne» (Rome, 6–8 octobre 1994)*, Collection de l'École française de Rome 226 (Rome, 1996), 123–42

## The Letters of the Cairo Genizah

Highly important source for impact of Norman conquest of Sicily and—to a lesser extent—of the crusades upon maritime commerce between Egypt, North Africa and Sicily.

*Editions:*

M. Ben-Sasson and others, eds., *The Jews of Sicily, 825–1068: documents and sources* (Heb.) (Jerusalem, 1991)
　　Edition of most of the Genizah letters relating to Sicily before 1068. Hebrew critical apparatus etc. Historical judgement, especially regarding date, tends to be sounder than Gil's.

M. Gil, *In the Kingdom of Ishmael during the Gaonic Period* (Heb.), 3 vols. (Jerusalem, 1997)
　　Includes most of the Genizah letters relating to Sicily. Hebrew critical apparatus and translation. Bombastic approach conceals frequently poor historical judgement, especially bizarre conclusions based on misdating documents (e.g. Norman conquest of Sicily began in 1056).

*Translations:*

S. Simonsohn, *The Jews in Sicily. Volume 1: 383–1300* (Leiden, New York, Cologne, 1997)
　　Immensely useful but slapdash English translation of all Genizah letters relating to Sicily. Dates assigned to documents and other critical apparatus not reliable.

*Secondary Literature:*

A selection of the most relevant material in English. Goitein alone is unaffected by Gil's misdating of individual documents and consequent bizarre historical conclusions. The present author is preparing a study of the last years of Islamic Sicily and the Norman conquest (*c.* 1040–95), which addresses the problem.

S.D. Goitein, *A Mediterranean Society. The Jewish communities of the Arab world as portrayed in the documents of the Cairo Geniza*, 5 vols. and index (by P. Saunders) (Berkeley, Los Angeles, London, 1967–93)

—— 'Sicily and Southern Italy in the Cairo Geniza documents', *Archivio storico per la Sicilia orientale* 67 (1971) 9–33

M. Gil, 'The Jews in Sicily under Muslim rule, in the light of the Geniza documents', in *Italia Judaica I. Atti del I Convegno internazionale, Bari 18–22 maggio, 1981* (Rome, 1983), 87–134

—— 'Sicily 827–1072 in light of the Geniza documents and parallel sources', in *Gli ebrei in Sicilia sino all'espulsione del 1492: atti del V Convegno internazionale, Palermo, 15–19 giugno 1992* (Rome, 1995), 96–171

N. Zeldes and M. Frankel, 'The Sicilian trade—Jewish merchants in the Mediterranean in the twelfth and thirteenth centuries', in N. Bucaria, ed., *Gli Ebrei in Sicilia dal tardoantico al Medioevo. Studi in onore di mons. Benedetto Rocco* (Palermo, 1998), 243–56

M. Gil, 'Institutions and events of the eleventh century mirrored in Geniza letters (Part I)', *BSOAS* 67 (2004), 151–67

—— 'Institutions and events of the eleventh century mirrored in Geniza letters (Part II)', *BSOAS* 67 (2004), 168–84

—— 'Sicily and its Jews, 827–1072, in the light of the Geniza documents and parallel sources', in M. Gil, *Jews in Islamic Countries in the Middle Ages* (Leiden and Boston, 2004), 535–93 (Eng. tr. by D. Strassler of Hebrew original by M. Gil, Tel Aviv, 1997)

## Arabic Inscriptions from Sicily

In addition to personal epitaphs of Sicilian Muslims, these include: Arabic hymn to the Virgin from George of Antioch's church, St Mary's of the Admiral; trilingual—Arabic, Greek, and Latin—inscription from Roger II's water-clock; trilingual foundation inscription in name of King Roger II's eunuch Peter; quadringual—Arabic, Greek, Judaeo-Arabic and Latin—and trilingual epitaphs for Anna and Drogo, mother and father of royal priest Grisantus.

M. Amari, ed. and trans., *Le epigrafi arabiche di Sicilia, trascritte, tradotte e illustrate. Parte prima: iscrizioni edili* (Palermo, 1875); *Parte seconda: iscrizioni sepolcrali*, Società siciliana per la storia patria, Documenti per servire alla storia di Sicilia, 3rd ser., vol. 1 (Palermo, 1879); *Parte terza: iscrizioni domestichi*, Società siciliana per la storia patria, Documenti per servire alla storia di Sicilia, 3rd ser., vol. 2 (Palermo, 1885)
Indispensable first edition of most of the Arabic inscriptions of Sicily. The so-called second edition—F. Gabrieli, ed., *Le epigrafi arabiche di Sicilia, trascritte, tradotte e illustrate* (Palermo, 1971)—contains very few of the original plates, makes few significant revisions, and gives only some up-dated bibliography.

*Secondary Literature:*
J. Johns, 'Die arabischen Inschriften der Normannenkönige Siziliens: eine Neuinterpretation', in W. Seipel, ed., *Nobiles officinae: die königlichen Hofwerkstätten zu Palermo zur Zeit der Normannen und Staufer in 12. und 13. Jahrhundert: Kunsthistorisches Museum, 31. März bis 13. Juni 2004: Palermo, Palazzo dei*

*Normanni, 17. Dezember 2003 bis 10. März 2004* (Milan, 2004), 37–59. English and Italian versions of catalogue, including much material not in the German catalogue, forthcoming: M. Fontana, ed., *Nobiles officinae: perle, filigrane e trame di seta dal Palazzo Reale di Palermo* (Catania, 2006)
Includes up-to-date bibliography for original inscriptions and secondary literature.

# 14

# Jewish Sources

## NICHOLAS DE LANGE

THE JEWISH MINORITY FORMS A DISTINCT and largely self-contained element in the population of Byzantium, with its own religion, culture and written language, and perhaps for that reason it is often ignored by historians. An articulate and relatively literate community, it has left behind a not inconsiderable literary and documentary heritage, which is rich in information of a historical nature. The period under scrutiny coincides almost exactly with that of the documents recovered from the so-called Cairo Genizah (a kind of lumber room on the roof of a synagogue in Old Cairo): these are a resource of the first importance, about which more will be said below.[1] A travelogue compiled by a western Jew, Benjamin of Tudela (in Spain), in the 1160s is one of the few Jewish sources relatively familiar to Byzantine historians. Less well known is the extensive literature in Hebrew consisting of hymns, biblical commentaries, and other writings, many of which are unpublished and most untranslated. Some other sources of information about individuals, such as manuscript colophons and funerary inscriptions, although rare for our period, are not to be overlooked.[2] Serious research on all these sources demands specialised linguistic skills, but a sizeable corpus of materials is now accessible in translation. The writings relate mainly to the internal life of the Jewish community and its relations with Jewish communities in countries outside the Empire, but there are some incidental references to Byzantine society generally. In what follows I shall briefly introduce the Byzantine Jewish community, and shall then present the various types of writing that have come down to us. While the main focus is on Byzantine or 'Romaniote' Jews as such, Greek-speakers born on Byzantine territory, we shall also take account of sources written by foreign Jews, or mentioning foreign Jews residing in the Empire.

[1] On the Cairo Genizah and its importance for historians, see the introduction to S.D. Goitein, *A Mediterranean Society*, vol. 1 (Berkeley, 1973).

[2] For examples, see bibliography s.v. Nathan b. Makhir, Abraham b. Meir.

## THE BYZANTINE JEWISH COMMUNITY

It is impossible to estimate how many Jews there were in the Byzantine empire, but from the occasional statistics and the number of localities where they lived it is clear that they were a definite and widespread presence.[3] The largest concentration was in the capital, where they inhabited their own quarters, from *c.*1044 to 1203 in Galata or Pera, across the Golden Horn.[4] There were important communities too in Thessalonike and Thebes, and we hear of other localities, such as Kastoria, Attaleia and Seleukeia. Benjamin of Tudela mentions twenty-seven Byzantine towns which he visited personally and where there was a Jewish community—the clearest indication of the widespread presence of Jews in the Empire. (Yet Benjamin's tour was very incomplete, omitting for example Kastoria and the whole of Anatolia.) The Jews appear to have been more or less confined to the towns, although some of those mentioned were very small. Only in one place, near the north shore of the Gulf of Patras, did he find a farming community of two hundred families working their own land.

The Jewish communities, particularly the larger ones, were torn apart, literally in some cases, by conflict between two main groups, the Karaite minority, and the majority grouping, generally designated 'Rabbanites' because unlike the Karaites they revered and upheld rabbinic tradition. There was a good deal of mutual animosity and polemic, and according to Benjamin of Tudela in Constantinople a physical barrier divided the two communities.[5] However there is other evidence of members of the two communities mixing socially, and to a large extent both shared a common culture. We know the names of a number of participants on both sides of the rift, and there is a common but unjustified assumption that if we do not know someone was a Karaite he must have been a Rabbanite. Some other sects existed: in Cyprus, for example, Benjamin notes the presence of another religious sect, whom he terms 'Epicureans'. From the point of view of the state, however, all these groups were considered as part of a single community.

So far as we can judge from our sources the Jews led a largely self-contained existence, determined partly by their condition as a religious

---

[3] See Map 10 in this volume and the maps in Nicholas de Lange, *An Atlas of the Jewish World* (New York and London, 1984), 40–1; A. Sharf, *Byzantine Jewry from Justinian to the Fourth Crusade* (London, 1971), 106.

[4] See David Jacoby, 'Les quartiers juifs de Constantinople à l'époque byzantine', *Byz* 37 (1967), 167–227; 'The Jews of Constantinople and their demographic hinterland', in C. Mango and G. Dagron, eds., *Constantinople and its Hinterland* (Aldershot, 1995), 221–32; 'The Jewish community of Constantinople from the Komnenan to the Palaiologan period', *VV* 55 (1998), 31–40.

[5] For all aspects of Byzantine Karaism and the conflict with Rabbanism in our period, see Z. Ankori, *Karaites in Byzantium: the formative years 970–1100* (Jerusalem and New York, 1959).

minority and partly by imperial, ecclesiastical and rabbinic legislation which limited contacts with outsiders. Since late antiquity they had been banned from careers in the civil service and the army and from the state educational system, from owning Christian slaves and from exerting any formal authority over Christians. Many documents refer to their role as traders, both internally and internationally. Constantinople occupied a central place on the trading routes of Jewish merchants, whose interests extended from China and India to Spain. Such activities kept the Jews of Byzantium in close touch with Jewish communities overseas, and this in turn had an impact on their Hebraic culture, which knew no boundaries. Their trading role also brought them into some limited contact with non-Jews. Many of the Genizah documents relate to trading activity, and related matters, such as the danger of pirates and the ransoming of those they have taken captive (which was a religious obligation for Jews).[6] Benjamin of Tudela may have been on a trading journey from Spain to the Middle East when he compiled his itinerary, which consists in the main of brief descriptions of the places he visited, together with the distance from one place to the next and some details about the Jewish community, usually its size and the names of its leaders.

Most of the Hebrew texts from Byzantium arise, however, from the scholarly and religious activities of the local Jews. From an unknown date, certainly long before the starting-point of our period, the liturgical and scholarly language of the Jews in Byzantium was Hebrew, even if their spoken language was usually Greek. (Some Jews spoke and perhaps also wrote Arabic; these were foreign immigrants or Byzantine Jews who had lived in Arabic-speaking regions.) Primary education was directed to inculcating an understanding of the Hebrew Bible and prayer-book; at a more advanced level students engaged with the classical rabbinic texts, the Mishnah and Talmud (which also required a reading knowledge of Aramaic), and with the complex and voluminous *halakhic* (legal) literature.[7] A rabbi was a Jew who had mastered these sources and was able (in theory) to deliver independent legal rulings. The rabbis were the supreme spiritual, legal and perhaps administrative authorities of Rabbanite communities; an equivalent role was played by the Karaite sages. These men were also in a position to teach advanced students, preach and expound the scriptures. Since the title 'rabbi' is used very freely in the sources, it is not clear in any particular case what education or authority an individual enjoys. Thus Benjamin of Tudela, naming the heads of the various communities he visited, gives them the title 'rabbi', but it

---

[6] See Starr, *Jews in the Byzantine Empire*, index s.v. 'Ransoming of captives', and bibliography to this chapter s.v. Abū 'Alī b. Abu'l Mānī, and further entries listed under 'Brief References'.

[7] See N.R.M. de Lange, 'Jewish education in the Byzantine empire in the twelfth century', in G. Abramson and T. Parfitt, eds., *Jewish Education and Learning* (Chur, Switzerland, 1994), 115–28.

cannot necessarily be inferred in most cases that they were religious and legal authorities rather than prominent local worthies. Again, the Jewish hymnographers of Byzantium, many of whose compositions are extant, display considerable erudition, and impressive mastery of the Hebrew language; they may well have been rabbis, but it has been suggested that they held the somewhat subordinate position of congregational cantors.[8] The community will have required the services of teachers at various levels, as well as scribes to copy books for the school and private study[9] and scrolls for the synagogue and home, and while these must have commanded an appropriate level of education they were not necessarily rabbis. The free use of Hebrew in merchants' letters is an impressive indication of the extent of literacy in Hebrew, which was clearly not restricted to an élite class. On the other hand there is no real indication of literacy among women, although it is not impossible that some letters by women were written by themselves rather than by professional letter-writers.[10]

The only other learned profession open to Jews at this time was medicine. However, while we have a number of Hebrew medical texts from an earlier period, associated with southern Italy, there are none from the period under scrutiny, and the very rare Jewish physicians mentioned in the sources seem to have studied abroad, notably in Egypt.[11]

## EXTANT WRITINGS FROM THE PERIOD

The prosopographical materials in Hebrew relating to our period are of various kinds. Dated Hebrew manuscripts from the years 1025–1204 are very rare, although not completely unknown.[12] There is a very strong presumption in the case of Cairo Genizah texts of certain recognisable types, however, that they were written around this time, based on a large number of dated documents from other areas. Very few Genizah texts can be shown to have been

[8] L.J. Weinberger, *Jewish Hymnography* (London and Portland, Oregon, 1998), 195. Cf. ibid. p. 197 for a poet who was also a rabbi.

[9] Many learned works were copied by scholars for their own use; others were written to order. There were no scriptoria.

[10] For an example, Nicholas de Lange, *Greek Jewish Texts from the Cairo Genizah* (Tübingen, 1996), 11ff.

[11] e.g. an unnamed physician of Seleukeia (see bibliography s.v. Anonymous), or Rabbi Solomon the Egyptian (see below).

[12] We have, a little earlier, a marriage deed from Mastaura dated 9 March 1022 (de Lange, *Greek Jewish Texts*, no. 1). In our own period a fragment of a Pentateuch with a colophon and masoretic notes dated 1092 is unlocalised, but ascribed to Byzantium on codicological grounds (see M. Beit-Arié, *Hebrew Codicology. Tentative typology of technical practices employed in Hebrew dated medieval manuscripts* [Jerusalem 1981] 19, n. 18).

written in Byzantium, but some texts written elsewhere refer to Byzantium. (And many relate to the Holy Land and the Middle East generally at the time of the crusades.) In a few cases internal evidence suggests a date. The texts that concern us fall into two main categories, letters and documents. Many of the letters are commercial in content; some are personal in nature. In a few cases we have a number of letters from or to the same individuals. The most useful documents are marriage deeds, as they give us information about two families, and can be made to yield valuable social and economic data, particularly when a dowry list is attached.[13] Not all the Genizah texts have been published, or even adequately inventoried, but a good deal of work has been achieved since the end of the nineteenth century, when the materials were brought to Europe and North America. Substantial portions of the deposit are now accessible in libraries in Cambridge, St Petersburg, London, Oxford, and elsewhere.

The epigraphic record for Jews in our period, by contrast, is very sparse, at least so far as published inscriptions are concerned. This is an unsatisfactory situation, that contrasts sharply with that prevailing for antiquity, late antiquity, and even the earlier Byzantine period. An up-to-date corpus of Byzantine Jewish inscriptions is a desideratum.

Narrative texts are a very useful source for prosopography, although they must be used with caution as the editions and translations are not necessarily reliable. A case in point is Benjamin of Tudela's travelogue, which has already been mentioned. The standard (in fact the only) edition and translation, published in 1907, has been much criticised, and a replacement is long overdue. The information given by Benjamin is also frustratingly lean. He makes a point of naming prominent individuals, but only rarely does he give any personal information about them (even their patronyms or surnames). For example in Constantinople he states: 'The Rabbanites include scholars: their leaders are the Chief Rabbi, Rabbi Avtalion, Rabbi Obadiah, Rabbi Aaron Bekhor Shor, Rabbi Joseph Sergero (or Sargeno), and the head of the community, Rabbi Eliakim . . . No Jew is allowed to ride a horse except for Rabbi Solomon the Egyptian, who is the emperor's physician, and through whom the Jews find much relief in their oppression.' In the absence of any other information about these individuals such references are tantalising in the extreme. Much the same problems arise with the other narrative sources cited in English translation by Joshua Starr in his classic work *The Jews in the Byzantine Empire*, published in Athens in 1939 and woefully out of date.

---

[13] For an example of the uses that Genizah texts can be put to, see David Jacoby, 'What do we learn about Byzantine Asia Minor from the documents of the Cairo Genizah?', in *Byzantine Asia Minor* (Athens, 1998), 83–95.

Finally, prosopographical research cannot afford to ignore the authors of literary works that have come down to us in manuscript. These can all be broadly classified as religious texts, ranging from synagogue hymns to commentaries (on scripture, rabbinic texts and hymns) and legal treatises. The surviving literature is relatively rich, and in some cases internal evidence about the authors is supplemented by letters and by external information. These scholars are the best known and best documented of Byzantine Jews, although in no case do we have sufficient materials for a full biography.[14] Other authors, whose works are lost, are known to us through references in other writings.[15]

No Byzantine Jewish archives have been preserved from our period, nor, outside the Cairo Genizah, do we have much in the way of personal or family documents, such as deeds of marriage or divorce, wills or genealogies. Private archives may well have been assembled by individuals and by families, and indeed by synagogues and lawcourts, but if so they have left little or no trace. The family chronicle compiled in the mid-eleventh century by Ahimaaz of Oria (in southern Italy), and extending back some two hundred years, may well have been based in part on family records. It is impossible to be certain whether or not the Byzantine written texts (documents, prayer-books and scholarly texts) recovered from the Cairo Genizah represent the remains of one or more personal archives, although it does seem at least that we have copies of the personal correspondence of one of the foremost Byzantine Karaite scholars, Tobias ben Moses. No Jewish cemetery from our period has been excavated. The shortage of archival materials means that only in very rare cases can we form an impression of the life of a Jewish family or community, or even reconstruct the career of an individual.

From what has been said so far it is no surprise that the persons mentioned in Hebrew texts from our period are almost without exception male adult Jews. Women are named very rarely; gentiles and children hardly ever. A good majority of people named in the texts are scholars, and it is only about scholars that we have any substantial personal information. In other words the information relates mainly to an educated élite, and only very rarely do we learn about members of non-élite groups. Thus if the material is in any way representative, it is representative of a particular stratum of Jewish society. And indeed it is scarcely abundant enough for us to derive any meaningful generalisations from it. (Some further information about Jews may be gleaned from Greek sources, but this too tends to relate to members of the élite.)

[14] For some examples, see Starr, *Jews in the Byzantine Empire*, ch. 5, and bibliography to this chapter s.v. Benjamin b. Samuel, Judah b. Elijah Hadassi, Samuel of Rossina (Rossano), Tobias b. Moses.
[15] For examples, see bibliography below s.v. Isaac b. Melchizedek, and Starr, ibid.

Onomastic study can enhance our understanding of Byzantine Jewish society and culture. The names of male Jews preserved in the sources are mainly well-known biblical names, recalling key figures in the biblical narrative, such as Abraham, Isaac, Jacob, Judah, Reuben, Joseph, Benjamin, Aaron, Moses, Samuel, Elkanah or Elijah. Some names of biblical origin are more common than their place in the Bible might have led us to suppose, e.g. Caleb, Eliezer, Michael, Mordecai. The last of these is the hero of the book of Esther, associated with the festival of Purim. Michael, the archangel, was a name used by Christians too, which may have been a factor in its use. The same is true of Emanuel. Eliezer was the name of a well-known early rabbi, and some other rabbinic names, such as Avtalion, Hillel, Eleazar, Meir and Hiyya, are also attested, but some equally familiar ones (e.g. Akiva, Gamliel) are not. With the exception of Caleb, which may be considered a typically Byzantine Jewish name, all the others mentioned so far are names that could easily have been found anywhere in the Jewish world, although some were relatively rare in some places (for example Mordecai, popular in Byzantium down the centuries, was not common in Egypt).

Of the repertoire of Jewish names that were common among Greek-speaking Jews in antiquity many are notable by their absence or rarity at this period. These include Simeon and its Greek equivalent Simon, and the group of 'theophoric' names considered typically Jewish in the Hellenistic period (Jonathan, Mattathias, Theodoros, Dorotheos and suchlike). One name considered distinctively Jewish in the ancient papyri, Sabbataios, enjoyed enduring popularity in Byzantium in its Hebraised form Shabbetai. Of the names characteristic of the extra-biblical writings, we find Tobias, but not Tobit, Raphael, Sira or Enoch. Among rarer Hebrew names not found much if at all outside Byzantium we may mention Avishai, Eliakim, Guri, Kuti, Meyuhas, Namer, Navon, Shalom and Shelahia.

This is a representative rather than an exhaustive account of Byzantine Hebrew names. It illustrates some of the continuities and discontinuities with other Jewish societies, both diachronically and synchronically viewed. Its distinctive features are striking, but hard to explain in most cases. Naturally in a relatively small and not necessarily representative sample the absence of any particular name cannot be considered definitive. However, it is striking that some biblical names popular in other regions or periods (such as Simeon, Joshua, Solomon or Isaiah) do not seem to have been favoured in Byzantium at this period.

Greek names are very rare in the Hebrew sources. Leaving aside the many names that could be either Hebrew or Greek, we may note in particular the popularity of Leon, the Greek equivalent of Judah (Genesis 49:9). Why the Greek name is found so commonly in Hebrew documents is a matter for speculation. In at least one case both names are given.[16] Another, much less common, Greek name is Parigoris (Paregorios), the equivalent of the Hebrew name Menahem (meaning 'consoler'), which is also attested. It is reasonable to extrapolate from other times and places and suppose that Jewish men in Byzantium had two names, a Hebrew patronym that was given to them at their circumcision and a Greek name for everyday use. We have an example of this in a Greek deed of sale from Taranto dated 1033, where one of the parties is named as 'Theophylaktos, also called Chimaria, a Hebrew by race',[17] where the Hebrew name, Shemaria, meaning 'protected by God' or 'God protects', has a similar meaning to the Greek. Very often, as in the cases just cited, there would be a regular, direct connection between the Greek and Hebrew names.[18]

Women are so rarely named in the sources that it is hard to make any generalisations; in line with Byzantine Jewish practice at a later date (particularly well documented for Venetian Crete) they do not have Hebrew names but only Greek ones.[19] Names such as Archondou, Zoe and Evdokia are attested (the last more than once).

Normally personal names are followed by patronyms, but in a minority of cases surnames are used. Some of these are Greek (Kalomiti, Korsinos, Megas, Psaltiri, Spatha), others Hebrew, Aramaic, Arabic or Italian; many are hard to explain (e.g. Dava, Tirutot). Occasionally they suggest a geographical origin, e.g. Lombardo, or Hadassi, which some have associated with Edessa. There does not seem to be any particular logic in the use or absence of a surname. Benjamin of Tudela, for instance, never cites a patronym, although he does occasionally give surnames.

Very occasionally we are afforded a glimpse of Byzantine Jewish naming customs, and particularly the practice of naming sons after their grandfather. Thus we find an Eliezer son of Judah son of Eliezer 'the Great' (perhaps so called to differentiate him from his grandson),[20] and an Eleazar son of Hanukkah son of Eleazar son of David.[21] In the latter case, while the son has his grandfather's name his father does not. Perhaps the rule, as in some other Jewish societies, was that the eldest son is named after his paternal grand-

---

[16] See bibliography s.v. 'Judah, called Leon'.

[17] Starr, *Jews in the Byzantine Empire*, no. 137, p. 194.

[18] For a study of this question based on material from antiquity, see Milka Cassuto, 'La corrispondenza tra nomi ebraici e greci nell'onomastica giudaica', *Giornale della Società asiatica italiana* n.s. 2 (1930–4), 209–30.

[19] In a marriage deed from Cairo the bride, whose father was from Byzantium, has the biblical Hebrew name Rebecca (Hebrew Rivka: see bibliography s.v.). It may well be that Byzantine Jewish women were sometimes given biblical names, but this particular document is not clear evidence for Byzantine practice.

[20] Starr, *Jews in the Byzantine Empire*, 204.

[21] Scribe of MS Bodley Heb.c.6.

father. Unusually in a Jewish milieu, a son could bear the same name as his living father.

Prosopographical information, taken in conjunction with other evidence, can help to shed light on the social history of the Jewish population of Byzantium, which, it must be stressed, is very poorly documented at this period. We are able to observe, for example, the presence of numbers of foreign Jews, of various origins, in Byzantium, some attracted by advantages on offer, others fleeing turmoil. Some foreigners married local wives, both Jewish and Christian. We also find Jews born in Byzantium living abroad, either temporarily or permanently. The Cairo Genizah texts reveal the presence of Greek-speaking families living in Egypt, indeed there is a mention of a 'Cretan quarter' in Alexandria. The dangers posed by piracy and banditry are also abundantly evident from these texts, which also provide some indications of relations between Jews and gentiles, including conversion to the dominant faith. In one letter, a Christian priest whose mother was a convert from Judaism conveys some merchandise for a Jewish trader.[22] Conversion in the opposite direction is also documented.[23]

The principal caveat that needs to be borne in mind, as with most prosopographical material, is that, as already observed, we are dealing with an educated élite. By and large we hear nothing of the less prominent or less prosperous members of society.

[22] See de Lange, *Greek Jewish Texts*, 22.
[23] See bibliography s.v. Obadiah the Proselyte.

# JEWISH SOURCES: A BIBLIOGRAPHY
## JOSHUA HOLO

### NOTE ON TRANSLITERATION AND ORGANISATION

IN THE ABSENCE OF A UNIVERSALLY ACCEPTED SYSTEM of transliteration, Hebrew proper names such as Benjamin, Tobias, Isaac, Melchizedek and Nathan are anglicised when possible. Similarly, more recent Hebrew publications that are catalogued under English titles bear only a parenthetical note indicating that the text is in Hebrew.

Despite inconsistencies, most electronic catalogues recognise a simplified, phonetic system of Hebrew transliteration. Though this system sometimes represents more than one Hebrew letter with a given Latin character, its use increases the probability of a successful search. Some letters of note: *h* is *het* (ח, elsewhere *ḥ*), as in *Yohasin*, and it doubles as *he* (ה), as in *Hadassi*; *k* is both *kof* (ק, elsewhere *ḳ* or *q*), as in *Eliakim*, and it also represents *kaf* (כ), as in *Eshkol ha-kofer*; *v* is the aspirated *bet* (ב), as in *Ovadyah*, elsewhere transliterated as *b* or *ḅ*; *z* is both *zadi* (צ and ץ, elsewhere *ts*, *ṣ*, or *tz*), as in *Ahimaaz*, and also *zayin* (ז), as in *Mahzor*; the gutturals *aleph* (א) and *ayin* (ע) do not appear, while other systems represent them with apostrophes or superscript symbols (' is *aleph*) and (' is *ayin*).

**Handbooks, surveys and prosopographies,** organised by author's last name, includes the major modern histories, regesta, translations, and source-lists. These works contain the bulk of Byzantine-Jewish prosopographical information.

**Byzantine-Jewish authors and scribes,** ordered by first name, lists literary and legal works, letters and colophons written by Byzantine Jews. Some works are of interest for the prosopographical data they contain, while others were authored by influential scholars. Those listed are either absent from, difficult to find in, or have been reconsidered since the publication of, the works under Handbooks, surveys and prosopographies.

**Brief references** lists individuals and groups who appear in the primary sources either very briefly or in contexts otherwise unconcerned with the Byzantine empire. Here, too, overlap with 'Handbooks' was avoided when possible.

*Abbreviations:*
T-S     Cambridge, University Library, Taylor-Schechter Collection
ULC     Cambridge, University Library, University Library Collection

### HANDBOOKS, SURVEYS AND PROSOPOGRAPHIES

Z. Ankori, *Karaites in Byzantium: the formative years 970–1100* (New York, 1959)
Compendious historical study, but relies heavily on analogy with other Jewish Mediterranean cultures for historical generalisations. Rich in prosopographical information and full notes.

S.W. Baron, *A Social and Religious History of the Jews*, 18 vols. (New York, 1956–93), index, s.v. 'Byzantium'
Sweeping history, touches on Byzantine history and individuals, with the relevant periods being found in the text and notes of vols. 3–8.

S. Bowman, *The Jews of Byzantium: 1204–1453* (Tuscaloosa, Alabama, 1985)
Modelled on the format of Starr, *The Jews in the Byzantine Empire* (below). The most comprehensive compilation of translated sources available and the starting-point for its period, even touching on the period prior to the Fourth Crusade. Includes substantial historical introduction.

I. Davidson, *Thesaurus of Medieval Hebrew Poetry*, 4 vols. (New York, 1924–33; repr. with new supplement and introduction, 1970)
Compendious list of poems, by incipit. Still the basic resource for the totality of medieval Hebrew poetry, but updated for Byzantium by subsequent works such as Schirmann's *New Hebrew Poems*, and Weinberger's various editions (below).

N.R.M. de Lange, 'Greek and Byzantine fragments in the Cairo Genizah', *BJGS* 5 (1989), 13–17
Review and update of S. Reif, *Published Material from the Cambridge Genizah Collections* (below). Lists Byzantine Genizah documents by call number, with brief descriptions.

—— 'The classical tradition in Byzantium', in D. Cohn-Sherbok, ed., *A Traditional Quest: essays in honour of Louis Jacobs* (Sheffield, 1991), 86–101
Primarily intellectual history, but also including a section dedicated to the name of a certain Herakles, mentioned in the *Itinerary* of Benjamin of Tudela (below).

—— 'Byzantium in the Cairo Genizah', *BMGS* 16 (1992), 15–32
Lists relevant Genizah mss. with descriptions; publication information in footnotes. Overlaps largely, but not entirely, with de Lange, 'Greek and Byzantine fragments in the Cairo Genizah'. The two articles are the only lists of Byzantine-Jewish Genizah sources, complementing Reif's *Published Material* and authoritative in tandem with it.

—— 'Jewish education in the Byzantine empire in the twelfth century', in G. Abramson and T. Parfitt, eds., *Jewish Education and Learning* (Chur, Switzerland, 1994), 115–28
Introduction to Jewish scholarly culture, with very useful prosopographical appendix of individual scholars and notes. Particularly noteworthy are the numerous individuals from Crete who figure in the local Jewish community's statutes from the year 1228. Additionally, de Lange specifies individuals from Benjamin's *Itinerary* for convenient reference.

—— *Greek Jewish Texts from the Cairo Genizah* (Tübingen, 1996)
Selected mss., introduced, transcribed, translated and annotated, with images. Important prosopographical and, especially, lexicographical data. Mostly literary and liturgical, but also including four documents. Includes data on previous editions.

—— 'A thousand years of Hebrew in Byzantium', in W. Horbury, ed., *Hebrew Study from Ezra to Ben-Yehuda* (Edinburgh, 1999), 147–61
Discusses, among other things, scholars of note in the middle Byzantine period, with references to major editions.

N.R.M. de Lange, 'Hebrew scholarship in Byzantium', in N. de Lange, ed., *Hebrew Scholarship and the Medieval World* (Cambridge, 2001), 23–37
Discusses major Jewish scholars throughout Byzantine history with notes and bibliography.

M. Gil, *Palestine during the First Muslim Period: 634–1099* (Heb.), 3 vols. (Tel-Aviv, 1983)
Comprehensive, authoritative assembly of relevant mss. from collections around the world, of great prosopographical interest. Includes historical analysis (vol. 1), editions of mss. (vols. 2–3), tr. into Hebrew when necessary, and bibliographical, palaeographical and historical notes. English tr. of vol. 1: E. Broido, *A History of Palestine: 634–1099* (Cambridge, 1992).

N. Golb and O. Pritzak, *Khazarian Hebrew Documents of the Tenth Century* (Ithaca, NY, 1982)
An historical and palaeographical examination of the documents concerning the Jewish Khazars, including those from and relating to the Byzantine empire.

S.D. Goitein, *A Mediterranean Society*, 6 vols. (Berkeley, 1973–93)
Magisterial overview of the society represented in the Cairo Genizah, including frequent references to individuals throughout, with notes and cumulative indices.

R.J.W. Jeferson and E.C.D. Hunter, *Published Material from the Cambridge Genizah Collections* (Cambridge, 2004)
A continuation of Reif's bibliography (below), listing mss. published from 1980–97.

S. Krauss, *Studien zur byzantinisch-jüdischen Geschichte* (Leipzig, 1914)
The seminal narrative history on Byzantine Jewry, though no longer up-to-date.

J. Mann, *The Jews in Egypt and Palestine under the Fatimid Caliphs*, 2 vols. (London, 1920, 1922; repr. with new introduction, New York, 1970)
Seminal study of the Cairo Genizah combining historical analyses with editions of mss. Errors are not infrequent, but still a major source for Palestinian and Egyptian Jewry, and an important font for Starr, *Jews in the Byzantine Empire* (below).

—— *Texts and Studies in Jewish History and Literature*, 2 vols. (Cincinnati, 1931–5)
Important texts and references to texts of considerable prosopographical interest, among other historical considerations, particularly vol. 1, 45–59.

A. Neubauer, *Aus der Petersburger Bibliotek: Beiträge und Documente zur Geschichte des Karäerthums und der karäischen Literatur* (Leipzig, 1866)
Outdated résumé of Karaite works in the Saltykov-Shchedrin Public Library, formerly the Imperial Public Library of St Petersburg. Despite its shortcomings, still an important source for orientation in the Firkovitch collection, especially chap. 3, which deals with Byzantine Karaites.

S. Reif, *Published Material from the Cambridge Genizah Collections* (Cambridge, 1988)
Consummately useful and easily cross-referenced list of mss. published to 1980. References in *Published Material* naturally overlap with some of those listed here. However, as the first step for research on any Cambridge Genizah document, it has not been cross-referenced.

J. Schirmann, *New Hebrew Poems from the Genizah* (Heb.) (Jerusalem, 1965)
Major study of Genizah poetry, including one section, pp. 421–6, on Byzantine poets. Includes brief textual introductions and editions.

A. Sharf, 'Jews in Byzantium', in C. Roth, ed., *World History of the Jewish People*, ser. 2, vol. 2, *The Dark Ages* (Tel-Aviv, 1966), 49–69
Byzantine-Jewish history to the twelfth century in short order, with some prosopographical mentions and notes.
—— *Byzantine Jewry: from Justinian to the Fourth Crusade* (London, 1971)
Organised along the major trends in Byzantine-Jewish history, prosopographical information present throughout.
—— *Jews and Other Minorities in Byzantium* (Ramat-Gan, 1995)
Collected articles dealing with Jews from the early and middle Byzantine periods, most notably the latter for prosopography.
C. Sirat, *Hebrew Manuscripts of the Middle Ages*, ed. and tr. N. de Lange (Cambridge, 2002)
Comprehensive overview of the Hebrew manuscript, including codicology, palaeography, illumination, etc. from throughout the Jewish world.
J. Starr, *The Jews in the Byzantine Empire: 641–1204* (Athens, 1939)
Full-length treatment of Byzantine Jewry in the middle period, including an historical introduction and partially translated, annotated sources. No longer authoritative in all respects, but the most thoroughgoing work to date and still the starting-point.
—— *Romania: Jewries of the Levant after the Fourth Crusade* (Paris, 1949)
Narrative history, useful in tandem with Bowman, *The Jews of Byzantium*.
L.J. Weinberger, 'New poems from the Byzantine period' (Heb.), *HUCA* 39 (1968), Heb. sec., 1–52
A collection of fourteen poems from the eleventh to sixteenth centuries, with black-and-white images. Including six poets (nos. 1, 2, 6, 10–12) either definitely or probably of Byzantine origin from the eleventh and twelfth centuries.
—— *Anthology of Hebrew Poetry in Greece* (Cincinnati, 1975)
Editions and commentary on poetry from the eleventh to thirteenth centuries and beyond, including brief notes about the personalities in the introduction.
—— *Early Synagogue Poets in the Balkans* (Cincinnati and Tuscaloosa, Alabama, 1988)
Authoritative editions of three Kastorian poets from the eleventh to twelfth centuries: Moses b. Hiyya, Joseph b. Jacob Kalai and Isaac b. Judah. Includes introduction and notes.
—— *Rabbanite and Karaite Liturgical Poetry in South-eastern Europe* (Cincinnati, 1991)
Diachronic, authoritative collection of Byzantium Hebrew poems, including first editions and previously unknown poets. Weinberger's three major collections exhibit only minimal overlap, and thus must be used in tandem.
—— *Jewish Hymnography* (London and Portland, Oregon, 1998)
Includes a descriptive section on the major poets of the middle Byzantine period, with significant literary analyses and incidental personal data.
H. Zimmels, 'Scholars and scholarship in Byzantium and Italy', in C. Roth, ed., *World History of the Jewish People*, ser. 2, vol. 2, *The Dark Ages* (Tel-Aviv, 1966), 175–88
Helpful overview of Byzantine-Jewish scholarly achievements with notes; cf. de Lange, 'Hebrew scholarship in Byzantium'.

L. Zunz, *Literaturgeschichte der synagogalen Poesie* (Berlin, 1865)
Seminal work, tracing the compositions of many individual poets, with comments and occasional, brief excerpts. Compendious but no longer up-to-date and difficult to use. Most helpful in conjunction with Davidson, *Thesaurus of Hebrew Poetry*.

## BYZANTINE–JEWISH AUTHORS AND SCRIBES

Abū 'Alī b. Abu'l Mānī
Letter, T-S Misc. 35.8, sent from Abū 'Alī b. Abu'l Mānī to Joseph al-Baghdadi: 'We were sold in Constantinople and we were redeemed with the help of the Creator . . .'

*Mentions:*
S. Assaf, 'New documents concerning proselytes and a Messianic movement' (Heb.), *Zion* 5 (1940), 115, n. 12; repr. in S. Assaf, *Texts and Studies in Jewish History* (Heb.) (Jerusalem, 1946), 145
S. Shaked, *A Tentative Bibliography of Geniza Documents* (Paris, 1964), 155

Ahimaaz b. Paltiel, *Sefer Yohasin,* or the *Chronicle of Ahimaaz*
Chronicle of a southern Italian, Byzantine-Jewish family, purporting to span the ninth to mid-eleventh centuries. One of the major sources for Byzantine-Jewish history and prosopography. Author's name also transliterated 'Ahimaas'.

*Editions:*
A. Neubauer, 'Sefer Yohasin', in *Medieval Jewish Chronicles and Chronological Notes* (1887–95; repr., Amsterdam, 1970), vol. 2, 111–32
The first edition of the story, from a *unicum* found in the cathedral of Toledo.
B. Klar, *Megilat Ahimaaz* (Heb.), (Jerusalem, 1944; 2nd edn., 1975)
Authoritative edition with descriptions and evaluations of the literary traditions outside the *Chronicle* itself.

*Translations:*
M. Salzman, ed. and tr., *The Chronicle of Ahimaaz* (New York, 1924)
Edition, introduction and complete English tr. that favours meaning and flow over literal faithfulness. Summarises scholarship to date and offers historical background.
Starr, *Jews, passim*
Partial tr., with various sections of the chronicle placed in the chronological sequence of the other sources.
C. Colafemmina, *Sefer Yuhasin: libro delle discendenze* (Cassano delle Murge, 2001)
Italian tr., introduction, notes and bibliography.

*Scholarly Treatments:*
D. Kaufmann, 'Die Chronik des Achimaaz von Oria (850–1054)', *MGWJ* 40 (1896), 462–73, 496–509, 529–54
Rich, though outdated, study of the various personalities in the *Chronicle*.

J. Marcus, 'Studies in the Chronicle of Ahimaaz', *PAAJR* 5 (1933–4), 85–94
   Discusses and edits the work of the poet Silano, who figures somewhat promi-
   nently in the *Chronicle*.
M. Cohen, *Jewish Self-Government in Medieval Egypt* (Princeton, 1980), *passim*
   Important, up-to-date historical revision of the role of one of the *Chronicle*'s
   heroes, Paltiel, in the foundation of the Egyptian leadership. Ch. 1 includes an
   outline of research to date.
R. Bonfil, 'Can medieval storytelling help understanding Midrash? The story of
   Paltiel', in M. Fishbane, ed., *The Midrashic Imagination* (Albany, 1993), 228–54
—— *Tra due mondi* (Naples, 1996), pt. 1
   Bonfil's studies provide important perspectives on the relationship between
   Byzantine Italy and the two primary centres of Judaic learning in Baghdad and
   Palestine.
S.D. Benin, 'Jews, Muslims, and Christians in Byzantine Italy', in B. Hary and others,
   eds., *Judaism and Islam* (Leiden, 2000), 27–35
   An outline of aspects of social history embedded in the *Chronicle*.

## Anonymous
An unnamed Jewish doctor, living in Seleukeia but originally from Egypt, writes in the
twelfth century to his landsmen, encouraging them to come to the Byzantine empire.

*Editions:*
S.D. Goitein, 'A letter of historical importance from Seleucia (Selefke)' (Heb.), *Tarbiz*
   27 (1958), 521–36
   In this first edition of T-S 13 J 21, Goitein identifies Seleukeia with the Syrian
   town of that name.

*Translation:*
S.D. Goitein, 'A letter from Seleucia (Cilicia)', *Speculum* 39 (1964), 298–303
   Goitein revisits his identification of Seleukeia, claiming it to be the well-known
   Byzantine regional capital.

## Benjamin b. Samuel the Constantinopolitan
Poet and scholar, probably from the eleventh century.

*Edition:*
Weinberger, *Anthology*, 38–70

*Scholarly Treatments:*
Zimmels, 'Scholars and scholarship', 176–7
L.J. Weinberger, 'A note on Jewish scholars and scholarship in Byzantium', *JAOS* 91.1
   (1971), 142–4
—— 'On the provenance of Benjamin b. Samuel Qustani', *JQR* 68–9 (1977–9), 46–7
*Mentions:*
I. Davidson and L. Ginzburg, *Mahzor Yannai* (New York, 1919), xvi
Schirmann, *New Hebrew Poems*, 421

## Benjamin of Tudela, *Sefer Masaot* or *Itinerary*
Benjamin names, describes and quantifies a number of Byzantine-Jewish communities, their leaders, and in some cases their professions. His famous work has inspired
studies too numerous for inclusion here. The relevant section is conveniently

excerpted, translated and discussed by Starr, *Jews*, 228–34, and Bowman, *Jews of Byzantium*, Excursus A.

*Translations:*

M.N. Adler, tr. and ed., *Sefer Masaot: the Itinerary of Benjamin of Tudela* (London, 1907)
> The standard edition and tr., though a new critical edition is warranted.

R.P. Schmitz, *Buch der Reisen* (Frankfurt and New York, 1988)

J.R. Magdalena Nom de Déu, *Libro de viajes de Benjamin de Tudela* (Barcelona, 1989)

S. Benjamin, *The World of Benjamin of Tudela: a medieval Mediterranean travelogue* (Madison, 1995)
> Introductory material, tr., and a running commentary on the *Itinerary*.

H. Harboun, *Benjamin de Tudèle* (Aix-en-Provence, 1998)

*Scholarly Treatments:*

Ankori, *Karaites*, 155–63
> Valuable critique of the problem of Benjamin's census.

Z. Ankori, 'Viajando con Benjamín de Tudela', in C. Carrete Larrondo, ed., *Actas del III Congreso internacional encuentro de las tres culturas* (Toledo, 1988), 11–28
> A useful attempt to explain the motivation both for Benjamin's travels and his particular style of recording them.

J.A. Ochoa, 'El imperio bizantino en el viaje de Benjamín de Tudela', in G. Busi, ed., *Viaggiatori ebrei: atti del Convegno europeo dell'AISG, San Miniato, 4–5 novembre 1991* (Bologna,1992), 81–98

G. Busi, 'Binyamin da Tudela: nuove avventure bibliografiche', *Materia giudaica* 3 (1997), 39–42
> A sobering call to appreciate the *Itinerary*'s limitations for historians.

D. Jacoby, 'Benjamin of Tudela in Byzantium', *Palaeoslavica* 10.1 (2002), 180–5
> A brief, helpful overview of the date and reliability of Benjamin's description of the Empire, linking it with other, well-established historical events.

## Isaac b. Melchizedek

Early twelfth-century scholar of Mishnah from Siponto, mentioned by Abraham b. David of Posquières as 'the Greek scholar', and in contact with the sages of Rome on legal issues.

*Mentions:*

H. Vogelstein and P. Rieger, *Geschichte der Juden in Rom*, 2 vols. (Berlin, 1869), vol. 1, 223–4; 355, n. 4; 368, 371, n. 1

H. Albeck, *Introduction to the Mishna* (Heb.) (Jerusalem, 1959), 245

Weinberger, *Early Synagogue Poets*, 8

de Lange, 'Jewish education', 125

## Judah b. Elijah Hadassi, *Eshkol ha-kofer* or *The Cluster of Henna*

Mid-twelfth-century Karaite legist and leader of Byzantine community.

*Editions:*

M. Tirishkan, *Eshkol ha-kofer* (Gozlov, 1836; repr. with additional material and introduction, 1971)
> The only complete version available in print.

W. Bacher, 'Inedited chapters of Jehuda Hadassi's *Eshkol hakkofer*', *JQR* 8 (1896), 431–44
Supplement to the standard edition.

*Scholarly Treatments:*
A. Scheiber, 'Manuscript material relating to the literary activity of Judah Hadassi', in A. Scheiber, ed., *Jubilee Volume in Honour of Professor Bernhard Heller* (Budapest, 1941), 101–29
Z. Ankori, 'Some aspects of Karaite-Rabbanite relations in Byzantium on the eve of the First Crusade', *PAAJR* 24, 25 (1955–6), 1–38, 157–82
—— *Karaites*, index s.v. 'Yehudah Hadassi'
D. Barthélemy, 'La tradition manuscrite d'*Eshkol ha-Kofer*', *Bulletin d'études karaïtes* 2 (1989), 5–22

*Mentions:*
G. Margoliouth, 'Ibn al-Hītī's Arabic chronicle of Karaite doctors', *JQR* 9 (1897), 435, 443 (tr. L. Nemoy, *Karaite Anthology* [New Haven, 1952], 235)
de Lange, 'Jewish education', 125
J. Olszowy-Schlanger, *Karaite Marriage Documents from the Cairo Genizah* (Leiden, 1998), 248–9

## Nathan b. Makhir

Hebrew colophon in Parma, Biblioteca Palatina, de Rossi 12 (2004), by Nathan b. Makhir b. Menahem of Ancona b. Samuel b. Makhir of Oria b. Solomon. Nathan copied a Pentateuch, transliterating the vocalisation from the Babylonian to the Tiberian system. Uncertain date.

*Edition:*
A. Neubauer, 'The early settlement of the Jews in southern Italy', *JQR* 4 (1892), 616

*Mention:*
Zunz, *Literaturgeschichte*, 161
Distinguishing this Nathan from another of similar name.

## Obadiah the Proselyte

An autobiographical account of Johannes, a Norman priest born *c.*1073 in Oppido, in formerly Byzantine southern Italy. He took the Hebrew name Obadiah and converted to Judaism in 1102, partially under the influence of the example of Archbishop Andreas of Bari, his elder contemporary, who had similarly converted to Judaism and subsequently fled to Constantinople. The autobiography is pieced together from six mss., discovered over time (Oxford University, Bodleian Library, Heb. a. 3 fol. 1; Jewish Theological Seminary of America, New York, Adler ms. 4208; T-S Loan 31; T-S 10 K 21.1; Hebrew Union College, Cincinnati (HUC), no. 8; Hungarian Academy of Sciences, Budapest, Kaufmann 134). The scholarly treatments listed are necessarily selected, as Obadiah has inspired an entire bibliography of his own; among those aspects of his career omitted is his liturgical music.

*Editions:*
S.A. Wertheimer, *Ginze Yerushalayim*, 2 vols. (Jerusalem, 1901; 2nd edn. with new material, 1991, 2000), vol. 2, 286–9

First, partial edition of Barukh b. Isaac's letter of recommendation, Bodleian Heb. a. 3 fol. 1 (= Neubauer Catalogue 2873). Incomplete and without the advantage of later discoveries. The second edition did not correct the shortcomings of the first, which J. Mann pointed out in his 1930 complementary edition (below).

E.N. Adler, 'Obadiah le prosélyte', *RÉJ* 69 (1919), 129–34

Edition and French tr. of Adler ms. 4208 (= 3098b in article); seminal but lacking in accurate historical context, later furnished by further discoveries and studies. Reproduced in *Catalogue of Hebrew Manuscripts in the Collection of Elkan Nathan Adler* (Cambridge, 1921), 156b, fig. 1.

J. Mann, 'Obadya, prosélyte normand converti au Judaïsme, et sa meguilla', *RÉJ* 89 (1930), 245–59

First edition of T-S Loan 31 and HUC 8; revision of T-S 10 K 21.1 (first edition in J. Mann, 'Obadya le prosélyte', *RÉJ* 71 [1920], 89–93); revision of Adler 4208; and continuation of Wertheimer's incomplete edition of Bodl. Heb. a. 3 fol. 1. Contains numerous errors.

A. Scheiber, 'Fragment from the chronicle of Obadyah, the Norman proselyte', *AOH* 4 (1954), 271–96

Very useful article, including first, unvocalised edition of Kaufmann 134, with English translation and historical context. Includes black-and-white facsimiles of the following mss.: Kaufmann 134; T-S 8.271; Adler 4208; HUC 8; T-S Loan 31; T-S 10 K 21.1. This and other articles by Scheiber, regarding Obadiah and other topics, are reprinted in A. Scheiber, *Geniza Studies* (Hildesheim, 1981).

—— 'Ein aus arabischer Gefangenschaft befreiter christlicher Proselyt in Jerusalem', *HUCA* 39 (1968), 168–72

Edition of T-S 8.271.

Z. Malaki, *Chapters in Medieval Hebrew Literature* (Heb.), (Tel-Aviv, 1971)

Complete, relatively recent, publication of the mss., though the Hebrew is left unvocalised even when originals are vocalised.

N. Golb, 'Megilat Ovadyah ha-ger', in S. Morag and others, eds., *Mehkere edot u-genizah* (Jerusalem, 1981), 77–107

Revised, authoritative editions of all the fragments that comprise the autobiography, in addition to the letter from R. Barukh b. Isaac of Aleppo vouching for Obadiah. Comparative palaeographical and historical analysis. Supersedes all previous editions.

*Translations:*

S.D. Goitein, 'Obadyah, a Norman proselyte', *JJS* 4 (1953), 74–84

Partial translation, without Hebrew text, of T-S 8.271, with historical comments.

J.L. Teicher, 'The origins of 'Obadyah, the Norman proselyte', *JJS* 5 (1954), 32–7

English translation, without Hebrew text, of Kaufmann 134, with introduction by A. Scheiber. Later slightly revised by A. Scheiber in 'Fragment', *AOH* 4.

*Scholarly Treatments:*

B. Blumenkranz, 'La conversion au judaïsme d'André, archevêque de Bari', *JJS* 14 (1963), 33–7

Argues for the attribution of the anonymous T-S 12.732 to Andreas of Bari, though most consider it unrelated to either Andreas or Obadiah. The fragment in question was first published by S. Assaf in *Zion* 5 (1940), 118–19.

N. Golb, 'A study of a proselyte to Judaism who left Egypt at the beginning of the eleventh century' (Heb.), *Sefunot* 8 (1964), 102–4
Useful bibliographical appendix.

A. Scheiber, 'Some notes on the conversion of Archbishop Andrea to Judaism', *JJS* 15 (1964), 159–60
Brief notes on Andreas and his flight to Constantinople in 1066.

Goitein, *Mediterranean Society*, vol. 2, 308–9 and notes

P. Borraro, ed., *Antiche civiltà lucane: atti del Convegno di studi di archeologia, storia dell'arte e del folklore, Oppido Lucano, aprile 1970* (Galatina, Italy, 1975), 203–60
Articles on various topics of Obadiah's life and career, including useful bibliography.

J. Prawer, 'The autobiography of Obadyah the Norman', in I. Twersky, ed., *Studies in Medieval Jewish History and Literature* (Cambridge, MA, 1979), 110–34
Careful, recent consideration of the life and autobiography of Obadiah, with notes.

N. Golb, *Jewish Proselytism—a phenomenon in the religious history of early medieval Europe* (Cincinnati, 1988), 9–31
Useful and up-to-date overview of the mss. sources for Obadiah's biography, with important conclusion that he converted in Italy, as opposed to Syria.

## Samuel of Rossina (Rossano)

Twelfth-century commentator on the Pentateuch, originally thought to be from Russia, more recently, from Rossano in former Byzantine Italy.

*Edition:*

M. Weiss, *Sefer Rushaina*, 3 vols. (Jerusalem, 1976–93), vol. 1, 12–13

*Mention:*

D. Sperber, 'Contributions to Byzantine lexicography from Jewish sources', *Byz* 46, 48 (1976, 1978), 58–61, 244–8
Also discusses Hillel b. Eliakim, a twelfth-century poet and commentator.

B.D. Weinryb, 'The myth of Samuel of Russia, twelfth-century author of a Bible commentary', in A. Neuman and S. Zeitlin, eds., *The Seventy-fifth Anniversary Volume of the Jewish Quarterly Review* (Philadelphia, 1967), 528–43

*Scholarly Treatment:*

I.M. Ta-Shma, 'Sefer Rossina—a southern Italian Bible commentary of the late eleventh century' (Heb.), *Tarbiz* 72.4 (2003), 567–80
Accepts Rossano as Samuel's home town and further develops his relationship with contemporary commentators and classical rabbinic literature.

## Tobias b. Moses

Karaite leader and translator of the mid-eleventh century. Travelled to Palestine and Egypt, and is credited with being a major force in transplanting the intellectual spirit of Karaism from Palestine to his native Byzantium. His correspondence, of considerable prosopographical interest, is divided among six fragments that constitute four mss. (Smithsonian Institution, Washington DC, Freer Gallery Hebrew mss. 31–2; T-S 12.347; ULC Or. 1080 J 21; Hungarian Academy of Sciences, Budapest, Kaufmann 166; T-S AS 153.82).

*Editions:*

R. Gottheil and W.H. Worrell, *Fragments from the Cairo Genizah in the Freer Collection* (New York, 1927), nos. 31–2
Edition and English tr. of two mss., Freer Gallery 31–2.

J. Mann, *Texts*, vol. 1, 373–4, 383–5
Partial edition with brief discussion (Freer Gallery 31–2 and T-S 12.347).

S.D. Goitein, 'Letters from the land of Israel in the period of the crusades' (Heb.), *Yerushalayim: Review for Eretz-Israel Research* 2.5 (1955), 68–9
Hebrew tr. of Arabic ULC Or. 1080 J 21.

Z. Ankori, 'The correspondence of Tobias ben Moses the Karaite', in J. Blau and others, eds., *Essays on Jewish Life and Thought Presented in Honor of S.W. Baron* (New York, 1959), 1–38
Consideration of Tobias's letters and life, including an edition of three fragments (Freer Gallery 31–2 and T-S 12.347).

A. Scheiber, 'Ein aus arabischer Gefangenschaft befreiter christlicher Proselyt in Jerusalem', *HUCA* 39 (1968), 163–7
Scheiber did not yet connect this document, Kaufmann 166, with T-S AS 153.82, which is part of the same document, or with its author, Tobias b. Moses.

Z. Pelek, 'From the Cairo Genizah' (Heb.), *Sinai* 85 (1979), 145–7
Combined edition of T-S AS 153.82 and Kaufmann 166.

M. Gil, *Palestine during the First Muslim Period*, nos. 293–6
Complete edition of correspondence, with a Hebrew tr. of ULC Or. 1080 J 21. Authoritative in all respects.

*Mentions:*

Zunz, *Literaturgeschichte*, 162

Neubauer, *Aus der Petersburger Bibliotek*, 55

E. Bashyatsi, *Adderet Eliyahu* (*Elijah's Mantle*) (Odessa, 1870), introd. p. 4 (tr. L. Nemoy, *Karaite Anthology* [New Haven, 1952], 249)

Starr, *Jews*, 242–4, Appendix A

Z. Baras 'Jewish–Christian disputes and conversions in Jerusalem' (Heb.), in B.Z. Kedar, ed., *Perakim be-toledot Yerushalayim bimei ha-beinayim* (*Jerusalem in the Middle Ages*), (Jerusalem, 1979) 34–5

A. Scheiber, 'New texts from the Geniza concerning the proselytes', *HUCA* 50 (1979), 277

S.D. Goitein, *Mediterranean Society*, vol. 3, 200, n. 190

E. Fleischer, 'On the identity of the scribe of *ha-Sheelot ha-atiqot*', *Kiryat Sefer* 55 (1980), 185

*Scholarly Treatments:*

S. Poznański, 'Karaite literary opponents of Saadiah Gaon', *JQR* 19 (1907), 78–82
Part of the seminal English-language work on Karaite–Rabbanite polemics beginning in the tenth century, reprinted as a book with same title in London, 1908.

Z. Ankori, 'Some aspects of the Karaite–Rabbanite relations in Byzantium on the eve of the First Crusade', *PAAJR* 24 (1955), 1–38

—— *Karaites, passim*

## BRIEF REFERENCES

### Aaron and Shabbetai
Hebrew letter, T-S 12.179, addressed to Aaron, care of Shabbetai, in Seleukeia. Goitein dates the letter, on the basis of palaeographical analysis, to the tenth or eleventh century.

*Editions:*
S.D. Goitein, 'Letters from the land of Israel in the period of the crusades' (Heb.), *Yerushalayim: Review for Eretz-Israel research* 2.5 (1955), 69–71
—— *Palestinian Jewry in Early Islamic and Crusader Times* (Heb.) (Jerusalem, 1980), 277–8

### Abraham b. Meir
In the minaret of the Seyh Kutbeddin Mosque, Iznik (Nicaea), Turkey, is the Hebrew epitaph of Abraham b. Meir. Thought to be datable to the twelfth or thirteenth century, no later than the fifteenth.

*Edition:*
A. Schneider, *Die römischen und byzantinischen Denkmäler von Iznik–Nicaea*, Istanbuler Forschungen 16 (1943), 36–7

*Mention:*
Bowman, *Jews of Byzantium*, 89

### Anonymous
In the 1030s, a captive boy found himself in Constantinople, where he was recognised years later and redeemed, after which his story figured in a responsum of Moses b. Isaac of Vienna.

*Edition:*
Moses b. Isaac of Vienna, *Or Zarua,* 4 vols. (Zitomir, 1862), vol. 1, 196, no. 694

*Translation:*
Starr, *Jews*, 193
    Partial, dealing only with the account of the boy's capture and redemption.
I. Agus, *Urban Civilization in Pre-Crusade Europe*, 2 vols. (New York, 1965), vol. 1, 104–7
    Partial, but including both the story and the surrounding legal questions.

*Mention:*
S. Assaf, 'Slavery and the slave-trade among the Jews in the Middle Ages' (Heb.), *Zion* 4 (1939), 106, n. 104

### Cretan Quarter
T-S Arabic 18(1).113 mentions the 'Cretan quarter' of Fustat, Egypt.

*Edition:*
J. Blau and S. Hopkins, 'Judeo-Arabic Letter', *JSAI* 6 (1985), 417–76
    Edition with English tr.

*Mention:*
Goitein, *Mediterranean Society*, vol. 1, 398

Ibrāhīm ibn Fadānj
Judaeo-Arabic letter, T-S 13 J 9.4, written in Palestine by Simon b. Saul in 1053 to his sister in Egypt. Deals with Ibrāhīm ibn Fadānj and Ibrāhīm al-Hārūnī, and refers to the former's capture in Constantinople.

*Editions:*
S. Assaf, 'Sources for history of the Jews in Spain' (Heb.), *Zion* n.s. 6.1–2 (1940), 40–4
   Includes Hebrew tr. Reprinted in S. Klein and others, *Sefer ha-yishuv* (Jerusalem, 1939–44), vol. 2, 41–2, and S. Assaf, *Texts and Studies in Jewish History* (Heb.) (Jerusalem, 1946), 108–13
E. Ashtor, 'Documentos españoles', *Sefarad* 24 (1964), 47–59
   Includes Spanish tr.

*Mention:*
E. Ashtor, *The Jews of Moslem Spain*, tr. A. Klein and J.M. Klein, 3 vols. (Philadelphia, 1973, 1984; paperback edition with new introduction, 1992), vol. 2, 227, 342, nn. 103–4

Judah, called Leon, b. R. Elhanan
Certain students of the academy of Siponto in the mid-eleventh century studied under the Baghdadi sages Sherira Gaon and his son Hai Gaon of Pumbedita: Judah, called Leon, b. R. Elhanan, son of R. Judah; R. Menahem ha-Cohen; R. Elhanan; R. Anan ha-Cohen; R. Melchizedek; R. Moses ha-Cohen. Preserved in London, British Library Or. 1054.

*Edition:*
M. Grossberg, *Abraham ibn Ezra, Sefer azamim* (London, 1901), 46
   The reference to the Byzantine scholars in fact comes, not from Ibn Ezra's *Sefer azamim*, but from a responsum of Hai Gaon (d. 1038) of Pumbedita, contained in the same ms.

*Mentions:*
V. Aptowitzer, 'Unterschungen zur gaonäischen Literatur', *HUCA* 8–9 (1931–2), 435, n. 36
S.D. Goitein, *Jewish Education in Muslim Countries Based on Records from the Cairo Genizah* (Heb.) (Jerusalem, 1965), 182, no. 14
A. Grossman, 'From Father to son' (Heb.), *Zion* 50 (1985), 207, 43, nn. 2–3
M. Gil, 'Between two worlds' (Heb.), in D. Carpi and others, eds., *Shlomo Simonsohn Jubilee Volume* (Tel-Aviv, 1993), 50

Rivka
Karaite marriage contract, T-S 16.67, from Cairo in the year 1201, identifying the bride as 'Rivka, the daughter of the dear elder Joseph, who was from Byzantium'.

*Edition:*
J. Olszowy-Schlanger, *Karaite Marriage Documents from the Cairo Genizah* (Leiden, 1998), 342–9
   Most recent edition and consideration of the text with English tr. and notes.

# Index

Note: diacriticals are ignored for purposes of alphabetisation